Michael McCallister

openSUSE Linux

UNLEASHED

SAMS | 800 East 96th Street, Indianapolis, Indiana 46240 USA

openSUSE Linux Unleashed

ISBN-13: 978-0-672-32945-6
ISBN-10: 0-672-32945-X

Library of Congress Cataloging-in-Publication Data:

McCallister, Michael.

OpenSUSE Linux unleashed / Michael McCallister.

p. cm.

Includes index.

ISBN 978-0-672-32945-6 (pbk. w/dvd)

1. Linux. 2. Operating systems (Computers) I. Title.

QA76.76.063M37486 2007

005.4'32–dc22

2007033555

Printed in the United States on America

First Printing October 2007

Trademarks

Warning and Disclaimer

Bulk Sales

Sams Publishing offers excellent discounts on this book when ordered in quantity for bulk purchases or special sales. For more information, please contact

U.S. Corporate and Government Sales
1-800-382-3419
corpsales@pearsontechgroup.com

For sales outside of the U.S., please contact

International Sales
international@pearsoned.com

Associate Publisher
Mark Taber

Development Editors
Damon Jordon
Michael Thurston

Managing Editor
Patrick Kanouse

Project Editor
Mandie Frank

Copy Editor
Jill Batistick

Indexer
Ken Johnson

Proofreader
Susan Eldridge

Technical Editor
Tim Boronczyk

Publishing Coordinator
Vanessa Evans

Multimedia Developer
Dan Scherf

Designer
Gary Adair

Composition
TnT Design, Inc

Contents at a Glance

Table of Contents

About the Author

Michael McCallister has spent all of this century and a part of the last making computing easier for the full spectrum of user levels and experience. He is currently a technical writing consultant with Compuware.

Michael has run a SuSE Linux desktop at home since version 5.3 and knows firsthand how far the distribution has come over the years. Besides *SUSE Linux 10 Unleashed,* he is the author of *Computer Certification Handbook,* published by Arco Press (2000), and his technology stories have been published in places such as *Linux Journal, SearchEnterpriseLinux.com, Java Developer's Journal, Internet Voyager,* and *Isthmus.* He is a senior member of the Society for Technical Communication and the National Writers Union. He blogs about working, writing and open source at *Notes from the Metaverse* (http://metaverse.wordpress.com).

Dedication

To Jeanette, who keeps pushing me forward and still keeps everything together.

Acknowledgments

Writing can be a lonely endeavor, but in the course of writing a book like this, there are all sorts of people whose paths you cross and who make the result better. Many thanks to Jenny Watson, my original acquisitions editor, who gave me the chance to do this, and Mark Taber, who allowed me to continue down this road. Also thanks to my agent, Carole McClendon at Waterside Productions. Endless props to Rob Shimonski, who tech edited the bulk of the first edition of this book and to Tim Boronczyk for his tech edit of the entire text of the second edition. Scott Meyers offered excellent advice, Mandie Frank shepherded the review process, and Jill Batistick did a marvelous copy edit.

Special and everlasting thanks to Don Bangs, who got me my first computer and *always* responds to hardware emergencies.

To all the developers, testers, documenters, and users of openSUSE Linux and all the wonderful applications that go with it: Thank you isn't enough, but I hope it'll do for now. To the participants on all the mailing lists: Your helpfulness to me and all the other users should never go unnoticed. To my friends in the Boulder and Milwaukee Linux Users Groups: Couldn't have done any of this without you.

Finally, to my wife Jeanette, who always believed I was a writer and my two favorite distractions, Hannah and Ben (and their parents, Bev and Bob): May you grow up happy and in a Linux world.

We Want to Hear from You!

As the reader of this book, *you* are our most important critic and commentator. We value your opinion and want to know what we're doing right, what we could do better, what areas you'd like to see us publish in, and any other words of wisdom you're willing to pass our way.

You can email or write me directly to let me know what you did or didn't like about this book—as well as what we can do to make our books stronger.

Please note that I cannot help you with technical problems related to the topic of this book, and that due to the high volume of mail I receive, I might not be able to reply to every message.

When you write, please be sure to include this book's title and author as well as your name and phone or email address. I will carefully review your comments and share them with the author and editors who worked on the book.

E-mail: opensource@samspublishing.com

Mail: Mark Taber
Associate Publisher
Sams Publishing
800 East 96th Street
Indianapolis, IN 46240 USA

Reader Services

Visit our website and register this book at www.samspublishing.com/register for convenient access to any updates, downloads, or errata that might be available for this book.

Introduction

Welcome to *openSUSE Linux Unleashed*! This book is going to help you get the most out of your SUSE Linux system, and it includes a fully functional copy of the operating system distribution.

Since SUSE Linux A.G. was acquired by networking pioneer Novell in 2003, more North Americans are becoming familiar with the SUSE Linux distribution that has long been popular in Europe. SUSE Linux offers an incredibly easy installation and a large number of applications that have been tested for stability.

openSUSE marks a new way of doing things for both Novell and SUSE, and this book can help you join the excitement. openSUSE 10.3 is now the fourth SUSE release built and tested through the openSUSE project. Many thousands of people around the world have downloaded and run beta releases and have contributed bug reports, feature wish lists, and postings on the openSUSE mailing list. Novell has committed to opening up the process even further in the future. You'll read more about the openSUSE project in Chapter 1.

Whether you're completely new to Linux or coming to openSUSE Linux from another distribution, you're going to find solid information in a slightly more relaxed style than you're used to in a computer book.

SUSE Linux has always been known as a distribution packed with applications, and openSUSE 10.3 is no exception. This book, as always, includes a complete copy of the distribution on a DVD. The Linux kernel forms the core of a truly modern operating system that can power anything from wrist watches to supercomputers. openSUSE Linux can run on computers running processors ranging from the Intel 486 through 64-bit processors from AMD and Intel.

This book will be especially helpful to the millions using Linux as their everyday desktop system. After first sweeping over the server landscape in the late 1990s, Linux is gaining ground in the desktop arena. More Linux developers have become interested in writing software for the masses of ordinary users. You'll learn how to use several open-source office productivity applications, access the Internet, work with digital music and video, and even play a few games.

openSUSE Linux Unleashed contains everything you need to get started and be productive.

NOTE

This book includes a copy of openSUSE 10.3, but readers owning earlier versions of SUSE Linux should find nearly all the advice contained here useful.

You'll get a little bit of Linux history before jumping into the preparation needed for a successful installation and long-term operation of openSUSE Linux. Then you'll get step-by-step instructions in using the SUSE Linux standby, Yet another Setup Tool (YaST), to install the distribution and configure your hardware. Next, you'll learn about the everyday applications you need to run Linux on the desktop, and then you'll learn about using the Internet, creating websites, and running web and FTP servers.

System administration is the next major topic; in this topic, you'll learn how to manage your files, users, and data, and how to keep your system current by updating it with the same tool you used to install the system.

Finally, because Linux has always been a playground for programmers, we'll cover both the classic tools for creating new programs and the newer scripting languages.

Why Use Linux?

More than a decade has passed since Linus Torvalds put his operating system code on the Internet, and millions have been putting Linux to good use. It's been a while since Linux was viewed as a "toy operating system" used only by geek computer hobbyists.

Big corporations, colleges, governments, school districts, nonprofit organizations, and everyday users are all turning to Linux to boost productivity at a low cost. If you're still thinking about whether to join them, here are a few good reasons:

- Linux puts you in control of your computing environment. Although much of the buzz around "free software" revolves around cost (and we'll get to that argument in a moment), what's really important is that the user is really in charge. Choices abound in the Linux space. If you're not happy with the way one application works, there's usually something else out there that can make you happy. Most applications are also endlessly customizable, so if there's an annoying feature included as a default, you can always turn it off or modify its functioning.

- Linux is inexpensive to install, run, and update. Unlike proprietary operating systems, you can take the DVD from this book and install openSUSE on as many computers as you need to. Configure Linux individually for your file servers, routers, web servers, and desktops. All these systems will run crash-free with little maintenance required and (if you like) automated updates that don't even need user intervention to install.

- Linux is ready for the desktop. Nearly everything you can do on a Windows machine can be done on openSUSE, from creating professional office documents and presentations to getting files on the Internet. It's also not that hard to get used to after you've made the switch. When Grandma is running Linux, she's less likely to see error messages and crashing programs, too.

- Linux is a rock-solid server performer. The operating system (OS) made its first impression as a fast, secure, stable, scalable, and robust server OS. The current kernel easily handles multiprocessor machines, gigabytes of system memory, and terabytes of data. Most enterprise-level applications have Linux versions. Although this book does not cover the Novell Open Enterprise Server (OES), openSUSE serves as a proving ground for new enterprise applications to be included in OES.

- Linux thrives in a variety of environments. Linux drives many personal digital assistants, laptops, desktops, and specialized computers. You can put your ancient 486 processor to work as a router or file server with openSUSE. It also runs on AMD 64-bit Opteron processors, and did so for a year before 64-bit Windows XP was released.
- Linux offers a royalty-free development platform for several operating systems. Because of the open-source development model and the high-quality, free tools available to developers, anyone from 13-year-old budding programmers to massive development shops can produce quality software relatively inexpensively.
- Linux now offers big player support. Although the Linux community is still the best place to go for support when things go wrong, the presence of IBM, Novell, and other big companies in the support space can make even the most uneasy bean counter relax a little.

Who This Book Is For

This book will get you going on openSUSE Linux. When Novell began the openSUSE project, this distribution became targeted for the computer enthusiast and personal user. The contents are aimed at the intermediate to advanced user, but even the newest Linux users should find much useful information, especially in Part 1. The end of each chapter offers pointers to excellent resources on the World Wide Web (WWW) to keep you current and help you delve deeper into the subject areas covered here.

The YaST installer is better than most at identifying and configuring hardware, but you should have at least some familiarity with your system and the types of hardware it contains before installing any Linux system. Knowing your way around the command line never hurts either. This book will help you gain and refine those skills and show you how to learn more about your computer, Linux, and the applications included in the distribution.

System administrators of all experience levels will be able to use this book to install, set up, and run common network services, including the Apache web server, FTP servers, and Samba for cross-platform networking. You'll also get comfortable with using YaST to update your systems.

Programmers will learn about the tools available to help them be productive, with summaries of many professional-grade text editors, integrated development environments, and web programming languages and tools.

What This Book Contains

openSUSE Linux Unleashed is organized into six parts, covering installation and configuration, everyday usage, Internet access and usage, basic and advanced system administration, and programming. The idea is to work from the very basics of using the OS into more difficult and advanced tasks. With the accompanying DVD, you have everything you need to get started.

New Linux users will find the first three parts most helpful. You'll get valuable information on the following topics:

- An overview of SUSE Linux.
- Getting help through the printed and online documentation provided with openSUSE, through the Internet, and through Linux User Groups (LUGs).
- Planning for your installation by looking at the tasks you have for your computer, and then examining your hardware.
- A detailed walk-through of the installation process.
- Preserving an existing Windows installation for dual-boot launching.
- Configuring and using the X Window System, the Linux graphical interface, and the two primary desktop environments for Linux—KDE and GNOME.
- Making friends with your command line.
- Printing in Linux.
- Running OpenOffice and other productivity tools.
- Accessing the Internet.
- Managing email, Usenet, and file transfer with both FTP and peer-to-peer protocols.
- Playing music, video, and games.
- Burning CDs and DVDs.
- Turning your PC into a personal video recorder like TiVo.
- Creating your own websites and weblogs.

Parts 4 and 5 are about system administration. New users should at least review Part 4 to learn how to manage data and users and use YaST and other tools to keep the system updated. Professional system administrators can go deeper, with material on the following:

- Managing the boot process.
- Securing your system and network.
- Managing the kernel and its modules.
- Setting up networks.
- Working with Samba to network Linux and Windows systems together.
- Running the Apache web server.
- Managing Internet domains.

Part 6 covers programming in SUSE Linux. You'll learn about these topics:

- Tools for the C, C++, and Java programmer.
- Managing databases and using them in programming.
- The LAMP web programming suite: Linux, Apache, MySQL, and the scripting languages Perl, Python, and PHP.

The appendixes describe the various permutations of SUSE Linux offered by Novell and deliver an expanded list of Internet resources for learning about the topics introduced here.

Conventions Used in This Book

openSUSE Linux Unleashed is intended to be as complete as possible, but with all the applications included in the distribution, it's impossible to cover every option. You'll find a lot of lists and tables to help you through, however.

Where there are graphical tools to use, you'll find screenshots giving you visual cues to the steps you're working through.

To help you better understand code listing samples and the command-line interface, several formatting techniques are used to show input and responses. For example, where you have to type something in, the typeface looks like this:

```
ls
```

If typed input is in response to a prompt, what you type will also be in bold:

```
Delete files? [y/n]  y
```

Words in commands that are between brackets are placeholders. If you see

```
<username>
```

enter the username at that spot.

The following elements give you useful tidbits of information that relate to the surrounding text.

NOTE

Notes give you additional information that may help you perform a task, give you some ancillary detail, or point to another spot in the book, or online, for more information about the current topic.

Longer notes, or sidebars, will help you with specific tasks, related technologies, and events on the horizon.

TIP

A tip will have a timesaving technique, a special insight, or some bit of information designed to make you a smarter user.

CAUTION

Cautions will warn you about potential mishaps or steps to take before doing something potentially dangerous, such as running a command, editing configurations, or choosing a setting.

You should know that everything in this book was developed using openSUSE Linux and open-source tools.

As you work through this book and learn more about the OS and its tools, always keep in mind the admonition SUSE Linux developers try to remind us of at the end of every installation: "Have a lot of fun!"

PART I

Installation and Configuration

IN THIS PART

CHAPTER 1

Welcome to openSUSE

IN THIS CHAPTER

And it is a fine place to begin! Whether you are brand new to Linux or moving from another distribution, you will find openSUSE easy to use and powerful to work with. *openSUSE Linux Unleashed* is here to help you get the most out of this distribution. This chapter will give you a brief overview of openSUSE, with hints on how to use the rest of this book.

What Is openSUSE?

The first thing anyone wants to ask is, "Where does this SUSE thing come from, why is it written in all uppercase letters , and how do I pronounce it?" These are all fair questions.

- The Gesellschaft für Software-und System-Entwicklung (Corporation for Software and System Development) was founded in 1992 in Nuremberg, Germany, and it released its first distribution of the Linux kernel and associated software a year later. SuSE began publishing its distribution in English in 1997; it opened an office in Oakland, California at that time.
- The spelling, as you can see, is not derived from some marketer's branding idea. It really is the corporate acronym. However, since being acquired by Novell in 2004, the distribution is now called SUSE (no lower-case letters) Linux, and the acronym no longer stands for anything.
- In German, there are no silent letters, and the letter E is almost always short (as in "the"), so the company's name is pronounced "Sue-suh." More often than not, though, you'll hear it referred to as "Susie" or some other variation.

But what is Linux? More properly known as GNU/Linux, it is an operating system born in 1991, when Linus Torvalds, then a computer science student at the University of Helsinki, wanted to run a variation of Unix on his home computer. At that time, Unix ran only on big workstations with lots of power and memory, not Intel-based personal computers. Using tools from the GNU (GNU's Not-Unix) project, Torvalds was able to port a usable operating system to PCs. He then made the source code available on the Internet, licensed under the GNU General Public License (GPL).

As a result of that generosity, Linux now runs on nearly every platform and architecture, from cell phones and personal digital assistants to Intel- and Macintosh-based PCs to mainframes and workstations running global enterprises.

openSUSE is one of dozens of distributions of Linux. What does this mean? The Linux kernel is really just the central piece of any distribution. Each distribution bundles different pieces of compatible software (most, if not all, licensed under the GNU GPL or another free software license), an installation program, perhaps some documentation, and some level of support.

TIP

Want to learn more about other distributions? See http://distrowatch.com/ for listings of more than 300 distinct offerings.

SUSE offers a variety of versions of its core distribution to meet differing needs. This book focuses on openSUSE Linux 10.3, which Novell calls the "community supported" product targeted to home and home-business users. This is the version now created by the openSUSE project, which launched in August 2005. The next sections include descriptions of the other versions available.

All these versions use the openSUSE install program, YaST (Yet another Setup Tool), to install, configure, and update your Linux installation. Besides being one of the tools that makes the SUSE distributions unique, YaST is such a useful and pervasive tool that you'll find mention of it in nearly every chapter in this book. YaST simplifies nearly all your administrative tasks: managing users and groups, updating applications, installing new hardware, and maintaining security. YaST also manages your printers through the Common Unix Printing System (CUPS), which contains drivers for more than 1,000 printers.

openSUSE Linux

openSUSE Linux and its predecessors have always been well known for having the biggest distribution among the "majors." Hundreds of open-source applications are bundled with openSUSE—so many that it takes six CD-ROMs (or one DVD) to hold them all. Nonetheless, consider this: If you have instant access to all these programs, you are less likely to be a prisoner of your installed applications. If you find an application installed with openSUSE that isn't doing the job right, chances are there's another application you can install that will be more to your liking.

If your business needs change and you need some other software tool to get things done, odds are you don't have to pull out your checkbook to get the functionality you need. You just need to fire up YaST and search for the appropriate tool, and in minutes, you're ready to go.

Both Unix and Linux began as systems oriented toward the command line (or *shell*), and the command line is often the fastest and easiest way to get computing tasks done. But just as DOS begat Windows, Unix begat the X Window System. Proprietary X servers later begat the XFree86 project, which became the default GUI for Linux systems. In 2004, the X Consortium, which originally oversaw the development of X, revived and put out its own free server. SUSE Linux opted to use this (referred to as X.org) as the basis for its X Server beginning with v9.1.

Sitting on top of most copies of X these days is a desktop environment: the K Desktop Environment (KDE) or the GNU Network Object Model Environment (GNOME—pronounce the G). Both provide the same sort of look and feel and functionality of proprietary desktops, but each has its own personality. Historically, the SUSE team has been involved in developing KDE practically from the beginning, and so KDE has been the default SUSE desktop, although GNOME was always an option. With openSUSE Linux 10.3, you can choose your preferred desktop. You'll learn more about X, KDE, and GNOME in Chapter 6, "Launching Your Desktop."

openSUSE also comes with two complete office suites (OpenOffice.org and KOffice), two minisuites (GNOMEOffice, with a word processor, database, and spreadsheet; and SoftMaker Office, with a word processor and spreadsheet), two industrial strength open-source relational database management systems (PostgreSQL and MySQL), two financial programs (GnuCash and KMyMoney), two personal information managers (Ximian Evolution and Kontact), and just about everything else you need to be productive.

When you consider that the Internet largely runs on Unix, there should be no surprise that you can find on your openSUSE DVD just about anything you need to connect with or do work on the Internet. In addition, many functions have a selection of tools: multiple web browsers (all the browsers you've heard of, except for Internet Explorer, and many you haven't), email clients, chat and instant messaging tools, and newsreaders (for both Usenet and RSS feeds). Web developers and designers also have two web-page creators in Bluefish and Quanta Plus.

Programmers at all skill and experience levels will find almost all the necessary tools for their craft. These tools include text editors galore, starting with the venerable GNU Emacs and vim and including many others of more recent vintage. The tools also include the GNU Compiler Collection (gcc), support for Perl, Python, Ruby, PHP, Java (and just about any other language you can think of), and at least two integrated development environments (IDEs) in KDevelop and Eclipse. You can even manage your large projects with the Concurrent Versioning System (CVS) or Subversion.

Generally, openSUSE is updated with point releases twice a year, but because applications get revised with bug fixes, security fixes, and feature enhancements all the time, you can stay on the cutting edge using package management tools. Many developers package their applications using the Red Hat Package Management System (RPM). SUSE has always used this method to build its distribution, and many SUSE-specific RPMs have been written. Use the openSUSE Online Updater or the Smart Package Manager to keep your system current.

With openSUSE, you can create many types of systems: a networked file server, a Web server, a DNS server, a mail server, a router, or a plain old desktop workstation.

You can string together several machines to make your own super computer, known as a Beowulf cluster. The choice is yours.

The openSUSE.org Wiki

On August 9, 2005, Novell announced the openSUSE project at the LinuxWorld conference in San Francisco. For the first time, the SUSE community participated in the testing and development process for SUSE Linux. Novell's stated goal in this venture was to make it easy for anyone to get access to what they call "the world's most usable Linux distribution" and to welcome new open-source developers into the SUSE fold.

The openSUSE process offers a freely downloadable distribution that contains only open-source software, with the ability to add non–open-source packages (like the Java Runtime Engine) separately. In addition, openSUSE serves as the basis for the boxed, retail version of SUSE Linux, which is the traditional distribution.

To participate in the project and get the latest installable version of openSUSE, visit www.opensuse.org and click the download link (see Figure 1.1).

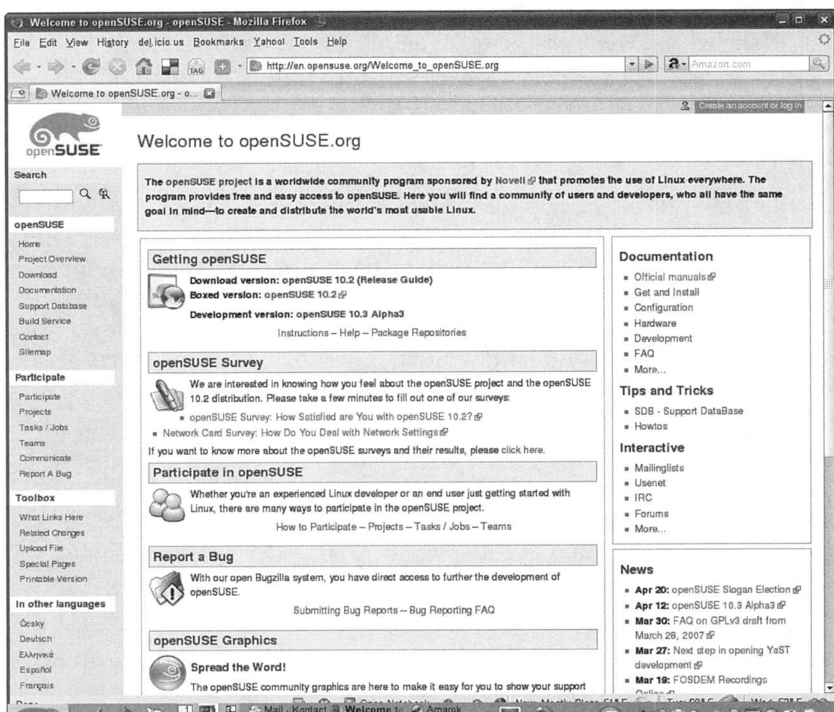

FIGURE 1.1 The openSUSE.org website, available in several languages, lets you participate in the openSUSE Linux development process.

This site contains useful content, in addition to the latest release and the latest test version of openSUSE.

On the openSUSE.org site, you can learn more about the distribution. You can view official documentation and read posted articles from the Novell website and elsewhere on the Web. Other things you can do include viewing the roadmap for the next release, subscribing to the openSUSE discussion/support mailing lists, and peruse the FAQs. One of the more interesting aspects of openSUSE.org is that it is a wiki. This means that you—and every other user of the page—can submit content to any page on the site. You are especially encouraged to add content to the Documentation page, so that as you learn more about openSUSE, you can share that knowledge with other users. openSUSE.org uses the same engine (MediaWiki) that powers the most famous wiki of them all, Wikipedia. You'll learn more about wikis in Chapter 16, "Collaborating with Others."

Users will also be the driving force in future development. Like Red Hat's Fedora Core project, openSUSE will be the place where new features and applications first appear. What works will then appear in the regularly updated boxed version of SUSE Linux. In addition, where appropriate, Novell will also add features in the corporate SUSE Linux Enterprise Desktop (SLED) and SUSE Linux Enterprise Server (SLES).

The openSUSE Install Program

There are several ways to install openSUSE, but the easiest is to boot from the DVD that accompanies this book. Your initial install is not the only thing you can do with this DVD. You can use it to do the following:

- Test your computer's memory—This test confirms that your installed RAM chips are working properly.
- Rescue a troubled system—If you cannot boot your computer at all, booting from the DVD gives you access to an emergency command line that can help you access your files and troubleshoot the problem.

File Systems in openSUSE

After several generations of using the ReiserFS file system written by Hans Reiser and maintained by the Namesys team as the default file system, openSUSE Linux 10.3 installs ext3 by default. This decision was made thanks to ext3's improved speed, scalability, and a combination of stagnation in ReiserFS development and the incompatibility of Reiser4 with earlier versions of ReiserFS.

By default, openSUSE uses the ext3. file system. ReiserFS, ext3, and other journaling file systems make crash recovery much simpler. When changes (such as creating, deleting, saving, or executing a file) are about to be made to the file system, ext3 writes this information in a journal file that exists on the disk. Should the system crash before the change is finished, the repair utility need only search the journal, rather than the entire disk surface, to locate the problem. This makes it easier to repair and preserve your data.

What if you don't like ext3? No problem. The install program will create volumes in ext2, ReiserFS , the IBM Journaling File System (JFS), and XFS, which was originally developed for the SGI Irix. You will learn more about file systems in Chapter 18, "Managing Files, Volumes, and Drives."

64-Bit openSUSE

Personal computers are getting more powerful as time goes on. A decade ago, the 32-bit microprocessor, and the new operating systems that could support it, were the focus of attention. The transition from 16-bit processors, like the Intel 80286 and its predecessors, to 32-bit processors and the graphical operating systems that supported them, was rapid and changed our lives. These processors could support four gigabytes of memory, which was just a phenomenal amount in the days when RAM was measured in megabytes. We got genuine multitasking, prettier interfaces—and yes, the ability to think about running Unix-like systems on PCs.

We are now standing at the dawn of the next revolution in personal computing; 64-bit processors have come down in price to the point where it's quite possible that your next computer will have one. Servers have been running 64-bit processors for some time now. Since September 2003, AMD has been selling 64-bit Opteron and Athlon chips for ordinary PCs, and the Apple G5 is a 64-bit processor.

What does this mean? A couple of things for the average user. First, your system will (theoretically) support up to 16 million gigabytes of RAM. In practice, however, your system will probably be limited to a mere 256 terabytes or less. This still means, however, that applications will run much faster. Chances are they will also be larger, because they can now have more code running at the same speed.

The Linux kernel has supported 64-bit processors from the beginning, and SUSE Linux has run on the x86_64 architecture since version 9.0. If you install the 64-bit version of openSUSE (not included with this book's media), nearly all the applications you install will be the 64-bit versions. openSUSE will still run 32-bit applications as well, but you are a little more likely to run into problems. Some of the known problems will be mentioned in Notes in this book.

Getting Help: Documentation and Other Sources

With more than 1,000 programs included in the distribution, even a book of this size cannot cover everything in your copy of openSUSE.

There are plenty of places to go to learn more about Linux and help you troubleshoot problems with applications. Many of these are included in the references at the end of this and the other chapters of this book.

Printed Documentation and the openSUSE Help Center

SUSE is one of the few software companies anywhere that still provides printed manuals that try to help users learn the product beyond installation. Buying the boxed version of

SUSE Linux gives you two thick books, the *Administration Guide* and the *User Guide*. Although you can sometimes tell that they have been translated from German, these books have a fairly easy-to-read style that will get you using the product in short order.

Both manuals were also converted into HTML pages and integrated into the electronic openSUSE Help Center. This is a boon in two ways: You don't have to rummage around the office to find the books, and you can run a full-text search of both books for the information you're looking for.

The online versions of the manuals are updated regularly, so check for updates at least a couple times a year to be sure you have the latest version.

Searching the Help Center

Open the Help Center by typing **`susehelp`** from the shell, or click the life preserver icon in KDE or GNOME. Putter around the Table of Contents to see what is included, or click the Search tab to find something specific. Help-Center search uses the ht://dig engine used on many websites (see Figure 1.2).

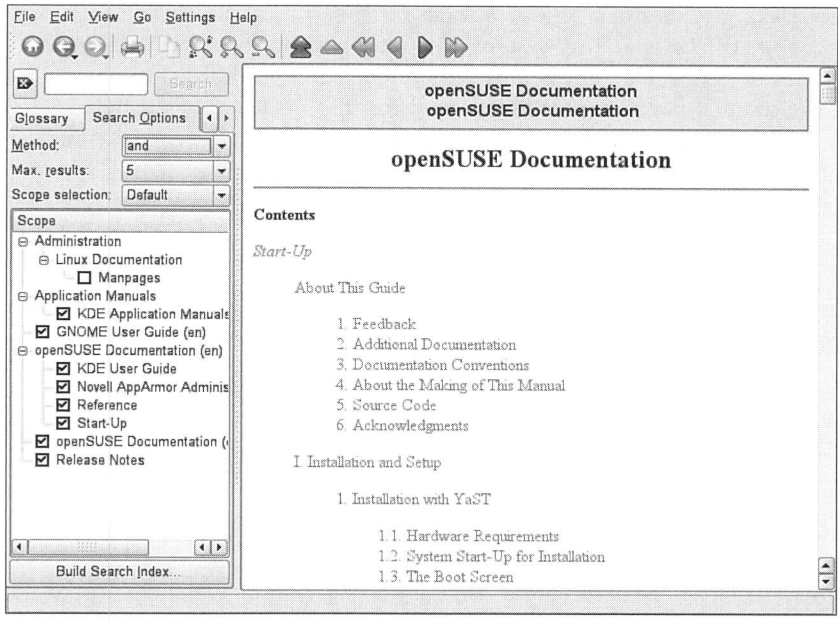

FIGURE 1.2 The openSUSE Help Center offers the full text of the SUSE Administration Guide and User Guide. It's searchable, too.

The first time you want to run a search, click Create Search Index first so that the engine has something to look at. You'll see a set of online books to index; check them all so that you can access everything. If you happen to be on a slower machine, results may come faster if you just index the two guides. Click the Search tab, then click Build Search Index.

The list of available documentation appears in the Search Scope column, with its status (OK or Missing). Check the boxes of the items you want to index, and click Build Index to create the index.

The search screen is much like an advanced web search screen where you can select what to search, how many results to return, and how to treat multiple word searches. By default, if you ask Help Center to find the terms "spam" and "filter," the engine will search for documents with both words in it (a Boolean AND). If you want to find either term, choose OR in the Method box. The default search scope includes the two manuals, the release notes and the KDE Application Manuals. To search all the components, choose All. If you think your answer may be in an info or man page (more on these later), check these boxes, too; the Scope Selection box will switch to Custom automatically. Click Search to find your answer. Results will appear in the right window. Click a hyperlink to see the pertinent article.

Man and Info Pages

One of the earliest forms of online help was the humble Unix man page.

In the early days of Unix, the manual came as a series of three-ring binders sent out from Bell Labs with each copy of the operating system. The manual would expand with each new tool or command included. At some point, someone got the bright idea to create electronic files of the manual pages so that everyone running the OS could get help without having to roam the lab to find the page they needed. This is how the man(ual) page was born, along with the `man` command.

Man pages are compressed text files, located in `/usr/share/doc`. They are usually tersely written (usually by the application's programmers), with information listed under particular categories specified by convention. These categories include a command reference, a summary of what each option/switch does, and the author of the page and/or the program. Occasionally, there are even known bug statements.

To learn more about using the `man` program to read man pages, type `man man` at the command line. When you press Enter, a paging program called groff will load and display the page. Press the spacebar to scroll from screen to screen. When you're done reading, press the q key to return to the shell prompt.

More complex programs can tax the man page format, so the info help format was created. These pages, created with a version of the TeX document formatting system, include a hierarchical structure, hypertext links for easy navigation between documents, and keyboard and mouse navigational tools. The first time you use info (often when looking for help in the Emacs text editor), it can be a little overwhelming, but it is not too hard to deal with after you have a feel for it. Read the info tutorial (type `info info`) to learn more.

Many man pages are on the web, and you can search both man and info pages in the openSUSE Help Center. Start looking for man pages at the Linux Documentation Project. Then try going to http://www.google.com/linux to search.

TIP

Use apropos and whatis to find what you need. If you know what you want to do but are not sure about the tool to use, type `apropos <keyword>` at the shell prompt. Apropos will search the NAME section of each man page (which includes a brief description of the tool's purpose) and display a list of programs and commands that may help. It's not foolproof, but even if you don't find exactly the right tool, you may get on the road to finding what you really need.

The *whatis* program does the inverse of *apropos*. Suppose you couldn't remember what the acronym "bash" stood for. Type `whatis bash` and then you'll know!

openSUSE Online Support

The openSUSE support database at http://en.opensuse.org/SDB:SDB is a great resource for getting help.

When you're trying to find a solution for a problem, use the Search box in the upper left corner of the Support Database site. You can also view and search by Categories and view the most recently updated articles on the History page.

NOTE

If you can't find a page listed here, check the http://www.opensuse.org and http://www.novell.com/linux home pages to see where it may have moved to.

The Documentation page links to some interesting HOWTO documents, showing you step-by-step how to accomplish many tasks, from partitioning your hard drive to comparing HTML editors to encrypting email.

Novell also offers what they call "Cool Solutions Communities" for the Enterprise Server and Desktop products on their website. This is an area where assorted experts offer tips, most of which are helpful to openSUSE Linux users, on a regular basis. This is located at http://www.novell.com/coolsolutions; select either the Desktop or Data Center categories.

The Linux Documentation Project

The place to start for more user-friendly guides to Linux tools and applications is the Linux Documentation Project. Frequently Asked Questions (FAQ) lists, HOWTO pages, and more detailed guides to applications are written, reviewed, and edited by a team of volunteers and compiled at the LDP site, which is www.tldp.org.

Because all the documents there are formatted in DocBook XML, everything is presented in a variety of formats; at least one should meet your needs. Site search is powered by Google and is right on the home page, so finding items related to your question is quick and easy. You can also easily see the most recently updated documents or just browse through categories to educate yourself.

The howto packages included on the openSUSE disk are not updated often, but they can be helpful. They are not installed by default, so if you want them, use YaST.

The openSUSE Mailing Lists

The openSUSE project sponsors 34 electronic mailing lists in multiple languages to allow users to help each other with problems and questions. The general list in English, opensuse, generates some 150 messages per day on all topics, but most lists are more specialized. Read descriptions of all the lists, with links to the list archives, at http://en.opensuse.org/Communicate. Each list has a mailto link to subscribe to that list. You must subscribe to a list to post a question.

The list archives, located at http://lists.opensuse.org are searchable via the Search box. This is a gigantic improvement over the old SUSE list archives. You can also browse the monthly archives, which are sorted by thread. To search just suse-linux-e, change the site to lists.opensuse.org/opensuse.

TIP

Before posting your question, also check the openSUSE Bugzilla database at http://bugzilla.novell.com for a solution. See "Filing a Bug in openSUSE's Bug Tracker" in the next section for information on how to do this.

Because these lists are high traffic, make sure to check the archives before posting a question yourself. Chances are that whatever you are experiencing, someone else is, too. To get the best help from the list, keep these things in mind:

- When you ask a question, describe any problem as specifically as possible. Include pertinent sections of log files, along with the error messages you received.
- Describe your efforts to solve the problem. "I've searched the Help Center and the archives. I saw the discussion about a similar problem and tried the solution, but it didn't work (or here's why my problem is different from that one)."
- Be patient! Although some questions can be answered in minutes, that's not the norm. If people don't respond, wait a few days (if you can) before asking again. The person who has your answer just may be busy at that moment. If you can't wait for a solution, try another list, or contact your local Linux User Group (see the next section).
- After you have asked a question, hang around for a while. Perhaps you can answer someone else's question—what goes around comes around.

There is also a SUSE Users Yahoo Group. Sign up or view the archives at http://tech.groups.yahoo.com/group/opensuse-users/.

Filing a Bug in openSUSE's Bug Tracker

How often have you run into a problem that might be a bug, and asked yourself whether the software company is aware of the problem, and on the road to fixing it? With openSUSE, now you can check. Novell has opened up its SUSE bug database, Bugzilla; if you run into trouble, you can search the database, and if necessary, submit the problem directly to Bugzilla.

Searching for Existing Bugs

Before filing a bug, you should confirm that the problem is not already known. It may even be good to check before consulting the mailing lists.

1. Go to http://bugzilla.novell.com.
2. Log in.
3. Click Search Reports.
4. You can search Open, Closed (unfixed), or All bugs with the Status drop-down menu. Select openSUSE Linux 10.3 from the Product menu, and your search terms. Click Search (or press Enter) to search the database.

   The Advanced Search page offers a full page of options for narrowing or expanding your basic search.
5. The Bug List page appears. You'll see the Severity, Priority, Type and the person assigned to fix the bug on this page, along with a one-line summary of each bug. Click the ID number to get more detailed information about any bug.
6. The top of the detailed bug screen recaps the information from the list. To see what's actually going on, scroll down to the Comments section. You'll see the initial description of the bug, along with any further comments from the developers and/or other users. Depending on when the bug was filed, there may be helpful information that may apply to your problem. You can reply to any comment with relevant information or add a new comment at the bottom of the page. If a bug is exactly (or pretty near) your problem, you can have any future comments emailed to you; click the Add me to the CC list of this bug box just under the Comment window.
7. If you want to keep looking through the bug list after looking at one screen, click the Show Last Search Results link that appears at both the top and bottom of the bug detail page.
8. If you find your bug, ideally there will be a solution (or at least a suggestion for one). Try it. If it works, return to the bug and let people know. If it didn't, post a comment explaining what happened. This will help the team get the bug fixed.

Filing a New Bug

If you don't find a bug report that matches your problem, you can add your bug to the database. This is a three-step process.

1. Click Enter a Bug at the Bugzilla home page. You must have a Novell account to file a bug. If you are not yet logged in to the site, you will be asked to log in. To create an account, you will be asked for some personal information, and identify a username and password. This account will be valid at all Novell sites requiring a password.
2. Select openSUSE Linux 10.3 from the Product page. Click Submit.
3. Describe your bug. Read the Bug Writing Guidelines linked to from this page, then describe your bug as clearly as possible. Click Submit Report when you are finished.

Linux User Groups

When you really want a live, knowledgeable human being to help you with a problem or teach you something, most users have just two choices: hire a consultant for big bucks or find your closest friend who knows something about computers. Problem is, that tech-savvy friend is probably pretty well versed in working with one or another of the proprietary operating systems produced on the West Coast, but might not know a lot about Unix or Linux. What do you do then?

Fortunately, if you live reasonably close to a decent-sized population center or town with a college campus, there is likely to be a gaggle of Linux-savvy people just a few mouse clicks away—your local Linux User Group (LUG). These people usually meet once a month for speakers, demonstrations, occasional door prizes, and general camaraderie. Most active LUGs have websites, and many have email lists where problems get solved, equipment gets traded, and opinions about various technical and Linux-related issues are shared. If you are slightly intimidated by the thought of installing Linux on your computer, LUGs frequently hold "install fests" where experienced folks will install openSUSE or another distribution (your choice) on your system and give you pointers along the way. As with most everything Linux, this all comes free of charge.

Now you can't just pick up a phone book and call the LUG office to get started, but it is not especially hard to find one either. You can check your daily newspaper for meeting notices (these are often found on the business pages) or call your public library for information. Some communities still have specialty computer magazines left over from the tech boom days that list user groups of all kinds.

The fastest way to find a LUG is probably online. Linux Online hosts a directory at http://www.linux.org/groups/. They are organized geographically, so you can browse through the. Every group has an email contact, and many have a URL listed. If a website is not listed here, do not assume the group doesn't have one. Searching is an option. Both Google and Yahoo have Linux User Group directories, but rather than sort through a complicated directory structure, just type "<yourtown> Linux User Group" into the regular search box.

References

Each chapter in this book includes a reference section with links to additional or related information about the subject of the chapter. Use it to build a set of bookmarks to help you learn more about Linux in general, and openSUSE in particular.

- http://www.ibm.com/linux—This is the Linux portal at IBM, which has news, reports, and white papers related to this important Linux player. Check the SUSE Linux link under "Linux Distributors" for material related to IBM support for SUSE Linux products.
- http://en.opensuse.org—This is the English-language home of the openSUSE project. Download the latest version for testing and use. Sign up for a mailing list and contribute to the openSUSE wiki. For other languages, start at http://www.opensuse.org.
- http://www.novell.com/linux—This is the English-language home of openSUSE's commercial siblings, SUSE Linux Enterprise Server and Desktop. It offers news, downloads, and support.
- http://en.opensuse.org/SDB:SDB—This is a direct link to the openSUSE support database.
- http://www.namesys.com—Learn about the ReiserFS file system here.
- http://www.tldp.org/—This is the Linux Documentation Project. This is where to go for general Linux questions and to learn about many of the applications included in your openSUSE distribution.
- http://www.linux.org/groups —This is Linux Online's global list of Linux User Groups.
- http://www.google.com/linux—This is The Google Linux-specific search page.
- http://linuxgazette.net/—*The Linux Gazette*, "making Linux just a little more fun," is oriented toward new Linux users. Ask The Answer Gang your question.
- http://linuxjournal.com—The *Linux Journal* is the oldest monthly print magazine covering all things Linux. Most of the archives are available only to subscribers, but there's much valuable content for everyone on the site.
- http://www.linux-mag.com—This is the US-based *Linux Magazine*. Print articles appear online 60 days after its release. They have weekly email newsletters too.
- http://searchenterpriselinux.com—This site is focused on enterprise Linux, but is still a good resource for Linux news.
- http://www.linuxpromagazine.com—This is the Germany-based *Linux Magazine,* a print magazine featuring a monthly distribution disk.
- http://www.lwn.net—This is Linux Weekly News, one of the oldest sources of Linux news online.
- http://www.newsforge.com—This is "the online newspaper for Linux and Open Source."
- http://www.tech.groups.yahoo..com/group/opensuse-users—This is the SUSE Users Yahoo Group page.

- http://distrowatch.com—News and information on hundreds of Unix distributions, including openSUSE.
- http://bugzilla.novel.com—The SUSE Linux bug database.

CHAPTER 2

Preparing to Install openSUSE

IN THIS CHAPTER

- Planning Your openSUSE Installation
- System Requirements
- References

It is easier to buy a Linux PC today than it was a few years ago, but manufacturers still don't see the need to preload Linux, even if they are strong Linux proponents (such as IBM and Novell). So the odds are very good that you will have to install openSUSE yourself, especially if you want to use it as your everyday desktop system.

Even if you are not planning to install openSUSE on 10 different servers and 47 desktops, changing operating systems is not a matter to be taken lightly. You should give as much consideration to the questions of meeting hardware requirements, whether you want to dual-boot with another operating system, what applications to install, and how your new openSUSE system relates to the other machines on your network as any Chief Information Officer (CIO) would.

If you are approaching this installation with some trepidation, relax! Although some of the horror stories of the bygone past may have been true, your experience installing openSUSE is likely to be a pleasant memory later on down the road. If you have a typical system with reasonably modern hardware, installing should be a snap. To make that even more likely, it is important to plan ahead. This chapter and the next two will help you make an easy transition.

In this chapter, we will think carefully about all the things that you need to consider before installing openSUSE. We will go over the minimum and recommended system requirements for using openSUSE and try to help you avoid some of the potential driver-related problems with some peripherals.

Finally, there are the questions of partitioning your hard drive(s), which you should definitely think about before starting to install. openSUSE is very flexible and can meet most any computing need you have. This chapter is about figuring out what those needs are.

Planning Your openSUSE Installation

Even if you are installing openSUSE on a single computer (which is a basic assumption in this book), there may be some business-related considerations to make before getting started with openSUSE.

If you know ahead of time what you need and want from your new system, you will save time. You can always make changes down the road.

The most important consideration is: What do you want to do with your openSUSE system? Will it run just the Apache web server or will it be your network file server? Will the computer be connected to the Internet? If so, how? Do you want to launch a web-hosting business? Will it be just a toy to practice on, or a full-time tool?

Will you have to access Windows files on other computers or on the same machine? If you have some other operating system (OS) now performing the task(s) you want Linux to do, you should think about why you want to make a change.

There is a cost in time and training to migrating, although in most cases, Linux makes that cost very worthwhile.

TIP

As you plan for your install, keep a notebook handy to write things down as you think of them, and always keep it around to make notes as things happen while you're running Linux. Text files typed into the machine are handy, as are sticky notes. But when something breaks and you can't get to those electronic notes, you'll be happy you have something to refer to.

I got this tip from Matt Welsh's *Running Linux* when I was starting out, and it is still one of the best tips I ever got.

Another thing to consider is what to do with your existing OS. Later on in this chapter, you'll learn about setting up your machine to dual boot Windows and openSUSE.

This is an easy thing to do, assuming you have the space. Before you decide, though, make a list of all the things you use your computer for and the applications you use. Look at the list of applications in your Windows Start menu to be thorough; it's easy to forget some of the things that are second nature to use. Try to find a Linux counterpart. Start with the list at http://www.linuxrsp.ru/win-lin-soft/ and match the Linux applications to your Windows list.

To get you started, look at Table 2.1. The list of applications features some of the best-known applications for their category, but the list is not comprehensive by any means.

TABLE 2.1 Selected Computing Tasks and Linux Applications

Task	Windows Application	Linux Application
Browsing the Web	Seamonkey, Flock, Opera Internet Explorer, Firefox,	Mozilla Firefox, Seamonkey, Opera, Konqueror, Galeon, Epiphany, Flock
Budget stretching	Quicken, Money, QuickBooks	Gnucash, KMyMoney
Developing websites	Dreamweaver, FrontPage, HomeSite	Quanta, Bluefish, emacs
Editing photos and graphics	Photoshop, Paint Shop Pro	The GIMP
Editing plain text	Notepad/WordPad, jEdit, NoteTab	KWrite, Emacs, XEmacs, vim, jedit, gedit
Number crunching	Excel, Paradox OpenOffice.org Calc	OpenOffice.org Calc, KSpread, Gnumeric
Opening and creating Zip archives	WinZip, ZipMagic, PKZip	Ark, GNOME File Roller, command-line
Playing MP3 and other multimedia content	WinAmp, MusicMatch, RealPlayer, Windows Media Player	XMMS, Xine, Kaffeine, Amarok, RealPlayer, rhythmbox, JuK
Playing RealAudio streaming audio files	RealPlayer	RealPlayer (Helix Community version), XMMS
Reading and writing email	Outlook/Outlook Express, Mozilla Thunderbird, Eudora, Pegasus Mail	KMail, Mozilla Thunderbird, Evolution, Sylpheed
Word processing	Word, WordPerfect, OpenOffice.org, Writer, Abiword	OpenOffice.org Writer, Abiword, KWord
Managing personal information (contacts, calendar)	Outlook, Lotus Notes, Groupwise	Evolution, Kontact, Groupwise

System Requirements

The first thing to know and understand is that the days of worrying whether your current hardware setup will run Linux are largely over. openSUSE will run on most any Intel-based hardware, including PowerPCs and Itanium chips. Novell/SUSE promises full support on anything Pentium-classed, including Celerons and AMD K5 processors.

Two ends of the aging process present difficulties; aging 486 machines and brand-new machines with 64-bit processors and the high-performance gaming video card released just last week may have problems (though perhaps fewer than you might think).

NOTE

Do you have a 64-bit processor on your PC? See the 64-bit openSUSE section in Chapter 1, "Welcome to openSUSE."

Hardware problems generally stem from vendors not writing Linux drivers for their equipment. This is distinctly true for laptop manufacturers. Because of Linux's recent gain in popularity, the biggest hardware vendors are beginning to support Linux with their hardware, either providing drivers directly or providing open-source developers with software development kits (SDKs) for writing open-source drivers. The drivers often wind up directly in the Linux kernel for all distributions.

SUSE recommends three basic system requirements for running openSUSE Linux 10.3:

- Processor—Pentium 1–4; AMD Duron, Athlon, Athlon XP, Athlon MP, or Athlon 64; Intel Celeron or EMT 64
- Main memory—At least 256MB; 512MB recommended
- Hard disk—At least 500MB; 2.5GB recommended for standard system

Before installing openSUSE, you should spend some time comparing your existing hardware with the openSUSE Hardware pages at http://en.opensuse.org/Hardware.

The openSUSE Hardware Compatibility List is a well organized list of hardware, organized by function. You can see comments from other users on openSUSE's overall compatibility with server, desktop and laptop systems, and check a variety of peripheral components against the list. There is no hardware-specific search, but you can use the site search located at the left side of each page to get information about your hardware.

TIP

If you are migrating from Microsoft Windows and are unsure of the details (manufacturer, type, and so on) of your hardware, go to the Device Manager to find out. Right-click My Computer and choose Properties from the context menu. Go to the Hardware tab and click Device Manager. Select the system at the top of the list. Click Print to get a list of all your devices.

This list can be quite lengthy. For something a little more configurable, try downloading the shareware product mvPCinfo or using another third-party system utility.

When searching the database, here are some of the categories you'll want to confirm:

- Network cards—Generally not an issue, but if you're planning on Linux managing your network resources, it would be bad to have a non-supported card.
- Printers—Consult the OpenPrinting project at the Linux Foundation (http://www.linux-foundation.org/en/OpenPrinting) in addition to the openSUSE list for current information about printers on Linux.
- Sound cards—Most popular cards are fine, but might not have every feature.
- Universal Serial Bus (USB) devices—Consult the USB-Linux device page at http://www.qbik.ch/usb/devices/ for current information.
- Video cards—Occasional problems occur running the X Window System. You may not get the highest resolutions the card is capable of. Proprietary Nvidia and ATI drivers must be downloaded separately via YaST.

Linux on Laptops

openSUSE Linux 10.3 has improved support for the Advanced Configuration and Power Interface (ACPI) standard, so your laptop battery will last longer.

If you plan to run Linux on your laptop, be aware that manufacturers include many proprietary drivers for their hardware, and Linux support may be spotty at best. But don't be completely discouraged. The Linux on Laptops page at http://linux-laptop.net/ has the latest news and HOWTOs on its subject.

TIP

If you are in the market for a new Linux laptop, a few companies have sprung up to preinstall openSUSE, or any other distribution you want, on a name-brand portable. Browse the ads in your favorite Linux magazine or head over to http://www.linuxcertified.com/ or http://emperorlinux.com/.

openSUSE and Legacy Hardware

The problem with older hardware and Linux is, as stated earlier, a general lack of device drivers. This is somewhat reasonable, in that the operating system was being built from the ground up, both in terms of people hacking on the Linux kernel and in (often the same) people using it. As Linux grew in usage, at least on the server, more hardware manufacturers took notice, and more active support existed for server-side cards and peripherals. Only recently have advanced video cards, dial-up modems, and printers started shipping with Linux drivers.

Do not fret if you have an ancient Pentium box with a 33MHz processor, built-in sound and video cards, and a 1-gigabyte hard drive. Although you may not be able to install a GUI on it, there are several valuable modern-day uses you can put that box to. These include the following:

- Save tons of space on your other machines by installing all your fonts on this one and attaching it to the network.
- Store and play your MP3 (or Ogg Vorbis) music collection.
- Store data backups from CD or tape.
- Build a hardware firewall for your network.
- Make it a web server for your intranet.
- Make it your email box with fetchmail, postfix, and a text-based email client (mutt, pine, or emacs).
- Put a fax modem in it and make it your fax machine.
- Host a remote printer.
- Build an FTP server.

With pre-Pentium processors (386/486), you will probably not be able to run openSUSE. You should be able to install a basic Debian GNU/Linux, though. Check out the Debian Project at http://www.debian.org.

Avoiding Potential Hardware Problems

It should come as no surprise that no operating system is perfect. Within every Windows service pack, some software breaks, and that often includes hardware drivers. The same is true with Linux. Many devices will work out of the box or at the point of install. More and more, manufacturers are providing Linux drivers for their equipment. But some pieces of hardware always seem to have at least some trouble working under Linux. This section is designed to help you through the special minefields.

Software-Based Modems

Most computer peripherals handle whatever task they are built for by themselves; all that's needed is a device driver that integrates with the operating system. Tell an application you want to print the file on your screen, the application tells the OS, which tells the driver, which tells the printer. Done!

An exception to this rule exists, and you may never realize it until you install Linux on their computers. Suddenly the modem doesn't work anymore, and you can't access the Internet. Welcome to the world of Winmodems! Many popular dialup modem models, both the internal and the external varieties, work as you would expect. Driver support for modems is excellent under Linux. Some modems, though, move much of the functioning to software—software designed for Microsoft Windows.

The argument for this setup is that it is easier and cheaper to update software than hardware, but making hardware functioning dependent on having a specific operating system seems difficult, at best. This is somewhat like Michelin deciding to make tires only for General Motors. They would then tell Ford owners they'd have to make their own Michelin-like tires if they wanted to use the features Michelin had, only they won't tell you how they did it.

Nonetheless, many open-source software developers have taken on the challenge of making Winmodems work under Linux. Not that many years ago, the only choice available to users was to buy another modem, but that is no longer true. Some Winmodem makers have helped provide details and development kits to create open-source drivers. IBM has integrated support for software-based modems on the ThinkPad 600/E and 770 in the Linux kernel.

It's always best to check for Linux compatibility before buying a modem, but you don't always get that choice. The place to turn for information on Winmodems on Linux is http://www.linmodems.org.

Universal Serial Bus Devices

The Universal Serial Bus (USB) specification was designed to allow PCs to support more peripheral devices without adding serial or parallel connections to an already overburdened pile of cables. It also allows devices that don't need a permanent connection to the PC (such as digital cameras and audio players) to plug in and out only as needed, without having to reboot.

Nearly all PCs produced since the late 1990s have included at least two ports based on the USB 1.1 specification. Devices built to this specification move data to and from the device to the PC at speeds between 1.5 and 12 megabytes per second (MBps). USB 2.0 permits much faster transfer speeds (up to 480 MBps). Now you see even portable hard drives plugging into USB 2.0 ports and moving data swiftly.

Among the types of devices you'll see that plug into a USB port are keyboards, mice, modems, scanners, printers, digital cameras, webcams, and network cards (both wired and wireless).

The Linux kernel has supported the USB standard since v2.2.18, so all recent versions of SUSE Linux support at least USB 1.1 through the uhci kernel module. Developers working on the 2.6 kernel created the ehci module to support USB 2.0 and have since included compatible modules for earlier kernel versions, going back to v2.4. Some USB devices still have problems, though. These devices include wireless (802.11b) network adapters, scanners, and some webcams.

Visit http://www.qbik.ch/usb/devices/ to search an excellent database of USB devices, and visit http://www.linux-usb.org/ for general information on this topic.

Peripherals on the Motherboard

Most laptops and some less-expensive desktop PCs include built-in video, audio, and network support right on the motherboard. This practice lowers power requirements and simplifies the design, although these units often don't have all the power and features of more expensive PCI cards.

If these are new devices, Linux support can be flaky. When buying these machines, be careful to check for Linux support. Ask the vendor questions, and get answers. That's good advice for anything, but especially if you have a new, cutting-edge notebook, because you can't replace just one piece of a notebook yourself. It almost always has to go back to the factory.

Dual Booting, Partitioning, and Other Worries

The last thing you need to think about before beginning your openSUSE installation is what to do with your current installed OS. Chances are that you have perfectly good data on your computer that you want to keep. This should already be backed up on some other media (CD-ROM, Zip drive, or tape) in any case. But what about that copy of Windows XP under which you have created all that data? Do you want to start over from scratch, or should you keep it around? This goes back to the original question asked at the beginning of the chapter—what do you want to do with your PC?

Unless you have a small hard drive packed with applications and data, installing openSUSE alongside your existing Windows and using a boot manager to switch back and forth is a simple matter. Installing a standard Office package with X, KDE, and OpenOffice would not take up more than 1 gigabyte of space. Table 2.2 shows you what openSUSE recommends in the way of partition sizes for various uses:

TABLE 2.2 Recommended Partition Sizes

Type of Install	Partition Size
Minimum install (no X Window System)	180MB
Minimum with X Window System	500MB
Standard graphical install (one desktop environment, OpenOffice, and a web browser)	1–2GB
Storing multimedia (music and video clips)	2GB
CD burning	1GB
All of the above	4GB

As you can see, openSUSE won't eat up your 80GB drive all at once—or even after a lot of usage. And even if you're a glutton for choices, it's not really a problem. A system with both KDE and GNOME desktop environments, three office suites, five browsers, six text editors (both graphical and plain), a couple of personal information managers, and a fair amount of data still barely takes up 10GB.

So if for any reason you want to keep Windows around, this is easily done.

Dual Booting with Windows

When the YaST installer finds Windows on the system, a new extended partition is created for openSUSE. Windows retains a primary partition.

NOTE

On any dual-boot machine, Windows must *always* be installed first.

openSUSE comes with a free software disk-partitioning tool, GNU Parted, that works much like the commercial products Partition Magic and Partition Commander. This makes it easier to create and organize data on your drive. Unlike the `fdisk` tool (both the DOS/Windows and UNIX/Linux versions) that destroys data when modifying partitions, Parted protects the data on partitions that are being resized. YaST uses a version of Parted called Expert Partitioner during the initial install, and the root user can run it directly from YaST at any time to resize, delete, or add partitions. Learn more about Parted/Expert Partitioner in Chapter 18, "Managing Files, Volumes, and Drives."

CAUTION

Anytime you want to play with the partition table, be aware that you are putting your data at some risk, even if it is a small one. Power surges, fuse burnouts, and temporary blackouts happen, and never at a convenient time. Always back up critical data. Have an emergency boot disk on hand. Create one when the openSUSE install asks you to. See Chapter 20, "Managing Data: Backup, Restoring, and Recovery," for more information.

The downside to dual booting is that you must reboot every time you want to use a different OS. Shutdown and startup time can add up when you are trying to get things done. The good news is that you don't have to do this to access and use a data file on the Windows side of your box. openSUSE will read and open (with an appropriate application) any file on your system. Linux supports both FAT and NTFS file systems. When detecting the presence of a Windows file system, openSUSE creates a `/windows` directory where it stores and displays your directories and files. How much you can move and copy files to and from these directories depends on the underlying Windows file system. Linux permissions won't transfer from a Linux file system to the Windows File Allocation Table (FAT), and copying from a Linux file system to the NT File System (NTFS) used by default in Windows NT/2000/XP/Vista is nearly impossible. Unfortunately, no Windows OS supports any Linux file system. Third-party Windows utilities allow you to view and copy files from a Linux ext2 file system, but none will let you open a file directly from your `/home` directory.

NOTE

Want to work with files on a Windows box on your network? For that, you need Samba. See Chapter 25, "Setting Up Networks and Samba."

How to Partition Your Drive(s)

Whether you dual boot or not, you will need at least two partitions to run openSUSE properly. You can do this before the install with a commercial product if you're comfortable doing that, or YaST will help you with the process during the install. If you are not planning to dual boot, you are probably better off waiting for the install, as YaST will reformat the drive for you.

The two minimum partitions are the root partition, signified with a forward slash (/), and a swap partition, which Linux uses as virtual memory. Traditionally, the size of the swap partition is equivalent to (or a multiple of) the amount of hardware RAM you have installed. So if you have 256MB of RAM, your swap should be 256MB (or even 512MB) as well. YaST will configure this automatically during the install.

If you have only these two partitions, YaST will put all the other standard directories on the same partition as /. These are:

- /bin—Binary files.
- /boot—Files to boot Linux.
- /dev—Device drivers.
- /etc—Configuration files.
- /home—Each user gets a data directory under this one.
- /lib—Libraries, the underlying code for many applications.
- /media—Removable disks and drives (floppy discs, CD-ROMs, and Zips).

- /mnt—The mount directory, where all partitions (mount points) are listed.
- /opt—Some applications install to this directory instead of /usr.
- /proc—A dynamic directory where all running processes are logged; this is constantly changing.
- /root—Not to be confused with plain / (also called "root"); this is the home directory for the root user.
- /sbin—System binaries, usually files that need to run during startup.
- /srv—Services.
- /tmp—Temporary files.
- /usr—Most applications install themselves here.
- /var—Variable files and programs, including print spoolers, mail clients, and security logs, are stored here.

You may want to consider putting one or several of these directories on a separate partition (mount point), because doing so can make a drive more efficient and ready for expansion. Candidates for separate mount points include `/home` (especially with multiple users on the same system), `/opt` (if you find several applications installing here, setting aside a gigabyte as a mount point could improve performance), and `/usr` (this would enable you to further separate programs from data and may improve performance; make this partition up to 6GB if you plan to install everything on the SUSE install disks).

References

This set of links points to useful resources on partitioning, installing Linux on a variety of hardware, and other installation tools.

- http://linux.dell.com—Home of the Dell Linux Community. Dell is focused on Enterprise Linux and will sell you servers with either SUSE Linux Enterprise Server or Red Hat Enterprise Server, but the community site offers mailing lists to support Linux users on desktops and laptops as well.
- http://www.linuxrsp.ru/win-lin-soft/—Look here for Linux equivalents of Windows applications.
- http://en.opensuse.org/Hardware—The openSUSE hardware compatibility database.
- http://www.linux-foundation.org/en/OpenPrinting—Want to see if your printer works in Linux? Here's the place.
- http://www.linux-usb.org—The Linux-USB project, with information on supported devices and drivers.
- http://www.qbik.ch/usb/devices—The Linux USB devices database to search for compatible devices.

- http://www.linmodems.org—Linux drivers for software-based modems.
- http://www.linuxcertified.com and http://emperorlinux.com—Two companies that deliver laptops with Linux preinstalled.
- http://linux-laptop.net—More information on Linux-friendly laptops.
- http://www.linux1394.org—The Linux FireWire project with information on drivers for these devices.
- http://elks.sourceforge.net—The Embeddable Linux Kernel Subset is an attempt to build some Linux functionality that will run on an Intel 286 and earlier processor.
- http://www.lnx-bbc.org—Home of the Linux Bootable Business Card project, producing a Live CD in the shape of a standard business card.
- http://www.knoppix.org—Another Live CD project; stick the CD in the drive and run Linux, no matter what OS is installed on the hard drive.
- http://www.gnu.org/software/parted/parted.html—Home of GNU Parted, the free software disk-partitioning tool.

CHAPTER 3

Installing openSUSE

IN THIS CHAPTER

- Methods of Installing openSUSE
- Preparing to Install from a CD-ROM or DVD
- Installing openSUSE with YaST
- Logging In and Shutting Down the First Time
- References

Installing openSUSE is a simple process. The openSUSE YaST application (Yet another Setup Tool) walks you through the process, detects and configures your hardware, and generally takes charge. In this chapter, you learn how to complete a basic installation of openSUSE using the DVD included with this book.

At this stage of the game, you're probably anxious to get started, but a brief introduction helps you make sure everything is ready. Then you can begin the installation and follow this chapter's advice all the way through.

By the end of the chapter, you will have logged in for the first time, ready to use openSUSE.

Methods of Installing openSUSE

openSUSE can be installed on a workstation through a plethora of possibilities. The installation can be done from a central server, across the network, or using any of the media types available (CD ROM/DVD).

Because this book includes the operating system on accompanying media, we will focus on installing it using those. While the method is different with the other types of installation, most follow the same steps, and you can easily find information specific to those installations on the website.

Preparing to Install from a CD-ROM or DVD

The media included with this book is bootable and will install openSUSE directly when you start your computer. The main thing you need to know before starting the process is whether your BIOS is set to boot from your CD-ROM or DVD-ROM drive.

NOTE

If you have Windows installed on your system, instlux lets you simply insert the DVD into your running Windows system and begin the openSUSE install process. You will have the choice to have openSUSE Linux replace Windows as your operating system (Be sure to have all your data backed up!) or to dual boot using grub.

CAUTION

Changing BIOS settings can be dangerous, and it's not hard to make a computer unbootable with the wrong setting. Follow these instructions carefully and don't change any other setting unless you know what you're doing.

To check this, reboot your computer. Among the first things you see on your screen as the computer starts up is the method of accessing your BIOS settings. Often this is the Delete or Escape key; other times, it is one of the function keys at the top of the keyboard. Each BIOS manufacturer does things differently. Press this key as soon as you see it. Shortly, the settings will appear.

Look for a setting title called Boot Sequence, Boot Order, or something similar. This setting determines where the BIOS looks for a bootloader code that tells it the volume is bootable. The setting itself should look something like this if the CD-ROM is to be checked first:

```
CD-ROM, C:, floppy
```

TIP

Change the order accordingly if you have both a DVD drive and CD-RW drive.

Every drive that may be bootable should be listed here. This order points first to the CD drive, then the hard drive (which may be identified as either IDE or SCSI instead of the Windows drive letter), and then the floppy. It's possible that either the hard drive or the floppy may come first in the sequence. In this instance, you should adjust the setting so that the CD is checked before the hard drive. To change the setting, use the Tab key to highlight the Boot Sequence, and then press Enter to change the setting. This process, again, varies from BIOS to BIOS. You should get a list of possible sequences from which you can choose, or you may have to select each drive in the order you want.

NOTE

Checking other drives before the hard drive will slow your boot time a few seconds, so you may want to reset the Boot Sequence after your openSUSE installation is completed. Learn more about your BIOS and the boot process in Chapter 22, "Managing the Boot Process and Other Services."

Select a sequence similar to the one listed in this section, and save your new choice. If the first openSUSE CD or DVD is in the drive, it should now boot. If not, and another operating system is installed, the computer may boot to that OS. If the computers boots to another OS, make sure the SUSE CD/DVD is in the drive and then restart your computer.

Installing openSUSE with YaST

The installation begins when you insert the openSUSE DVD (or the first openSUSE CD) into your drive and boot up. A menu appears with several startup choices (see Figure 3.1). Select Installation. YaST will identify and initialize the hardware it needs to begin, and then display the list of languages supported in this version. Select your preferred language and click Next. Next up is the Novell Software License Agreement. Click Yes, I Agree to the License Agreement to continue to the first installation screen.

NOTE

This book was completed before openSUSE 10.3's final release. The order of steps in the final installation may differ somewhat from what appears here, and the figures may not be completely accurate. The installation process will cover all the steps listed here, however.

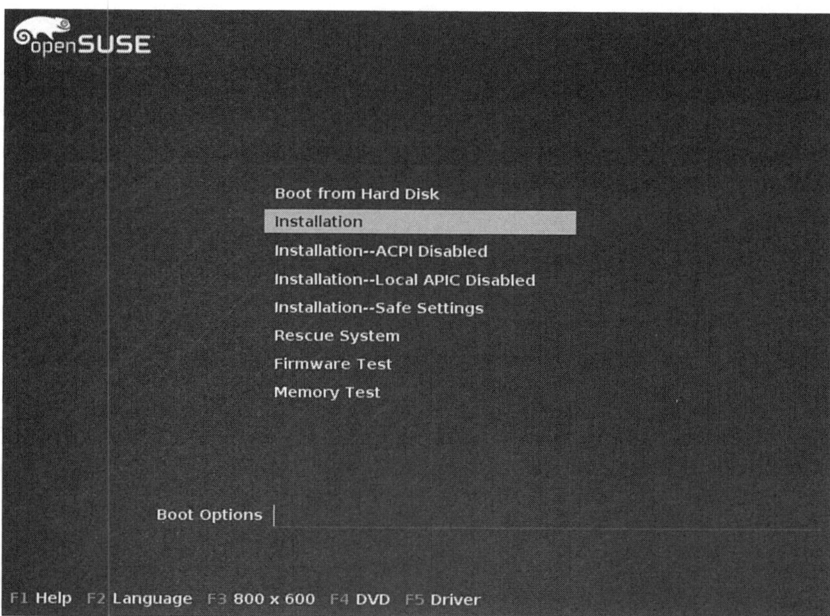

FIGURE 3.1 Select an Installation option from this initial screen.

In the next screen, tell YaST whether this is an update or a new installation. YaST will check to see if another version of SUSE Linux is installed. If there is, you'll get the Update and Other Options choices in the Installation Mode screen. If you happen to be installing openSUSE Linux over another Linux distribution, this still qualifies as a New Installation. If you are using CDs to install, you'll also get the option to include the non-open-source "Add-On Product," but the openSUSE DVD has this stuff too. Click Next.

YaST will also ask to test your network/Internet connection at this point. This will help in setting up update and other software installation sources, but is not required at this stage. If you happen to be installing on a laptop with only a wireless Internet connection, the test will likely fail due to the wireless card not yet configured. Wired LAN and broadband connections should work, however. Don't panic if your system doesn't pass this test, though. You'll get another chance at configuring your network later in the install.

Setting Your Time Zone

Use the Time Zone section to identify your location so that the system time will be correct for your time zone. Learn more about date and time in "Setting Date and Time" in Chapter 4, "Further Configuration with YaST2 and SaX2."

Selecting a Desktop Environment

There are two teams vying for control of your Linux desktop, GNOME and KDE. If you're brand new to Linux, this may be a difficult choice this early in the installation process. You may want to skip over to Chapter 6, "Launching Your Desktop," before making this decision—or maybe not. At this stage, you may just want to pick one, knowing that it's easy to switch from one to the other and that virtually every application written for one desktop environment works just as well in the other.

Initial Installation Settings

YaST loads the kernel modules for your hard drive and then displays a list of Installation Settings The Overview tab contains just the highlights, while the Expert tab (Figure 3.2) goes into more detail. Review carefully all the settings for accuracy and click either the heading of each section or the Change button on the bottom to correct any errors.

This is the last screen before beginning your openSUSE Linux installation. The next few sections point to things to consider before you click Accept at the bottom of this page.

TIP

If you have a two-button mouse, notice that YaST will automatically emulate a three-button mouse. This lets you access many middle-button features by clicking both buttons at the same time.

Partitioning

You learned most of what you need to know about how disks are partitioned under Linux in Chapter 2, "Preparing to Install openSUSE." YaST creates a Root, home, and swap partition by default. If you want to add partitions or use a different file system than ext3, select the Partitioning heading and make your changes.

TIP

If YaST detects the presence of another operating system, it will ask whether you want to replace that OS with openSUSE or dual boot both. YaST will use its partitioning tool to shrink the existing partition and allow openSUSE to install. If you have two physical hard drives and want to install Linux on the second drive, it will format that drive accordingly.

See "Dual Booting, Partitioning, and Other Worries," in Chapter 2, and Chapter 11, "Going Cross-Platform," for more information.

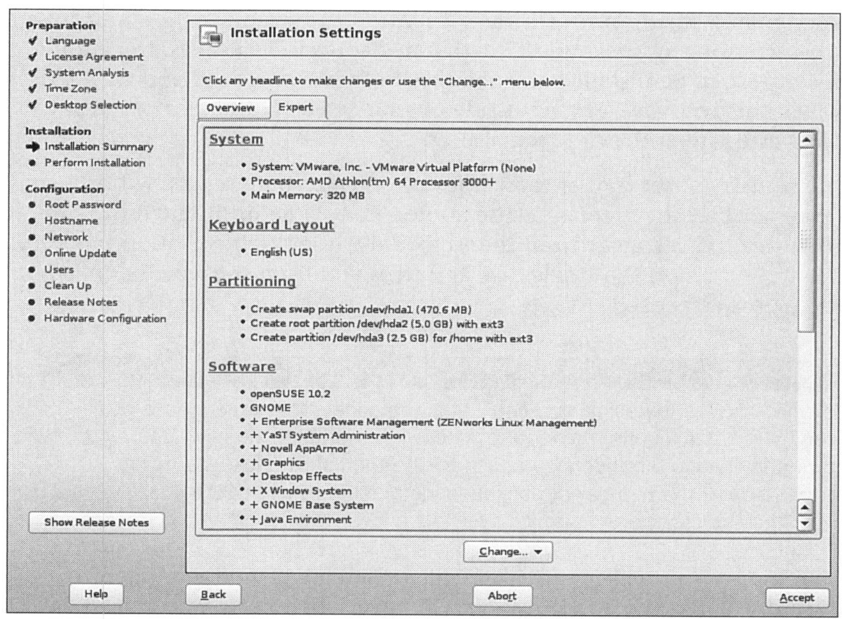

FIGURE 3.2 YaST autodetects your hardware and makes some default choices about your installation. Edit any default selection by clicking the heading or using the Change button.

Installing Software Packages

The Expert page tells you the basic types of packages it will install. You may still want to peruse the Software section to check for specific packages in which you may be interested. You can also change your mind about your basic desktop (or decide to install both if you're so inclined) here.

If you open the Software page, you'll see packages organized by function, in what openSUSE calls "patterns." To turn your openSUSE box into a free software development engine, check the Development pattern (or some subset of it). Deciding to install something is just a matter of checking a box from the thousands of individual programs included in your openSUSE Linux DVD.

Click Accept when you are ready to install the base system. Depending on the software packages you selected, you may have to view and accept other license agreements for certain applications (for example, the Adobe Flash player).

CAUTION

YaST will also warn you that it is formatting a partition and that any data on that partition will be destroyed. This gives you one more chance to turn back in case you have data on your computer that you want to preserve. Click Install to begin the process.

YaST formats the designated partition for the data drive and the swap partition and then begins installing the operating system and the designated software packages. Depending on the amount of software to be installed and the speed of your processor and CD drive, the time it takes to do this will vary. The right side of your screen contains a progress bar that gives you a total estimate of the time remaining.

If you are installing from a CD set (rather than from the DVD), you'll see a few horizontal bars crossing the progress bar; they represent the approximate time until you'll have to swap CDs again. Feel free to walk away from the keyboard while the installation proceeds. The DVD contains all the files on the single disk and frees you from the worry of needing to be ready to swap media as needed.

NOTE

To pass the time while YaST is installing, you can watch the slide show, which (as is traditional in lengthy software installations) presents a rundown of some of the new features in this version, or click the Details tab (see Figure 3.3) to see the list of packages being installed (and an overview of the number of packages installed from each CD).

After the base system and boot manager are installed, YaST reboots your computer to make sure things are in good shape to begin (you will have a 10-second warning when you can stop the reboot, if necessary). Leave the disk in the drive for the reboot. When the reboot is complete, the Package Installation screen appears, and you'll be asked to insert the second CD (with the DVD, everything installs before the system reboots).

Packages will continue to install, and the blue progress bar will continue to shrink. You'll be asked again to swap out CDs occasionally until the installation is complete.

Creating the Root User

When all the packages have been installed, you will become the system administrator for the first time. Your task is to create the first user on the system: Root. This is done simply enough. In Unix and Linux, a user equals a password.

The first password you create, for the Root user, is by far the most important. The Root user has complete control over the system, for good or evil. Therefore, the Root password must be secure and easy to remember. If you forget the Root password, it becomes extremely difficult (although not impossible) to access any system files. At minimum, the Root password must be at least five characters and should have a mixture of letters, cases, and numbers.

TIP

See "Selecting Passwords" in Chapter 19, "Managing Users, Managing Security," for tips on creating secure passwords.

Click Expert Options to choose the encryption method for your passwords (see Figure 3.4). By default, openSUSE uses the Blowfish encryption standard because it allows for up to 72 characters in the password string. This is much harder to crack randomly. You could choose the less safe (but more widely used) DES standard, or the MD5 standard as well. When you have typed and confirmed the root password, click Next.

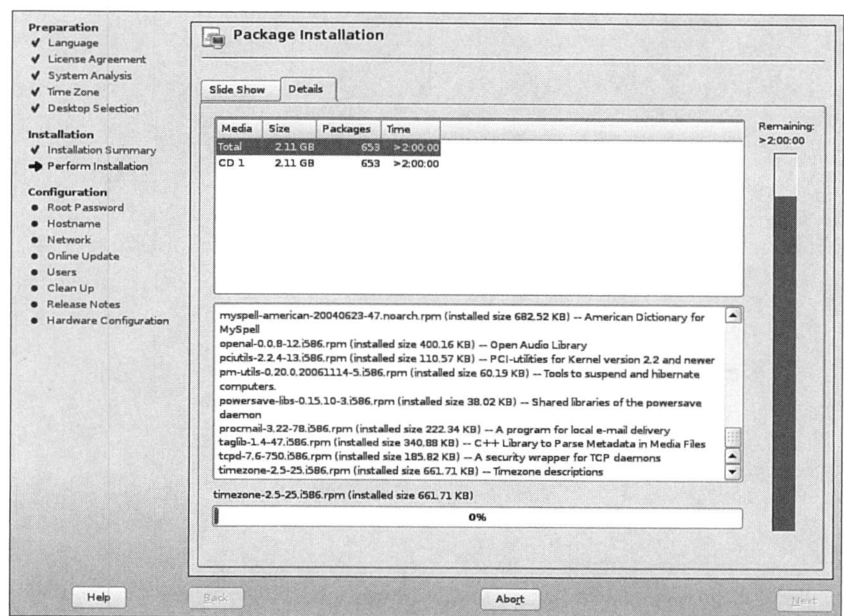

FIGURE 3.3 View the details of the software package installation in this screen.

Setting a Hostname and Domain Name

Whether you have a local area network in your home or have an Internet connection—or ever plan to have either—you need a unique identifier for this machine. You set this identification in this screen. YaST proposes a hostname and domain name, but you can change either of these to anything you want.

Choose your own names, or accept YaST's defaults.

Configuring Network and Internet Connections

Next, YaST checks for networking hardware: Ethernet cards, dial-up modems, or high-speed connections. You have the option to configure these yourself later (click Skip Configuration), but it is a good idea to set this up during the installation. YaST will use this connection to go online to update your installation in the next step.

Figure 3.5 shows the default network settings screen. As before, if YaST failed to detect all your networking hardware, or misidentified something, click the appropriate heading or use the Change button to make adjustments.

NOTE

If more than one network interface card (NIC) is found, you may be asked to configure the second card. This might be the case if this computer is going to function as a router or Internet gateway. One card, labeled eth0, will be the first active interface when you boot.

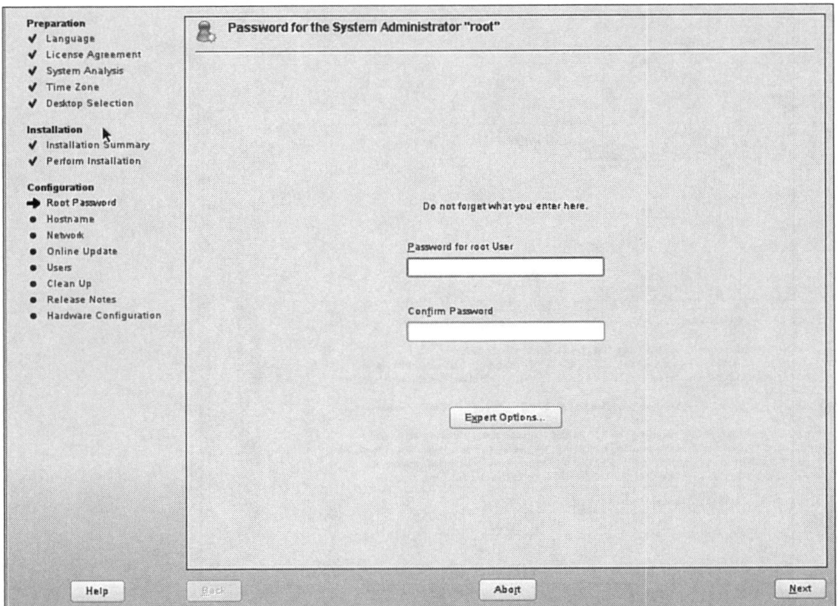

FIGURE 3.4 Strengthen the encryption of your Root password by clicking Expert Options.

Note that the SUSE Firewall is turned on by default. This is a good thing, unless you are already protected by a hardware router, which is included with many Digital Subscriber Line (DSL) accounts, and in business network settings. Click Next to confirm the network settings.

NetworkManager is a Novell tool designed to keep laptops connected to a network. When you take your laptop to a place you've been before, NetworkManager is designed to find and login to the network you connected to last time. If you are installing openSUSE Linux on a laptop, you can configure this in the Network Mode page. Desktop machines will generally not need this.

Version 6 of the Internet Protocol (IPv6) is the next generation of the protocol that allows computers and other things on the Internet. IPv6 allows more devices to have Internet connections, but is not yet in wide use. Some browsers have trouble reaching sites with traditional IPv4 addresses when searching for IPv6 addresses, so you may find it useful to disable IPv6 support. Click Disable IPv6 if it might be a bother. If you leave this on here, and later change your mind, you can make the change in YaST later on. See Chapter 25 for more information.

After you have confirmed your network, YaST tests your connection as you set it up. It connects to a nearby openSUSE update server to retrieve the latest Release Notes and any updates to your installed software. It will set up your installation sources for future updates as well (See Figures 3.5, 3.6, and 3.7). You can get more information in Chapter 21, "Keeping Your System Current: Package Management." If you have any problem connecting, review the network settings and make sure everything is correct.

TIP

Learn more about your Internet connection in Chapter 12, "Connecting to the Internet."

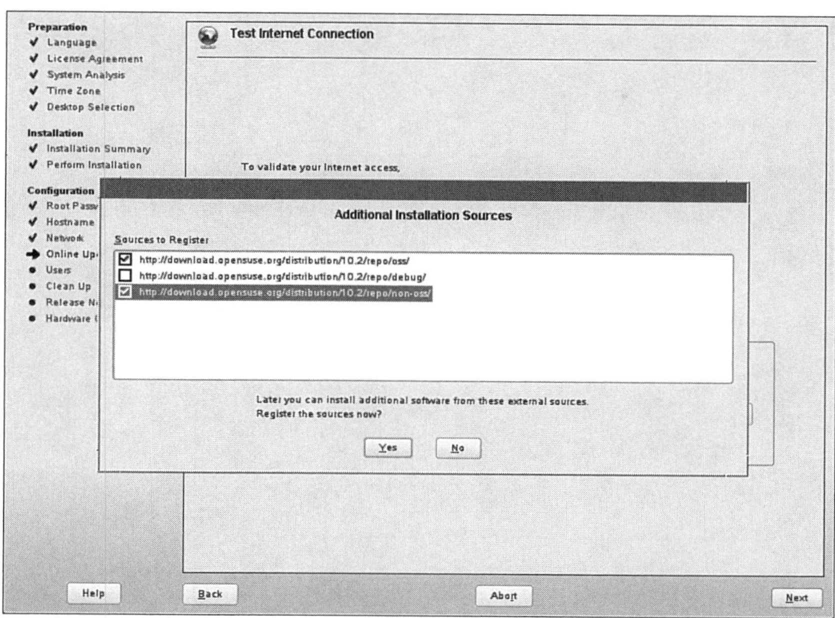

FIGURE 3.5 Set up your initial software installation sources on this screen.

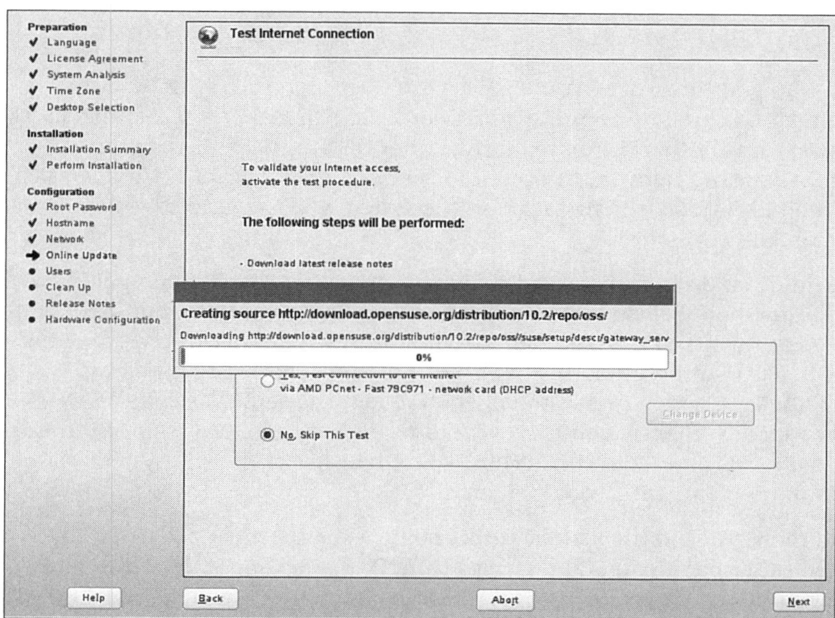

FIGURE 3.6 When you select the installation source, YaST will download a list of packages from the source.

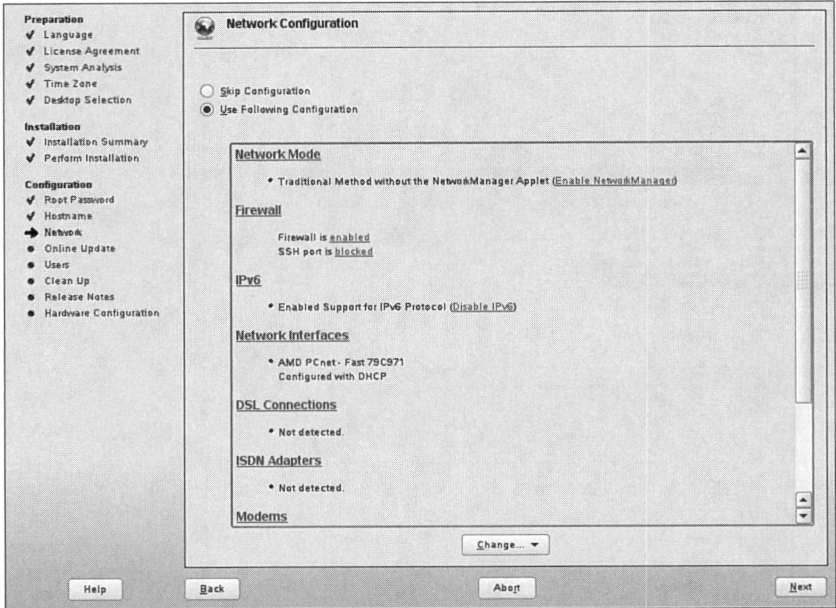

FIGURE 3.7 Confirm or edit your network hardware and configuration on this screen.

Creating a User

Now it's time to set up your first user—you! As with the Root user, the central task in creating a user on a Linux system is to make a password. YaST first asks whether this user will log in locally or from another computer, using either the Lightweight Directory Access Protocol (LDAP) or the Network Information Service (NIS), or from a Windows PC through Samba. In all likelihood, the first user on the system will log in locally on this PC; select this option and click Next.

Type the relevant information into the New Local User screen (see Figure 3.8), including the user password. This should always be different from the Root password, but use the same general rules. For further information and advice on New User settings, see "Setting Up User Accounts in YaST" in Chapter 19. YaST checks the Automatic Login box by default, allowing ordinary users to bypass the openSUSE login screen. This choice sacrifices some security for convenience; you may wish to reconsider. Similarly, the first user is likely to be you (that is, also the Root user). Thus, you might like to get the System Mail that may alert you to problems with your system.

If you want to add more users to the system at this point, click User Management. You can also add and edit user permissions and groups in YaST at any time. Click Next when finished to create your users.

YaST now runs the `SUSEConfig` file to add the user and confirm the other changes made to this point (see Figure 3.9). This can take a minute or longer, depending on your system. It then displays the Release Notes, with current information on new features and known problems. Click Next when you have reviewed this information.

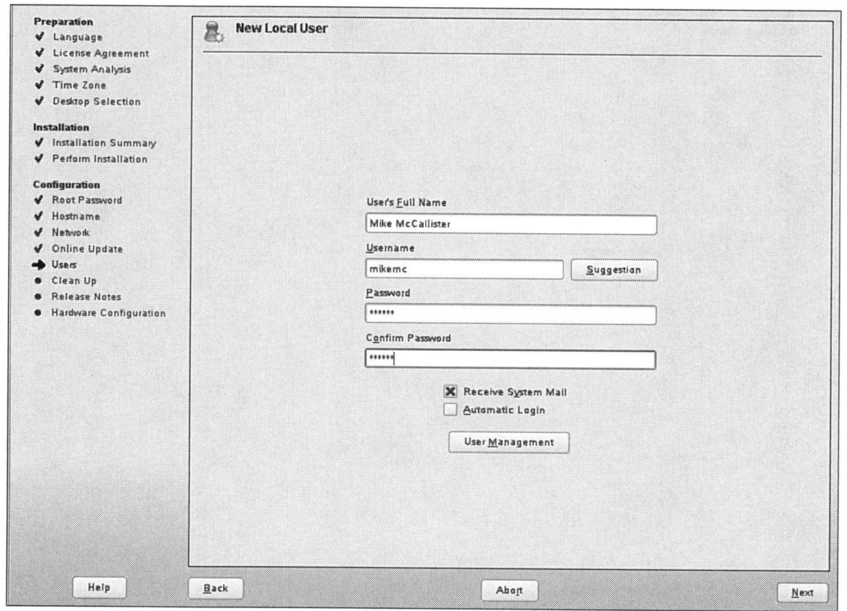

FIGURE 3.8 Add your first user (usually you) in this screen.

Configuring Hardware for the X Window System

The last step in the installation is identifying and configuring the hardware you'll need for the graphical X Window System and your chosen desktop environment. YaST autodetects your graphics card, connected printers, sound card, and a few miscellaneous peripherals. Again, if the autodetection failed or misidentified a card, select the appropriate heading or click the Change button and make any necessary changes. Click Next when you're ready. YaST confirms the changes and writes the default configuration files.

CAUTION

While you may think that because you've had a smooth installation so far, and all the screens have appeared normal, there won't be any problem after your reboot, you may be wrong. Occasionally, YaST will misidentify a card or not have the proper specifications configured. If your display suddenly goes haywire, try pressing Ctrl+Alt+Backspace to restore your screen to the last settings. Open YaST's Graphics Card and Monitor module (under Hardware), and adjust your settings. You can then test the new setup before confirming.

You will now see the Congratulations! screen (see Figure 3.9), signifying the end of the installation process. You are ready to log in for the first time. If you want to use these settings as the basis of another openSUSE install on another computer, check Clone This System for Autoyast before clicking Finish. You may remove your CD at this time.

The system will then begin the boot process, finishing by displaying the blue screen with the login prompt.

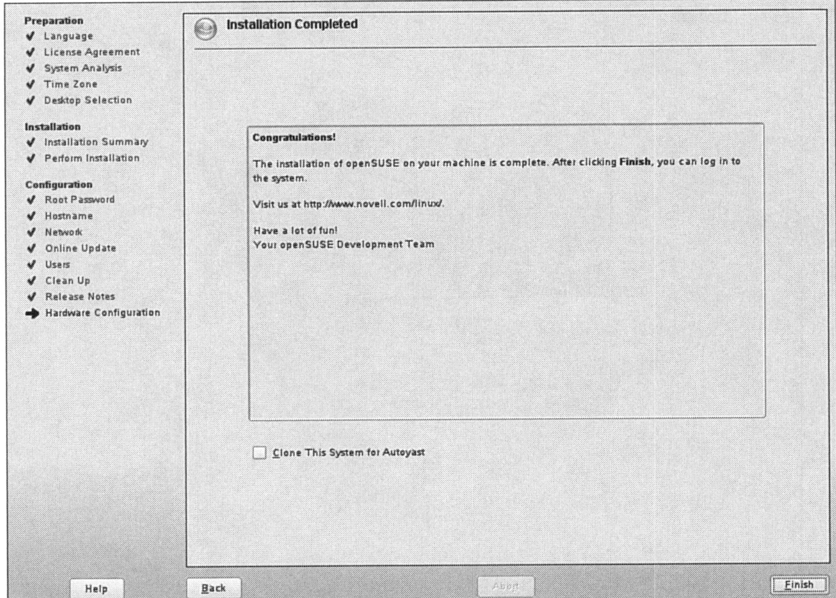

FIGURE 3.9 You've finished!

Logging In and Shutting Down the First Time

When you boot your openSUSE system after running the startup scripts, your Linux kernel will display the login screen (Figure 3.10 displays the GNOME login; if you installed the KDE desktop environment, the login screen will look a little different). You'll be asked to type the username and the password. Only rarely should you log in as Root, and then only for specific purposes.

Looking in the lower-left corner of the login screen, you'll see that you have some options in logging in. You can change the language of the display manager by selecting your language from the menu. By clicking the appropriate choice, you can choose to shut down or reboot your computer instead of logging in.

The Session menu allows you to change your desktop environment for this session if you have other window managers or desktop environments installed. Although this is probably not the case in your first login, if you like variety in your computing experience, you may want to play with this function later.

TIP

For the first login, it is always recommended to keep it as simple as possible. Your primary purpose is to make sure that the installation was successful and there are no problems. After you have assured yourself that this is the case, you can get more creative with login choices.

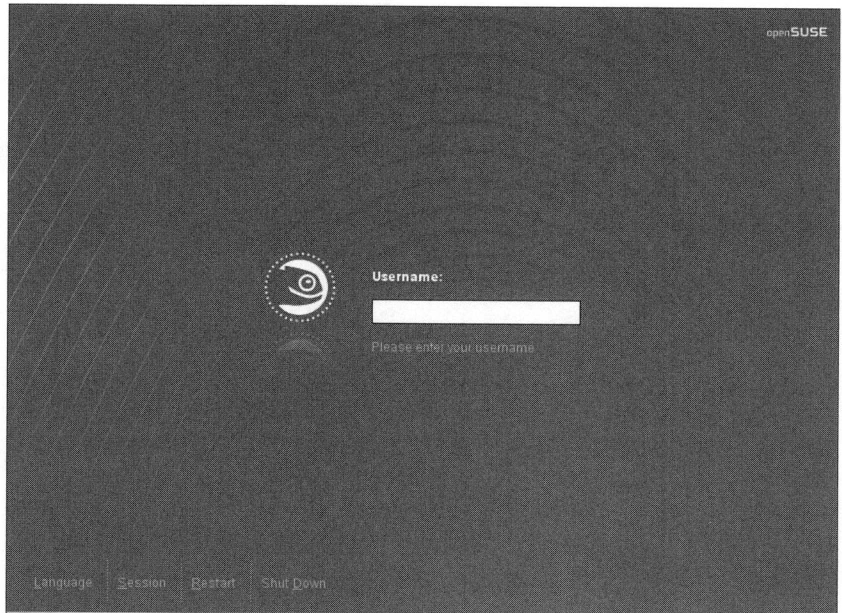

FIGURE 3.10 Log in here.

When you have entered your username and password, your selected desktop environment loads. Take a look around; click and right-click to your heart's content. Visit the Novell SUSE or openSUSE.org websites and get comfortable. You should then log out and reboot your system to make sure everything is in proper order.

Find the Logout command from the desktop menu and click Restart Computer. That's all there is to it. The computer will shut down and then restart.

Welcome to Linux! You have now begun the journey.

References

- http://en.opensuse.org/installation—Tips and other instructions on installing openSUSE.
- http://www.novell.com/linux/—Always the place to start if you want to know something about SUSE Linux.
- http://tldp.org/HOWTO/Installation-HOWTO/index.html—From 2002, this Linux Installation HOWTO was written by programming guru Eric S. Raymond.
- http://www.pcguide.com/ref/mbsys/bios/set—A detailed description of most BIOS settings. Go to the Advanced Settings page to review the boot sequence/order options.

- http://www.pcworld.com/howto/article/0,aid,107870,00.asp—This article from *PC World* magazine runs through various BIOS settings in a more popular style.
- http://www.gnome.org/projects/NetworkManager—Basic information on NetworkManager.
- http://www.gnu.org/software/grub—The GRUB bootloader home page.
- http://grub.enbug.org/—The GRUB wiki, with information on the forthcoming GRUB2.

CHAPTER 4

Further Configuration with YaST and SaX2

IN THIS CHAPTER

- Troubleshooting Installation Problems
- Configuring Hardware with YaST
- Setting Date and Time
- Power Management
- Portable PC Issues
- Configuring CD, DVD, and Rewritable Drives
- References

In the previous chapter, you saw how easy it was to get openSUSE up and running. In this chapter, you'll learn more about configuring hardware after the installation. You'll start with the no-longer-inevitable but still trouble-some post-installation glitches, and you'll finish with peripherals and portables.

Troubleshooting Installation Problems

Linux applications, and the kernel itself, are much more fault tolerant than they used to be. It's hard to render a system completely unbootable. At the same time, it's much easier to overlook certain problems that may be affecting performance on a system that seems to be running well. Services may not start, modules don't load, or the hard drive does not respond as quickly as it should. It's a good idea to run the `dmesg` program occasionally to review the information the kernel is getting during bootup. Also review `/var/log/messages` regularly to see everything that goes into the log. Anyone can view this file in a text editor, but you can also view it in YaST. Go to the Miscellaneous page and click View System Log.

TIP

Besides `/var/log/messages`, you can view other logs, such as `/var/log/warn`, and several process tables from the `/proc` directory in this YaST module. Use the drop-down menu to change the file you're viewing.

Messages in `/var/log/messages` are generated by the kernel and other applications run by `sysinit`. Many errors noted here are not really errors. If the system has configured a device you don't have, it will generate an error, but that's harmless. But look for errors that appear to affect devices and processes that you use. Investigate the causes of these errors.

When you're troubleshooting problems, search the SUSE help pages and check the man page for the problem application (along with `modules.conf` for kernel modules that are not loading). Paste the error message (up to 10 words) into an Internet search engine and see what comes up. Then head over to the "Getting Help: Documentation and Other Sources" section of Chapter 1, "Welcome to openSUSE," to look deeper into the problem.

Configuring Hardware with YaST

YaST autodetects and configures many types of peripheral hardware. But it's not really Linux if you can't tweak the default settings. In this section, you look at the YaST Hardware page and learn what you can configure, and how.

Gathering Information About Your Hardware

Before tweaking away, you may want a snapshot of what hardware is already recognized and functioning. The YaST Hardware Information module is a graphical version of the `hwinfo` command-line utility. It probes your system and displays a comprehensive report on what hardware (cards, controllers, devices, and the like) is on your system, along with fairly in-depth information about most of the items. To start this program, open YaST and go to the Hardware page. Click Hardware Information and you're on your way. Figure 4.1 gives you an idea of what it looks like.

Click the plus (+) sign next to an item to see detailed information on that item. To save the results to a file readable in a text editor (and thus printable as well), click Save to File. Name the file (`hwinfo<date-run>`, for example) and put it somewhere in your home directory. Click Close to return to YaST.

Modifying Disk Controller Settings

Your hard disk controller (HDC) is located on the motherboard. The Linux kernel loads the disk controller early in the boot process. You can set optional parameters here to improve system performance, if you know what you're doing. These parameters and modules will vary depending on your system. Your motherboard's manual may have some suggestions, and Googling **`"<module_name> parameters"`** may offer valuable advice.

CAUTION

Always test the loading of modules when changing disk controller parameters! If your hard disk does not load when you boot, you will be able to launch Linux only from the DVD and will not have access to any files on your hard drive!

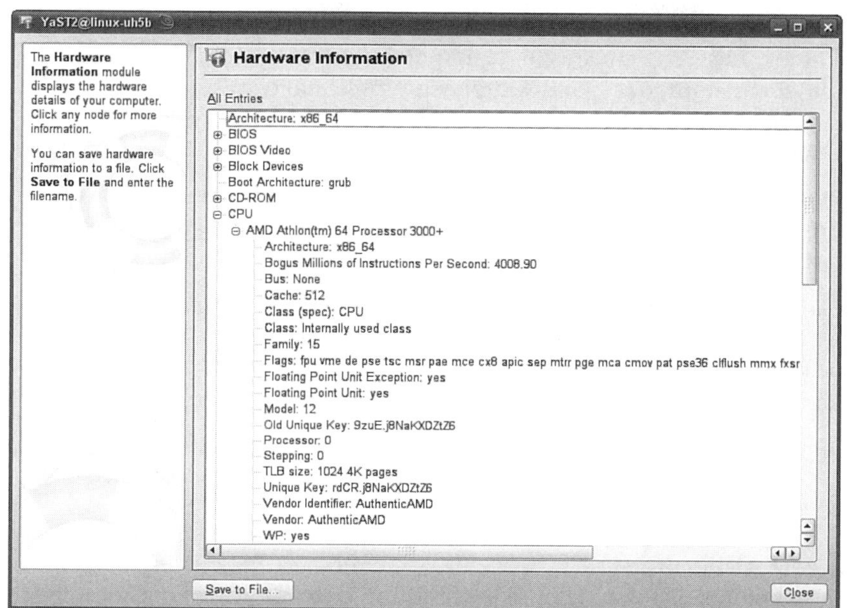

FIGURE 4.1 The YaST Hardware Information module provides detailed information on your system.

If you have more than one HDC on your system, you can use the Move Up or Move Down buttons to choose what loads first. If you don't want an HDC to load on boot, uncheck the Load Module in initrd box. `Initrd` is a file the kernel accesses to determine what modules it should load at boot.

Click Finish to confirm your settings and return to YaST.

▶ Learn more about the Linux boot process in Chapter 22, "Managing the Boot Process and Other Services."

Configuring Your Sound and Video Cards

An impression exists that Linux is weak in multimedia (especially sound card) support. This is largely because of some early mixed results for the very popular Creative Labs (SoundBlaster) products under Linux. Today, multimedia support is great and continually improving.

openSUSE Linux supports most current sound cards out of the box. During the openSUSE Linux installation, YaST should recognize and give you a default configuration for both your sound and video cards, enough to get you up and running. Although you can further configure both cards during the setup, it's better to get your system going and then tweak later through YaST.

Default sound support for openSUSE Linux is provided through ALSA, the Advanced Linux Sound Architecture. ALSA began as a simple project to write better drivers for a single sound card, and it blossomed. It has been supported in the kernel since v2.5 and has been the default sound system since v2.6. It supports everything from consumer sound cards to multichannel interfaces and will play multiple audio streams simultaneously if you want. YaST handles all the configuration tasks for ALSA, and you are no longer required to load the kernel modules manually. This is the topic of the next section.

Most settings for audio and video are set in YaST. To do this, open YaST and click Hardware to start the configuration. When you click Sound, YaST checks your current configuration and displays all detected sound cards.

You can set some advanced options for the card, but unless you are trying to solve some problem and know what to change, you should leave these alone. Click Volume to change the default volume settings for every channel on your card. The Start Sequencer check box loads kernel modules for MIDI sounds at boot, and is checked by default.

If YaST does not automatically recognize your card, you can add it manually in this dialog box. Choose the card from the menu or use the Search tool to find your card. Click Next to confirm the changes.

Configuring Audio with AlsaConf

Occasionally, YaST has trouble with certain audio cards. In cases like these, the command-line AlsaConf tool can be a savior. This application is not installed by default, so use YaST to install. From your desktop, open a shell (Konsole in KDE, Terminal in GNOME), log in as the SuperUser, and type `alsaconf` at the prompt. The introductory screen (Figure 4.2) will appear. Click OK.

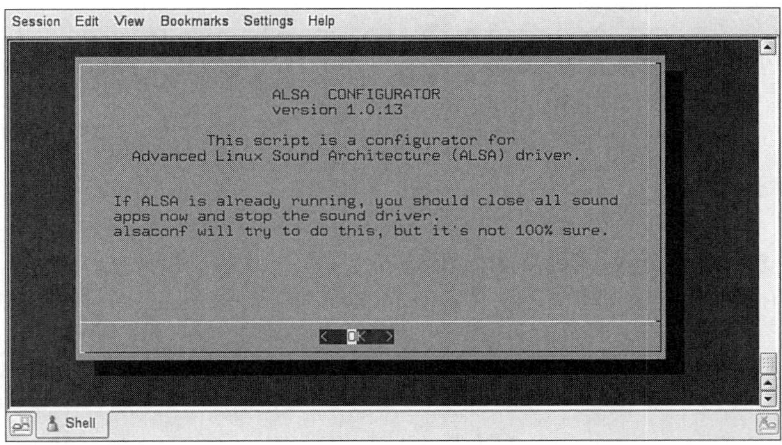

FIGURE 4.2 AlsaConf can configure sound cards that YaST can't.

AlsaConf will probe your hardware and identify your sound card(s). Select one to configure in the second screen (Figure 4.3) and click OK.

The program will configure the card and ask you to test the sound. If it passes the test, you should always use AlsaConf if anything goes wrong with the sound.

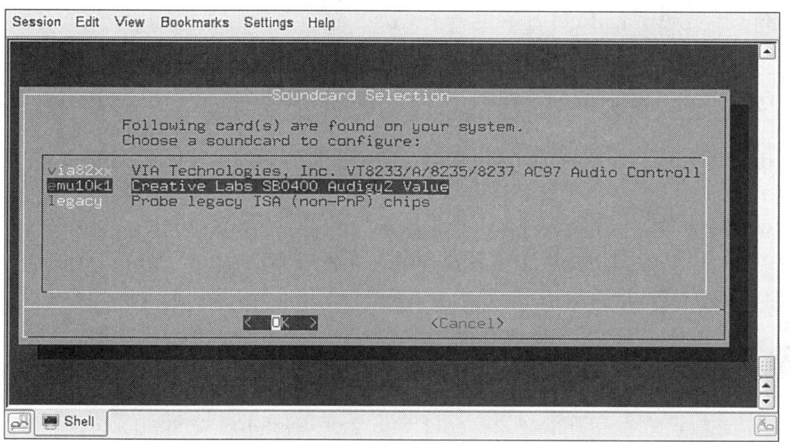

FIGURE 4.3 Select your card in this AlsaConf screen. The program does the rest.

Configuring Video Cards

Video in Linux is a little trickier than audio, as this often involves installing proprietary kernel modules. The two dominant video card manufacturers, ATI and Nvidia, have been particularly reluctant to release open source drivers. The good news is that both manufacturers now offer a software repository for Linux drivers that integrate with YaST. This makes it a little easier to install and update these drivers. You'll learn more about adding third party repositories to YaST in Chapter 21, "Keeping Your System Current: Package Management," but here's the process for getting and installing these drivers.

1. Open a Root shell, and type the following text (for Nvidia only):

   ```
   rpm -import 'ftp://download.nvidia.com/opensuse/10.2/repodata/repomd.xml.key'
   ```

2. Go to YaST Installation Sources on the Software page. Click Add, and the Media Type screen appears.

3. Choose Specify URL and click Next. Enter the URL for your card in the next screen

   ```
   Nvidia: ftp://download.nvidia.com/opensuse/10.3
   ATI: http://www2.ati.com/suse/10.3.
   ```

   When you click Next, YaST probes the source to confirm it has the installation packages and creates the package database on your system. This can take some time, especially if you have a slow connection.

4. When the installation source is configured, you'll be asked to Agree to the openSUSE license agreement. Do that, and click Next.

5. You should see the mirror site added as an additional installation source. Ensure the Status of the mirror site is set to On. Set the Refresh Status to On, so that you get new drivers as they appear. This should be the default, but if it is not, select the source and click Source Settings. Choose Refresh On or Off to toggle this setting. Click Finish to confirm.

6. Open Software Management and get the relevant packages for your card:

```
Nvidia: x11-video-nvidia and nvidia-gfx-kmp-default.
ATI: x11-video-fglrxG01 and ati-fglrxG01-kmp-<kernel-flavor>
```

7. Exit out of your desktop and restart X. Your new drivers should be installed.

Reconfiguring your video card and monitor should also be done automatically if you change your hardware. Clicking Graphics Card and Monitor in YaST's Hardware section opens SaX2 and tells you the current settings.

TIP

Need to test your sound quickly? Head for the KDE or GNOME Control Center and set a system notification. In KDE, go to Sound & Multimedia, and then System Notifications. In KDE System Notifications, select KDE Is Starting Up and click the > icon to play the sound. In GNOME, open System (if necessary) and then Sound. Select the Sounds tab and pick a random sound (you must have the gnome-audio package installed for the default sounds to work).

Configuring a Joystick

If YaST did not detect your joystick, use the Joystick module to select one yourself. It has a Test button, so you can confirm that the joystick works properly with the selected driver.

NOTE

Joysticks connected via your USB port do not need to configure a driver. Just plug your joystick into the USB port and fire away!

You can further configure joystick behavior (even without SuperUser access) in the settings for your desktop environment. In the KDE Control Center, go to Peripherals, Joystick. The GNOME desktop does not have a special configuration tool.

Adjusting Your Keyboard Layout

Do you occasionally type in a different language from your primary tongue? Do you use a Dvorak keyboard? The YaST Keyboard Layout module can change how the OS and all applications respond to your individual keystrokes. Open the module and you will see a long list of layout styles. Select a different language and tab to the Keyboard Test. Chances are that most of the letter keys will be the same as what you are used to, but the punctuation and symbol keys will be different. In some languages, even the number keys will be changed. The changes generally involve accented letters and common symbols used in a particular language.

NOTE

Changing your keyboard layout to a different character set (such as Russian-Cyrillic or Japanese) will not load that character set. You will need to install the appropriate language font set first.

Click the Options tab to change certain system defaults. If you don't use the keypad on the right of your keyboard to enter numbers and don't like the NumLock light on all the time, you can turn off NumLock on startup here. The same is true for Caps Lock. You can even disable Caps Lock completely (click None in this section). These settings are written to `/etc/sysconfig/_keyboard`, so you can review and adjust them manually if you prefer.

TIP

You can further configure keyboard behavior (even without SuperUser access) in the settings for your desktop environment. In the KDE Control Center, go to Peripherals, Keyboard. In the GNOME Control Center, go to Hardware, Keyboard. One nice thing about the GNOME keyboard settings is that you can tell the system to force you to take breaks from your keyboard to forestall repetitive motion injuries.

Configuring Your Mouse

In all likelihood, YaST autodetected your mouse and loaded appropriate drivers during the installation. If your mouse worked during the installation, it should be installed properly. Feel free to check what driver openSUSE is using in the YaST Mouse Model module. If your mouse is not working properly, press Alt+C on your keyboard or use your tab key to select Change to see other mouse drivers.

Although many drivers are included in the list, options are minimal. Consult the documentation for your mouse to check for appropriate drivers. If you don't have a working mouse, use the Tab key to maneuver to the module and then to the list. If you see your model, arrow down to select it. Click OK (or press Alt+K) to return to the main screen to test the new driver. Click in the Test area, and the display should show you the click. If this driver fails the test, you will have to work your way through the list, testing one by one to find a working driver.

TIP

You can configure (even without SuperUser access) many more mouse options in the settings for your desktop environment. These include selecting left-handed mouse behavior, cursor themes, and acceleration settings.

In the KDE Control Center, go to Peripherals, Mouse. In the GNOME Control Center, go to Hardware, Mouse.

Configuring Your Scanner

If YaST did not autodetect your scanner when you first installed (or when you hooked it up to your PC), you've got problems. Manual configuration of USB-connected scanners is complex and dangerous (it is possible to damage your scanner with the wrong settings). Manually configuring a SCSI scanner is a little easier, but you can't do it without shutting down your system first.

Before manually configuring any scanner, consult with your local Linux User Group (LUG) for help. See the "Getting Help: Documentation and Other Sources" section of Chapter 1 for information on finding a LUG and other resources to help you.

Common reasons for a scanner not being detected include the following:

- The scanner is not supported. Check http://en.opensuse.org/HCL/Scanners for a list of Linux-compatible devices.
- The SCSI controller was not installed correctly.
- There are termination problems with your SCSI port.
- The SCSI cable is too long.
- The scanner has a SCSI light controller that is not supported by Linux.
- The scanner is defective.

If you use a Hewlett-Packard scanner, or an HP All-in-One device, make sure the hplip package is installed on your system. This is available in YaST. Even if YaST doesn't recognize the scanner immediately, use the Add button to configure the hplip driver for your model.

Configuring Your TV or Radio Card

With a TV card, you can turn an ordinary PC into a home entertainment system. You'll learn more about this, including how to make your own personal video recorder, in the "Watching TV and Video" section of Chapter 10, "Sights, Sounds, and Other Fun Things."

As with the other cards and peripherals in this chapter, YaST should have recognized your TV or radio card on installation. If not, you can install it manually with the TV Card module. Open the module in YaST and click Add. A list of manufacturers and models (see Figure 4.4) appears. Select yours.

Depending on your card, you may also have to select a tuner model. Click Select Tuner and choose from the list. To get a list of TV stations and channels available to you, click TV Channels and use the drop-downs to set your location and type (TV Standard) of signal. North Americans should set the TV Standard for NTSC and choose one of the US Frequency Tables. Click Scan the Channels to get the list. You can then use the Add, Edit, or Delete buttons to customize the list.

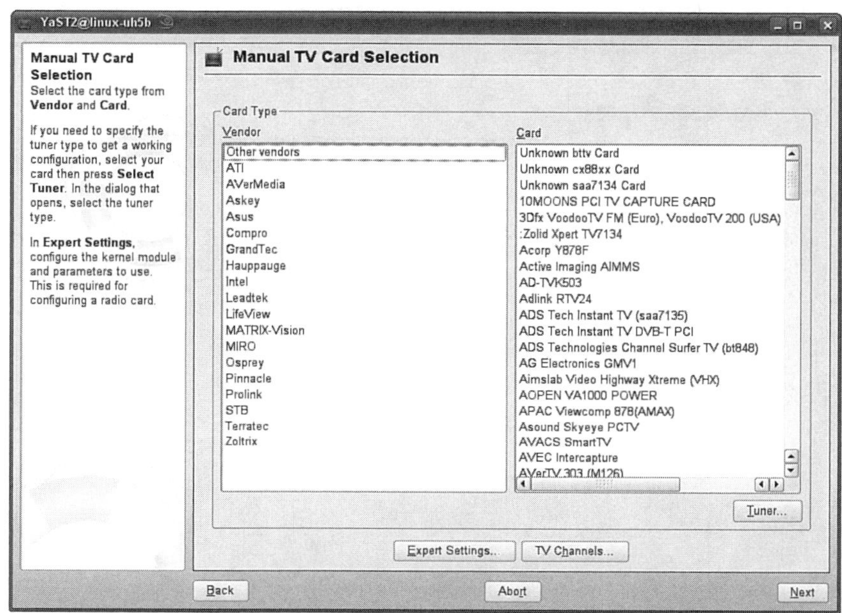

FIGURE 4.4 Select your TV card from the list.

Click Next to specify how to manage audio output. By default, openSUSE sends it to your sound card. If you have multiple sound cards, you can select one here to work with your TV card. If no sound cards are set up, click Configure Sound Cards to open that YaST module and follow the steps outlined in the earlier section. Click Next to continue.

This screen configures the infrared control mechanism for your card. You can choose from two different kernel modules to load and then click Test to see which one works. Click Next to complete the process. You can also chose "Do Not Configure IRC" if you want.

Setting Date and Time

During the installation, YaST will ask for your time zone and set your clock accordingly. If you move, or if you have a laptop that travels with you, it's easy to change time zones with the YaST Date and Time module (see Figure 4.5), which is located on the System page. When you open it, select your region in the left pane and your time zone in the right.

If you prefer to have your clock set in relation to the Universal Time (also known as Greenwich Mean Time), click the Etc region. The Global region includes several non-standard zones, such as South Pole time and Navajo time.

In this module, you can also specify how the kernel sets your hardware clock at boot. If you are dual booting with Windows, this should be set for Local Time. Otherwise, it is good to use the Unix Universal Time standard.

When your settings are correct, click Accept to confirm.

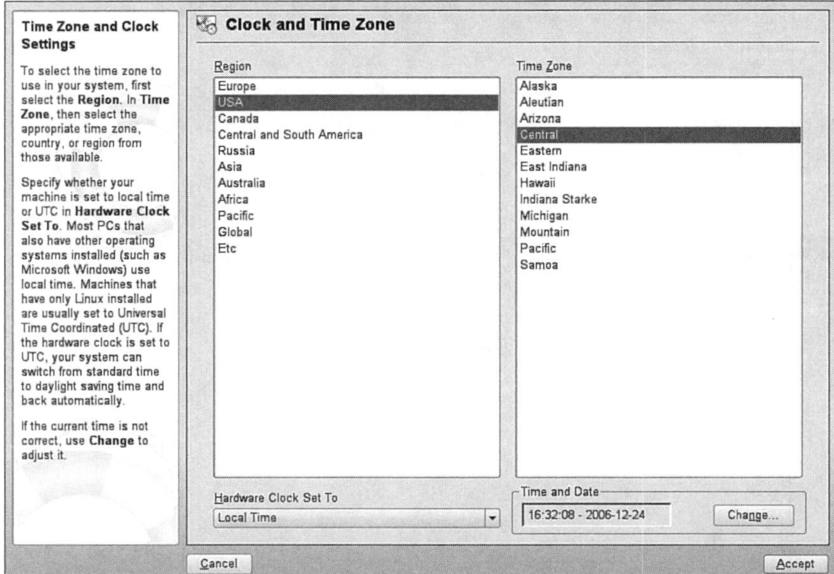

FIGURE 4.5 Select the desired time zone in the Date and Time module.

You can also configure your time and date settings in your desktop environment. Change time and clock settings in KDE by right-clicking on your taskbar clock, usually located on the right end of the taskbar. This context menu gives you the option to change your time-zone, manually adjust the time, and change the display settings. If YaST configured your system to display 24-hour time, you may want to switch this to AM/PM right away. You have to reboot for the changes to stick, though.

In GNOME, right-clicking the clock opens the Clock Preferences dialog box. You can choose from four display types: the traditional 12-hour (AM/PM) and 24-hour standards, or the less traditional UNIX or Internet times. UNIX Time counts seconds since January 1, 1970, while Internet Time was invented by the Swatch watch company. Here's how they describe the format on their website:

"Internet Time is a new universal time created by Swatch. With this new way of timekeeping, there are no more time zones, as the entire world is happening at the same time, at the same moment. Internet Time divides the 24 hours of a day into 1,000 units called beats. 1 beat represents 1 minute, 26.4 seconds. Internet Time is displayed by @ and three digits, ranging from @000 to @999. The internet day starts at midnight (@000) in Biel, the home of Swatch."

Use the checkboxes to decide whether to display the passing seconds and/or the current date on your clock, and whether to use Universal Time (called UTC here).

Using the Network Time Protocol (NTP) to Keep Accurate Time

If you have an always-on connection to the Internet, either through a LAN or broadband modem, consider running a Network Time Protocol (NTP) client. You can use NTP to connect to public servers attached to an atomic clock. These clocks, which measure the resonance of a cesium atom, will lose a second every million years. The NTP client included with openSUSE checks with a specified public time server and resets your system's clock accordingly.

Go to the YaST Network Services page to open the NTP Client module (see Figure 4.6). Turn the client on by clicking During Boot where it asks when to start the client. This will load the NTP client daemon. To make it work, the daemon needs a time server to connect to.

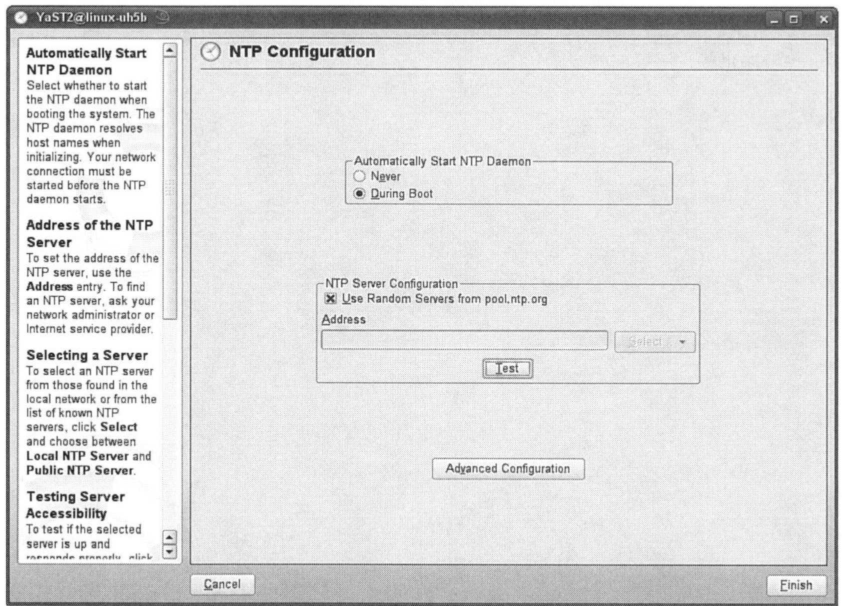

FIGURE 4.6 Set up your NTP client to use the pool NTP servers to reduce the load on high-traffic servers.

There are two ways to set up your NTP connection, simple and advanced. The easiest way is to choose Random Servers from pool.ntp.org, identify another machine on your LAN (which, presumably, is then connected to a time server), or choose from a selection of public time servers that SUSE has found.

To ease the burden on public time servers—and keep them going—the Server Pool Project was created. This is a system where the client points to a nearby pool server (such as north-america.pool.ntp.org) and this site points to a different public server every hour. It is most courteous to do this, so leave this box checked unless you have a good reason not to. Click Test to confirm that this connection is working.

NOTE

YaST works with pool.ntp.org to deliver the appropriate time server for your area, but if you're curious, visit http://ntp.isc.org/bin/view/Servers/NTPPoolServers for the current list of subzone pool servers.

If you prefer to choose a server to which to connect, uncheck the Pool box and use the drop-down menu to define the type of server (local or public). Choose Public NTP Server, and you will see a list of predefined servers for your country. Select one geographically close to you. It's a little better if the server is in your time zone, but it does not matter greatly. Click Test to confirm the server is active and then click OK to confirm the selection.

Click Advanced Configuration to set up a backup server. Click Add from the first screen (Figure 4.7). After choosing Server from the Peer Type choices (Figure 4.8), click Next.

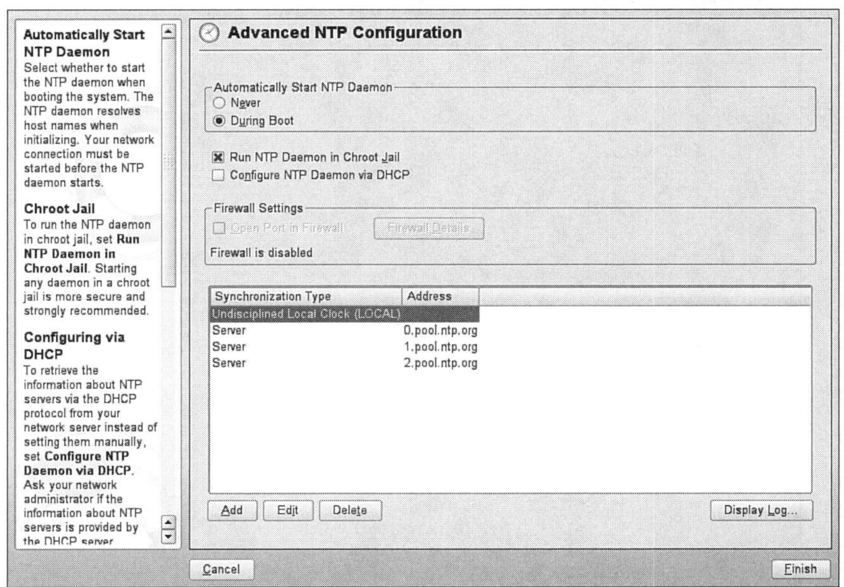

FIGURE 4.7 Configure the Network Time Protocol daemon in YaST.

There are other settings in the Advanced Configuration dialog box. Accepting the defaults, as always, is OK.

- Run NTP Daemon in chroot jail—Never underestimate the creativity of bad guys who want to interfere with your system. When you are contacting remote public servers, there is a risk (however slight) that malware could exist on that server that could compromise security on your system. Checking this box (which is the default setting) puts the NTP daemon in a special `/home/jail` directory, from which it cannot access any part of your system.
- Configure NTP Daemon with DHCP—If there is a DHCP server on your network, it may help you connect to NTP servers. This provides another security layer, because the information passes through another secure machine before getting to you. Check with your network administrator to see if the DHCP server is set up to look for NTP servers before turning this option on.

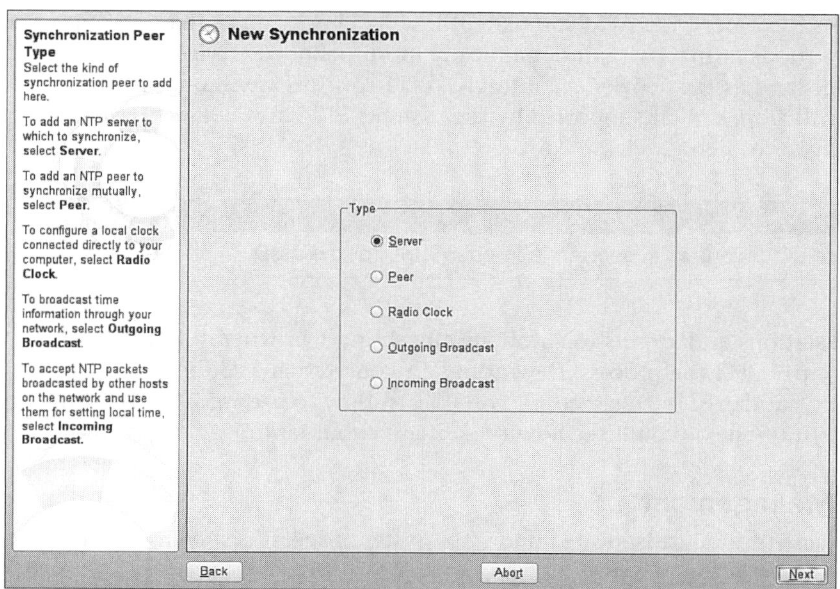

FIGURE 4.8 You can select from many types of timekeepers, but most likely you will choose a public time server to manage your clock.

- Open Port in Firewall—Say you're traveling with your laptop, and want to connect to this machine through a Wide Area Network to set your laptop time. You must first open the firewall to get access. Do that by checking this box. Click Firewall Details to choose a network interface that you'll use. It's best to only open one port in the firewall.

Click Finish to confirm your choices. The NTP daemon will connect to your designated server(s) the next time you boot to Linux. If you change settings while the daemon is running, YaST will restart it when you click Finish.

Power Management

There's no getting around this fact: Computers and peripherals consume a lot of electricity. With dwindling supplies of fossil fuels leading to ever-higher energy bills, it's good to minimize the power drain.

We are in a transition phase for power management on PCs and laptops, with one standard replacing another. Advanced Power Management (APM) is supported by most hardware manufacturers and BIOS routines.

Advanced Configuration and Power Interface (ACPI) is a power-management specification that allows the operating system (OS) to control the amount of power distributed to the computer's devices. Devices not in use can be turned off, reducing unnecessary power expenditure. ACPI is the latest generation of DOS-based power management software for

PCs. ACPI replaces the older Intel APM software utility. ACPI does more than just manage timeouts during periods of inactivity; it dynamically monitors power usage within the computer's systems and assigns power accordingly. ACPI controls are found in your PC's BIOS, and ACPI will work only if supported by the systems BIOS and your systems OS, such as SUSE Linux as of Kernel release 2.6.

NOTE

One place where ACPI alone is supported is in openSUSE for the AMD 64-bit processor.

APM allows workstations and servers to automatically shut down when told to. ACPI provides more control over the process. Depending on your system, you may want to configure for both standards. In this section, you'll learn how to use YaST to configure your desktop PC. In the next, you'll see how to configure your laptop.

YaST Power Management

The Power Management module is located under the System page. It is shown in Figure 4.9.

By default, a PC is set for best performance, but you can adjust this scheme in favor of Powersave (for the least energy consumption) or Acoustic (for quiet operation). You can add your own scheme or edit existing ones by clicking Edit Schemes.

The Test scheme lets you check custom settings without adjusting one of the standard schemes. Select this scheme and click Edit to view the complete power management settings. After naming the scheme, you see the Hard Disk and Cooling Policy settings (see Figure 4.10).

Standby Policy tells openSUSE Linux what to do when the machine comes out of Standby mode. Set it for Maximum Performance (the hard disk will spin up fast); you can also set it to Power Saving or Aggressive Power Saving (for degrees of slow waking). You can also disable this completely.

Acoustic Policy attempts to make your hard disk quieter by slowing down movement of the disk heads. Settings here are Maximum Performance, Quiet, and Maximally Quiet.

Cooling Policy addresses the fan that dissipates the heat your processor generates. To save power, the fan does not fire up automatically if the PC overheats. Change the Status setting to Active if overheating is a problem with your machine.

The Overheat Temperature Action and Critical Temperature Action menus define what openSUSE Linux should do when things get hot. These choices include:

- Notify—Puts a warning message onscreen.
- Shutdown—Turns your machine off.
- Switch to Standby—This shuts down power to your screen, turns off the fan and any other system power drains until you power back up. Designed for brief respites, data is not saved before going to Standby.

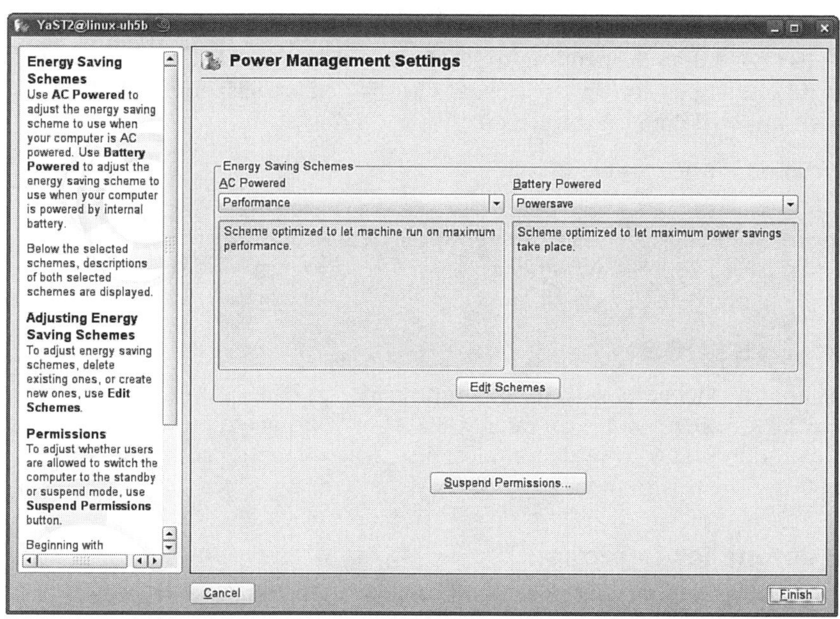

FIGURE 4.9 YaST offers several power management schemes, or you can adjust it your own way or even make your own.

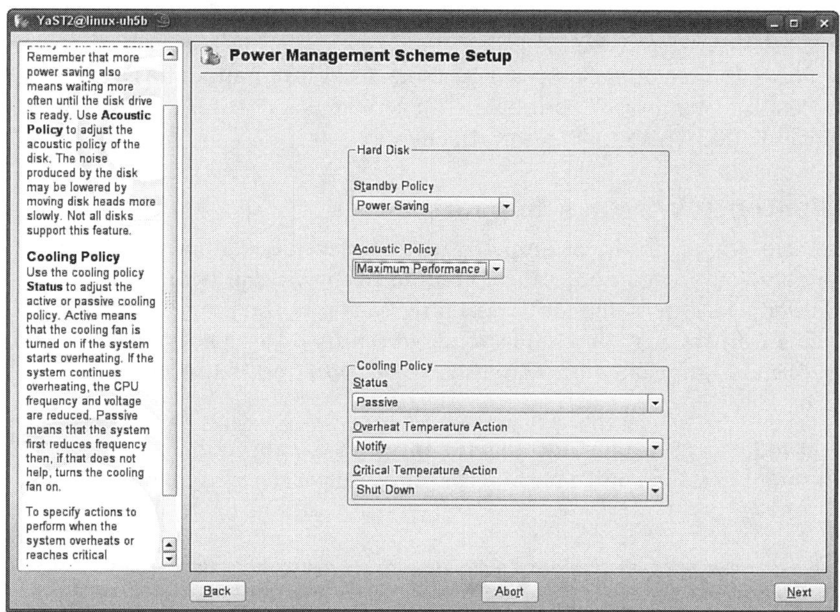

FIGURE 4.10 Edit Schemes lets you play with your power management settings.

4

- Suspend—Two choices here. Suspend to Disk protects your data most effectively, but takes longer to revive than Suspending to RAM. Suspending to RAM recovers quickly, but if you happen to run out of power while you are suspended to RAM, you could lose unsaved data on the screen.
- Ignore—Carries on blithely as before.

Click Next to confirm your changes. Select the Power Scheme you want to use going forward, and click Finish to apply these settings.

Portable PC Issues

Laptop computers are finicky beasts with many proprietary bits of hardware and software. These issues can make it difficult to install openSUSE. After you have the OS installed and running, though, you don't have to settle for a lesser system when you're on the move. This section will offer some tips to help.

Power Management for Laptops

openSUSE configures laptops for saving power and prolonging battery life, regardless of whether you have an APM or ACPI system (see the earlier "YaST Power Management" section if you missed these definitions). The YaST Power Management module, also covered in "YaST Power Management," lets you tweak those settings.

Working with PCMCIA Cards

Laptops often use PCMCIA (Personal Computer Memory Card International Association) cards to add functionality, memory, or peripherals. To activate support for PCMCIA cards, use the YaST Runlevel Editor. This module is on the System page.

Configuring Bluetooth Wireless Support

When the Swedish telecommunications company Ericsson developed a new wireless tool that allowed different electronic components to communicate without being attached by heavy cables, it wanted a snappy name for it. Reaching back into the Scandinavian past, someone discovered a Danish king, Harald Blaatand, who united Denmark and Norway in the tenth century. Blaatand translated into English is *Bluetooth*. And that is how this trademark was born.

openSUSE should autodetect your Bluetooth device and load the appropriate drivers. YaST should also install the `bluez-libs` and `bluez-utils` software packages to manage your connection.

TIP

Install `bluez-cups` if you need to print via Bluetooth.

You can enable Bluetooth support manually through the YaST Bluetooth module, which is located on the Hardware page. This tells the kernel to hot-plug the Bluetooth kernel module and its daemon at boot. Click Advanced Daemon Configuration to further set up Bluetooth support (see Figure 4.11).

If you want Bluetooth communication channels to be encrypted, click Security Options. First, enable Authentication to force users to enter a password before making a Bluetooth connection; then enable Encryption to further protect data passing through the connection.

NOTE

Not all Bluetooth devices support authentication or encryption. You may have to turn these options off when connecting to a device that does not authenticate users or encrypt data.

Click Finish to confirm your changes.

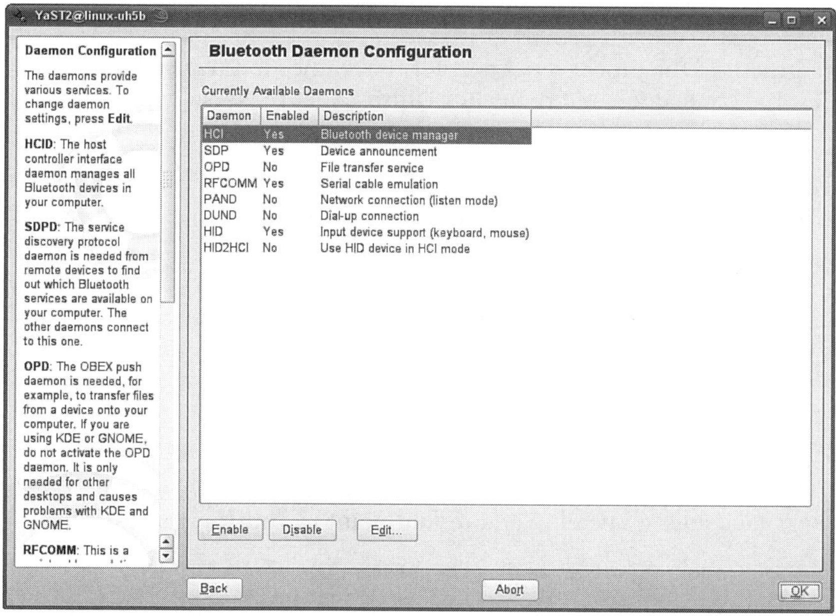

FIGURE 4.11 Configure the Bluetooth daemon here.

Configuring Infrared Interface (IrDA) Mode

Chances are good that your laptop uses either Bluetooth or Infrared Data Association (IrDA) to communicate with other devices. IrDA's differences with Bluetooth are minimal, but significant:

- In Bluetooth, the individual devices do not need to see each other directly.
- In Bluetooth, several devices can be connected in a network. However, the maximum data rate is 720 Kilobits per second (in the current version 1.2). The next version of Bluetooth is expected to improve that rate to more than 2 Megabits per second.
- Theoretically, Bluetooth can even communicate through walls. In practice, however, this depends on the properties of the wall and the device class. There are three device classes with transmission ranges between 10 and 100 meters.

There are two IrDA operation modes. The standard mode, SIR, accesses the infrared port through a serial interface. This mode works on almost all systems and is sufficient for most requirements. The faster mode, FIR, requires a special driver for the IrDA chip. Not all chip types are supported in FIR mode because of a lack of appropriate drivers. Set the desired IrDA mode in the BIOS of your computer. The BIOS also shows which serial interface is used in SIR mode.

IrDA is a major drain on your battery, so openSUSE does not automatically turn IrDA on at boot. You must go to the YaST Infrared Device module located on the Hardware page.

Click Start IrDA and then set the proper serial port for the connection (consult your laptop manual). Test the connection and then click Finish to get to work.

Configuring CD, DVD, and Rewritable Drives

So much of our entertainment now comes on compact disks of various types, it is essential for our computers and operating systems to keep up. Although it has had some obstacles to surmount, Linux developers have made it relatively easy to run CDs, DVDs, and the gamut of recordable CD formats. This section focuses on the technical end of providing device drivers for these types of drives and disks. To learn more about the Linux multimedia experience, including how to burn CDs and DVDs, see Chapter 10.

Integrating CD and DVD Drives into Your System

openSUSE Linux simplifies the process of mounting your CD and DVD drives. The system identifies your drive(s) and adds a reference and mount point to your `/etc/fstab` file.

▶ Learn more about mounting drives and `/etc/fstab` in Chapter 18, “Managing Files, Volumes, and Drives.”

References

- http://www.bluetooth.com—The Bluetooth website.
- http://www.holtmann.org/linux/bluetooth—Marcel Holtmann's Linux and Bluetooth page. Articles in English and German, plus downloads.
- http://www.cs.ucl.ac.uk/staff/s.zachariadis/btpalmlinux.html—A guide to connecting your Palm PDA to your PC with Bluetooth.
- http://tuxmobil.org—The place to get information on Linux on all sorts of mobile hardware: laptops, PDAs, and cell phones. A monthly newsletter is available as well.
- http://tuxmobil.org/howto_linux_infrared.html—The Linux Infrared HOWTO. Configuring and using IrDA.
- http://linux-laptop.net—Another portable Linux site.
- http://www.sane-project.org—Home of the Linux scanner driver project "Scanner Access Now Easy." Search to see if your scanner is supported by Linux.
- http://www.ntp.org—Network Time Protocol home.
- http://support.ntp.org/bin/view/Servers/WebHome—The Public NTP Server list. Find a Network Time Protocol server to connect to. Contains much more helpful information, too.
- http://ntp.isc.ort/bin/view/Servers/NTPPoolServers—Information about the NTP Pool servers.
- http://www.cpqlinux.com/acpi-howto.html—The Linux ACPI HOWTO.
- http://en.opensuse.org/HCL/Scanners—Provides a list of Linux-compatible devices.

PART II

Using openSUSE

IN THIS PART

CHAPTER 5

Getting Started with openSUSE

IN THIS CHAPTER

- Logging In to openSUSE
- Working with the Linux File System
- Essential File System Commands from the `/bin` and `/sbin` Directories
- Using the `/boot` and `/dev` Directories
- Editing Configuration Files in the `/etc` Directory
- Where All the Good Stuff Goes: Your `/home` Directory
- Finding Desktop Programs in `/opt`
- Where Most of the Programs Go: The `/usr` Directory
- Variable Data: The `/var` Directory
- Changing User Information and the Finger Program
- Choosing and Using a Shell
- Editing Text
- Why Can't I Edit This File? How Permissions Work
- Working as Root
- References

In the days before the X Window System made things a little more soft and cuddly, Unix was labeled the most user-unfriendly operating system known to humanity.

There was the cold, forbidding command-line interface (CLI) with seemingly millions of obscure commands to learn. Today both Unix and Linux have an assortment of terrific graphical interfaces to give you point-and-click ease for your computing tasks, but even if you use them all the time, it is good to have access to and an understanding of that command line (usually called the shell or console). When you want something done quickly, or want to understand what's going on under the hood when you ask Linux to do something, the shell is the place to go.

In this chapter, you will learn the basics of interacting with openSUSE, from logging in to understanding the file system to dealing with file permissions.

You'll pick out the best shell for your working style and play with some text editors, too. By the end of the chapter, you'll be able to handle the power of being the Root user and know when and how to wield that power.

Read this chapter in particular if you are transitioning from a proprietary operating system, even more so if that operating system was Windows 98 or earlier, which had no conception of logging in multiple users and dealing with security via file permissions. Read this chapter whether you are the administrator (Root user) of your system, have some administrative privileges (via `sudo`), or are just an ordinary user in an office with an IT staff. If you are more experienced using Unix or another Linux distribution, you may still find some new tricks, or just get a refresher on the basics.

Logging In to openSUSE

After you have installed openSUSE and created at least one user (yourself) on the system, you must log in. The standard login is pretty straightforward. By default, openSUSE boots to a KDE-based graphical login screen, known as the display manager. You enter your username (or click the icon representing you) and password. By default, you will start in the same desktop environment you were in the last time. Click Session Type to choose a different environment (your choices will depend on what you have installed). Click System if you want to shutdown or restart your system. Press Enter to log in.

Logging In from the Shell

What about those times when you don't need to load graphics just to log in, get a piece of information, and shut down? Or what if X has a problem loading? The text login is a simple process. openSUSE boots to a login shell. Type your username and press Enter to get the password prompt. Enter your password, and you have full access to your system (or at least as much access as you have with the graphical interface).

NOTE

In this book, you will see some terms for the Linux command-line interface used somewhat interchangeably.

Most often, you'll see *shell* or *command line* to refer to this interface. When you read about a command to run at the shell prompt, you can run that command whether or not you have a graphical interface loaded.

Occasionally, you will see a reference to a `console`, or `X Terminal` (`xterm`, for short). These refer to graphical shells within an X environment. Some consoles have additional tricks they can do that a standard shell can't. When you see these terms, understand that the instructions apply only to the graphical shell.

NOTE

If you get the text login prompt as a result of something bad happening and X won't boot, it is always better to log in as Root because you will have more tools to fix what went wrong. If you are not Root (the system administrator), go get the person who is.

Logging Out of the Shell

Typing **`exit`** or **`logout`** logs you out of the shell. At this point, another user can log in, or you can shut down your computer. Depending on your settings, users may be able to use the `shutdown` or `reboot` commands to perform these tasks.

Working with the Linux File System

As the Internet has just a few specific but well-known top-level domains (.com, .net, .org, .edu, and the like), so too are Linux files organized in a particular hierarchy, with specific directories that hold specific types of files.

Virtually all Linux distributions have the same structure, and this is likely to become more entrenched with the Linux Standard Base specifications becoming more universal. The Linux Standard Base (http://www.linux-foundation.org/en/LSB) is an effort to make all Linux distributions more compatible with each other, and with most applications. Novell/SUSE is a longtime supporter of this effort, and has been compliant with LSB standards since LSB v1.0. In addition, the Filesystem Hierarchy Standard seeks specifically to standardize the contents of the top-level Unix/Linux directories. This structure is beautiful for software developers because they can know what directories will be present on each user's machine and can install programs into the appropriate directory. It also enables programmers to build more modular programs, which depend on other standard libraries. It helps packaging systems—such as the Red Hat Package Manager (RPM) that openSUSE uses—check and confirm that a file on which a package depends is present on a user's system. Testing goes easier, too, because fewer things can go wrong.

We went over that structure briefly in Chapter 2, "Preparing to Install openSUSE." To have another look and get your first lesson in using a shell, open the KDE Konsole and type **`ls /`**. You should see the following:

```
bin    dev    home    media    opt    root    srv    usr    windows
boot    etc    lib    mnt    proc    sbin    tmp    var
```


For a more detailed view of the file system from the shell, use the `tree` command. This program might not be installed by default, but it is on the DVD. The results displayed by this program include all the top-level directories listed in "How to Partition Your Drive(s)" in Chapter 2, along with a few levels of subdirectories.

NOTE

When you're typing into the KDE Konsole, you're using the `bash` shell in an X Terminal (or `Xterm`). You'll learn more about shells and terminals, including how to change the defaults, later in the chapter.

In Windows, you have the capability to create, delete, and rename as many top-level directories and subdirectories as you want, and very few bad things can happen to you as a result. Renaming the Program Files or Windows directories would cause problems, but the system won't come to a halt if you installed a program to a directory outside of Program Files. Although you have the same technical ability to manipulate the directory structure in openSUSE, at least if you have Root privileges, *don't*!

The sole exception to this otherwise ironclad rule is in your home directory. As a user, you can and should organize your documents and other data any way you see fit. You will see several recommendations in this book to put particular files and programs in your home directory because it can be the best place for them. If you find it useful, put every file you create in its own directory (although that might be a little extreme).

This recommendation extends to putting files of your own creation into one of the system directories. Say you create a text file that has a collection of tips and tricks you've learned about the `bash` shell over the years, called `BashTips`. Because you know that man pages and other documentation for bash goes in the /usr/share/doc/bash directory, you might be tempted to store the file there. No problem—unless somewhere down the road one of the developers or documentation writers adds a BashTips file to the bash package. When that file gets installed, your file is replaced with no questions asked, never to be recovered. No program will ever try to copy a file in your home directory, so put things that are yours there.

TIP

If you ever find the need to have files in two places at once, use symbolic links, usually called *symlinks*. In the preceding example, keep the file in /home/documents/bash. Then open a shell and type **ln -s /documents/bash/BashTips /usr/share/doc/bash/MyBashTips**. Now if you look for MyBashTips in this directory, it will open your file. More about this later.

Essential File System Commands from the /bin and /sbin Directories

The /bin (short for binary) directory holds your shell applications and many essential shell commands you need when running and booting Linux. The /sbin (or system binary) directory contains the various installed file systems, YaST, the SUSE Firewall, and other commands needed at boot or for the Root user to solve systemwide problems. On the average system, each directory will have 5–8MB worth of files in them, with /sbin a little bit bigger than /bin. Many, if not all, of these commands are statically linked, not dependent on other software libraries located in other directories (mostly /lib and /usr/lib). Nearly every other application on your system relies on one or more of these external (or shared) libraries to run. These dynamically linked applications create a software ecosystem that ties an application to its operating system. Statically linked applications and commands, along with the kernel, represent the operating system itself.

Using the /boot and /dev Directories

The /boot directory contains a compressed version of the Linux kernel that loads at boot (earlier versions of the startup script delivered a message that the kernel was "exploding," which undoubtedly unnerved more than a few novices in those days). When you rebuild or install a new kernel, the new kernel and related files go first into this directory (see Chapter 24, "Kernel and Module Management," for more information on updating your kernel).

Linux device files are located in the /dev directory. As noted earlier, nearly everything in Linux is represented as a file. No further proof is needed than a peek into this directory. There you will find about 7,500 files representing devices that are or may someday be attached (or not) to your system. The more commonly used devices include the following:

- IDE and SCSI hard drives, represented as hda and sda, respectively.
- CD-ROM, CD-R, and CD-RW drives (and their DVD counterparts), some of which are IDE; others are viewed by the system as SCSI.

- Serial ports, marked `tty`.
- Pointing devices, such as `/dev/input/mouse`.
- Universal Serial Bus (USB) devices, in the `dev/usb` directory.
- Printers, marked `lp`.

If you're running short of disk space, you might think cleaning out some of these files would help you. Closer inspection reveals that they are all 0-byte files. Leave them alone.

Editing Configuration Files in the /etc Directory

One of the beauties of Linux applications is the way you can make software your own. Whether it's changing the behavior of a command, adding a keyboard shortcut, or changing the color of the application title bar, there are lots of ways to make the applications you use work the way you want them to. Often, you don't even have to open the application you want to modify to make the changes you want. Most applications store their configurations in a simple text file located in the `/etc` directory. Scroll through the directory to see exactly what is there. Check permissions to see which user owns a file before trying to edit it—if Root owns the configuration file, you'll have to log in as the SuperUser to make changes.

Some of the more important system-related configuration files in this directory are as follows:

- `fstab`—This file system table lists each mountable storage device on your computer. These include hard drives, floppy drives, CD and DVD drives, and removable drives. The file displays each device's mount point, its location on the partition table, instructions on whether it should mount automatically on boot, and a few other options. See the section "Mounting a File System" in Chapter 18, "Managing Files, Volumes, and Drives," for more information on `/etc/fstab`.
- `inittab`—The system initialization table defines the different runlevels that the system uses at boot to start your computer. Changes to this file (which can be made manually, but also in YaST's `suseconfig` editor) can determine whether you boot to a graphical or text login screen, as well as whether someone can log in to the machine remotely with a dial-up modem. You will learn more about the boot process and runlevels in Chapter 22, "Managing the Boot Process and Other Services."
- `modprobe.conf` and `modprobe.conf.local`—The main `modprobe.conf` file contains directions and options used when loading kernel modules to operate various pieces of hardware, such as sound cards, USB devices, network cards, and the like. The contents of this file are used during boot. SUSE engineers update this file from time to time and recommend that if you want to do your own editing, you use `modprobe.conf.local` to keep those changes from being overwritten. You will learn more about `modprobe.conf` in Chapter 24.

5

- passwd and shadow—The passwd file and its more secure counterpart, shadow, contain the list of all users on the system, along with their account information. It's often said in Unix circles that a user doesn't exist until she has a password. This is one of the reasons why. You will learn more about users and passwords in Chapter 19, "Managing Users, Managing Security."

Where All the Good Stuff Goes: Your /home Directory

Ultimately, the most important data on any desktop or workstation computer belong in this directory—the files you create for yourself. While many important files may be stored elsewhere (or in a database) if you are using your system as a server, the /home directory is essential for desktop users. Every real user (in contrast to a system user) on a Linux system gets a /home directory labeled with his or her username. That user has complete control over folders and files created in this directory and control over all access to those files except for the Root user.

In an effort to be helpful, openSUSE adds a few subdirectories to the /home directory by default:

- /bin can hold binary (program) files, but is usually empty to begin with.
- /Desktop holds your KDE desktop icons. GNOME users tend to have a cleaner look, but the subdirectory is there if you want it.
- Documents is a lovely place to store word processing files and other, well...documents.
- /public_html is a place to store your website. If you have a web server, such as Apache, installed, this directory links directly to your localhost URL. Read more about building websites in Chapter 14, "Creating Basic Websites," and Chapter 31, "Programming Dynamic Websites." Learn more about the Apache web server in Chapter 26, "Managing Web and FTP Servers."

You can work with these subdirectories, create more, or delete some—your /home is your playground. But remember, back up your /home directory regularly. It's designed for that.

Finding Desktop Programs in /opt

The Filesystem Hierarchy Standard (FHS) says, "The /opt/ directory provides storage for large, static application software packages." In practice, this seems to mean applications oriented to the desktop. Confined within /opt are all the built-in KDE and GNOME applications, Mozilla and its Firefox progeny, Softmaker Office files, and the Zope web application server. Depending on what you have installed, your mileage may vary.

Where Most of the Programs Go: The `/usr` Directory

The `/usr` directory is somewhat surprising when you look at it, because it has a parallel structure to the main (/) directory. This is why some folks give `/usr` its own mount point (that is, in DOS/Windows it would have its own drive letter). This directory is usually quite large (in the multigigabyte range, depending on how many applications you install) and contains many shared files and applications. It also houses the X Window System for graphical and remote computing. This directory is the place to start when looking for a particular application on your system, to handle troubleshooting, desktop icon placing, and everything in between.

Variable Data: The `/var` Directory

The `/var` directory holds subdirectories used by various system services for spooling and logging. Some of the files in this directory are temporary, like a printer queue spooler file. System and kernel logs keep much longer and so are renamed and rotated through periodically. Incoming local email is usually directed to `/var/spool/mail` as well.

Linux also uses `/var` for other system services. YaST keeps backup boot sectors and YaST Online Update files, among other things, in `/var/lib/YaST2`. The RPM package database is also stored in `/var/lib/rpm`.

Changing User Information and the Finger Program

Unix was born in a multiuser environment at Bell Labs and was widely used in university computer science labs with a bunch of students floating in and out using whatever terminal was available. Defining users in a system was a necessity in the early days of Unix. As more users came on to systems with the advent of the PC, requiring users to log in was the touchstone of security measures. Today, because of viruses, worms, and assorted evildoers trying to almost constantly break into networks, named users and passwords are essential elements in any secure computing environment.

The Root user, who is responsible for all administrative tasks on the system, creates an account for each user. This involves assigning a username and creating an initial password for that user. You created the first user account for your system during the installation in Chapter 3, "Installing openSUSE."

The Root user can delegate responsibilities to a single user or a group of users by sharing the Root password. Those users can then run the SuperUser program (su) to act as the Root user. You will learn more about SuperUsers in Chapter 19.

Individual users cannot change their usernames. System administrators of large user communities like to have some consistency in usernames, especially considering that a username is a central element of that user's email address. Users can, however, change the information associated with their name and contained with other login information in `/etc/passwd` and in the public finger file. This is generally phone-directory information that may need to be public, but that otherwise may be an artifact of a bygone era.

Finger was a program developed to help Unix users find each other, both electronically and physically. Typing **finger** <username> delivered whatever was in that user's finger file. To see what's in yours, type **chfn** (change finger information) at the shell prompt. By default, openSUSE does not create additional user information with new users, but it is easily configured by Root. You'll see something like this:

```
Name:
Office:
Office Phone:
Home Phone:
```

You're led through a series of prompts to enter new or updated information. Feel free to leave items blank (or change them appropriately).

Choosing and Using a Shell

The shell is perhaps the most underappreciated feature of a modern Linux system. New users try to avoid it, preferring the GUI tools that they are used to. Old-timers are wedded to the shell they learned at school. There's no real reason to give the shell a second thought, is there? Of course there is!

By default, openSUSE (and pretty much all the other Linux distributions) installs the `bash` (Bourne Again SHell) shell as the standard command-line interface. There's certainly no reason not to take this fine choice and run with it. But this is Linux, and there's absolutely no reason not to explore some or all of the alternatives to `bash` included in openSUSE. This section will introduce you to these options, tell you how to change shells temporarily and permanently, and then offer pointers on how to use a shell productively.

NOTE

Learn even more about using shells, including writing shell scripts to automate tasks, in Chapter 8, "Shaking Hands with Your Shell."

Cool Stuff That All Shells Have in Common

The shell is not just a keyboard-based program launcher. It is a powerful tool you can use to get lots of things done quickly—if you know how to use it. Some shells are designed for running scripts to automate tasks, and others work best interacting with its favorite user—you! Following are some of the things that all shells have in common:

- Command history—The shell stores every command you enter (up to a limit, which is configurable). This feature lets you easily access and repeat commands from the history. Press the up-arrow key to see the last command and keep pressing the key to view each previous command. Pressing the down-arrow key moves forward in time, as it were, returning you back to an empty prompt. To reuse a command, locate it and press Enter to run the command. This works over sessions, too. Even if you run the shell only once a month (or once a decade), the command history stays current.

- Filename completion—Another terrific tool for lazy typists. Start typing a filename and press the Tab key. The shell checks the path for files that start with the characters you typed, and a suggestion appears. This is especially helpful when performing actions on files with long names, or deep in a directory. Some shells will also complete commands. See the sections on running `tcsh` and `zsh` later in the chapter.
- Command-line editing—Did you mistype a letter in a command and get an error? Don't retype the whole thing; use the command history and left- and right-arrow keys to get to the error, or change the options.
- Many utilities —Tools such as `sed` and `awk` can help with commands and scripts.
- Aliasing—Another typing shortcut, similar to a symlink. One command (or set of letters) stands in for another. This is set up in the shell configuration file. Among other things, aliasing allows bash to run when you type `sh` and the `tcsh` shell to run when you call `csh`.
- Background processing—If one command is taking a long time to complete, you can move it to the background and run another command.
- Multiple sessions—You can have more than one shell (and multiple instances of the same shell) open at the same time, even without a graphical interface, and switch back and forth.
- Programmable everything—The shell is a programming environment with languages on par with any other programming language.

5

These are just some of the advantages of most all shells. But how does one shell differ from another? We will look at the three most popular shells—`bash`, `tcsh`, and `zsh`—in some detail, and then look at Midnight Commander (`mc`), a specialized shell for managing files and directories. Finally, there is a very brief introduction to the Korn (`ksh`) and the Almquist (`ash`) shells.

Running `bash`

Just about every Linux user has used `bash` at least once. As one of the original GNU projects, it has been in development since 1987. Version 3.0 was released in July 2004 and is included in openSUSE Linux. As you might guess from the name, `bash` (Bourne Again Shell) is the logical successor to the venerable Unix shell (`sh`) written by Steve Bourne. This is a shell best adapted for running scripts to automate tasks.

You can tweak `bash`'s performance by editing the `.bashrc` configuration file. Root can edit the systemwide `.bashrc`, and each user on the system may have his or her own configuration file, although a user cannot override the system configuration.

Looking at a configuration file provides both a sample of the kinds of things you can do with a shell and offers a glimpse at the syntax each shell uses to perform its tasks. The default system configuration in openSUSE, `bash.bashrc`, is located, like other configuration files, in the `/etc` directory. Let's look at some of the settings defined here.

This section lets you display directory listings in different colors.

The colors are set in another file, `DIR_COLORS`. In this setting, `bash` looks for `DIR_COLORS` first in the home directory, then in `/etc`.

```
#
# Colored file listings
#
if test -x /usr/bin/dircolors ; then
    #
    # set up the color-ls environment variables:
    #
    if test -f $HOME/.dir_colors ; then
    eval `dircolors -b $HOME/.dir_colors`
    elif test -f /etc/DIR_COLORS ; then
    eval `dircolors -b /etc/DIR_COLORS`
    fi
fi
```

Note the hash mark (#) in front of some of the lines. This indicates a comment line. The line is not processed by the shell, but usually describes what the next batch of code is supposed to do.

The next section defines some aliases. As mentioned before, aliases are command-line shortcuts that allow you to substitute one command for another.

```
    #
    # Set some generic aliases
    #

    alias rd=rmdir
    alias md='mkdir -p'
    alias which='type -p'
    alias rehash='hash -r'
    alias you='yast2 online_update'
```

This alias is a nice one. If you often mistype a command, you can specify a little reminder. You may think that the opposite of the `mount` command to display a drive or partition is unmount, but really it's `umount` (no n). This alias tells `bash` to remind you of the right command every time you add the extra n. Sure, you could just have unmount replace umount on your system, but what if you are working on someone else's system that does not have this alias? You may just forget the real command.

With this method, you might train your fingers to type the right thing after a few gentle nudges.

```
    alias unmount='echo "Error: Try the command: umount" 1>&2; false'
    test -s $HOME/.alias && . $HOME/.alias
    fi
```

This section modifies how the command history is handled, by making sure the History file doesn't get too big with many duplicate listings of the same file.

```
    # Do not save dupes and lines starting by space in the bash history file
    HISTCONTROL=ignoreboth
    if test "$is" = "ksh" ; then
    # Use a ksh specific history file and enable
        # emacs line editor
        HISTFILE=$HOME/.kshrc_history
        VISUAL=emacs
    fi
    ;;
esac
```

SUSE recommends not editing this default system file, because it can be overwritten in a system update. With this bit of code, bash checks for a local configuration file edited by the system administrator, saved as `/etc/bash.bashrc.local`:

```
if test "$is" != "ash" ; then
    #
    # And now let's see if there is a local bash.bashrc
    # (for options defined by your sysadmin, not SuSE Linux)
    #
    test -s /etc/bash.bashrc.local && . /etc/bash.bashrc.local
fi
```

As noted at the beginning of this section, bash is a shell environment for scripting. Other shells are designed to be more interactive. Let's look at the leading example: the C shell.

Running `tcsh`

Bill Joy (later to become a founder of Sun Microsystems) wrote the original C shell in college. He aimed to provide a more interactive work environment, with a syntax more like the C programming language.

Interactive shells are focused on directly processing commands you type in, rather than running scripts or files. Script-oriented shells such as bash can be used interactively, but it is rarely a good idea to make a C shell run scripts.

The version of the C shell included in openSUSE is called `tcsh`, a tribute to the TENEX mainframe operating system. It has programmable command completion and a referable command history.

The best thing about `tcsh`, though, is its command spell checker. If you type **`frotune`** at a `tcsh` prompt, it will ask if you mean **`fortune`**. A yes answer gives you a fortune cookie. Configuration options are set in two files: `etc/.tcshrc` and `etc/.tcshrc.conf`.

5

Running zsh

The Z shell strives to be the best of both worlds, enabling you to safely write scripts or use it interactively. It is based on the Korn shell (ksh) written by David Korn, with tons of extra features. Many folks love zsh for its power and flexibility, but with great power comes great complexity. This shell's Info file has 21,530 lines of documentation in 11 subnodes. We won't cover all of that here.

zsh has virtually all the neat features previously listed and works quite well with the default configuration file (etc/zshrc).

Some features, such as command spell check, are not set by default, but it is a fairly easy task to edit them.

This shell also checks your default text editor, and if it is emacs or vim, it will adopt that editor's key bindings (a.k.a. keyboard shortcuts) in addition to its own.

Managing Files with Midnight Commander

Whatever shell you choose for your everyday use, you may find the Midnight Commander a handy tool for moving files around. Suppose you don't need to load a full GUI desktop to move a batch of files, but even all the wildcards and completion shortcuts offered by your shell won't let you easily copy a set of files from different directories into one other directory. You need something else—something that will display two directories side by side and let you drag or move things from one place to another. You need Midnight Commander!

To open Midnight Commander, type **mc** at the shell prompt. Figure 5.1 shows the initial default display of your home directory on both sides of the screen. Use the arrow keys to navigate in the left pane. Use the Tab key to move from one side to the other, and then move around. Select a file or folder and press Enter to open that item. Mouse support is excellent; click any menu at the top to see your choices. Along the bottom are the F-key bindings: pressing F1 brings up the Help file, F2 displays a context-sensitive menu of choices for the selected file or directory, and so on.

To copy a set of documents with the .odt extension from ~/Documents to a directory on a remote server called /backup/mikemc, follow these steps:

1. In the left pane, use the arrow keys to navigate to the /Documents directory. Press Enter to open this directory.
2. Tab to the right pane. At the bottom of the Midnight Commander, you will see a flashing cursor. This is a shell prompt. Type **cd /backup/mikemc** to navigate to this directory. You could use the parent folders, marked .., to find the directory, but this is faster.
3. Tab back to the left pane. Press **Alt-+** to open the Select Group dialog. Type ***.odt** and press Enter to select all files with the .odt extension.
4. Press F5 to open the Copy dialog box. Confirm that the correct files are going to the correct directory. Select any options you want by navigating with the Tab key and selecting with the spacebar. Press Enter to complete the operation.

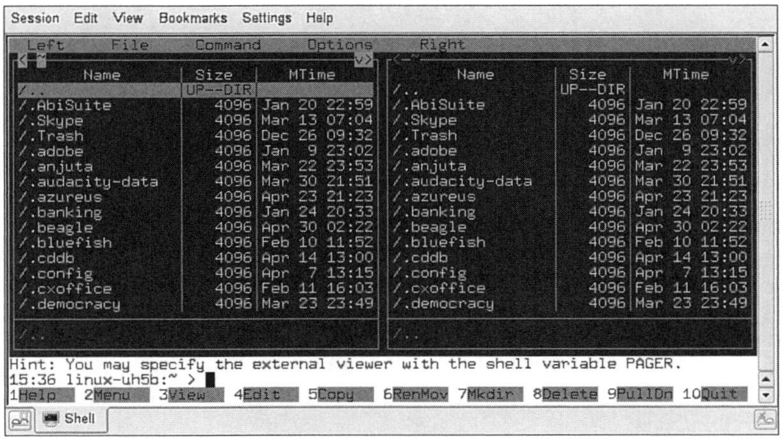

FIGURE 5.1 The Midnight Commander shell.

Midnight Commander is a program ripe for exploration. The first few times you work with it, play around a little. Go to a menu, or press an F key to see what a command does.

The help files are indeed helpful! This is a full-featured file manager. View hidden files if you like, access FTP sites, upload or download files (at the same time, if you want to), run executables, and change permissions (if you can) and owners with the `ChMod` and `ChOwn` commands. In short, just about everything you can do with a file in a shell, you can do with Midnight Commander. It even has a command history.

TIP

The KDE Konsole lets you open a new Midnight Commander session from the Session menu. Choose regular or Root (with your password).

`ksh` and `ash`

The other shell choices may be less popular, but are still valid. Here's a quick overview:

- Korn shell (`ksh`)—This shell, written by David Korn, was the first popular shell to try to combine the scripting features of the Bourne shell and the interactive features of the C shell. AT&T tried to turn `ksh` into a commercial product, with limited success. There are two versions of the pure Korn shell: `ksh88` and `ksh93`. openSUSE includes both the latest version of `ksh93` and the public domain `pd-ksh`. The latter has reproduced most of the features of `ksh88`, with a few new ones of its own. The Z shell is also one of the Korn shell descendants, and if you know `ksh` well, you should be able to function well with `zsh`.
- Almquist shell (`ash`)—This lightweight Bourne-like shell has but 17 built-in commands, so as a shell, it's perfect for embedded and other tight spaces and login shells. In fact, it is the SUSE login shell.

Choosing a Shell

You now know a little bit about each shell. How do you decide which to use? The easiest thing is, of course, to stick with what you know. If you have used a shell before, there should be some compelling reason to switch. Similarly, if you don't ever intend to do anything fancy with your shell, you might as well stick with `bash`. You can certainly do very fancy things with `bash`, but why change from the default?

`bash` is also a great tool to learn scripting from. Resources abound on the Net to help you do that, and you'll learn more about that in Chapter 8 as well. If you don't want to write scripts, use an interactive shell such as `tcsh`, `pd-ksh`, or `zsh`.

If you are a lousy typist, you should certainly consider one of the shells with a spell checker. `tcsh` spell checks by default; `zsh` spell checks with a very quick configuration file edit. The fancier you want to get with file and command completion, the more you'll probably want `zsh`.

As recommended at the beginning of this section, try out all the shells, at least once. All you have to do is type the name of the shell at any other shell prompt. When you're done and want to return to `bash`, type **`exit`**. Look over the documentation. All the shells have extensive man or info pages. After you've settled on a shell, run the Change Shell (`chsh`) program to identify your choice. Then take some time to read those docs thoroughly.

Now that you've settled one of the interminable Linux wars to your satisfaction, you can choose a text editor.

RUNNING YaST FROM THE SHELL

YaST is a tool older than most GUI desktop environments, and it runs beautifully from any shell. Log in as the SuperUser with the `su` command, and then type **`yast`** at the prompt. Figure 5.2 shows the opening screen in a KDE Konsole.

This is especially useful in an emergency, when the system won't boot to the GUI login screen. To restore your system from a previous backup (see Chapter 20, "Managing Data: Backup, Restoring, and Recovery," for more information on backing up and restoring your system), follow these steps:

1. Run YaST by typing **`yast`** at the rescue prompt.
2. Use the arrow key to select System from the listing on the left.
3. Tab to the module section on the right, and then arrow down to Restore System.
4. Follow the instructions on the page or view details in the "Using System Restoration" section of Chapter 20.

To maneuver around the menus and choices, use the accelerator keys highlighted on each screen. Press the Alt key with the highlighted letter to move to the item you want. For example, in any screen, press Alt+H to get Help on that screen. When finished, press Alt+Q to Quit and return to the shell prompt.

All YaST modules that are in the GUI version work in the command-line version as well, although Online Update (YOU) is dependent on the state of your Internet connection.

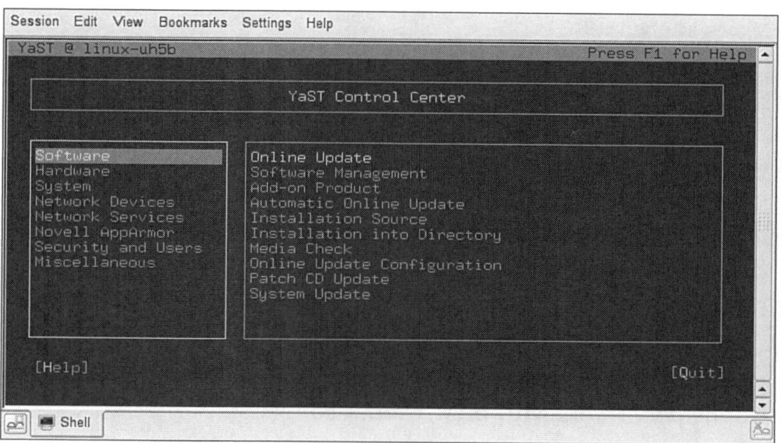

FIGURE 5.2 YaST works just as well from the shell as from a GUI environment.

Editing Text

Because Unix and Linux are rooted in the hacker/geek/programmer culture, where coding was (and is) the most important function of any computer, having robust shells and editors were essential parts of the experience. It is no accident that Bill Joy wrote both the C shell and the `vi` editor, nor that Richard Stallman created the GNU Project and the `emacs` editor (and that each has completely different views about how to create and license software).

Of course, that was in the bygone early days of Unix. Why does it matter what text editor you should use now? And why do you need one, anyway? Consider this: Word processors are wonderful things, but often they are the very essence of overkill. One of the beauties of Linux is that nearly all the configuration and customization options for applications are contained in simple text files. This is true whether the program has a GUI or not. So making changes in the way a program works doesn't necessarily have to require opening the program; just open the config file in a text editor!

There's one other reason to be at least somewhat comfortable with at least one nongraphical editor. One of the truly cool things about Linux is the capability to access many different computers regardless of where you happen to physically be located at a given moment.

Remote access to other servers and workstations is another beauty of Linux, but most times, those remote machines (especially the servers) don't even have X installed. To get any work done, you need a text editor.

openSUSE offers no fewer than 19 text editors through YaST, as shown in Table 5.1. Don't be overwhelmed by the number of choices, though. Basically, text editors fall into one of two major camps: editors that behave like `vi` and editors that behave like `emacs`. This list also has a few line editors that work directly in the shell.

TABLE 5.1 Types of Editors in openSUSE

Vi-type	emacs-type	Other
Vim	emacs	Ed
Gvim	Xemacs	Joe
Nvi	TeXmacs	Pico
Kvim/Yzis	Uemacs	E3
	Zile	FTELeaf
	Qemacs	Mined
		THE (the Hessling Editor)
		JEdit

The next few sections will help you work with these various editors.

Working with `vim` and Its Clones

They say that `vi` is hard to learn, but once you get there, you can do amazing things with it. That hard-to-learn part is evident from the first time you use it (unless you have a `vi` user nearby). When you first open the `vi` editor (and these days, typing `vi` actually opens its "improved" version, `vim`), you cannot type anything. By default, `vi` opens in its command/viewing mode. You can maneuver around a file, provided you know that commands in `vi` begin with a colon (`:`). To edit a file, you must press the Insert key (or `Esc+i`) first.

After you know this secret handshake, `vim` can be very useful and, with practice, very powerful. It also comes with extensive documentation. The documentation page at the Vim.org site says it best: "The most useful software is sometimes rendered useless by poor or altogether missing documentation. Vim refuses to succumb to death by underdocumentation."

To quickly get up to speed in `vim`, you don't have to run the editor. Run `vimtutor` from the shell prompt to get a brief tutorial, estimated to take about 30 minutes to complete.

Following are a few commands that will help you get started with `vim`:

Simple navigation: Your arrow keys work fine, but these characters also move the cursor:		
	`h`	left
	`l`	right
	`k`	up
	`j`	down
Delete character	`x`	
Delete line	`dd`	
Copy (yank) selected text	`y`	
Paste (put)	`p`	
Undo	`u`	
Save	`:w` (write)	
Find text in file	`/<string>`	
Changing mode from Insert to Command	`Esc`	
Quit	`:q`	
Quit without saving	`:q!`	

Vi and Yzis run inside your shell. Gvim offers a GUI for the basic editor. Nvi is a slightly different version of vi from the University of California at Berkeley.

Working with `emacs` and Its Clones

GNU `emacs` is the infinitely customizable, everything-but-the-kitchen-sink editor/work environment. It was the first product of the GNU Project, and so is beloved by many free-software purists.

It is the text editor that keeps your hands busy over the keyboard with seemingly odd multiple keybindings (Ctrl+X to begin a command and another combination to complete it). Learning `emacs` is a supremely geeky thing to do.

If `vim` has everything an editor should have in one pretty, if sometimes impenetrable, package, `emacs` is a modular monster. `emacs` reads email and Usenet newsgroups, browses the web, and composes web pages in HTML, XHTML, XML, and sundry other formats as well. It offers a development environment for practically every extant programming language. You can even see a sublimely odd conversation between Zippy the Pinhead and a psychoanalyst. But to do all this, you must have the proper mode installed. `emacs` is a big program (taking up to 30MB), but it does not include every mode that has been written. Sometimes you have to go hunting for the thing you need.

5

`emacs` is easy to start up (type **`emacs <filename>`** from the shell prompt), and navigation can be pretty easy.

Unlike `vim`, `emacs` has its own interface (vim shows up just in the shell) with menus and mouse support, although it is not quite as pretty as under X. Unless you include a mode command when you launch it, `emacs` assumes you want to write text and loads in text fill mode. If you don't want words to wrap at the end of a line, go to the Options menu or type `Alt+X+auto-f[TAB]` to change the mode.

`emacs` also has a tutorial that will walk you through the basic commands and navigation tools. In `emacs`, use Ctrl+H, and then press "T" to get to it. Here are some examples:

Simple navigation: Your arrow keys work fine, but these characters also move the cursor:

Left (backward one character)	`Ctrl+b`
Right (forward one character)	`Ctrl+f`
Up (previous line)	`Ctrl+p`
Down (next line)	`Ctrl+n`
Delete character	`Ctrl+d`
Delete line	`Ctrl+k` (kill)
Transpose 2 characters	`Ctrl+t`
Transpose 2 words	`Alt+t`
Cut character	`Ctrl+d`
Cut word	`Esc+d`
Copy selected text	`Esc+w`
Paste	`Ctrl+y`
Undo	`Ctrl+x, u`

Save	`Ctrl+x, Ctrl+s` (one right after the other)
Find text in file	`Ctrl+S <string>`, (Forward) `Ctrl+r <string>` (Backward)
Changing mode from Insert to Command	`Ctrl+x`
Quit without saving	`Ctrl+x`, `Ctrl+c`

Most of the other clones of `emacs` (aficionados use the plural `emacsen`) are subsets of the original designed for specific uses. XEmacs began as a plain GUI version of `emacs`, but has a separate group of developers. XEmacs does some things differently from its command-line parent. Generally speaking, XEmacs is faster for adding new features and does not require packagers to assign copyright to the Free Software Foundation, which administers the GNU Project.

Some of the Others

You don't need to follow the crowd when choosing an editor. Choices are not limited to the big two. Take these for a spin:

- `ed`—The first Unix line editor. It opens by default in viewing/command mode and is the reason `vi` does the same. You could put it in the `vi`-clones category, if it didn't predate `vi`. If you need a shell script to edit or perform commands on some text, `ed` is the editor to invoke. It's fast and functional for basic line editing.
- `Joe`—You say you can't decide whether `emacs` or `vi` is cooler? Do you still remember all those WordStar commands and macros? You just might love Joe's Own Editor. `Joe` is a flexible beast that wants to work the way you want it to. It can emulate any of the previously mentioned editors with a simple command switch. You can open and edit multiple files at once and provide different environments for each one. Like `emacs`, it can read email and news, too. Help is extensive and can put a command template right on your screen so that you don't have to think about how to save a file (Ctrl+K, and then D, if you must know).
- `JEdit`—This is a Java-based graphical editor that many folks swear by. Although powerful by itself, it also has a plug-in architecture that can bulk it up even more. The nice thing is that it is incredibly easy to add and update any plug-in you have with the built-in plug-in manager. The commands are relatively easy to learn, and the user's guide is helpful.
- The Hessling Editor (`the`)—This is a specialized editor for people used to working in VMS/CMS and another example of how niches get served in an open-source environment. There may not be millions of VMS veterans with wallet in hand transitioning to Linux, but it takes only one person with some programming skills to write that editor and make it available to the rest of us.

Why Can't I Edit This File? How Permissions Work

If there's one thing that is important to know about Linux, it is that everything on your computer exists as a file. There is a file on your system that represents each device on your system—printer, sound card, hard-drive partitions, monitor, and directories. Each file has rules about who can access it and in what manner.

In this section, you will get an introduction to permissions. You'll learn about permissions in more depth in Chapter 19. No matter what your skill level is, you should read the "User Accounts and Permissions" section of that chapter.

Linux is a multiuser operating system, with a minimum of two users on any machine: the Root user and a generic user.

NOTE

The Root user is also the SuperUser when logged in as such, and other users can become the SuperUser with the Root password.

Each file (again, that means everything on your system) has an owner and is assigned to a group when it is created. Read, write, and execute permissions are set for three types of user: Owner, Group, and Others (that is, the rest of the world).

The `ls -l` (long format) directory listing command displays the permissions for each file. To see the system default permissions for a file, use the `touch` command to create an empty file and then run `ls -l`, like this:

```
touch file
mikemc@linux:~> ls -l file
-rw-r--r--    1 mikemc   users           0 2004-12-08 09:43 file
```

TIP

`touch -t` will also change the access time of any existing file.

Looking at this listing, you see a 10-character block of dashes and letters (`-rw-r--r--`). These characters identify the permissions for this file.

The first character in the block indicates whether the referenced file is a special file in some way (`d` identifies it as a directory, `c` is for a character device, and `b` is for a block device, such as a hard drive). We know this is a plain data file because there is a dash that indicates that the file is not any of these special types. You'll learn more about the other types of files and devices you may encounter in Chapter 18.

The default permissions for this file show us that the Owner of the file can Read and Write it (`rw-`); it is Read-Only (`r--`) for both the Group and Others (the rest of the world). If this was supposed to be an executable program file, a problem would exist, because no one has permission to execute it.

The next columns tell us other important things about this file:

- The number next to the permissions block shows the number of hard links to a file. You may better understand this as the number of copies of this file that exist on the system. Files almost always have just one link/copy. Directories nearly always have at least two because each directory is linked in its parent directory.
- After the link counter, you see the Owner of the file. Because we created the file logged in as user `mikemc`, `mikemc` is the owner. In this case, this user is the only person who can edit this file (that is, make changes to and write back to the hard drive). The Owner can be changed by either the current Owner or by Root using the `chown` command.
- After the Owner is identified, you see the Group (users) assigned to this file. This means that all users on the system can read the file, but cannot write (save changes) to it. As with any read-only file, other users can save changes in a different location or with a different filename. The Group assignment can be changed by the Owner or by Root using the `chgrp` command.
- The file size and creation date are defined in the last columns. This file is empty; if the file had content, the size would be defined in bytes.

Changing Permissions

When you are the owner of a file (or the SuperUser), you have the right to make that file more (or less) accessible by adjusting its permissions. You do that with judicious use of the `chown` (Change Owner), `chgrp` (Change Group) and `chmod` (Change Mode) commands.

NOTE

You can make these changes in any of the GUI file managers (Konqueror, Nautilus, and so on) by opening the Properties dialog box of a file (or group of files). This is covered in more detail in Chapter 18.

To make user2 the owner of the file we created in the last section, type the following:

```
chown user2 file
```

CAUTION

If your system administrator has imposed disk quotas for users, only Root can change owners. This prevents you from exceeding your quota by fobbing off your excess files on another user. Disk quotas are covered in Chapter 18.

This trick works for multiple files, too. Name each file or use wildcards to specify similar files. For example, if you have a bunch of files in this directory that begin with "file" and you want to change ownership of them, modify the previous command to

```
chown user2 file*
```

As with many Linux commands, when you run this command, the shell prompt will reappear unless there is a problem or error.

Our file allows only the owner to make changes (write) to the file. If you want anyone in the writers group to be able to edit it directly, you should change the group assigned to this file from users (which are all system users) to writers (a previously defined select group of users):

```
chgrp writers file
```

CAUTION

chgrp works only if you are both the Owner of a file and a member of the group you're changing to. If you want to change permissions to a different group, you may be able to use the newgrp command to temporarily join that group, if you know the group password. Otherwise, Root must make the change.

But we're not done; the group permission is still set for Read-Only. We complete the task here:

```
chmod g+w file
```


As noted in the previous section, permissions are defined as Read, Write, and eXecute—rwx. With the `g+w` switch, we've told `chmod` to add (+) Write (w) privileges to the Group (g).

The choices for chmod include the following:

u—User

g—Group

o—Others

a—All users

Plus sign (+)—Add a Read, Write, or eXecute permission

Minus sign (-)—Remove a Read, Write, or eXecute permission

Some people prefer using octal (base 8) numbers when using `chmod`. This way, instead of adding or subtracting individual permissions, you can specify exactly what you want them to be when you complete the command. Using octals to make the same change we made previously, the command looks like this:

```
chmod 664 file
```

Why these numbers? Each digit represents one set of permissions: Owner Group Others. Each number represents the rights each entity has:

4 = Read permission

2 = Write permission

1 = Execute permission

Add each permission number to signify the permission level the file should have. So, as shown, the Owner and Group has Read and Write (4+2=6); Others just has Read.

To confirm the changes you've made, just run `ls -l` again.

Directory Permissions

Directories also have permissions assigned to them. Use `ls -dl` (`d` for Directory, `l` for Long version) to see the permissions of your current directory (most likely, the `home` directory). You should see something like this:

```
drwxr-xr-x    64 mikemc    users         4056 2004-12-09 15:02
```

The distinguishing mark here is the leading `d` in the permissions block. This tells you that you are looking at a directory. Looking carefully, you can see that the Owner (`mikemc`) can do everything (`rwx`), whereas the users Group and Others can only read a list of the directory's contents. You have to have execute rights (`r-x`) to view directory contents. Looking at this octally, permissions are set at `755`.

You can perform the same permission changes on directories as with files, using the same tools, provided you have the rights to do so.

Working as Root

Permissions, or more importantly, the lack of them, mean a lot on a Linux (or Unix) system, especially if you're just a user. Permissions are all about security—keeping the system safe from harm. In this case, harm can come from many directions. When you think about computer security, the vision that comes to your head is mostly likely that of the evil hacker who attempts to steal your passwords, credit card numbers, critical data, or even your identity. Security on the Internet is certainly an important consideration, and protecting your networks and systems against that type of criminal activity is essential.

TIP

If you spend any time hanging around the Linux community, you will probably get a lecture about the hacker previously described. Don't be put off; Unix and Linux were both forged out of the more noble "hacker culture" devoted to making better technology, not to busting into other people's machines.

In Linux and Unix, however, security and permissions also keep you from the more mundane harm and the bad things that can happen to any user at any time, such as the time you accidentally deleted an entire folder of documents relating to your company's latest merger from your machine, and it took the IT staff a week to reconstruct it from backups.

As Root, you have inestimable power at your fingertips. You can keep the system humming, or you can bring it down with a few keystrokes. All you have to do to destroy a system is type this command (*Don't* try this at home!):

```
rm -fr /
```

This command removes (`rm`) all files and directories recursively from the root of the tree. If you're dual-booting with a mounted Windows partition, that partition will be gone, too. If you happen to be logged in to some remote machine somewhere that is now part of your system, it's best to get on the phone now. The remote files are disappearing, too.

TIP

This scenario is another reason to not mount your Windows partition(s) automatically at boot time.

So don't take chances. Even if you are the all-powerful Root on your machine, always log in as the humble user unless you have system work to do. Even though you can add the Root user to your openSUSE graphical Login screen, don't. Save it for emergencies.

Now that you're properly terrified, let me tell you that there are essential tasks that must be performed by the Root user. You can do these things safely, too. We will go into detail about many of these things in Parts 3 and 4, but for now here is a small list:

- Install and update most software
- Run YaST
- Set the clock
- Turn the firewall on and off
- Add and delete users
- Kill some services

The best way to perform all these tasks is to use the `su` (SuperUser) command and type the Root password. You can do whatever tasks you need to, return to the shell prompt, and type **`exit`** to return to your user prompt.

NOTE

When you run YaST and some other graphical programs that need Root access, they will sometimes offer to remember the Root password for you. If there is any chance that some day you will forget the Root password when you need it the most, don't take them up on this offer. Just keep typing it in. For more tips on passwords, see Chapter 19.

As Root, you can allow specific users to perform specific tasks using the `sudo` command. This is described in detail in Chapter 19.

Creating and Deleting Users

A user is not a user until he or she has a password. All user passwords (and occasionally some other information) are stored in the `/etc/passwd` file. You can create new users in openSUSE in two ways—through YaST or through the shell.

When you first installed openSUSE, you created your first user—you. If different people use the computer, giving them their own accounts is essential. If you happen to be the only one planning to use Linux, why would you need to create another? Think about the different roles you play when you're at your computer. You might want to create different users to play those roles, without distraction.

In YaST, managing users and groups comes under the Security and Users tab. To add a user, go to User Management and click Add. You'll be asked to supply a username and an initial password. You'll also be asked if you want to set an expiration date for that password. Changing passwords regularly is a good idea, especially on networked computers, including ones that access the Internet.

From the shell, adding users is a two-step process. After logging in with `su`, use the `useradd` command to quickly create a user:

```
useradd drone77
```

You must now create an initial password (remember: no password, no user) by running `passwd`:

```
passwd drone77
Changing password for user drone77
New password:
Retype new password:
passed: all authentication tokens updated successfully.
```

Enter the new password twice. If you don't do this, drone77 will not be able to log in. The first time drone77 logs in, she will be given the opportunity to create her own password.

Type **`useradd -D`** to confirm the new user's default settings. You will see the Group ID, home directory, account and password policy, default shell, and the directory holding the configuration file for that shell.

As you might expect, if `useradd` adds users, `userdel` will delete users from your system. It is best to delete the user's home directory when you remove the user from the `passwd` file as well. Do this using the `-r` (recursive) switch:

```
userdel -r drone77
```

This also removes the user from the mail queue.

Shutting Down and Rebooting the System

By default, only Root can shut down the system. This is especially important when the system is a server, but it is also good for any networked device where people may depend on a file being available.

Root can allow users to perform this function, which is a good idea when you are using your computer as a desktop or a dual-boot system. This is done in YaST.

To shut down the system from the shell, log in as su and run the shutdown command. The fastest way to do this is with the -h (halt) switch:

```
shutdown -h now
```

or

```
shutdown -h 0
```

If you are on a network, you may want to specify a time for shutdown, and send the other users a message:

```
shutdown -h 18:30 "System is going down for maintenance this evening"
```

The message will go out 15 minutes before shutdown (in this case, at 6:15 p.m.).

To reboot a system, you use the same shutdown command, this time with the -r (reboot) switch. Set the time as you did previously.

If this system is a server, make sure you don't shut it down while something else is happening (such as a backup). Again, with awesome power comes awesome responsibility.

References

This chapter covered a lot of ground. The references will help you go into more depth on the Linux file system, shells, editors, and permissions. When choosing a shell or an editor, I highly recommend reviewing their man (or info) pages, as well as their websites.

File System

- http://www.pathname.com/fhs—Probably more than you want to know about the new Linux Filesystem Hierarchy Standard.
- http://www.linux-foundation.org/en/LSB—The Linux Standard Base page.
- http://standards.ieee.org/regauth/posix—The IEEE POSIX information page.

Shells

- http://cnswww.cns.cwru.edu/~chet/bash/bashtop.html—Chet Ramey's bash page. He is the current maintainer of the bash project.
- http://www.tldp.org/LDP/Bash-Beginners-Guide/html/—The Bash Beginners Guide as a web page. If you visit you can get this in other formats, along with other excellent Linux resources.
- http://web.cs.mun.ca/~michael/pdksh/—The Public Domain Korn Shell home page.
- http://www.tcsh.org/Welcome—The tcsh Wiki. Learn more and contribute your own knowledge about this C Shell.

- http://www.zsh.org/—Home of the Z Shell. Select a nearby mirror.
- http://www.ibm.com/developerworks/linux/library/l-z.html—Good introduction to the Z shell from IBM.
- http://www.ibiblio.org/mc/—Home of the Midnight Commander. Includes screen shots, FAQs, and a TODO list for the developers.
- http://www.dotfiles.com/—Explore contributed configuration files for various shells, editors, and other tools.
- http://www.shelldorado.com/—Heiner's Shelldorado. Includes scripting information for all shells, and a good introduction, too.

Editors

- http://www.gnu.org/software/emacs/emacs.html—The GNU/`emacs` home page.
- http://www.dotemacs.de/—The "very unofficial dotemacs home." Explore the many ways to configure your `emacs`.
- http://www.emacswiki.org—Find new modules and helpful people here.
- http://lpn.rnbhq.org/tools/xemacs/emacs_ref.html—A helpful reference for `emacs` commands.
- http://www.vim.org/—The Vim home page.
- http://vimdoc.sourceforge.net/—Where to find documentation of all sorts for Vim.
- http://www.yzis.org/—The new project from the developers of Kvim for the K Desktop Environment.
- http://joe-editor.sourceforge.net—The home for Joe's Own Editor.
- http://jedit.org/—The Java-based editor.

Working as Root

- http://linux.about.com/od/embedded/l/blnewbie_toc.htm—A basic overview of the Linux Newbie Administrator Guide.
- http://www.gratisoft.us/sudo/—The sudo main page. Includes downloads, documentation, and resources for this command.

CHAPTER 6

Launching Your Desktop

IN THIS CHAPTER

- Understanding the X Window System
- 3D Video with Xgl
- Choosing a Desktop Environment: KDE and GNOME
- Managing Files from Your Desktop
- Configuring Your Desktop Environment
- What Is a Window Manager and Why Would I Want to Use It?
- References

When you normally log in to openSUSE, you use a graphical login screen. That screen, a display manager, is your first taste of the X Window System, more often called X11, or just plain X. X has a much longer history than Microsoft Windows, but it is similar in many ways. It has also gone through more than a few changes along the way. The most recent change is a revival of development from the X.org Foundation, the official owners of X. Earlier versions of SUSE Linux included an open-source version of X for the Intel platform called XFree86; openSUSE uses X.org version 7.2.

X uses a client/server model in its architecture, but it's a little different from what you may think. Normally, you are working with a client on your PC that makes requests on your server, which is remote. With X, the server is installed on your machine. It accepts requests from any number of clients, which can also be on your machine, or connected from a remote location (like a Telnet session). X Servers supply the graphics drawing protocols and much of the network communication to support clients' libraries.

Most openSUSE users boot to an X-based graphical desktop environment. By default, that has always been the K Desktop Environment (KDE). SUSE developers have long worked on KDE, and continue to do so. But in recent years, many users have gravitated toward the GNU Network Object Model Environment (GNOME, pronounced with a hard G sound). Among those were Miguel De Icaza, Nat Friedman, and their Ximian development team. Novell purchased Ximian shortly before acquiring SuSE, Inc., and has been working to promote compatibility between the two desktops and their applications. The SUSE Linux Enterprise Desktop (SLED) seeks the best of both worlds, and openSUSE offers you the choice to install either or both desktop environments.

This chapter covers the basics of the X Window System and how it works in openSUSE. You'll learn about the primary desktop environments, KDE and GNOME. You'll also learn about the new advanced 3-D display system called Xgl. Finally, you'll get a brief introduction to some other X Window managers, if you don't need all that overhead.

Understanding the X Window System

The X Window System represents two primary concepts. The X Window System was created to keep the UNIX kernel and GUI code separate. It was also designed for distributed processing based on the client/server model. That is, with X, you don't need to have a computer with massive amounts of hard drive space and RAM to run graphical applications. A thin client with a connection to an X server is all you need. Nonetheless, if you have the aforementioned massive hard drive and hundreds of megabytes of RAM, you can host both the X server and many clients on your own machine.

The X server's primary job is to create and manage windows, dialog boxes, buttons, and other graphical elements on a screen. That screen can be located practically anywhere in the world, and perhaps even on a laptop on the International Space Station. X is extremely portable, too. After you have configured X the way you (or your system administrators) want it, you can take that configuration file with you and copy it into any other X-capable machine and it will run the same way.

Dozens of applications have been developed to manage windows for X, and hundreds of X client programs exist to help users work in the graphical environment X provides. It all begins, however, with the fundamental question: What do you want your window decorations to look like?

Configuring X in openSUSE

SaX is the X configuration tool for openSUSE. It runs for the first time during the initial openSUSE installation, where it identifies your graphics card, installs the graphics drivers, and sets up X to its default configuration. The settings are stored in the `/etc/X11/XF86Config` file. You can edit this file manually, but that would be unnecessary and risky behavior.

Depending somewhat on your card and driver, SaX is much less configurable in openSUSE than in previous versions. To open SaX after the initial installation, go to YaST, Hardware, Graphics Card and Monitor. A second window will open with your initial monitor and card listed, along with the resolution and whether the card supports 3D acceleration, and possibly some other settings. Click Change to open SaX and configure X.

When you open SaX, you can see that it manages much more than your video settings (see Figure 6.1). If your driver supports multiple monitors, you can set that up in Dual Head Mode. Other SaX2 modules include your keyboard, mouse, touchscreen, and graphics tablet. Remote Access covers Virtual Network Client (VNC) access and XAccess, a tool for controlling your mouse with the keypad (especially useful for people who can't see the screen).

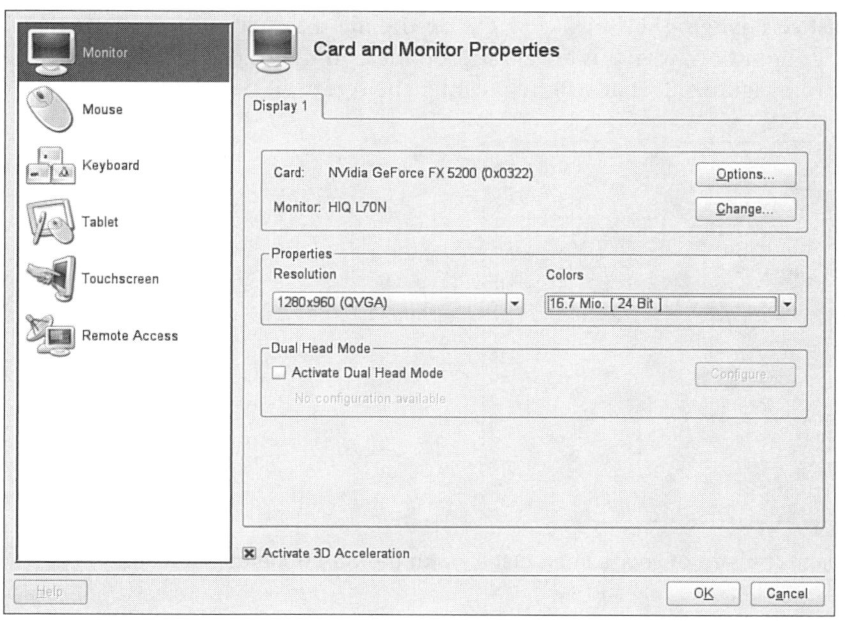

FIGURE 6.1 SaX2 offers a safe and graphical way to configure the X Window System.

If SaX has incorrectly identified your monitor, click Change. You will get a list of manufacturers and models from which to select. Select the correct one; if you have a Linux driver disk for the item, click the Utility Disk button to install the new drivers. In the Options dialog box for your card, you can read and make changes to the frequency range and other settings, but don't do this unless you are absolutely sure you know what you're doing. Click OK and Finish to confirm your choices.

CAUTION

With the wrong Monitor Frequency settings, it is possible (although quite rare) to blow out your monitor.

NOTE

As you make changes in each SaX component, be aware that nothing is written into the configuration file until you click OK and test the new setup.

Use the Color and Resolution sections to define the color depth and resolution (how big your icons are) of your screen. SaX does attempt to identify the best settings for its defaults, but these are adjustable. Where possible, you should select a 24-bit color depth, for the best experience.

When you're finished changing settings, click OK on the main SaX screen. You'll be asked to test the new configuration, which is always a good idea. In the test, you will see the Geometry screen (see Figure 6.2) that will help center the screen, if necessary.

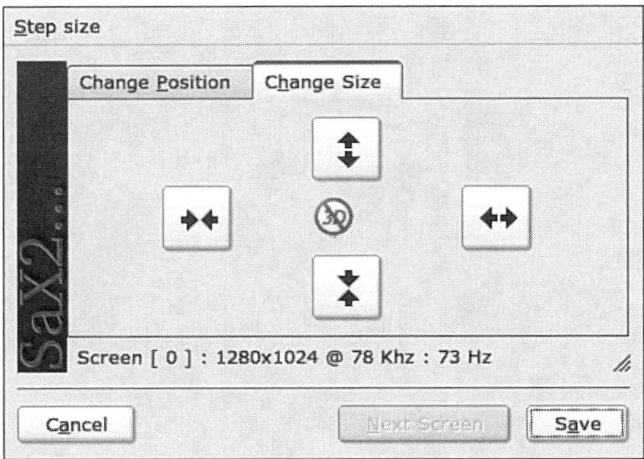

FIGURE 6.2 Adjust the size of your screen display with the SaX Geometry screen.

Change the position if the desktop is large enough in width and height but is still displaying empty space on one side or both sides. Keep pushing the appropriate arrow buttons on the screen until it looks right; then click Save.

If everything looks good, click Save; if the desktop image fails, click Ctrl+Alt+Esc to kill the X server and review your selections.

TIP

In most cases, you'll be using a display manager to log in and start X, but there may come a time when something breaks and you can't get into the display manager. Don't panic! You may still be able to get into X.

If this happens at boot, you will get a text-based login prompt. Log in as user, and you should be sitting in your home directory (type **pwd** to make sure). Look for the .xinitrc file: `ls -a .xinitrc`.

openSUSE puts a default file in your Home directory called `.xinitrc.template`. Make a copy of this file to activate it: **`cp .xinitrc.template .xinitrc`**

Now, type the magic word: **`startx`**.

This should get you in and may help you solve the original problem.

3D Video with Xgl

Video hardware has long supported 3D graphics, but the X Window System architecture predates 3D by a long while. The Mesa project offered an open source version of the OpenGL standard for 3D graphics, but as a software interface, it can only scratch the surface of 3D acceleration available in modern cards. What to do?

Novell developer Dave Reveman worked on this problem for a long time, and in January 2006, he felt he had at least the beginnings of a solution. Reveman built an X server to run on OpenGL (thus Xgl), and released a window manager for this system called Compiz. This technology was included for the first time in SUSE Linux 10.1 and is enhanced in openSUSE 10.3.

Xgl is a work in progress, but much of its promise is on display in openSUSE. You'll see a much faster desktop, to be sure. You can zoom in on portions of your desktop with a keyboard command. Put applications on separate virtual desktops that emulate a cube on your screen. You can also arrange a rainstorm on your screen, and then use a windshield wiper to clear it off!

This section will cover what you need in order to enable Xgl on your system, and how to use the default Compiz Xgl window manager.

Enabling Xgl

Purists who demand only open source software on their systems will have trouble running Xgl. Nearly all open source graphics drivers cannot deliver OpenGL with enough performance to make Xgl run properly. Reverse-engineered 3D drivers for ATI Radeon 300–500 series cards are included in both X and Mesa, but otherwise, you will need to install to install proprietary drivers from your card manufacturer.

The good news is that graphics card manufacturers are producing excellent drivers for Linux. Nvidia and ATI now offer repositories to download drivers in YaST. See the "Configuring Video Cards" section in Chapter 4, "Further Configuration with YaST and SaX2" for details. The other bit of good news is that Intel has released open source drivers for its 965 Express chipset, and plans to expand its open source driver program.

Check the wiki at http://openSUSE.org to see how to install your video card driver before enabling Xgl. When you have completed the driver install, reboot the system to add the driver to your kernel.

CAUTION

When installing the proprietary video drivers for your card, know that you're installing a special kernel module. The driver may require you to install a different kernel. For this reason, it's a good idea to back up your data before installing the drivers, even if you're using YaST.

When you have installed your driver, open YaST and go to Hardware, Graphics Card and Monitor. Confirm that 3D Acceleration is active. Now you can run Xgl.

Go to the YaST Software Management module, and search for the Xgl package. By default, YaST will also install the Compiz compositing window manager, which will become the default, regardless of what desktop environment you choose.

NOTE

A second compositing window manager for Xgl, called Beryl, has also been developed. See the Beryl page on the openSUSE wiki (http://en.opensuse.org/beryl) for installation and usage information. The Compiz and Beryl projects have reunited and should have a single Xgl window manager sometime in 2008.

Configuring the Compiz Window Manager

Generally speaking, GNOME has better support for Xgl and Compiz than KDE at this point. For this reason, the easiest way to set up Compiz and Xgl effects is by using the GNOME Control Panel Desktop Effects module. When you do this, GNOME will check your video card against its database of Xgl-compatible hardware. You may get a caution if your hardware isn't listed as fully compatible, but as long as you support 3D graphics, you'll be allowed to use the tabs to configure Compiz.

Click Window Effects to make your windows wobble when they appear or are moved, among other things.

The Cube is one of two very slick ways Compiz has to deal with clutter on your desktop. If you tend to have too many applications open at a time, and waste time minimizing and maximizing windows, Linux desktops have always had virtual desktops, or workspaces, to ease the burden. Just put related applications on a separate desktop for easy viewing. With the Cube, switching desktops lets you see the edges of each desktop swoosh by while the display shifts. Click Desktop Cube to use the 3D Cube, define how many sides you want the cube to have, and use the other settings to define how to maneuver among them.

Click Other Features to activate the other clutter cleaner, called the Window Picker. When you have more than one application on a desktop, the Window Picker lets you see all the windows with one keyboard command (Ctrl+Alt+UpArrow, by default), and then select the window you want to work on with a mouse click. This tab also lets you define Zoom settings for your desktop, and the "water effect" bit of eye candy, if you want that rainstorm on your desk.

When you've made your selections, click Close to confirm.

NOTE

When you have both GNOME and KDE on your system, turning Desktop Effects on in GNOME automatically activates Compiz in KDE as well. To switch between Compiz and the Kwin standard window manager for KDE, go to Personal Settings, KDE Components, Session Manager. Click the drop-down menu under Preferred Window Manager to change this setting.

Choosing a Desktop Environment: KDE and GNOME

With Windows and the Macintosh, the desktop is just that—the desktop. Linux is all about choices, and so is X. We'll talk about your choices in more lightweight window managers later, but chances are you are going to spend a good chunk of your computing time in one or another of these two desktop environments: KDE or GNOME.

One of the cool things is that you can remain indecisive your whole life: You can choose what desktop to load every time you log in. Of course, you don't have to choose that often either; openSUSE will load whatever desktop you loaded last time by default.

When you first install openSUSE, YaST will give you the option to install either the KDE or GNOME desktop. You can always change your mind, or even install both with YaST if you have enough disk space.

NOTE

If you'd like a portable, single-CD installation of openSUSE Linux, consider downloading the KDE or GNOME ISO. Go to the Download page of the openSUSE website, choose your preferred desktop, and burn your CD.

With very few exceptions, all software designed for one desktop will happily run on the other, and will even show up in the other's Start menu. A trivial example is that openSUSE installs identical default wallpaper for both desktops. You might find that one application designed for GNOME runs a little slower on KDE (or vice versa), but these types of issues are rarely catastrophic. All the Linux products not designed with either desktop (like OpenOffice.org and the Mozilla family) will also run beautifully in both.

Another key similarity is the capability to display multiple virtual desktops. If you regularly run one of those other operating systems and if you're a busy person, the desktop can get awfully crowded with a web browser, email client, word processor, and project manager all up at the same time. You can wind up Alt+Tabbing between apps, resizing and minimizing windows, or heavily working the taskbar to keep up. Wouldn't it be nice to have each application in its own desktop, away from the others? By default, GNOME and KDE offer you two virtual desktops (GNOME calls them workspaces). You can have up to 16 in KDE and 36 in GNOME. You can switch between them by pressing the Ctrl key along with the F key corresponding to the desktop number (that is, to switch to Desktop 2, press Ctrl+F2; for Desktop 3, press Ctrl+F3, and so on). For the incurable customizers, you can use descriptive names for each desktop, and even have different wallpaper on each one! You can have some applications (such as your schedule or time tracker) appear on all desktops, and choose whether you want to see the applications on other desktops in the taskbar. The taskbar will always show you your desktop lineup, with representations of the windows, as shown in Figure 6.3.

In openSUSE 10.3, GNOME does not set up workspaces by default unless you have Xgl; then it will display the Cube. They are relatively easy to create, though. Right-click on the bottom panel and select Add to Panel from the menu. Scroll down to Workspace Switcher, select and click Add. This will display a single workspace on the panel. Right-click on the Workspace square and select Preferences. Identify the number of workspaces you want, name them if you like, and identify whether you want the workspace icons in one or more rows on the panel. Click Close, and you're done. To set up the keyboard switchers to your liking, open the GNOME Control Center and click Shortcuts in the Personal section. Find Switch to Workspace X, click on the word Disabled, and use the keyboard combination you desire (whether it's the Ctrl+F-Key combination listed above or something else you like).

NOTE

If you have Xgl activated, and Compiz is your window manager, virtual desktops are called Viewports. By default, the Cube has four viewports, but in GNOME Desktop Effects, you can configure as many as you like.

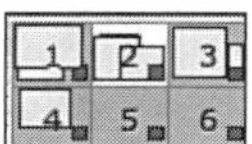

FIGURE 6.3 One busy desktop displayed as four busy desktops. This diagram shows active applications in virtual Desktops 1–4, with one small window in all six. Click any of the images to work on that desktop.

In this section and the next, you will learn more about each desktop environment and the tools specifically designed for it. This should guide you in selecting the right desktop for you. Try them both, though. As with most things, choosing a desktop is largely a matter of personal preference.

KDE is older, more stable, and has more applications designed for it. Its technological underpinnings come from the commercial Qt libraries from Trolltech, and for a long time, Qt's licensing scheme was not open source.

GNOME is the relative newcomer and has only recently become a stable system. openSUSE installs GNOME v2.19. Its technological underpinnings come from the first Linux killer app: The GNU Image Manipulation Program (The GIMP). (See the "Editing Images" section in Chapter 10, "Sights, Sounds, and Other Fun Things.") It began as an open-source rebellion, but has the support of many leading Linux-oriented corporations.

GNOME was the first desktop project to put usability at the top of its concerns, producing a truly admirable Human Interface Guidelines (HIG) document that has been a model for later efforts (including KDE's forthcoming HIG project). It has ambitions beyond the desktop as well. Many of its most partisan developers believe it provides a model framework for all software development.

TIP

One more common function for both desktop environments is a very handy application launcher. Press Alt+F2 to bring up a dialog box. Enter the name of an application to launch it. If you enter a URL, the default browser (Konqueror in KDE, Epiphany in GNOME) opens on that site. This way, you save time browsing through menus or opening new shells.

KDE: The K Desktop Environment

The KDE project began in 1996 and has been the default desktop environment for openSUSE for nearly all that time. openSUSE 10.3 includes KDE 3.5.7. openSUSE also uses the KDE Display Manager to provide a graphical login screen after it has booted.

When you first log in to KDE, it will take a few seconds to load, but when it's finished, you will see the basic elements of the desktop looking much like Figure 6.4. Windows users should feel pretty comfortable with this opening experience—a few icons on the desktop, a taskbar (called the Kicker in KDE parlance) along the bottom with assorted applications ready for quick access, and a clock in the right corner (optionally configured to show the seconds passing by).

PREVIEWING KDE 4.0

KDE 4.0 was scheduled for release a few weeks after openSUSE 10.3. The distribution has some "preview" KDE 4 applications, but did not incorporate the bulk of the desktop at release time. Thus, the screen shots included in this book are all of KDE 3.5.

Highlights of the new version include:

- An ambitious new desktop interface called Plasma. This dynamic desktop is expected to facilitate creation of widgets, small programs that display useful (and occasionally useless) and customizable information.
- A new, simpler, file manager called Dolphin. This will replace Konqueror as the default file manager, but both applications will continue to be developed.
- Better identification and support for different types of hardware.
- And all of this in a faster, less memory-intensive environment.

Perhaps by the time you read this, you can use YaST to upgrade your KDE desktop.

By default, KDE loads any applications that were running when your last session ended, so you can pick up where you left off. The openSUSE icon in the left corner of the Kicker opens the application menus. To its right, the icons on the left side give you access to your home directory (via the Konqueror file manager), the Konsole Xterminal shell, the openSUSE Help Center, the Konqueror web browser, and the Kontact personal information manager (the Outlook-style combined email, address book, and calendar program).

If you've used KDE before, you'll be in for a little surprise when you access the menus in openSUSE. Instead of a standard hierarchical setup, there is a series of tabbed menus not unlike Windows XP. The Favorites tab includes OpenOffice.org Writer, Firefox, the KDE Control Panel, and other standard applications. The History menu gives quick access to recent programs and documents. The Computer tab points you to YaST, system folders, and other storage media. The Applications menu is the standard setup, with newly installed applications at the top of the menu. The Leave menu lets you end your session and/or reboot your computer.

Should you decide to return to the old-style menu, open Personal Settings. Go to Desktop, and then to Panels. Click the Menus tab. At the top, you'll see Start Menu Style; use the drop-down menu to change from SUSE to KDE.

You will notice that KDE developers have a fetish for naming their programs with a K in front. This can be kreative, or just a little too kute, but it is a handy way of identifying what applications are K-specific. The Kicker panel is highly customizable; right-click anywhere to add or remove icons from the panel. The Configure Panel screen also lets you put the panel on a different side of the screen and set several other options.

In the right corner of the Kicker, next to the clock, are more application icons that always run. Mouse over each to see what they are. The blue globe icon is the openSUSE Software Updater application, which checks the YaST Online Update (YOU) servers regularly to see if updates are available. These fix security problems and give you new versions of installed applications. This icon will change color when new updates are available; click once to begin the update process. See Chapter 21, "Keeping Your System Current: Package Management," for more information on YOU.

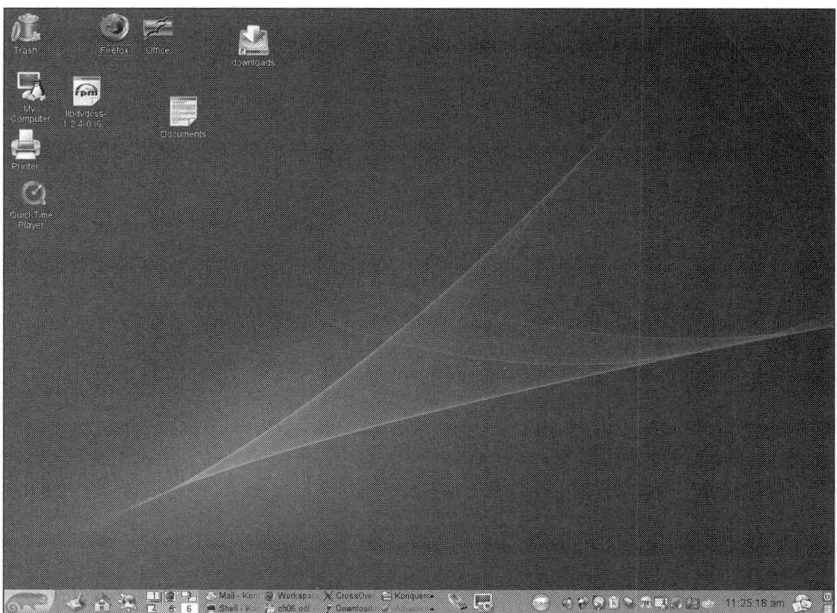

FIGURE 6.4 The SUSE default KDE desktop. Along the bottom are the standard application icons, virtual desktops, and applications that run at startup.

The Klipper clipboard utility offers much more than its Windows counterpart. Among other things, Klipper stores your last seven cut/copy actions by default, so you can paste several items in sequence if you choose. Klipper will remember your clipboard actions over sessions, too.

So many applications have been written for KDE that the YaST initial installation menu separates out some from the default KDE installation. It's all there if you want it, though. KDE includes a complete office suite (KOffice, see Chapter 9, "Being Productive: Office Suites and Other Tools"), a programming integrated development environment (KDevelop, see Chapter 28, "Programming Tools"), a CD/DVD burning utility (K3b, see Chapter 10), and an outstanding printer support tool (KPrint, see Chapter 7, "Printing with openSUSE"). The Konqueror file manager is also a web browser with its own interface. All these tools are covered in greater depth in their relevant chapters.

GNOME: The GNU Network Object Model Environment

When you open GNOME for the first time, you may notice two differences between it and KDE: There are no desktop icons, and there's not much that's visible in the taskbar either. GNOME is all about the DIY ethic—if you want something, you've got to do it yourself. The right corner offers the time, the volume control, the Software Updater, and an indicator of your network status. Over on the left, it says Computer; it's really your applications menu. Then there's the Tomboy Notes application that allows you to write notes to yourself.

The menu is a GNOME version of the KDE menu structure described above, with Favorites on top. Click More Applications to see the complete list, categorized or not.

FIGURE 6.5 The default GNOME desktop is much cleaner than KDE, with a smaller and more configurable set of panels.

The GNOME panels are highly configurable with a curious collection of applications over which you have much more control than in KDE. Displaying many of the same characteristics and applications by default as KDE, the whole look is a bit more pristine (and with much smaller icons). See Figure 6.5 for a look.

To add an icon to either panel, right-click exactly in the spot where you want the item to appear and choose Add to Panel. You can then select your item from the menu. Among the choices is a weather report with the current temperature and conditions for many global cities. Select your own location—or the place you want to be.

TIP

To get quick access to the standard GNOME menus, add the Traditional Main Menu to your top panel. This is much more extensive, and GNOME-specific, and comes complete with the GNOME footprint logo.

Managing Files from Your Desktop

Sooner or later, you will need to move or copy files from one directory (or device) to another. Chances are, at one time or another, you have used Windows Explorer (and/or its slightly less useful companion, My Computer) to perform this task. Perhaps you've thought that there has to be a better way to do this than Microsoft's way. Thus, even in the Windows world, there are third-party file managers that reinvent that task in several ways.

Both Linux desktop environments have file managers that seek to ease this task. In this section, we'll look at both of them, plus a third KDE-based file manager included in openSUSE, Krusader.

Using Konqueror in KDE

KDE's Konqueror takes a Microsoft Explorer-like approach (to the point of being a web browser as well), with mount points (drives) and directories in the left pane and the contents of the selected directory displayed as large icons with the file or subdirectory name on the right. The toolbar runs across the top. If you're comfortable working in the Windows file manager, you should find Konqueror easy to work with, but it won't take long for you to see that Konqueror has more to offer than Explorer. You will also see that Konqueror can be configured to work in whatever style you want.

There are several ways to launch Konqueror:

- To see the contents of your `/home` directory, click the House icon on the left end of the KDE Kicker taskbar.
- Clicking the My Computer icon opens a Konqueror browser window in `sysinfo:/`. This contains many useful links to different places on your system, including your hard drive(s), other mounted storage devices, and your floppy drives.
- Press Alt+F2 and type in a path to a directory. Konqueror will open in that directory (typing a web address will open Konqueror in browser mode).
- From the Kicker menu, go to the Computer tab for quick access to any folder. In the Applications tab, you can go to System, File Manager as well. Among the listed options, see File Manager–Super User Mode in this menu. This mode is especially helpful when you're troubleshooting permissions problems while you are the SuperUser.

The first time you open your `home` directory, you'll see something similar to Figure 6.6.

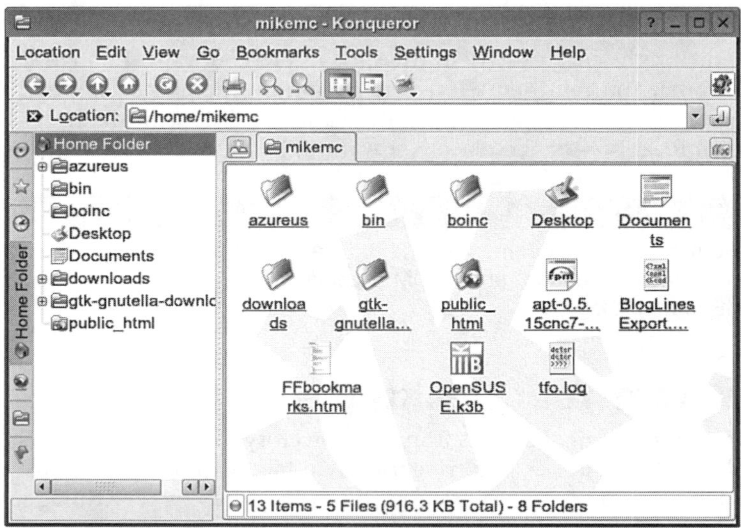

FIGURE 6.6 The KDE Konqueror file manager offers an Explorer-like interface with lots of extras.

This is Konqueror's default File Management profile, in Icon view. On the left side is the familiar directory tree, focused on the `/home` directory, with the files and folders in that directory displayed with icons on the right. To see more details on your files, click the Tree View icon in the toolbar, or go to the View menu at the top, and select View Mode, Tree (or Detailed List) View. On the far left of the Konqueror screen, you can also change what you see in the left pane of the window. Click each icon to display various system services, the Root (/) folder, your network (including FTP sites configured by Konqueror's own team or added manually), or your current Konqueror web browser history and bookmarks. What's nice about this is that changing the display in the left pane does not automatically change the display in the right File pane—until you click something in the new left pane. This makes dragging and dropping files just a bit easier when you have quick access to nearly every place to which you'd want to send a file.

Konqueror takes another cue from modern web browsers by enabling tabbed navigation even on your file system. To open a new, empty tab, press Ctrl+Shift+N (for New), or right-click in the tab area and select New Tab from the context menu. You can then use the Location bar to type in a destination, or use one of the left-pane options to open a folder in the new tab. Should you desire, you can detach the tab and put it in its own window. Unfortunately, you cannot drag files from one tab to another, but there's a way around that. Go to the Window menu, select Split View Top Bottom, and then select another location. You'll see something like Figure 6.7.

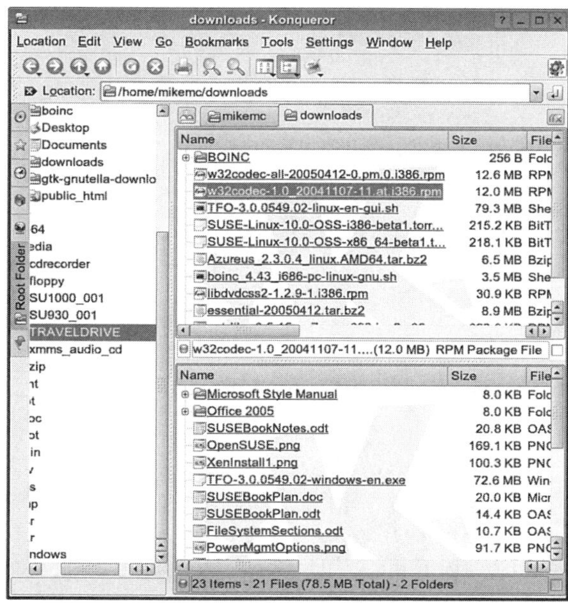

FIGURE 6.7 Drag and drop items from one pane to another in Konqueror.

Now you can drag from one pane to another. Should you happen to have something in the other tab to send to the bottom folder (in this case, a USB keychain drive), you can drag that down as well. By default, Konqueror always asks you what to do (copy, move, or create a link) when you drop something, so you are always in control of what happens.

When you get Konqueror configured the way you like it (or at least in one of the ways you like it), go to Settings, Save View Profile. By default, the current profile name comes up in the Profiles screen (see Figure 6.8). Unless you want your new setup to become the default File Management settings, change the name as shown.

NOTE

When saving a profile, you can tell Konqueror to remember the directories you are currently in by checking the Save URLs in Profile box. Do the same thing for the Save Window Size box.

Using Krusader in KDE

When you look at a power user's file manager, such as Midnight Commander and others like it, one thing that makes it stand out is this notion of double panes. When you're moving files from one place to another, it is comforting to be able to see both the original location and the target at the same time. This way, you know that things worked out as you intended. This is Krusader's mantra.

FIGURE 6.8 Set a desired configuration as a profile in Konqueror, and you can load that configuration with a few mouse clicks.

When you open Krusader (see Figure 6.9), it will certainly remind you of the Midnight Commander interface. Krusader does dual panes by default—in fact, you can't get rid of them. It has the `mc`-like F-key command menu on the bottom, along with the standard GUI menus and toolbars on top. But that's only the beginning of this feature-rich file manager.

Although it will not browse the Web for you, it will do just about everything else Konqueror does, and more:

- Compare and synchronize two directories.
- Create compressed archives in one of several formats (including standard tarballs, gzip, and bzip).
- Mount a drive.

- Open and edit a file as Root (if you have the rights to do that).
- Split one file into smaller pieces (to fit on a portable drive), or combine several files into one.

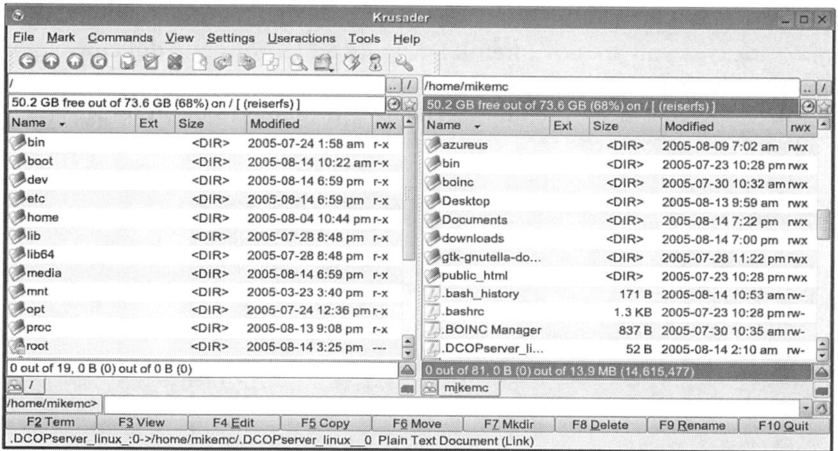

FIGURE 6.9 Krusader gives you a dual-pane interface and will synchronize the files in each pane if you want it to.

Krusader also has a fairly fast search engine that will locate files and directories using a specified pattern. For example, in Konqueror, you can search your entire computer or individual directories, but not selected multiple directories. In Krusader, you can specify multiple directories to look in or directories to not search in (such as `/proc` or `/var`). You'll learn more about finding files in Chapter 18, "Managing Files, Volumes, and Drives."

You can be quite productive with Krusader if you are busy with files all the time. You might even find Krusader fun to use, even if it won't burn a new CD for you.

Using Nautilus in GNOME

Once upon a time at the turn of the millennium, a group of former Apple developers were converted to the open source cause. They founded a company called Eazel and announced their determination to make Linux as easy to use for the ordinary person as the Mac OS. Their plan was to begin with a simple file manager and work from there. However, the economy turned bad, and venture capital was no longer throwing money at even promising startups. Just 16 months after announcing their big plans, Eazel was dead, but not before their file manager, Nautilus, was born. Through the miracle of open-source licensing, Nautilus lives on as the default file manager for the GNOME desktop.

Nautilus is a bit more adaptable in openSUSE 10.3 than in previous versions. In its earlier incarnations, Nautilus seemed to operate from the principle that if two windows make file management easier, more windows are even better. As you drilled down a directory structure, each new directory opened in a separate object window, rapidly filling your screen. Now directories all open in the same window by default. If you prefer the old behavior, you can adjust this in Preferences. As with just about every GUI file manager, Nautilus opens in

Icon view, which has a set of icons representing files and folders and a small menu bar, by default. Figure 6.10 shows the Nautilus List view, which you can access by choosing View as List from the View menu. Whatever your view, you'll see that directory hierarchies are downplayed somewhat in Nautilus, with parent directories accessible only in the drop-down menu in the lower-left corner.

Drag-and-drop can be tricky if you are not careful. Dragging a file from one directory to another only moves the file. If you want to copy files, you must first select your files, right-click, and choose Copy Files from the menu. Then open the destination folder and right-click again to Paste.

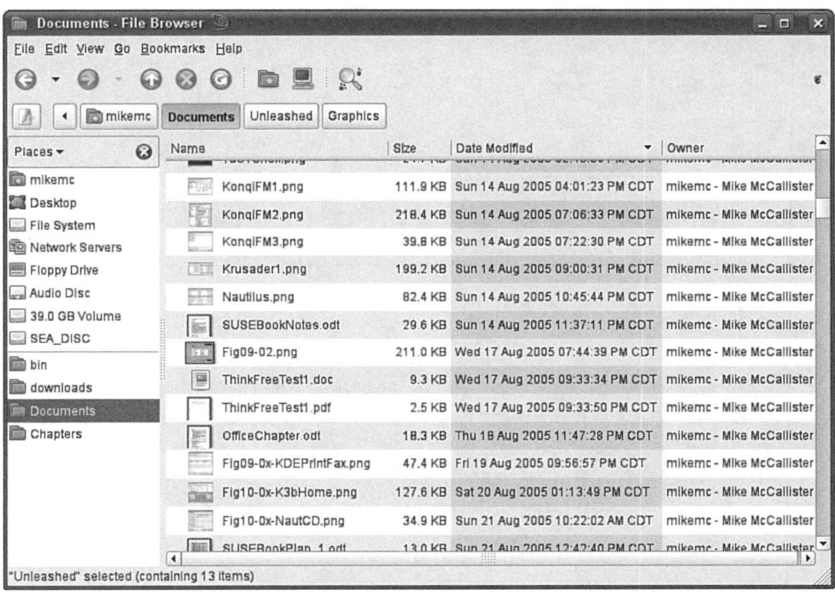

FIGURE 6.10 Nautilus has a clean interface with multiple windows.

The Places menu on the left of the Nautilus window points to several common starting points (Computer, Home, Trash) and will also open the GNOME CD Creator for easy CD burning.

Configuring Your Desktop Environment

You can choose to customize your experience with both desktops as much as you like. KDE has a simple and comprehensive Control Center where this happens. GNOME gives you a choice in how and where to customize. The following is a brief guide to some of the highlights.

KDE Control Center

When you open the KDE Control Center by clicking Configure Desktop in the Favorites menu, you get a quick summary of your system information: versions for KDE and the

Linux kernel release, the machine name, and your username. Down the left side are the configuration categories.

In Appearance and Themes, you can set the wallpaper (called Background here), the screensaver, window colors, and other look-and-feel items. Each can be set individually, or themes can do this all at once. Go to the Theme Manager and click Get New Themes to visit http://www.kde-look.org for downloadable themes, wallpaper, and screensavers. The Background and Screen Saver pages show you what each option looks like in a test screen, so you don't have to commit before seeing it.

The Desktop area lets you set up the number of virtual desktops you want and sets various options for the Kicker panels and taskbar. Choose the Device Icons tab under Behavior to include links to devices and directories on your desktop.

The Internet and Network area lets you configure Konqueror's web-browsing functions, share your desktop with other KDE users on the network, and set up your Samba client configuration for accessing Windows shares on your network (SuperUsers can also configure a Samba server). If you're on a laptop with Bluetooth capabilities, you can add and manage your Bluetooth services here as well.

In KDE Components, you can set default applications for mail, Konqueror's embedded text editor (for viewing text files in the file manager), instant messaging, and Xterminal. You can also change the default web browser from Konqueror so that Internet links open in your browser of choice. The Session Manager also sets the behavior for shutdown and startup.

Peripherals sets mouse, keyboard, and joystick behaviors. The Power Control settings, which turn off the screensaver and monitor when not in use, are located under Display (and laptop power controls are in Power Control). Regional and Accessibility settings define your keyboard layout and how times, dates, and money are displayed depending on the norm for your country. Set keyboard shortcuts for various KDE functions in the Keyboard Shortcuts section and define other keyboard shortcuts and mouse gestures in Input Action. Figure 6.11 shows the Keyboard Shortcuts screen.

Security and Privacy lets you take some security measures for yourself. The KDE Wallet function will remember website passwords and other private information if you choose. This is kept in a password-protected file that only you have access to.

Don't like the startup music that KDE plays? Head over to Sound & Multimedia, System Notifications. You can turn off or replace many automatic sounds associated with various actions—and not only sounds. You can assign a log file to an action, display a message, or specify any combination of notifications for any action. The Audio CD section also lets you specify how you want to rip songs from your CDs.

Most of the System Administration tools and all the YaST tools require SuperUser (SU) access to manipulate, but the Administrator Mode button is a handy way to make that happen.

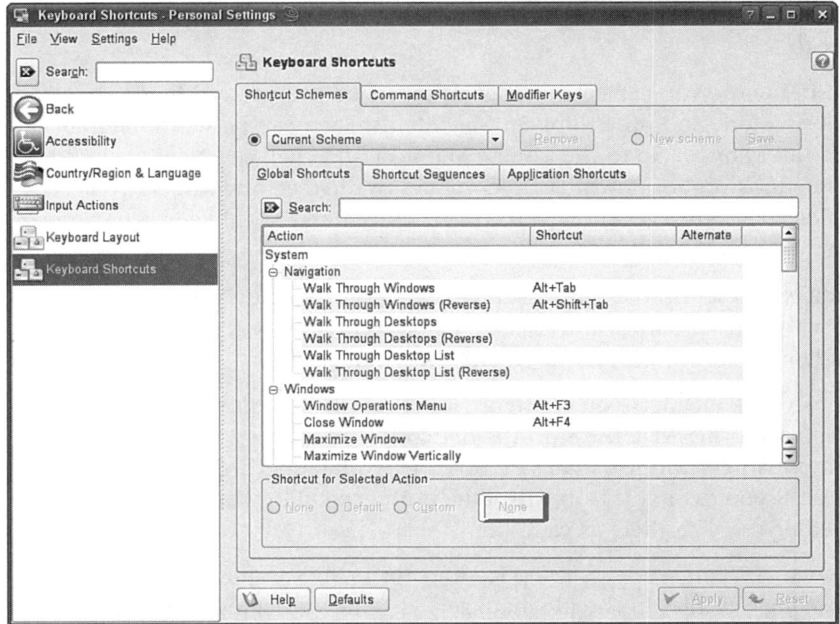

FIGURE 6.11 Define keyboard shortcuts for several KDE applications in the Control Center Regional and Accessibility area.

If you are dual booting Windows and openSUSE, the Font Installer lets you include all your Windows fonts in Linux. Click Add Fonts and then navigate to `/windows/c/Windows/Fonts`. Select all (or only the ones you want) and click Open.

When making changes in the Control Center, you must click Apply before moving away from that window. If you forget, you'll get a message asking if you want to apply the changes you made. With a few exceptions, all changes take place immediately.

Customizing GNOME

Making the desktop work the best way for you is one of the stated goals of the GNOME project. If something doesn't look or work right, right-click it, and you should see a way to fix it. In the panels, you can add or remove items and panels easily enough, and you can set the size, color, and autohide capability in the Properties screen. Want to use a 24-hour clock instead of the AM/PM variety? Right-click the clock and you can make those changes.

The centralized Settings customization tool is in the System menu in the top panel (see Figure 6.12). Click any of the Settings icons to open the relevant screen.

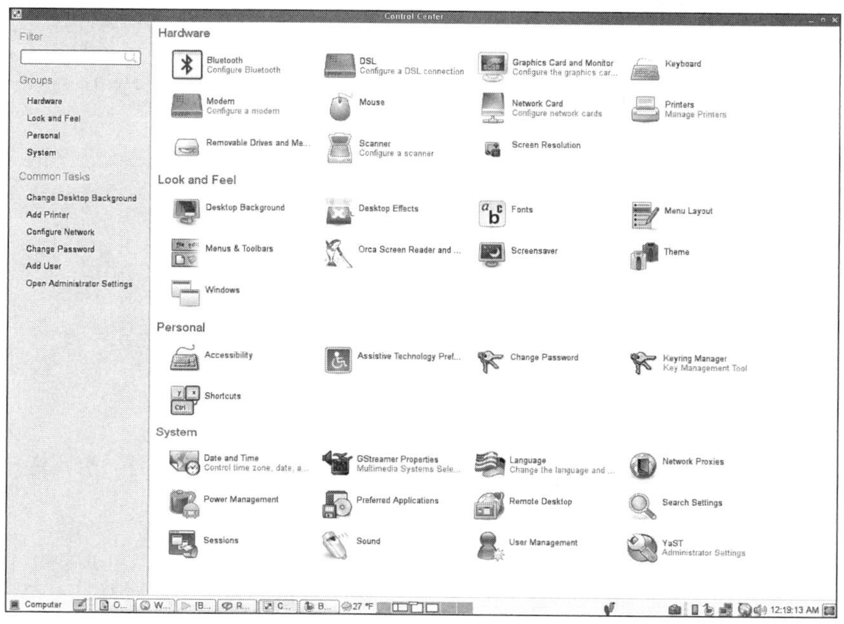

FIGURE 6.12 The GNOME Settings Control Panel gives each area its own page.

The Hardware section offers links to several relevant YaST hardware modules, but any user can configure the keyboard, the mouse, removable drives, and the screen resolution. The keyboard settings here are the same as in the Accessibility area (and there's a link to those preferences, too), but one tab is of note to those of us who don't want to be disabled: GNOME will enforce a three-minute typing break every hour (by default, this is configurable, of course) to keep you away from repetitive stress syndrome. You can postpone the break, but I don't recommend that you do. Screen resolution should generally not be changed.

The Look and Feel section covers the usual window decorations and such. GNOME is famed for its dashing GTK-based Themes, which are really more about color schemes than wallpaper and screensavers. Some themes come with suggestions for these elements as well. As with KDE, you can select screen fonts, wallpaper (Desktop Background), and screensavers separately. The Window preferences let you select a window just by passing the mouse cursor over it.

Click Desktop Effects if you want to see how Xgl works in this environment. If Xgl is not set up on your system, GNOME will check to see if your hardware is supported before giving you access to this menu. See "Configuring the Compiz Window Manager" earlier in this chapter for more information on these settings. The Menu Layout screen is much improved over earlier versions. Just check boxes to add items to the main menu, and uncheck them to remove items. You can add new items and even new sub-menus from a dialog box, and move things up and down a menu. In this area, you can also activate the built-in Orca Screen Reader and Magnifier if you have trouble reading screens.

The Personal section allows you to change your system login password without having to open YaST. The Accessibility and Assistive Technology Support pages confirm the GNOME project's commitment to usability. Some of the tools here can even help people with ordinary abilities and without physical disabilities get more done.

The shortcuts screen is much like the KDE screen shown in Figure 6.11. It's easy to create a new shortcut (highlight the action on the screen and then press the key[s] you want to use as the shortcut), but there's only one option. In KDE, you can choose an alternative.

The System section covers Sound events, applications associated with file types, and whether you're using a proxy server to access the Internet. The Sessions page lets you define what applications should run at startup. It shows you the currently active programs and gives you the option to save that configuration for your next session start. You can also add applications manually to the startup.

What Is a Window Manager and Why Would I Want to Use It?

Full-blown desktops for X did not come around until the mid-1990s. Before their arrival, there were window managers. From the humble Tabbed Window Manager (TWM) that is about as basic as you can get, to the very ambitious nearly complete desktops WindowMaker and FVWM, there are X window managers to fit every taste. Most of the widely used window managers are still in active development, and some work on top of the desktop environments as well as with just plain X.

Window managers are essential to any X installation. While X draws the window, it relies on a window manager to move, resize, minimize, or maximize the window.

This section covers some of the window managers included in openSUSE and describes how they work. Like the desktop environments, window managers can be quite customizable and offer several goodies on their own.

Why Run a Window Manager?

The following are a few reasons to know at least one window manager, even if you normally run a full desktop environment:

- Window managers are generally lightweight; they don't take a long time to load and don't suck up memory.
- If you just need X to connect to a remote machine and move some files, you don't need to load all the libraries for all the KDE utilities.
- If you ever have to connect to a remote X server halfway around the world on a phone line that transfers data at 33Kbps on a good day, knowing how to navigate in a window manager can save time and your sanity.
- Window managers tend to focus on performance at the expense of eye candy.
- OpenOffice.org, your favorite text editor, and your graphical browser work just as well under a window manager as they do in a desktop.

Starting Up with a Window Manager

When you install a window manager with YaST, another entry is put into the display manager's boot menu. When you log in, click Session Type and choose your window manager.

Running FVWM

This window manager, which started life as the Feeble Virtual Window Manager (but is no longer an acronym), is a favorite of more than a few alpha geeks. Gushing quotes from such Linux stars as Eric Raymond, Alan Cox, and Linus Torvalds himself appear on FVWM's website.

The default FVWM desktop (see Figure 6.13) is somewhat plain, but clearly you can get some work done on it.

The FVWM menu bar at the top displays the multiple workspaces FVWM supports; it loads an analog clock and the playful "Eyes" toy that follows your mouse around while you're working. FVWM loads an Xterm by default for command-line work, but the SUSE menu gives you access to most of the same applications that run on the meatier desktops, including OpenOffice.org. The Graphics menu will run The GIMP (which took the screenshot), and the Tools menu runs Mozilla.

TIP

Right-clicking anywhere in an FVWM workspace brings up the SUSE Applications menu for easy program launching.

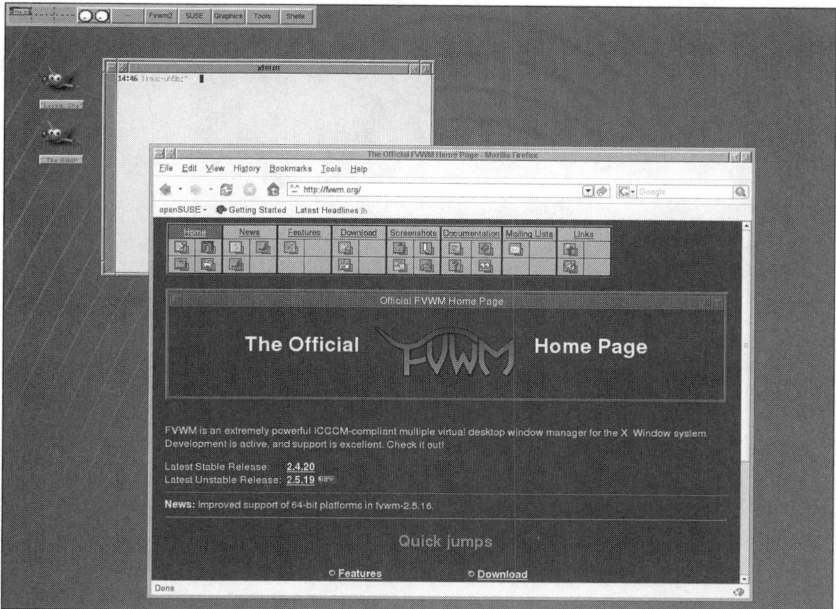

FIGURE 6.13 FVWM can run Firefox, and its menu bar helps you get to work.

When you launch a program in FVWM, a shadow window attaches to your cursor so that you can place it exactly where you want it on your screen (or in another workspace). Clicking the mouse draws the application window at the spot you select.

FVWM is a modular program. To view the currently available modules, click Modules from the FVWM menu. The Config module helps you customize your `.fvwm2rc` configuration file. You can also edit it manually, from /etc/X11/fvwm2 (for a systemwide configuration). If you want your own, copy the systemwide file to your home directory and edit it.

Running WindowMaker

WindowMaker's roots are deep in the alternative-OS world. It is an attempt to re-create the look of NeXTSTEP, the operating system for the NeXT Cube. NeXT was the second big idea from Apple Computer co-founder Steve Jobs. It may not have been great from a marketing standpoint, but it certainly has its fans.

WindowMaker (you'll find that the team of developers has not yet fully resolved whether the application is one word or two) takes a little getting used to, but is a fast and powerful system.

When you load WindowMaker for the first time, the main thing you'll notice is that you don't have to wait. Log in and before you blink your eyes, it's up and ready for work. This may depend somewhat on your processor and RAM, but it should be quick. WindowMaker, by default, loads just two things on the desktop: the Workspaces Clip (Clip) on the left and the Applications Dock (Dock) on the right (see Figure 6.14).

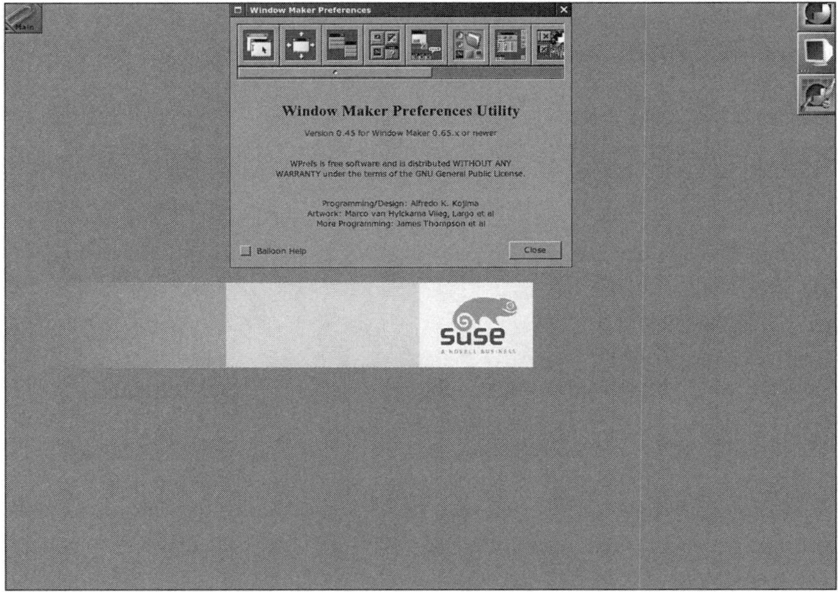

FIGURE 6.14 The Workspaces Clip and the Applications Dock (right corner) make WindowMaker distinctive. Customize your WindowMaker in the separate WmakerPrefs package.

The Dock is a place to quickly launch applications, although there is not much there to start with. The Clip manages workspaces and applications. To create a new workspace, right-click anywhere on the desktop and choose Workspaces, Create New from the context menu. The context menu is also where you will see the familiar SUSE Applications menu from which to launch apps.

When you launch an application in WindowMaker, an icon square will appear in the lower-left corner of the screen; it may have the application's real icon or just a generic one. Drag that application icon to the Dock to add it to the Dock for this session. To put it on the Dock permanently, right-click and go to Workspaces, Save Session. You also get that opportunity when you exit WindowMaker. Saving a session also saves the number of workspaces you have open.

Use the arrows in the corners of the Clip to navigate between workspaces and applications, or use Alt plus number keys. Alt+2 moves you to Workspace 2, Alt+3 moves you to Workspace 3, and so on. The Clip will tell you what workspace you're in.

Customize WindowMaker with the Prefs utility that installs separately from the main WindowMaker package; download the `wmakerconf` package. Prefs is fairly easy to understand and gives you no fewer than 13 categories of settings. Novices should activate the button help located in the main window. The Expert category is where you can set WindowMaker to always save the session at shutdown. You can also customize the context menu in the Applications Menu Editor.

Running IceWM

IceWM is another straightforward window manager that SUSE does not dress up too much in its representation. The SUSE menu is there, of course, and the multilingual Welcome wallpaper used in the KDM login screen is used instead of something more scenic.

Otherwise, IceWM behaves like the others. It's effective without being flashy. It is highly configurable, thanks to a separate configuration package with an interesting history.

This is another open source success story. When David Mortenson, the original developer of IcePrefs, stopped updating the program without formally relinquishing control of the project, the program lay dormant for three years. As Erica Andrews explains on the project website: "I love IceWM and IcePref...and IcePref needed a SERIOUS upgrade—so I did it, as everybody else seemed too lazy to do it."

IcePref2 is now a component of the IceWM Control Panel, a series of utilities for this still-active window manager. Install the IceWMCP package in YaST (see Chapter 21 for more information).

Log in to IceWM and you'll get that nice clean screen. Open an Xterminal and type **`icepref`** at the prompt. The instantly-familiar IceWM Control Panel (Figure 6.15) appears. Configure to your heart's content.

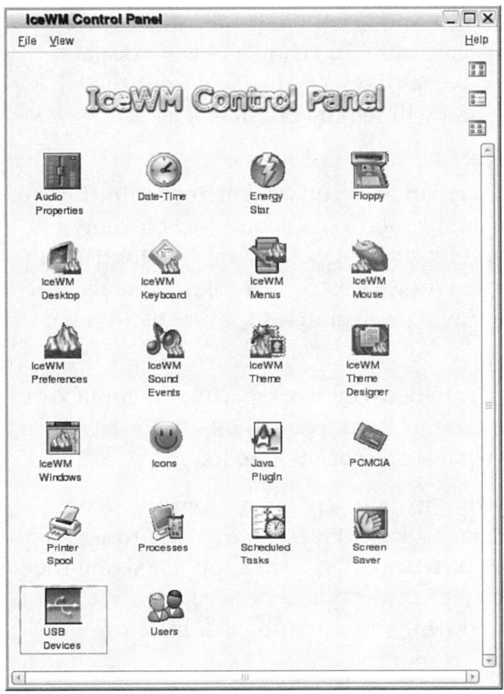

FIGURE 6.15 Use IcePref to customize just about anything you want in IceWM, including keyboard shortcuts.

A look along the row of tabs shows you the types of changes you can make. Some options will be confusing to novices, but window managers are for the more sophisticated users anyway.

References

- http://www.x.org—The X.org Foundation, the hub of X Window System development activity.
- http://freedesktop.org—The effort to produce minimum standards for free desktop software. Not a formal standards body, but a "collaboration zone" where projects are hosted and KDE and GNOME developers can discuss concerns. Also hosts the Xgl source code.
- http://www.novell.com/products/desktop/features/xgl—Novell's Xgl page. Check out the Spinning Cube and other video demonstrations.
- http://en.opensuse.org/Compiz—The openSUSE page on the Compiz Xgl window manager.

- http://www.suse.de/~sndirsch/nvidia-installer-HOWTO.html—The SUSE NVIDIA installer HOWTO, with instructions in setting up the NVIDIA YaST repository and more information on installing proprietary NVIDIA drivers.
- http://www.kde.org—The home of the K Desktop Environment. A well-organized site, with links to nearly everything relevant to KDE.
- http://dot.kde.org—The KDE News site, with links to online articles about KDE and its applications, along with press releases and the like.
- http://www.gnome.org—The GNOME home.
- http://www.gnomedesktop.org—"Footnotes," the GNOME News site.
- http://www.novell.com/linux/ximian.html—The Ximian area of Novell.com. Information about Evolution, Mono, and the Ximian Desktop.
- http://konqueror.kde.org/—The Konqueror site, covering both the file-management and web-browsing functions of this versatile tool.
- http://krusader.sourceforge.net/—The Krusader dual-pane file manager for KDE.
- http://www.gnome.org/projects/nautilus/—Nautilus, the GNOME file manager.
- http://xwinman.org—An Internet hub for learning about and trying Window Managers for X.
- http://www.gnomefiles.org/app.php?soft_id=599—Metacity.
- http://sawmill.sourceforge.net—Sawfish.
- http://www.windowmaker.info—WindowMaker.
- http://www.icewm.org—IceWM.
- http://www.phrozensmoke.com/projects/icewmcp/IcePref2—IceWM Control Panel configuration tool.
- http://www.fvwm.org—FVWM.
- http://blackboxwm.sourceforge.net—BlackBox wiki.
- http://icculus.org/openbox/2—OpenBox.
- http://enlightenment.org—Enlightenment.
- http://www.xfce.org—Xfce.

CHAPTER 7

Printing with openSUSE

IN THIS CHAPTER

Until relatively recently, printing in Linux has been something of a chore. As the hardware got cheaper, the proprietary drivers got more specialized and more valuable to their vendors. Open-source drivers for the most popular inkjet printers were hard to come by, and different distributions did printing differently, even though the protocol they used was the same. This situation has changed dramatically since the advent of the Common Unix Printing System (CUPS), a protocol that simplified things greatly.

Today, openSUSE supports hundreds of printers to one degree or another, and YaST makes it easy to set up, test, and configure your printer. In this chapter you will walk through a printer setup, learn to manage multiple printers on your system, and use the command line to print documents directly.

You will also learn a little about PostScript, the primary UNIX/Linux printing language, and its cousin, the Portable Document Format (PDF). Linux has always had applications that read PDF files, and Adobe has occasionally released Linux versions of Acrobat Reader. Several Linux applications (chief among them OpenOffice.org) now support making PDF documents as well.

Printing: An Overview

The most important thing to understand about printing in Linux is that it is largely a conversion process. Whenever you issue a print command in an application, you are actually creating a PostScript (.ps) file that is sent to the printer. The problem is that most printers, except for relatively high-end laser printers, do not have the power to process PostScript commands directly.

To solve this problem, Peter Deutsch of Aladdin Enterprises wrote a program called Ghostscript and released it under an open source license, the Aladdin Free Public License (AFPL).

Subsequently, another version was released under the GNU General Public License. The primary difference between the two licenses is that the AFPL does not allow for commercial distribution. Both versions (and a commercial version produced by Artifex) are still being produced, with AFPL Ghostscript at v8.11 and GPL Ghostscript at v7.05. CUPS incorporates a specially patched version of GPL Ghostscript, called ESP Ghostscript, that openSUSE uses in its distribution.

Ghostscript lets you view raw PostScript and Portable Document Format (PDF) files. With the right drivers, it can also convert them into files that non-PostScript printers can process.

The following steps describe what happens when you press Print:

1. The data you want to print is stored in the print queue.
2. The print spooler retrieves the data and sends it on to the print filter.
3. The filter then determines whether the data is already in PostScript; if not, it converts it to PostScript.
4. The PostScript data is then sent on directly to a PostScript printer (if that's available), or the filter runs Ghostscript.
5. Ghostscript, in turn, uses its driver to convert the PostScript into another standard printer language. That data is then sent to the printer.
6. When all the converted data is in the printer, the spooler deletes the data from the print queue.

Common Unix Printing System (CUPS)

CUPS made printing a lot easier for ordinary users. Before CUPS, printing could involve navigating around the Internet trying to find the right drivers. For system administrators, it was worse because the admin had to set up all printing configurations for each system.

Developed by Easy Software Products, CUPS pulled all the drivers together in one place. It also allows users to set different printing options on a job-by-job basis, at least within the context of general limits set by the administrator.

CUPS is a standards-based print system. It uses the Internet Printing Protocol (IPP) developed by the Internet Engineering Task Force (IETF) Printing Working Group. It runs as a server daemon that receives print data from Ghostscript and then communicates with the printer.

The CUPS daemon on your computer can also communicate with other printers on its dedicated communications port 631. This makes it possible for your computer to "see" other printers without having to configure them.

You can configure a printer with CUPS with a built-in web-based administrative tool (open a browser to localhost:631, or go to Utilities, Printing, Manage Printing in the new KDE menu system), but the potential exists for a security breach because you are typing the Root password into your browser. As always, doing your configuration through YaST is safer, and probably easier.

Configuring Printers with YaST

YaST attempts to detect active printers on install, and if you have a fully supported printer, it should find it. Do not give up hope if YaST does not detect it, because it is a simple task to configure your printer manually in YaST as well. To set up a local printer, follow these steps:

NOTE

YaST will let you manually configure your printer even if it is not connected to your computer. Obviously, you won't be able to run any of the tests, but go ahead and walk through the steps.

1. Open YaST, go to Hardware, Printer.
2. YaST checks its settings and tries to detect any active printer(s); then it displays the first Printer Configuration page (see Figure 7.1).

TIP

In some cases, YaST will hang up when rebuilding the printer database. If this happens, kill the process (either from the command line or using KSysGuard, as the SuperUser). Then (also as the SuperUser) rename the YaST printer database file with this command:

```
mv /var/lib/YaST2/ppd_db.ycp /var/lib/YaST2/ppd_db.bad
```

The next time you run the Printer module, YaST should successfully rebuild the database, and you'll be back in business.

3. If YaST finds no active printers, it will display the basically blank screen you see in Figure 7.1. Click Add to start manual installation of a local printer.
4. The first step in adding a printer queue is identifying how your printer is connected to your system. First identify whether this printer is directly connected to your computer, or if it is on the network. For this exercise, we'll focus on connecting a local printer. Older printers use the parallel port, and newer printers usually plug in to your system via a USB port (see Figure 7.2) or perhaps a Bluetooth connection. If you are trying to attach a network printer, you need to know the protocol the printer uses: If it's on a Windows network, use the Samba (SMB) option; if it's on an older Novell NetWare network or you otherwise need to use this protocol, choose IPX. When you have selected the type, click Next.
5. This screen lets you test your connection before loading a driver. Figure 7.3 shows the parallel printer test screen. Your screen may differ slightly, depending on your printer type. Make sure your printer is on before testing the connection. When you click Test Printer Connection, YaST sends a message ("Hello World") to the printer. Depending on your printer, it should light up, print the message, or just send a form feed (that is, move the paper down). If it does, click Next.

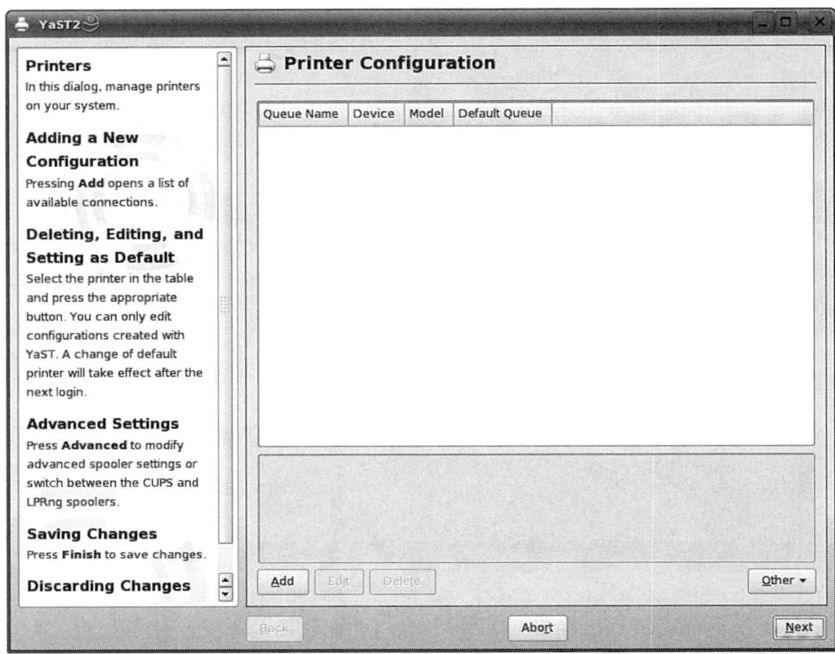

FIGURE 7.1 If YaST cannot detect your printer, it displays this empty screen. You can then manually configure your printer.

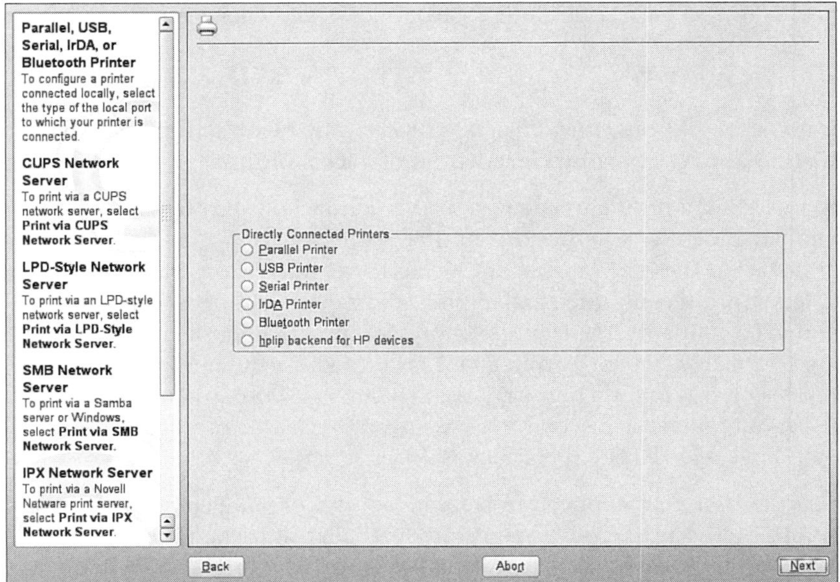

FIGURE 7.2 You should know how your printer is connected to your system: parallel port or USB for most local connections, or the protocol your network printer uses.

6. In this screen, shown in Figure 7.4, you name the printer (actually, the print queue). The first field, Name for Printing, is how the machine identifies the printer. By default, YaST assigns the name "printer," but you should name it something else, especially if it is a network printer. This is usually the model name or location. The queue name cannot have spaces in it (you can do that in the Description line). The Description is what you call the printer and has no rules. The Location is optional, but can help you figure out which printer is yours. You also have the option to share your printer with other users, which is the default setting.

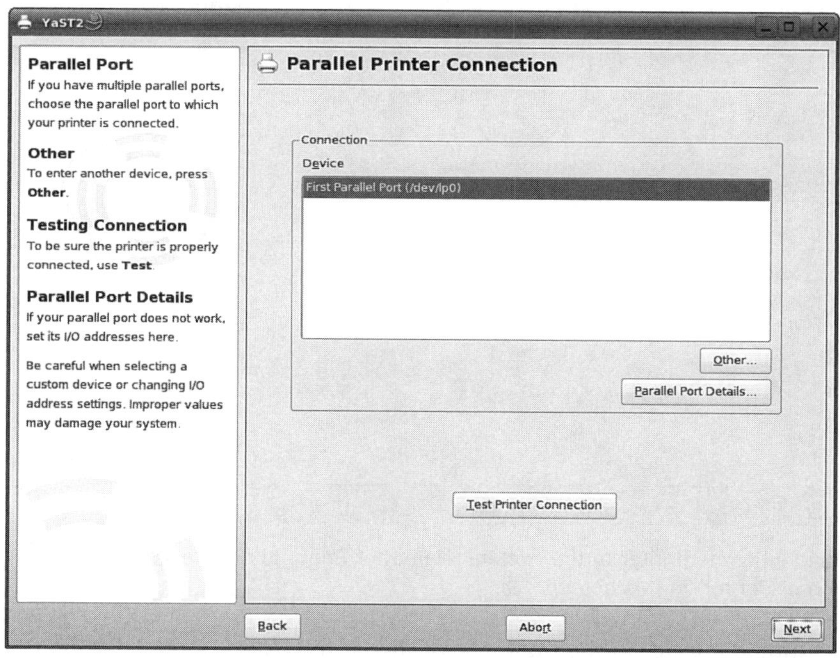

FIGURE 7.3 Test your parallel printer connection on this screen. YaST sends a test message, and your printer should respond.

NOTE

All local printers "Do Local Filtering," so leave this box checked and do not click Test Printing on this page. You'll do that after you identify your printer model.

7. Figure 7.5 shows where you identify your printer model. Select one of the 49 manufacturers on the left side, and then select a model on the right. If you have a PPD file from your manufacturer, click Add PPD File to Database. You'll get the choice to install from a local file or download from the manufacturer's FTP site (you have to enter the site name). Click Next to confirm your settings and test your configuration.

NOTE

Although the model list seems pretty thorough, don't panic if you don't see your model. There are often common drivers for many manufacturers. Check the printer database at http://www.linux-foundation.org/en/OpenPrinting for the right driver for your model.

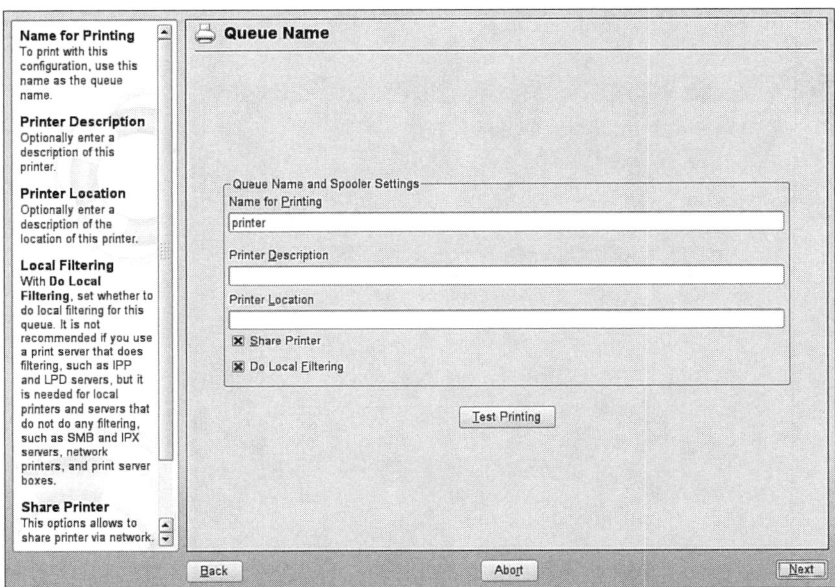

FIGURE 7.4 You identify the printer to the system (Name for Printing) and describe it for yourself (Description of Printer) in this screen.

8. Your settings should appear on the final screen, shown in Figure 7.6. Make sure everything is correct in the Current Values list, and then check (double-click) the Printing Filter Settings. These may be set to A4 paper and other items that may not work for your printer in this test. Click Test to send a test page to the printer, and select one of the test versions from the dialog box. Ideally, the page should print. Click OK when it does.

Your printer should now be set up for all applications. If you need to make changes in your configuration, you can always come back here to do that.

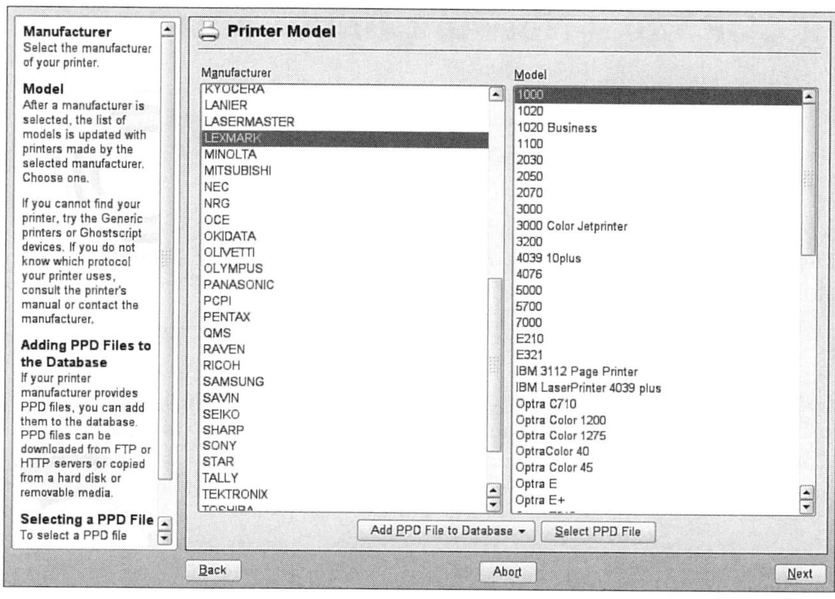

FIGURE 7.5 Select your printer from the list.

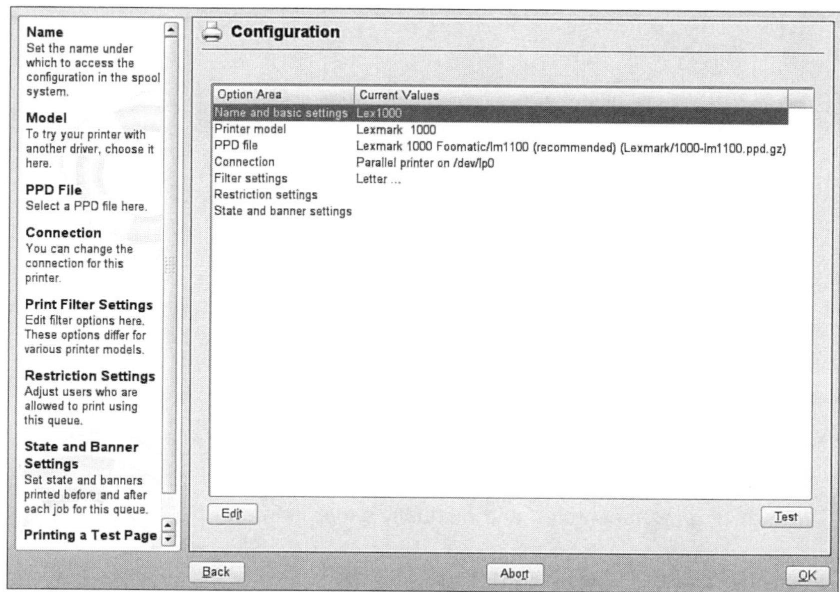

FIGURE 7.6 Test your printer here.

Configuring CUPS and Network Printers with KDEPrint

Setting up remote network printers is not substantially different from the local setup process, but because openSUSE Linux 10.3 gives you a choice, let's show you how to set this up in the KDEPrint wizard.

To open KDEPrint, open the KDE Control Panel (also known as Configure Desktop/Personal Settings) and go to Peripherals, then Printers. Figure 7.7 shows you the existing printers it has autodetected.

Click Administrator Mode at the bottom to take control of your printers. Click and hold down Add to see a pair of choices: Choose Add Printer/Class. The KDEPrint Wizard appears. You have several choices of network printer interfaces. Both Network Printer and Network Printer w/IPP options allow you to scan your network for printers to connect to. The Remote CUPS Server and Remote LPD Queue (which you should only use if the printer you are trying to use does not support CUPS) require you to enter an IP address manually.

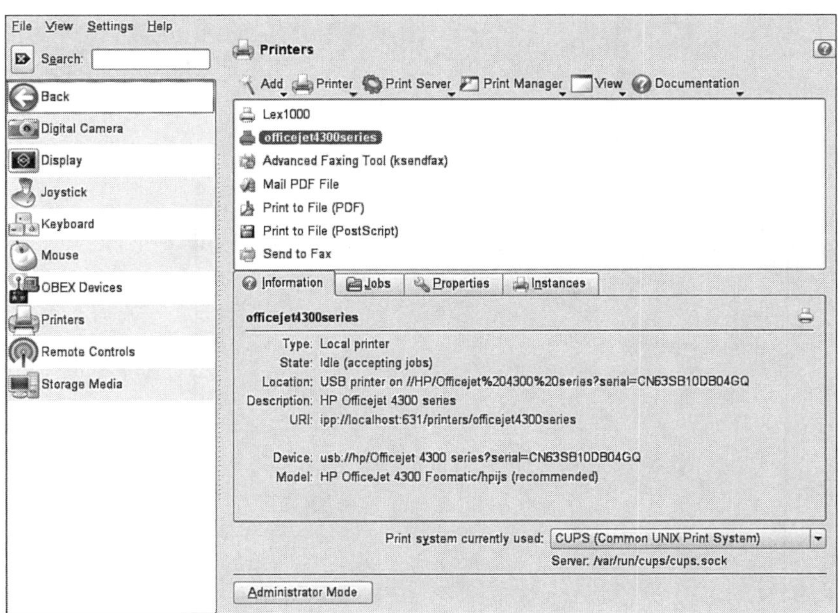

FIGURE 7.7 KDEPrint displays autodetected and manually added printers.

When you select Network Printer, Figure 7.8 appears.

Click Scan to check your network for printers, which will appear in the main window on the left. If you know the location of the printer already, you can also enter the address and port manually. Click Next to confirm your settings.

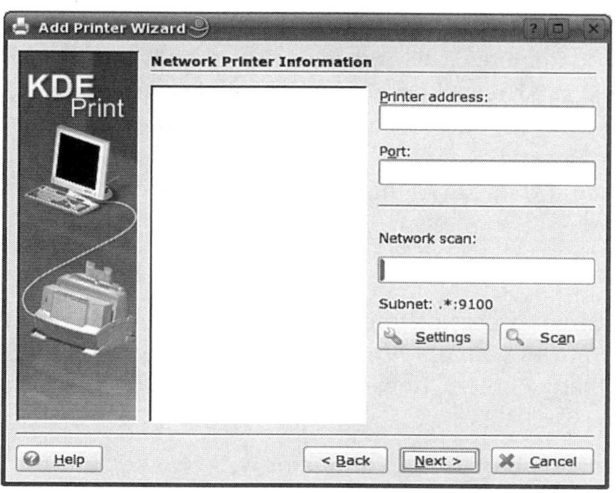

FIGURE 7.8 Scan your network for available printers with this wizard screen.

To connect to a remote CUPS server, you must know the IP address of the server. You will first be asked if the remote server requires authentication, or is anonymous. If necessary, type your username and password for the CUPS server (which may be the same as your openSUSE login). Click Next, and enter the IP address of the server; the wizard will connect to the address. Confirm your settings, and you're in.

You can also connect to Windows printers through Samba. See Chapter 25, "Setting Up Networks and Samba," for more information on this.

As a last resort, openSUSE also will try to connect with remote CUPS servers that may be available on the Internet. As noted previously, CUPS uses the Internet Printing Protocol to connect to printers. Network printers can thus communicate with CUPS clients via port 631. If configured properly, the network printer can send out broadcast packets when it is available for printing jobs. In the YaST Printer Configuration dialog box (refer to Figure 7.1), you can set your computer to Listen to Remote CUPS Servers to Get Comfortable Access to Remote Queues.

The problem with this method is that you risk the possibility that an attacker sends IPP broadcasts to your computer announcing available print queues, and you accidentally print to a counterfeit queue. You may believe the job is sent to a local server, whereas in reality it is sent to the attacker's server.

To use this method, port 631/UDP must be open for incoming packets from the network, but not from outside your network or the Internet. The way to solve this problem is to configure the SUSE Firewall appropriately. This means enabling listening only via the Internal Network interface, not the External (Internet) interface.

If your firewall is not turned on when you configure your printer, you are putting your print data at risk. If necessary, open the YaST Firewall module and turn it on before setting up Listen mode (you can have two YaST modules open simultaneously). Pay attention to how the Firewall has identified your Internal and External interfaces, because you will need to know the External interface in the Printer setup.

When you have the firewall turned on, go back to the Printer setup and click Change next to the line telling you Port for Listening to Remote CUPS Servers is Closed by Firewall. Now check the Open Port in Firewall box; the Firewall Details button will become active. Click the button; both interfaces will be checked, but won't be identified as Internal and External. Uncheck the box matching the External interface. Click OK to confirm your choice and return to the main Printer menu; then click Finish to complete the operation.

Printing with CUPS

After you have set up your printer, printing is an easy chore from the user's standpoint. In most cases, you'll just click Print (Ctrl+P) from your application, bring up the print dialog box, and accept the defaults. You have many choices, however, when that dialog box appears.

Take a look at Figure 7.9. It is the Print dialog box in the Konqueror web browser, but the options are common to many applications. At the top is the Printer ID section, with the default printer showing. By default, this is all that shows when you first click Print.

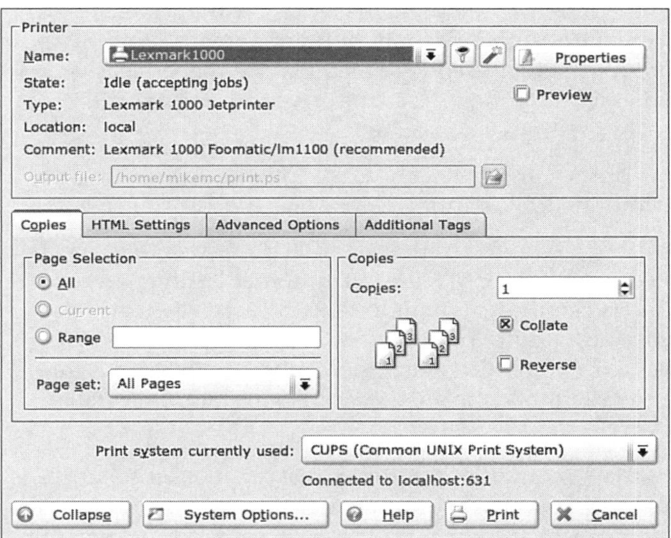

FIGURE 7.9 CUPS enables the user to make lots of choices on-the-fly, as shown in this Konqueror print dialog box.

TIP

Need to add a printer? Just click the icon that looks like a magic wand to the left of the Properties dialog box. This opens the KDEPrint application.

You can change many of the default settings by clicking the Properties button at the top, but Konqueror makes nearly all of them available in this dialog box when you click

Options. The tabbed properties pages let you choose a page range if you don't want to print the whole document, and you can print them last-page-to-first if you have an inkjet that spits out paper print-side up.

In the Advanced Options page, you can schedule a print job for later. If you're in a networked setting and need to enter a job or budget code into the printer, you can enter that information here, too, under Billing Information.

Working with the Portable Document Format (PDF)

You have no doubt seen and worked with Adobe Acrobat documents in the Portable Document Format. Software manuals, government documents, and electronic books of all kinds have been published and distributed on the Web for years. The idea behind PDF is simple: create and distribute electronic documents in a manner in which the layout of the page is controlled (that is, every reader sees it the same way) and there are no barriers to reading it (a free Reader exists for every system).

Adobe Systems, the owners of the Acrobat software and inventors of the PDF format, has been inconsistent in its Linux support over the years. The Reader supplied with openSUSE is version 7.0.8, though version 8.0 should be available by the time you read this. There has never been a Linux version of the full Acrobat product, either. Ghostscript has become the default Linux PDF reader over time, but its interface is a bit more clunky than Adobe's own product.

Considering that PDF is a slight variation on the UNIX/Linux PostScript print standard, it's a little surprising that free, open source PDF creation tools have not been forthcoming. The exceptions are the TeX publishing tool and a pstopdf shell utility that did not produce a quality transformation from plain PostScript (ps) to PDF. You can indeed make PDF files with TeX, but this publishing behemoth is notoriously difficult to learn and operate.

Making PDF documents got a whole lot easier with OpenOffice.org v1.1. Finally, there was an easy-to-use method of creating good-looking PDF documents in Linux. All you need to do to create a PDF is click the PDF Export tool on your default toolbar.

Suppose you have a holiday letter with graphics that you send out to friends and family every year. You can easily create a PDF version right in OpenOffice.org that you can send to your email buddies or put on your personal website by doing the following:

1. Create your document as you would normally.
2. Insert graphics and watermarks and position them where you want.
3. Save the document as OpenDocument Text first so that you have an "original" copy that you can edit.
4. When everything's ready to go, click the Acrobat toolbar button to create the PDF directly, or go to File, Export as PDF for more control over your presentation.
5. A dialog box will come up. If you want to give the PDF file a distinct name, that's OK. OpenOffice.org will automatically add the `.pdf` extension to your file.

6. If you chose Export as PDF from the File menu, a PDF Options screen will appear, allowing you to choose how many pages of your document to include in your PDF, how to handle graphics, and a couple of other options. If you have a long document with headings, you may want to check the Tagged PDF box. Your headings will then appear as Bookmarks in the PDF, making for easier navigation. Click the Initial View, User Interface, and Security tabs to fine-tune exactly how your readers will view and interact with your document. When you've made your choices, click Export to create the PDF.

7. Your OpenOffice.org file will still be onscreen so that you can edit it. To open your new PDF document, locate it in your favorite file manager. Acrobat Reader (or Ghostview, depending on how your system is configured) will display your exported file.

Figure 7.10 shows a PDF created with OpenOffice.org in Acrobat Reader.

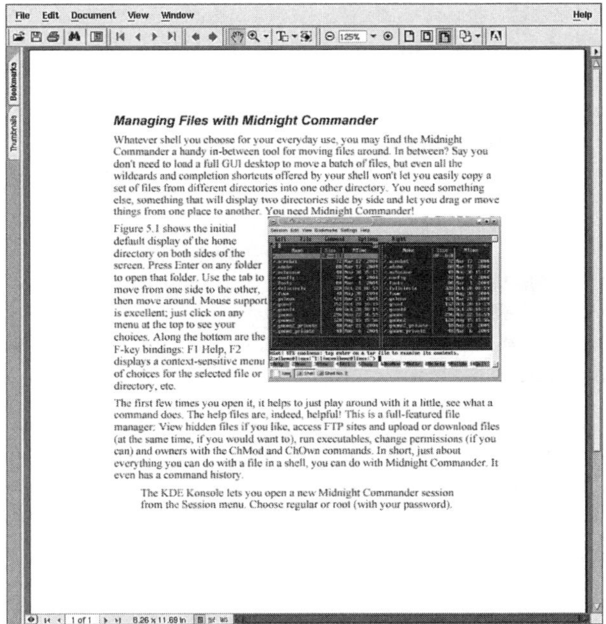

Managing Files with Midnight Commander

Whatever shell you choose for your everyday use, you may find the Midnight Commander a handy in-between tool for moving files around. In between? Say you don't need to load a full GUI desktop to move a batch of files, but even all the wildcards and completion shortcuts offered by your shell won't let you easily copy a set of files from different directories into one other directory. You need something else, something that will display two directories side by side and let you drag or move things from one place to another. You need Midnight Commander!

Figure 5.1 shows the initial default display of the home directory on both sides of the screen. Press Enter on any folder to open that folder. Use the tab to move from one side to the other, then move around. Mouse support is excellent; just click on any menu at the top to see your choices. Along the bottom are the F-key bindings: F1 Help, F2 displays a context-sensitive menu of choices for the selected file or directory, etc.

The first few times you open it, it helps to just play around with it a little, see what a command does. The help files are, indeed, helpful! This is a full-featured file manager: View hidden files if you like, access FTP sites and upload or download files (at the same time, if you would want to), run executables, change permissions (if you can) and owners with the ChMod and ChOwn commands. In short, just about everything you can do with a file in a shell, you can do with Midnight Commander. It even has a command history.

The KDE Konsole lets you open a new Midnight Commander session from the Session menu. Choose regular or root (with your password).

FIGURE 7.10 Create your own PDF documents with OpenOffice.org.

TIP

Learn more about the things you can do with OpenOffice.org and other Linux office suites in Chapter 9, "Being Productive: Office Suites and Other Tools."

Console Print Control

As with nearly everything else in Linux, you don't need X running to print a file. CUPS answers shell commands very well, and if for some reason the CUPS daemon won't run, you still have access to the old UNIX/Linux print standard, LPRng, which responds to the same commands. This section will cover how to print from your command line.

TIP

If you don't know much about the shell or console, there's much more in Chapter 8, "Shaking Hands with Your Shell."

Using Basic Print Commands

It's good to know these five basic shell commands if you just need to print something quickly without having to launch a program or wait for a GUI to load. These will work from any shell prompt, whether you have X running or not. In some cases, you need to be logged in as the SuperUser to have access to all options.

- `lp <options> <filename> <printer>`—The basic "line printer" spooling command.
- `lpq`—Tells you what print jobs are currently being processed. It will also give you the name(s) of the line printer queue(s) installed on this machine if you do not know what's available.
- `lpstat`—Statistical information from the server and printer.
- `lprm`—Cancels the current print job.
- `lpadmin`—The CUPS line printer administration system. You must be Root (or SuperUser) to use. This command manages spooling, the print daemon, and all printer activity.

All these commands have reasonably good man pages, and you can also examine the CUPS Administration Guide in `/usr/share/doc/packages/cups/sam.html`.

Don't be afraid to use wildcards when using the `lp` command to print from the shell. To print all OpenOffice.org Writer documents in the current directory to a printer called "lp," type the following:

```
lp -dlp *.odt
```

Now if you run the queue command, `lpq`, you will see the file(s) being printed. This includes other pertinent information, such as the owner, the job number, and size of the job. CUPS uses the job number to handle multiple orders.

Armed with a job number, you can cancel that specific job with `lprm` <jobnumber>.

7

Avoiding Printing Problems

Before buying a new printer, always research its Linux compatibility first. openSUSE and CUPS can run most current printer models, especially if they are standard printers connected by a parallel cable. Some vendors support Linux better than others, and it is always a good idea to visit http://www.linux-foundation.org/en/OpenPrinting to get the current thinking on each printer vendor.

The following sections contain a few tips on the more problematic devices.

Multifunction (Print/Fax/Scanner) Devices

The more you try to do, the harder it is to succeed. These printing triathletes need the full support of the manufacturer to make a go of it in Linux, and that support has been spotty, but improving. In response to a clamor from Linux users, the leading producer of budget-priced multifunction devices, Brother, has begun writing Linux print and scan drivers. See http://solutions.brother.com/linux/en_us for current information on Brother drivers.

Consider yourself lucky, however, if you have an HP OfficeJet multifunction device. openSUSE supports these devices out of the box with the open source (but fully supported) hplip drivers.

USB and Older Inkjet Printers

More printers run from the USB port these days. You learned something about Linux and vendor support for USB devices in Chapter 2, "Preparing to Install openSUSE." Although there's nothing special to note about USB printers, you should still check out http://www.linux-usb.org if you have or are considering one of these printers.

Generally, you should avoid inexpensive older inkjet printers that came out at the end of the last century. Manufacturers didn't know much about Linux when these printers were new, and they certainly aren't going back to add support now.

Like the Winmodems that rely on software to perform many essential communications tasks, quite a few of these printers shaved a few bucks off their cost by using the Microsoft Graphic Device Interface (GDI). Essentially, the printers run only because they have access to this Windows-only interface.

The openSUSE Administration Guide offers a partial list of these printers, and http://www.linuxprinting.org has a broader listing in its database.

References

- http://www.linux-foundation.org/en/OpenPrinting—Formerly LinuxPrinting.org, this is a central compendium of information on printing in Linux. Download official and unofficial open source drivers. Read the recommendations in the Suggested Printer List when you're in the market for a new printer. Ask questions in the forums.
- http://hplip.sourceforge.net/—Hewlett Packard's Linux Imaging and Printing driver.
- http://www.tldp.org/HOWTO/Printing-HOWTO—From the page, "A collection of information on how to generate, preview, print and fax anything under GNU/Linux."
- http://www.cups.org—The place to keep up with the Common Unix Printing System.
- http://www.ghostscript.com/awki— The Ghostscript news and community page. New release announcements and a community component based on "diary entries."
- http://www.cs.wisc.edu/~ghost—The Ghostscript home page.
- http://www.adobe.com/products/acrobat—Learn more about Acrobat and PDF from the official site. You can also download the free Reader here.
- http://solutions.brother.com/linux/en_us—The Brother Linux support and driver status page.
- http://www.linux-usb.org—The site to visit when considering a USB printer for use with Linux.

CHAPTER 8

Shaking Hands with Your Shell

IN THIS CHAPTER

- What Is the Shell?
- Using the Shell in openSUSE
- The Power of the Command Line
- Basic Shell Programming
- Advanced Shell Programming
- References

"In the beginning was the command line," sayeth Neal Stephenson in his wonderful essay on the history of computer operating systems. And so it is true. The easiest and fastest way to get things done in Linux is directly from the command line; the command line is known as the *shell*. Why "shell"? Well, if the heart of the operating system is the kernel of the nut, clearly you have to crack the shell to get at it.

The point-and-click graphical interface is easy, once you've learned it. Yet there is so much power behind a couple of keystrokes in the shell that it's sometimes hard to think of an easier way to do things. The big difference is the learning curve. In the GUI, after you've figured out how a mouse works, you're well on your way to getting work done. As opposed to this, that cold empty shell prompt gives you no advice on what to do with it.

No matter how expert you are with the graphical interface, there may be times when you have to rescue a system and a shell prompt is all you have to work with. It's important to know at least a few commands to get things going. Throughout this book, you'll find plenty of ideas on using your shell to quickly get computing tasks done.

In this chapter, we will focus on understanding the shell as a programming language. Most of the shells included in openSUSE Linux allow you to string commands together in an editor and save them as a script. Knowing the shell's syntax, you can define variables, assign values, create functions, and evaluate different results—most everything a "real" programming language such as C, Java, or C++ can do. Many of the standard shell commands are really just shell scripts. Perhaps your script will one day find itself in common usage, too.

What Is the Shell?

Before you can start writing shell scripts, it's a good idea to first have a clear idea as to what the shell is, and what it can and can't do. The shell is a term that is thrown around a lot in the Unix world, and is not often clearly defined.

The core of the Linux operating system is the kernel. All of the program processing, device handling, and memory control happens within the Linux kernel. The kernel is off in its own world running the Linux system. To start new programs on the system, you must somehow tell the kernel what program to start. The trick is interfacing with the kernel to start the programs you want to run.

The shell is an interactive environment that allows Linux users (and administrators) access to the kernel. The shell interacts with an input device (usually the console keyboard) and an output device (usually the console monitor). The shell allows users to type commands at the console, which are read and processed by the shell. Internal shell commands are processed by the shell, while commands to start programs are passed to the kernel to run. Figure 8.1 demonstrates how the shell interacts with the kernel and users.

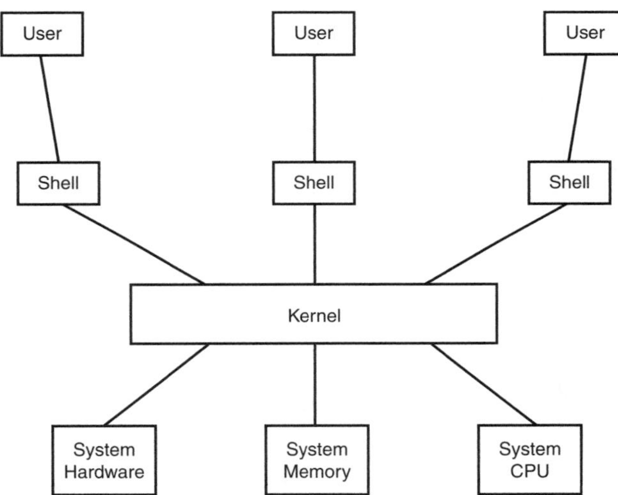

FIGURE 8.1 The Linux shell interacting with the kernel and the user.

As an interactive environment, the shell allows you to enter commands at what is called the command prompt. Often, the commands entered are program names. When a program name is entered, the shell attempts to find the program in the file system and then passes the executable program to the kernel to be run on the system.

Besides allowing you to start programs, the shell command prompt also provides a compilation of special commands used by the shell to interact with the Linux system. These commands are used to work with files and directories contained in the file system, display programs that are running in the kernel (called processes), and control user accounts used to log into the Linux system.

The shell structure also provides a rudimentary programming environment that can be used to help provide structured scripts for automating shell commands. This is where shell scripting comes in. By combining shell commands, program statements, and programs within a script, you can simulate a complete programming environment with just the shell.

There are several shells available for the Linux operating system. The different shells have different capabilities, such as the commands they provide and the way commands can be scripted. The openSUSE Linux 10.3 Linux distribution supports many types of shells, as shown in Table 8.1

TABLE 8.1 Linux Shells

Shell	Description
sh	The Bourne shell, the original shell written by Steven Bourne for Unix
bash	The Bourne-again shell, an Open Source project to emulate the functionality of the Bourne shell
csh	The C shell, written by Bill Joy, that emulates the C programming language
ksh	The Korn shell, written by Dave Korn, that combines features of the C shell and the Bourne shell
tcsh	An Open Source modification of the C shell
zsh	The Z shell, an Open Source shell which provides advanced programming techniques, such as processing floating point numbers

By far the most common shell used on Linux systems is bash. This provides a robust scripting environment while maintaining a simple command interface. The bash shell is the default shell used in openSUSE. The next section describes how to get to the bash shell from your openSUSE desktop.

Using the Shell in openSUSE

Back in the old days, accessing the shell was easy. Once you logged into a Linux system, you were immediately greeted by the shell command prompt. From there, all you could do is enter shell commands.

8

With the invention of fancy graphical user interfaces (GUIs), things have changed. Now when you log into a Linux system, most likely you will be greeted with a full-featured graphical desktop, similar to what you see on a Microsoft Windows system.

The default desktop environment in the openSUSE Linux 10.3 Linux distribution is either the GNOME or KDE graphical environment. While both of these desktops provide excellent interfaces for starting programs at the click of a button, if you are working with shell scripts, you'll need access to the bash command line.

This section walks you through how to get to the shell, and how to build and run shell scripts using the tools available in openSUSE.

Getting to the Shell

Fortunately, both openSUSE GUI environments provide a few different methods that can be used to access the Linux shell. Both desktops provide a menu item for accessing the console, which interacts with the shell. KDE provides two different ways to access the shell command prompt:

- The KDE Konsole program
- The X Terminal program

Both programs provide a simple graphical access the shell command prompt. The X Terminal program provides a bare-bones terminal within a graphical window. The Konsole program provides a few more bells and whistles. It is shown in Figure 8.2.

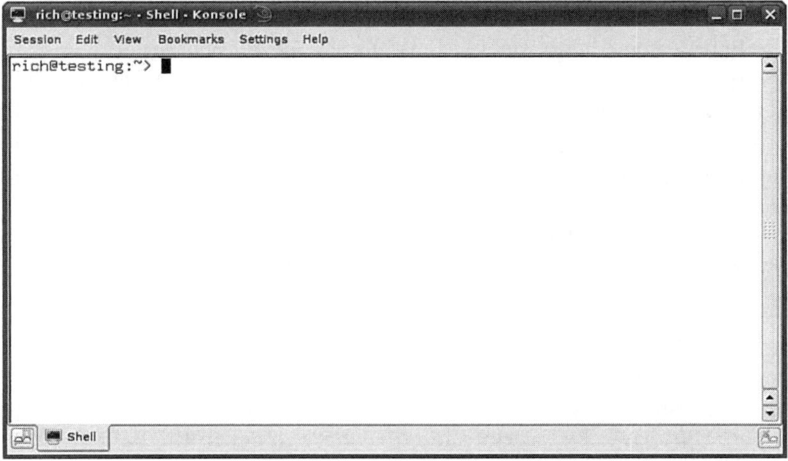

FIGURE 8.2 The Konsole command prompt interface.

The Konsole main window shows the shell command prompt, which by default shows your userid and the name of the openSUSE system. From this prompt you enter shell commands. The Konsole application also provides a few extra fancy features, such as the ability to copy and paste text from the command prompt window to the clipboard area, and the ability to start multiple command prompt windows at the same time within the Konsole window.

Running Shell Commands in Konqueror

Do you want to combine the power of the shell with the relative convenience of a GUI file manager? The KDE file manager, Konqueror, lets you run any shell command from its interface.

Go to Tools, Execute Shell Command (or press Ctrl+E). If you have a file or directory selected, you will see its name in the edit box, but running a command on that file isn't necessary. Type any command (or series of commands) and it will run; any messages pop up in a separate window.

If you have opened Konqueror as the SuperUser, you will have all the privileges of rank when you run commands, but you cannot log in as SuperUser (or run any command that requires extra input) from a plain Konqueror window.

Creating Scripts

The key to a shell script is the ability to process multiple commands. Instead of manually entering one command, checking the output, and then entering another command, the shell allows you to chain commands together in a single step.

If you want to run two commands back-to-back, you can enter them both on the same command prompt line, separated with a semicolon:

```
rich@testing:~> date ; who
Mon Dec 11 17:44:35 EST 2006
rich     :0        2006-12-11 15:23 (console)
rich     pts/1     2006-12-11 15:24
rich     pts/0     2006-12-11 16:42
barbara  pts/2     2006-12-11 17:30
katie    pts/3     2006-12-11 17:39
rich@testing:~>
```

Congratulations, you just wrote a shell script! This simple script uses just two bash shell commands. The `date` command runs first, displaying the current date and time, followed by the output of the `who` command, showing who is currently logged on to the system. Using this technique, you can string together as many commands as you wish, up to the maximum command line character count of 255 characters.

While using this technique is OK for small scripts, it has a major drawback—you have to enter the entire command on the command prompt every time you want to run it. Instead of having to manually enter the commands onto a command line, you can combine the commands into a simple text file. When you need to run the commands, just simply run the text file.

In the old days, creating a text file in Unix meant you were stuck having to use a clunky text-based editor such as vi or emacs. Because these editors were text-based, programmers had to use key sequences for editor commands. Using these editors meant having to memorize strange key combinations to cut, paste, add, and modify text in the file.

Fortunately, things have changed in the Unix world. GUI editing programs are now available that allow you to create and edit script files on your openSUSE system using the mouse. Both the GNOME and KDE desktops include simple text editors that are excellent for creating shell scripts.

The Kate editor is my favorite graphical editor for Linux. It is available in the openSUSE KDE desktop under the Utilities menu area. Figure 8.3 shows an example of a Kate session.

Kate allows you to cut and paste text using the mouse, as well as handle multiple versions of a text file. Kate was designed for programmers. It incorporates easy editing features with extra features such as highlighting programming elements within the text.

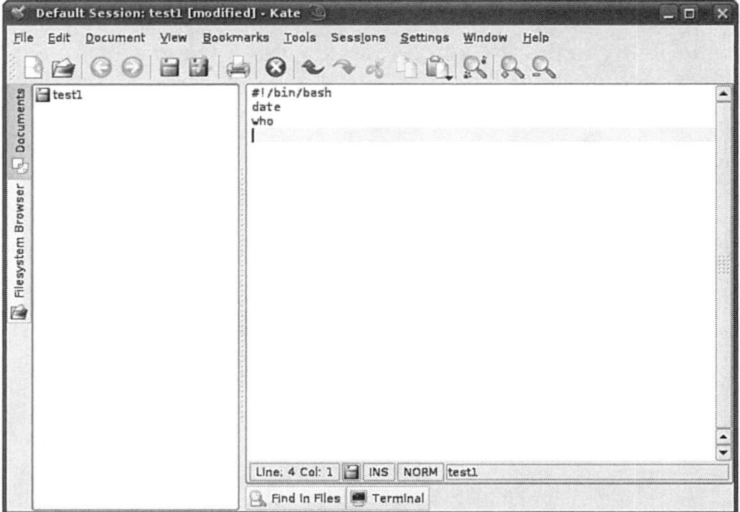

FIGURE 8.3 The Kate text editor.

When creating a shell script file, you must specify the shell you are using in the first line of the file. The format for this is:

```
#!/bin/bash
```

In a normal shell script line, the pound sign (#) is used as a comment—the line isn't processed by the shell. However, the first line is a special case, and the pound sign followed by the exclamation point tells the shell what shell to run the script under (yes, you can be using a bash shell and run your script using another shell).

After indicating the shell, commands are entered onto each line of the file, followed by a carriage return. As mentioned, comments can be added by using the pound sign. An example looks like this:

```
#!/bin/bash
# This script displays the date and who's logged on
date
who
```

And that is all there is to it. Save this script in a file called `test1`, and you are almost ready. The next section describes how to run the new script on the system.

Running Scripts

Once your text shell script is created, you'll want to run in on your system. The next step is to tag the shell script file as an executable file so that it can be run on the Linux system.

In the Windows world, you can tell if a file is executable by its file name extension. It is common knowledge that files that end in .com or .exe are binary executable files, and files that end in .bat are text batch files that can be executed.

Linux doesn't use filename conventions to identify executable files. You can have script files called testing, myscript.txt, or even this.is.a.test.script. Instead, Linux uses file properties to tag whether a file is executable.

If you use the KDE desktop environment, the Konqueror application allows you to graphically modify the properties of a file. After finding the file in Konqueror, right-click the file icon, and select Properties.

In the Properties window, select the Permissions tab. This tab shows what permissions are allowed for the file. Check the Is Executable checkbox to make the file executable.

If you prefer to work within the command prompt, you can also set the executable feature using the `chmod` shell command:

```
chmod +x test1
```

This command makes the shell script executable by anyone on the system. If you are working in a controlled Linux environment with other users, you may need to be more restrictive.

Once the file is marked as being executable, manually running a shell script from the command prompt is an easy task. As mentioned, the shell attempts to find programs in the file system when they are entered at the command prompt. This is done using the `PATH` environment variable. The shell searches the directories listed in the `PATH` environment variable for the program.

NOTE

openSUSE Linux automatically creates a `/bin` subdirectory in your home directory. This is a good place to store your scripts because this is the first item in your search path.

If you place the shell script file in a directory that is not listed in the `PATH`, you must manually specify where it is located in the shell command. This can be done using either a full pathname or shortcuts. Using the full pathname looks like this:

```
rich@testing:~> /home/rich/scripts/test1
```

If you want to run a script that is in the current directory, you can use the shortcut:

```
rich@testing:~/scripts> ./test1
Mon Dec 11 18:21:15 EST 2006
rich     :0       2006-12-11 15:23 (console)
rich     pts/1    2006-12-11 15:24
rich     pts/0    2006-12-11 16:42
barbara pts/2     2006-12-11 17:30
katie    pts/3    2006-12-11 17:39
rich@testing:~/scripts>
```

Look familiar? It is the same output that was produced by entering the two commands directly on the command line. Now any time we run the `test1` script, we can get the results without having to manually enter both commands.

The Power of the Command Line

Understanding the shell's capabilities is the first step to writing good scripts. The shell is much more than a program launcher, although it does do that very well. The shell is also called the command interpreter because it takes your typed command and does several things with it:

1. First, the shell determines whether the command is something built into it. If it is, the shell runs the command.
2. If not, it checks the search path environment variable to find the command (unless you've located the command yourself by typing in the full path).
3. When it locates the command you've asked for, the shell makes a fork call on the Linux kernel to copy the program (so that it will return to the shell prompt after the program completes its task). The program then makes another exec call on the kernel to execute the command.
4. Finally, the shell uses some rules to determine what a command like `cat *.txt *.sxw > doclist` is trying to accomplish (this is, where the interpretation comes in) and delivers a result.

A shell can run several commands included in a single string, as in the preceding example. This is a relatively simple command, but while executing it, the shell does several things:

- Launches a program—It runs cat, a program that displays files on the screen.
- Does job control and gets out of the way—The shell pretends it isn't there while cat searches for the text of all files in the current directory with `.txt` and `.sxw` extensions and then displays the results.
- Redirects output—Before the text display hits the screen, the shell leaps back into action and intercepts the system call, putting the display (that is, the text of all files with those extensions) into a file called doclist and saving it to the same directory.

Among the other things a shell can do (besides the "Cool Stuff That All Shells Have in Common" listed in Chapter 5, "Getting Started with openSUSE") are the following:

- Search files and directories for patterns or regular expressions using locate, gawk, or grep
- Feed the results or output of one program into another program for further processing
- Run multiple commands separated by a semicolon

- Create five empty files with a single command:

  ```
  touch file {a,b,c,d,e}
  ```

- Run a program in the background

You will use all of these little wonders when writing your scripts in this chapter.

NOTE

The examples in this chapter will be for bash shell scripts, as bash is by far the most popular (and the default) shell in openSUSE Linux. You can write scripts to perform practically all the tasks included here on other shells as well. Consult the man page for your shell to check the proper syntax. You might also want to check out *Sams Teach Yourself Shell Programming in 24 Hours* by Sriranga Veeraraghavan or *Linux Shell Scripting with Bash* by Ken O. Burtch.

Pattern Matching in the Shell

The shell command line allows you to use strings of specially constructed patterns for wildcard matches. This is a different but simpler capability than what is supported by GNU utilities such as `grep`. Most GNU utilities use more complex patterns, known as expressions, to search through files or directories or to filter data input to or out of commands.

The shell's pattern strings can be simple or complex, but even using a small subset of the available characters in simple wildcards can yield constructive results at the command line. Some common characters used for shell pattern matching are as follows:

- *—Matches any character. For example, to find all files in the current directory ending in `.txt`, you could use:

  ```
  ls *.txt
  ```

- ?— Matches a single character. For example, to find all files in the current directory ending in the extension `d?c` (where ? could be 0–9, a–z, or A–Z):

  ```
  ls *.d?c
  ```

- `[xxx]` or `[x-x]`— Matches a range of characters. For example, to list all files in a directory with names containing numbers:

  ```
  ls [0-9]*
  ```

  To find only those with characters 1, 5, or 8, the pattern would be:

  ```
  ls [158]*
  ```

8

- `\x`—Matches or escapes a character such as ? or a tab character. For example, to create a file with a name containing a question mark:

```
touch foo\?
```

Table 8.2 shows a few more common special characters. For a more comprehensive list, see the Advanced Bash Scripting Guide, listed in the References section.

TABLE 8.2 Special Characters in bash

Character	Meaning
#	Beginning of a comment line (except when it's part of a `#!`).
$	Shell variable name.
;	Command separator.
.	Current directory.
..	Parent directory.
~	Home directory. This character is located to the left of the number 1 on your keyboard; hold down the Shift key to use it.
`	Command substitution. This character tells the shell to use the results of the upcoming command as part of the next task.
>	Redirects the output of a script to a file. If the file exists, it will be overwritten.
>>	Appends the output of a script to an existing file. If the file does not exist, it will be created.
¦	Pipe. Helps to chain commands and scripts together and passes the output of one command as an argument in the next.
&	Run this in the background; it allows you to return to the shell prompt.

Always be careful when using special characters. As you can see, some special characters have different meanings depending on their context, so your script may not behave if you don't use the character properly. Some characters can also be destructive, so make sure you use the right one.

If you want to use a special character in a normal way, use the backslash (\) as an *escape character* in the script. To display the result of some calculation involving U.S. or Australian money, for example, include this string:

```
echo \$(5153.27 + 654863.15)
```

Note that mixing wildcards and regular expressions in shell scripts can lead to problems if you're not careful. For example, finding patterns in text is best left to regular expressions used with commands such as `grep`; simple wildcards should be used for filtering or matching filenames on the command line. Although both Linux command expressions and shell scripts can recognize the backslash as an escape character in patterns, the dollar sign ($) will have two wildly different meanings (a single-character pattern matching in expressions and a variable assignment in scripts).

Redirecting Input and Output

You can create, overwrite, and append data to files at the command line, using a process called input and output redirection. The shell recognizes several special characters for this process, such as >, <, or >>.

In this example, the output of the `ls` command is redirected to create a file named `textfiles.listing`:

```
ls *.txt >textfiles.listing
```

Use output redirection with care because it is far too easy to overwrite existing files. All you need to do is redirect a different command to any existing file. The shell will perform the task you ask it to without checking for a file with the same name, or prompting you about your wishes concerning the soon-to-be-departed file.

On the bright side, you can redirect output to add content to an existing file with the `append` operator, >>. So if you find something interesting to add to your textfiles collection, use two angle brackets instead of one in your command:

```
ls /usr/share/doc/packages/emacs/doc/gnus-tut.txt >>textfiles.listing
```

You can also turn your angle bracket around to take data and feed it to a command with input redirection, like this:

```
cat < textfiles.listing
```

Piping Data

Many Linux commands can be run together in a single, connected command line to transform data from one form to another. Stringing commands together this way is known as using or creating pipes. Pipes take the output of one command and use it as input for the next command. This can be done nearly endlessly.

Use the bar operator (|) to create pipes in the shell (it is used most often in this role, so many folks know the bar operator as the pipe already). Say you were the system administrator and needed to know who was currently logged in at a given moment. A piped command like this would give you a nice, tidy list:

```
who | cut -ci-8 | sort -u | pr -l1 -8 -w78 -t
```

You can see four commands at work here:

- `who`—Tells you the users who are logged in.
- `cut`—Processes the `who` command results and outputs only the usernames to the screen (instead of the whole line)
- `sort`—Puts the names in alphabetical order prior to the output screen, and removes from the list those users who are logged in more than once.
- `pr`—Takes the list, one per line, and delivers it to the screen in eight columns.

This is simple, and as your shell wizard skills improve, you will be able to do amazing things with a few keystrokes and some pipes.

Background Processing

Often in this book, you'll see a shell command with an ampersand (&) at the end of it. This is especially true when you use the shell to launch a graphical application. You may wonder what this is there for. The & takes advantage of the shell's ability to process commands in the background, while still running other programs from the same command line.

Let's say you want to run the GKrellM system monitor from the shell. If you just type **`gkrellm`** at the prompt, the program will run, of course. But if you look at the shell, you'll see a dead cursor that cannot complete any more commands, at least until you exit out of GKrellM.

If you then exit out of the monitor (right-click anywhere in the program and select Quit), your shell prompt returns, and you can type commands again. Using the up arrow to recall your last command from the command history, `gkrellm` again appears at the prompt. This time, add the background processing operator `&`, and press Enter. GKrellM runs as before, but `bash` now tells you the process number for this application, and then returns you to the prompt. You can now enter any other command you like.

Basic Shell Programming

Now that you are familiar with the way the shell operates, you can start working on your shell scripts. This section walks though the basics of the shell programming statements that are used to write full-featured shell scripts.

Displaying Messages

Most shell commands produce their own output, which is displayed on the console monitor where the script is running. Many times though, you will want to add your own text messages to help the script user know what is happening within the script. This is done using the `echo` command. The `echo` command can display a simple text string by adding the string following the command:

```
rich@testing:~> echo This is a test
This is a test
rich@testing:~>
```

Notice that, by default, you don't need to use quotes to delineate a string. However, sometimes this can get tricky if you are using quotes within your string.

The echo command can also use either double or single quotes to delineate text strings. If you need to use one type of quote within the text, you can use the other type to delineate the string:

```
rich@testing:~> echo "This is a test to see if you're paying attention"
```

```
This is a test to see if you're paying attention
rich@testing:~> echo 'Mike says "scripting is easy".'
Mike says "scripting is easy".
rich@testing:~>
```

The echo command is a crucial piece of shell scripts that interact with users. You will find yourself using it in many situations, especially when handling script variables.

Using System Variables

Just running individual commands from the shell script is useful, but it has its limitations. Often you will need to incorporate external data in your shell commands to process information.

The shell maintains system variables that track specific system information, such as the name of the system, the name of the user logged into the system, the user's system id (called UID), the default home directory of the user, and the search path used by the shell to find programs. You can display a complete list of active system variables available by using the set command:

```
rich@testing:~> set
BACKSPACE=Delete
BASH=/bin/bash
EUID=1000
HISTFILE=/home/rich/.bash_history
HISTFILESIZE=1000
HISTSIZE=1000
HOME=/home/rich
HOSTNAME=testing
HOSTTYPE=i586
LANG=en
LANGUAGE=en_US:en
LINES=24
LOGNAME=rich
...
```

You can tap into these system variables from within your scripts by using the system variable name preceded by a dollar sign. This is demonstrated in the following script:

```
#!/bin/bash
# display user information from the system.
echo "User info for userid: $USER"
echo UID: $UID
echo HOME: $HOME
```

The $USER, $UID, and $HOME system variables are used to display the pertinent information about the logged in user. The output should look something like this:

```
rich@testing:~> ./test2
User info for userid:  rich
UID: 1000
HOME: /home/rich
rich@testing:~>
```

Notice that the system variables in the echo commands are replaced by their current value when the script is run. Also notice that we were able to place the $USER system variable within the double quotes in the first string, and the shell script was still able to figure out what we meant. There is a drawback to using this method though. Look at what happens in this example:

```
rich@testing:~> echo "The cost of the item is $15"
The cost of the item is 5
```

That is obviously not what we intended. Whenever the script sees a dollar sign within quotes, it assumes you are referencing a variable. In this example the script attempted to display the variable $1 (which was not defined), and then the number 5. To display an actual dollar sign, you must precede it with a backslash character:

```
rich@testing:~> echo "The cost of the item is \$15"
The cost of the item is $15
```

That is better. The backslash allowed the shell script to interpret the dollar sign as an actual dollar sign, and not a variable. The next section shows how to create your own variables in your scripts.

Creating User Variables

Besides the system variables, a shell script allows you to set and use your own variables within the script. Setting variables allows you to temporarily store data and use it throughout the script, making the shell script more like a real computer program.

User variables can be any text string of up to 20 letters, digits, or an underscore character. User variables are case sensitive, so the variable Var1 is different from the variable var1. This little rule often gets novice script programmers in trouble.

Values are assigned to user variables using an equal sign. No spaces can appear between the variable, the equal sign, and the value (another trouble spot for novices). Here are a few examples of assigning values to user variables:

```
var1=10
var2=-57
var3=testing
var4="still more testing"
```

The shell script automatically determines the data type used for the variable value. Variables defined within the shell script maintain their values throughout the life of the shell script, but are deleted when the shell script completes.

Just like system variables, user variables can be referenced using the dollar sign:

```
#!/bin/bash
# testing variables
days=10
guest="Katie"
echo "$guest checked in $days days ago"
days=5
guest="Jessica"
echo "$guest checked in $days days ago"
```

Running the script produces this output:

```
rich@testing:~> ./test3
Katie checked in 10 days ago
Jessica checked in 5 days ago
rich@testing:~>
```

Each time the variable is referenced, it produces the value currently assigned to it. It is important to remember that when referencing a variable name to assign a new value, you do not use the dollar sign. Use the dollar sign only when you want to reference the value the variable contains.

The Backtick

One of the most useful features of shell scripts is the lowly backtick (`). Be careful, this is not the normal single quote character you are used to using for strings. While it is not used very often outside of shell scripts, you should become familiar with where the backtick is located on your keyboard, because it is a crucial component of many shell scripts (*Hint:* On a PC, it is usually on the tilde key.).

The backtick allows you to assign the output of a shell command to a variable. While this doesn't seem like much, it is a major building block in script programming. Here is an example of how the back quote typically is used:


```
#!/bin/bash
# copy the /usr/bin directory listing to a log file
today=`date +%y%m%d`
ls /usr/bin -al > log.$today
```

The `today` variable is assigned the output of a formatted `date` command. This is a common technique used to extract date info for log file names. The `+%y%m%d` format instructs the `date` command to display the date as a two-digit year, month, and day:

```
rich@testing:~> date +%y%m%d
061213
rich@testing:~>
```

The script assigns the value to a variable, which is then used as part of a file name. The file itself contains the redirected output of a directory listing. After running the script, you should see a new file in your directory:

```
-rw-r--r--    1 rich     rich           769 Dec 13 10:15 log.061213
```

The log file appears in the directory using the value of the `$today` variable as part of the file name. The contents of the log file are the directory listing from the /usr/bin directory. If the script is run the next day, the log file name will be `log.061214`, thus creating a new file for the new day.

Arithmetic

Another crucial feature to any programming language is the ability to manipulate numbers. Unfortunately, for shell scripts, this process is a bit awkward.

Originally, the Bourne shell provided a special command that was used for processing mathematical equations. The `expr` command allowed for processing equations. This was extremely clunky:

```
rich@testing:~> expr 1 + 5
6
rich@testing:~> expr 5 \* 2
10
```

Note that the multiplication symbol (*) must be preceded by a backslash to prevent the shell from recognizing it as a wildcard character.

Using the `expr` command in a shell script was equally cumbersome:

```
#!/bin/bash
# An example of using the expr command
var1=10
var2=20
var3=`expr $var2 / $var1`
echo The result is $var3
```

To assign the result of a mathematical equation to a variable, you had to use the back quote to extract the output from the `expr` command.

While the bash shell fully supports the `expr` command, it also includes a much easier way of performing mathematical equations. In bash, when assigning a value to a variable, you can enclose a mathematical equation using square brackets ([]). The shell interprets anything within the square brackets as a mathematical equation to evaluate:

```
rich@testing:~> var1=$[1 + 5]
rich@testing:~> echo $var1
6
rich@testing:~> var2 = $[$var1 * 2]
```

```
rich@testing:~> echo $var2
12
rich@testing:~>
```

Using square brackets makes shell math much easier. Also notice that when using the square brackets, you don't need to worry about the multiplication symbol. The shell knows that it is not a wildcard character because it is within the square brackets.

NOTE

Unfortunately, the bash shell does not have the ability to perform floating point arithmetic, only integer arithmetic. If you must do floating point arithmetic, there are few tricks that programmers have used, such as redirecting the numbers and operators as strings to the bc program, which is a calculator provided by the bash shell. You can also try using the Z shell (zsh) included in openSUSE. It handles floating point values just fine.

Advanced Shell Programming

Now that you have the basics of shell programming down, it's time to dig deeper into some other commands and techniques available. The commands and techniques presented in this section will help make your shell scripts more like real programs.

User Input

Often shell scripts must interact with whoever is running them. There are two ways for a script to retrieve data from a user:

- Process command line arguments and options supplied by the user
- Interactively query the user for data while the script is running

Command line arguments and options allow the user to enter data on the command line when the shell script is executed. An option is a dash followed by a single letter. Options are often used to control the behavior of a script, such as whether or not to produce an output.

A command line argument is a string value that can be a single text string, a number, or a string with spaces enclosed in double quotes. Each argument or option is separated by one or more spaces. The shell script assigns variables to each argument and option that is specified. These variables are shown in Table 8.3.

TABLE 8.3 Shell Command Line Variables

Variable	Description
$0	The name of the shell script
$1	The value of the first argument (continuing for $2, $3, and so on)
$#	The number of command line arguments specified
$*	A string containing all of the command line arguments
$-	A string containing all of the options specified

8

These argument values can be used anywhere in the script you would use a normal variable:

```
#!/bin/bash
# testing command line paramters
# enter your name, then two numbers on the command line
echo Hello $1,
result=$[$2 * $3]
echo The answer to your problem is $result
```

When running the program, you just include the arguments on the command line (in the proper order):

```
rich@testing:~> ./test4 Rich 140 3
Hello Rich,
The answer to your problem is 420
rich@testing:~>
```

Sometimes, though, instead of making your users supply information up front in the command line, you need to ask questions on the fly. This can be done using the `read` command:

```
#!/bin/bash
# asking for user input within the script
echo Please enter your name:
read name
echo "Welcome, $name, pleased to meet you!"
```

Note that the variable is used without the dollar sign in the `read` command. When the value is referenced in the `echo` command, you must use the dollar sign. When the read command is processed, the script halts and waits for an entry from the user:

```
rich@testing:~> ./test5
Please enter your name:
Ima Test
Welcome, Ima Test, pleased to meet you!
```

Notice that the text input was a string with a space. The `read` command accepts all text entered on the input line.

Flow Control

In a shell script, commands are executed in the order they appear in the text file. In many programming situations though, you need to alter the program execution flow. This is where the flow control commands come in handy.

The most common flow control common is the `if-then` statement. This statement allows you to check a condition and then execute commands based on the result of the condition. The basic format of the `if-then` statement is:

```
if [ condition ]
then
    commands
else
    other commands
fi
```

The *condition* is enclosed in square brackets. It is also important to include spaces between the *condition* and the square brackets. If *condition* evaluates to a `TRUE` value, the *commands* listed between the `then` and `else` are executed. If *condition* is `FALSE`, the *other commands* are executed (you may omit the else section if it is not needed). Make sure you end the `if-then` block with an `fi` statement.

There are many conditions that can be tested in the shell script. The most basic is checking the values of numbers. Table 8.4 lists the format for checking number values in an `if-then` statement.

TABLE 8.4 Number Evaluation Conditions

Format	Description
n1 -eq n2	Check if n1 is equal to n2
n1 -ge n2	Check if n1 is greater than or equal to n2
n1 -gt n2	Check if n1 is greater than n2
n1 -le n2	Check if n1 is less than or equal to n2
n1 -lt n2	Check if n1 is less than n2
n1 -ne n2	Check if n1 is not equal to n2

Here is a handy way to check to make sure the user entered the proper number of command line arguments:

```
#!/bin/bash
# check the command line arguments entered
if [ $# -lt 3 ]
then
    echo "Sorry, you did not enter enough arguments for this"
    echo "Usage: test6 name num1 num2"
else
    result=$[$2 * $3]
    echo "Hello, $1"
    echo "The answer to your problem is $result"
fi
```

Running the script with the correct number of command line arguments produces the following results:

```
rich@testing:~> ./test6
Sorry, you did not enter enough arguments for this
```

8

```
Usage: test6 name num1 num2
rich@testing:~> ./test6 rich 140 3
Hello rich,
The answer to your problem is 420
rich@testing:~>
```

One of the most useful test conditions available in the shell is the ability to test the status of a file or directory. These test conditions are often used in system shell scripts to determine if a software package has been installed. Table 8.5 shows the file tests that are available in the bash shell.

TABLE 8.5 Testing for Files and Directories

Test	Description
-d *file*	Checks if the specified file is a directory
-e *file*	Checks if the specified file or directory exists
-f *file*	Checks if the specified file is a file (rather than a directory)
-r *file*	Checks if the specified file is readable
-s *file*	Checks if the specified file size is greater than zero
-w *file*	Checks if the specified file is writeable
-x *file*	Checks if the user has execute permissions for the specified file

These simple tests provide great control when checking on the condition of installed software on the system:

```
#!/bin/bash
# check the status of the Z shell program
echo "Checking for the Z shell..."
if [ -e /bin/zsh ]
then
    echo "  The Z shell is available"
    if [ -w /bin/zsh ]
    then
        echo "  Hmm, we can write to the zsh file, that's a security problem"
    else
        echo "  As expected, we can't write to the Z shell file"
    fi
else
    echo "Sorry, the zsh shell is not available"
fi
```

This simple script uses the -e condition to check if the Z shell file (/bin/zsh) exists on the system. Next, a simple security check is made to see if the zsh file is writeable (for security purposes all executable files on the system should be locked).

References

- http://www.cryptonomicon.com/beginning.html—The Neal Stephenson essay, "In the Beginning Was the Command Line." See also an authorized update by Garrett Birkel, "The Command Line in 2004," at http://garrote.bdmonkeys.net/commandline/.
- http://www.gnu.org/software/bash—The official bash site at the GNU Project. Download the latest, and read the "Introduction to Bash" section.
- http://cnswww.cns.cwru.edu/~chet/bash/bashtop.html—Chet Ramey's bash site. Ramey is the current bash maintainer. Looks very much like the official page, but also has the bash FAQ list.
- http://www.tldp.org/LDP/Bash-Beginners-Guide/html—A bash guide for beginners.
- http://www.tldp.org/LDP/abs/html—The Advanced bash scripting guide. Read online, or download the PDF or the SGML source of this complete guide to bash shell scripting.
- http://www.filibeto.org/sun/lib/development/shell/config_the_bash_shell.html—Configuring the bash shell.
- http://www.justlinux.com/nhf/Shells/Basic_Console_Commands.html—Learn these commands and you can be comfortable saying you know bash well enough.
- http://www.kornshell.com/doc—Assorted documentation for the commercial Korn shell, ksh.
- http://web.cs.mun.ca/~michael/pdksh—The public domain Korn shell site. This is the version included with openSUSE Linux.
- http://www.tcsh.org—The tcsh wiki. Although it does not contain a wealth of information, check out the FAQ and TipsNTricks page. You can also subscribe to the two tcsh mailing lists.
- http://www.faqs.org/faqs/unix-faq/shell/csh-whynot—Perl guru Tom Christiansen's famous 1996 essay, "Csh Programming Considered Harmful." It tells you why it's a bad idea to script in the C shell.
- http://www.zsh.org—Home of the Z shell. Very useful.

CHAPTER 9

Being Productive: Office Suites and Other Tools

IN THIS CHAPTER

- Comparing Linux Office Suites
- Connecting with PDAs and Smart Phones
- More Tools to Make You Productive
- References

We are at the dawn of the age where businesses and ordinary people are using Linux as their everyday computing platform. There have been Linux tools for word processing, making presentations, managing finances, personal calendars, and other such tasks for a long time. Productivity tools are now coming into their own, and more people are starting to recognize that.

SUSE has always been in the forefront of desktop Linux, marketing the first Linux Office Suite in 1999. Based on the Applixware suite now produced by VistaSource, this suite didn't exactly set the world on fire, but it did mark the beginning of the Linux desktop revolution.

There is hardly a task you can complete in Windows that cannot be done in Linux, and often you will find that your Linux application does it better, or faster, or easier. This chapter explores the office productivity applications included in openSUSE and shows you how to get started with them. Many of these applications install by default with the Office install option, and others can be added through YaST. These tools will make you a more productive user.

Comparing Linux Office Suites

Today, four competitive open-source suites operate under openSUSE. They each come with a word processor and spreadsheet program, and some have additional elements. Some have versions for Windows and/or the Apple Macintosh. All will help you get your work done.

OpenOffice.org (and its commercial sibling StarOffice) is probably the best known of the four. Its backing from Sun Microsystems, its variety of applications, and its multiplatform character make it a very big player. But it is not the only game in town. Both KDE and GNOME desktop environments have associated office suites that may not get all the publicity OpenOffice.org gets, but are fine tools nonetheless. A new suite from German company Softmaker made its debut in SUSE Linux 9.2, and there are other commercial choices for your consideration.

This chapter gives you a quick rundown on all the office suite choices available under openSUSE to help you decide what you need. As always, play around with each of them.

Running OpenOffice.org

If your primary concern when choosing an office suite is the capability to read and write Microsoft Office-compatible files, OpenOffice.org (OOo) is probably your best bet. The notoriously finicky proprietary formats remain dominant in modern business, and OOo offers the best filters currently available. Although it is impossible to be 100% compatible without access to the format's structure, OOo does a terrific job. Microsoft Office users will also find OpenOffice.org's interface quite familiar, making the transition a little easier as well.

But OpenOffice.org is not just a Microsoft clone. There are some things it does differently, and more than a few things that it does better. We'll explore these in the next section.

What Is OpenOffice.org?

This product began its life as a fully integrated productivity suite for the OS/2 operating system. Produced by the German company StarDivision, it had everything wrapped up in one desktop interface. StarOffice 5 was the first major suite produced for Linux (just beating out WordPerfect for that honor). It was important for Linux to have this type of software available, but there were problems with it. Chief among these problems was that it took forever to load. The interface took over the entire desktop and loaded all its components—word processor, spreadsheet, database, presentation, even a web browser, calendar, and email client—into memory at once.

When Sun Microsystems bought StarDivision in 2002, it made two decisions that put the product on the very successful path it is now on. First, it released the StarOffice code under an open source license (the Lesser General Public License, or LGPL), creating the OpenOffice.org project and allowing developers and users to contribute. Second, it scrapped the integrated features that bogged down its predecessors. Although it would always be easy to access different parts of the suite and put data from a spreadsheet into a document, the desktop interface would disappear, and not all components would load simultaneously. Sun also scrapped some of the feature creep that had set in and focused on delivering the core elements of a suite.

OpenOffice 2.x produces documents in the ISO standard Open Document Format (ODF). This standard makes it easier to produce documents that anyone can read or edit. OpenOffice.org 2.3 ships with openSUSE 10.3. It has the following programs:

- Writer—This word processor should be very familiar to users of just about any other similar application. It creates documents with amazing complexity, handles collaborative tools such as Comments, and exports to a variety of non-native formats. You can even turn any document into a Portable Document Format (PDF) that anyone with the Adobe Acrobat Reader (or the open source Ghostview) can open and read. The Writer/Web tool offers a slightly different toolbar layout, but delivers much cleaner HTML code than its Microsoft counterparts (Word and FrontPage).

- Calc—This spreadsheet program is the number-cruncher's delight. Although it uses a different macro language than Microsoft Excel uses, nearly all standard functions are supported. Calc supports several data exchange formats, as well.
- Impress—The presentations you make with this tool may not be any more informative than its PowerPoint counterpart, but they are just as professional. When you start Impress, a wizard walks you through the steps to create a new presentation. Impress comes with two presentation templates: Introducing a New Product and Recommending a New Strategy.
- Draw—This vector drawing program is similar to CorelDraw or Adobe Illustrator. Create polygonal drawings for your documents, presentations, or web pages. Use connectors for Visio-like flowcharts and brainstorms. You can even do Flash animations if you're so inclined. See Chapter 10, "Sights, Sounds, and Other Fun Things," for more information on this and other drawing programs.
- Math—This is a formula editor for higher math equations. Create and edit formulas for insertion into a spreadsheet or for display in a document. Math includes a number of fonts and symbols rarely needed in standard word processing documents, but essential for academic science and math writing.
- Base—The first effort at a database product by the OpenOffice.org team will create new databases and import from a selection of database formats, including Microsoft Access, MySQL, and Java Database Connectivity (JDBC)—even the flat-file dBASE database. Learn more about Base in Chapter 29, "Managing Databases."

Installing OpenOffice.org

When you install openSUSE with the Office components included, YaST will install the English version of OOo by default. If you prefer to install OOo later, this is easily done through YaST. Run YaST and choose Software Management. Either Search for the OpenOffice package or use the Package Groups to locate Productivity, Office, Suite. You will find several language versions of OOo on the openSUSE DVD.

YaST takes care of all the details related to an install, which is good. Installing a downloaded version can be messy. If you download a new version directly from the OOo site, you must run the installer twice. First install OOo as Root (that is, using `su`). This will allow all users to run OOo and install some files that are owned by Root. Each user who wants to use OOo should then install the client, using the same process. The second install places many OOo files into your home directory.

As you might expect from a Sun product, OOo uses Java-based files for some tasks and requires that the Java Runtime Environment v1.4 or later be installed for best results. However, the OOo install program doesn't always look in the right place for the JRE. In openSUSE, the JRE is stored in the `/usr/lib/SunJava2` directory.

TIP

OpenOffice.org updates frequently. New and tested versions eventually show up in YaST, but if you're anxious to see what's new (at a risk of some system stability), use the preceding process to install OOo yourself.

Starting OpenOffice.org

You can start OpenOffice.org in any of several ways. OOo is integrated into both the KDE and GNOME menus, under `Office`. In KDE, each application is listed under the appropriate type (word processor, spreadsheet, and so on). At the bottom is the Office Suite icon with the OOo logo. This opens the Documents and Templates window.

OOo also provides a QuickStarter program that places an OOo icon in both the KDE and GNOME taskbars. Turn this on in the OOo Options dialog box, under Memory. Double-clicking the QuickStarter icon brings up a new Writer document by default. This is configurable. Choose Configure OpenOffice.org QuickStarter from the QuickStarter menu.

With either method, you are presented with the OOo menu. Depending on your OOo version, you may be presented with either the list of programs or the type of document you want to open or create: Text Document, HTML Document, Spreadsheet, Drawing, Database, or Presentation. Choosing From Template brings up a list of existing templates, and Open Document lets you choose from existing documents.

Configuring OpenOffice.org

Regardless of the method, after you have OOo installed, you are ready to go and can begin creating documents and other files. You may, however, want to customize standard OOo behavior before you begin. Go to Tools, Options in any OOo application to open the dialog box.

As you can see in Figure 9.1, there are many choices to make in configuring OOo, to the point where some users complain this dialog is too complex.

Following are some of the many choices you can make in the Options dialog box:

- Define your mail client in the Internet section (should you want to email a document directly from OOo) . See more about setting up and using email in Chapter 13, "Using the Internet: Browsing the Web and Writing Email," and Chapter 15, "Managing Email Servers."
- Tell OOo to automatically save your work at regular intervals in the Load/Save General section.
- Tell OOo if it should save a backup copy of your work in Load/Save General.
- Turn on (or off) the automatic spell checker in Language Settings/Writing Aids.
- Use a Direct Cursor tool to put text wherever you click (and not just at the beginning of the next line). This is set in the Writer section, Formatting Aids.
- Define your default document fonts in Writer, Basic Fonts.

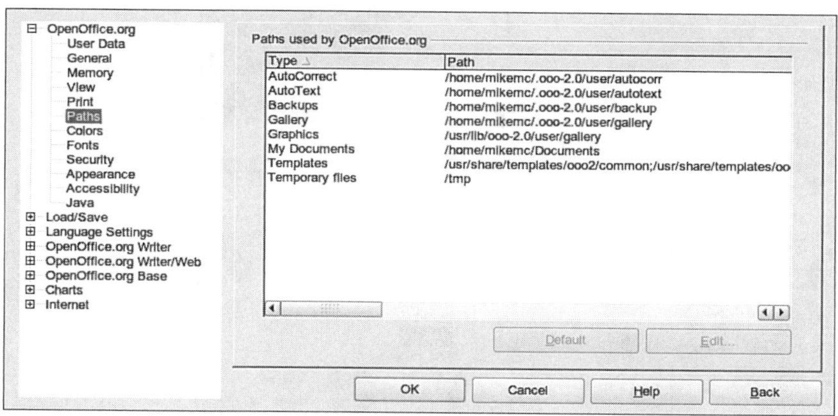

FIGURE 9.1 The OpenOffice.org Options dialog box lets you set up OpenOffice.org and its various tools the way you want.

You may also want to set up and customize your toolbars and keyboard shortcuts at some point. Do this by going to the Tools, Customize menu.

Suppose you needed to keep track of the word count of a document and wanted to check it periodically. You can find this information under the Tools menu, but not in the standard toolbar. To change the toolbar, go to Tools, Customize. Click the Toolbars tab. The dialog box shown in Figure 9.2 appears.

At the top, you see a listing of the various toolbars in a drop-down menu, with the standard toolbar displayed. In the middle are the available commands for this toolbar.

Notice that some items in the Commands window don't have a check next to them. If you click the check box, it becomes active. Looking over the list, you'll see that there's no Word Count there. Fortunately, there's an Add button on the right. This brings up the Add Commands dialog box, with Categories on the left and related Commands on the right. There are a lot of categories, and they don't match up completely with the menus, but if you click the Options category, Word Count appears, but it does not have an icon.

Select Word Count on the right, and click Add. Click Close to return to the Customize menu. You can then drag the new icon where you want it on the toolbar.

If an item you want on the toolbar doesn't have a default icon (or maybe you have a different one in mind), click Modify and Change Icon. A selection of icons will appear, and you have the option to import any 26x26 pixel image and apply it to your command. Use the Modify drop-down menu to create new groups of icons with separators or to rename or delete items from your toolbar.

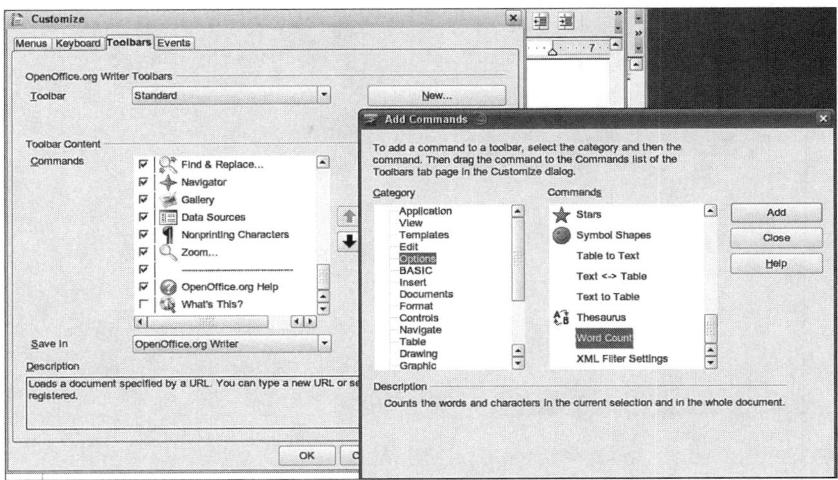

FIGURE 9.2 The Customize Toolbars page is a little tricky to deal with, but will put nearly any OpenOffice.org command a click away.

Click OK to return to your document. Done! To see your word count, click the new Word Count icon.

Using OpenOffice.org

For the most part, this is an interface that should be familiar to anyone who has used a word processor. A few things are different about OOo that may take some getting used to, especially if you are migrating from Microsoft Office. Some of these are shown in Figure 9.3, which shows the face of a typical Writer document.

Have you ever wondered where a signature line is supposed to start in a letter? How to properly do a block quote in a school paper? How much space is supposed to be between the number and the text in a list? Have you ever spent a half-hour trying to get any of these things to line up right in a document? If so, you need to start working with styles and the Stylist.

What is the Stylist? It is a handy way to apply standard formats to blocks of text or spreadsheet cells. In Microsoft Word, styles are easy to ignore and most people don't ever change from the Normal style. In OOo, you can continue to go through life using only the Default style, but the Stylist is there to at least make you think about using it.

NOTE

In earlier versions of OpenOffice.org, the Stylist opened by default in any document. In version 2.0, a Styles drop-down menu was included with the Formatting toolbar. You can use this to apply existing styles to any paragraph or characters in a document. To open the Stylist, go to Styles and Formatting in the Format menu, or just press F11.

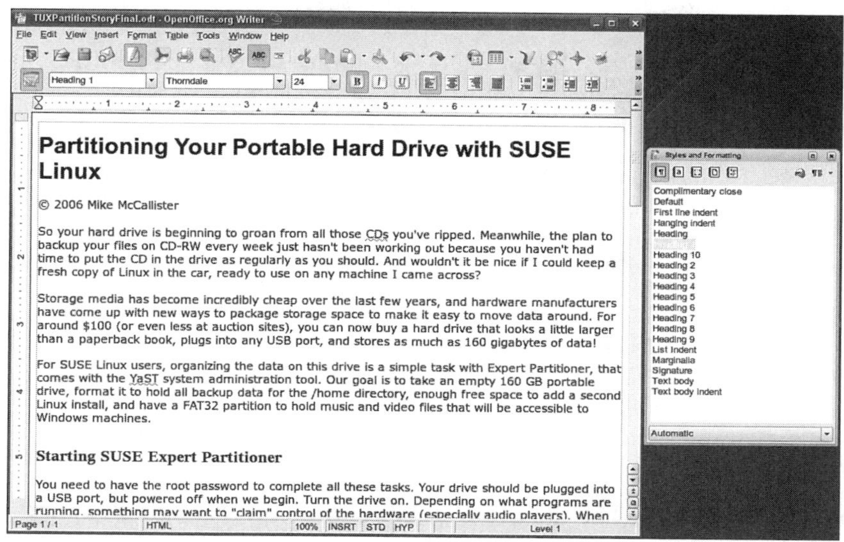

FIGURE 9.3 A typical document window in OpenOffice.org. Note the Stylist on the right.

Use the Stylist to set up paragraphs (the most often used styles), characters (such as a book title), pages, and whole documents. If you have a certain way you want your styles to look, you can edit the properties of existing styles or create new styles of your own.

One default setting in OOo that takes more than a little getting used to (if you don't put it to pasture early) is autocompletion mode. As you type, you will suddenly find green-highlighted letters on the screen. Press Enter to accept Writer's suggestion or keep typing or hit the space bar to make it go away. Lazy typists may love this as much as autocompletion in their favorite shell, but Writer is frequently wrong in its guesses, and that can make for complications or embarrassing typos.

You can make it work for you, but if it's just too maddening, turning autocompletion off is fairly simple: Go to Tools, AutoCorrect. Click the Word Completion tab and uncheck Enable Word Completion. You can make other tweaks in this dialog box, too.

TIP

There are two boons for formal or academic writers in OpenOffice.org that are not obvious to the casual observer:

- You can use the Navigator tool to build outlines of your documents. Your Headings are listed in the Navigator, and you can drag them around, promote, and demote them. Turn the Navigator on in the Edit menu, or press F5.
- You can also create a bibliographic database for use in either a single document or across documents. Go to Tools, Bibliography Database to give it a spin.

Running KOffice

The K Desktop Environment (KDE) team began building an office suite in 2001. Although it does not have all the polish (and certainly not the level of publicity) of OpenOffice.org, it is a very good suite. KOffice v1.6 ships with openSUSE.

KDE users should especially appreciate KOffice and its tools. KOffice is designed to integrate well with this popular desktop and with the other tools in the suite. Although each component launches separately from either the shell or the KDE Kicker menu, there is also a launch interface, called the KOffice Workspace, that includes icons for all the office tools.

KOffice uses a technology, called KParts, that allows for integration of many tools under one umbrella, but does not require every piece to be present for everything to work. Thus, although you have to download and install the entire OpenOffice.org suite, you may need only the word processor. Each KOffice tool is a single KPart, and if you want only KWord, that's all you need to get.

The primary weakness of KOffice is its lack of compatibility with most modern Microsoft formats. The KOffice tools will read the vast majority of Microsoft Office documents, spreadsheets, and so on, but cannot produce complex documents in the current Office formats, although it can do Rich Text Format and WordPad (that is, Microsoft Word 6). Communicating with Office users is not impossible, as KOffice will save to the OpenOffice.org OpenDocument format, WordPerfect, and standard HTML or XML.

What's in KOffice?

The KOffice tools rival OOo in number, if not always in quality. As with many things related to KDE, they also tend to run the "K" references into the ground. The following is what you'll find if you install the entire suite:

- Koshell—The integrated KOffice Workspace launch tool for all KOffice tools. Use this if you need access to all the tools in the kit.
- KWord—A frames-based word processor that also serves as a fine desktop publishing tool. If you have experience with Adobe PageMaker, InDesign, or FrameMaker, you will find much that is familiar in KWord.
- KSpread—This spreadsheet is scriptable and can handle complex formulas as well.
- KPresenter—Another presentation program.
- Kexi—An Access-like desktop database management tool.
- Kivio—A flowcharting and diagramming program similar to Visio under Windows.
- Karbon14—The basis for all life on earth, it is also the KOffice vector drawing program. See Chapter 10 for more information on this and other drawing programs.
- Krita—This paint program hopes one day to replace the GIMP in the hearts of Linux designers everywhere.

- KPlato—A project management tool.
- Kugar—Something different for an office suite under any OS: a business report developer/generator.
- KChart—A chart generator.
- KFormula—A formula editor.

Installing and Configuring KOffice

YaST does not install KOffice by default, even if you choose KDE as your primary desktop. To install KOffice, follow these steps:

1. Go to the YaST Software page and click Software Management. Have your openSUSE DVD ready.
2. Either Search for KOffice (which is faster) or go to the Package display under Productivity, Office.
3. Select the KOffice modules you want to install. They are listed by function (word processing, spreadsheet, and so on).
4. Check for compatibility (if that was not done automatically) and then click Accept to install the selections. You may get a notification that other files are being installed as well.
5. YaST will install KOffice and, barring any problems, will return to the main screen.
6. Run YaST Online Update (YOU) to check for updates to the software.

Customizing and configuring KOffice tools is very much like configuring any KDE tool. Go to the `Settings` menu and choose from any of five `Settings` dialog boxes. Opening the `Configure KWord` dialog box displays something similar to Figure 9.4.

Using sliders to change settings is a little unusual and is just one option for making changes in this dialog. Click each icon on the left to view and edit settings related to those items. Use different dialog boxes to edit toolbars, keyboard shortcuts, and automatic word completions and corrections.

Using KOffice

When you launch a KOffice application, you get choices from some basic templates, recent documents, and the contents of your Documents directory (see Figure 9.5).

TIP

Download additional KWord templates at http://www.koffice.org/addons/.

9

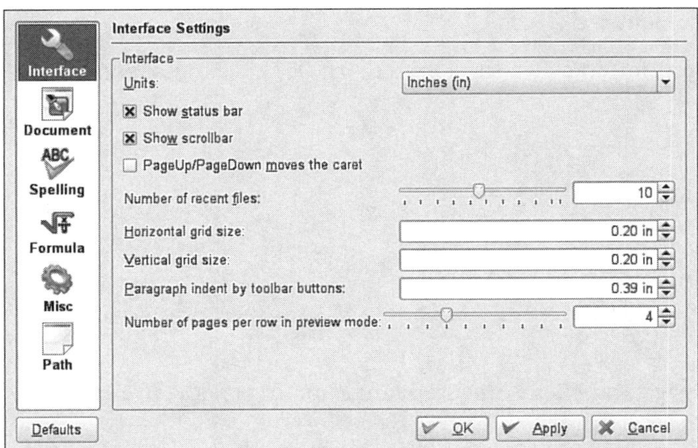

FIGURE 9.4 The KWord configuration dialog box lets you use sliders to change settings.

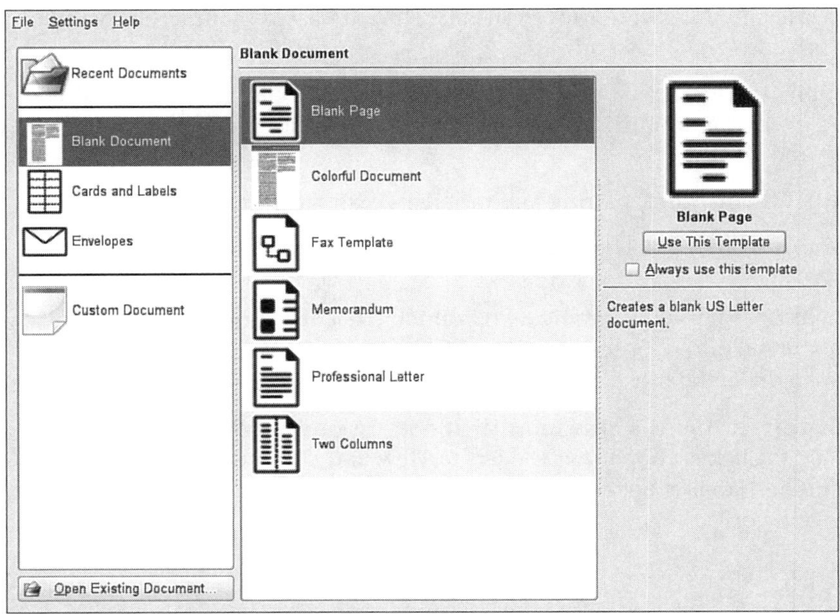

FIGURE 9.5 The KWord Open dialog box lets you select from several blank templates or from existing documents.

What makes KWord stand out is its page layout formats. Inspired by the indispensable technical writer's tool, Adobe FrameMaker, KWord helps you create frames to hold text, graphics, white space and other design elements with relative ease.

The KWord interface includes a document structure map that lets you quickly add frames to fill in later. The software isn't yet ready for really long documents, but is certainly up to the task of a company newsletter or holiday message.

KSpread also has templates for many standard tasks—invoices, balance sheets, and tracking credit cards. You can even use KSpread to calculate your body mass index.

Running GNOME Office

Despite having a pair of fine and well-built applications, GNOME Office (GO) is still a work in progress. As of this writing, GNOME Office is a very loose confederation of tools, with no common interface or direct integration. The applications are built on the GTK widget set that underlies everything in the GNOME desktop.

What's in GNOME Office?

For now at least, GNOME Office consists of three key applications:

- AbiWord—A cross-platform word processor with a pluggable architecture allowing you to have just the functionality you want, and not so much bloatware.
- Gnumeric—A spreadsheet with all the features you would expect. It will read your Excel files, too.
- GNOME-DB—A GUI front end to all popular open source databases that can also connect to LDAP directories, mail data, and the like. The libraries associated with this project provide data management functions to many GNOME applications.

Other productivity tools running under the GNOME desktop may one day be part of the GO project, but today this is it. We will cover Evolution, the GNOME personal information manager, in Chapter 13; we will cover GIMP in Chapter 10.

Installing and Configuring GNOME Office

GO has no single install, but all the components are installable from YaST. There are three GNOME-DB files to install: libgda, libgnomedb, and mergeant.

TIP

Are you running KDE as your main desktop? You can still run any or all of the GNOME Office tools. YaST will install any of the necessary GNOME libraries if you choose to install AbiWord or Gnumeric. Both of these tools have Windows versions, should you want to try them out there. GNOME-DB will also run on Macintosh OS X.

Using GNOME Office

AbiWord has a very nice, clean interface based on the Microsoft Works word processor. It has a pretty good Save as Word function, so it should be easy to trade documents with the Microsoft world. As always, some of the more esoteric functions are hard to reproduce.

AbiWord 2.4.5 is a word processor with a difference: its default file format is the Extensible Markup Language (XML). Any document created by AbiWord can be viewed in a web browser that supports XML or any text editor. In the latter, you can see the markup tags. AbiWord will export documents to standard HTML or with PHP instructions and display the results in a browser with a default or custom cascading stylesheet.

AbiWord handles right-to-left text with ease, giving support to those who craft words in Arabic and Hebrew. You can even manipulate this feature paragraph-by-paragraph if you are writing for multiple audiences.

You can use styles in AbiWord, and you can modify them on-the-fly. AbiWord also comes with a few templates, including a most interesting Resume template, using their mascot, Abi the Ant.

Gnumeric delivers on its promise to be Fast, Free, and Accurate. It will import your Excel files and should also handle most other popular spreadsheet formats (including OpenOffice.org Calc and Quattro Pro). It boasts of more than 100 functions that are unique to Gnumeric (that is, not available in Excel).

There is fine documentation at http://www.gnome.org/projects/gnumeric/doc/gnumeric.shtml. Newcomers to spreadsheets should certainly read Chapter 3 of the online manual, which is a Quick-Start tutorial in using Gnumeric.

Running Softmaker Office

Softmaker Office was first added to openSUSE Linux 9.2, and it continues in openSUSE. This small commercial suite promises a small memory footprint, fast loading, and seamless conversion to and from Microsoft formats. As with GNOME Office, Softmaker is a very loosely connected collection of two applications: word processor Textmaker and spreadsheet Planmaker.

Like KOffice, Textmaker offers some desktop publishing features as well as ordinary word processing. Its Object Mode makes it easy to create and place new text or graphics frames (see Figure 9.6). The built-in templates are interesting, with several business card designs, letters, faxes, memos, and a phone list template.

Planmaker is a perfectly serviceable spreadsheet—nothing fancy—but with all the features you would expect from this application. It does a great job of importing Excel worksheets (see Figure 9.7) and has 320 built-in functions.

Other Commercial Suites

Although not included with openSUSE, a few other commercial products in this category might interest you.

ThinkFree Office for Linux was released just days before the openSUSE project was announced in August 2005. Its chief claim to fame is even easier document sharing with Microsoft Office tools. ThinkFree saves files to the Microsoft format by default and also makes Acrobat PDF files for use in the Adobe Reader. ThinkFree Office contains a word processor (Write), a spreadsheet (Calc), and a presentation (Show) package. You can try it out free at the ThinkFree website: http://www.thinkfree.com.

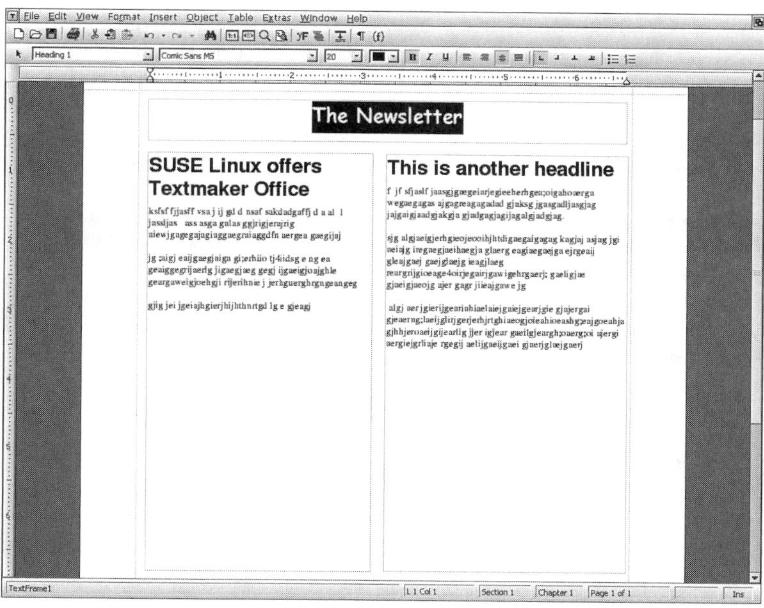

FIGURE 9.6 Textmaker lets you easily create multicolumn layouts with text and graphics frames.

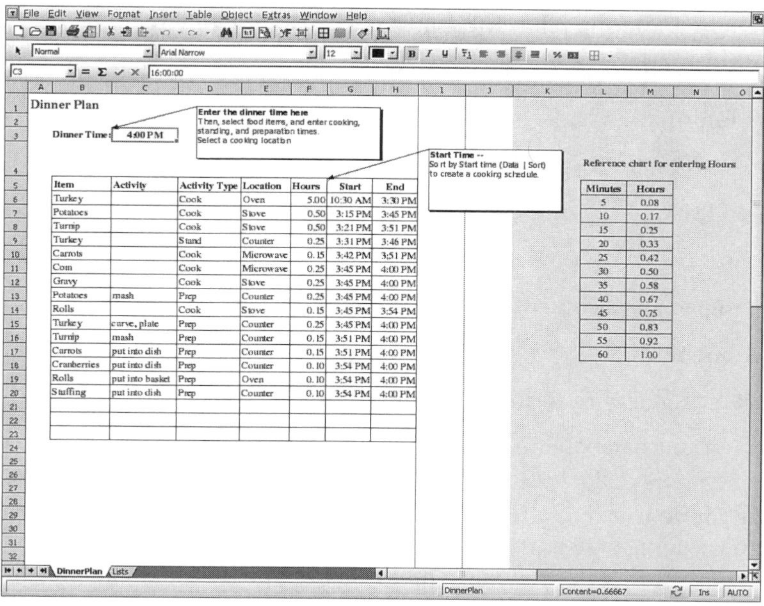

Item	Activity	Activity Type	Location	Hours	Start	End
Turkey		Cook	Oven	5.00	10:30 AM	3:30 PM
Potatoes		Cook	Stove	0.50	3:15 PM	3:45 PM
Turnip		Cook	Stove	0.50	3:21 PM	3:51 PM
Turkey		Stand	Counter	0.25	3:31 PM	3:46 PM
Carrots		Cook	Microwave	0.15	3:42 PM	3:51 PM
Corn		Cook	Microwave	0.25	3:45 PM	4:00 PM
Gravy		Cook	Stove	0.25	3:45 PM	4:00 PM
Potatoes	mash	Prep	Counter	0.25	3:45 PM	4:00 PM
Rolls		Cook	Stove	0.15	3:45 PM	3:54 PM
Turkey	carve, plate	Prep	Counter	0.25	3:45 PM	4:00 PM
Turnip	mash	Prep	Counter	0.15	3:51 PM	4:00 PM
Carrots	put into dish	Prep	Counter	0.15	3:51 PM	4:00 PM
Cranberries	put into dish	Prep	Counter	0.10	3:54 PM	4:00 PM
Rolls	put into basket	Prep	Oven	0.10	3:54 PM	4:00 PM
Stuffing	put into dish	Prep	Counter	0.10	3:54 PM	4:00 PM

Minutes	Hours
5	0.08
10	0.17
15	0.25
20	0.33
25	0.42
30	0.50
35	0.58
40	0.67
45	0.75
50	0.83
55	0.92
60	1.00

FIGURE 9.7 Planmaker smoothly imports Microsoft Excel worksheets.

9

Applixware, by VistaSource, has been around for a while. The recently released v4.3.3 has a word processor, a spreadsheet, a presentation product, a graphics generation toolkit, a database management integration client, and an email client.

WordPerfect, one of the first big-name products to enter the Linux market, no longer develops a Linux version, but you can still buy a copy of Corel WordPerfect Suite 2000 for Linux.

NOTE

Will nothing less than Microsoft Office do for you? Crossover Linux from Codeweavers lets you install and run Word, Excel, Powerpoint and Outlook 2003 (and earlier) under Linux for a reasonable sum. Download a free 30-day trial at http://www.codeweavers.com. See Chapter 11, "Going Cross-Platform" for more information on Crossover.

Connecting with PDAs and Smart Phones

openSUSE provides programs and clients you can use with your Palm-style personal digital assistants (PDAs). Sync up your PDA data with your PC, send and retrieve mail, keep your calendar in order, and more.

Command-Line PDA Software for openSUSE

The most popular PDA-related applications are bundled in a single package, called pilot-link. You can organize and work with your Palm OS-compatible PDA directly from your shell prompt—no GUI required. Among pilot-link's amazing capabilities are the following:

- Extracting and uploading addresses from your address book(s)
- Installing datebook information
- Transferring text memos to and from the PDA
- Managing your to-do lists
- Managing user settings
- Sending and retrieving email documents
- Installing new PDA programs
- Backing up, synchronizing, and restoring the contents of a PDA
- Acquiring expense-account database information

The suite has 31 tools for you to use, and after you've connected your Palm cradle to your PC, you should be able to use any of them to manage your information. For example, to back up the contents of your Palm device to your Linux system, type this command at the shell:

```
pilot-xfer -p /dev/ttyS1 -b backupdirectory
```

This command creates a directory called `backupdirectory` and then downloads and saves the contents of the PDA to `backupdirectory`. Explore the range of pilot-link tools in the suite's man page, or visit http://www.pilot-link.org to connect with the pilot-link community.

Connecting with Your PDA in KDE and GNOME

If you want to know how good a tool pilot-link really is, all you need to know is that all the GUI tools mentioned here are just different ways of putting a pretty face on the underlying command-line tools offered by pilot-link. KPilot and Gnome-Pilot are the official Palm interfaces for their respective desktop environments (although KPilot is considerably more powerful than its counterpart), and a third, J-Pilot, also works well.

J-Pilot will manage, retrieve, install, back up, and sync any information for your Palm-compatible PDA. Click the Date Book, To-Do List, Address Book, and Memo Pad buttons to perform related tasks. Use the Sync and Backup buttons to update or preserve a copy of a PDA's data. KPilot integrates with the Kontact personal information manager for KDE, allowing you to quickly transfer mail and contact information between your devices.

NOTE

If you need to sync up information only periodically, the GNOME-based Multi-Sync and KDE-based KitchenSync may be just what you need. Both of these tools are based on the new OpenSync standard, and they come with assorted plug-ins to connect to various devices.

Managing Your Finances

For even the most rabid Linux fan, financial software was (and maybe still is) the final frontier for the Linux desktop. Many people keep Windows around just to run Quicken (and maybe a couple of games).

Now there are two open source projects that want to make you feel comfortable managing your (or your business's) money in Linux. GnuCash is the veteran, with KMyMoney the upstart challenger. Both are set up to do standard double-entry bookkeeping and can import Intuit Quicken OFX and QIF files. Both tools support scheduled transactions and will alert you to bill-sending due dates.

GnuCash and KMyMoney handle all the major tasks of modern financial software:

- Tracking your savings and checking accounts
- Tracking credit card debt, mortgage payments, and other long-term debts
- Tracking your assets (house, car, and so on) and expenses related to them
- Reminding you when your bills are due
- Helping you identify your expenses and develop budgets based on what you already spend money on
- Managing your stock portfolio and other investments
- Managing accounts for a small business

Using the banking package, both GnuCash and KMyMoney can perform online banking, but only with European financial institutions. At some point down the road, perhaps this will change. In the meantime, with both products you can download and import account information from financial institutions in either the QIF or the newer OFX format.

Running GnuCash

GnuCash 2.0.5 is a double-entry accounting system for Linux generally and GNOME in particular. While clearly inspired by Quicken, it's not a reverse-engineered job or feature-for-feature clone either.

GnuCash has a very nice account setup wizard that, by default, creates a set of "Common Accounts" that covers most typical personal financial situations. GnuCash supports creating accounts in nearly every currency imaginable. After you've set up at least one account, the opening screen gives you a list of your accounts, a description, and your current balance. To open an existing account, select it from the list and click Open.

Quicken users will be very comfortable with the register interface, as seen in Figure 9.8.

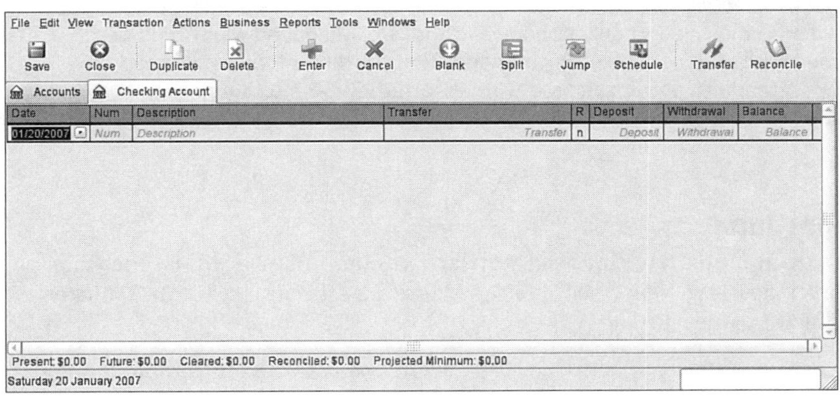

FIGURE 9.8 The GnuCash register screen is very similar to Quicken's.

Organizing your income and expenses into categories is a little different in GnuCash than in its Windows counterpart, however. This is related to GnuCash's double-entry system. Let's say you have set up your checking account and downloaded some transactions from your bank. For GnuCash to track your expenses, you need to identify what kind of expense it is. Both Income and Expenses exist as separate accounts alongside your bank account, and to enter and categorize these items, use the Transfer column in the "checkbook" to create and identify the category (called a subaccount in GnuCash) for each expense. If you import an existing Quicken file into GnuCash, assigned categories may transfer over, but you might have to create subaccounts manually. GnuCash does not have any default subaccounts built in, but that means you can identify as many categories as you want to track.

You can download and import transactions from your financial institution and/or credit card company using either the QIF or OFX standard. This can save you hours of manual-entry time, but you still have to assign subaccounts. If you need to print checks, GnuCash will do that.

TIP

The first time you download banking information, you can save some subaccount-creation time by just getting a month's worth of transactions first. Flag all your regular bills in their appropriate categories (for example, phone, gas, and electric bills in the Utilities subaccount). Once you've created your standard subaccounts, assigning later bills to those accounts is easy.

Running KMyMoney

KMyMoney 0.8 works pretty much the same way as its counterparts do, but it is definitely a work in progress. This should be a fine application by the time it gets to v1.0.

When you open KMyMoney for the first time, you can set up a new data file or see a tutorial first. The initial data file setup wizard to do this is straightforward, and though the terminology may be a little off-putting at first, it is easy to get started. After entering your identifying information and the base currency unit, choose a template from the folder dialog presented. For the United States, click the <font>en_US</font> folder and select <font>default_accounts.Kmt</font>.

Once you've created your data file, click the Institutions button on the left side. This is where you identify the financial institution(s) that hold your accounts. Right-click again on the Institution you've named, and select New Account. You'll walk through another wizard to set up your account.

The Ledgers screen that displays your data is not as attractive as GnuCash (see Figure 9.9), but manually entering transactions is less confusing. KMyMoney will not automatically add a new payee when you enter it in the Edit box, but if you import a QIF file, it will automatically create missing payees if you check the appropriate box.

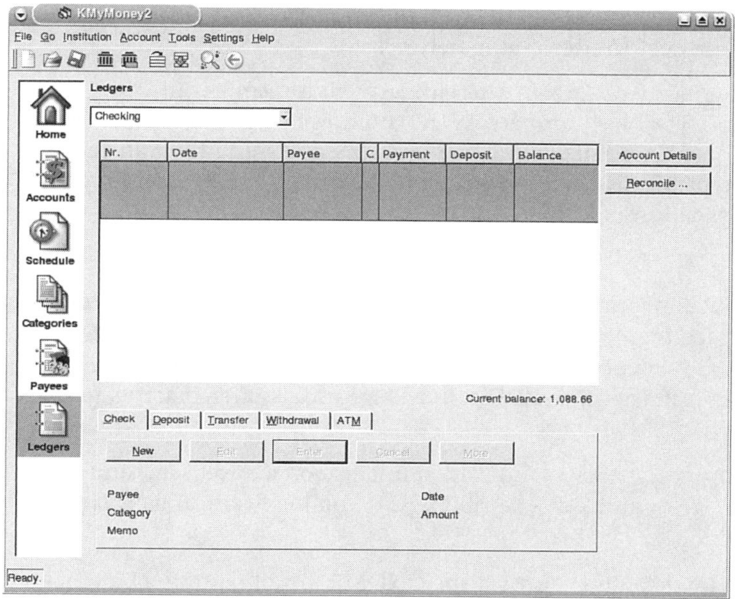

FIGURE 9.9 KMyMoney's Ledgers screen displays your account information and lets you enter transactions manually.

As with GnuCash, you can import Quicken data files and QIF/OFX account information from your financial institution(s). KMyMoney will also import GnuCash files (GnuCash does not return the favor). When you do this, however, you may be in for a small shock. Imported transactions that haven't been categorized appear in blinking red text. This is a good thing if you miss putting one or two manual entries in a category, but this is not so good for several hundred imported entries. This particular annoyance is scheduled to disappear in the next version.

More Tools to Make You Productive

To round out this chapter, here are a few more tools that will help you get more done, and often in less time. Some of these tools are alternatives to others already in a suite; others are unique in their categories.

TIP

Managing personal information is essential to a productive life. Because so many of the Linux tools for managing personal information include email clients, these tools are described in Chapter 13.

Voice-over-IP (VoIP) with Skype and Ekiga

Paying too much for your landline telephone, or running out of minutes on your cell? If you can attach a microphone to your openSUSE system, you can make telephone calls (often free of charge) via the Internet. Your openSUSE DVD contains the Ekiga (formerly GnomeMeeting) soft phone and videoconferencing application. You can also download a free client to access the Skype peer-to-peer phone network.

Both these clients (and other less well known alternatives) will transmit your voice (and your picture, if you configure your webcam) across the Internet to either another computer or a physical phone. These clients include text-messaging and file transfer capabilities and other features typically associated with mobile phones. In this section, you'll learn more about these applications and the networks they access.

Ekiga

Ekiga is an open source VoIP application created by Damien Sandras as a college project modeled on Microsoft NetMeeting. It is now a robust client supporting both the SIP phone protocol and the H.323 videoconferencing protocol. It is integrated into the GNOME desktop, but works just as well in KDE. Every Ekiga user is offered access to the Ekiga network, as well.

You need a working full-duplex–capable sound card, a microphone, a webcam, and a video device to take advantage of all Ekiga's capabilities. If you just want to listen in, the sound card is all you need.

YaST does not install Ekiga by default, even with the GNOME install pattern. Nonetheless, it's easy to install via YaST. The first time you run Ekiga, the setup wizard walks you through all the information needed to make phone calls with your computer.

In the first screen, Ekiga asks your name for purposes of the phone directory. In the next screen, you are asked to set up your acccount at Ekiga.net. A browser window opens, where you deliver a minimal amount of personal information, define a username (which is also added to the directory as <username>@ekiga.net), and a password to access the network. You'll be sent a confirmation email at the address you specify. Once you have set up your account, enter your username and password and move to the next screen.

Here, Ekiga checks for a network router and firewall, and discovers whether the router uses a Network Address Translator (NAT) for security purposes. In the likely event this is true, the wizard will ask you to enable STUN support. This acronym stands for Simple Traversal of UDP (User Datagram Protocol) through NATs, and it basically allows Ekiga to get through your firewall.

The fourth screen identifies your audio manager (ALSA by default) and indicates what application handles audio input and output. You should have your microphone plugged in by this point. Click Test Settings to confirm that these are correct. You'll be asked to speak into the microphone, and seconds later you should hear your voice coming out of your speakers. If you don't, play with the options some more.

The final screen locates your webcam and configures video accordingly. The setup wizard is then complete, and the Ekiga phone displays. You can adjust any of these settings.

Once set up, Ekiga will put an icon in your GNOME or KDE taskbar, announcing your availability to the network. To place a call, right-click the icon and select Call from the menu. If you don't want an interruption while you're working, you can select Do Not Disturb from this menu. You won't receive calls while this flag is active.

Skype

Skype is a very popular commercial VoIP application, with millions of users around the globe. This network developed a Linux client only recently, but it works quite well.

If you find the Ekiga setup wizard a little intimidating, you'll be glad to know Skype does not demand information about your hardware during your initial configuration. All it does is ask you to set up your Skype account, and you're up and running. You can then make a Skype Test Call to confirm that everything works right. You'll connect to Skype and be asked to speak into the microphone for 10 seconds. The service will then play your message back to you.

TIP

Skype has a great feature that taps into the sheer novelty of making phone calls over the Internet. Skype-Me Mode turns off your normal privacy controls and allows anyone in the Skype network to contact you via Skype.

Click the Find icon in the Skype client to open the directory, and then click Advanced Search. Use the drop-down menu to select the Language you want to speak in, and perhaps a country or city (though this narrows the possibilities dramatically—there usually aren't many folks in this mode). Finally, check the "Search for people who are in 'Skype Me' mode" box, and click Find. A list will appear. Use the icons at the bottom of the Search window to make your call.

If you have a sense of adventure, you can put yourself in Skype Me mode by changing your Online Status from the File menu.

Desktop Publishing with Scribus

Several of the word processing applications we've discussed here have had some desktop publishing features, but if you've got experience with dedicated publishing software such as Quark Xpress, Microsoft Publisher, or Adobe PageMaker/InDesign, you may find that Scribus is the tool you want. You may even find yourself abandoning these other apps for good!

You can create newsletters and magazines, and even complete books have been published with Scribus. It will do heavy-duty, high-resolution, print-production work, interactive PDF forms, and other high-end publishing tasks, and it can also do simple PDF flyers and posters. You can also produce HTML files for posting on the Web.

Curiously, Scribus adds itself to the KDE menu as a word processor (under the Office menu). This is the wrong way to view this tool. Scribus is a page designer. It is best suited for taking already written text and graphics, adding formatting to the text, adding headlines, and placing all these elements on a page. As a workflow, it's best to create plain text in your favorite editor, bring it into Scribus for formatting and placement. Scribus will import OpenOffice documents, but with spotty formatting.

If you're not familiar with desktop publishing concepts, be sure to visit the Scribus wiki site, http://wiki.scribus.net, and work through the Get Started with Scribus tutorial. You will walk through the entire process of producing a print magazine with Scribus, using all the tools and learning a bit about page design as well.

Scribus comes with several templates for you to play with, including several newsletters, advertisements, brochures, calendars, menus and programs. Choose New from Template from the File menu to select a template to work with. Figure 9.10 shows a basic newsletter template. If you prefer to work from scratch, just click the New Document from the toolbar, and select from the basic blank templates.

TIP

Users in the United States might skip over the fact that the default page size in Scribus is A4, regardless of what template you use. Unless you are regularly producing content for European audiences, you should change this default.

Go to Preferences in the File menu, and click the Document page. Use the drop-down menu to change Size from A4 to Letter (for the US standard 8.5 x 11-inch paper) or whatever default paper size you prefer. Click OK to confirm your changes.

Once you have set the default, you can still change paper size for each publishing project.

Whether you're working with a contributed template, or the plain choices, you'll need to display several windows (from the Windows menu) to get your work done. The main window opens by default, and is where your document lives. You can create and place frames, which are the building blocks to bring in text and graphics, in this window. Once you have your frames set up and objects inserted, you can drag the frames around the page, and tweak them (and any objects within) using the Properties dialog box (in the lower-left).

Use the Outline tool (lower-right) to plan the elements of your document and where you want to place them. You can easily change your mind and move each element around when using this tool.

The page map in the upper-left lets you easily navigate among multiple pages. Keep frequently used clips of text or graphics in the Scrapbook, and drag them into your new document at any time.

Play with Scribus and get your documents out.

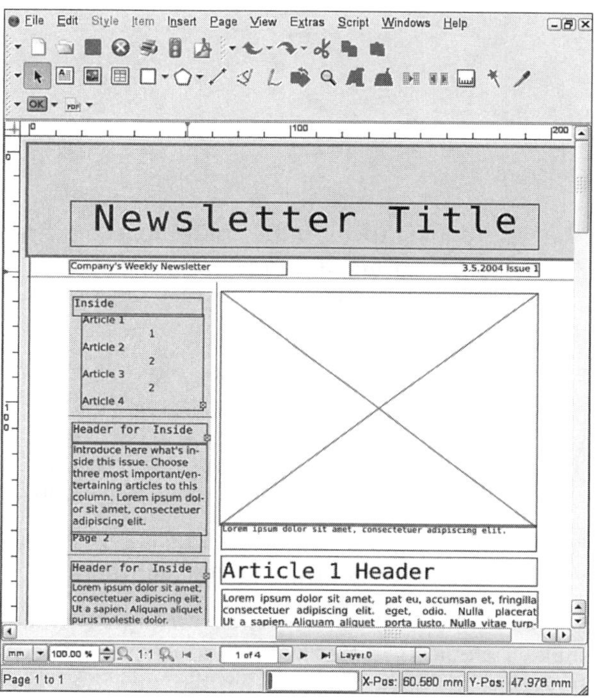

FIGURE 9.10 Scribus makes it easy to create and publish professional documents.

Diagramming and Flowcharting with Dia and Kivio

Dia seeks to be the Linux version of Microsoft Visio, the business tool that enables IT managers to diagram their networks and enables human resource folks to build their organizational charts. And it does a pretty nice job of it.

Dia is a GNOME application with dozens of default shapes, from general polygons to network diagrams to Uniform Modeling Language programming charts that can be quickly slapped together and connected with each other in no time. Figure 9.11 shows a very simple network configuration created in less than five minutes.

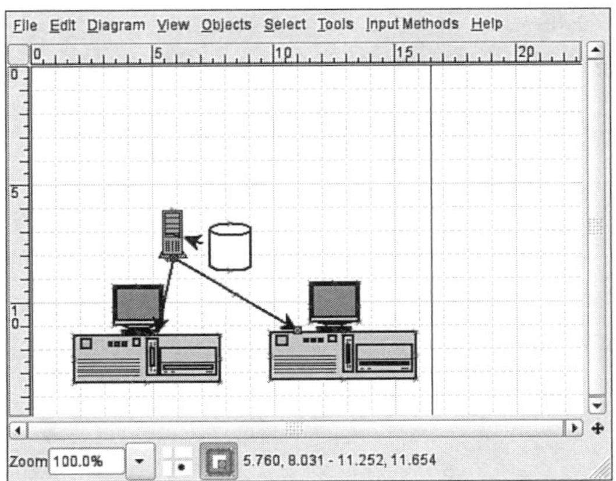

FIGURE 9.11 A simple Dia networking diagram.

Making connections between objects—that is, grouping them so they move together—is two clicks away. Select an object, right-click, and choose Select, Connected from the context menu. Dia works much better in GNOME than in KDE, but it is easy to work with, whatever your environment.

KOffice's counterpart, Kivio, is a little less usable out of the box, but is a fine tool. When you run Kivio for the first time, there's just a single template for basic flowcharting. To do anything else, go to the Tools menu and select Add Stencil Set. This gives you access to dozens of different sets. Choose directly from the menu, or select Show Stencil Chooser to view them all. Pick a stencil, and click Add to Document to add these shapes to your toolbar.

Both Kivio and Dia support creating layers in your diagrams. Layering allows you to create a single diagram that can display different objects and relationships at different times.

To create a layer in Kivio, click the Layers tab in the right side and the New Layer (white document) icon. Add your objects. To make the objects in this layer disappear, click the View icon to the far left of Layer 2. It grays out, and the layer is not visible.

The Layer tool in Dia is a little harder to find. It sits in the Diagram menu. A new Layers window opens. Click Add to make a new layer. Add your objects. Click the Eye icon in the Layers window to make it disappear.

You'll see Dia again in Chapter 14, "Creating Basic Websites," as we use it to brainstorm a design for a basic website.

Mindmapping with VYM

View Your Mind is a nifty little tool that is similar to Dia, but with a specific purpose: helping your brain make the connections it needs to resolve all those little ideas running around in it.

VYM lets you develop your ideas on things great and small. It can serve as a visual document outline or help you develop a plan for your next job search or career change. Your maps can be deeply hierarchical or with thought balloons randomly strewn around the screen. Connect headings with more detailed musings, or attach other documents to your map.

Fax and Scanner Applications

As the countless owners of multifunction printers can attest, scanning documents and faxing documents are just other ways of printing. Although email and FTP may now be the document-transfer methods of choice for many, digitizing paper documents and sending them across phone lines as a fax are still widely used methods of getting information into the hands of your clients. Linux can easily handle both tasks, and openSUSE provides the tools to handle them.

Scanner Applications

The use of a scanner provides a wealth of options to enhance productivity. You can manipulate scanned images in graphics applications such as GIMP, and then print, fax, or embed them in a word processing document or presentation. You can scan paper documents for archival purposes, or you can process them with optical character recognition (OCR) software to translate images into words that can be put in an editable form. openSUSE offers the SANE and Kooka applications to assist you with scanning.

Scanner support under Linux is provided by Scanner Access Now Easy (SANE). If your scanner is supported, it is listed on the SANE support page at http://www.sane-project.org/sane-supported-devices.html. You can find it using the search engine or browse the list of supported scanners before you make your purchase.

NOTE

If you have a newer scanner, check the latest development versions of SANE. Each new version adds support for more devices. If your scanner is supported only in the development version, you need to download and compile the CVS version. This is a complex operation suitable for advanced Linux users only, and it is beyond the scope of this book. For information on that process, see the CVS HOWTO at the Linux Documentation Project: http://www.tldp.org.

Kooka is a KDE application that provides standard scanning capabilities along with OCR functions and its own image gallery. Because Kooka is a KDE application, it can also provide scanning services to other KDE applications, such as the KOffice suite.

Fax Client Software

openSUSE provides several clients that handle different aspects of composing, viewing, and sending faxes. KDE has two graphical applications: Kfax, which views incoming electronic faxes, and KDEprintFax, which writes them. The actual sending and receiving of faxes is handled by the command-line fax server HylaFax.

You can use any text editor or word processor to create a document to fax. OpenOffice Writer even has a wizard that will create a fax cover sheet template for easy use. Go to File, Wizards, Fax to set that in motion. KDEprintFax also lets you write a cover page in its interface, which you can see in Figure 9.12.

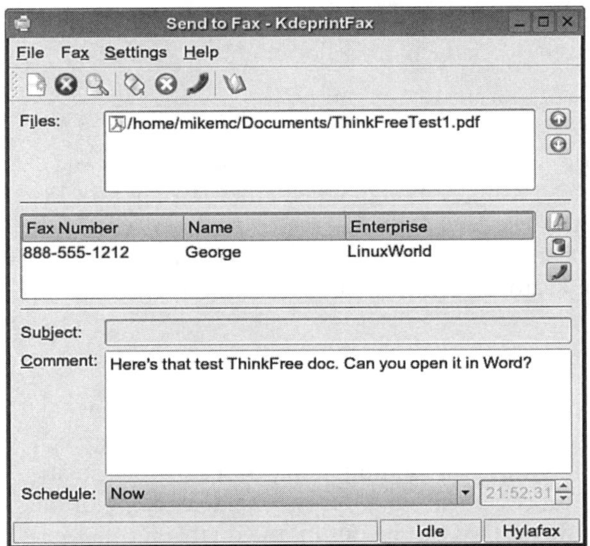

FIGURE 9.12 KDEprintFax lets you send faxes directly from your desktop. It serves as a graphical front-end to the command-line HylaFax fax server.

To open KDEprintFax, go to the Utilities menu in KDE and select Printing. Click Add File from the toolbar to locate the file(s) you want to fax. View the file with the View File button. To select a recipient, you can either retrieve the information from your address book or type in a name, company, and fax number using the Add Recipient dialog box. Click Send Fax to complete the operation.

NOTE

Using multiple fax applications might seem unnecessarily complicated if you're used to sending and receiving faxes with the same interface and/or with a modem connected to the fax machine. The Unix/Linux approach is more complicated because it is network focused. A single computer can be set up to send and receive faxes for the entire network of hundreds of computers. Not every machine on the network needs a fax modem to send faxes if one machine can. All any one node on the network needs is a way to view faxes and send them via the fax server. In some ways, that's simplicity itself.

Besides HylaFax, which is capable of handling faxes for a large network, the traditional way of handling faxes is with the command-line combination **`mgetty+sendfax`**. Although openSUSE includes the RPM packages for both of these tools, configuration is a bit complex and too big a subject for our context.

References

- http://www.OpenOffice.org—The home of the open source productivity suite. Contains extended documentation, a knowledge base, and links to the various mailing lists that keep this project running.
- http://wwws.sun.com/software/star/staroffice/—OpenOffice.org's commercial big brother, produced and marketed by Sun Microsystems. This version includes a database and a few other closed-source widgets and tools.
- http://www.learnopenoffice.org—Free tutorials on OOo Calc and Impress.
- http://www.taming-openoffice-org.com/—Aimed at the person who wants to get more out of OOo. Contains many valuable tips, links, and pointers to other books that cover OOo in depth.
- http://openoffice.blogs.com/openoffice—Solveig Haugland was the leader of the StarOffice/OpenOffice.org documentation team at Sun. Her blog includes all sorts of useful tips.
- http://www.KOffice.org—The KDE Office Suite home. Downloads, news, mailing lists and archives.
- http://www.gnome.org/gnome-office—The umbrella home for the GO Suite.
- http://www.abisource.com—The AbiWord page.
- http://www.gnome.org/projects/gnumeric—The Gnumeric page.
- http://www.softmaker.com/english/index_en.htm—Softmaker Office.
- http://www.vistasource.com/vs2/en/applixware.php—Applixware.
- http://kmymoney2.sourceforge.net—KMyMoney.
- http://www.gnucash.org—GnuCash.
- http://www.ekiga.org—Ekiga's home.
- http://www.skype.com—Skype.
- http://www.scribus.net—Home of the Scribus desktop publishing tool. Be sure to check out the documentation page at docs.scribus.net and the detailed and very helpful tutorial at http://wiki.scribus.net.
- http://www.gnome.org/projects/dia/—The Dia diagramming tool. Useful documentation not included in the package.
- http://www.insilmaril.de/vym/—The View Your Mind page. Written in VYM and exported to HTML. This is a nice way to see how the program works.

CHAPTER 10

Sights, Sounds, and Other Fun Things

IN THIS CHAPTER

- Playing Music and Listening to the Radio
- Creating Music with the Linux Multimedia Studio (LMMS)
- Burning CDs and DVDs
- Watching Video
- Watching TV on Your Computer
- Linux and Your Digital Camera
- Editing Images
- Gaming on Linux
- References

There is more than work to be done on your openSUSE machine. Your desktop can play music and serve as a radio. Movies are indeed made on Linux boxes. You can create and edit images of all types and move pictures from your digital camera to your PC. You can even watch TV on your monitor (with the right video card)!

Linux is not yet the gamers' OS of choice, but there are more ways to have fun on Linux than you may have thought. You'll learn what's available in this chapter, too.

Because most of this is visually oriented, we'll emphasize the tools for GNOME and KDE, but there are some interesting command-line tools for multimedia to learn about, too.

Playing Music and Listening to the Radio

After your sound card is working, perhaps the only thing you want to do, audiowise, is to play your CDs and MP3s, and access your favorite Internet radio stations. openSUSE provides a wealth of ways to do this and more.

Sound Formats

Digital sound recordings appear in several formats. You can create and listen to files in the following formats with openSUSE out of the box:

- Raw—More properly known as the headerless format, audio files using this format contain an amorphous variety of specific settings and encodings. All other sound files have a short section of code (the header) that identifies the format type.

- WAV—These days, WAV (Windows Audio Visual format) files are mostly used as brief sound effects to accompany error messages and other computer events. This is because WAV files are not compressed and take up a lot of room even for a short clip.
- Ogg-Vorbis—This format is the open source competitor to MP3. You'll enjoy better compression, better audio playback, and you can't be sued for using it.

You may notice that one particularly popular audio format is missing from this list, and it's true that Windows Media Audio isn't there. Oh, you want to know about MP3 is it? You've got hundreds, perhaps thousands of songs ripped in MP3 format, and you're fearing they are unplayable on your new openSUSE system. Unfortunately, this is true out of the box. The good news is this can be fixed.

TIP

Want to learn more about these and other audio formats? Head over to the Audio Format FAQ at http://www.cnpbagwell.com/audio.html.

Why isn't MP3 officially supported in openSUSE? It may be a small surprise to you, but this format isn't open source. MP3 uses a commercial, proprietary compression scheme, creating a big licensing issue for both creators and users. This is especially true for the openSUSE community, which publishes a nearly complete open source distribution. While there are some applications included in the non-OSS portion of openSUSE Linux, those applications (like Java) usually had an owner. MP3, of course, does not. Thus, the decision was made to officially support the completely open source Ogg-Vorbis audio format by default.

TIP

Should you need to convert an audio file from one format to another, various utilities can help you do that. The best known is Sound Exchange (SoX). This command-line utility is not installed by default, but you can get it via YaST.

Timidity is a cross-platform MIDI-to-WAV converter and player. It handles karaoke files, too, displaying the words so you can sing while it plays.

This leaves many users out in the cold, but thanks to others in the community, it is not especially hard to get support for proprietary and semi-proprietary media formats in openSUSE Linux. You even get pretty good Windows Media support in the bargain.

To turn your openSUSE machine into a fully functional multimedia player, follow these steps:

1. Go to http://opensuse-community.org/Package_Sources/Packman and select an appropriate mirror for the Packman software repository. This source has assorted multimedia-related packages that are not crippled.

2. Open YaST and go to Installation Sources. Click Add, and the Media Type screen appears. Choose Specify URL, click Next, and paste the URL for your mirror. Click Finish to complete adding the Packman repository.

3. Go to Software Management and install these packages (if they don't appear in the search box, check that Packman has been added): w32codec-all, ffmpeg, libxine1, and libdvdcss.

NOTE

If you are running a 64-bit processor, you need to compile libdvdcss manually. Download the tarball from http://download.videolan.org/pub/libdvdcss/1.2.9/libdvdcss-1.2.9.tar.gz. If you need help compiling, go to http://www.softwareinreview.com/cms/content/view/60/ and scroll down to "DVD playback on 64-bit machines."

4. When the installation is complete, test the system by playing an MP3 file and inserting a DVD in your player.

TIP

This process has been simplified greatly by a package called KonvenientSUSE. Go to http://KDE-Apps.org to find this script that will automate this task, and solve some other common problems as well.

Now that this is resolved, let's learn more about the audio players. All of these are installable via YaST. Most are on the openSUSE DVD, with some only in the Packman repository.

Audio Player Overview

Table 10.1 is a basic roundup of the features of the players covered in this section.

TABLE 10.1 Audio Players in openSUSE Linux

Feature	Amarok	Banshee	JuK	Rhythmbox	XMMS
User-developed Playlists	x	x	x	x	x
Smart Playlists	x	x	x	x	
Song Ratings	x	x		x	
Artist Information	Wikipedia	Last.fm (plugin)			
Lyrics	x			x (plugin)	
Cover Art	x	x	x	x (plugin)	
MP3 Tag Editor	x	x	x	x	
Streaming/Radio	x			x	x
Podcasts	x	x (plugin)		x	
Last.fm Integration	x	x (plugin)		x (plugin)	
Portable Player support	x	Indirect		x (plugin)	Indirect
CD Burning	Indirect	x	x	x	x
CD Ripping		x		x	

10

The basic process of playing music is very similar in each player. All the players except for XMMS build a music library from folders you identify on first launch. All can play audio files from CDs and on your hard drive. Search and select the tunes you want to hear, and they will play. All the players give you the option to play the songs in the order you select, or choose a random/shuffle order. You can save playlists for future entertainment and CD burning.

Nearly all these players also support programmable "Smart" Playlists. You set some conditions based on genre, personal ratings, number of plays and the like, and the player selects some matching tracks.

Some can also play streaming audio from Internet radio stations and audio clips distributed by RSS, also known as podcasts. This is an exciting way to find new music, as well as familiar tunes packaged in different ways. You can also keep up with the news—or your friends—through podcasting.

Many of these players work with the Last.fm web music service. The idea behind Last.fm is to use the songs you listen to, compare your favorite music to other users, and use the results to recommend new music that you might like. The service can also introduce you to others with similar musical tastes. You can learn more about artists, albums, and songs at the site as well, both from "authorized" sites and the community wiki pages. Last.fm has its own Linux player, available at its site, if you'd like to try it out.

You can use your iPod or other portable music player with your Linux computer as well, courtesy of the libgpod library. Some of these applications have stronger support for portable players than others, but it's all outlined here.

All the players can burn tracks from your hard drive onto CD, if you have a CD-RW drive. Only a couple can rip music from a CD to your hard drive.

Amarok

Developers have come up with a horde of audio players for KDE, but Amarok is by far the most ambitious. It will do nearly everything you might ever want to do with an audio player. Want to hear your CDs, MP3s, radio streams, and podcasts all in a single application? Want to learn song lyrics, or more about the artists you listen to? Connect with other fans of similar music? With Amarok, you can. It is so amazingly configurable, it can be a playground, good for hours of entertainment, all by itself.

NOTE

Amarok 2.0 is scheduled for release with KDE 4.0. The developers of this application are planning a major overhaul of the user interface, but the functionality should be quite similar to what is described here.

Building a Music Collection

On first launch, Amarok asks you where your music is located on your system. In minutes, all the audio files in your specified folders are organized in the Collections tab of the player. You can organize collections by Artist (the default), Album, Genre, Year, or using different levels.

> **TIP**
>
> You can play music files in Amarok that are not in a collection, but you'll miss some of the better tricks this player can perform (like viewing lyrics and band information).

You can filter the view of your collection so that you can easily play the newest material. Click the drop-down menu called Entire Collection. Select the desired time frame, and Amarok will display only those tracks added within that time.

Playing Music in Amarok

The Amarok player window is that big empty thing on the right in Figure 10.1. Drag and drop anything from the left side of the window (songs, playlists, streams, podcasts—Amarok doesn't care) to play. Use the standard controls at the bottom of the player to start listening.

FIGURE 10.1 Learn more about songs and artists in the Amarok Context window.

Now click the Context tab. The first thing you'll see is basic information on the song you're listening to (how many times you've played it, other songs on that album, etc.). You can also add tags to a song to further define and classify genre, instruments, or whatever else you fancy. Click Lyrics and the first time you'll be asked to identify a source (the default is perfectly fine, of course), and magically, the lyrics for the current song appears. Click the appropriate icon and you can view the lyrics in your default web browser, search for a word or phrase, and even edit the received lyrics. Click Artist and you'll see the current Wikipedia entry about that artist.

NOTE

Amarok gets its song information from the Last.fm website. While you do not need a Last.fm account to get this information, should you want to secure your data from Last.fm, you can turn this feature off. Go to the Last.fm Settings and uncheck the appropriate box in the Last.fm Services section. See more about Amarok's integration with Last.fm later in this section.

TIP

There's even more fun in the Context window. If you're connected to the Internet, click the generic CD graphic. Amarok will pull the album cover art from Amazon.com and associate it with the track! Right-click on the album, and you can buy the CD from Amazon as well. Use the Cover Manager to add covers all at once. This feature is located in the Tools menu.

You can (and should) rate your music using a 5-star system; click a star in the player window. Sitting on the fence between 3 and 4 stars? Click the fourth star twice, and your half-star gets recorded. Use your ratings to help select playlists.

Playlists

Playlists are the heart of any music player, and Amarok offers several options besides the mixes you create yourself. Click the Playlists tab on the left navigation tab. The Playlists folder holds existing manually-created playlists, including any .m3u files that Amarok found while building your Collection. To create this type of playlist, drag the songs you want into the player window and press Ctrl+S (or go to the Playlist menu and select Save Playlist As). You'll be prompted to name the playlist.

Smart Playlists are collections of songs that conform to a set of rules. There is quite a variety of these included by default, but it's pretty easy to create your own as well. Right-click on Smart Playlists and select Create Smart Playlist from the menu. Name the playlist, and then set up your rules. Start with choosing from the Any or All Conditions options. Then use the drop-down menus to define what it is you want to hear. Click the + sign at the end of each condition to add another. Limit the number of tracks in the playlist if you like (unfortunately, you can't limit by time). Click OK to create the playlist. Double-click or drag the Smart Playlist to the player window to get it going.

Dynamic Playlists are the equivalent of the iTunes "Party Mix." The Suggested Songs Playlist uses the recommendation engine from the last.fm music service. Pick at least one song from your collection, and Amarok will consult last.fm to find other songs in your collection similar to the track(s) you selected. Random Mix is what it suggests: It just randomly draws songs from your collection into the playlist. You can create these as well. Right-click on Dynamic Playlists and select New Dynamic Playlist.

Radio and Podcasts in Amarok

You can listen to many Internet-based radio stations directly in your Amarok player window. The player comes with a couple dozen or so "cool streams" to get you started, but if a stream has a direct URL, Amarok will play the station at will. You can create folders to organize your radio streams as well. Visit the website of the station you want to add. Copy the URL of the stream (look for a link that points to an MP3 stream, sometimes marked "Winamp") to the clipboard. In Amarok, right-click the Radio Streams folder (or the folder you want the stream to appear in) and select New Radio Stream from the menu. A small dialog box appears; fill in the desired name for the stream, and then copy the URL into the other box.

Amarok also supports podcasting, regular broadcasts on a variety of topics with producers ranging from ordinary do-it-yourself radio stars to established mainstream media outlets like the British Broadcasting Company, National Public Radio, and *The New York Times*. It does not offer a podcast directory like iTunes does, but you can import any podcast URL into Amarok. Find a podcast you want to subscribe to on the web and copy the URL. In Amarok go to the Advanced menu and select Add New Podcast. Copy the URL and add the name in the box provided.

Right-click on a podcast entry in the Playlists page to tell Amarok how to handle that podcast, including its transfer to your portable device.

See Chapter 16, "Collaborating with Others," for more information on listening to podcasts.

Integration with Last.fm

Last.fm is a web service and community that helps you find new music based on what you already like and what others with similar tastes like. Besides getting some track information from Last.fm, Amarok will send the music it plays into your personal Last.fm account. This fine-tunes the service's recommendations., and those recommendations play as the Neighbor Radio stream in Amarok.

Go to Settings, Configure Amarok and click the Last.fm tab near the bottom. You can visit the Last.fm website to check it out and/or register a new account directly from the Settings page. Once you have an account, type in your username and password, and select the services you want to enable.

Want to know what other Amarok users are listening to? Join the Amarok group at Last.fm with the link at the bottom of the settings page (you must have an account to join). Should you just want to know what this particular user is listening to, visit http://www.last.fm/user/workingwriter/.

Plugging in your Portable Player

Perhaps what you really want to know is this: "Does it work with my iPod?" All Linux audio players, including Amarok, support moving files to and from assorted devices, including portable music players. Plug in your player into a USB port, and Amarok will ask if you want to configure Amarok to support the device. Configure the settings and Amarok will become the default application for the device.

In Amarok, the Devices tab (in the lower- left corner of the screen) lists the devices it supports. When you have the device plugged in, the files on the device will appear in the window. Drag and drop to add songs to your collection, or transfer items from your hard drive to the player.

Burning CDs from Amarok

Amarok is integrated with the KDE CD-burning application, K3b, so burning playlists from inside Amarok is reasonably straightforward. Create Playlist of songs to burn, then insert a blank CD into the drive. Go to the Playlist menu and choose Burn to CD. K3b takes over, and notes whether there is enough space on the CD to have all the songs. You can even convert the format of the music files from one format to another. There's more information on burning CDs with K3b later in this chapter.

Amarok will not rip copies of music on CD to add to your collection, but you can use K3b or the Kaffeine multimedia player to do this in a KDE environment and Amarok will gladly add these new tracks to your collection the next time you load it.

Banshee

Banshee is the default audio player for GNOME, and is based on the Helix audio player from Real Networks. Users of the Apple iTunes application will feel instantly at ease with the Banshee interface (Figure 10.2), and it certainly seems like that's the model.

FIGURE 10.2 Banshee looks similar to Apple iTunes.

This player does most of the things Amarok does, but is geared more toward the music fan who just wants to hear tunes without a lot of the more obsessive information-gathering features.

Playing Music in Banshee

As with the other players, Banshee will ask you initially where your digital music is stored and create a Music Library with those files. You can import new files and directories as required.

Select songs from the library to play directly, or create a playlist. Banshee will also play random tracks from your library if you select that option from the Playback menu. Banshee doesn't organize the library in a tree format, but presents the library in columns, so you can sort the columns in a way to find the songs you want. There's also a search function.

Banshee can also work with Last.fm to provide some information about the music you're listening to, with recommendations of similar artists to the one you're listening to. You'll need to install the Banshee-plugins packages to get this and other tools outside the core Banshee package. Once installed, go to Plugins from the Edit menu to activate and configure your plugins.

Playlists

Click New Playlist from the Music menu to create a playlist. Select the songs you want from the library, and there you are. These playlists stay in Banshee until you remove them.

Click New Smart Playlist to set appropriate criteria for a mix you want to hear. This dialog box includes four predefined lists, as seen in Figure 10.2: Neglected Favorites, 700 MB of Favorites (handy for CD burning), 80 minutes of Favorites (ditto), and Unheard (so you can help define your Favorites).

Radio and Podcasts

Banshee includes 22 Internet radio stations for your listening pleasure. These stations are organized by style. Adding a new station is a matter of clicking a button in the upper right corner and putting in the URL for the stream, and assigning a group.

Banshee will help you find podcasts of interest, as well as letting you enter a URL for a podcast feed. Right-click on the Podcasts entry on the left side of the Banshee player and select Find New Podcasts.

Integration with Last.fm

Several Banshee plugins integrate your player with the Last.fm service. The Audioscrobbler plugin reports the songs you play in Banshee to Last.fm, to help them analyze your tastes and recommend more new music that will suit you.

The Music Recommendation plugin adds some Artist information generated at Last.fm into the Banshee player. It will show you similar artists and the top songs and albums by that artist on the Last.fm site.

Plugging in Your Portable Player

The player doesn't have any direct support for iPods and other portable music players, at least beyond the support of the kernel and desktop environment. Nonetheless, transferring files back and forth between the two is not any harder than any other storage volume.

To import songs from your player to your Banshee music library, go to Import Music from the Music menu. Select the location from the window. To export songs to your player, create a playlist and copy it to your player.

Burning and Ripping CDs

If Banshee has a particular talent, it is for working with audio CDs. It will rip tracks from any inserted CD into standard WAV files, Ogg Vorbis, Flac, or MP3. Burning CDs from a playlist is also child's play for this tool.

To import a CD's contents into Banshee, insert the CD with Banshee active. An Audio CD icon will appear in the left side of the player. Click this icon to see the CDs contents. Banshee will identify the CDs tracks and the Import CD button will appear in the right corner of the screen. Click this button, and Banshee will go to work. A progress bar will appear in the lower-left corner. Feel free to play the CD (or any other playlist) while the import takes place.

To burn a CD, create a playlist or just select the songs you want to burn. Go to Edit, Preferences and select the Output Format for the files on the CD. Insert a blank CD into the drive. Click Write CD, in the upper- right corner of the player. Banshee "transcodes" the files, if necessary, and then writes them to the CD.

JuK

Don't need anything fancy from your music player? Just a quick-loading tool that will play individual songs or albums in an order you select (or at random)? Little or no configuration required? Maybe burn a CD from your music? JuK can help.

JuK is very straightforward in simple jukebox mode (Figure 10.3). Pick some songs, or an album, and click the Play icon to play the list. It hides many of its powerful features in its menus, though. While not as loaded (some might say bloated) with features as Amarok, JuK does some things better than its counterparts.

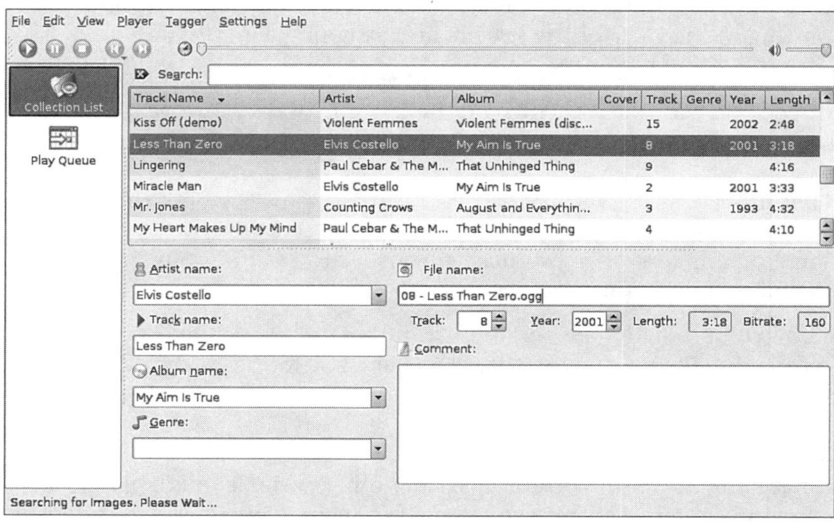

FIGURE 10.3 JuK simply plays music.

You may have a need to correct tags attached to the MP3 file you're playing. Go to the View menu and click Show Tag Editor. A box appears in the bottom of the player window with the tag information on the currently selected track. Make your changes, right-click the track in the player window, and select Refresh to confirm your changes.

What other applications call Smart Playlists, JuK calls a Search Playlist. Go to the File menu, select New, Search Playlist. Define your search criteria and the results show up in the Album/Playlist window on the left side of the player.

JuK doesn't play radio streams, have a plugin architecture, or do any of the things some of the fancier players do. It is a jukebox; it plays music. You might wish for a rating scheme, but other than that, it follows the Unix principle: do one thing, and do it well.

Rhythmbox

Rhythmbox is another ambitious GTK-based audio player, with features somewhere between Amarok and Banshee. Some features that Banshee implements as a plugin are part of the core Rhythmbox application, including radio and podcast support. Amarok features like cover art and song lyrics are plugins in Rhythmbox.

Playing Music in Rhythmbox

As with the other players, Rhythmbox asks you first where you store your music. It then builds a music library (Figure 10.4) and displays a three-pane window with Artists, Albums, and Song Titles. On the left side are your sources of audio. Select or search for songs to play. These will appear in the Play Queue window. You then have the option to save the queue as a playlist.

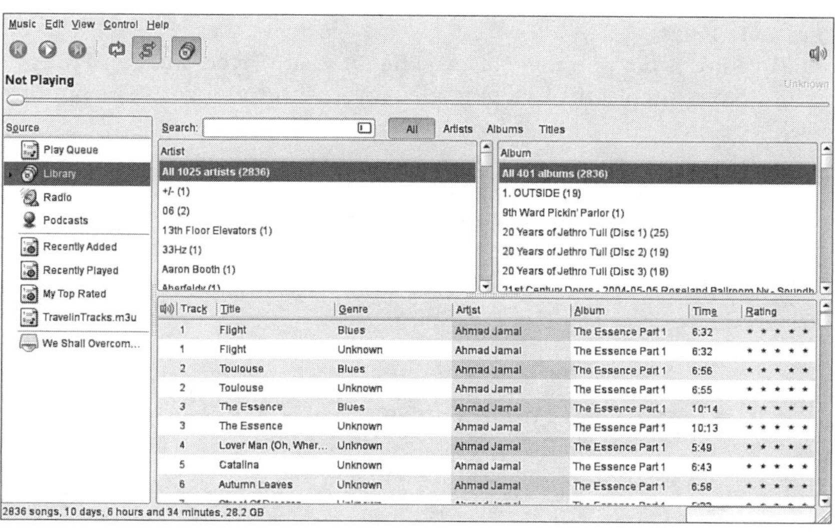

FIGURE 10.4 Rhythmbox uses a three-pane layout to access your music.

Rhythmbox will play your library in a random/shuffle fashion (as do the others). Click the icon that looks like an S with arrows coming out each end.

Playlists

It's easy to create a playlist in Rhythmbox. Go to Music, Playlist, New Playlist. Name the playlist, and then return to the library. Drag tracks to the playlist on the left side of the player.

The automatic playlist feature seems more sophisticated than others. There are three of these playlists created by default: Recently Added, Recently Played, and Top Rated. Create more from the Playlist menu. Add your criteria and Rhythmbox will keep an eye out for anything new that matches that criteria for adding to the playlist.

Radio and Podcasts

Rhythmbox supports both Internet radio and Podcast listening. It provides a small list of Shoutcast stations, but it is easy to add new stations by providing the URL of the stream.

There are no sample podcasts included with Rhythmbox, but these are also easily added. You can specify a directory to store podcasts in, but the application will not delete old episodes automatically, so you will need to clean out the Podcast directory from time to time to keep your hard drive from filling up (those one-hour audio files start adding up after a while).

Integration with Last.fm

Submit your listening habits to Last.fm with a Rhythmbox plugin. Go to Edit, Plugins. Enter your Last.fm username and password, and the plugin will notify Last.fm.

Plugging In Your Portable Player

Rhythmbox will pull in songs from portable players. Plug in your player, and go to Music, Scan Removable Media. Save any playlist to a portable player with the Save as File option in the Playlist menu.

Burning CDs

This is a two step process. Assemble a playlist or gather some songs in a Play Queue. Right-click on the list name on the left side of the player and select Create Audio CD (or just click the silver CD icon in the toolbar). Insert your blank CD, and Rhythmbox does the rest.

XMMS

The most mature all-purpose media player for Linux (and all X Window Systems) is the X Multimedia System (XMMS). XMMS modeled its GUI after Winamp, the popular media player for Windows.

Its display is very modular, so you can have as much (or as little) eye candy to visually enhance your audio experience. Figure 10.5 shows what happens if you display everything in a default installation. In addition, there are close to 20 XMMS plugins available in YaST.

XMMS plays most every audio format. It will play your audio CDs out of the box, as well as MPEG movies.

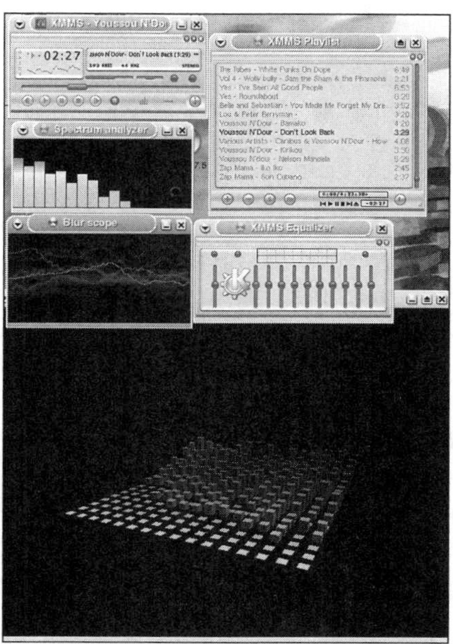

FIGURE 10.5 Arrange the XMMS display any way you like to enhance your audio experience. Equalizers, playlists, sound analyzers, and oscilloscope meters are all showing here in addition to the simple player in the upper left.

If you have a live Internet connection, XMMS will contact the CD Database (CDDB) of your choice (XMMS defaults to FreeDB) to deliver track information when you play a CD.

Playing Music

XMMS doesn't collect your music to store in a database; it handles things in a much more transitory state. Click in the upper-left corner of the player and select Play to see your options. Activate the Playlist Editor to select and play multiple songs, unless you want to hear everything in a selected directory.

Playlists

Open the Playlist Editor to create temporary or permanent lists of songs. Use the icons at the bottom of the Editor to bring in particular songs or directories. It may be easier to open a file manager and drag the files you want into the Editor.

Right-click in the editor and select Save from the Playlist menu to create an m3u list, which is then portable into any player that supports MP3 files.

Radio and Podcasts

XMMS supports all types of streaming audio, but you need to go to the Play menu and select Open Location. Type (or paste) the URL of the station, and you're on your way.

TIP

Want to find interesting radio stations to play on XMMS? Get the Streamtuner via YaST. It offers a list of stations, both Internet-based and terrestrial (that is, they also broadcast over the air in some location). The directory is organized by genre for easy sampling. Streamtuner works with other players, but XMMS is the default.

XMMS does not support podcasting, at least to the point of retrieving broadcasts when new ones are produced. Since all audio podcasts are in formats that XMMS understands, it can stream these live. Do not paste the XML feed address into the Open Location box, though.

Internet Radio and Other Streaming Media

One of the best things about your Internet connection, even under dial-up, is the capability to hear hundreds of radio stations broadcasting music, news, and information globally through the World Wide Web. What was once the province of hobbyists with expensive radio equipment is now available to anyone with an Internet connection.

Streaming audio comes in four formats: RealAudio, MP3, Ogg Vorbis, and Windows Media (wma). openSUSE media players handle all these formats. except for Windows Media. XMMS does streaming audio quite well, though occasionally it will ask you for a file to play.

The Linux player made for streaming audio is the Helix Community Player. RealNetworks open-sourced the code for its various media formats and the RealPlayer client some time ago. openSUSE 10.3 includes RealPlayer 10.0.8 in the non-oss section of the distribution.

If you happen to be fond of the built-in browser included in the Windows version of RealPlayer, you may be disappointed with the Linux version, but even though it may lack visual appeal, it performs its actual function—playing audio—quite well.

Both versions of the Helix player have the plug-in architecture that should, in time, yield a player that does what every user wants it to. This depends on whether enough users make their wishes known.

Creating Music with the Linux Multimedia Studio (LMMS)

openSUSE has a number of tools to help you record your own sounds.

Professional musicians and engineers know the Fruity Loops digital audio workstation has produced and enhanced a lot of good music over the years. Garageband for the Apple Macintosh has created quite a stir as well. The Linux Multimedia Studio (LMMS) does a pretty good job of bringing the ability to create electronic music to the home user. Of course, you have to bring your own talent.

LMMS is available from the Packman installation source, making installation through YaST (or another package manager) a simple task. When you first launch LMMS, it will ask you where to store your audio projects, defaulting to your home directory. Then a Settings dialog box appears. Look at the various settings, and decide which, if any, defaults you want to change. When you've completed that, click OK. You will then see the LMMS workspace in a maximized window. This includes the Song Editor, the Beat+Baseline Editor, and a Notepad for project notes.

Our first task is to build the baseline. For a start, LMMS provides a pair of drumbeat templates. Coming down the left edge of the workspace are a bunch of icons. Click the second one from the top, marked My Projects. Now click Templates. You'll see two options. The first, Acoustic Drumkit, offers electronic representations of Max Weinberg's, Larry Mullen's and Meg White's favorite instrument. The other, ClubMix, handles the rave crowd. Be sure the Beat + Baseline Editor is selected in the main work area, and double-click your favorite. You'll see a series of tracks appear in the editor. Look at the bars on the right side of the player; see where LMMS suggests turning the drum on. Click them, and then click Play to see what they sound like by default. Feel free to set the volume on each channel, or adjust when a note is struck by clicking the bars on the right side of the player.

Now we need some other instruments and sounds to support the basic beat. How about a bass line in the baseline? Back to the icon bar on the left side. This time click the green note labeled My Samples. You'll see Basses and Bassloopes. Click the Note icon next to any of these samples to hear what it sounds like. Double-click your favorite to add to the song, and a Settings box appears. Feel free to make adjustments, and then repeat the clicking of the bars. For a fuller sound, add another instrument to the mix. Save the Project whenever you have something you like. You can have multiple baselines; click the icon to the right of the Beat/Baseline box to add another.

With the rhythm section settled, perhaps you'd like some other instruments or patterns in this song. You have all kinds of choices in My Samples, and you can also look in My Presets (the Star icon) for other tools. Throw these into the Song Editor and open a Piano Roll to set up the melody. Keep playing the song until you've got something to show the world.

When you're done building your song, click Export Project. You can save as an uncompressed WAV file or a compressed OGG file. Either is playable on any computer. Only WAVs will play on standard stereo equipment.

LMMS allows you to import other tracks into a project, and pretty much lets you do anything you can imagine.

Burning CDs and DVDs

Burning your own CDs is a fundamental skill for Linux multimedia enthusiasts. Compact discs and digital versatile discs (DVDs) are the standard media for multimedia data of all types because they are cheap to produce, ultra portable, and can hold the large files that carry audio, and especially video, signals. Even the standard three-minute pop song requires a few megabytes of space to store. For multimedia, you can use CD/DVDs to do the following:

- Record, play, and store graphical images, music, video, and playlists
- Rip audio tracks from your own music CDs and create mix tapes to your liking

Of course, CDs can store many other types of files, not only audio and visual files. They are an excellent medium for storing backups of all data stored on your hard drives. See Chapter 20, "Managing Data: Backup, Restoring, and Recovery," for more information.

It may be obvious to state, but if you want to record multimedia (and other) data on a CD, you must have a drive that supports writing data to discs. A simple CD-ROM player does just that—plays already-recorded material that is read-only. What you need is a CD-RW (Read/Write) or DVD-RW/DVD+RW drive. The discs themselves must also be writable (CD-R or CD-RW and the corresponding DVD formats). YaST will configure your hardware at installation; see Chapter 4, "Further Configuration with YaST2 and SaX2," to see how that is done. To ensure that your hardware is configured properly, use `cdrecord -scanbus` to get information on using the CD drive under SCSI emulation. When you type the following in openSUSE Linux:

```
cdrecord -scanbus
```

You should see something like this:

```
Using libscg version 'debburn project-0.8ubuntu1+debburn1'.
wodim: Warning: using inofficial version of libscg (debburn project-0.8ubuntu1+deb-
burn1 '@(#)scsitransp.c       1.91 04/06/17 Copyright 1988,1995,2000-2004 J.
Schilling').
wodim: Warning: using inofficial libscg transport code version (cdrkit-team-scsi-
linux-sg.c-1.86 '@(#)scsi-linux-sg.c   1.86 05/11/22 Copyright 1997 J. Schilling').
scsibus1:
        1,0,0   100) 'LITE-ON ' 'COMBO SOHC-5232K' 'NK07' Removable CD-ROM
        1,1,0   101) *
        1,2,0   102) *
        1,3,0   103) *
        1,4,0   104) *
        1,5,0   105) *
        1,6,0   106) *
        1,7,0   107) *
```

The CD writer is present and is known by the system as device `1,0,0`. The numbers represent the scsibus/target/lun (logical unit number) of the device. You will need to know this device number when you burn a CD from the command line, so write it down or remember it.

When you're first getting started with CD burning, it's good to have the comforting approach of a GUI wizard to walk you through the process. You can tackle the command-line approach eventually, but because openSUSE offers a pair of very good GUI tools for burning multimedia discs, you are indeed in good hands. In this section, you'll first learn about the CD creation tools that come with KDE and GNOME. Then you'll see the shell tools that let you burn at your keyboard.

Creating CDs and DVDs from Your Desktop

KDE's graphical CD/DVD Kreator is called K3b, and it makes CD burning pretty much a matter of dragging and dropping files into a project and going about your business. Perhaps it's not quite that simple, but close enough for rock 'n' roll (or whatever style you prefer).

When you open K3b (see Figure 10.6), you see a familiar three-pane interface. On the upper left is your directory structure, with your last directory selected. In the upper-right are the files contained in the selected directory. At the bottom is where the action happens. K3b offers four options in the main window:

- New Audio CD Project
- New Data CD Project
- New Data DVD Project
- Copy CD

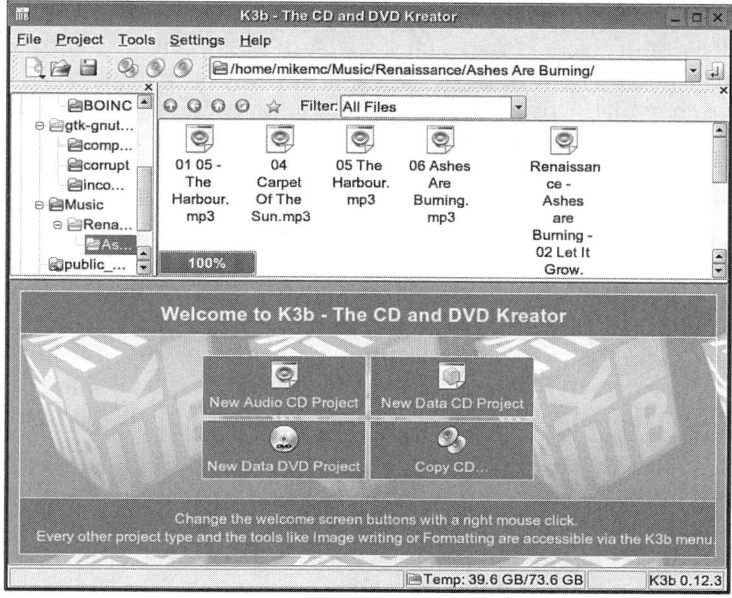

FIGURE 10.6 K3b knows what the typical CD-burning projects are and puts them in easy reach on the main screen.

These tasks are not the only things you can do with K3b, but they are the most typical. Click Further Actions in the same window to see your other selections.

TIP

The Copy CD feature in K3b is pretty cool. Want a copy of a favorite CD to play in your car while the original sits in your home stereo? Put that CD in your computer's drive. Run K3b and choose Copy CD (you may have to turn off the default CD player first). K3b will first copy the tracks of the CD to a temporary directory on your hard drive. It will then prompt you to insert a writable CD and burn the tracks to the blank CD.

Let's make an audio CD. Click the appropriate button and the bottom pane effectively becomes a representation of your CD. Find your digital music files using the two upper panels, and drag the files you want to burn into the bottom pane. K3b should identify the track information from the tags included in every digital music file. If you don't see the title, artist, or other information for a track in the pane after you drag them in, select the track and click Query Cddb if you are online to check the CD Database, or type the information in yourself.

As you drag files into the bottom pane, the progress bar tells you how much room you have remaining on the disk. When you have dragged all the files you want (or have reached the end of the disc), you can rearrange them in any order you want. To create an ordered M3u playlist file for your MP3 audio files, click the Convert Audio Tracks icon from the toolbar and check the box. You can also use this dialog box to convert files from one audio format to another if you choose.

When all is well, and you have your tracks in order, click the Burn button on the toolbar. Another dialog box will appear. If you want to give your CD a title, click the Description tab in this dialog box. There are many settings available here, but accepting the defaults is the way to go for the novice. Click OK to start burning. A progress bar will appear to let you know how the burn is going. When the burn is complete, K3b will eject your new CD and play a happy bugle tune to announce its success. Your new CD will now play in any computer, stereo, or other CD player.

Burning CDs with Nautilus in GNOME

In GNOME, basic CD burning is built right in to the Nautilus file manager. Insert a blank CD in your CD-RW drive. Go to the Places menu in Nautilus and select CD/DVD Creator. Open a second (or more) Nautilus window(s) containing the files you want to burn to the CD. Drag and drop the files into the CD/DVD Creator window (which is really a special directory called `burn:///`).

When you have your files selected, select Write to Disc from the File menu in the CD/DVD Creator window. This opens a dialog box (see Figure 10.7) where you can name the CD. There are no special features for building multimedia collections (such as playlist orders), but if you just want to get some files (music or otherwise) onto a CD or DVD, Nautilus gives you the tool to do that.

Creating a CD from the Shell

Under the hood of the CD writing process, you'll find that this takes two steps. First, you create the iso9660-formatted image, and then you burn (or write) that image onto the CD. The iso9600 is the default file system for CD-ROMs.

Use the mkisofs command to create the ISO image. This command has many options (see the man page for a full listing), but use the following for quick burns:

```
mkisofs -r -v -J -l -o /tmp/our_special_cd.iso /source_directory
```

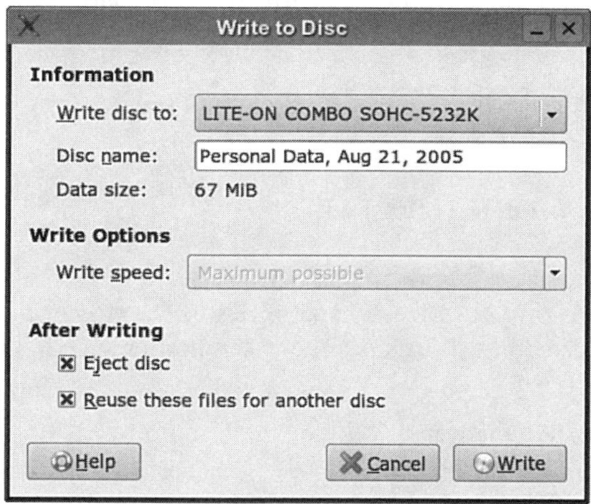

FIGURE 10.7 Nautilus gives you a simple tool to create CDs.

The options used in this example are

-r—Sets the permission of the file to more useful values. UID and GID (individual and group user ID requirements) are set to zero, all files are globally readable and searchable, and all the files are set as executable (for Windows systems).

-v—Displays verbose messages (rather than terse messages) so that you can see what is occurring during the process; these messages can help you resolve problems if they occur.

-J—Uses the Joliet extensions to ISO9600 so that Windows can more easily read the CD. The Joliet (for Windows), Rock Ridge (for Unix), and HSF (for Mac) extensions to the ISO9600 standard are used to accommodate long filenames rather than the eight-character DOS filenames that the standard supports natively.

-l—Allows 31-character filenames; plain DOS will not like it, but everyone else does.

-o—Defines the directory where the image will be written (that is, the output) and its name. The /tmp directory is convenient for this purpose, but the image could go anywhere that you have room and write permissions.

10

`/source_directory`—Indicates the path to the source directory, that is, the directory containing the files you want to include on your CD. There are ways to append additional paths and exclude directories (and files) under the specified path; it is all explained in the man page if you need that level of granularity. Our simple solution is to construct a new directory tree and populate it with the files we want to copy, and then make the image using that directory as the source.

Many more options are available, including options to make the CD bootable.

After you have created the ISO image, you can write it to the CD with the `cdrecord` command.

```
cdrecord -eject -v speed=12 dev=0,0,0 /tmp/our_special_cd.iso
```

The options used in this example are

`-eject`—Ejects the CD when the write operation is finished.

`-v`—Displays verbose messages.

`speed=`—Sets the speed; the rate depends on your drive's capabilities. If the drive or the disc itself does not support a faster speed (or burns poorly at the higher speed), you can use lower speeds to get a good burn.

`dev=`—Specifies the device number of the CD writer (I told you that you'd need this).

TIP

If you have CD-RW (read/write) discs, you can use the `cdrecord blank=` option to erase all the existing files on the CD.

`cdrecord` also gives you the option (when the disc supports it) of making multisession CDs. Without this option, when you remove a CD from the drive after writing files to it, your disc can no longer be written to, even if it still has space available. Using `cdrecord -multi` gives you the choice to put more files on the disc later.

Current standard capacity for a CD is 700MB of data, or 80 minutes of music. Some CDs can be overburned; that is, recorded to a capacity higher than the standard. You can overburn with `cdrecord` as long as your drive supports it. Find out more at http://www.cdmediaworld.com/hardware/cdrom/cd_oversize.shtml.

Creating DVDs from the Shell

Many new computers now come with DVD-writing drives, and costs have come down to where ordinary users can buy them as well. Unfortunately, the standards-making bodies have not kept up with the increasing availability of these drives, so there are two competing formats for writing DVDs. Commonly known as the + and – formats, DVD+R, DVD+RW, DVD-R, and DVD-RW are the ones we have to live with for now.

Differences between the two have mostly to do with how the data is modulated onto the DVD itself, with the + format having an edge in buffer underrun recovery. How this is achieved impacts the playability of the newly created DVD on any DVD player. The DVD+ format also has some advantages in recording on scratched or dirty media. Most drives support the DVD+ format, and some support both.

This section will focus on the DVD+RW drives because most drives sold support this standard. The software supplied with openSUSE supports both formats. It will be useful to read the DVD-writing HOWTO at http://fy.chalmers.se/~appro/linux/DVD+RW before you use these command-line tools. You can skip over the part in the HOWTO with a detailed explanation of how things are done in the kernel to record DVDs. Read the stuff on the tools, though.

You need to have two packages installed to make DVD recording possible: `dvd+rw tools` and `cdrtools`. The `dvd+rw tools` package includes the `growisofs` application, which acts as a front end to `mkisofs` as well as the DVD-formatting utility.

You can use DVD media to record data in two ways. The first is much the same as that used to record a CD in a session, whereas the second way is to record the data as a true file system using packet writing.

Session Writing

To record data in a session, you use a two-phase process:

- Format the disc with `dvd+rw-format /dev/scd0` (necessary only the first time you use a disk).
- Write your data to the disc with `growisofs -Z /dev/scd0 -R -J /your_files`.

The `growisofs` command simply streams the data to the disc. For subsequent sessions, use the `-M` argument instead of `-Z`. The `-Z` argument is used only for the initial session recording. If you use `-Z` on an already used disk, it will erase the existing data.

CAUTION

Some DVDs come preformatted. If this is the case and you format them again, the disc may become useless. Always be sure to read the fine print on the packaging on the DVD+RW before formatting.

TIP

When you write your first session on the DVD, cover at least one gigabyte (1GB). This helps ensure compatibility with other optical drives. DVD players calibrate themselves by attempting to read from specific locations on the disc. Data has to be present for the drive to read it and calibrate itself.

Also, because of limitations in the standard ISO9660 file system in Linux, do not start new sessions of a multisession DVD that would create a new directory past the 4GB boundary. If you do, it will cause the offsets used to point to the files to wrap around and point to the wrong files.

Packet Writing

Packet writing treats the DVD like a hard drive, where you create a file system (like ReiserFS) and format the disk. You can then write to it randomly as you would a hard drive. This method, although common on Windows computers, is still experimental for Linux and so is not covered in detail here.

It is possible to pipe data to the `growisofs` command:

```
your_application | growisofs -Z /dev/scd0=/dev/fd/0
```

It's also possible to burn from an existing image (or file, named pipe, or device):

```
growisofs -Z /dev/scd0=image
```

The DVD+RW Tools documentation, found in `/usr/share/doc/dvd+rw-tools`, is required reading before your first use of the program. Try experimenting with DVD-RW media first; DVD-R discs are not quite as cheap as CD-R disks, thus making the penalty for making mistakes somewhat higher.

Watching Video

Broadband Internet connections, cell phones, and cameras that take moving images as well as stills: These are the things driving the increasing ubiquity of digital video as an essential piece of a modern desktop system. openSUSE Linux users will not be disappointed when visiting YouTube. You have several choices for viewing video content.

Before beginning your search for quality video clips, be sure to follow the steps listed in the Sound Formats section of this chapter to get all the tools necessary to view proprietary video formats.

All the players listed below use one of two underlying frameworks for playing various multimedia files: xine or GStreamer. GStreamer is, as you might guess, based on GNOME/GTK+, while xine is a more generic, X-based engine. Both have extensive collections of plugins that can do assorted things (GStreamer has a plugin that functions as a telestrator, so you can draw on your playing movie, just like a TV sports analyst), and you might choose a multimedia engine based on a plugin you want to use. As always,

GStreamer can serve as the backend of any or all of the players here, including the KDE-based Kaffeine, and you can generally choose your engine in the preferences of the tool you are using.

These players are the more popular choices, but are not the only movie players available in openSUSE Linux.

Totem

Totem is the GNOME default movie player, and as such is pretty easy to use. It plays DVDs and ordinary film and video clips. You can resize the screen manually by dragging the edge(s) of the player, or use the View menu to adjust the screen using various methods. Press 2 to see the clip in double-size and F to view the movie full screen. The Escape key returns the display to the standard size.

You can take a "still photo" of the current screen (helpful if you're going to upload a clip to a video-sharing website) by pressing Ctrl+S or going to the Edit menu and selecting Take Screenshot (Figure 10.8). You can save the PNG screenshot to your Desktop (the default), or to another directory. Screenshots saved to the Desktop are given a generic file name; you can select the directory and give the file a different name with the other option.

FIGURE 10.8 Save a screenshot of a video clip in Totem.

Use Totem's Playlist feature if you have a number of clips to see. The playlist appears in a sidebar on the right that you can make disappear by pressing F9 or clicking the Sidebar button. Open a file manager and drag clips to the Sidebar, or use the standard Open dialog to add clips. Save a Playlist for later showings by clicking the Save icon at the bottom of the sidebar.

The arrow keys perform interesting functions in Totem. Turn the volume up or down with the appropriate keys. Skip ahead or rewind a short period (a few seconds or a minute, depending on the length of the clip) with the left (backward) and right (forward) arrows. For a more expansive fast-forward or rewind, just drag the indicator in the Time bar.

Kaffeine

Kaffeine is a full-service multimedia player that plays audio and video files simply and efficiently. It uses a tabbed interface, so different aspects of the player don't interfere with each other.

When you open Kaffeine from the Multimedia, Video Player KDE menu, you see a set of choices (Figure 10.9), including playing audio or video CDs, encoding (ripping) audio CDs, and playing DVDs.

FIGURE 10.9 The Kaffeine media player for KDE handles several different tasks.

Playback is a simple affair. As with Totem, you can size your screen any way you like, either by dragging the player window (which can lead to some distortion of the image) or using the View menu tools. These menus are a little more complicated than Totem's (there is another layer of Enable Auto Resize to get to the double- and triple-sized views), but still do the trick.

TIP

Not to discourage your office productivity, but Kaffeine comes equipped with a Boss button for when you are watching video clips. Changing desktops or minimizing Kaffeine automatically pauses video playback. Restore Kaffeine to pick up where you left off. Change this behavior by going to Settings, Configure Kaffeine, Behavior, and unchecking the Pause video... box.

Kaffeine will not only save a screenshot image of a video clip, but also it will save a stream as a file. Press Ctrl+S to save a screenshot. Kaffeine will save the screenshot anywhere on your system (with your Documents folder being the default) in PNG, BMP, or XBM format. Pressing R (for Record) will save streaming audio or video on your system.

NOTE

All keyboard shortcuts in Kaffeine are configurable, so you can change any of these to suit your own style. Go to Settings, Configure Shortcuts to open this dialog box.

Kaffeine puts all the tools for creating and organizing Playlists in one interface. When you open the Playlists tab, in addition to the main window, a Konqueror pane is also present. Navigate to the proper folder and drag your clips into the Playlist window to create a new list. If you then want to save that playlist for later, go to Save Current Playlist in the Playlist menu. Name the playlist and navigate to the folder you want to save it in. Incidentally, if you have a clip playing and want to look at the Playlist tab, a thumbnail of the video will play in the lower-left corner of the Playlist Editor, below the file manager.

Kaffeine is a typical KDE application: quite powerful, endlessly configurable, and more than adequate for its task.

Watching TV on Your Computer

Standard video cards let you see most video resources, as you would expect. What you may not know is that you can turn your monitor into a television screen to receive TV signals with a TV or TV/video combo card. This section describes a sampling of Linux software that works with these content types.

Make sure your cards are properly configured. (See Chapter 4 to configure your hardware cards with YaST and SaX. See Chapter 6, "Launching Your Desktop," for configuring X.)

TV and Video Hardware

Video support in Linux comes through the V4L (Video for Linux) API, or directly through the X Window System. Support for TV display from video cards with a TV-out jack is poor at this time. TV-only cards are well supported, but you must know the chipset name of your card, not the manufacturer's brand name. The most common chipset is the Brooktree Bt series; the Linux driver is called bttv.

YaST should recognize your card, if it is supported, and load drivers, whether the card is present at your initial openSUSE install or is added later. If this doesn't happen, you can always configure the card manually.

To configure the card, you need to identify the chipset. Check YaST. Go to Hardware, then Graphics Card and Monitor, or TV Card.

Building Your Own Personal Video Recorder

Personal video recorders like TiVo and ReplayTV have changed the way people use television. The VCR introduced the idea of time-shifting broadcast television, but developed the reputation of being so complicated to program that nontechnical folks threw up their hands and gave up. Technical advances have made this easier, but the image of the "guy who can't program his VCR" persists. PVRs automate the hardest part of this task and make it a virtual no-brainer to record both analog and digital TV signals to a hard drive for later viewing. TiVo itself runs Linux on a PowerPC processor to record shows on its hard drive.

Several open-source projects have been launched to create PVRs on Linux. The most successful of these is the mythTV project. The goal of mythTV is to bring the "mythical digital convergence box" to life, so it has the TiVo features, a web browser, an email client, games, and a music player.

Installing mythTV under openSUSE is much easier than in earlier versions, though still not for the faint of heart. YaST will help along the way, dealing with various software dependency issues that might not be solved through compiling packages one by one.

NOTE

Another PVR package, Freevo, also runs under SUSE Linux.

Hardware Requirements

Generally speaking, your mythTV box should be dedicated to this purpose. This is not a project to give your old Pentium II machine a new life. Processing TV signals requires a big and fast microprocessor chip and a good monitor. To make this work, you need modern equipment. Check the PVR Hardware Database at http://pvrhw.goldfish.org/tiki-pvrhwdb.php and compare these systems to the SUSE Hardware Database to pick the best PVR system for you. Hauppage, the maker of several popular TV cards, recommends a Pentium III processor at 733MHz (or 1.8GHz to make DivX video) for its PVR cards. You should also have a high-speed (DSL or cable modem) connection to the Internet to access TV schedule information. In addition, mythTV sets these guidelines:

- 256MB memory
- 40GB (or larger) hard drive
- XFS or JFS file system (which handles large files better than other file systems)
- A video card with a TV-out port
- A video capture card

You have two basic options for video capture: a frame grabber that is software driven or a more expensive MPEG encoder. The frame grabber does its encoding using the PC's resources, whereas the onboard encoder does it itself. The trade-off is that the IvyTV drivers needed for the encoder are somewhat troublesome to install.

If you have the right machine, let's start setting it up.

Setting Up Your PVR

Follow these steps to build your personal video recorder. Read the online mythTV installation guide before or during your setup. It will be very helpful. Find it at http://www.mythtv.org/docs/mythtv-HOWTO.html.

TIP

These instructions make use of two online tools to update and install software on your openSUSE system: YaST Online Update and Apt. Find out more about these in Chapter 21, "Keeping Your System Current: Package Management."

1. If you haven't already, install openSUSE. Make sure you have the `qt4`, `qt4-devel`, `qt4-mysql`, `gcc`, `freetype2-devel`, `ivtv`, and `mysql` packages installed.
2. Run YaST Online Update to confirm that everything's current.
3. Add the Packman software repository to YaST. See Chapter 20 for detailed instructions on adding repositories to YaST, and the Sound Formats section of this chapter for a quicker version.
4. Open YaST Software Management.
5. In the Search dialog, type myth. You'll see all the packages related to mythTV, along with a few others. At minimum, install these packages: `mythtv`, `mythtv-backend`, `mythtv-frontend`, `mythtv-setup`, `mythtv-themes`, `mythbrowser`, and `mythplugins`. Scroll through the list to see other options you may wish to include. Click Accept to begin the installation. You may be asked to install other dependent packages; if so, say Yes.
6. Start MySQL in a shell by logging in as the SuperUser and typing **/etc/init.d/mysql start**. If you haven't worked with MySQL yet, you need to set up a Root password for MySQL. Type **mysqladmin -u root password <yourpasswordhere>**.
7. Set up a MySQL database for mythTV. Type **mysql -u root -p < /usr/share/doc/packages/mythtv/database/mc.sql** (and key-in the previously entered password). If nothing happens, this is a good thing!

   You have now created a MySQL user called mythtv and the mythconverg database that mythTV uses to store your video data. For more information on MySQL and other database management systems, go to Chapter 29, "Managing Databases."

10

8. Go to http://www.mythtv.org/docs/mythtv-HOWTO-5.html#ss5.3 and follow the instructions on setting up Zap2It DataDirect to handle your scheduling needs.
9. Decide where in the file system you want to store your recorded video. By default, mythTV stores files in `/mnt/store`. You may have to create this directory; make sure that at least one user can write to that directory. You may also want to create a user mythtv to be that user. If you prefer to store the files elsewhere, you'll need to edit the mythTV configuration file later.
10. Go back to the shell (as the SuperUser) and type **`mythtv-setup`**. Follow the prompts to go through the initial configuration. Accepting the default settings should get you in no trouble. You'll be asked for the information in the last two steps.
11. After you have completed the setup, it's time to go back to being an ordinary user. If you have created a separate user, mythtv, log out and log back in as mythtv (otherwise, just exit the SuperUser shell).
12. Running mythTV is a two-step process. First, run `mythbackend` to open the database, and then run `mythfrontend` to view your content.

And so you have your own PVR, with no service to buy. There are lots of other options in setting up mythTV; read more about them in the mythTV manual.

Linux and Your Digital Camera

A digital camera combined with your personal computer is a powerful tool to create, store, edit, print, and share images. You can take your pictures, store them initially on the camera's disk or memory card, and then transfer them to your PC with the camera's USB cable. View or edit the file with your favorite image editor, email photos to friends and family, post them on your photo blog, or preserve the images on a recordable CD. No fuss, no muss, no film.

Unfortunately, some of the pleasure and convenience associated with digital cameras are lost when running Linux. Most, if not all, of the software bundled with your camera runs only on Windows.

Do not despair, however. openSUSE offers many tools to organize and share your photos, and because the digital imaging industry is organized around very common standards, Linux can handle most any task involving your camera.

To begin with, you should have no trouble connecting your camera to your Linux system. Just connect the camera with its Universal Serial Bus (USB) cable to your PC. openSUSE should recognize the camera instantly and install the proper drivers.

After you have the camera connected, use any file manager to see the image files on your camera. They should be located in `/media/camera`.

GNOME has a camera-support tool called `gtkam`. This is a GTK+ front end to the command-line `gphoto` software. To run it, go to the Graphics menu and click Digital Camera Tool. The first time, it will ask you to identify your camera model from the list of 500+ cameras it supports. After you have your camera configured, gtkam will help you download your images from the camera to your PC. Just click the thumbnail to select.

KDE fans can use the digiKam tool to handle similar tasks. It also is a KDE-based front end to `gphoto`, but includes an image editor as well. DigiKam will attempt to autodetect your camera, or you can add it manually. You can create photo albums for specific events.

When your images are on your computer, feel free to run them through The GIMP to enhance them. The GIMP can reduce red-eye problems, crop your photos, change colors, brightness, and contrast, and otherwise doctor up your pictures. See the next section for more fun with The GIMP.

Webcams

Webcams are typically small low-resolution cameras connected to your computer via a parallel or USB port. The camera can act in two modes: streaming (for a series of images or a moving object) and grabbing (for a single still image). The most common use for webcams includes videoconferencing and the widespread phenomenon of looking in on what's happening on a street corner where a local news organization has set up a camera. Webcams can be used to send almost-live images of assorted people, places, and things to an online correspondent. Perhaps even you've sent off a quick image of yourself—because you can!

You can use any of the video applications that can access a video4linux device to view webcam or still-camera images in openSUSE. You can also use Ekiga (discussed in Chapter 16) as a webcam viewer.

Not all webcams are supported in Linux, and the drivers are based on the chipset used, rather than on the model or manufacturer. Some of the kernel source documentation files in `/usr/src/linux-2.6/Documentation/usb` contain information about USB webcams and drivers supported in openSUSE, including the following:

- `ibmcam.txt`
- `ov511.txt`
- `phillips.txt`
- `se401.txt`
- `stv0608.txt`

A good place to start with your webcam is, as always, the Linux Documentation Project. The Webcam HOWTO is located at http://www.tldp.org/HOWTO/Webcam-HOWTO.

Editing Images

Let us begin with a truism: It is hard to create a great graphical interface without great graphics. While it may not be true that the Linux desktop would not exist without The GIMP (although it is the case with ONE Linux desktop), the quality of this image editor marked the first great step toward widespread acceptance of desktop PCs running Linux. Editing digital images is an essential task now that the photographic darkroom is becoming a relic of the last century, and even folks who take vacation pictures deserve high-quality tools to remove the finger from the edge of the image.

But photographs aren't the only images that can be created and modified in Linux. Vector images, or line drawings, are also an essential part of the PC toolkit, and openSUSE Linux has a couple of tools worth talking about as well.

Editing Photos with The GIMP

The GNU Image Manipulation Program (GIMP) use to be touted as the "killer app" that would drive ordinary desktop users to Linux. A professional image editor whose features rivaled the fabled Adobe Photoshop on Windows but that didn't cost several hundred dollars is just what people needed, some analysts thought. It didn't happen exactly that way, but it remains reasonable to say that Linux for the masses wouldn't be here if not for The GIMP.

TIP

To learn more about the role of The GIMP and the toolkit that spawned dozens of GUI products, see the section on GNOME in Chapter 6.

Photographers, animators, web designers, and other artists use The GIMP in all sorts of ways. The nonhuman characters in the *Scooby Doo* movies were created with the help of a GIMP spinoff now called CinePaint.

So what can you do with The GIMP? Just about any photo or other graphic-editing task. The GIMP can import and export more than 30 image formats, including Photoshop's native format. It supports layers (letting you easily add and remove text or other effects from an image) and has all the tools people expect from a modern image editor.

Version 2.2 of The GIMP, released in December 2004, features a more usable interface, better drag-and-drop support, and a shortcut editor.

To run The GIMP from the shell, type **`gimp &`**. The ampersand (&) launches The GIMP in the background and returns you to the shell prompt.

Otherwise, The GIMP can be found in the Graphics menu in the KDE or GNOME start menus. The first time you run The GIMP, you'll be asked a few startup configuration questions, but then you're on your way.

When you open The GIMP without an image, you'll see a pair of separated panels (not terribly unlike Photoshop). To the left is the toolbox; these icons offer the basic utensils for editing an image. Depending on the version installed on your system, more than 30 tool icons could be available to you. All these tools, from Crop to Lasso to Erase, will be familiar to the experienced image editor. On the right (also not unlike that other tool) is a layer and color-channel manager.

To create a new image, press Ctrl+N (or go to File, New). To open an existing image for editing, press Ctrl+O and an image window appears. Both the toolbox and the image window have their own menus. Open the File menu in either window to open and save graphics and perform other file-management tasks. The Toolbox Extensions menu (Xtns) contains the plug-ins and other enhanced functionality that make The GIMP special.

Right-clicking anywhere in an image window also gives you access to a context menu with a wealth of choices to work with your image (see Figure 10.10).

FIGURE 10.10 Just a hint of the choices you have available when right-clicking in a GIMP image.

In the right edge of the menu are two important options, Python-fu and Script-fu. Both offer ways to automate tasks and do all sorts of cool things. Script-fu is the original GIMP scripting language, but because it's based on a relatively obscure programming language, Scheme, it's hard to learn. GIMP 2.0 introduced Python-fu, based on the famous (and famously easy to use and learn) Python scripting language.

The GIMP's Help files are quite good. It doesn't hurt for newbies (either to The GIMP or to image editing in general) to read the manual.

PHOTOSHOP VERSUS THE GIMP

Two large obstacles prevent The GIMP from becoming a standard prepress format for dead-tree printers.

The first is Photoshop's licensing for Pantone colors to ensure accurate color matching. Adobe can pay to license Pantone's patented color specification; the all-volunteer GIMP Project cannot. There are GIMP palettes that approximate Pantone colors, but no one can say with certainty if these educated guesses are 100% right.

The second problem relates to the differences between how colors look on a computer screen and how they look in a magazine. The GIMP separates colors based on a combination of red, green, and blue (RGB) values. Print publishers use a scheme called CMYK (cyan, magenta, yellow, and "key," or black). In the short term, there is a GIMP plug-in called Separate that provides "minimal support for CMYK." For the long term, developers are working on a new technology, the Generic Graphics Library (GEGL), that will fully support CMYK color separation and other "deep color" issues.

If you produce images for print, these two issues may be critical, and you may need to keep a copy of Photoshop around. Be aware that you can run Photoshop under Crossover Office, the Codeweavers cross-platform tool.

Drawing Pictures

Painting pictures is often one of the first things a new computer user tries. It's a great way to learn how to use a mouse by clicking and dragging around a blank canvas with assorted tools that emulate spray paint, colored pens, and polygonal rubber stamps. It's also hard to imagine the World Wide Web without vector graphics decorating every page, since they load so much faster than photographs with millions of colors available to the palette.

Vector graphics are so important and common to modern communication that all the office productivity suites, regardless of supported operating systems, contain a vector drawing application (often in the guise of a presentation program). In this section, we will look at two standalone vector graphics programs, Inkscape and Skencil.

Inkscape

This editor is incredibly easy to use and reasonably intuitive for the task at hand. Open it from the KDE Office menu, under Flowchart.

Select a tool from the toolkit running along the left side of the screen and start drawing. Click inside an object with the selection tool (the arrow) to resize or rotate the object (be it a simple rectangle or a hand-drawn free shape). Change colors? Select the object and choose from the palette at the bottom. Want more precise control over the color shade, or put a red border around your shape? Right-click on the object and open the Fill and Stroke dialog.

In some ways, drawing a straight line or arrow may be the hardest thing to do in Inkscape. There is no distinct line-drawing tool; you must use the bezier curve tool. Click once to start the line, drag the line along and double-click to end the line. To add an arrow, right-click on the line and select Fill and Stroke. Click the Stroke Style tab, and go to the End Markers drop-down menu. Choose your arrowhead from the multitude of options.

When you open Inkscape, you see a piece of paper sitting in a much bigger canvas. You can place objects outside the paper (as in Figure 10.11), but they won't print. Inkscape provides these default shapes: rectangles, circles/ellipses, stars and spirals and freehand polygons. You can also use Inkscape for calligraphy and ordinary text in your image as well. All these are endlessly adjustable, but don't always behave the way you'd like them to.

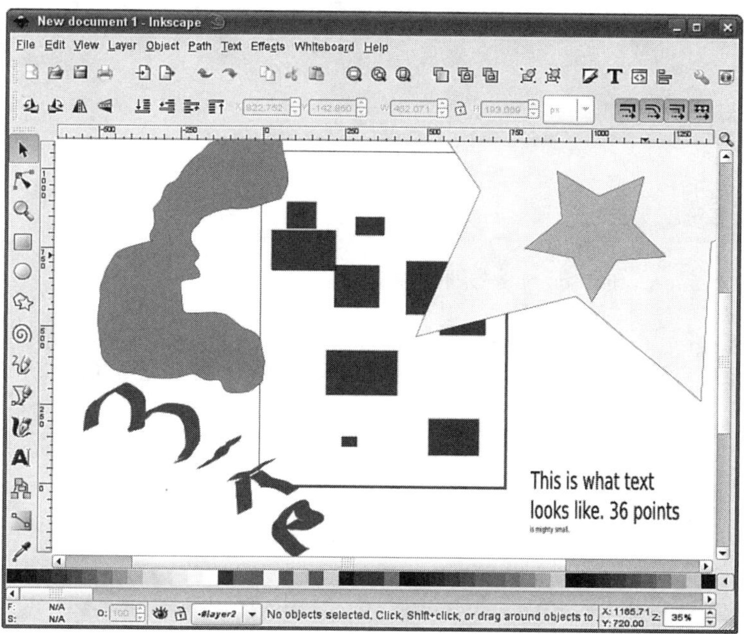

FIGURE 10.11 You can color outside the lines with Inkscape.

You can group shapes together and create connectors between shapes (a la Visio) that link them together. This last feature may be the reason Inskcape sees itself as a Flowchart application.

Inkscape creates web standard Scalable Vector Graphics (SVG) files by default. This means the information used to create the drawing is contained in a simple text file tagged in the eXtensible Markup Language (XML). You can even open an internal SVG editor (Figure 10.12) in Inkscape to "view source" as you would in a browser or WYSIWYG HTML editor.

You can also export your drawings as plain bitmaps, or save them in a variety of formats for display on the web, or for further editing in, say, OpenOffice.

If you like to pull different elements into a base graphic for multiple purposes, you'll be happy to learn that Inkscape supports Layers. Create a background image, then go to the Layer menu and select Add Layer. To make a layer "disappear," click the eye icon in the lower-left of the Inkscape screen.

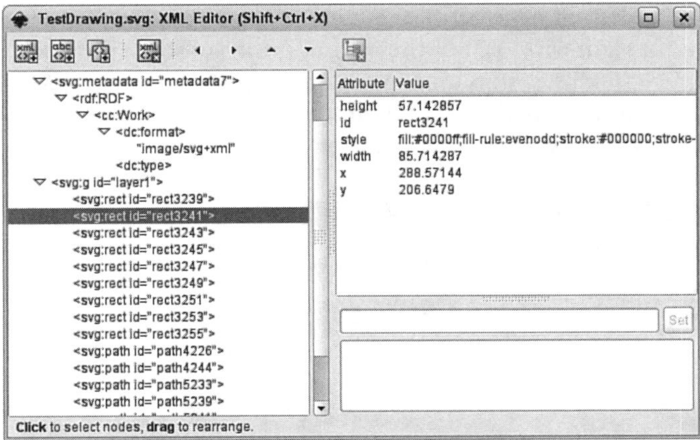

FIGURE 10.12 Inkscape creates valid Scalable Vector Graphics (SVG).

Should you be one of those graphics people who remain mouse-averse, you can do just about everything in Inkscape via your keyboard. Check out the enormous zoomable list of keyboard shortcuts in Keys and Mouse under the Help menu.

In an admirable display of confidence in their tool, Inkscape's tutorial files are published as SVG files, even with large amounts of text. These tutorials, accessible from the Help menu, are indeed useful for beginners just getting started.

Skencil

This drawing application, originally known as Sketch, is very similar to Inkscape, but much less user friendly. There is no help file or other documentation included with the application (though a User's Guide is posted online).

Experienced graphic artists should like the interface (Figure 10.13), and should be able to get much out of the tool. Skencil creates SVG, Adobe Illustrator, and PDF files in addition to its own format.

Creating a straight line is a bit easier in Skencil than in Inkscape. Select the Draw Poly-Line tool (a yellow pentagon in the toolbar) and click in two spots to create a simple line. Dragging the mouse with this tool creates a fuller, more freehand-style line. Right-click on the line and select Line from the context menu to choose an arrowhead (in the right section of the dialog box, under the Width setting).

Skencil does not support layers, but you can group and arrange objects and set the level of opacity (which is whether objects can bleed through other objects).

Graphics Formats

When you work with digital images, there seems to be a million different formats. Despite what you may believe, each format exists for a specific reason, be it technical, aesthetic, or legal/financial. Some formats are patented or have patented technology included.

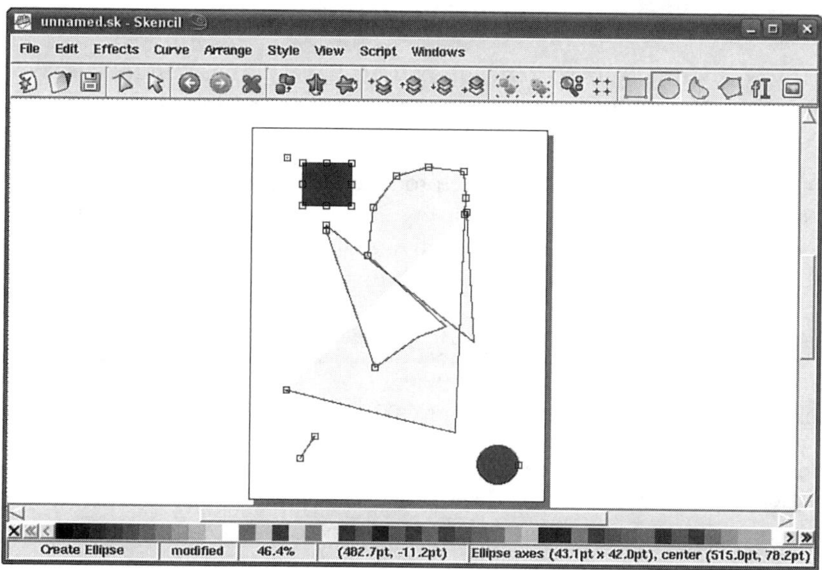

FIGURE 10.13 Skencil is another vector drawing tool.

When you're working with editors such as The GIMP, choose the right format for the task at hand. Following is a list of some of the more popular formats, followed by an explanation of why you might want to use (or not use) them.

- BMP—Bitmapped graphics, which are commonly used in Windows. They are large and uncompressed files, good for icons and wallpaper.
- GIF—Graphics Interchange Format. Most graphics on the web once used this format, developed by CompuServe, one of the original online services. GIF uses a patented lossless compression algorithm (LZW) that requires a license to use.
- JPEG—The Joint Photographic Experts Group developed this format for electronic photographs. All digital cameras produce this format by default. The compression scheme loses some data, but provides a sharp image nonetheless.
- PNG—Portable Network Graphics. The open source replacement for GIFs.
- SVG—Scalable Vector Graphics. The Next Big Thing, this XML web graphics standard is being developed by the World Wide Web Consortium (W3C).
- TIF—Tagged Image File. Often used for printing and publishing.

Sometimes you may not be able to work with a file in its current format. Coming to your rescue are a host of separate image-converter applications that can change an image's format almost instantly. The best known of these, ImageMagick, even does its thing from the command line!

Gaming on Linux

As the original "hobby" operating system, some Linux users have all their fun just tweaking the OS and their applications. Others need more traditional entertainments. openSUSE is fully equipped with assorted options for the gamer in you.

Very few shrink-wrapped commercial PC games are produced for Linux. For the most part, games are developed these days for Windows PCs using the Direct3D graphics engine. The cross-platform OpenGL engine is used for many popular games (like Doom III), but there's a perception that OpenGL is not as muscular.

TIP

TransGaming Technologies has an engine, Cedega, that converts Direct3D games to OpenGL. This enables Linux users to play as many as 300 Windows and online games, including multiplayer role-playing games such as Everquest and Star Wars Galaxies. View the supported games database, with some player ratings, at http://transgaming.org/gamesdb/.

You must subscribe to TransGaming's service, at $5 per month, to get Cedega. Depending on what you play and how often you play it, this might be worth it. See http://www.transgaming.com/ for more information.

Crossover Linux also supports several popular Windows games, most notably World of Warcraft. See Chapter 11, "Going Cross- Platform," for more information.

Many dedicated fans have worked on open-source clones of some classic games, like PacMan, Tetris, and SimCity (called LinCity). And it wouldn't really be a computer without a solitaire game, would it (see Figure 10.14)?

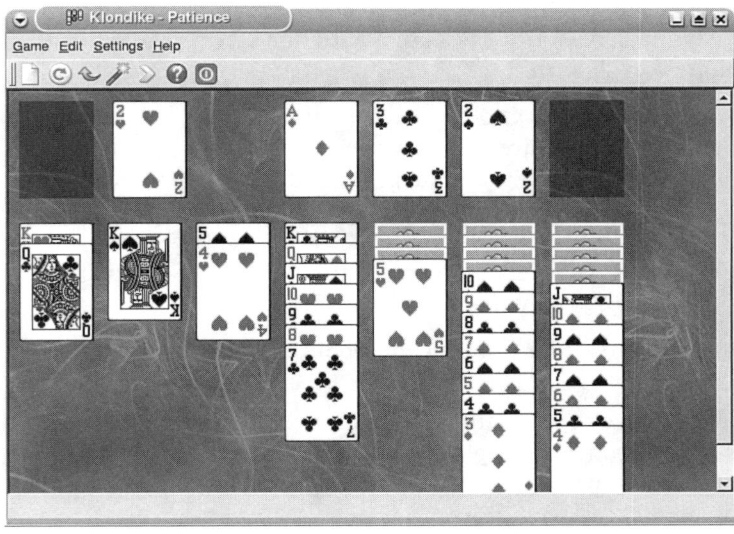

FIGURE 10.14 Patience is just one solitaire game in openSUSE.

openSUSE gives you two solitaire games, KPatience for KDE and PySol—the latter is written in Python. KPatience is installed by default with the KDE-Games package. It has 14 standard games for your amusement. One nice feature is that it will automatically play aces and other scoring cards.

PySol is much flashier, with musical accompaniment (yes, you can turn that off), dozens of games and card sets (sorted by type), and gobs of statistics. It is endlessly configurable to stave off boredom.

Games with your Desktop Environment

Whatever desktop environment you choose for your openSUSE system, you'll have a variety of gaming choices. The KDE-Games packages contains 31 games in four categories: Arcade (with 11 games, including adapted classics such as Asteroids and Tron), Board (another 10 choices including chess and backgammon), Card (just three: Poker, Patience, and Skat), and Strategy/Tactics (seven games that make you think).

The package of games that comes with GNOME is smaller than the KDE collection (just 17), but equally challenging. There's also some overlap, with the usual Tetris clones, disk-flipping, and solitaire games.

One standout is the Yahtzee clone, Tali. This game has great graphics, and you play against five computer opponents by default. This is, of course, configurable. The five dice roll automatically. You click the dice you want to roll (which turn into pumpkins) and click Roll to try to improve your score. After your third roll, you click the category you want to count your score.

GNOME also has a blackjack table for your gambling pleasure. Learn to double-down, split your hand, and other tricks of the trade without risking any real cash. The dealer plays under any of four sets of rules, called Vegas Strip, Vegas Downtown, Atlantic City, or Ameristar. This is set in the game's Preferences.

To play games, go to the KDE or GNOME Applications menu, and click Games. All your choices will come up, organized by type.

Freeciv: A Free Strategy Game

Sid Meier's Civilization is one of the most popular games ever. The chance to build a society from scratch, fight wars, and get to space is irresistible for some. Naturally, some game players run Linux for more serious pursuits. What is interesting is that for some of those players, one of their serious pursuits became creating the game.

The Freeciv project was born in November 1995, about a year after the release of Civilization 1. Freeciv 1.0 came out six weeks later, though a flurry of updates produced v1.0f three weeks later. By the time Civilization III came out in October 2001, Freeciv was up to v1.12, and v2.0 was released in May 2005. openSUSE 10.3 includes a beta of v2.1.

You can play by yourself with the computer as your opponent(s), play with friends across a local area network, or use the Freeciv metaserver to play with other folks across the

Internet. If you have played the commercial version, you'll be impressed with the similarities, although the quality of the graphics may vary depending on your video card. New players should not be intimidated, because there is a fair amount of help available, both in the game itself and at the Freeciv website (http://www.freeciv.org).

In Freeciv, you are the absolute ruler of your race. You marshal and manage resources to build cities. As in other city-simulation games, you must keep your citizens happy while getting them to produce more wealth, which you then can tax. Meanwhile, you try to increase your scientific and military capacity as you aim to either achieve world domination or build the first rocket to Alpha Centauri.

When you run Freeciv, you are launching two separate applications, a server (which creates your AI opponents) and a client, where you play. You can also connect to a remote server to play with others.

New players (especially those who haven't played Civilization) should read the online manuals at the Freeciv website to get a feel for how things work. There are three manuals: more technical, command-oriented manuals for the client and server and a game-playing manual that describes the forces and conditions of the game. The manuals are not complete (especially the client manual), but give you enough of a start to keep going. There is a Tutorial scenario option to help you out as well.

References

- http://bugtrack.alsa-project.org/main/index.php/Matrix:Main—The Advanced Linux Sound Architecture sound card matrix. Check here for more information on support for your card.
- http://en.opensuse.org/Hardware—The openSUSE Hardware Compatibility List. Search here first for your sound and video cards before installing openSUSE. Get instructions on installing proprietary drivers.
- http://www.linux-sound.org—From music made with Linux to musician mailing lists to player and production software, the jumping-off point for sound and music under Linux.
- http://lau.linuxaudio.org—The Linux Audio Users Guide.
- http://amarok.kde.org—News and information about the Amarok audio player for KDE. Check out the wiki for howtos and plugins.
- http://www.banshee-project.org—The Banshee music player for GNOME. Forums, FAQs, and other information.
- http://ktown.kde.org/~wheeler/juk.html—The JuK jukebox player.
- http://www.gnome.org/projects/rhythmbox—Rhythmbox music management program for GNOME.
- http://www.xmms.org/—Home of the X Multimedia System (XMMS). News, downloads, plug-ins, skins, and support for this multifaceted media player.

- http://last.fm—The last.fm social music and radio site.
- http://www.pandora.com—Discover new music based on an algorithm related to instrumentation, sound, beat, and other characteristics of the music you like.
- http://www.live365.com—A collection of hundreds of radio stations on the Web.
- http://www.jamendo.com—A musical sharing site where artists upload music for free, legal, sharing.
- https://helixcommunity.org—Many projects related to the open source Helix player, server, and producer for RealPlayer content.
- http://www.vorbis.com—Hows and whys for the Ogg Vorbis audio format.
- http://www.exploits.org/v4l/—Video for Linux information page. Technical information on the V4L APIs, drivers for supported cards, and personal video recorders. Links to software for making video of all types. When typing this URL, note that the last character is an L (as in Video4Linux), not a numeral 1.
- http://pvrweb.com—Guides to setting up PC-based personal video recorders with mythTV and the VDR system.
- http://www.mythtv.org—The mythTV personal video recorder software. Contains installation instructions and examples of mythTV in action.
- http://www.mythtv.org/wiki/index.php/Opensuse_10.2—Documentation from the mythTV wiki on installing mythTV in openSUSE Linux. Good info on dealing with specific TV cards.
- http://anandtech.com/linux/showdoc.aspx?i=2190&p=1—A detailed and honest explanation (from 2004) of a successful mythTV installation on SUSE Linux.
- http://www.gstreamer.net—The GStreamer multimedia engine that serves as the backend for many Linux audio and video players.
- http://www.gnome.org/projects/totem—Totem movie player for GNOME.
- http://kaffeine.sourceforge.net—Kaffeine multimedia player for KDE.
- http://www.mplayerhq.hu—The MPlayer headquarters for that varied and full-featured video player.
- http://xinehq.de—The Xine headquarters. News and downloads for this video player.
- http://www.gphoto.org/—Linux Management software for digital camera images.
- http://www.gphoto.org/proj/libgphoto2/support.php—The gphoto list of supported cameras.
- http://www.teaser.fr/~hfiguiere/linux/digicam.html—Digital Camera Support for UNIX, Linux, and BSD. If your camera is not on the gphoto list, this site may help you find out why and offer suggestions.
- http://www.digikam.org—The KDE digiKam front end for gphoto. Look here for plugins and new versions, which seem to come out every two months.

- http://www.gimp.org—The very well-organized home of the GNU Image Manipulation Program (GIMP). Check out the Tutorials section, with walk-throughs for all skill levels, beginner to expert.
- http://www.gegl.org—Home of the Generic Graphics Library, better CMYK support for The GIMP.
- http://gug.sunsite.dk—The global GIMP User Group. Mailing lists, a large gallery of images and textures, tutorials, and articles to help make you a better GIMPer.
- http://www.skencil.org—Home of the Skencil vector drawing program. Sign up for the support mailing list, read the User's Guide, and download scripts and other add-ons.
- http://www.inkscape.org—News, tutorials and community for Inkscape users.
- http://icculus.org/lgfaq—The Linux Gamers' FAQ. Get your questions answered.
- http://www.happypenguin.org—The Linux Game Tome, a catalog of Linux games of all sorts. Player ratings, news, forums, and links.
- http://linuxgames.com—LinuxGames, with all sorts of news related to the topic.
- http://games.kde.org—The KDE Gaming area, with descriptions of all the games included with KDE.
- http://www.ggzgamingzone.org—Play Linux games online for free.
- http://freeciv.wikia.com—The Freeciv wiki site. All things Freeciv, with translations in 19 languages.
- http://www.cnpbagwell.com/audio.html—An audio format FAQ site useful for learning more about various audio formats.
- http://opensuse-community.org/Package_Sources/Packman—A list of mirrors for the Packman software repository, a great source for multimedia software.
- http://download.videolan.org—Download the VideoLAN player, and libdvdcss (that allows you to play DVDs on Linux) here.
- http://www.softwareinreview.com/cms/content/view/60/—Jem Matzen's "Hacking openSUSE 10.2" article, helpful in adding MP3 and other multimedia support to the default openSUSE setup.
- http://KDE-Apps.org—A community directory of applications written for KDE. Among other things, you can pick up the KonvenientSUSE package to add multimedia support to your openSUSE system.
- http://www.cdmediaworld.com/hardware/cdrom/cd_oversize.shtml—Learn how to "overburn" CDs.
- http://fy.chalmers.se/~appro/linux/DVD+RW—FAQ and kernel patch for writable DVDs under Linux.
- http://pvrhw.goldfish.org/tiki-pvrhwdb.php—PVR Hardware database.
- http://www.tldp.org/HOWTO/Webcam-HOWTO—The Linux Documentation Project's Webcam HOWTO.

CHAPTER 11

Going Cross-Platform

IN THIS CHAPTER

- Viewing Files from the Windows Side of Your Computer
- Emulating Other Operating Systems in Linux: An Overview
- Using Wine to Run Windows Applications
- Running Windows Applications with Win4Lin
- Running Windows Applications with VMware
- Emulating a Mac with Basilisk II
- Using dosemu and DOSBox
- Xen: The Future of Virtualization?
- References

Truly one of the great things about Linux is its flexibility. You are not always forced to abandon your old platform or your favorite applications when you make the move to Linux. With enough hard drive space, you can dual boot Windows on a separate partition and share files across file systems. Tools exist that allow you to run many Windows applications directly in Linux. You can even emulate MacOS Classic without a PowerPC.

This chapter is all about using these tools. Some are built into your openSUSE installation, others are freely available for download, and some commercial products are available to purchase as well.

You will learn about the Wine project and its Crossover Linux commercial spinoff, that allows you to run many Windows applications in Linux. Win4Lin is another commercial product that allows you to run Windows 98 or Windows 2000/XP applications directly in Linux. VMware uses a virtual machine approach to installing and running other operating systems and applications. Basilisk II is the MacOS emulator, and DOSBox recaptures some of the earlier days of personal computing. Finally, you'll take a peek at a new project that's been gaining a lot of attention recently, the Xen Virtualization Project.

Viewing Files from the Windows Side of Your Computer

When you install openSUSE on a computer that already has some form of Windows running on it, YaST will offer to run the two operating systems side by side. Linux will then repartition the computer, and the GRUB bootloader adds Windows to its list of boot options.

In this instance, openSUSE also creates a `/windows` directory to make all Windows files accessible to you directly in Linux. Depending on the file systems you are using on either side of your computer, you may not even notice a difference in how a file behaves.

MS-DOS and all versions of Windows up to the introduction of Windows NT ran on the File Allocation Table (FAT) file system. All Linux file systems (ext2, ext3, ReiserFS, XFS, and JFS) fully support FAT. That is, you can open files from a FAT formatted volume, edit them, and save them either on the Linux volume or back to the FAT formatted volume. If you edit a Windows file in Linux and save it back to the same directory, you can open that file again in Windows.

The main reason this works so well is that FAT is not a permission-based file system. If you copy a Linux file to a FAT partition, the copy won't have permissions attached to it, but it will be completely readable in the other OS.

Starting with Windows NT, Microsoft created a proprietary permissions-based file system called NTFS, which is the default file system in Windows 2000, 2003, XP and Vista. The transition to this file system has been good for Windows users because NTFS uses disk space more efficiently than FAT, and having permissions on files and directories is more secure. Because Microsoft has not shared many of the details of the file system, Linux support is somewhat less transparent.

Thus, most files on an NTFS volume are read-only on Linux. You can still open and edit these files in a Linux application, but you cannot save the changes back to the NTFS volume. You can, however, save or copy a Linux file to a FAT-formatted floppy, USB storage, or Zip disk, and then open and save to an NTFS volume.

NOTE

You can play most multimedia (music and video) files stored on an NTFS partition in Linux. Because there's no editing/saving going on, the only potential problem lies in support for the format. Linux multimedia player applications such as MPlayer and Helix support some Windows Media features. See Chapter 10, "Sights, Sounds, and Other Fun Things," for more information.

If you edit a lot of files in both operating systems, you should strongly consider creating a small FAT partition to store your data files.

On the other side of the computer, Windows has no native support for reading any Linux file system. Some applications, like the Ext2 IFS for Windows, enable you to view files on the Linux Extended File System (ext2 and ext3), but none of these currently support other file systems like ReiserFS.

Learn more about Linux file systems in Chapter 18, "Managing Files, Volumes, and Drives."

Emulating Other Operating Systems in Linux: An Overview

Essentially, there are two methods to accomplish the task of running applications across platforms. In the first method, an emulator translates an application's calls to one operating system (such as Windows) to another (Linux). In the second method, an application builds a virtual machine that creates a second computer inside your computer. The virtual machine then hosts a file system and operating system just as any physical computer does.

In this section, you will learn about three emulators (Wine, DOSBox, and Basilisk II) and two virtual machines (VMware and Win4Lin).

A Few Misconceptions About Cross-Platform Tools

Nothing's perfect, and it's very hard to reach seamless cross-platform computing nirvana. Before looking closely at each of these tools, you should know a few things that may diminish your excitement at this newfound capability:

- Whatever tool you run from Linux, you won't run your existing Windows applications from the Windows side of your computer. You will install a new instance of the application and will probably have to re-create your settings from scratch.
- You cannot automatically use the same data (such as your Eudora mail queue) for both the Windows side and the Linux side. In many applications, you can import data from one side to the other, but changes made in one copy will not be reflected in the other copy.
- Don't install an emulator or virtual machine to run an application you don't have. All these products will let you "run Word on Linux," but you will need your own copy of Word to install and run. If all you need is a Linux application that will let you open and edit Word documents, use OpenOffice or another of the Linux office suites.

Using Wine to Run Windows Applications

The Wine project chose its name in the fine GNU recursive-acronym tradition: *Wine Is Not (an) Emulator*, or so it says. Nonetheless, this open source project has been helping Linux users run Windows applications for a long time.

As mentioned in the overview, Wine works by attempting to turn Windows system calls into Linux kernel calls, in part by making the Windows application think it is resting comfortably in a Windows directory.

The Wine environment is targeted for Windows 98, and so applications behave as though they were running under Windows 98.

So far, this is not a problem, but now that Microsoft has dropped support for this operating system, other companies are likely to follow suit. Nonetheless, be careful when buying new applications that you want to run under Wine. Confirm that they will run under Windows 98, and then check the Wine applications database.

Installing and Configuring Wine

Getting Wine going is a two-step process. First, you must install the Wine package from YaST. This makes the Wine commands available, but does not create the environment or install any software.

An easy way to get things underway is to install the WineTools package. This is included in your openSUSE DVD, and is also available from http://www.von-thadden.de/Joachim/WineTools. This gives you a simple GUI tool to configure Wine and install a few essential applications. It comes in both RPM and tarball packages. Install this package via YaST or command line.

NOTE

Depending on your system and version of Wine, you may get a dependency error for `xdialog`. You can safely ignore this and install anyway.

When you have WineTools installed, go to a shell prompt (as user) and type **`winetools`**. The WineTools menu (see Figure 11.1) appears.

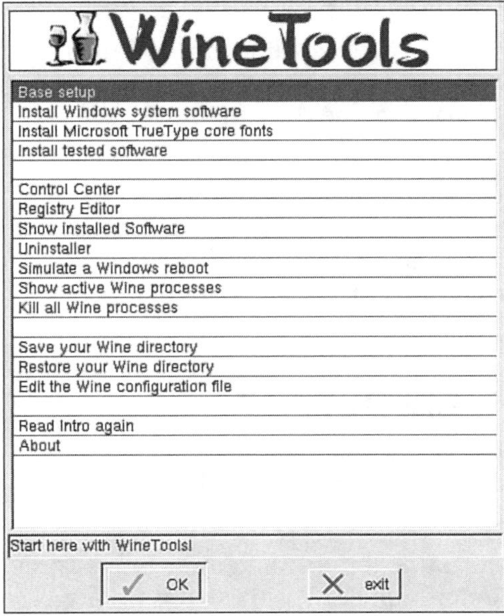

FIGURE 11.1 WineTools simplifies your Wine installation.

The WineTools menu is organized so that you run each tool in order and have a fully capable basic installation at the end. Begin with the Base Setup, which will create your `fake_windows` directories and handle the basic Wine configuration (see Figure 11.2).

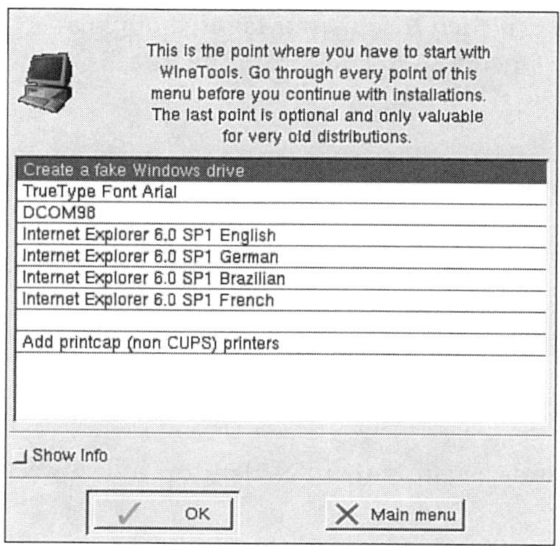

FIGURE 11.2 Create your base Wine configuration with this menu.

In addition to creating your Wine drive, use this menu to install DCOM98, an essential component for Microsoft Component Object Model (COM) applications, and Internet Explorer. When you've worked your way through this menu, click Main Menu to return.

TIP

An alternative way to install Internet Explorer 6 using Wine is with the IEs4linux package. This package installs IE in your /home directory and puts an icon on your desktop. See the tip in Chapter 14, "Creating Basic Websites" for more information.

Continue working through the WineTools menus to install Windows system tools and fonts. Then explore the list of tested software for common, downloadable applications. Although broken down into categories, the list is not comprehensive, but it will give you a good start.

Installing Windows Applications Under Wine

When you have Wine up and running, installing new applications is no different from installing any others, as long as you remember to keep it within the Wine framework.

Before installing any new Windows application, consult the Wine Applications database at http://appdb.winehq.org. Search for the application you want to install, or browse through the categories. You'll learn here what applications have worked for those who have tried; often included are helpful comments on imperfections, problems installing, and the like. Most, if not all, entries include links to the product website. This is especially helpful for downloadable applications.

Armed with information from the database, you can then install your favorite application. To do so, insert your installation CD-ROM. Open a shell and locate the install program with `ls`.

```
ls /media/cdrom
```

If the install program is `setup.exe`, type the following to launch it in Wine:

```
wine "D:\setup.exe" &
```

The installation program should run the same as it would in Windows. It's probably best to accept the program's default settings during the installation. You can always experiment later.

Downloading applications in Internet Explorer and installing them is identical to the way you would do so in Windows.

Running Wine

Starting Wine applications can be tricky. Some applications conveniently store an icon in your desktop environment's Wine menu. Others (QuickTime and Opera, for example) even place an icon on your desktop. More often, however, you are going to be working from the shell.

As indicated in the previous section, you then enter something of a land betwixt and between, including drive-letter references. To run Internet Explorer, for example, you need to type the following:

```
wine "C:\Program Files\Internet Explorer\IEXPLORE.EXE " &
```

Make sure the quotation marks, the Windows-style backslashes, the spaces, and the capitalization are all exactly as you see it here.

Two other GUI alternatives exist. The first, the Wine package, comes with a very rudimentary file manager called Winefile, and locating and launching files is all it's really good at. Unfortunately, you can't change the display so that it shows only executables. However, the free and powerful Windows file manager, PowerDesk 5, works nicely (although somewhat imperfectly) in Wine, as you can see in Figure 11.3.

The third option for the GUI-inclined is to go to your desktop environment's Control Panel and associate files with the EXE extension with Wine. You can then use Konqueror or Nautilus to locate and run your Wine applications.

Crossover Linux

Crossover Linux is a commercial spinoff of the Wine Project. Codeweavers is a company founded by several Wine developers that first created the Crossover Plugin, allowing Internet Explorer plug-ins to run in all the major Linux browsers. This project was followed up with the Crossover Office suite, now called Crossover Linux because of the expanded variety of Windows products, including games, it now supports.

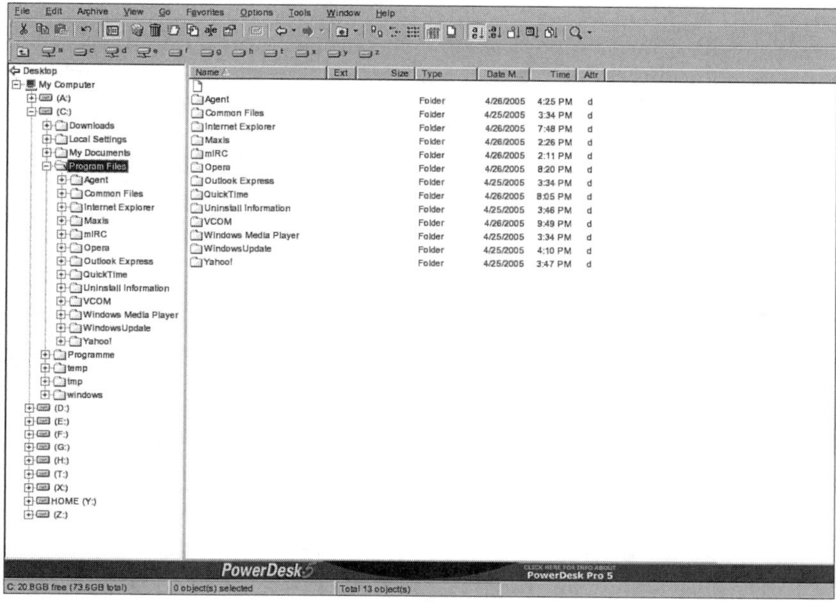

FIGURE 11.3 You can manage your Wine files easily with this third-party Windows file manager, VCOM PowerDesk.

Crossover allows its users to run Microsoft's flagship products—Office, Internet Explorer, and Visio—along with several other high-profile Windows applications. The current version even plays a few games, including World of Warcraft. Early versions of what is now the SUSE Linux Enterprise Desktop included Crossover Office.

Installing Windows Applications with Crossover

Running Windows programs under Crossover takes some resource overhead, so Codeweavers recommends downloading the free 30-day trial before buying directly. Download the install shell script, and run it (as a user) to get things started.

Once you've completed the initial install, you can install your applications one at a time. From the KDE menu, go to Applications, then Crossover, then Install Windows Applications. You'll see the list of supported applications. Most of these require a CD-ROM to install, but some are free applications downloadable over the Internet, like Internet Explorer 6. Select the application you want to install and click Next.

Crossover puts applications in (Wine) "bottles," representing different Windows versions. It's a very good idea to stick with the developers' recommended choice of bottle. Older applications generally go into the Win98 bottle, while Microsoft Office 2003 goes into the Win2000 bottle. These bottles will be created once by the installer and used by other applications as needed.

Insert your install CD, and follow the prompts to install your application. At the end of the process, you'll be asked whether you want to install other applications or exit the installer. If you're installing Microsoft Office, you'll want to pick up the relevant service packs before exiting entirely.

Running Crossover

Crossover integrates well with your favorite desktop environment. Go to the Applications menu, then Windows Applications (not Crossover—this is the administrative part, where you install and manage your applications). Select from the menu of installed programs.

Opening Word gives you a very standard interface, complete with Help panel, and the standard invitation to help Microsoft's customer satisfaction program in the taskbar. Click the Open File icon, and it opens in your ~/Documents folder (not the fake My Documents directory, which would be empty).

Running Windows Applications with Win4Lin

Win4Lin, formerly Netraverse, is a company that delivers Windows-on-Linux products for different audiences:

- Win4Lin 9x allows you to install and run a Windows 98 or Me virtual machine, along with any application.
- Win4Lin Pro is a virtual machine for Windows 2000 and XP that pledges to do for these permission-based operating systems what its sister products do for the consumer line of Windows.

You can order and download all three products directly from Win4Lin. All offer a free 30-day trial, after which you can buy a license code for permanent use.

TIP

Both Win4Lin Pro and VMware require kernel headers for your existing kernel. Although some distributions have a separate package for the headers, openSUSE is not one of them. Install the full kernel-source package from YaST before installing either of these virtual machine creators. Aside from pointing the installer to the location of the kernel headers (which is /usr/src/linux-<full_kernel_version_number>/<architecture>/default/include), you will not have to do any other manipulation of the sources.

See Chapter 24, "Kernel and Module Management" for more information on kernel sources.

Installing Win4Lin Pro

After registering and downloading the RPM package from http://www.win4lin.com, you have choices for installing Win4Lin. The easy way is to let YaST (or your favorite package manager) handle it. KDE users can open the Win4Lin package in Konqueror and find a big button labeled Install Package with YaST. GNOME/Nautilus users can right-click the same package and choose from any of your installed package managers. These applications, which you'll learn more about in Chapter 21, "Keeping Your System Current: Package Management," simplify the process of installation and updates.

You can also do the install the old fashioned way, at the command line. Open a shell and log in as the SuperUser. Go to the directory you downloaded the package to. Type **`rpm -ivh Win4LinPro-`*`<version>`*`.i386.rpm`**. This would be for the 32-bit version; Win4Lin also comes in a 64-bit package if you have the right processor. This is one of those times when the shell's file completion feature comes in handy, so entering the first few letters of the filename and then tabbing should work.

Regardless of the method you chose to install the Win4Lin RPM, you'll be asked a few questions about how you want to configure Win4Lin. Generally, it's OK to accept the defaults. You should think about how much physical memory you want to allocate to Windows. The default is 128 MB, but if you plan to install any large applications (like MS Office apps), you should have at least 256 MB. This consideration is partially dependent on how much memory you have, but even if you are blessed with multiple gigabytes of memory, you don't want to allocate it all to your Windows client, leaving poor Linux starving in the process.

In just a few minutes, you'll see the One-Click-2-Windows application ready to install your Windows client. That one click will create the GUEST.IMG file that acts like a separate partition and allows you to install your client OS. Have your Windows CD and product key ready. As with any Windows installation, it will take some time to complete.

After completing the Windows installation, your desktop-within-a-desktop will appear. Use the Start button to shut down Windows. You should back up the Win4Lin image file immediately. Go to the `~/winpro` directory, and type **`cp GUEST.IMG GUEST.IMG.backup`**. Do this periodically as well, before installing new software or updating Windows.

Running Win4Lin

Launching Win4Lin is simple enough. From the shell, type **`winpro`**. You can also use the SUSE menu; Win4Lin Pro is located under Utilities, More Programs. This will bring up the virtual machine (see Figure 11.4).

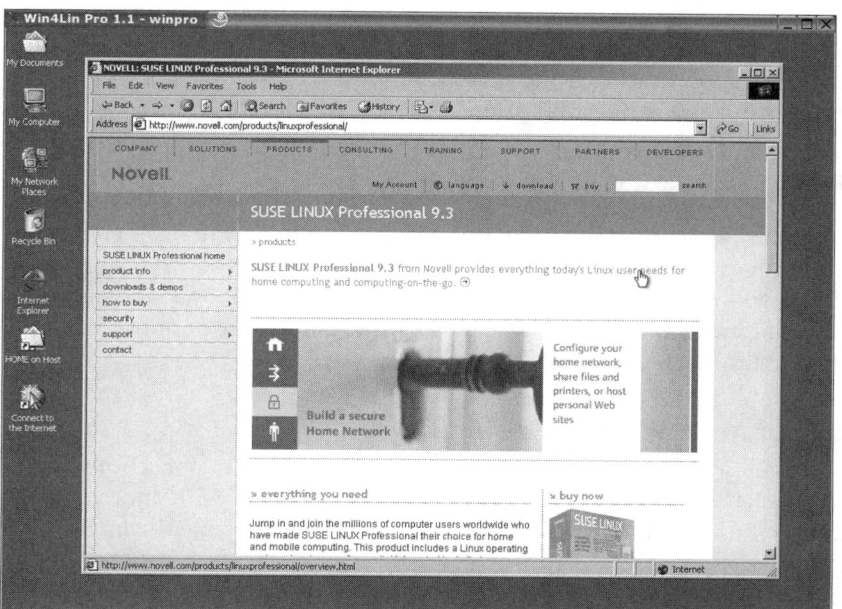

FIGURE 11.4 The Win4Lin Pro environment puts a complete Windows 2000 or XP virtual machine at your disposal.

Install your Windows applications as you would normally in Windows. CDs will not always launch the installation program, but you can open Windows Explorer to access CD contents.

Running Windows Applications with VMware

VMware offers a plethora of products designed primarily for enterprise customers to run and test applications and operating systems in a virtual machine environment. (hence the VM). Two of these products are of interest to the openSUSE user. VMware Server is designed as a server machine that "abstract(s) processor, memory, storage and networking resources" across different VMs/operating systems, according to the company website. VMware Player does the same thing for desktop systems. Both the Server and Player packages have separate host packages for Linux and Windows and support clients for all varieties of Windows and several other Linux distributions. The virtual machine is complete, down to its own BIOS.

The target audience for VMware primarily consists of cross-platform software developers and testers, along with system administrators. Developers can test their products on a single machine running Red Hat, Fedora Core, openSUSE, Novell NetWare, or any and all varieties of Windows. The system administrator can run tests to see what effect the latest Windows Service Pack or antivirus upgrade would have on his or her system.

This section will focus on running a Windows virtual machine on openSUSE.

Installing VMware

Go to the VMware website to download the Player software. You have a choice of installation packages, either RPM or standard tarball. You can use YaST to install the RPM or extract the tarball as the SuperUser from the shell. Consult the VMware User's Guide (available from the Documentation section of the VMware website) for instructions.

Regardless of how you do the initial package installation, you then run `vmware-config.pl`, the Perl script that will help you configure VMware's host program.

Read the configuration options carefully, accepting the defaults is okay, too. To ensure that your virtual machines use the same network and Internet access you have with openSUSE, use the default Bridged Networking. `Vmware-config.pl` tells you when it has completed its task and returns the prompt to you. When it's finished, exit out of your SuperUser shell and return to the plain user prompt.

Making Space for Your Virtual Machine

Unlike Win4Lin, VMware Player does not create its own space for a virtual machine. You need to make a virtual hard disk to hold the Player image. This is done with another virtualization tool called qemu. Install this with YaST, and go to a shell to create the image.

First, make a Guest directory in your /home:

```
mkdir ~/Guest
```

Change to this directory. You should put all files related to this virtual machine in this directory. The Player looks for a VMware Disk Image with a .vmdk extension, so let's make one. At the shell, in the Guest directory, type:

```
qemu-img create -f vmdk hd.vmdk 10G
```

This creates a 10 gigabyte image called hd.vmdk. This should be plenty of space for our Windows install, but adjust as necessary.

Next up is configuring our virtual machine. A sample configuration for a Windows machine is located at http://www.ffnn.nl/media/articles/linux/vmware-player-images/template-windows.vmx.

Edit this configuration file in any text editor. Most lines can be left as is. Some exceptions include the following:

- The first line of the configuration file should look like this to point to the Player:

  ```
  #!/usr/bin/vmplayer
  ```

- The displayName should indicate the type of virtual machine this is, and this setting appears in the Player window. Thus, if you're running Windows XP, this line should be Windows XP. If you're running a particular application, say GNOME, in this player window, the window should display that name.
- The guestOS defines the operating system that will be in charge here. In this example, you can define it as "WinXPHome" or "WinXPPro".
- As with Win4Lin, you must set the upper limit of the Player's memory use in the memsize line. For a Windows XP installation, you should enter at least 128 here (this is set in megabyte units), and probably much more. This will depend on how much physical memory you have, and the applications you want to run in the virtual machine.
- We're installing Windows from its CD-ROM. To do this, we have to make some changes in the ide1:0 section of the file. This section should look like this:

  ```
  ide1:0.present = "TRUE"
  ide1:0.deviceType = "cdrom-raw"
  ide1:0.autodetect = "TRUE"
  ide1:0.startConnected = "TRUE"
  ide1:0.fileName = "auto-detect"
  ```

- The ide0:0.fileName line should point to the VMware Disk Image we made earlier:

  ```
  ide0:0.fileName = "hd.vmdk"
  ```

Save this edited configuration file as windows.vmx to the Guest directory, and you're ready to run the VMware Player.

Running VMware

The next step is running VMware and installing a guest OS. Put your Windows CD in the drive. From the Guest directory in the shell, type **`vmplayer windows.vmx &`** (or press Alt+F2 in your desktop environment and type the same command) to launch the application. The home screen with the initial Windows install screen will appear.

> **TIP**
>
> You can also launch VMware Player from the KDE System menu. Look under Other Programs.

When you have finished installing your guest OS, you can work in it, or shut it down. The next time you run VMplayer, you'll be asked to locate the guest again.

The virtual machine will take control of your mouse, but you can regain control by pressing Ctrl+Alt. When the installation is complete, run Windows Update so you can see what updates are required for your computer's operating system, software, and hardware.

To install a new application in your virtual machine, power up the VM and then insert your CD. In Windows, the CD should autorun and install as per usual. If it doesn't, run Windows Explorer and locate the installer on the CD.

Running applications may not be 100% as responsive in the VM as in a more normal environment, but it's pretty good. You will be able to discover the same errors in an application that would appear in the standard environment, which makes it good for testing. But games play well, too.

Always remember to shut down your client operating system before exiting VMware.

Emulating a Mac with Basilisk II

The Apple Macintosh operating system, and the computers it powers, generates intense loyalty from its many users.

Many applications programmed for the Mac are indeed great. But because the MacOS was never designed to run on Intel PC chips, building an emulator, or even a virtual machine, is a difficult task. Credit Christian Bauer, the creator of Basilisk II, a free GPLed and stable MacOS Classic emulator, with rising to the challenge.

Basilisk II works on Linux, Solaris, FreeBSD, Windows, Amiga, and BeOS and will emulate any 68K version of MacOS up to 8.1 (although a port has been written for OS X). You need a valid ROM image from your Mac to make this work. This ROM image contains several applications, including the Mac Toolbox and QuickDraw, and is otherwise indispensable.

Basilisk II supports various Mac color displays and peripheral drivers. It will also connect to the Internet and your LAN.

However, the task is not for the faint of heart. You will need to create Linux-readable Mac floppies to copy the ROM image. You will need to compile Basilisk II from source. You may have to download and install a new copy of the MacOS. Fortunately, you will find an excellent companion for this journey in "Basilisk II for Linux—Getting It Going from Start to Finish," a tutorial from Marc Hoffman at http://os-emulation.net/basiliskII/system753_tutorial/linux/. Several support forums exist at the Sourceforge project page, http://sourceforge.net/projects/basilisk/. Click the Forums tab.

Using `dosemu` and DOSBox

DOSBox and the venerable `dosemu` are DOS emulators you can install with YaST. `dosemu` can run all sorts of DOS programs, and it comes with a GPL version of DOS, called FreeDOS. DOSBox comes with a graphics package, making it particularly suitable for running games. If you are lucky enough to have a spare copy of Windows 3.x, you can install it under `dosemu` as well. Both applications can be installed by YaST, and DOSBox inserts itself into the KDE System menu.

`dosemu` is a little harder to run because it must run outside of X Window System the first time. This is done somewhat easily by launching a virtual console. Press Ctrl+Alt+F1 (or any of the F keys except 7, which belongs to X).

You'll be asked to log in with your password as User. To launch `dosemu`, enter the program name **`dosemu`** at this shell prompt.

You'll be asked for a copy of DOS; pressing Enter will install FreeDOS. By default, your Home directory will be your C drive. You'll then be presented with your C:\ prompt and can run any default program or install your copy of WordPerfect 5.1.

When you're done with the Virtual Console, type **`exit`** and then press **`Ctrl+Alt+F7`** to return to your X desktop.

Xen: The Future of Virtualization?

Since 2003, researchers at Cambridge University in Britain have been working on a new method of virtualizing operating systems. Their project, called Xen, reached a critical mass of support in early 2005.

Unlike VMware, which builds a complete virtual machine, Xen is a *hypervisor*, a layer that doesn't quite go that far. This technology vastly improves the performance of guest operating systems in tests to nearly native performance. This requires a special Xen version of each supported OS kernel. openSUSE implements this is by using the standard kernel for a standard installation, putting the Xen kernel into `/boot`, and then using the grub bootloader application to boot to either the Xen kernel or the standard kernel.

Xen developers have ported several open source kernels, including the 2.4 and 2.6 Linux kernels, NetBSD Unix, FreeBSD Unix, and the Plan9 OS, so you can use Xen today to run several Linux distributions side by side with a copy of FreeBSD to spare. This might be entertaining for some users, but is especially useful to programmers hoping to solve distribution-related problems. It's also useful when testing pre-release versions of distributions like openSUSE.

The key question for many users is whether Windows will join the list of supported OSs at some point. As of this writing, Windows Server 2003 will run on SUSE Linux Enterprise Server 10 with newer processors from Intel (Dual Cores and Xeons with Virtualization Technology) and AMD (AMD-V). You should not see all the performance you get with directly ported kernels, but the application support on these processors may well exceed Wine's.

SUSE Linux 9.3 was the first Linux distribution to include a copy of Xen, even integrating it into YaST. In openSUSE, however, installing the Xen packages automatically adds the Xen kernel to your grub bootloader menu. In this section, we will install the Xen server packages, and then install a fresh disk image.

CAUTION

You can install Xen as part of an openSUSE install, but be sure to complete the openSUSE install and at least one initial update before running Xen the first time. Both your Xen and Linux kernels should be up to date before booting to Xen. In addition, you may find you need to install proprietary video drivers (nVidia and ATI) to run the Xen server properly.

Installing the Xen Server

In previous SUSE Linux releases, installing Xen was a combination of downloading kernels, configuring YaST, and then modifying the grub menu.lst by hand, and hoping Xen recognized everything when you booted. While still not perfect, the install is much easier in openSUSE Linux.

If you didn't install the Xen packages as part of your original openSUSE install (these packages are not installed by default), open the YaST Software Management module, and select Patterns from the Filters drop-down menu. Scroll to the Server Functions pattern, and you'll see the Xen Virtual Machine Host Server. All nine packages in the pattern should be checked. Click Accept to install the Xen Server packages.

YaST will then download and install these packages. Included in the set is the YaST VM module that will automatically install the Xen kernel and configure the grub bootloader to include the Xen kernel.

When the installation is complete, take a look at the YaST Bootloader module, located on the System page. You'll see the Xen kernel is the new default OS, meaning that if you start your machine up, and don't select something from the grub menu, you'll boot to Xen (and whatever client OS is running there). This setting may be fine for installing a fresh OS in Xen, but you may want to reconfigure this later.

Meanwhile, select the Xen kernel in the menu and click Edit. It's good to know where this kernel is stored, and you'll see it's in the /boot directory. You may be surprised to see this is just a 1.6MB file (and a symlink that isn't tied to the kernel version). This kernel will, in turn, serve as the host for its associated virtual machine.

Close YaST, and restart your computer. If not already selected, click the Xen kernel from your grub menu on reboot. The Xen server should soon appear.

NOTE

If you cannot boot to a graphical login screen with the Xen kernel, you may be having a problem with your video driver. Login as Root from the shell prompt, and type **startx**. If you get an error message about not being able to load the video driver into the kernel, contact your video card manufacturer for a solution.

Installing a Guest OS in Xen

Once the server is set up, go back to YaST. In the System page, the Virtual Machine Management (Xen) module awaits your configuration. When the Manage Virtual Machines screen comes up, click Add. If you have a disk image to apply to the Xen server, that's an option. For this example, however, you'll do a new installation.

Review the default settings for your Xen guest installation on the Virtual Machine (Installation Settings) screen. As with the other virtual machine packages, you have to define the size of the virtual partition, how much memory it will use, your network card settings, and identify where your OS installation program is located (ISO images, CD/DVD, or network installation). You should name the guest machine as well. If you are installing from DVD, put the disk in the drive before clicking Next.

The OS installation program launches. Proceed with the installation, and you're in business. The installation should go normally, though possibly a little slow, depending on how much memory you allocated to the VM.

Installing a Guest OS from Multiple CDs or CD Images

If you want to install a pre-release alpha or beta in Xen for testing, you may run into problems. Generally speaking, the openSUSE project offers only downloads of separate CD images, instead of one simple DVD medium. At some point, the installation program will want you to change CDs. If you try to do this from the YaST module, though, the install will end prematurely. You must follow these steps before changing CDs:

1. Open a terminal window and type **`xm list`**. Note the name and the ID of the VM you are creating.
2. Type **`xm block-list`** ***<vm_ID>*** where *vm_ID* is the ID number of the VM. Decide which device is the mounted ISO image (or CD) and note its Vdev number. Usually the last device displayed in the list is a mounted ISO image because the first devices are usually disk drives.
3. Type **`xm block-detach`** ***<vm_ID> <Vdev_number>***. This command allows the VM to eject the CD from the drive.

4. Type **`eject`** to eject the CD.
5. Put the next CD in the drive.
6. Type **`cat /etc/xen/vm/`*`<vm_name>`*` ¦ grep disk`** where *`vm_name`* is the name of the VM you are creating. Note the attach string of the CD reader, which is usually listed towards the end of the output string and prefaced with phy: (for example, `phy:/dev/sr0,hdb,r`). You will need it in the next step.
7. Enter **`xm block-attach`** ***`<vm_ID>`*** ***`<attach_string>`*** where *`vm_ID`* is the VM's ID number and *`attach_string`* is the attach string for the CD drive (for example, xm block-attach 1 phy:/dev/sr0 hdb r). Put spaces instead of commas between the `attach_string` parameters.
8. Return to the VM's installation program window and press OK to continue. Repeat process as required.

You should now have a working system in Xen.

References

- http://www.winehq.org—The Wine Project headquarters. Be sure to vote for your favorite Windows application to be ported using Wine in the Applications Database section.
- http://www.von-thadden.de/Joachim/WineTools—WineTools offers a relatively painless installation of Wine and a number of well-known free applications, including Internet Explorer.
- http://www.codeweavers.com—Codeweavers, Inc., the makers of Crossover Linux.
- http://frankscorner.org—This site helps you get the most out of Wine. It includes FAQs and HOWTOs to get you through most problems.
- http://www.fs-driver.org—The ext2/3 IFS driver for Windows lets you open and copy files from your ext2/3 partition to a FAT or NTFS partition. It even creates a drive letter for that system.
- http://www.vmware.com—VMware Inc., where you can get information the free Server and Player products, and a free 30-day evaluation copy of the workstation virtual machine.
- http://www.win4lin.com—Win4Lin, building Windows virtual machines.
- http://dosbox.sourceforge.net—The DOSBox site. Check on support for your DOS game and even find downloadable copies of some ancient games.
- http://dosemu.org—The home of `dosemu`, the DOS emulator.
- http://www.freedos.org—The FreeDOS project. Assorted applications to use in DOSBox or `dosemu`.

- http://basilisk.cebix.net/—Home of the Basilisk II MacOS emulator.
- http://os-emulation.net/basiliskII/system753_tutorial/linux—A tutorial on installing and running Basilisk II on Linux.
- http://xensource.com—The commercial side of Xen development.
- http://www.cl.cam.ac.uk/Research/SRG/netos/xen—The Xen virtual machine monitor project home.
- http://www.ffnn.nl/pages/articles/linux/vmware-player-image-creation.php—Creating a VMware Player image, with links to empty images you can download.
- http://sourceforge.net/projects/basilisk—The Basilisk II Project page. Find user forums here.

PART III
Using the Internet

IN THIS PART

CHAPTER 12

Connecting to the Internet

IN THIS CHAPTER

As it has over the last decade, the Internet is a prime driver of computer sales all over the world. People want to get access to the treasures of the World Wide Web, send email and instant messages to friends and family, learn more about this spam thing they keep hearing about—well, maybe not that.

With all due respect to the SUSE employees in Germany, it is difficult to imagine Linux existing without the Internet bringing together programmers from around the world to work on the kernel and all the other packages that make Linux what it is today. For that reason alone, it makes sense that making a connection to the Internet is a priority and a relatively simple proposition in openSUSE.

openSUSE provides many tools to access and manage your Internet experience. In the next few chapters, we'll go over the ways to create websites, manage email, upload and download files, and collaborate with others using Instant Messaging, mailing lists, Usenet news, Wikis, and video conferencing.

In this chapter, we will focus on the basics of getting connected, be it through an ordinary dial-up modem or a high-speed Digital Subscriber Line (DSL).

Basic Connectivity Information

If you already have an Internet connection running under Windows, it is best to gather some information beforehand to make your Linux Internet setup go a little easier. There are still not enough Linux users for many ISPs to pay attention to them. Some ISPs remain ignorant of or hostile to the Linux users they already have. This leads to a general lack of Linux support, especially from the main players.

This means you are not likely to get a shiny CD from your ISP with everything to get you started, but YaST will be there as always to handle that function. The things you need to know most are the following:

- How your IP address is determined—Static or Dynamic (DHCP)
- The IP address(es) for your Domain Name System (DNS) server, especially for dynamic connections
- The DNS names and IP addresses for your mail and news servers
- The dial-up phone number for your ISP if you're using a dial-up connection
- Your credentials, such as your username and password

Every computer connected to the Internet must have a unique Internet Protocol (IP) address. The vast majority of standard ISP connections use the Dynamic Host Configuration Protocol (DHCP) to assign each logged-in user with an unoccupied server.

NOTE

You'll learn more about TCP/IP and DHCP networking in Chapter 25, "Setting Up Networks and Samba."

An ISP will then get a range of IP addresses that allow it to connect to the Internet. As a user about to configure your system, you may need to find out what that range is. Often this will be in your ISP's documentation booklet. If it's not there and you have a Windows XP box already connected, check the Network Connections in your Control Panel. You should see your connection listed. Double-click to open it, and then click the Support tab. This will tell you whether you are using DHCP for access or DNS service and should tell you all the necessary IP address(es).

You can also get to this information from a Windows command prompt. Go to Programs, Accessories, and then Command Prompt. Type **`ipconfig`** and you will get the IP Address, Subnet Mask, and Default Gateway addresses. This command is the Windows analog to the Linux `ifconfig` utility, which you will learn more about in the next section and in Chapter 25.

NOTE

Depending on your ISP, the range may not be required to make your connection.

If you have a high-speed connection, you may receive a static IP, but even these are often handled by DHCP. Regardless of your connection type, many ISPs will offer you a static IP address, for a price. Unless you want to directly host a server (mail, FTP, DNS), this is not required.

Starting with a `localhost` Interface

Before setting up any kind of Internet connection, you'll need to create a dummy interface that the TCP/IP protocol uses to determine the network capability of your machine. This is called the *loopback (lo) interface*, or `localhost`. Many network-aware applications reference this interface as well, so it is important.

What is a loopback interface? To a Linux networking driver, this is a network composed of exactly one computer. The kernel loops back network traffic to and from itself using the 127.0.0.1 IP address.

openSUSE should create the `localhost` interface during the initial installation. To confirm this, open a Root console and run the `ifconfig` utility to identify your setup. Running this command should generate a response similar to this:

```
lo        Link encap:Local Loopback
          inet addr:127.0.0.1  Mask:255.0.0.0
          inet6 addr: ::1/128 Scope:Host
          UP LOOPBACK RUNNING  MTU:16436  Metric:1
          RX packets:2187 errors:0 dropped:0 overruns:0 frame:0
          TX packets:2187 errors:0 dropped:0 overruns:0 carrier:0
          collisions:0 txqueuelen:0
          RX bytes:114362 (111.6 Kb)  TX bytes:114362 (111.6 Kb)
```

This output tells you that the local loopback interface is active and is assigned the standard IP address for local connections, 127.0.0.1, and a broadcast mask of 255.0.0.0 is used. You even take a small peek into the future, as this version of ifconfig lists an IPv6 address of `::1/128`. This next version of the Internet Protocol (IP version 6) offers exponentially more IP address space than the existing IP version 4.

Configuring `localhost` Manually

In the off chance `localhost` was not created during your openSUSE installation, it is easy to do yourself.

The `localhost` interface address is stored in a text file called `/etc/hosts`. This file stores all network IP address and hostname information. The kernel and other network utilities read this to understand how this computer is connected to others.

TIP

You can also access and edit the Hosts file in YaST. Go to Network Services, then Hosts. Add, edit, or delete hosts here.

When you open this file, you will see a comment that describes the file and the syntax you should follow: `IP-Address [tab] Full-Qualified-Hostname [tab] Short-Hostname`.

If `localhost` is not already there, you may add this line:

```
127.0.0.1        localhost
```

You can leave the `Short-Hostname` blank. Save and exit. Reopen your Root console and use `ifconfig` and `route` to create the interface:

```
ifconfig lo 127.0.0.1
```

This puts the `localhost` interface in memory, as with all other Linux network interfaces, like an Ethernet (`eth0`) or dial-up (`ppp0`) interface.

```
route add 127.0.0.1 lo
```

This adds the IP address to a routing table the kernel's networking code uses to track routes to different addresses.

Test the new connection by running **`ifconfig`** again.

You should now be able to run your own loopback test by trying to ping `localhost`. You should see something like this (we'll use the `-c` option to count out 3 packets to send):

```
 # ping -c 3 localhost
PING localhost (127.0.0.1) 56(84) bytes of data.
64 bytes from localhost (127.0.0.1): icmp_seq=1 ttl=64 time=0.087 ms
64 bytes from localhost (127.0.0.1): icmp_seq=2 ttl=64 time=0.087 ms
64 bytes from localhost (127.0.0.1): icmp_seq=3 ttl=64 time=0.081 ms

--- localhost ping statistics ---
3 packets transmitted, 3 received, 0% packet loss, time 2000ms
rtt min/avg/max/mdev = 0.081/0.085/0.087/0.003 ms
```

We have completed our prerequisites; now it's time to take on the main course.

Configuring Your Dial-up Internet Connection

Setting up a dial-up Internet connection under Linux used to be somewhat difficult without a deep knowledge of computer hardware, but YaST has greatly simplified this for the openSUSE user.

When you set up a dial-up connection, you're really just using several Internet standard protocols to enable your modem to connect to the ISP through an ordinary phone line. Most dial-up Internet connections use the Point-to-Point Protocol (PPP) because ISPs have found it a fast, efficient way to use TCP/IP over serial (that is, modem) lines. PPP is designed for two-way networking. The TCP/IP protocol suite moves the data.

If you couldn't really conceive of Linux as a successful operating system without the Internet, why was it so hard to set up a dial-up connection in Linux? It's true that Unix (and its Linux cousin) was network-aware from the very beginning, but these were assumed to be machines networked with wires and cards that could have static IP addresses. These workstations were located at research universities, corporate offices, and science labs, where users might log off the network, but the computer would always be there. Unix (and Linux) wasn't ready for computers that had intermittent connections. The protocols for personal computers to connect were kludged together and eventually made to work.

You may not need to entirely understand PPP anymore to dial up to the Internet, but following is a quick primer.

Setting up a dial-up connection is really installing the `pppd` daemon on your system. This daemon controls the use of PPP. Launching your connection runs two other processes.

The high-level data link control (HDLC) protocol controls the flow of information between your computer and your ISP's server, and the `chat` routine communicates with the modem, dials the number, and reports on the status of your connection (or occasional lack thereof).

If you want to confirm that `pppd` is installed, log in as SuperUser (**`su`**) and run **`pppd`** with the **`–help`** argument. You'll see the many parameters you can use to tune your connection, but veering from the defaults can be risky.

CAUTION

Some modems still have a software interface that will not work under Linux. See Chapter 2, "Preparing to Install openSUSE," for more information on Winmodems.

Using YaST to Set Up Your Dial-up Connection

YaST's Network Devices section manages setup wizards for several types of network connections:

- Modem
- Network card
- ISDN
- DSL

Although very similar, there are some distinctions. In this section, we'll cover the modem connection. The DSL connection will be in the next section, and the other networking protocols will be covered in Chapter 25.

Begin by opening YaST. In KDE, go to the Kicker menu and choose System, then YaST. You'll be asked for the Root password and YaST will load. Click Network Devices. You'll see the items previously listed. Click Modem to set up your connection.

YaST should have detected your modem, but you can easily do this if it hasn't. Click Configure under the top screen to launch the Modem Wizard. The first screen should look like Figure 12.1.

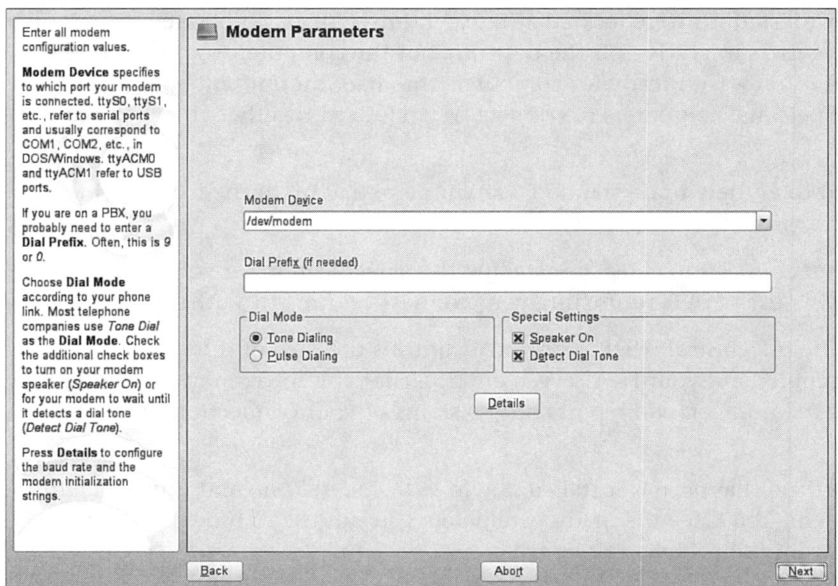

Enter all modem configuration values.
Modem Device specifies to which port your modem is connected. ttyS0, ttyS1, etc., refer to serial ports and usually correspond to COM1, COM2, etc., in DOS/Windows. ttyACM0 and ttyACM1 refer to USB ports.
If you are on a PBX, you probably need to enter a Dial Prefix. Often, this is 9 or 0.
Choose Dial Mode according to your phone link. Most telephone companies use Tone Dial as the Dial Mode. Check the additional check boxes to turn on your modem speaker (Speaker On) or for your modem to wait until it detects a dial tone (Detect Dial Tone).
Press Details to configure the baud rate and the modem initialization strings.
Modem Parameters
Modem Device
/dev/modem
Dial Prefix (if needed)
Dial Mode
Tone Dialing
Pulse Dialing
Special Settings
Speaker On
Detect Dial Tone
Details
Back
Abort
Next

FIGURE 12.1 The first modem configuration screen sets the mount point and dial mode.

This screen sets the mount point for the modem and a few initial settings. Using the default /dev/modem mount point is the easiest and should always work, but you can choose a different point from the drop-down menu. If you are in an office where you need to dial 9 to make an outside call, set the Dial Prefix. Modern phone systems nearly always use Tone dialing, so don't change this setting unless you are certain. If you don't like to hear the white noise that accompanies a connecting modem, turn the speaker off (although while you're doing the initial setup, it's a good idea to leave it on until you have confirmed that everything is working properly). If you have call waiting or some other service that changes your dial tone, you may want to uncheck the Detect Dial Tone box so that the modem always dials. Check the Details button only if you need to change the default initialization string. When you're finished, click Next to set up your ISP. YaST pulls up a list of Providers in several countries from which you can select. In Figure 12.2, we've selected Earthlink as our provider. Notice that the screen displays the provider's website and support line. If your provider is not listed, click New to add it. Click Next to identify the phone number and other access settings.

Figure 12.3 shows the ISP configuration screen. You should know at least one local access number for your ISP. Enter it here, along with your username and password. If you want to enter your ISP password each time you dial up, check the Always Ask for Password box. Click Next to configure your connection.

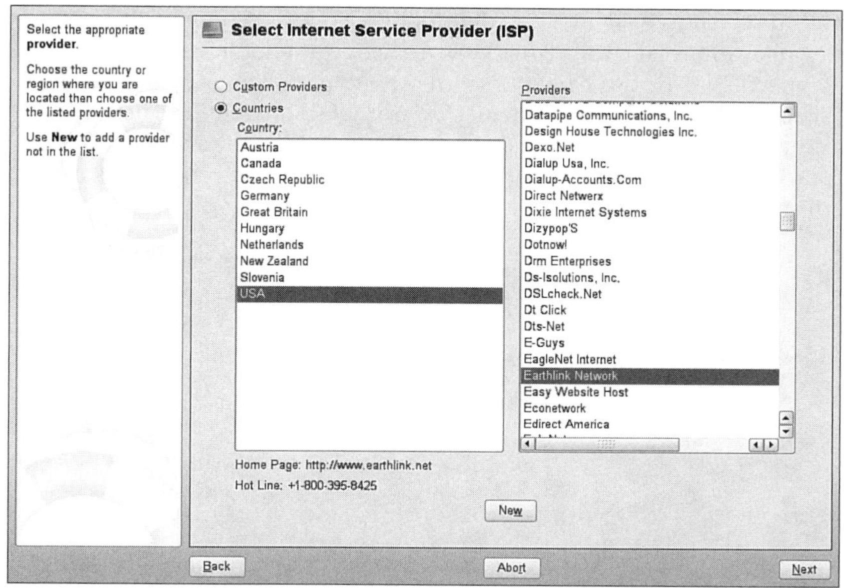

FIGURE 12.2 Select your ISP from the list of providers or click New to add yours.

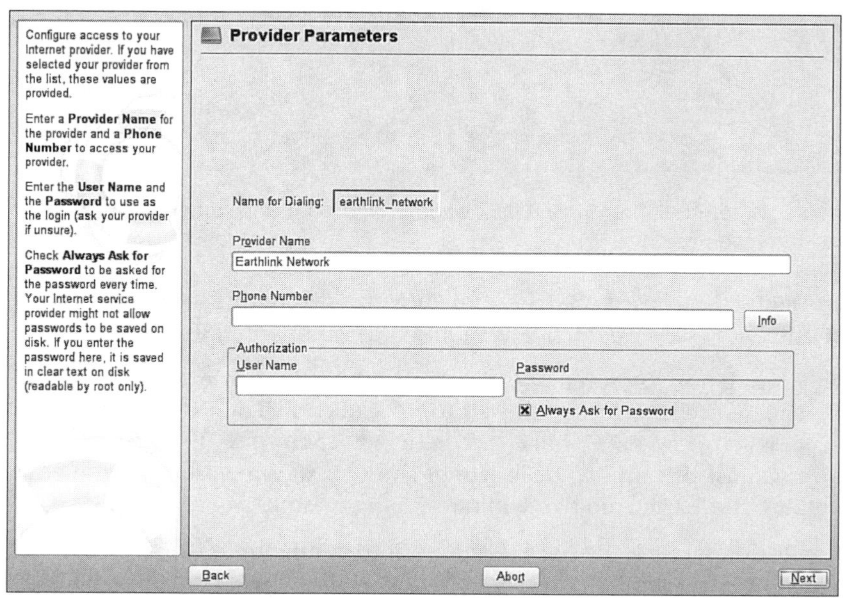

FIGURE 12.3 Enter your access number, username, and password on this screen.

The final configuration screen (see Figure 12.4) defines how you want to manage your connection. The key question to answer here is whether you want applications to be able to start a dial-up connection. This can be a nice thing when you ask your mail client to check mail and it dials up, but can be annoying if, for example, Software Updates wants to check for system updates at 2 a.m. daily and the modem speaker wakes you up. It is also not good if your ISP charges by the minute and an automatic connection does not hang up after completing its task.

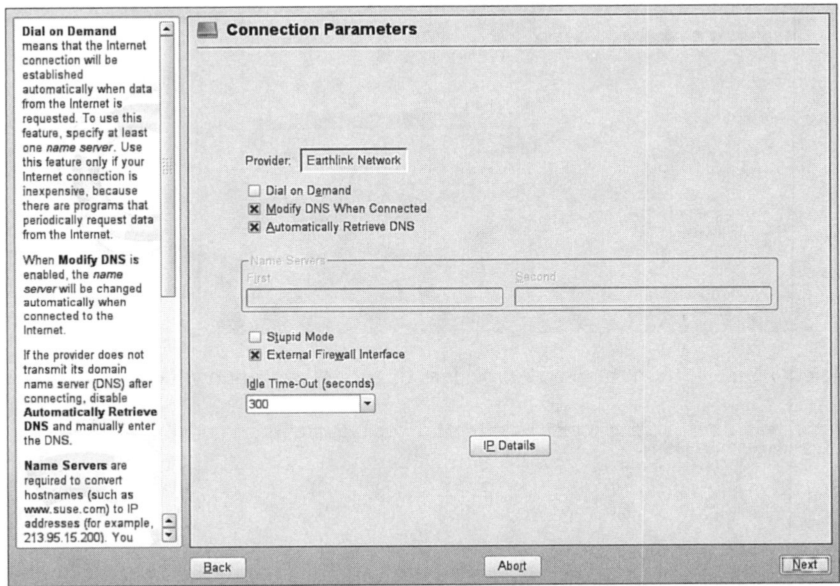

FIGURE 12.4 In this screen, tell openSUSE Linux whether you want applications to dial-up automatically or only when you ask.

By default, Dial on Demand is turned off. Check the box to activate this feature. You need to identify at least one name server (which you should have from your ISP).

Check the Activate Firewall box to prevent all incoming connections from attacking your computer. The Idle Timeout tells how long to wait for a dead connection to revive. By default, if the modem receives no data from the server for five minutes (300 seconds), it will hang up. You can adjust this time to be longer or shorter using the drop-down menu. Setting the Timeout at 0 means the modem will never hang up unless you tell it to.

If you have a static IP address, click the IP Details button to configure it. Uncheck the Dynamic IP box, and enter the static IP address in the Local IP Address box. Click OK to return to the previous screen. Click Next to complete the setup. You should now see your modem and provider listed in the appropriate windows. Should you have multiple ISPs, you must configure each separately. Click Add to start the wizard again.

When you click Finish, your new settings will be saved.

Test your new connection in KDE by running KInternet, or in GNOME by running GNOME PPP. It should use the new settings to dial up your ISP and get you going.

TIP

Another way to test your modem is through a terminal program such as `minicom`. This program is not installed by default, but if you are having problems connecting with your ISP, running `minicom` can help you troubleshoot problems with your modem.

Install `minicom` through YaST, and then run `minicom` from the shell with the `-s` argument to set your modem's serial port:

```
minicom -s
```

Tell `minicom` which serial port your modem is using, and then return to the main screen. Now you can send AT commands (check your modem documentation for examples) and see how the modem responds.

Configuring a Digital Subscriber Line (DSL) Connection

openSUSE supports all flavors of DSL connections, and they can all be set up in the YaST DSL configuration dialog boxes. DSL service generally provides 128KBps to 1.0MBps transfer speeds, transmitting over copper phone lines from a Central Office (CO) to individual subscribers, like you. Many DSL services offer asymmetric speeds, usually offering higher download speeds than upload.

DSL connections require you to have an Ethernet network interface card (NIC) in your computer. If you have multiple computers on a LAN that want to share the connection, you'll need to have at least one other NIC on the machine managing the connection.

Depending on your ISP, you may have a static IP address or use DHCP to assign a new IP address; it also uses a slightly different protocol called PPP Over Ethernet (PPPoE). This is difficult to configure manually through the shell, but YaST greatly simplifies this task.

Using YaST to Set Up Your DSL Connection

Setting up a DSL connection in YaST is very similar to setting up a modem connection. Begin by opening YaST. In KDE, go to the Kicker menu and choose System, then YaST. You'll be asked for the Root password and YaST will load. Click Network Devices. Click DSL to set up your connection.

NOTE

Many people get their high-speed Internet connection through their cable companies. Setting up these connections in openSUSE Linux is even easier than with DSL.

You should have a cable modem attached to a router when your service is installed. Connect your Ethernet network card to the router, then open YaST Network Devices. Go to the Network Card module (Figure 12.6) to confirm that your Ethernet card is configured properly, and you are set up.

The hardware devices involved in a DSL connection are a DSL modem and a network card (usually Ethernet). YaST handles configuring both of these in a DSL Devices page. When you open the DSL configuration page, YaST should have detected your devices during the install, but you can easily do this if it hasn't. Click Add under the top screen to launch the DSL Device Wizard. The first screen should look like Figure 12.5.

NOTE

To check or edit your existing DSL settings, select the device and click Edit. It will display the same options as the Add screen.

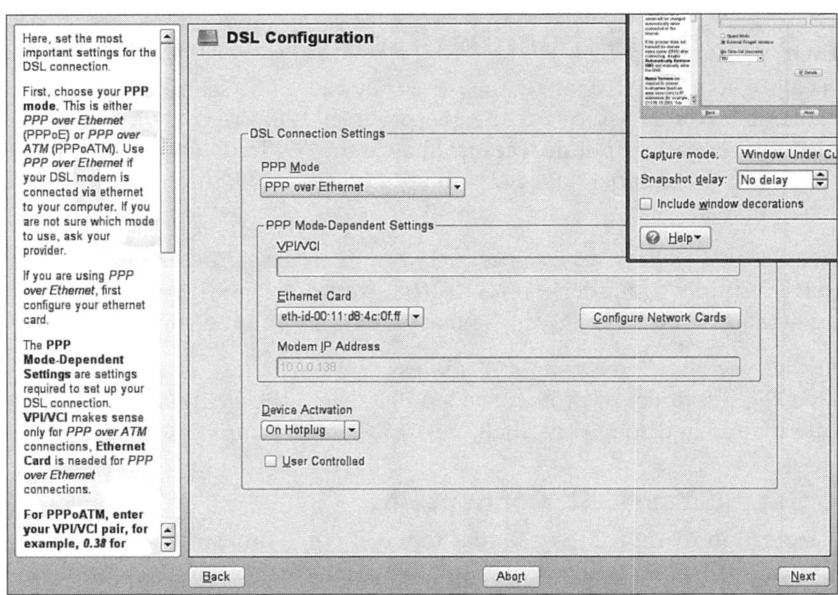

FIGURE 12.5 The first DSL configuration screen lets you identify the type of connection and the Ethernet card.

By default, YaST selects PPP Over Ethernet as the default PPP Mode. If your Ethernet card is not listed, you will need to set it up. Click Configure Network Cards to do so.

At first, you will see the overview screen. Figure 12.6 shows you this dialog box. If your card is not listed, click Add to open the configuration dialog box.

The configuration dialog box (see Figure 12.7) sets up your DSL card. It should be labeled as either `eth0` or `eth1`, depending on whether you have an Ethernet LAN card installed in addition to the DSL card.

Setting up for a static IP address is easy. Click the appropriate option button and enter your primary address and subnet mask. If your ISP uses DHCP to set addresses on bootup, you will need to configure other items on this screen.

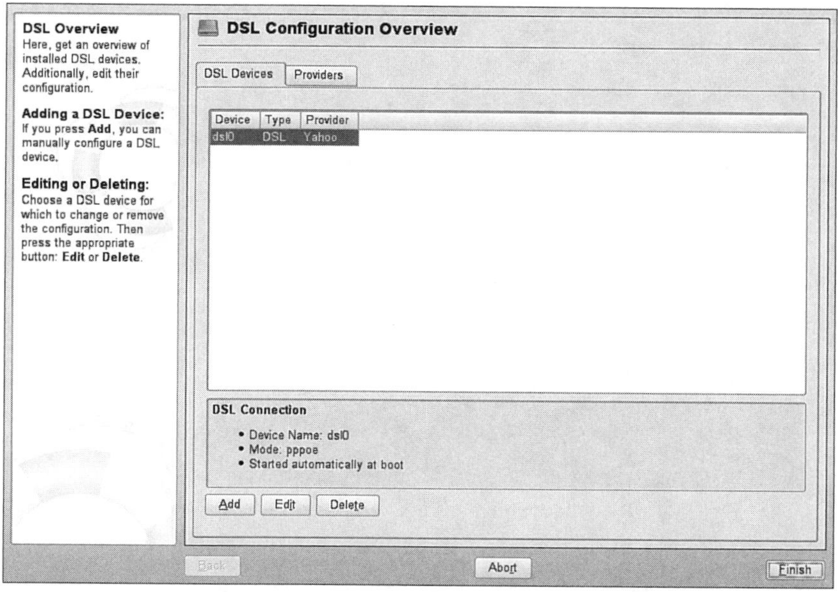

FIGURE 12.6 Use the Edit button on the Network Cards Configuration Overview page to change the existing settings for your DSL card, or use Add to define a new or undetected card.

Click DHCP Client Options and confirm that Host Name to Send is set to AUTO unless your ISP has specified a hostname. If your card is acting as a router, you may also want to look at the Routing page. You want to enable IP forwarding in this case.

Click Next to save your settings and return to the Network Card overview page, and click Finish to return to the DSL Setup page. When you're finished setting up your hardware, click Next to set up your ISP.

YaST pulls up a much smaller list of DSL Providers in several countries that you may select from in a screen like the one shown in Figure 12.2. If your provider is not listed, click New to add it. Click Next to set your username and password.

Figure 12.8 shows the ISP configuration screen. Enter your username and password. A DSL connection is always on, but when you reboot, the connection is dropped. If you want to enter your ISP password each time you connect, check the Always Ask for Password box. Click Next to configure your connection.

The final DSL provider configuration screen, which is identical to Figure 12.4, defines how you want to manage your connection. There is no real need to set up Dial on Demand, as you are always on. Similarly, you need not worry about the Idle Timeout setting. Do check the Activate Firewall box to prevent all incoming connections from attacking your computer.

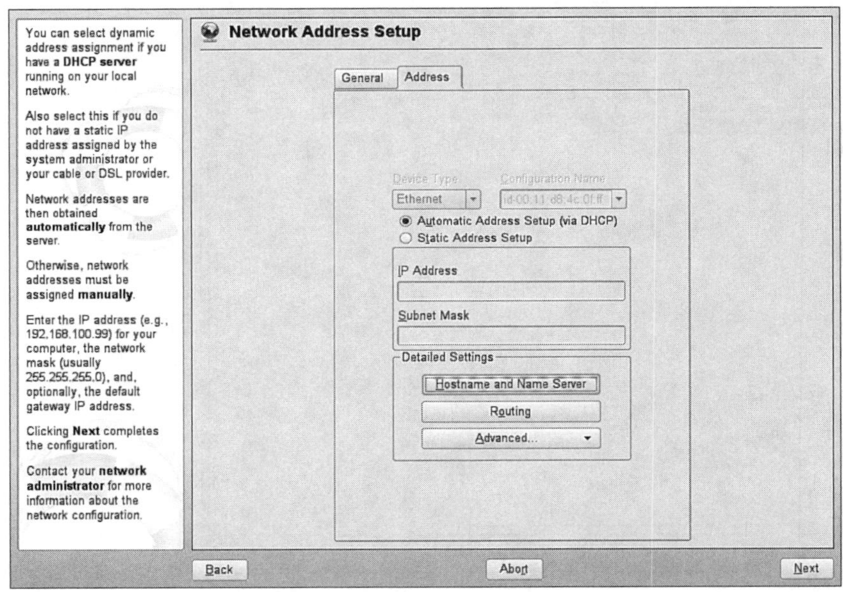

FIGURE 12.7 Configure your DSL Ethernet Card with this dialog box.

If you have a static IP address, click the IP Details button to configure this. Uncheck the Dynamic IP box and enter the static IP address in the Local IP Address box. Click OK to return to the previous screen. Click Next to complete the setup.

When you click Finish, your new settings will be saved.

NOTE

For static addresses, make sure the PPP Mode is set for standard PPP, not PPPoE.

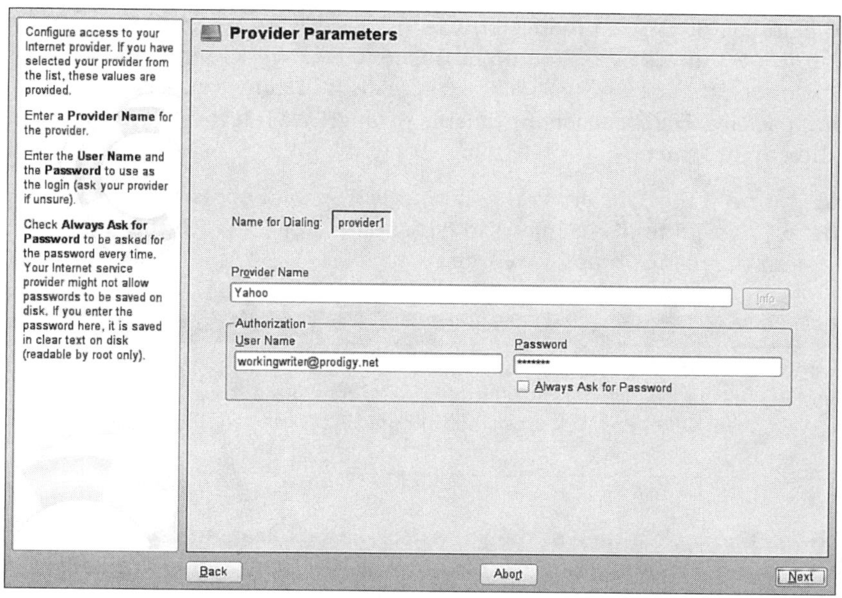

FIGURE 12.8 Enter your username and password on this screen.

Connecting Your Computer to a Wireless Network

So you're traveling with your openSUSE laptop and want to connect to your hotel's wireless network. This can be a problem, but the hurdles can be overcome.

You have basically three problems to deal with when trying to connect to a wireless network:

- Making sure your card is supported, and the proper drivers and firmware are in place
- Locating the access point
- Configuring a profile

This section will cover each of these issues.

Getting Firmware and Drivers in Place

The first issue can be the easiest to solve. Linux supports many different wireless cards, although not always with every feature that the card supports. Firmware (system code that communicates directly with the card) often must be downloaded separately from a Linux distribution. You can download firmware for ACX100, ACX111, and PrismQT cards directly through YaST Online Update, but these packages do not come with the distribution.

Most wireless card manufacturers still produce only Windows drivers, which can present a major headache for non-Windows users. Too often this requires manual setup and configuration of your network configuration file, `ifcfg-eth2`. This task, however, has been simplified. A second package, `ndiswrapper`, installable through YaST, lets you use the Windows drivers directly in Linux.

To make this work, you need the *.inf driver file. If your laptop dual boots, this file is likely in the \Windows\System folder. It may also have come on a CD with the card, and it is downloadable from the manufacturer's website.

NOTE

Downloadable hardware drivers often appear as *.exe files. Usually this is just a self-extracting archive. To pull the INF file out of the archive, you may need to run the program in Wine, Crossover Office, or Windows itself before using `ndiswrapper` to use the driver in Linux.

Once you have the INF file, open a shell as the SuperUser, and navigate to the directory where the INF file is. Run this command to confirm that `ndiswrapper` can identify the driver:

```
ndiswrapper -l <driverfilename>.inf
```

You should see a message confirming that `ndis` installed, and the driver is present.

Now you need to make the kernel recognize the driver. This is done through `modprobe`.

```
modprobe ndiswrapper
```

The final step is to add these two previous commands to your `rc.local` configuration file. The kernel will now load the driver each time at boot.

Finding an Access Point

Ideally with your drivers in place, you should now be able to scan the area for a nearby access point. If your wireless interface point is `eth2`, you can just type **`iwlist eth2 scan`** from the shell. You would then need to use `iwconfig` to configure your connection.

There is a KDE tool that can simplify this process, however. The Wireless Assistant will perform the scan and connect you. Download the Wireless Assistant openSUSE package from `http://wlassistant.sourceforge.net/` and install it through YaST. If you have the Guru repository configured as an installation source in YaST (see Chapter 21, "Keeping Your System Current: Package Management" for more information on installation sources), you can install this directly.

Launch Wireless Assistant from the KDE Kicker menu, or run it from the shell with `wlassistant`. The first time, it checks for your active network card. The card name should appear in the Device line at the top of the Wireless Assistant screen. It will then scan the area for access points, and display the results of the scan in the main window. Look carefully, as you will also learn the quality of the wireless signal with a star ranking. The WEP column indicates whether a connection supports the relatively secure Wireless Encryption Protocol. This requires a password, but is still a big improvement over allowing open access to whatever comes across the network transom (including any passwords you may send out while you're surfing the Web).

Click the access point you want, and you will be prompted for the Root password on your system. Enter it, click OK, and you're connected.

Configuring Your Wireless Card

YaST can help connect to your wireless network as well. If you know the network to which you want to connect, using YaST will set things up for you. In YaST, go to Network Devices, and then Network Card. YaST should identify your wireless card, but might not configure it directly. Select the card and click Configure.

The first screen in the setup identifies your address. The default setting is for a Dynamic Address set by DHCP. This should be the correct setting. Click Next. Figure 12.9 will appear.

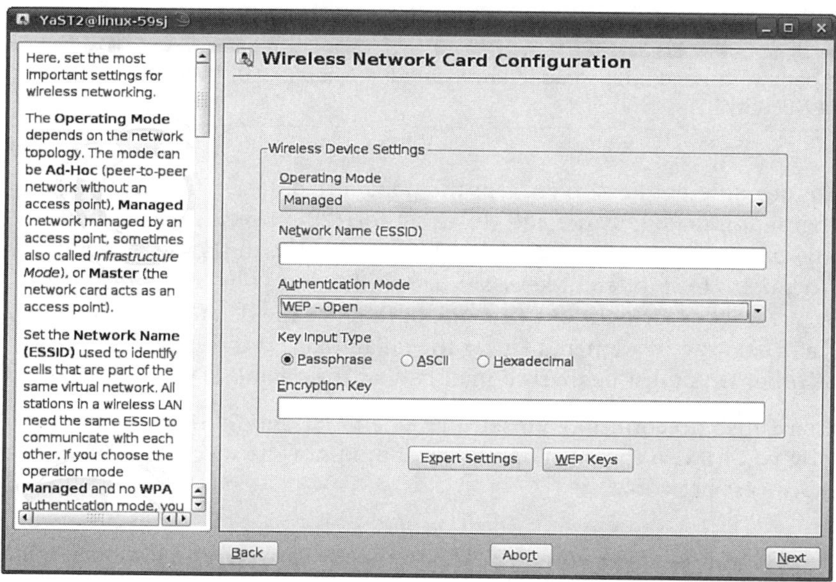

FIGURE 12.9 Configure your wireless card to connect to a stable network here.

At the top of the screen is the network Operating Mode. Nearly all the time, you want to choose Managed mode, as this is a connection with a wireless access point. An ad-hoc network is a peer-to-peer setup with no access point, and Master mode sets up your machine as an access point.

The next line indicates the name of the network to which you want to connect. In wireless networking, access points are identified with an Extended Service Set Identifier

(ESSID). You should enter the name of your network here; otherwise, the card will select the first access point it finds.

The last section deals with authenticating yourself to the network. There are three types of wireless networks. The first type, "open," is open to anyone (and that means anyone) without authentication. Generally speaking, you want to leave these networks to the bad guys who will invariably find them. WEP, or "shared key" authentication, is the prevalent, if not superior, option with many wireless networks. When severe holes were found in WEP, a new secure protocol was developed for wireless networks, WiFI Protected Access (WPA). This protocol is still not widely used, but is supported by the Linux kernel and openSUSE.

Select the appropriate protocol from the Authentication Mode drop-down menu, and then define your pass-key using the mode buttons and the Encryption Key edit box. Selecting a passphrase is the best way to proceed, if you want to have more control over your security. If you select Passphrase, enter a word or a character string from which a key is generated according to the length previously specified. ASCII requests an input of five characters for a 64-bit key and thirteen characters for a 128-bit key. For hexadecimal, enter ten characters for a 64-bit key or twenty-six characters for a 128-bit key.

TIP

Tips on creating passwords and passphrases are located in Chapter 19, "Managing Users, Managing Security."

You can keep up to four different keys to encrypt the transmitted data. Click WEP Keys to enter the key configuration dialog. By default, this is set for 128-bit security, but you can lower the level to 64 bit here if that is what your network is set for. In the list area at the bottom of the dialog, up to four different keys can be specified for your computer to use for the encryption. Press Set as Default to define one of them as the default key. Unless you change this, YaST uses the first entered key as the default key. If the standard key is deleted, one of the other keys must be marked manually as the default key.

Click Next, and then Finish, to confirm your settings. openSUSE should then find your access point, and log you in with the passphrase. You should now be successfully connected to your wireless network.

When to Call Your Internet Service Provider

The lack of official Linux support by the big players in the Internet access business can be a problem, but it can be sidestepped. Many connection problems can be solved by carefully reviewing the documentation in the YaST windows. Others can be solved by the many HOWTO documents at the Linux Documentation Project site, including the ones listed in the Reference section that follows. As always, consult with your Linux User Group (see the "Getting Help: Documentation and Other Sources" section in Chapter 1, "Welcome to openSUSE") to identify Linux-friendly ISPs in your neighborhood.

Dial-up connection problems are usually temporary or involve user error. So before you harass the tech support folks, make sure you haven't fallen into one of these traps.

- If you connect but can't log in successfully, your password could be mistyped. Remember that passwords are case sensitive.
- If the phone number and password are both right, but you still can't log in, check the authentication protocol.
- If nothing works, check the power cords. Is the modem plugged in and connected to the PC with the right jack in the right hole? Things do come loose.
- If everything works properly under Windows on your dual-boot system, but nothing works in Linux, you probably have a Winmodem. Try the Linmodem drivers, or go out and buy a hardware modem.
- This one's good for both dial-up and DSL: If nothing works, and it worked a few minutes/hours ago, and there's no smoke coming out of your machine, it could be a problem at the ISP. If it's a big ISP, they'll know about a glitch quickly. If they're a mom-and-pop local operation, call to report if it just happened; otherwise, give them some time to fix it. Call if the problem persists for hours.
- If you log in okay, but can't browse the Web, it could be a DNS problem. Double-check your DHCP settings and then contact the ISP.

When you contact your ISP, and you know they don't support Linux, try to explain the context of the problem outside of the operating system. It helps to know the Windows counterparts of the Linux (or YaST) dialog boxes with which you're working (the Internet Connection Wizard, Network Neighborhood, and the like).

References

- http://www.tldp.org/HOWTO/HOWTO-INDEX/hardware.html#HWMODEMS—Linux Documentation Project modems HOWTOs. What you need to know, sometimes in excruciating detail, about ordinary modems, Winmodems, DSL modems, and cable modems. Some of it is outdated, but the revision dates are always posted here.
- http://axion.physics.ubc.ca/ppp-linux.html—Trying to set up PPP manually? This is the place to go, as W. G. Unruh has worked hard to troubleshoot many PPP problems.
- http://en.opensuse.org/Hardware—The SUSE Hardware database. Check here to see if your modem is officially supported. If your DSL modem is not listed here, don't assume that it won't work. There are not many to choose from.
- http://linmodems.org—The place to visit if you have a software-based "Winmodem." This site might have information that may help you get this working.
- http://start.at/modem—Winmodems Are Not Modems. A large list of modem models to check for Linux compatibility.

CHAPTER 13

Using the Internet: Browsing the Web and Writing Email

IN THIS CHAPTER

When most of us talk about using the Internet, we're usually talking about one of two things: browsing the World Wide Web or reading and sending electronic mail. For some people, these two things are the reason to have a computer in their home. As an operating system that largely owes its success to the existence of the Internet, email and the Web are things Linux does very well.

This and the next few chapters cover openSUSE and the Internet. Here you will learn about your many choices in browsing the Web and managing email in openSUSE. After that, you'll learn about helping to create the World Wide Web by making a basic website. In later chapters, we'll cover email in depth and show you how to use the net to collaborate with others, transfer files, and administer a web server.

There are a lot of things to do on the Internet, and openSUSE is here to help you make the most of it.

Choosing a Web Browser

Chances are pretty good that you have some experience with browsing the Web and don't need anyone to tell you how to do that.

You should know, however, that several browsers are available to you in openSUSE. All are under active development and are more secure out of the box than Microsoft Internet Explorer (IE).

Here's a quick rundown of names and features.

Mozilla, Firefox, and SeaMonkey

This family of browsers represents the best known and most popular Linux browsers. As Netscape Communicator, the Mozilla suite was the first dominant commercial browser. Its developers eventually got the open source religion, and the suite became the first major commercial application to be open-sourced in 1998. While it took over four years to get to Mozilla 1.0, it quickly became the default Linux browser.

Some Mozilla developers believed the suite (with built-in email, chat, and an HTML editor) was overkill, and that users wanted a simple, quick-loading browser that didn't need much memory. The first test version of this browser, called Phoenix, was released in September 2002. After going through a few name changes and several beta releases, Mozilla Firefox 1.0 came out on November 9, 2004. In the first 99 days of availability, people downloaded more than 25 million free copies of Firefox (for all operating systems). Since then, Firefox's share of the browser market has been hovering around 15%. Firefox 2.0 was released October 24, 2006, and it is the default browser in openSUSE 10.3.

The growth of Firefox led the Mozilla Foundation to announce in March 2005 that it would no longer support development of the complete Mozilla Suite. Another group of developers then launched the SeaMonkey project to maintain and improve the suite code. SeaMonkey 1.0 was released on January 30, 2006. It is not installed automatically, but you can get it via YaST.

Both current versions of Mozilla and Firefox offer tabbed browsing (no more separate browser windows unless you want them), effective (and selective) popup ad blockers, and support for RSS and Atom webfeeds. The latter lets you create Live Bookmarks for blogs and other sites that deliver continuing updates. Look for the square orange icon in the address bar of Figure 13.1. Besides Live Bookmarks, Firefox 2.0 gives you the option of subscribing to sites via your favorite online newsreader (see the RSS section of Chapter 16, "Collaborating with Others") .

Personalizing and Enhancing Firefox and SeaMonkey with Add-Ons

Firefox is a terrific and quick-loading browser installed as is, but its modular design lets you make it more powerful (or just more personal) through the use of themes, search engines, and extensions. The Mozilla team created the XML User Interface Language (XUL, pronounced "zool") to facilitate the easy development of extensions. These are collectively known as Add-ons in Firefox 2.0. You can get a sense for the variety of these Add-ons at the Mozilla Add-Ons site. In Firefox, go to the Tools menu and select Add-Ons. A small box identifying your current extensions appears. Click the Get Extensions link in the lower-right corner to see the Extensions page.

The main Extensions page (https://addons.mozilla.org/firefox/extensions) gives you access to Add-ons by category and a list of the most popular and most recently added extensions. If you're new to Firefox, click the Recommended Add-Ons link from the left side menu. Choose among the frequently-updated selections to get started with extensions. Click Install Now to download an extension. A dialog box (Figure 13.2) appears warning you to download extensions only from trusted sources. It is reasonable to assume that anything included in the official site is OK, so click Install Now again. The extension will download, and nearly always will ask you to restart Firefox to complete the install. If you're planning to install several extensions at once, you may click Restart Later. In any case, when you do restart, Firefox 2.0 will save the session and restore the tabs that were open before. Some extensions will also load a page with information on how to use or configure the extension.

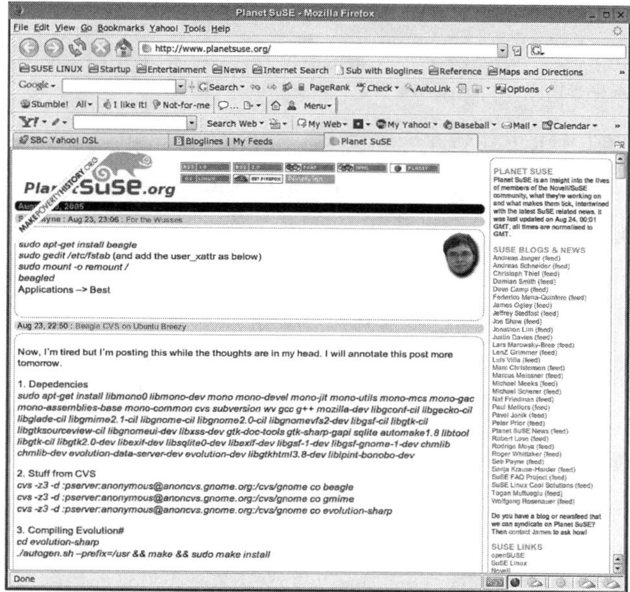

FIGURE 13.1 Mozilla Firefox reignited the browser wars in 2004, and it is the favorite of many Linux users.

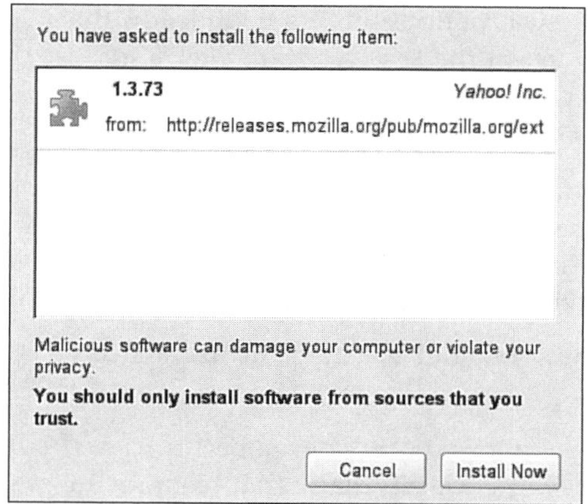

FIGURE 13.2 When adding extensions, Firefox gives you a chance to back out. Never install extensions unless you know who is responsible for them.

You can configure the way many extensions work in the Add-On window by selecting the extension and clicking Configure. Use the same dialog to uninstall add-ons that have outlived their usefulness.

Extensions useful to nearly everyone include the following:

- Search toolbars—One can easily get carried away with these, but both the Google and Yahoo toolbars have useful things besides just search.
- ScribeFire (formerly Performancing)—A great tool to simplify posting to your blog. This is a complete WYSIWYG editor for blog posts.
- FasterFox—Improves browser performance, even for broadband connections.
- Greasemonkey—A framework to personalize both your browser and the entire Web experience. Install Greasemonkey, and then visit http://userscripts.org to see the kinds of things you can do.

Some extensions are more about fun. These include the following:

- StumbleUpon—Designed to bring back the random search of sites that are personally interesting. Define your interests, and then vote thumbs-up or thumbs-down on sites presented to you. You can also find other users with interests similar to yours through the StumbleUpon site.
- FoxyTunes—Controls your music player from the bottom of the browser window.
- ForecastFox—Get your local (or any other location's) weather forecast in the bottom of your browser. Warns you when severe storms are headed your way too.

Besides extensions, you can use Themes to customize the look of your browser.

By default, Firefox uses Google as the engine used when you type something into the Search box to the right of the Address bar, and a few other options are included in the default install. Click the drop-down menu to the left of the Search box to view and change the current engine. The Add-On site lets you add other engines to the list. These range from the special narrow niches to the commercial to the outlandish.

Add-ons are updated frequently, so if you encounter a problem, use the Add-Ons window to check for updates periodically. Addicted to having the latest and greatest? Get the Update Notifier extension. It checks for updates daily and puts a very small icon in the upper right corner that turns colors when an extension or theme is updated.

Most Firefox extensions work just as well in SeaMonkey (but the site is https://addons.mozilla.org/seamonkey/extensions).

The open-sourcing of the Netscape/Mozilla browser allowed other developers to create their own visions of a Linux browser. So in many ways, we can thank that team for so much.

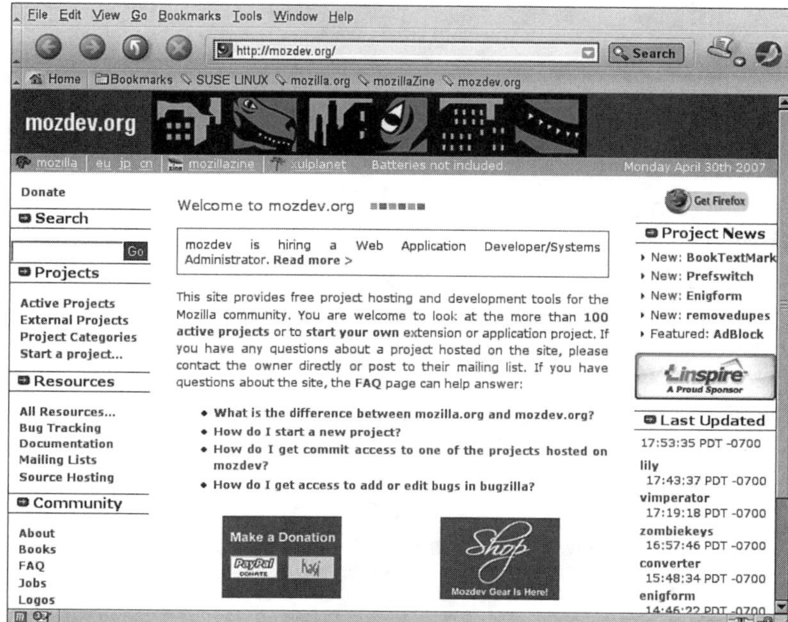

FIGURE 13.3 SeaMonkey is the independent project that continued the Mozilla Suite.

Konqueror

Your KDE file manager is also a fully functional web browser. Click the globe-ish looking icon in the KDE taskbar and Konqueror will open in Web Browsing mode (see Figure 13.4). It is also the default KDE browser (though you can change that in the KDE Control Center), so clicking links in most other programs in KDE will open Konqueror. Based on the KHTML rendering engine (also used in the popular Safari browser for the Macintosh), it also offers excellent cookie management to protect your privacy on the Web. Unlike Firefox, Konqueror asks you by default if you want to accept a cookie from a site. While you may find this behavior distracting at times, the privacy reminder is often useful. You can adjust these settings by going to the Settings menu, selecting Configure Konqueror, and going to the Cookies page.

TIP

If a site doesn't display properly in Konqueror, try changing the browser identification to Firefox. Many sites have a script that checks this ID and displays pages accordingly, skipping out on Web standards. Too often, those scripts only recognize the Big Two: Internet Explorer and Mozilla/Firefox.

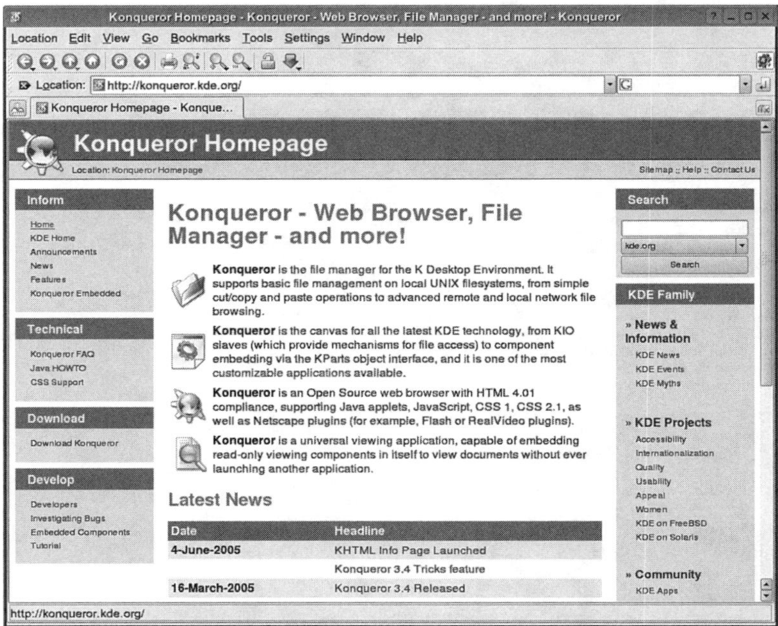

FIGURE 13.4 Konqueror, the KDE web browsing and file management king.

Konqueror is not a perfect browser, though it continues to improve. There was some talk of implementing XUL in KDE, but that proved difficult, so Konqueror does not import Mozilla or Firefox extensions or themes, though it does import bookmarks and multimedia plug-ins quite well. If you happen to have a file-manager window open and then open a URL, chances are the browser will open in a new tab in the file-manager window. You then have to detach the tab through the context menu. There is no direct support for social-bookmarking engines like del.icio.us. Yet overall, it provides an excellent experience, and is less of a memory hog than either Mozilla browser.

TIP

Maybe the best thing about Konqueror is its bookmark management tool. It is simple to categorize your bookmarks as you create them. Konqueror also imports bookmarks from IE, Mozilla, and Opera, making it easy to integrate all your bookmarks in one place, even if you aren't consistently loyal to one browser.

But if you've ever tried to prune your extensive bookmarks list, wishing to remove sites that may not have survived the dot-com era, Konqueror could just be a godsend. In the Bookmark manager, there's a tool that will visit all your bookmarks and let you know if they are still active. Go to Tools, Check Status: All. This can take some time, but it's well-spent if you have a lot of dead links. You can also check the status of a single bookmark in the Bookmark menu of the manager.

Epiphany

The default GNOME browser (Figure 13.5) runs on the same Gecko rendering engine as the various Mozilla projects, has many of the same great features, and a few of its own.

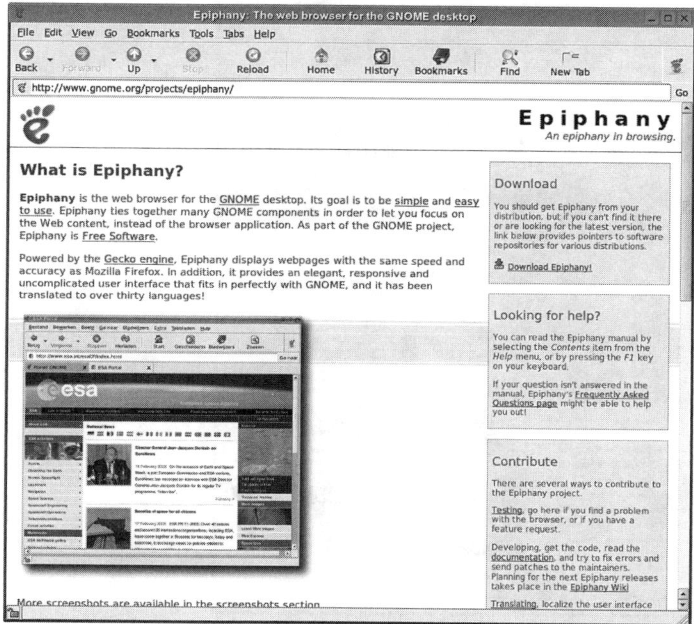

FIGURE 13.5 Epiphany, the GNOME default browser.

Epiphany's developers are keen on building a simple, usable browser. To that end, bookmarks in Epiphany can be placed in multiple categories, and the interface is as clean and customizable as GNOME's. You can move toolbar buttons and tabs around with a drag-and-drop action, and you can bookmark a set of tabs. Epiphany supports extensions in an optional package you can install through YaST, but does not let you pull in Firefox extensions directly.

Opera

This commercial browser has long been the home of much innovation in the browser market. Opera first employed the idea of tabbed browsing, with multiple sites displayed within a single browser window, pop-up ad blocking, strict adherence to standards, and (to somewhat lesser acclaim) advertising-supported software. In 2006, Opera Software celebrated its tenth anniversary as a company by making the browser free of charge (but not yet open source), and dropping the ad window from the top of the browser. This included version 9 for Linux.

Like SeaMonkey, Opera (Figure 13.6) has a built-in email client that also supports RSS feeds (see Chapter 16 for more on RSS) and an Internet Relay Chat client. Opera 9 introduced a BitTorrent client that works inside the standard download engine, and a Widget engine. Opera Widgets are more like desktop gadgets than browser extensions, with assorted diversions, games and RSS newsfeeds and podcasts. Nonetheless, the widgets are only active when browsing with Opera.

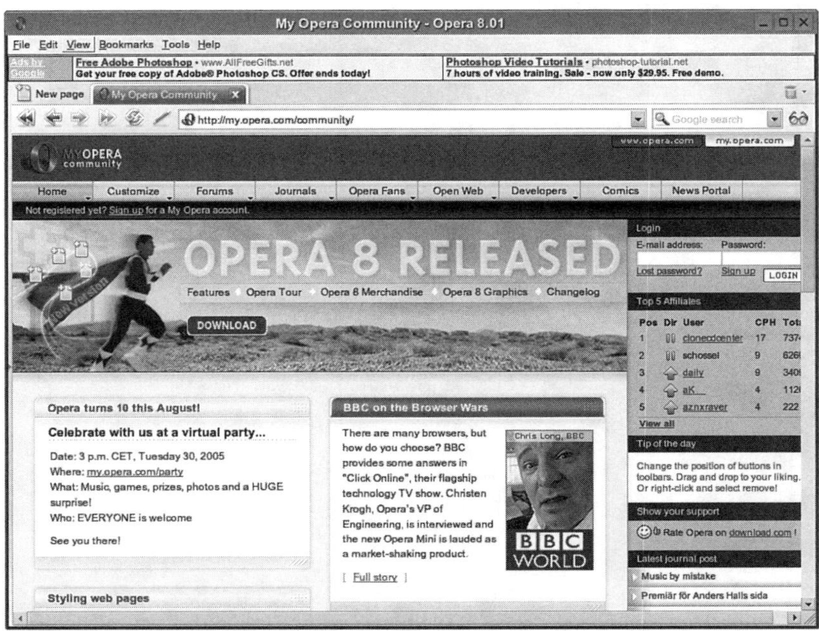

FIGURE 13.6 Opera brings its clean look and standards-based engine to Linux.

Flock

If Epiphany is the browser offering "just the Web," this social browser is all about the read-write Web. Sure you can just search and surf with the Gecko-based Flock as you would with any other browser, but this one comes with a built-in blog editor.

Flock, still in beta as of this writing, does not come with openSUSE, but is simple to install. Just go to http://www.flock.com and click the Get Flock Now link; Flock will recognize your operating system and download a nice tarball (a Linux archive with a .tar.gz extension). Use Ark to extract the file to your Home directory. Open the new /home/<username>/flock directory and click the flock-bin executable to run the setup wizard. This wizard allows you to import your Firefox bookmarks and settings.

That Flock is targeting social-network savvy youth is evident with the browser's default bookmark toolbar (as you can see in Figure 13.7): MySpace, MTV, and YouTube. Flock offers an easy way to upload your pictures to the Flickr and Photobucket photo-sharing services. Like Opera and Firefox, Flock has a built-in RSS/Atom newsfeed reader (see Chapter 16 for more on newsfeeds). The Accounts and Services setup lets you enter your blog address, and then when something interesting shows up in your browser, you can blog it instantly.

FIGURE 13.7 Flock is a social browser aimed to help you share your Web discoveries with others.

Their unusual Search tool may well be helpful to just about anyone. If you've ever been sitting on a page, wanted to search something and waded through pages of search results only to realize you can't get back to the page that prompted the search, Flock has a solution. Its Web Search tool in the upper-right corner of the browser searches your bookmarks, recent history, and the major engines for results in a drop-down box that doesn't even require you to press Enter to get results.

Flock will adapt most, if not quite all, Firefox extensions. Visit http://extensions.flock.com/extensions to sample the selections.

Choosing a Mail Client (Mail User Agent)

People spend a lot of time with their email programs. Many get to know their quirks and foibles as well as those of any human being around them. Attachments develop, as do love/hate relationships. Take Microsoft Outlook, for example. Nearly everyone has used it at one time or another.

Maybe you've never used anything but Outlook, but you're now thrown into the Linux world, either by choice or by corporate fiat. Maybe you're a little nervous about the change. Don't be. If you like the way Outlook does things, you can get something that mimics the same Outlook experience that you are accustomed to.

If you've left the Microsoft reservation and want something different, how about a text-based mail client like mutt or pine, or Emacs mail? Want a calendar/to-do list function in your mail client? Sure. Want a Usenet (or RSS) newsreader? You can do that, too. As always, you have choices.

In this section, you will become familiar with the leading Linux email programs: Evolution, Kmail/KOrganizer/Kontact, SeaMonkey Mail/Thunderbird, Claws, and mutt. Choose one that fits your style and your needs.

Evolution

Evolution was written by Nat Friedman and the Ximian team to be the Linux alternative to Outlook. Although it is not a reverse-engineering effort, Evolution looks and behaves as much like Outlook as possible. In one package, you have an integrated mail client, a calendar, a to-do list, and an address book.

Setting up Evolution is very easy, with a wizard to walk you through the entire process. To set up an email account, type in your name and email address to get things going (Figure 13.8). You can also identify a separate address for replies and an Organization that appears in your outgoing mail header. The first account you set up is your default account; you can set up a different account to be your default later.

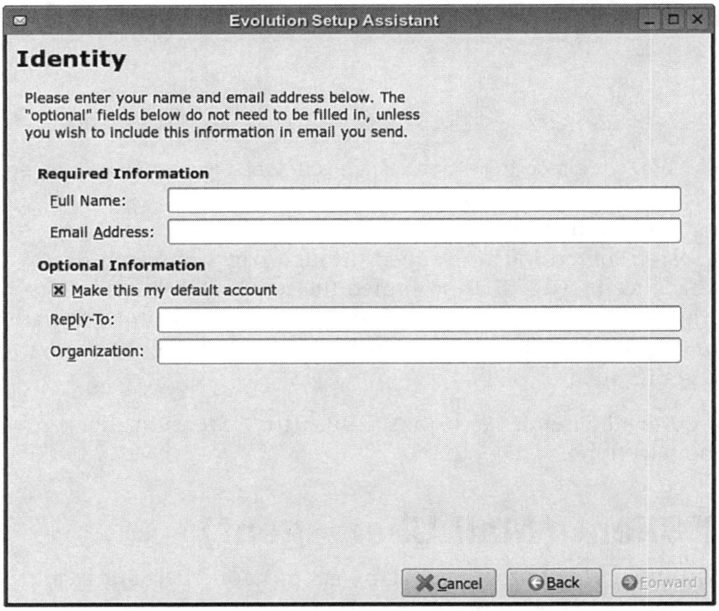

FIGURE 13.8 Setting up basic email information.

Click Forward and select your server type from the drop-down menu. As you can see in Figure 13.9, Evolution supports a variety of mail servers: POP, IMAP, and GroupWise, along with Usenet News.

Click Forward to fill in the third wizard screen (Figure 13.10). Enter the name of your email server in the Server box, and your email account's username. If your ISP permits mail to be sent via a secure connection, you can set this up here. If you want Evolution to remember your ISP password (at the risk of unauthorized people reading and writing email under your name), check the Remember Password box.

Click Forward again. The last Receive Mail setup screen (Figure 13.11) gives you some options: whether Evolution should check mail automatically, and how often; whether (and for how long) to leave retrieved mail on the server (good if your ISP offers a lot of space on the server and web access to your mail); and whether to disable extensions to the POP3 standard. These extensions are rarely needed.

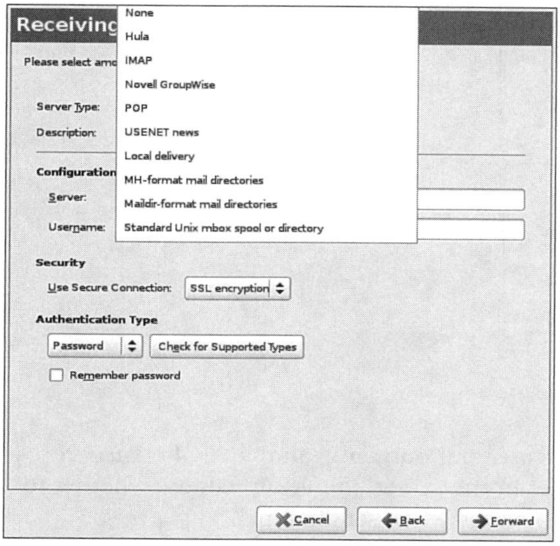

FIGURE 13.9 Select the type of mail server to which you are connecting.

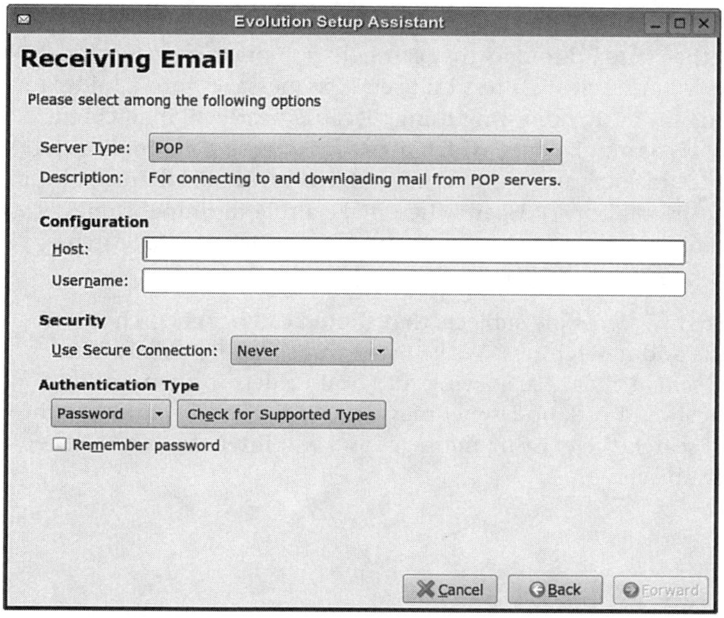

FIGURE 13.10 Set up your incoming mail server information.

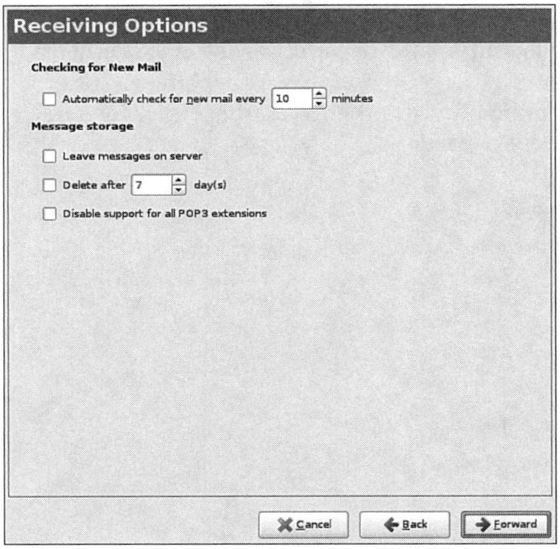

FIGURE 13.11 Select receiving mail options.

In the next screen (Figure 13.12), you configure your outgoing (Simple Mail Transport Protocol, SMTP) mail server. Name the server in the Server line. Again choose whether to have Evolution remember your password, this time when sending mail.

In the last two screens, you name your account and select your time zone (from a beautifully rendered world map). When you've completed all the setup tasks, click Apply to open Evolution, and then click Get Mail on the toolbar to get your mail.

Evolution supports creating the standard folders that can help you organize your mail, especially mailing list traffic. You can create filters that send list messages into a folder for reading and storing later. This isn't the interesting thing, because nearly all mail clients do this. Evolution also supports Search Folders, which allow for unique combinations of relevant data. Say you want to track discussions over several lists on email clients. You can search your existing mail for several keywords, and then make a rule to funnel copies of these discussions into a virtual folder. Go to the Search menu and click Create Search Folder. A dialog box appears (see Figure 13.13).

In this example, we've selected five possible subjects that should catch a good chunk of the relevant traffic in the lists and newsgroups. We've listed three leading email clients and two variant spellings of "email client." Choosing All Local Folders in the Search Folder Sources at the bottom should pick up Usenet messages, too. Click OK to create the Search Folder. Evolution will search the existing messages and will filter mail and Usenet postings with the matching subjects.

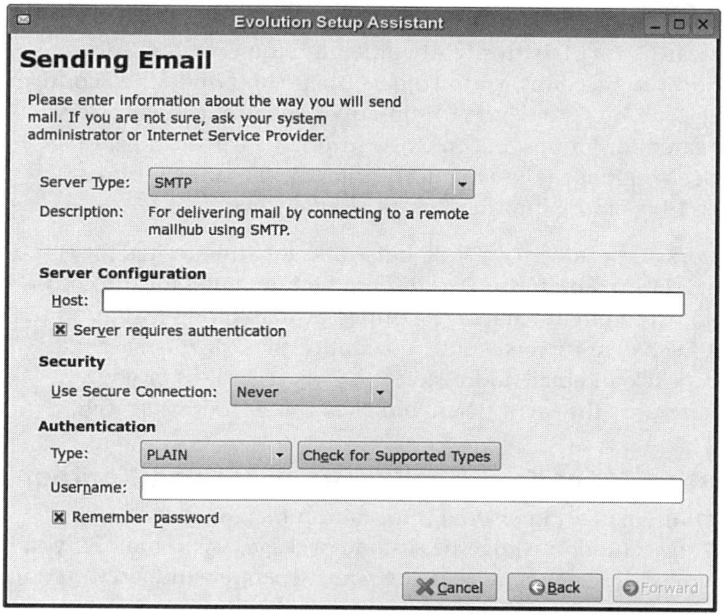

FIGURE 13.12 Configure outgoing mail server information.

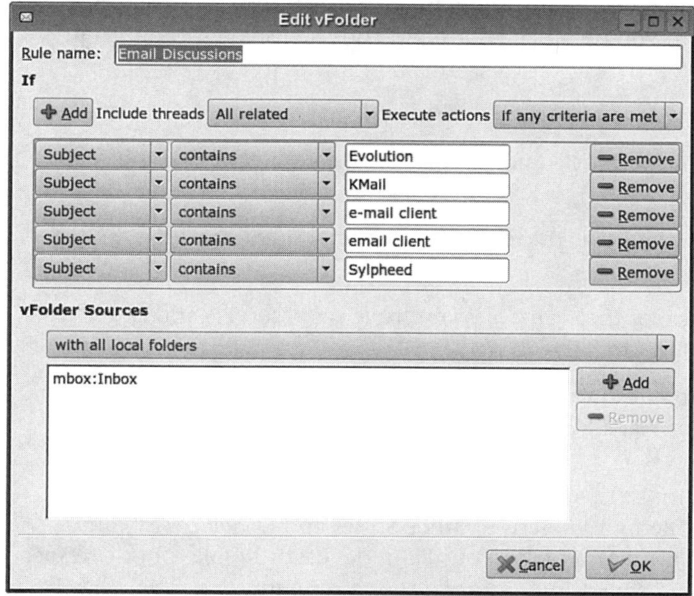

FIGURE 13.13 Configure vFolders in evolution.

Evolution also handles Usenet News in the same environment as mail. Setting up a Usenet feed uses the same wizard as mail, with slightly different requirements. To access newsgroups once you've set up your account, go to Folders, then Subscriptions to connect to your news server and to select groups to which to subscribe. The problem with this method is that you cannot search for groups, but must go through a threaded list of all the groups on the server. Once you make your selections, though, the display is just like your mail client. See Chapter 16 for more information on Usenet News.

Based on GTK+, Evolution works best under GNOME, but works just fine in KDE. It is the default mail client in the SUSE Linux Enterprise Desktop product designed for the corporate market, in part because of the Ximian Exchange Connector that allows Evolution to get messages from Microsoft Exchange Servers. You'll also notice that Mozilla Firefox launches Evolution when you click an email address on the web, regardless of your default mail setup. Evolution returns the favor when you click a web address as well.

KDE Personal Information Manager: Kmail/KOrganizer and Kontact

KDE offers two ways to get your email and personal information managed. If you like Outlook's way of keeping all these functions together in one package, try Kontact. If you prefer that all these things remain independent, and you want separate windows for your calendar and email, each component of the KDE-PIM package will still run separately.

Kontact has six basic components:

- KMail—A full-featured email client with some built-in spam and virus protection, configurable filters to help you organize your mail, and the usual customization features.
- KOrganizer—Calendar and to-do list for the busy person.
- KAddressBook—Holds your Kontacts and integrates with your calendar and mail clients.
- KNotes—A quick-opening, lightweight text editor for reminders and other bits of information.
- KNode—A Usenet newsreader that can access multiple news servers and filter out spam and other worthless material.
- aKregator—A new RSS/Atom feedreader that downloads information from weblogs and news sites for easy reading. You'll learn more about this component in Chapter 16.

Besides the main information tools, there are some handy accessories in the KDE-PIM lineup. KPilot (see Chapter 9, "Being Productive: Office Suites and Other Tools") and Kandy are tools to sync your information with your Palm device or mobile phone, respectively. KAlarm notifies you when something important is coming up (or you just have new mail), and KArm is your personal time clock, available to help you figure out where all the time goes (especially if you have billable hours).

Kontact has a Summary page, with calendar and to-do list highlighted, along with a configurable set of news feeds. You can choose the components that appear in the Kontact window (so if you don't read Usenet, you don't have to load KNode every time you want to read mail).

TIP

Want to have a Kontact-like experience in Windows? Try Aethera, a Windows PIM from theKompany.com based on the Kontact code. See http://thekompany.com/projects/aethera for more information and the free download.

KMail can deal with those with evil designs on your computer. The KMail Antivirus and Spam Wizards integrate with your installed antispam and antivirus tools. In addition, KMail has integrated encryption using the GNU Privacy Guard (GPG) available for those messages that need to be secure.

TIP

It's a good idea to keep traffic from each list you're subscribed to in a separate folder. It's much easier to follow threads of a discussion when they aren't interrupted by other messages.

If you use electronic mailing lists, you'll find KMail will help you immensely. KMail is very list-aware. That list-awareness is expressed in many ways:

- Right-click a list message and you can create a filter for that list from the context menu (Create Filter, On Mailing List, <name>).
- KMail will display messages in threads if you like. You can also perform some actions on whole threads: Delete Thread, Ignore Thread (which automatically marks messages in the ignored thread as Read, so that you can see them later if you want), and Watch Thread (which marks each new message in the thread with a Watch icon so that you don't miss them). You can set this globally in the KMail configure screen or folder by folder.
- Some lists are configured so that when you reply to a list message, it goes to the list; others send replies to the message author. In KMail, regardless of how things are set at the list, you can choose where it goes. Press L to reply to the list, press Shift+A to Reply to Author, and press A to reply to All.
- If you have a mailing-list folder selected, go to the Folder menu and select Mailing List Management. Check the Folder Holds a Mailing List box, and click Detect Automatically. The list's posting address should appear, as in Figure 13.14. Choose whether you want KMail or your default browser to handle your posts. Click Address Type for the list's subscribe/unsubscribe addresses, the posting address, and several other options.

Do you get buried in mailing list email to the point where you can't read it all, but don't have time to prune the Inbox either? KMail's Expire tool can help. Right-click a folder and select Expire to see Figure 13.14.

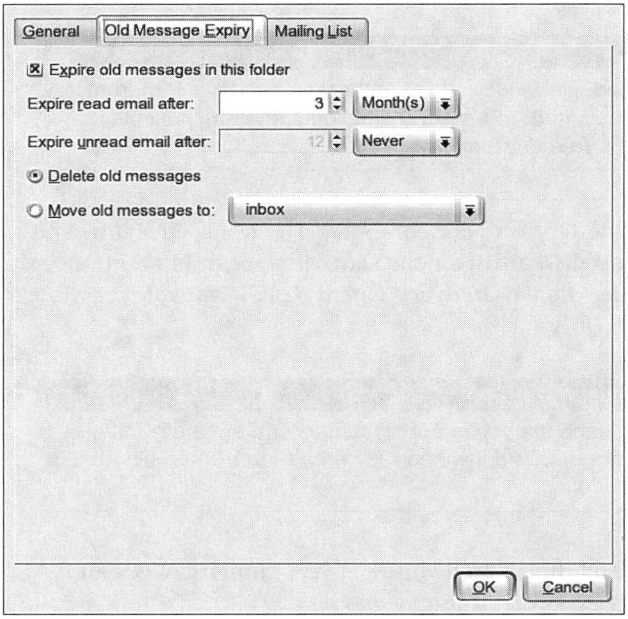

FIGURE 13.14 Prune your Inbox and other folders with the KMail Old Message Expiry screen.

When you check either Expire box (identifying read and/or unread email), you'll see the default settings. They are easily adjusted for your message-reading style. Suppose you're inclined to keep a good tip that you got from a list; leave the Read Mail box unchecked, and dump Unread after a proper period. You can also opt to put old messages in another folder if you are either required to keep email for a specified period or if you just can't bear to delete things entirely.

In older versions of KMail, you had to tell the application to expire a single folder or all folders at once. With KMail 3.3, the Expire function works constantly in the background, occasionally delivering a message in the lower-left corner: `Expired x messages in Folder Y`. You can still Expire messages manually; select Expire All Folders from the File menu.

SeaMonkey Mail and Thunderbird

The SeaMonkey suite is more than a browser. A mail and news client, an Internet Relay Chat (IRC) program, and an HTML editor are all included in the package.

Mozilla project developers are heading in a new direction, separating each of these functions into faster-loading applications with new names. The mail and news client is called

Thunderbird, and it is a thing of beauty. Designed to make Outlook Express users comfortable, the interface is very familiar. Setting up mail accounts is simple; creating folders and filters is even more so.

Thunderbird is very security conscious as well. To protect your privacy, the application will not load remote images in HTML-based messages unless you tell it to. Remote images often contain web bugs that tell the sender you've opened their message, confirming your email address. The Junk filters are very good.

New features are added first to the standalone products and then are brought into the SeaMonkey suite. If you prefer to have everything together, SeaMonkey Mail has all the Thunderbird features mentioned previously.

Claws-Mail

This fast and powerful mail and news client (originally known as Claws) was written by a Japanese programmer, Hiroyuki Yamamoto, with GTK+ for GNOME. Its clean interface is easy to read, although you may want to adjust the spartan default Courier fonts (see Figure 13.15).

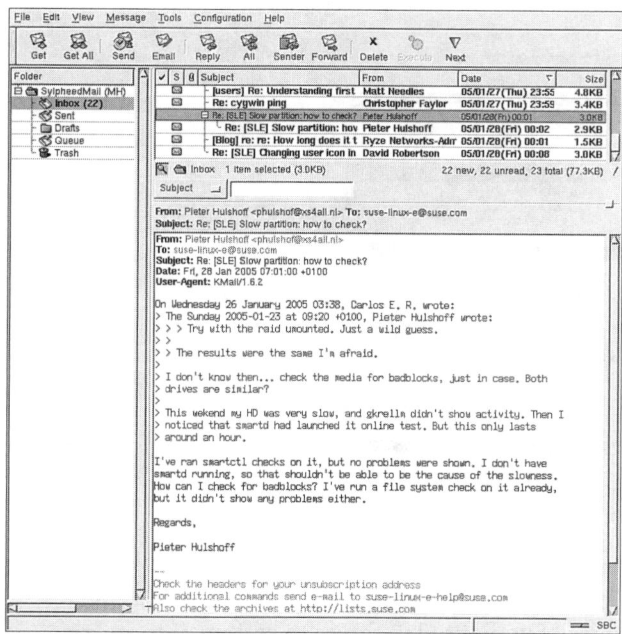

FIGURE 13.15 Claws-Mail's clean interface.

Claws-Mail has powerful filters, but the dialog boxes to create them are better suited for the technically adept. The same can be said for the other configuration dialog boxes. It also does Evolution-style Search Folders.

Claws-Mail will also read Usenet news, but has no calendar function. The address book supports multiple email addresses for one individual and has room for many free-form user attributes, such as physical addresses, company, title(s), birthdays, and the like.

mutt

`mutt` is a text-based mail client that runs directly in the shell.

Originally based on another mail client called elm, `mutt` has taken on features and ways of doing things from several of its brethren (hence the name). The interface is colorful for a text screen, and the colors are configurable. You can see it in Figure 13.16.

This client's fans emphasize the power of the client and the ease with which they move through their mail. Like KMail, `mutt` is highly attuned to mailing-list users, with threading and list-reply options.

openSUSE defines a basic systemwide `mutt` configuration file in `/etc/Muttrc`. Open it as root to configure `mutt` for all users on your system, but each user can have his or her own `Muttrc` in the home directory. It's a relatively big file as configuration files go, so you can see the kind of power you have. It comes well commented, so even newbies can play with some settings. Always make a backup file before you make changes.

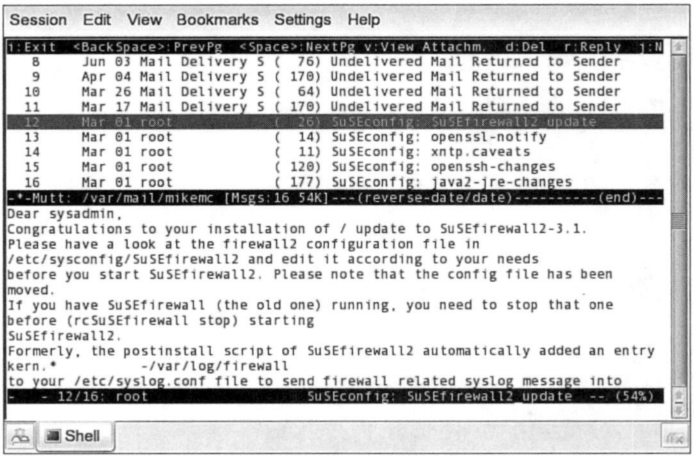

FIGURE 13.16 The mutt mail client combines features from several of its text-based brethren, such as elm and pine.

At a minimum, you will have to point `mutt` to your mail server to read mail from your ISP. Use your editor's Find command to locate the POP section of `Muttrc`; then uncomment and modify the file to your liking.

Navigation between messages in the Index pane and within messages in the Pager is accomplished with arrow keys, the spacebar, and PgUp and PgDown. There are prompts at the top of the pane to remind forgetful users.

Take advantage of the active development team and lively user community, should you get hooked on this client. Start at http://www.mutt.org.

Managing Your Calendar (and Other Life Tasks)

Recognizing that email often is the genesis of tasks, appointments, and other events, most email clients have expanded into the realm of personal information managers. These elements include to-do lists and calendars. This section takes a look at your options.

Evolution Calendar

Evolution is a complete personal information manager, with calendar and task (to-do) lists. You can convert email messages to either events or tasks, if you need to.

You can import calendars, from other individuals and from the Web, into Evolution. The calendar supports the iCal standard developed by Apple and the emerging webCAL standard. Visit http://icalshare.com to see user-contributed calendars on assorted topics, from holidays and history to local Linux User Group calendars. To import a calendar from iCalShare into Evolution, right-click on the Subscribe link on the website and copy the link to the clipboard. In Evolution, open the calendar and select New Calendar from the toolbar or File menu.

Choose On the Web from the Type drop-down menu, and then paste your copied address in the URL box (delete the default text in this box first). Name the Calendar, give it an identifying color, and decide how often you want to update it (every 30 minutes is the default, but this is probably overkill for the US Holidays calendar, among others).

If you have a dial-up connection, you can also download a calendar file that doesn't constantly ping the web for updates. Click Download Calendar on the website, and save it to a Calendars directory somewhere on your Home directory. When opening the New Calendar dialog box, select On This Computer from the Type drop-down menu (this should be the default). Point to the directory where you saved the calendar, and make it the default folder.

KOrganizer

Kontact also helps you manage your schedule with KOrganizer. Set up events, work on your to-do list, invite people to meetings, and do all the other things you expect to do in this type of application.

You can easily turn a to-do item into an event by adding start and end times for the to-do. Drag an email message to an event to attach it.

As with the Evolution calendar, KOrganizer supports the iCal standard, and you can subscribe to or download user-created calendars at iCalShare.com. You can also create your own and share them.

Mozilla Sunbird

Sunbird is something of the weak stepchild of the Mozilla family of applications. While Firefox (and perhaps Thunderbird) have reached version 2.0, Sunbird is still at version 0.5. At the same time, Sunbird is surprisingly robust even in its current state. You can install the MozillaSunbird package in YaST.

Its clean interface, with big print for day and date columns, makes it easy to glance at your calendar and get a sense for what's happening. Events and appointments can be scheduled by double-clicking anywhere in the calendar. The start time for your event is set depending on where you click. This is, of course, adjustable if Sunbird didn't guess right. Unlike many calendars that set appointments only at 15- or 30-minute intervals, you can set events to start at, for example, 9:35 AM in Sunbird.

There are no built-in calendars in Sunbird, so you can't add your country's holidays immediately, but the project has a Holiday Files page on its website. Meanwhile, importing calendars from this site or iCalShare.com is a three-step wizard process. Sunbird also supports the calDAV standard, though this is shakier in this version than the iCal support. To import a calendar from iCalShare, copy the link as discussed in the Evolution section. In Sunbird, go to the File menu and select Subscribe to Remote Calendar. The Create New Calendar wizard appears. Choose On the Network in the first screen, and click Next. In the next screen, choose the iCalendar (ICS) format, and paste the URL from iCalShare in the Location box. Click Next, and name the calendar and assign a color to events coming from that calendar. Use the same wizard to color-code your own internal events, should you choose.

Double-click in an empty area of the Tasks window to add a task to your list. You can optionally specify a location, a due date, a category, and a calendar to associate with the task. Click the More button to add a detailed description, Status labels (a.k.a. progress reports), alarms, and more.

Sending File Attachments

Some people get confused about email. "If email is just text, and only text, how do people send me fully formatted documents and all those family pictures?" The capability to attach binary files is one of the extensions to SMTP that makes it more useful.

There are several methods for turning a binary file into text for mailing; these methods are somewhat tied to the operating system you're running. The historic Unix method is called UUEncode/UUDecode (the UU standing for Unix-to-Unix), whereas Macintosh users made BinHex files. Later on, the Multipurpose Internet Mail Extension (MIME) format came in for all operating systems. Nearly every mail client now produced, for whatever OS, can read file attachments that use these formats, and they all can attach files using at least one of these methods without user intervention. That is, you don't have to decide how to encode your attachments.

One deficiency in this encoding and textifying of binary files is that the encoded files are much bigger than the original binary file. Recently, a new format called yEnc has taken the field, claiming to produce smaller, more compressed attachments. Client support for this format is spotty at the time of this writing, but that may change.

In the event you find yourself needing to decode one of these files manually, this section will help you with some pertinent details about each format.

When do you need to manually decode an attachment? If you get a message that has a large batch of random digits, characters, and apostrophes in 80-characters-per-line format, that's probably an undecoded attachment. If you see a line at the top of the randomness with a filename, you definitely have an undecoded attachment. See the section "Using UUDeview to Decode a File Attachment" to know what to do with it.

NOTE

Microsoft Exchange Servers use a proprietary format to attach files to Outlook messages. This format, the Transport Neutral Encapsulation Format (TNEF), is read beautifully in Outlook itself, but other clients (regardless of OS) sometimes have a problem with attachments being labeled with a generic winmail.dat filename.

Progress has been made in viewing these files in Linux mail clients. KDE (and KMail) has a built-in TNEF viewer. Other clients can use the shell utility TNEF to view these files. This utility is available through YaST.

BinHex

Apple Macintosh users have long used the BinHex format to wrap files. This hasn't changed with the advent of the FreeBSD-based OS X. openSUSE users can install UUDeview from YaST to decode these files. This shell utility decodes all manner of attached-file formats, including yEnc and MIME.

yEnc

This format, with a name derived from smushing together the words "My Encoder," is freely available. Mostly used in the Usenet binaries newsgroups, it can also be used for attaching files to email. The developer, Jürgen Helbring, insists that if you use it in email, you must include the word "yEnc" in the subject heading. This serves both to warn recipients that there is an attachment with this message and to spread the word about the format.

UUDeview will decode these attachments for you. You'll find a list of yEnc-friendly Linux applications at http://www.yenc.org/linux.htm.

UUEncode/UUDecode

These venerable utilities are included in the sharutils package installed by default in openSUSE. If you know you have a UUEncoded file, you can use UUDecode to extract the file. The telltale sign that an attachment has been UUEncoded is that in the top line, along with the filename, is the three-digit permissions indicator.

Suppose the first line in the attachment looks like this:

```
begin 664 vacation027.jpg
```

This tells us that when it's decoded, we'll have a single JPG image, vacation027.jpg, when we're done. You can UUEncode any number of files in a single instance.

When you get an email like this, save it as a file in your home directory. Leave it with no extension (attach1). Then go to your shell and run the UUDecode program:

```
uudecode attach1
```

This will decode the attachment and produce the vacation027.jpg image in your home directory. You should now see this file if you run the ls command, and you should be able to open it. After you've opened the decoded file, delete attach1.

MIME/Base64

MIME is the general Internet standard for formatting email. It includes the Base64 method for encoding file attachments, as well as messages using non-English characters.

Heinz Tschabitscher at About.com briefly describes what happens when you use Base64: "Base64 encoding takes three bytes, each consisting of eight bits, and represents them as four printable characters in the ASCII standard." Use UUDeview to decode Base64 attachments.

Using UUDeview to Decode a File Attachment

What do you do when you find yourself with an undecoded file attachment? Follow these steps:

1. As we did with the preceding UUEncoded message, use the Save As command in your mail client, save this message in your home directory, and call it **attach1** with no extension.
2. Go to a shell or console. Type this command:

   ```
   uudeview -p Documents attach1
   ```

   This will decode the attachment (whatever form was used to encode it) and place the decoded file(s) in your Documents directory. Type **uudeview** (with no switch) to see a list of all the options.
3. Go to the Documents directory (either by cd-ing in the shell or opening a file manager) and open the newly decoded file(s).

After you've opened the decoded file, there is no need to keep the original attachment.

NOTE

When you have decoded a file attachment, you have just turned it back to a binary file. To view or execute it, you still have to open the decoded file(s).

References

- http://www.mozilla.org—The home port for all things Mozilla, including Firefox, Thunderbird, the SeaMonkey Suite, and Sunbird. Get extensions and themes here.
- http://www.spreadfirefox.com—The community marketing effort for Firefox. Get a link for your own web page, and some ammunition for the war with Internet Explorer.
- http://www.mozilla.org/projects/seamonkey—The next generation of the Mozilla Suite.
- http://konqueror.kde.org—Learn more about both sides of Konqueror.
- http://www.gnome.org/projects/epiphany—Get your Epiphany extensions and learn more about its features.
- http://www.flock.com—Flock social browser.
- http://www.opera.com—Home of the Opera browser. Download the latest version, sign up for OperaMail, and do your own blog, too.
- http://www.gnome.org/projects/evolution—The Evolution home page.
- http://www.mozilla.com/en-US/thunderbird—The Mozilla Thunderbird page.
- http://pim.kde.org—Home of the KDE Personal Information Management suite: Kontact, KMail, Korganizer, and the ancillary tools.
- http://www.Claws-mail.org—Claws, the other GTK-based mail client.
- http://www.mutt.org—The mongrel of text-based email clients.
- http://wiki.mutt.org/?MuttGuide—A user-developed Getting Started guide for Mutt newbies.
- http://www.mozilla.org/projects/calendar/sunbird—The home of the Mozilla Sunbird calendar client.
- http://www.mozilla.org/projects/calendar/lightning—Thunderbird's integrated calendar.
- http://icalshare.com—A place to find user-developed calendars for your openSUSE client.
- http://www.fpx.de/fp/Software/UUDeview—The UUDeview multiformat file attachment decoder. Works with all encoding formats (BinHex, yEnc, MIME, and UUEncode). Enjoy the "Introduction to Encoding" document and get some useful history, too.
- http://www.yenc.org/linux.htm—Linux readers and writers for the yEnc coding format.
- http://email.about.com/cs/standards/a/base64_encoding.htm—An excellent description of Base64 encoding.

- https://addons.mozilla.org/firefox/extensions—Find extensions for Firefox here.
- http://userscripts.org—If you have the Greasemonkey extension to Firefox, SeaMonkey, or Flock browser, find scripts here to customize your web experience.
- https://addons.mozilla.org/seamonkey/extensions—Find SeaMonkey extensions here.
- http://extensions.flock.com/extensions—Find Flock extensions here.
- http://thekompany.com/projects/aethera—Get the KMail experience in Windows with this free software.

CHAPTER 14

Creating Basic Websites

IN THIS CHAPTER

- Choosing a Web Development Tool
- Practice: Building a Site with Quanta Plus
- Weblogging with openSUSE
- References

The Internet is not just a place to visit. More than ever, it's a place to contribute too. openSUSE can help you build your space on the web. There are tools for everyone to create impressive sites, regardless of your skill level and interest in learning the technology behind it.

The weblog revolution has changed the way many people think about the Internet. The rise of personal weblogs (blogs) has transformed how people communicate with each other, and how they relate to the world—or at least the part of the world that's online.

In this chapter, you will explore the tool choices available to you for producing web pages. Then you'll build a basic informational website with Quanta Plus. We will then explore the various Linux tools for making a personal weblog.

Choosing a Web Development Tool

The Linux web developer can choose among several good tools. What you choose depends on your skill level and what your comfort level with writing raw HTML is.

For the Beginner

For the absolute web page beginner, there's nothing better than OpenOffice.org's Writer/Web. To open a new HTML document, you can choose New Web Document from the File menu, or go the View menu and select Web Layout. You can then create new web pages by using Styles in text (see the OpenOffice section of Chapter 9, "Being Productive: Office Suites and Other Tools," for more information on styles), importing images, and adding other graphic elements. You can even create clickable image maps right in the word processor.

In addition, the Web Page Wizard, accessible from the File menu (under Wizards), will convert any existing OpenOffice or Word document (or set of documents) to an HTML page, and upload it to your web server if you like.

1. After a quick introduction, the second wizard screen (Figure 14.1) asks what documents you want to include on your site. Click Add to put OpenOffice or Word docs on your site. Use the arrows on the right to define the order in which documents appear. Edit the Document Information for each document as you see fit. Click Next when finished.

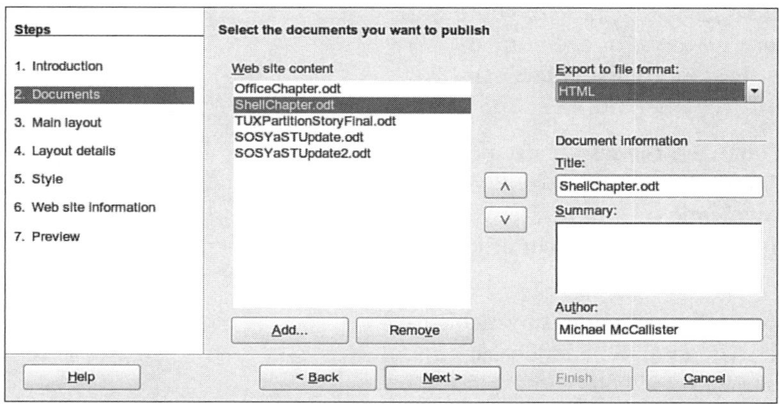

FIGURE 14.1 Transform your ordinary OpenOffice or Word documents into web pages with the OpenOffice.org Web Page Wizard.

2. On the next page (Figure 14.2), define the layout for your page. The wizard will even put the site's table of contents in a separate frame if you like.

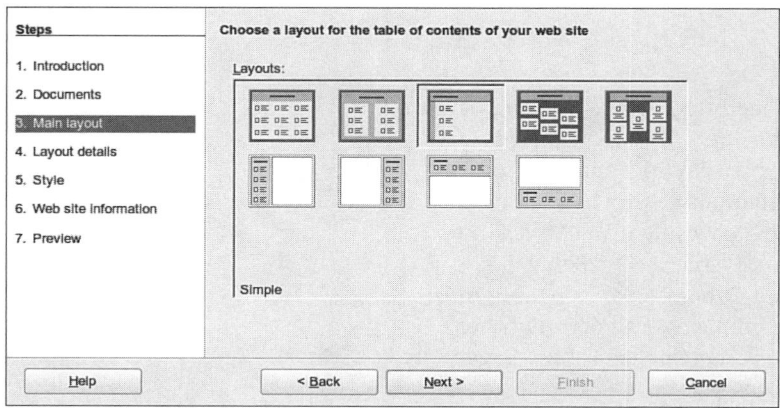

FIGURE 14.2 Select a layout for your page.

3. The third page (Figure 14.3) lets you set details for your layout. Note the option to "Optimize the layout for screen resolution." By default, this is set at 800×600. There's a good reason for this: Most people still use this resolution, even with the higher options available to them! This will change over time, with the continuing transition to flat-panel monitors, but we just aren't there yet. Nonetheless, if you are certain the only people visiting your site are on the bleeding edge, go ahead and optimize for 1024×768. Also, check the box that includes the Last Change Date on your page. This tells your visitors that the information on your site is current. Click Next.

Steps
1. Introduction
2. Documents
3. Main layout
4. Layout details
5. Style
6. Web site information
7. Preview

Customize the selected layout
Include the following information for each document in the table of contents:
File name
Description
Author
Creation date
Last change date
File format
File format icon
Number of pages
Size in KB
Optimize the layout for screen resolution:
640x480
800x600
1024x768
Help
< Back
Next >
Finish
Cancel

FIGURE 14.3 Select your optimal screen resolution and other details on this page.

4. The Style screen lets you select a color scheme, background, and icon set for your site. Figure 14.4 shows you the defaults, but you have a variety of colors to choose from for your basic style. Keep in mind the readability of the site when choosing a style. Click Next when finished.

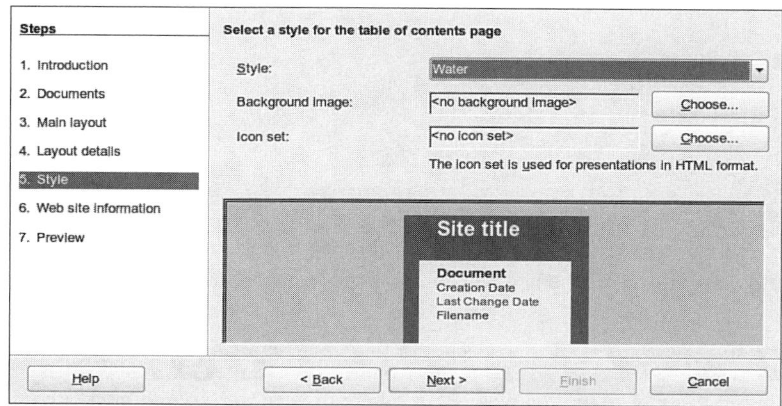

FIGURE 14.4 Watch for readability when selecting a Style here.

5. Define your site's metadata in this final settings page (see Figure 14.5). Search engines use your site's title and description to pick up keywords, so these are important. Click Next.

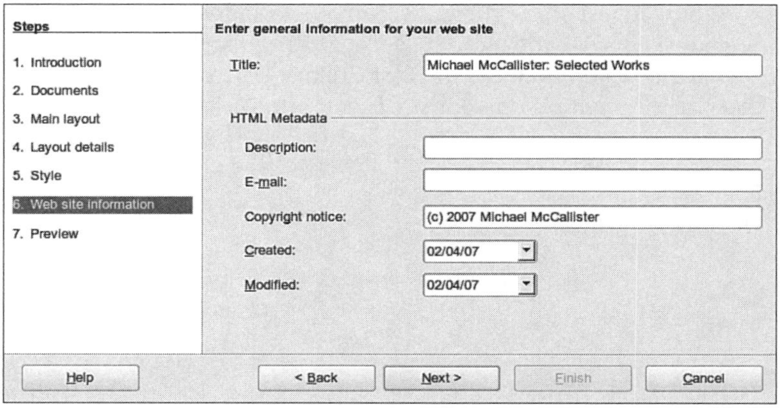

FIGURE 14.5 Describe and title your site accurately for proper categorization by search engines.

6. In the final screen, you can preview your site, and tell OpenOffice where to publish the site. If you have properly configured OpenOffice, you could upload the site directly to your web server. Otherwise you can save to a local folder (as shown in Figure 14.6), or zip it up for manual uploading to your server later. Click Finish to publish your site.

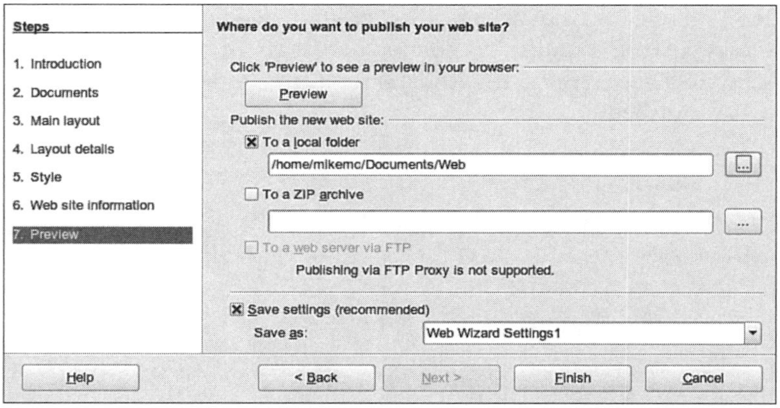

FIGURE 14.6 Complete your site by publishing to your server or a local directory.

NOTE

There are many schools of thought regarding whether a beginner is better served by a set of templates or by learning the basic HTML tags. OpenOffice's Web Page Wizard and similar programs are useful to a point, but you should still consider studying the basics of HTML if you expect to move beyond the very basics with your web skills.

Unlike Microsoft Word, Writer/Web delivers very clean and standards-based HTML code.

The advantage of using a word processor such as OpenOffice for website creation is that it's a familiar environment. Paragraph styles transfer easily from a standard document to the web, and for the most part it is more WYSIWYG (what you see is what you get) than a specialized editor.

Where the office suites fall short compared to more specialized web-development tools is in creating projects that link pages together in a coherent site. Applications such as Quanta and Bluefish offer advantages that we will explore later.

Browser-Based Page Creators

An alternative to word processors are the browser-based page-creation tools. The genesis for these was Netscape's early decision to include Composer in its suite of Internet tools. This tool is still present in the SeaMonkey suite.

When the Mozilla project decided to break the components of the Netscape suite into sleeker, faster individual applications that still worked well together, some thought Composer might die. Coming to its rescue was Michael Robertson and his team from Linspire (formerly Lindows). They have shepherded the development of a new, simple page-creation tool called nvu (pronounced N-View). It fills the need for a simple tool for new users who don't need to build massive sites with lots of Flash and glitter, but have something to contribute.

Specialized Web Tools

Next up on the scale are the special tools created for making websites. Like Microsoft FrontPage or Macromedia Dreamweaver, these applications handle all the relevant tasks in building a professional website, with the advantage of being free.

Two of these have become the standard applications for Linux web developers:

- Quanta Plus (now KDE-WebDev) started out as an independent project, but has since become integrated within the KDE desktop.
- Bluefish was created with the Gimp Toolkit (GTK), and is popular with GNOME users. It runs on KDE as well.

One difference between the Linux development tools and the Windows products mentioned earlier: These tools are proudly non-WYSIWYG, at least by default, preferring to show you the code first and testing the appearance later. What this means is that you have to know at least a little bit about HTML tagging and how it works before using these tools successfully.

In our forthcoming example, we will not dwell extensively on what specific tags mean, but you will get a sense of how tagging works.

Quanta is not as ruthlessly anti-WYSIWYG as Bluefish, though. With version 3.3, Quanta introduced the VPL (Visual Page Layout) editor, which can display in place of (or in) a dual view with the default (a.k.a. Source) editor. This is still a little buggy, but not bad for a first version.

This is not to say that the only help you get from these tools are some extra toolbars that add a tag when you tell it. Quanta comes with an assortment of templates to handle all the basics of page creation, as you can see in Figure 14.7. No navigation tools are included, though.

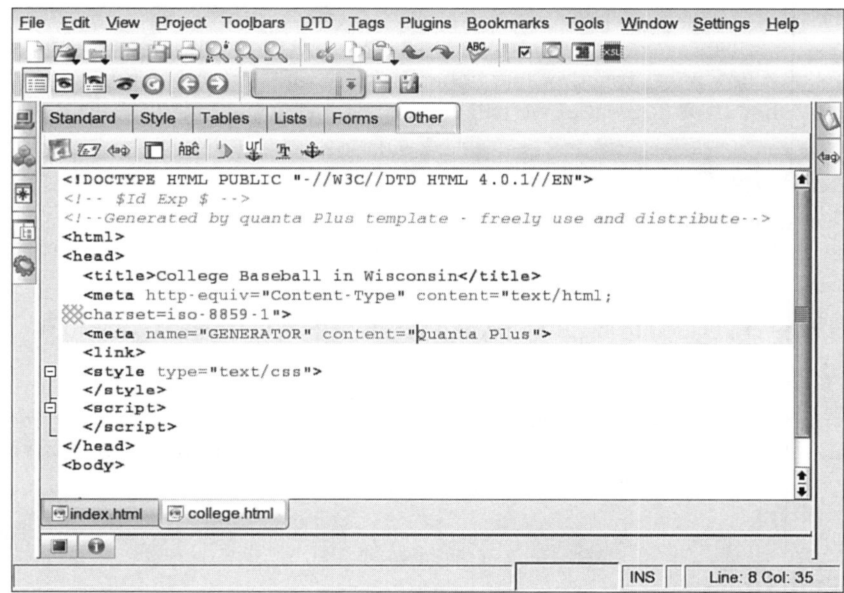

FIGURE 14.7 Quanta's basic HTML template creates a standard page heading and not much else.

One thing you get with a web tool that you can't get with an ordinary word processor is the support for a variety of web technologies. It is often as easy to create an interactive PHP-based site, or any of several varieties of XML, as it is a static HTML page, if you know what you're doing.

Both tools will also display your pages in most, if not all, prominent Linux web browsers. However, Bluefish and Quanta each handle this differently. Quanta displays pages in its own internal browser and in Konqueror, Firefox, Mozilla, Netscape, Opera, and Lynx (a text-based browser). Bluefish handles Mozilla, Netscape, Opera, Galeon, and the GNOME default browser. You can add other browsers in the external preferences dialog box. Of course, you must have each browser installed on your system for this feature to work.

Testing Pages in Internet Explorer

Do you want to test your pages on Microsoft Internet Explorer 6 without leaving Linux? This is not easy, but it is possible. One cannot say the same for the new Internet Explorer 7. IE7 will only run on Windows XP and Vista, which Wine does not yet support. With proper licensing, you can run IE7 inside a Windows virtual machine, like Win4Lin or VMware Player. See Chapter 11, "Going Cross-Platform," for more information on these applications.

Internet Explorer will run under Wine, the Windows emulator, but it takes some work. After installing Wine and the cabextract package (via YaST), download IEs 4 Linux at http://www.tatanka.com.br/ies4linux/page/Main_Page.

Extract the tarball to your home directory, open a shell and type **`./ies4linux`** to run the script. In addition to IE6, you can also install versions 5.01 and 5.5 of IE (if you want to be thorough in your browser testing). By default, it will also install the latest Flash Player plugin for that browser. When the script is finished, run /bin/ie6 in your home directory to confirm your install.

Now add Internet Explorer to the browser list in Quanta or Bluefish.

1. In Bluefish, go to Edit, Preferences, External Programs. At the top you'll see the browser list. See the line labeled Untitled? Double-click and type **`Internet Explorer`** there. Click Command, and type **`wine iexplore %s`** (for the current file). Click Add and this will appear in the browser list. Click OK to confirm.
2. In Quanta, go to Settings, Configure Actions. Expand the All tree, scroll down to the View with (browser) settings. This is what you'll base your new action on. Click New Action. Settings are as follows:

   Type: Script

   Text: View with Internet Explorer (You can choose an icon, too.)

   ToolTip (optional): View with Internet Explorer

   Shortcut (Custom): Alt+Shift+F6 (All the others are variations on F6.)

   Detailed Settings:

   `sh %scriptdir/externalpreview.sh %pid wine iexplore` (To save typing, copy and paste from one of the other Views with choices, and then add **`wine iexplore`** to the end.)
3. Leave the other boxes as they are. Click OK to confirm.

Both Quanta and Bluefish come with ample documentation for the product and reference manuals for HTML and PHP. Quanta also includes references for JavaScript and cascading style sheets (CSS).

Übergeek Web Page Tools

You know that a real Linux geek doesn't need a GUI tool to write for the web. It is just markup—hypertext markup at that. Maybe all you need is a text editor and a tag reference guide. Rest assured that every text editor included with openSUSE is fully capable of producing perfect HTML code just the way you like it.

`emacs`, as per its reputation, not only comes with a web browser, but also has a major mode for Standard Generalized Markup Language (SGML), which means it will help you write to any Document Type Definition (DTD): HTML, XHTML, XML, and so on. Open or create any file with an HTML extension and `emacs` will add the relevant menus to your display. All these things work in Xemacs as well.

Vim has a Convert-to-HTML syntax file called 2HTML. Jedit also has a Code2HTML plug-in and plug-ins that will insert tags into your text.

Practice: Building a Site with Quanta Plus

So you have a lot of knowledge about something and you think other people might be interested. There's no reason not to put up a website with all the stuff you know. In this section, we will work with Quanta to draw up a site with a few basic pages of information about baseball in Wisconsin.

Planning Your Site

Ideally, before you build your site, you should do some planning. Most importantly, you have to think about where to store your site; that is, you have to select a web host to keep your pages up. Chances are your ISP offers you some free space, and there are always the free web hosts such as GeoCities, Angelfire, and the like. If you're serious about building a web resource site, you will want to register your domain name and should consider paying for a host. A good web-hosting company will work hard to keep those servers running and your site available to web surfers around the globe.

Another option, particularly if you have a high-speed, always-on connection, would be to host your own site. openSUSE includes the Apache web server, so updating your site is a trifling matter. This would be a reason to get a static IP address from your ISP, because your site's availability would be hit-and-miss if the world's DNS servers had to re-locate your site every time you rebooted and got a new DHCP address. For our example, we will self-host the site. See Chapters 26, "Managing Web and FTP Servers," and 27, "Managing Domain Names," for more information on Apache and domain names.

The next thing to consider is what type of information you want to have on your site and how the pages will be organized. A mind-mapping tool like View Your Mind or a flow-charting tool like Dia or Kivio may help you think this out, but quite often, it's time for the old pencil and paper to work its magic.

Our site will have a home page that mostly links to subpages for NCAA Division 1 college baseball, minor league teams in Wisconsin, and the state's only Major League franchise, the Milwaukee Brewers. We'll have a history page, for information related to the Milwaukee Braves, the defunct minor league franchises, and the Milwaukee Bears of the Negro National League. Finally, we'll have a listing of folks with Wisconsin ties in the Baseball Hall of Fame in Cooperstown, NY. Figure 14.8 shows a very rough Kivio site plan diagram.

Now it's time to build the site.

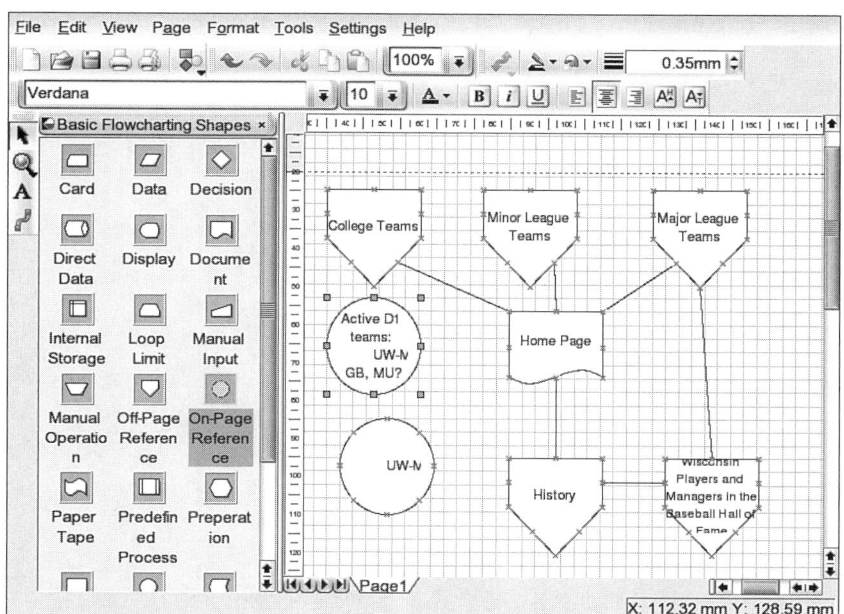

FIGURE 14.8 A site plan for the Wisconsin Baseball site.

Building the Site

The first task in creating our site in Quanta is to create a new project. Go to Project, New Project, and the wizard dialog box shown in Figure 14.9 appears.

Name the project and Quanta fills in the filename. If you already know who your web host is, adjust the Server Settings so Quanta can immediately upload updated files when you ask it. Set the Main Directory; you can store your working files anywhere, but the Documents folder is a fine place. The Templates and Toolbars directories will be placed underneath the Main Directory, although if you have multiple projects going, you may want to have only one of each of these. Finally, if you have an existing site that you want to pull into Quanta, choose Use wget to Download Files from a Site in the Project Sources area. Click Next to locate existing source pages.

What's on the second page (see Figure 14.10) is determined by how you answered the Project Sources question on the first page. Because we have no existing files to bring into the project, there's nothing to do.

Check the Insert Files box at the top, and then add selected files or the entire folder with the appropriate buttons at the bottom.

If you select the option to pull existing files online in the first screen, the New Project Wizard will ask where to look in the Site Source line (unless you've already identified the server in the first screen) and generate a `wget` command. You can edit the options if you want (run **`wget -h`** from a shell to see all the options for this program), but clicking `Start` will retrieve all the files in your site.

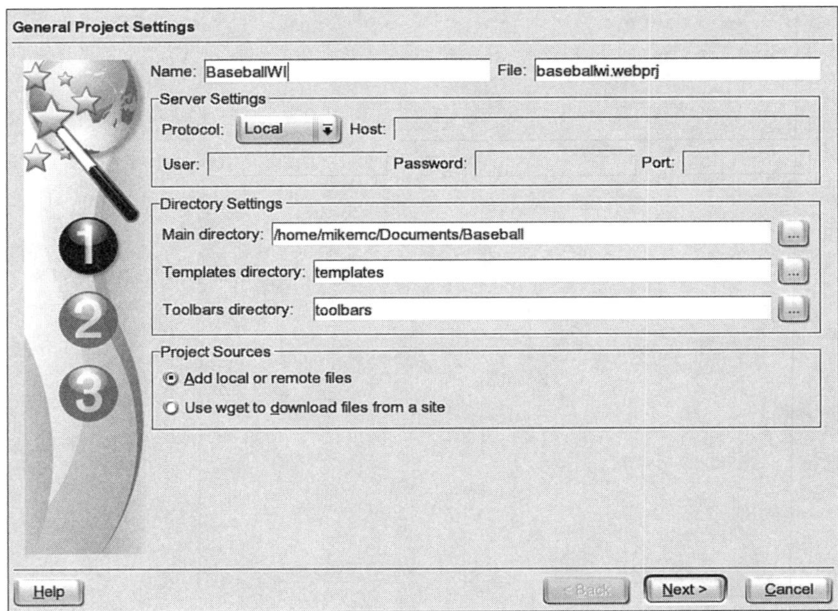

FIGURE 14.9 Creating a new project in Quanta is a three-step process.

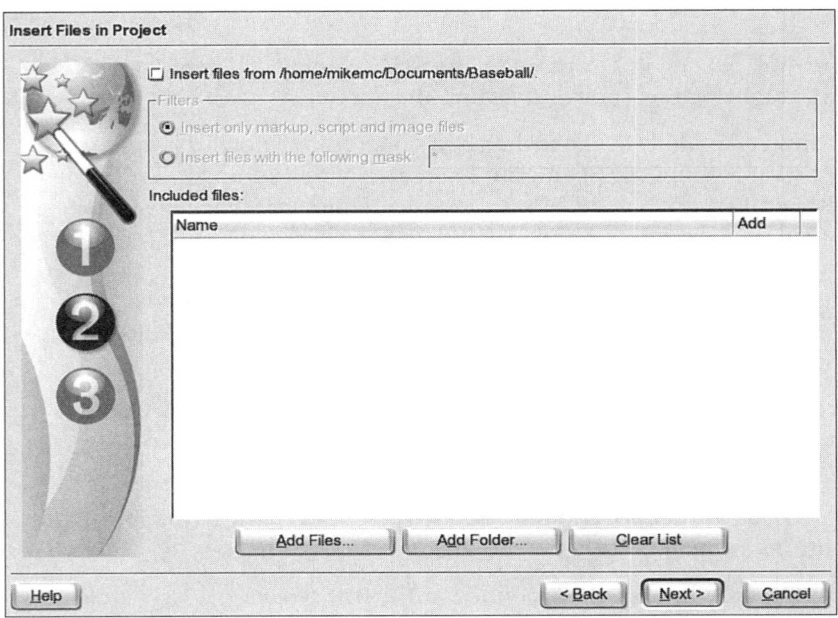

FIGURE 14.10 Pull existing local files into your new project with this dialog box.

When you've pulled all the existing files into the project, click `Next`. Your last task is to tell Quanta what type of site you're building. You may also identify yourself (or anyone else) as the site author.

In Figure 14.11, you can see the varieties of DTDs you can use for any given site. For our example, we will use the default HTML 4.0 (Transitional), but you can always select something different from the drop-down menu. We will also stick with the default UTF8 Unicode encoding; you'll rarely have to change that. Also check the Insert global templates box; this will give you quick access to different options for your site. Click Finish to complete your new project.

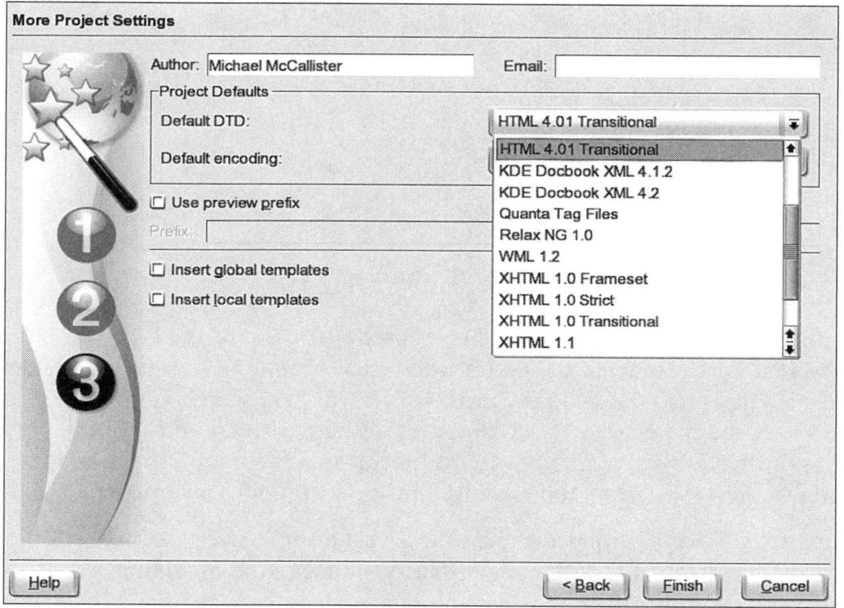

FIGURE 14.11 Quanta lets you select from different DTDs to describe the type of site you're putting up.

The first page in any website is the Index page, where people wind up if they access your domain name. Creating a new project does not automatically open a new page in Quanta, so we need to do that. There are three ways to do this:

- To open a blank page with no header information, click the `New Page` toolbar icon (or go to `File`, `New`).
- Click the `Templates` icon from the vertical toolbar located to the left of the editor. Go to `Pages`, `HTML_4.01`, `Basic`. Double-click to create the page. You can then fill in the page title yourself.
- Use the `Quick Start` dialog box. Click the first icon in the Standard toolbar above the editor space. This dialog box (see Figure 14.12) lets you define nearly everything about your page layout.

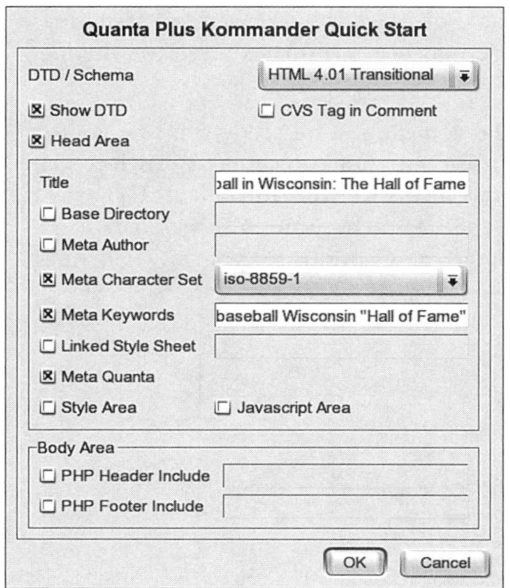

FIGURE 14.12 Create a new page with the Quick Start dialog box.

Enter the title of this page—that is, the title people will see at the top of the browser window when they visit (and also what comes up when they search for your page). Beside the default options, we have also entered keywords, which will help search engines identify the topics the site is about. Separate words and phrases here with commas. Don't overload this tag; if you have more than a few items here, a search engine's spider may decide you're trying to skew the results too heavily, and it may ignore you entirely.

Quanta makes it pretty easy for multiple authors to work on a site. As you can see, you can change several project defaults for each page from this dialog box, including the DTD, the base directory, and the author. If you don't check the boxes, Quanta will create the page using the Project defaults.

When you've finished with the page settings, click `OK` to confirm. Quanta may ask you if you want the new page to be part of the current project. You should see the editor page looking a lot like Figure 14.13.

CAUTION

The project must be open before you run the Quick Start dialog box; otherwise, you won't get the page created properly unless you identify the base directory where the templates are stored.

Adding content is simple. Use the existing toolbars to tag paragraphs either before or after writing your text. Use the Visual Page Layout WYSIWYG editor to see how it looks while you're still working. You can edit from either the Source or the VPL editor. Figure 14.13 shows the start of our page in the VPL editor.

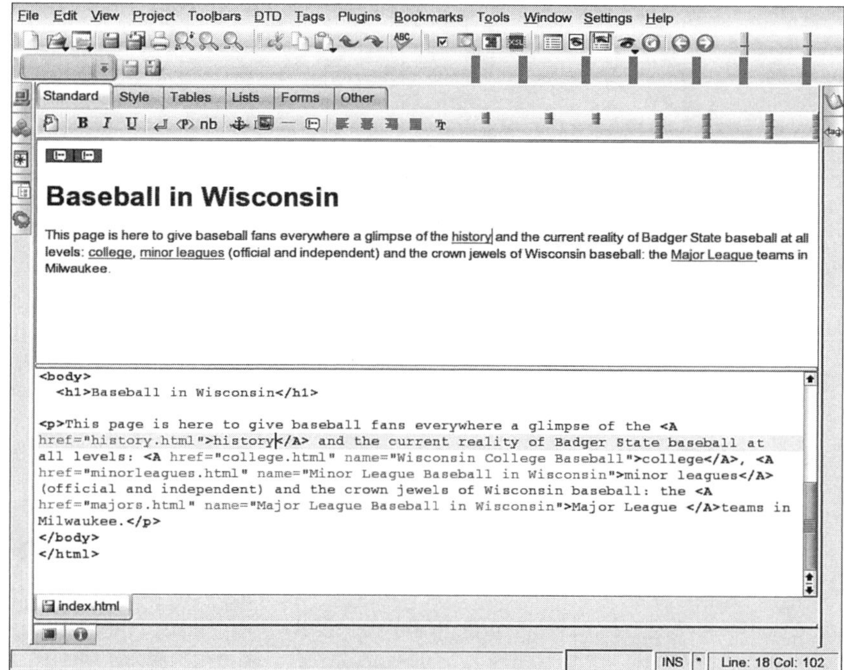

FIGURE 14.13 Insert images to liven up the page and include links to other pages on the site.

When you've got a page ready, test it in several browsers to make sure it looks good for everyone. Using the Lynx browser will also indirectly tell you how usable your site is for a blind person using a page reader.

When your site is ready, press F8 (or go to `Project`, `Upload Project`) to put your handiwork where people can see it. This dialog box shown in Figure 14.14 comes up.

Select (or define) a host server in the Profile Name box. Select the files to upload from the main window (all are selected by default) and click `Proceed`. Quanta will connect with and upload your files and give you a progress report at the bottom of the screen.

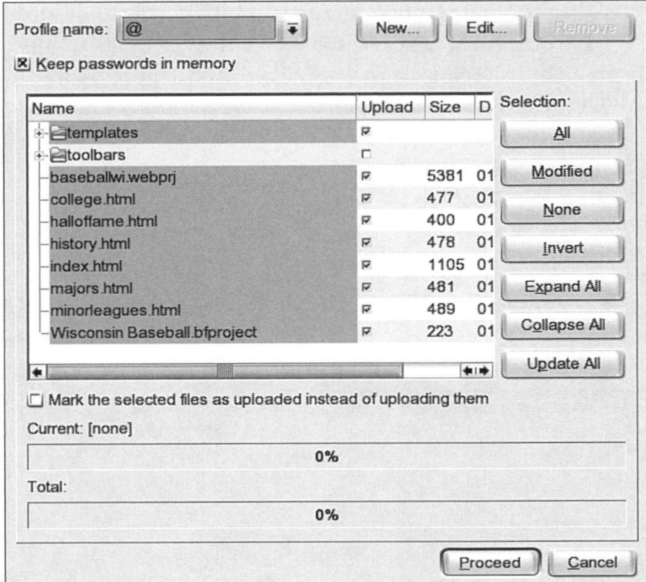

FIGURE 14.14 Upload your finished website to your host's servers automatically with Quanta.

Weblogging with openSUSE

Weblogging, or just plain *blogging,* has been around for a relatively long time. The practice managed to claw its way into broad public consciousness in 2004, and millions of blogs have been created, though a relatively small percentage are regularly updated.

Some observers believe that weblogs represent a new form of journalism, as ordinary folks bring their life experiences and perspectives to bear on events large and small and have a potentially global audience to read what they say.

Bloggers are many types of people, using their sites in all sorts of ways, serious and trivial:

- Many people post their personal journals online, to keep friends and family posted on the latest news.
- Enthusiasts about all kinds of things view their blog as a place to share new information (often gleaned from the web itself) about a shared passion.
- Businesspeople are increasingly using blogs to communicate with employees and customers.
- People on the scene at business or technology conferences and similar events report, often in real time, on what's happening to inform those who couldn't be there.
- Political commentators of nearly every persuasion imaginable share news, gossip, and commentary on current events.

- Journalists—professional, amateur, and inbetween—share information about stories they cover that may not make it into the paper or on the air.

Blogs can be one person's project or have multiple authors. They can be on one topic, broad or narrowly defined, or they can be on whatever pops into an author's head. There are great blogs and poor blogs in all categories. Some are read by thousands every day, but most are read by only a few.

For just a few examples in how to do a blog right, consider these:

- The Doc Searls Weblog (http://doc.weblogs.com)—Longtime columnist at Linux Journal magazine and co-author of *The Cluetrain Manifesto*, Searls puts a lot of interesting ideas out for consideration, and some pretty nice photography too. His blogroll will take you to interesting places as well.
- Linux-Watch (http://www.linux-watch.com)—Linux news and analysis, mostly from Steven J. Vaughn-Nichols of CNET News.
- Worldchanging: Tools, Models, and Ideas for Building a Bright Green Future (http://www.worldchanging.com)—A group blog promoting practical and visionary ideas for sustainable living and development.

Whatever you want to do with your blog, about the only rule that matters is that a blog home page features posts in reverse chronological order, with the most recent posts at the top of the page. Other characteristics that help differentiate blogs from ordinary websites include the following:

- Blog posts are usually archived and have a link to the URL where the post will be archived when it floats off the home page. This URL, called a *permalink*, is done because bloggers often link to other blog posts to comment on them. With permalinks, and a similar process called TrackBacks, readers can then follow the conversation between two or more blogs on the same topic.
- Blogs often have sidebars, called blogrolls, with listings of the bloggers' favorite blogs and other websites.
- Bloggers were among the first to use an XML technology called Really Simple Syndication (RSS) or a competing technology, Atom, to make postings easily accessible. More traditional news outlets are now adding these XML feeds to their sites, and browsers (Firefox, Opera) and portal sites (Yahoo!) are including RSS and Atom readers in their products. See the next section for more on syndication.
- Most blogs encourage interaction between reader and writer. Some blogs permit readers to comment on posts directly on the page. This practice has decreased as spammers began inundating popular bloggers' pages with their wares, but has not disappeared completely.

Not every blog has all these features, and some sites that have these features are not blogs.

Blogging, because it's on the web, is an activity that isn't terribly concerned with operating systems. Many blogs are written directly in a blogger's browser and hosted on the same site. Many bloggers, though, want to separate the writing from the posting, and so use editing tools that run locally on a desktop or laptop and then upload pages to a remote site, just like regular websites.

In this section, we'll review some of the more popular tools that Linux users blog with along with a quick review of some of the popular blog hosts (like Blogger, Typepad, and LiveJournal) that welcome bloggers with all operating systems to participate.

openSUSE does not include specific blogging tools in the distribution, although the Quanta team wants you to know that one of the biggest "A-list" blogs, WilWheaton.net, is produced with its tool. Some tools are easy to install; others require a little bit of database or Apache savvy.

TIP

Whatever blog engine you choose, Firefox users who tend to create a lot of links in their posts (or just like the convenience of one user interface for many blogs) should check out the ScribeFire extension for Firefox. This professional blogger's tool lets you write blog posts in a window at the bottom of the browser, and post them directly to many blog services, or your own server. Visit http://scribefire.com for information.

Blogging with Blosxom

Blosxom is an incredibly easy blog-creation tool written by Rael Dornfest, one of the blog founding fathers. Blosxom (pronounced "blossom") is a simple CGI script that sits on your web server and turns ordinary text files into blog posts.

For those with simple blogging needs (mostly plain text, with the occasional hand-created link and styled text), Blosxom is perfect. But don't think that it's just for basic users. With Blosxom's plug-in architecture and easily modified configuration dialog box, you can accomplish many things with your blog.

Blosxom runs as a Common Gateway Interface (CGI) script on your web server, so if you want your blog live on the web at all times, you need to have a host that permits running CGI scripts (most do). You may want to experiment with several tools before settling on one, though. For this, you have the capability to run Apache on your own openSUSE system. See Chapter 26 for a more detailed explanation of Apache.

To try Blosxom on your own Apache server, follow these steps to install:

1. Go to http://www.blosxom.com/downloads/blosxom.zip to download Blosxom.
2. Extract blosxom.cgi into the `~/public_html/cgi` directory and make it executable (**`chmod 755`**).
3. Create a local directory to store your Blosxom posts; Blosxom recommends `~/blosxom`, but you can choose anything you like.

CAUTION

Don't choose a common directory to store your posts in. Blosxom will post to your blog any file in the directory with the appropriate extension (*.txt by default).

4. Open `blosxom.cgi` in a text editor to configure your blog. The first 10 entries in the script describe what Blosxom should do. Name your blog. Give it a description, which can be prosaic (this blog is about growing marigolds) or creative (ruminations on canine lycanthropy and other wizardly things). Set the language. Tell the script where to look for posts (the directory you selected in Step 3). You can probably leave the remainder of the entries with their default settings, but consult the manual if you want to know more.
5. Write a test post. Open your text editor and write something. Save it with a .txt extension into the posting directory.
6. Open your favorite web browser and go to the directory where `blosxom.cgi` lives, such as

   ```
   http://home/<username>/public_html/cgi/blosxom.cgi
   ```

7. Your test post should appear, with your blog's title and description, along with the date and time of your post.

For more information on working with your blog, visit the http://www.blosxom.com site.

Movable Type and Typepad

Movable Type (MT) is considered by many to be the gold-standard weblog application. It has a reputation of being somewhat difficult to install, but it has so many features, it's worth the moderate pain. Many of the more technical-oriented blogs run MT, as do quite a few businesses and news organizations.

Typepad is the Blogger-type hosting service set up by Movable Type's developers. Typepad makes it easy to produce a high-quality MT-type blog without having to manage the installation. They've even made it a going concern by charging a minimal monthly fee ($4.95 as this is written) for basic users.

MT runs on just about every platform and can use any web server or database application you prefer. There is a free version for personal use, but if you want to have multiple authors for your blog, you'll need a paid version (less than $100). An Enterprise version is also available.

Go to http://www.sixapart.com/movabletype/pricing.html to download your desired MT version. You'll be asked to establish (or login to) your TypeKey account with minimal personal information. The free TypeKey account also allows you to leave comments on MT-based blogs. This is a security measure against comment spam, which is produced by spammers who spew their messages in blog comment logs.

Once you're logged in, download the MT tarball. While you're at it, you should probably pick up the Installation and User's Guides at http://www.sixapart.com/movabletype/docs.html.

Follow these steps to install Movable Type into your local Apache server.

1. As with Bloxsom, extract MT into the `~/public_html/cgi` directory. You may want to rename the resulting MT directory from `/MT-<version>-<language>` to just plain MT.

2. In a shell, type **`chmod 755 *.cgi`** to grant global read/write permissions to all the CGI scripts in the MT directory.

3. MT relies on a bunch of Perl modules to do its work. It ships with common modules that work in all its supported platforms, but you may not have all the modules installed that MT needs. To figure out what you may need to get, MT provides a script that checks your system. Open a browser and enter this url: http://localhost/cgi-bin/mt/mt-check.cgi. A list of required and optional modules will appear.

4. Install any necessary Perl modules through the Comprehensive Perl Archive Network (CPAN). See the CPAN section of Chapter 30, "Using Perl and Python" and the MT Installation Guide for more information on using CPAN.

5. Open mt-config.cgi-original in a text editor. Identify the URL that would point to the MT main directory in the CGIPath line; for example, you could identify the following: CGIPath http://home/<username>/public_html/MT.

6. Still in the text editor, configure MT to work with the database engine of your choice. This is where your posts will be stored. See the MT Installation Guide for sample database configurations, and Chapter 29, "Managing Databases" for more on MySQL and PostgreSQL configuration.

7. When you have completed the initial configuration, save the file as mt-config.cgi.

8. Now you're ready to launch MT for the first time. Open http://home/<username>public_html/MT/index.html. You'll be asked for a username, email address, and password to log in to the database. Click Finish Install. Your MT database will initialize for awhile.

9. When the MT database is initialized, you'll see the Main Menu. Now you can post!

Blogging with WordPress

WordPress is a very popular system, but a little complex to run. It is driven by a MySQL database, which must be running before you get started. Chances are your web host will support database-driven sites, but you should check in advance.

TIP

You can also use the free online WordPress blog service, www.wordpress.com to manage your blog. You don't have quite as many options as if you were hosting the blog yourself, but do not need to immerse yourself in the details if you don't want to. Wordpress.com also tries to foster a sense of community among its bloggers that isn't forced. For SUSE, Linux, and other sorts of open source news and commentary, check out a pair of WordPress.com blogs:

The Linux and Open Source Blog: http://linux.wordpress.com

Notes from the Metaverse: http://metaverse.wordpress.com

Similarly, if you want to try out WordPress on your local system first, you will have to get MySQL and PHP set up and running. Use YaST to install the PHP and MySQL packages. See Chapter 29 for more information on setting up MySQL.

To set up WordPress:

1. Go to http://wordpress.org/latest.tar.gz to download the current version.
2. Extract the tarball to any directory (your home directory will do nicely, as it will create a WordPress directory).
3. Open MySQL, and create a WordPress user. Call it `wpress`.
4. Create a new MySQL database. From a root shell, type **`/usr/bin/mysqladmin -p create wordpress`**.
5. Log in to the WordPress database: **`/usr/local/mysql/bin/mysql -p -u root.`**
6. Give the WordPress user access to the WordPress database: **`GRANT ALL PRIVILEGES ON wordpress TO wpress@localhost IDENTIFIED BY wppass;  GRANT ALL PRIVILEGES ON wordpress TO wpress IDENTIFIED BY wppass;`**. When this is completed, type **`exit`** to return to the shell.
7. Either from the shell or your favorite file manager, copy the contents of the WordPress directory that you created in Step 2 to the `~/public_html` home directory. If you already have content there (or want your blog to be part of your larger site), copy the whole directory over.
8. Open your favorite browser and go to the directory where you extracted WordPress to: `http://localhost/wp-admin/install.php`. The install screens check that everything is in order and will occasionally ask you a question.
9. WordPress generates a password for the administrator in the install process. Log in to post. You'll see a very nice interface that's pretty straightforward. Fire away!

The WordPress website offers, among other things, plug-ins and templates to further customize your experience.

Popular Blog Services

The biggest and best-known blogging services generally offer both live-in-your-browser posting and free storage space on their servers for your blog. Some offer the option to email posts, which can be a handy device. Here's a quick overview of what you can do with these services.

Blogger (www.blogger.com)

This is the best known and still the easiest way to get started in the blogosphere. Basic accounts are free, and there are lots of templates to choose from.

In many ways, Blogger is the America Online of the weblog industry; it's where people get started. Blogger blogs run the gamut of styles, but lean toward the personal-journal end of the spectrum.

There are three ways to post. The web-based interface and using email are the standard ways; you can also create an audio-post via telephone.

LiveJournal (www.livejournal.com)

LiveJournal started as a way for a group of friends to keep each other posted on their lives. It grew into a large, but still by-invitation-only, community of all kinds of journal-keepers. Now owned by Six Apart, the Movable Type company, anyone can get a LiveJournal account and start blogging.

LiveJournals are best known for their mood-indicator and other colorful graphics and lists of connections between users. The LiveJournal code is open source software (visit www.livejournal.org to contact the development team or download the source).

You can post via the web interface or use one of several Linux clients (Kluje for KDE, Logjam and Drivel for GNOME). They also have clients for personal digital assistants (Palm and PocketPC) and cell phones.

Typepad

As mentioned earlier, Typepad is the hosting service from Movable Type's developers. It is currently available for $4.95 a month for basic users.

WordPress.com

The WordPress hosting service is free of charge, and offers bloggers statistics on visitors and feed subscribers. You get a broad choice of themes, and can change themes whenever the mood strikes. The posting editor is also very nice.

Syndicating Your Blog

As you travel around the Web, you may have seen the little orange rectangles marked XML on certain pages. This is especially true for weblog sites, but increasingly true on regular news sites (CNET News.com, BBC News, Christian Science Monitor, CNN, and Alternet, among others) as well. Perhaps you've clicked the button and saw the equivalent of an HTML source page and wondered what that was for. What you're really seeing is a new way of delivering news and information to you: headline (or full text) syndication of website content.

Publishing a syndicated version of your blog is a great way to gain readers. Most blogging software does this by default, and it is otherwise easy to set up. With syndication, readers can find your blog through blog-search sites like Technorati, Weblogs.com, Daypop, Feedster, Bloglines, and Syndic8. As a blog reader, syndication also simplifies building collections of blogs to read.

Syndication is about delivering information (also called *newsfeeds*, or just plain *feeds*) from your site to other sites or applications. When you syndicate your site, you can deliver just headlines, full-text rendering of your postings, or some portion of them. Applications called *aggregators*, or *feedreaders*, ping the server periodically (typically hourly) to see what's new and deliver new content to readers who have subscribed to your feed.

NOTE

You'll learn more about feedreaders in Chapter 16, "Collaborating With Others."

There are two popular formats to syndicate with: RSS and Atom. This is another religious war you can choose to participate in, or not. RSS (also known as Rich Site Summary) is the older format. Development of this format is run by Dave Winer of Userland Software. A group of developers/bloggers decided that RSS wasn't providing the features they wanted and developed the Atom standard. Some blog software supports one standard or the other, and some support both. All the aggregators support both standards.

References

- http://www.openoffice.org—Participate in and get help from the OpenOffice.org project.
- http://www.nvu.com/—The nvu (N-View) project for a Mozilla-based web-authoring tool.
- http://quanta.kdewebdev.org/—Quanta Plus project page for the KDE web-authoring tool.
- http://kdewebdev.org—The KDE WebDev suite site, for Quanta and its subsidiary tools.
- http://bluefish.openoffice.nl—Bluefish, the GTK-based web-authoring tool.
- http://bfwiki.tellefsen.net—The Bluefish Wiki, where the development team keeps the rest of us posted on what's happening.
- http://www.screem.org—A GNOME/GTK editor for HTML and XML files.
- http://www.webmonkey.com—The all-purpose online web-design school. Tutorials on various web technologies for all skill levels, from basic HTML to Apache to ColdFusion. Like Wired magazine, occasionally the pages lean to the illegible.
- http://webdesign.about.com—Down-to-earth advice about website design. Free online classes in HTML and cascading style sheets, too.

- http://metaverse.wordpress.com—Notes from the Metaverse, the author's technology weblog. Lots of links and news related to open source software and openSUSE.
- http://www.planetsuse.org—Planet SUSE, a group blog of openSUSE developers.
- http://directory.google.com/Top/Computers/Internet/On_the_Web/Weblogs/Tools—The current directory of blogging tools and services. You'll find something useful here.
- http://www.blosxom.com—Download and learn about Blosxom, the CGI-based blogging tool.
- http://www.billstclair.com/blogmax—The Blogmax extension for `emacs`.
- http://wordpress.org—WordPress blog and content-management tool. Very busy and helpful support forums.
- http://www.wordpress.com—Hosted WordPress blogging.
- http://www.blogger.com—Still the easiest and cheapest way to start blogging. Now managed by Google.
- http://www.sixapart.com—The company behind Movable Type and Typepad. Access either product from the company blog page.
- http://www.livejournal.com—LiveJournal is a place for more personal blogs and building communities of kindred bloggers.
- http://radio.weblogs.com/0102385/2003/04/24.html#a329—A description of how to run the Windows blog program Radio Userland under Wine.
- http://www.xul.fr/en-xml-rss.html—A step-by-step guide to building and using an RSS feed.
- http://atomenabled.org—Whys and hows for the Atom feed standard.
- http://akregator.kde.org—The Akregator feedreader for KDE.
- http://www.tatanka.com/br/ies4linux/page/Main_Page—Download Internet Explorer for testing pages without learning Linux.
- http://doc.weblogs.com—Longtime columnist at Linux Journal magazine and co-author of *The Cluetrain Manifesto*, Searls puts a lot of interesting ideas out for consideration, and some pretty nice photography too. His blogroll will take you to interesting places as well.
- http://www.linux-watch.com—Linux news and analysis, mostly from Steven J. Vaughn-Nichols of CNET News.
- http://www.worldchanging.com—A group blog promoting practical and visionary ideas for sustainable living and development.
- http://www.scribefire.com—ScribeFire is a professional blogger's tool that lets you write blog posts in a window at the bottom of the Firefox browser, then posts them directly to your blog.
- http://linux.wordpress.com—The Linux and Open Source Blog.

CHAPTER 15

Managing Email Servers

IN THIS CHAPTER

Is there a single application more essential in making people want to be on the Internet than electronic mail? The idea of dashing off quick notes to colleagues, friends, and family without having to buy envelopes, find stamps, and locate a mailbox—and have the note in the recipient's hands in seconds, not days—it's almost magical, isn't it?

For many of us, that magic has worn off a little. We have to wade through piles of spam, forwarded jokes, and semi-pointless mailing-list postings to get to the really important stuff. And don't get us started on the weekly battle against the latest virus to hit the wild. Email is a blessing, but with its share of accompanying curses.

The magic of email happens thanks to a bunch of standards and protocols helped along by a network-aware operating system. In this chapter, you will learn a bit about the mechanics of how email gets from your mailbox to your recipient's mailbox. You will also learn how to configure a mail server in YaST to move message bits around the Internet.

How Email Works

When you send an email message to your Aunt Betty, it passes through several programs along the way. The Linux operating system breaks the different functions of Internet email into separate processes that are each handled by separate programs. Figure 15.1 shows how most Linux email software modularizes email functions.

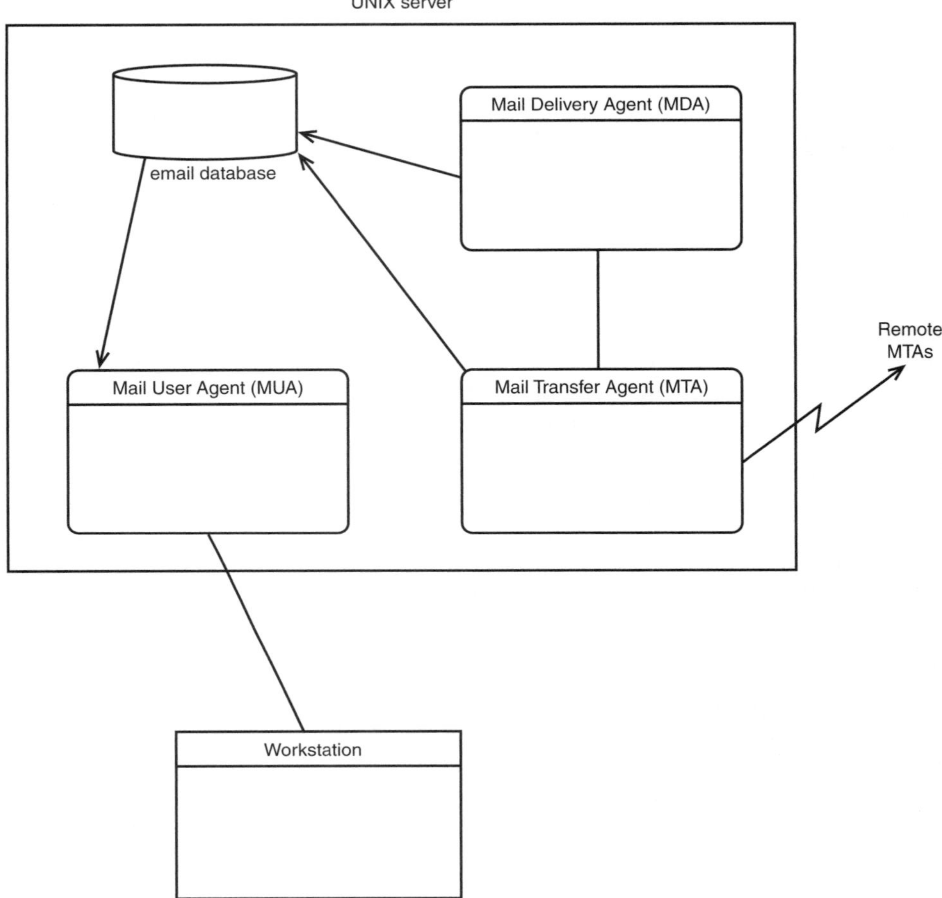

FIGURE 15.1 Linux modular email environment.

As can be seen in Figure 15.1, the Linux email server is normally broken into three separate functions:

- The Mail Transfer Agent (MTA)
- The Mail Delivery Agent (MDA)
- The Mail User Agent (MUA)

In a nutshell, the job of the MTA is to deliver mail messages between different mail servers on the Internet (most likely you and Aunt Betty use different Internet Service Providers [ISPs]). The job of the MDA is to move mail received by the MTA to the appropriate user's local mailbox, and the job of the MUA is to allow individual users access to their own mailboxes to read and send messages.

The lines between these three functions can sometimes be fuzzy. Some email packages combine functionality for the MDA and MTA functions, while others combine the MDA and MUA functions. The following sections describe these basic email agents and how they are implemented in Linux systems.

Mail Transfer Agent

The MTA software is responsible for handling both incoming and outgoing mail messages on a mail server. For each outgoing mail message, the MTA determines the destination of the recipient addresses. If the destination host is the local machine itself, the MTA can either deliver it directly to the local mailbox or pass the message off to the local MDA for delivery.

However, if the destination host is a remote mail server, the MTA must establish a communication link with the remote host to transfer the message. Similarly, for incoming messages, the MTA must be able to accept connection requests from remote mail servers and receive messages destined for local users. There are many different types of protocols that can be used to transfer messages between two remote MTAs. The most common protocol used for Internet mail transfer is the Simple Mail Transfer Protocol (SMTP). This protocol is used only for passing messages to mail servers. It's not used for retrieving messages from an individual mailbox.

The three most popular MTA packages used on Linux servers are:

- sendmail
- qmail
- Postfix

Each of these MTA packages provides the same basic functions of using SMTP to send and receive mail messages. However, there are a few differences between them. The following sections describe these three MTA programs.

sendmail

The sendmail MTA program is one of the most popular Linux MTA programs available. Originally written and supported by Eric Allman, the Sendmail Consortium (http://www.sendmail.org) currently maintains the source code for sendmail. Eric has moved on to Sendmail, Inc., which provides commercial versions of the sendmail program. Eric also provides support to the Sendmail Consortium.

The sendmail program has gained popularity mainly from its ability to be extremely versatile. Many of the standard features of sendmail have become synonymous with email systems—virtual domains, message forwarding, user aliases, mail lists, and masquerading.

sendmail can be used for many different types of email configurations, such as large corporate Internet email servers, small corporate servers that dial into ISPs, and even stand-alone workstations that forward mail through a mail hub. Simply changing a few lines in sendmail's configuration file can change its characteristics and behavior.

Besides being able to change its server characteristics, sendmail also has the ability to parse and handle mail messages according to predefined rule sets. As the mail administrator, it is often desirable to filter messages depending on particular mail requirements. To do this, all that is needed are new rules added to the sendmail configuration file.

Unfortunately, with versatility comes complexity. The sendmail program's large configuration file often becomes overwhelming for novice mail administrators to handle. Many books have been written to assist the mail administrator in determining the proper configuration file settings for a particular email server application.

qmail

qmail is a complete MTA program written and maintained by Dan Bernstein (http://www.qmail.org). It supports all of the MTA functionality of the sendmail program.

qmail takes the idea of modular email software one more step; it was written as a set of modular programs to perform the MTA function. It breaks the MTA functions down into several modules and uses separate programs to implement each function.

qmail requires several different user ids to be added to the mail server. Each program module runs under a different user id. If an intruder compromises one module, it most likely will not affect the other modules. The security features of qmail are often touted as the best feature of qmail.

Still another feature of qmail is its reliability. As each message enters the qmail system, it is placed in a mail queue. qmail uses a system of mail subdirectories and message states to ensure that each message stored in the message queue is not lost. As an added feature, qmail can use Maildir-style mailboxes. Maildir-style mailboxes separate user mail into folders, which helps messages not get corrupted or lost in the single message mailbox.

qmail also uses multiple configuration files, one for each feature of qmail. While this avoids the problem of one large configuration file, novice administrators often get confused as to which feature is configured in which file.

Postfix

Postfix is the default MTA package installed on openSUSE. Wietse Venema wrote the Postfix program to be a complete MTA package. Similar to qmail, Postfix is written as a modular program. Postfix uses several different programs to implement the MTA functionality.

However, Postfix requires only one separate user ID to be added to the mail server. Unlike qmail, which uses a separate user ID for each module, Postfix runs each module under one user ID. Although it uses only one user ID, if an intruder compromises a Postfix module, he or she most likely will not be able to control the mail server as well.

One of the nicest features of Postfix is its simplicity. Instead of one large complex configuration file like sendmail, or multiple small configuration files like qmail, Postfix uses two files that use plain-text parameter and value names to define functionality. However, in openSUSE, you don't need to worry about manually setting the Postfix configuration files. The openSUSE YaST application provides a great graphical interface for you to easily set your desired features. YaST then automatically updates the appropriate configuration file with the required settings.

Mail Delivery Agent

While each of the popular Linux MTA packages has the ability to deliver messages directly to users' mailboxes, Linux email implementations often rely on separate stand-alone MDA programs to deliver messages to local users. Because these MDA programs concentrate only on delivering mail to local users, they can add additional bells and whistles that aren't available on MTA programs that include MDA functionality. Some of these bells and whistles include:

- Automatic mail filtering
- Automatic mail replying
- Automatic program initialization

Possibly the nicest and most used feature of MDA programs is the ability to filter incoming mail messages. For users who get lots of email, this can be a lifesaver. Messages can be automatically sorted into separate folders based on a subject header value or even on just one word within a subject header. Figure 15.2 demonstrates this process.

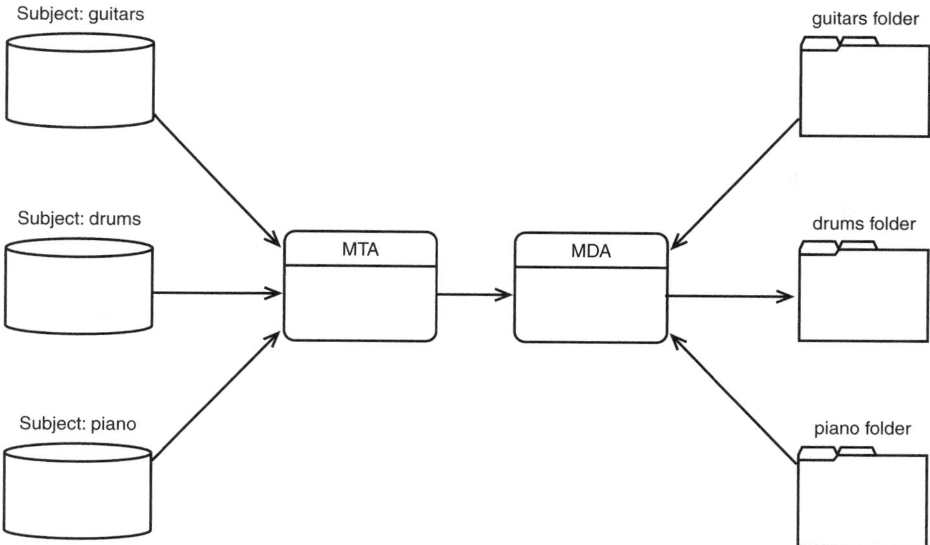

FIGURE 15.2 Sorting incoming mail messages to separate folders.

The MDA program utilizes a configuration file that allows the user to specify regular expressions to search fields in the incoming message header. As expressions are matched, the message will be saved in a predetermined folder in the user's mail area. An alternative feature similar to this is the ability to filter messages and throw away undesirable messages. This feature can also be used to help reduce spam.

MDA programs also provide the ability to run separate programs when email is received without the user having to do anything. If you have used commercial email packages in a work environment, no doubt you have seen the ability to leave out-of-office messages. This feature requires that the MDA automatically reply to any emails you received. This feature can also be used to run external anti-virus and spam detection software for each message that is received.

There are several open source MDA programs available for the mail administrator to incorporate with the email system. Three of the most popular programs are mailx, mail.local, and procmail. This section describes these programs.

mailx

The mailx program is the most popular MDA program used on Linux systems (and is the default MDA used in openSUSE). You may not recognize it by its official name, but you most likely have used it by its system name, `mail`.

Messages are passed from the MTA program to the mailx program, which delivers the messages to the standard `/var/spool/mail` directory. Each user on the system has a separate file there that contains only the user's messages (new messages are appended to the end of the file as they are received).

The mailx program also allows you to create a `.forward` file in your home directory. The `.forward` file can contain an email address where you wish to temporarily forward your incoming mail messages. This is an extremely handy way to allow individual users to forward their mail to external email accounts while they are out.

mail.local

While not found in Linux systems, Unix systems based on the Berkeley Software Distribution (BSD) Unix model (such as FreeBSD and NetBSD) use the mail.local program for local mail delivery. Similar to the binmail program, messages are passed from the MTA program to the mail.local program, which then determines how to deliver them.

The mail.local program also operates similar to the binmail program in that it uses the same standard format of mailboxes as binmail, although most BSD systems use `/var/mail` as the mailbox directory.

Cyrus

The Cyrus server provides a way for remote users to access their mailboxes. The Cyrus server delivers mail messages from the MTA program to an individual mail folder for each user. Users use the Interactive Mail Access Protocol (IMAP) to access the Cyrus server mailboxes through the network. Users can read mail messages, as well as store them within subfolders under their Cyrus mailbox folder on the server. This feature allows users to connect from any remote client to view mail messages.

The Cyrus server software isn't part of the standard openSUSE software installation, but can be added using the YaST software installer discussed in Chapter 21, "Keeping Your System Current: Package Management".

procmail

One of the more popular and most versatile MDA programs in use is the procmail program written by Stephen R. van den Berg. It has become so popular that many Linux implementations (including openSUSE) now install it by default, and many MTA programs utilize it in default configurations. The openSUSE 10.2 distribution installs the procmail program by default, but doesn't activate it in the default Postfix configuration. You'll learn how to do that later on in this chapter.

The popularity of the procmail program comes from its versatility in creating user-configured recipes that can allow a user to direct how received mail is processed. Similar to the mailx `.forward` file, procmail allows users to create a .procmailrc file in their home directories to redirect messages.

The procmail redirection utilizes complex regular expressions to filter incoming mail messages to separate mailbox files, alternative email addresses, or even to the /dev/null file to automatically trash unwanted mail. The procmail MDA is an excellent tool to help prevent spam and viruses in your email.

Mail User Agent

The Linux email model uses a local mailbox for each user to hold messages for that user. The next step in the process is for individual users to be able to read messages in their mailboxes. MUA programs became available to provide a method for users to interface with the mailbox to read messages stored there.

MUAs do not receive messages themselves; they only display messages that have already been placed in the user's mailbox by either the MTA or MDA program.

Because the basic features of all MUA programs are the same (that is, to read messages from a mailbox), MUA programs must use different features to distinguish themselves from other MUA programs. Two of the biggest features that separate MUA packages are:

- The location in which the MUA program stores read mail
- The method by which messages are displayed

Over the brief history of Internet mail, two different philosophies regarding where user mail messages should be stored have developed. Both philosophies have proponents and opponents. In reality, both philosophies can be beneficial in their own right—given a particular email environment.

One philosophy of message location is to download messages directly to the user's workstation, thus freeing up disk space on the mail server. While this makes the job of the mail administrator easier, it often leads to confusion for users who check their mail from multiple workstations (having your INBOX split between several computers is not fun).

The other philosophy for message location solves the problem of multiple workstations by keeping all of the messages on the mail server. As users read their mailboxes, only a copy of the message is sent to the workstation for display purposes. The actual messages are still stored in a file or directory on the mail server. No matter from which workstations the users check their mail, the same messages will be available for viewing. While this makes life much simpler for users, now the mail administrator's life has become more complicated. With all messages stored on the mail server, disk space becomes a crucial factor.

The second distinguishing feature in MUA packages is how messages are displayed. With the advent of fancy GUI devices, MUA programs have become more sophisticated in how they can display messages.

The original Linux MUA Programs used text mode from a console screen to display email messages. Of course, this limited what could be sent in an email message (no fancy fonts or backgrounds). However, with the popularity of Linux graphical desktop systems such as KDE and GNOME, many Linux MUA programs now have the ability to display rich text and HTML-formatted emails.

To accommodate these additional features, many email messages use the Multipurpose Internet Mail Extensions (MIME) format. MIME allows the message to contain multiple versions of the same message; each is formatted using a different display method. It's the job of the MUA to determine which display method to use to display the message. Thus text-based terminals can display the message in text mode, while graphical terminals can display the message in HTML mode.

The Open Source movement has created several very good MUA programs for Linux operating systems. This section describes some popular Linux MUA packages that are available in openSUSE:

- mailx for text terminals
- fetchmail for system-to-system access

The following sections describe each of these packages. The email section of Chapter 13, "Using the Internet: Browsing the Web and Writing Email" covers a variety of graphical MUAs for your evaluation.

mailx

While the mailx program was discussed as an MDA program, it does double duty as an MUA program as well. The `mail` program allows users to access their mailboxes to read stored messages and to send messages to other email users. Here's an example of sending a message to a user using the `mail` program:

```
rich@testing:~> mail rich
Subject: Test message
This is a test message.
.
EOT
rich@testing:~>
```

The first line shows the mailx program being executed with a single command line option, the email address of the mail recipient. If you are sending messages to other users on the same mail server, you can omit the hostname part of the email address; otherwise, be sure to use the full email address.

When the program starts, the mailx program automatically enters compose mode, querying you for a Subject line and then the body of the message. To exit compose mode, type a single period on a line by itself. This returns you to the command line and sends the message to the MTA for processing.

To read mail messages in your mailbox, just type **mail** on the command line by itself:

```
rich@testing:~> mail
Heirloom mailx version 12.1 6/15/06.  Type ? for help.
"/var/spool/mail/rich": 1 message 1 new
>N  1 rich@linux.lan     Fri Dec 29 18:58   18/546   Test message
?
Message  1:
From rich@testing.lan  Fri Dec 29 18:58:17 2006
X-Original-To: rich
Delivered-To: rich@testing.lan
Date: Fri, 29 Dec 2006 18:58:15 -0500
To: rich@testing.lan
Subject: Test message
User-Agent: Heirloom mailx 12.1 6/15/06
MIME-Version: 1.0
Content-Type: text/plain; charset=us-ascii
Content-Transfer-Encoding: 7bit
From: rich@testing.lan (Rich)

This is a test message.

?
```

After entering the `mail` command, a summary of all of the messages in the user's mailbox is displayed. Individual messages can be displayed, copied, or deleted using simple single letter commands within the `mail` prompt.

Fetchmail

The Fetchmail program is a slightly different type of MUA program. Instead of being a user MUA interface, it runs behind the scenes, allowing one mail server to contact another remote mail server to download user mail from a mailbox. You can purchase email services from a remote ISP and then download your messages to your local system using either version 3 of the Post Office Protocol (POP3) or the Interactive Mail Access Protocol (IMAP). Not only can you do that for yourself, but also you can do that for an entire company.

Instead of running their own full-time Internet email server, some companies opt to allow an ISP to host their email system. The problem then is that all of the employees would have to connect to the remote ISP to retrieve mail messages. Fetchmail helps solve this problem.

Instead of having multiple individuals connect to the ISP to download their messages, Fetchmail can be configured to download all of the messages at once and place them in local mailboxes on the server. For companies that don't have a full-time Internet connection, this can be a great savings.

The openSUSE mail configuration system allows you to utilize Fetchmail in this manner. The email configuration utility (discussed in the next section) provides an easy interface for configuring Fetchmail to perform these functions.

Email Server Configuration

Armed with the knowledge of how Linux email servers work, you are ready to start your email configuration. Fortunately for us, the openSUSE email system incorporates configuring the Postfix MTA and the Fetchmail MUA in one process.

The Mail Transfer Agent link in the Network Services section of YaST is where you need to go to configure your email server settings. In this section, we will deal with the configuration screens available in the YaST MTA Configuration Wizard. Novice users should stick to the defaults for these settings, but if you want to fine-tune your mail operations, read on.

General Settings

The first window to greet you in the wizard is the General Settings window. Here you must select the type of Internet connection your system has. If your system is not connected to a network, Postfix will be configured to just pass messages to local users (because you can't connect to a remote MTA).

If you have a dial-up Internet connection, indicate that by selecting the Dial-up radio button. A dial-up connection requires the server to queue outbound mail messages until the connection is established. You must manually run the `sendmail -q` command when you are ready to send and receive mail with the remote MTA.

NOTE

Even though openSUSE uses Postfix, the actual MTA executable program is called `sendmail`. This is a remnant from the old Unix days when the sendmail MTA was the only game in town. Many system script writers hard-coded the sendmail program in their scripts. In order not to break anything, new MTA programs such as Postfix link the sendmail executable program to their programs.

A permanent Internet connection allows the server to send messages in real-time as they are generated. Selecting the Permanent radio button enables Postfix to attempt message delivery as each individual message is created.

Also in this section, you can indicate whether you want an anti-virus program to scan your inbound and outbound messages. Enabling this feature installs and activates the Open Source AMaVIS virus detection software.

Outgoing Mail

The next wizard window determines the configuration for how mail messages will be sent by the Postfix MTA to remote sites. If your server is directly connected to the Internet, it can send its own mail directly to remote MTAs. No configuration is required here.

However, for dial-up connections, you must forward outbound messages through a single remote mail server. This is called a smart host. The smart host accepts messages destined for other MTAs and then forwards them to the proper destination MTA. If your ISP requires that you use a smart host, you can enter its address in the Outgoing mail server textbox, as shown in Figure 15.3.

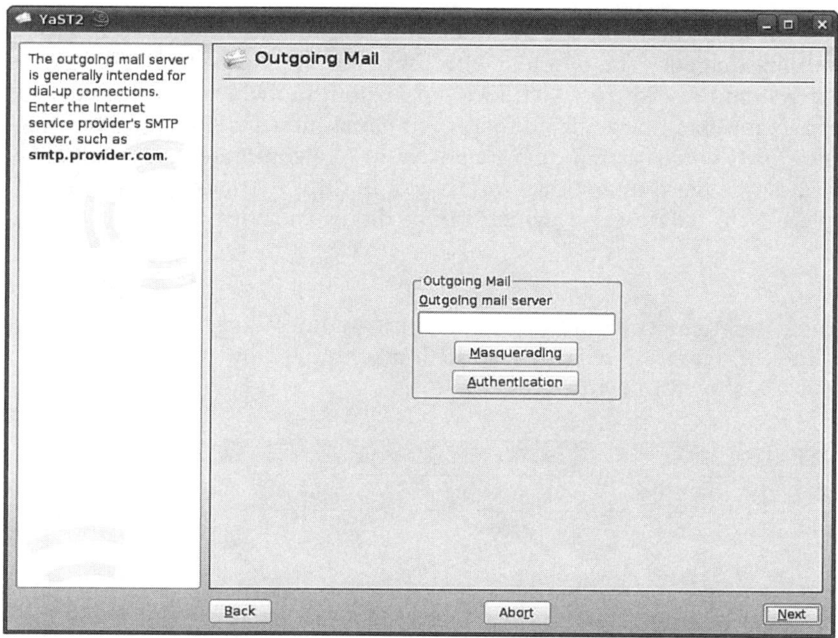

FIGURE 15.3 The Outgoing Mail configuration window.

Some smart hosts require remote clients to authenticate who they are before forwarding mail messages. This helps prevent what's called open relays, where spammers forward mass mail messages through smart hosts. If your smart host server requires authentication, click the Authentication button, and enter your username and password in the appropriate textboxes.

The final piece of the Outgoing Mail window is the Masquerading button. Just as in a masquerade party where you pretend to be someone (or something) you're not, mail masquerading allows you to fake the From and Reply-To addresses in your email messages.

While on the surface this feature sounds like an evil plot to trick people, it does come in handy in many practical situations. By default, the Reply-To address of your messages sent by the server will contain the full mail server name (such as barney@server1.mycorp.com). To make their email address look more professional, many companies prefer to use just their corporate domain name in their email addresses instead of the individual server name.

15

If outbound messages come from server1.mycorp.com, the remote MTA will automatically use that as the return address. The trick is to fake (or masquerade) the Reply-To address in messages to be just mycorp.com. The Masquerading window allows you to define the domain name used in your Reply-To addresses. When this value is set, all messages will be sent using the masqueraded name rather than the normal host name in the Reply-To address.

Besides masquerading a single domain, the Masquerading window also allows you to list multiple domains to masquerade. The problem with using multiple masqueraded domains is that the system must know which local user belongs to which masqueraded domain. Each user account must be assigned to a specific masqueraded domain. The listbox on this page allows you to assign each user account to a configured masqueraded domain. This feature is one piece that allows you to host multiple domains from one mail server (the other piece is virtual domains, which will be discussed shortly).

Incoming Mail

The next step in the configuration wizard is the Incoming Mail window. This is the most complicated of all the configuration windows, so we'll take things slowly here. The main configuration window is shown in Figure 15.4.

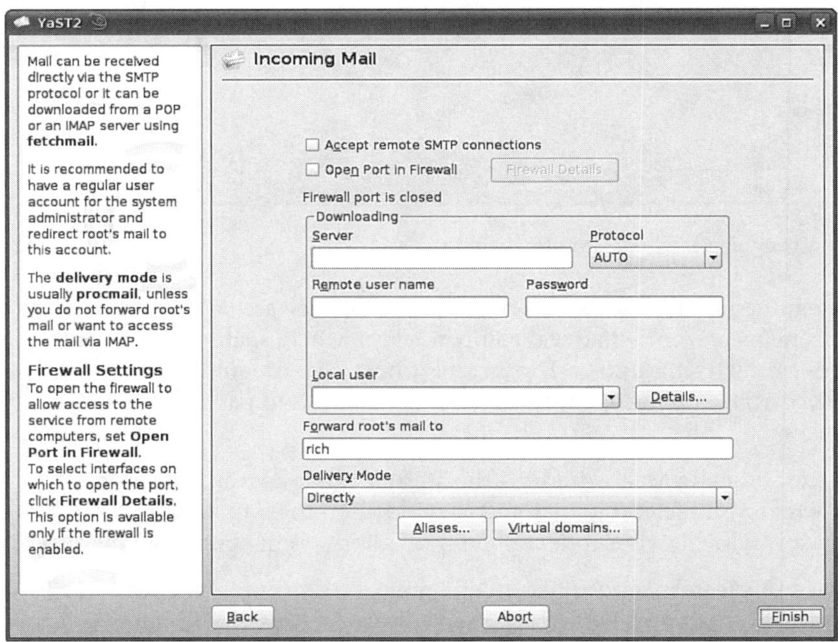

FIGURE 15.4 The Incoming Mail configuration window.

There are several mail features that are configured in this one window:

- The method used to accept inbound messages
- The firewall configuration
- Whether or not to manually retrieve mail from a remote server
- The mailbox used to receive mail for the root account
- The MDA method used
- Creating local alias accounts
- Creating virtual domains

The following sections describe each of these configuration processes in detail.

Accepting Inbound Messages

The first item in the window is a checkbox for accepting remote SMTP connections. Checking this box enables the Postfix server to listen for SMTP connections from remote MTAs. If your server is directly connected to the Internet and is the advertised mail server for your domain, you must check this checkbox. Remote MTAs will attempt to deliver messages directly to your server. Postfix will accept the SMTP connection. It will then accept the mail messages destined to either the local host or to any configured virtual domains (discussed later).

If your server is not directly connected to the Internet (such as when you are using a dial-up Internet connection) or your openSuSE system is not the advertised mail server for your domain, you can leave this checkbox unchecked.

Firewall Configuration

If you are accepting remote SMTP connections, you must configure the firewall to allow the inbound SMTP connections. The second checkbox takes care of this for you. Checking this box opens TCP port 25 (the standard SMTP port) for the selected interface (if you have more than one network interface, you can choose which one should be opened using the Firewall Details button).

Retrieving Mail

Some companies prefer to have their mail server hosted on a separate server, often provided by an ISP and external to the local network. If this is the case in your situation, you must use Fetchmail to connect to the remote mail server to download your mail.

The Downloading section defines the parameters required for Fetchmail to do its thing. Besides the standard POP and IMAP protocols, there are several other protocols that can be used to transfer mail from a remote mail server:

- POP2—Possibly still present on some mail servers, this version of the Post Office Protocol is really old.
- APOP, KPOP—More secure authentication than ordinary POP3.

NOTE

Though it is one of the most used services on the network, and has been for quite some time, email remains one of the most insecure services as well. Any security features you can add to the service—including more secure clients—help head off problems before they occur.

- SDPS—The special POP3-compliant protocol used by Demon Internet, an ISP in the United Kingdom.
- ETRN—Short for Extended Turn, an extension to the SMTP mail delivery protocol that allows an SMTP server to request from another SMTP server any email messages it has for a specific domain.
- ODMR—On Demand Mail Relay.

You can manually choose the protocol to use (such as POP or IMAP) or allow Fetchmail to automatically detect the appropriate protocol.

When a remote mail server accepts your mail messages, you must map which local user accounts use which email addresses. The Fetchmail program retrieves the email messages and then delivers them to the appropriate local user mailbox. The Details button allows you to map local user accounts to specific remote mail accounts on the mail server.

Root Mail

The root admin account on the system receives important system messages if things go wrong on the system. Because it is not usually a good idea to log in as the root user, you can choose to redirect mail destined for the root user to another user.

Select a user account that belongs to an admin on the system and remember to check it daily. It is important to read system mail messages as soon as possible to avoid costly problems.

MDA Method

The Delivery mode dropdown box allows you to select one of three MDA methods to use for delivering local mail:

- Directly— instructs Postfix to deliver inbound mail directly to the user's mailbox.
- Through procmail— instructs Postfix to pass inbound mail off to the procmail program for delivery.
- To Cyrus IMAP Server— instructs Postfix to place inbound messages in a Cyrus IMAP server mailbox system. The Cyrus IMAP server allows remote clients to use MUA software (such as KMail) to access their mailboxes.

The default method is for Postfix to directly deliver inbound mail to the user's mailbox.

Local Aliases

Just as you have the ability to redirect mail for the root user to another user, you can use aliases to redirect mail for other accounts to different users. Often this feature is used to define fictitious mail accounts. The aliases list allows you to create any type of email name and then point that address to a valid local user.

This feature allows you to create generic accounts, such as customercare@mycorp.com, and then redirect that mail account to a valid user. You can also change the user to which the mail is forwarded at any time using the same interface.

Virtual Domains

While aliases allow you to use fictitious usernames in an email address, virtual domains take that one step further by allowing you to accept messages for entirely different domain names.

This is the second piece required for hosting multiple domains (along with masquerading, as described earlier). The first step is to use masquerading to replace the outbound Reply-To message with another domain name. The second step is to allow your mail server to accept messages destined to that domain.

This is done by defining the domain name as a virtual domain. If you want to use your domain name as your email address, enter it as a virtual domain. When you register your domain on the Internet, you must also register your server as the domain mail server. Mail destined to a user on the virtual domain is redirected to a local user account on the mail server.

Fighting Spam and Viruses

Email is incredibly easy to use, and practically cost-free. That's why it's so popular with people. Unfortunately, those same factors are the reasons our mailboxes are inundated every day with dozens, or hundreds, of anonymous messages begging us to refinance our homes, buy various drugs, and enhance the body parts of our choice.

Email is also the favorite mechanism of spreading assorted attacks on our computers and networks through worms, Trojan horses, viruses, and other malware. Technology columnists, politicians, and ordinary users declare the death of email in the face of this attack. What can we do? Keep trying to fight the battle.

SUSE Linux 9.2 introduced a new antispam wizard that works with your email client to remove unwanted email before it even sullies your mailbox. Several open source projects aiming to battle spam have sprouted up, and each has its fans: SpamAssassin, Bogofilter, SpamBayes, Assistance-Filter, and GMX are the best known. KMail and Mozilla Thunderbird both include antispam tools. Thunderbird's is built in, and KMail creates filters to work with the previously mentioned antispam tools.

Finally, there are the old-school methods, using procmail.

procmail

procmail acts as a middleman, filtering each user's mail as it comes from the server, but before it is written to the mailbox. You can configure it yourself or have one of the other antispam tools work with it.

The procmail program is extremely versatile. You can configure the Postfix MTA to directly send all incoming messages to procmail for local delivery or just allow individual mail users to customize their mail environment to use procmail.

To allow individual users to use procmail, do the following:

1. Configure the mailx `.forward` file to send incoming messages to procmail.
2. Create a `.procmailrc` file to instruct procmail on how to process incoming mail messages.

The `.forward` file was discussed earlier in the mailx section. Instead of forwarding all incoming messages to a remote email address, you can forward your messages directly to the procmail program. This is done using a single line in the `.forward` file:

```
¦/usr/bin/procmail
```

This command instructs mailx to send all of your messages to procmail instead of the standard mailbox. Next, you must tell procmail what to do with your messages.

Mail delivery is defined by recipes defined in a `.procmailrc` file, located in each user's home directory. Each procmail recipe defines a matching expression value and an action for procmail to take when a message matches the expression. The format of a procmail recipe is:

```
recipe header line
condition line(s)
action line
```

The recipe header line defines the basic action of the recipe. All recipe lines start with the heading:

```
:0 [flags] [: locallockfile]
```

The flags identify the basic function that the recipe will perform. Table 15.1 lists the flags that are available.

TABLE 15.1 Recipe Flags

Flag	Description
A	Do not execute the recipe unless the conditions of the last preceding recipe are met.
a	Do not execute the recipe unless the conditions of the immediately preceding recipe are met.
B	egrep the body of the message.
b	Feed the body of the message to the destination (default).
c	Generate a carbon copy of this message.

TABLE 15.1 Continued

Flag	Description
D	Distinguish between upper and lower case (the default is to ignore case).
E	Do not execute the recipe unless the conditions of the last preceding recipe were not met.
e	Do not execute the recipe unless the immediately preceding recipe failed.
f	Consider the pipe as a filter.
H	egrep the message header (default).
h	Feed the header of the message to the destination (default).
i	Ignore any write errors on the recipe.
r	Do not ensure that messages end with an empty line (raw mode).
W	Wait for the filter or program to finish and checks the exit code. Suppresses any "Program failure" messages.
w	Wait for the filter or program to finish and check the exit code. Does not suppress any error messages.

The flags are listed in the recipe header line after the `:0` header. More than one flag can be entered on the recipe header line.

After the flags, if a lock file is required, the mail administrator can specify either a specific lock file by name or omit the lock file name to allow procmail to use a default lock file. For example, the recipe header line:

```
:0:
```

specifies procmail to use the default flags (`Hhb`) and to utilize the default lock file when processing the message. Alternatively, the mail administrator can specify a specific lock file to use:

```
:0 Whc: msgid.lock
```

After the header line, one or more recipe condition lines must be defined. Each condition line must start with an asterisk (*). After the asterisk, a normal regular expression is used as the matching condition. Besides normal regular expressions, procmail defines seven special conditions. Table 15.2 lists these special conditions.

TABLE 15.2 procmail Special Conditions

Condition	Description
!	Invert the condition.
$	Evaluate the condition according to shell substitution rules inside double quotes.
?	Use the exit code of the specified program.
<	Check if the total message length is less than the specified number of bytes (in decimal).
>	Check if the total message length is greater than the specified number of bytes (in decimal).
variable ??	Match the remainder of the condition against the environment variable specified.
\	Quote any of the special characters to use as normal characters.

The easiest way to learn how to write condition lines is to see a few examples. This condition line checks if the message subject header field contains the word guitars:

```
* ^Subject:.*guitars
```

The condition uses the caret (^) regular expression character to match any message header lines that start with the word "Subject:". Next, it checks to see if the word "guitars" is anywhere in that line.

You can also check on multiple words in a line. The next condition line checks if the message subject header field contains the words "guitars" and "bass":

```
* ^Subject:.*guitars.*bass
```

Received messages with both of the words "guitars" and "bass" in the message subject header field would match this condition line. Finally, this condition line checks the entire message for the word "meeting":

```
* meeting
```

Any received message with the word "meeting" anywhere in the message would match this condition line.

After the condition lines are defined, the procmail action line must be defined. The action line defines the action that procmail will take if the condition line is matched with a message.

Much like the condition line, the action line can start with a special character that describes the basic action that will be taken. Table 15.3 describes the action line special characters.

TABLE 15.3 procmail Action Line Special Characters

Character	Description
!	Forward message to the specified addresses.
|	Start the specified program.
{	Start a block of recipes checked if the condition is matched.
}	End a block of recipes checked if the condition is matched.
mailbox	Forward message to the mailbox defined by *mailbox*.

Each recipe has only one action line. The action line defines what procmail will do with any messages that match the condition lines. Again, the easiest way to explain this is to show some examples.

Here is an example of a simple `.procmailrc` file for a sample user on the mail server.

```
MAILDIR=$HOME/folders

:0 c
archive

:0
```

```
* ^From.*guitar-list
{
    :0 c
    ! rich@ispnet3.net

    :0
    guitars
}

:0 hc
* !^FROM_DAEMON
* !^X-Loop: rich@ispnet1.net
¦ (formail -r -I"Precedence: junk" \
-A"X-Loop: rich@ispnet1.net" ; \
echo "Thanks for your message, but I will be out of the office until 1/4") \
¦ $SENDMAIL -t

:0
* ^Subject.*pills
/dev/null
```

15

The first line in the sample `.procmailrc` file tells procmail where you want to keep your mail folders. Each folder will be created as a separate file under the `MAILDIR` directory specified. To read messages in folders using mailx, you can use the `-f` command line option:

```
rich@testing:~> mailx -f /home/rich/folders/testing
```

You can also configure KMail to read local mail folders in the KMail configuration window.

The sample `.procmailrc` file shown here contains four separate recipes that are processed by procmail. Each procmail recipe is separated by a blank line. The first recipe simply places a copy of all received messages in the mail folder "archive".

The second recipe demonstrates the use of recipes within a recipe. The main recipe first checks if the received message is from a user called "guitar-list". If it is, both of the internal recipes are checked. First a copy of all of the messages is forwarded to the email address rich@ispnet3.net. Next, a copy of all the messages is placed in the mail folder "guitar". Because these are only copies, the original message will still be placed in the normal INBOX folder.

The third recipe demonstrates redirecting messages to an external program. All messages that are not sent from either a daemon (system) process or from the original user are forwarded to the `formail` program. This program is included with the procmail distribution. It's used to help filter header information from messages. Two header fields are added to the message header by `formail`: a Precedence: line and an X-Loop: line. These lines are used by `formail` to help prevent message loops. After that, a simple shell command is used to generate a message and redirect it to the local MTA process, which is defined by the `$SENDMAIL` environment variable.

The last recipe demonstrates filtering messages based on a Subject header line. Any message with a subject containing the word "pills" is placed in the mail folder `/dev/null`. System administrators may recognize this as a special file. The `/dev/null` file maintains a 0 byte file size. Any information copied there is lost forever. Thus, this recipe deletes any messages with the word "pills" in the Subject line. While this technique can be used for blocking known spam messages from your email server, it is extremely dangerous. If any valid emails get caught by this recipe, they are deleted without your knowing it. It is much safer to just redirect suspected spam to a separate folder and manually sift through them.

Each message delivered by procmail is processed against each recipe. Any recipes whose condition line matches the message are processed. However, recipes that match a message but that are not specifically set to copy the message redirect the message from the normal INBOX. For example, the second recipe redirects messages from the guitar-list to the guitar folder. These messages will not appear in the normal inbox mail folder.

The third example shown above, creating auto-reply messages, is a great feature to use when you know you will be away from your mail server for an extended period of time. Any message sent to your email account will generate an automatic reply message to the sender with any text that you need.

Antispam Tools

Some MDA packages allow you to use prepackaged antispam tools, which are infinitely more sophisticated that any procmail recipes you could write. Modern antispam tools use Bayesian filtering to identify words and patterns that are typical in spam messages. They can work with either MTAs to scan incoming mail and filter it before it gets to the server or with MUAs to separate spam messages before they make it to your inbox.

The biggest problem with these filters is when they pick up *false positives*, which is good mail (also called ham) tossed as spam. Some will also still miss a good deal of spam in the bargain. However, they are trainable, in different ways, so that they improve their detection capabilities as you correct their mistakes.

While you are training your filter, make sure that detected spam gets sent to its own folder and is not deleted immediately. There's no telling how many false positives might be lost otherwise.

The openSUSE 10.3 implementation of KMail provides two different antispam tools for you to use:

- CRM114
- SpamAssasin

Both of these tools are Open Source projects that utilize multiple techniques for detecting spam messages. To configure them in KMail, click Tools, Anti-Spam Wizard. The Anti-Spam Wizard starts, as shown in Figure 15.5.

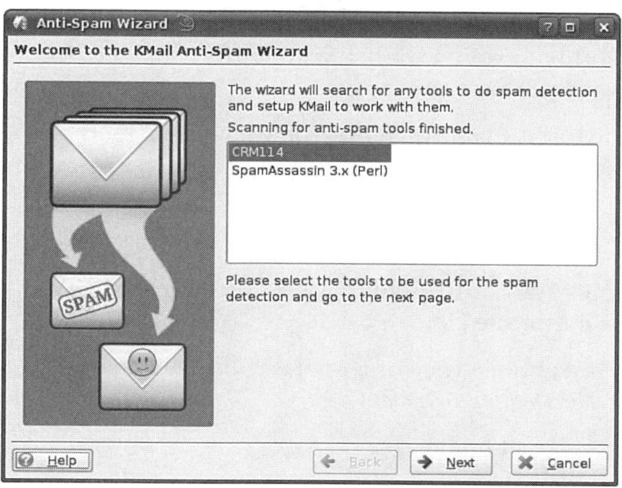

FIGURE 15.5 The KMail Anti-Spam Wizard to install antispam tools in KMail.

You can select either or both of the provided antispam tools to filter incoming mail messages. The wizard allows you to select how to handle identified incoming spam messages. Remember, antispam tools are not always 100% accurate, so be careful about discarding messages thought to be spam. It is safer to create a separate spam folder and have the tools redirect messages there.

NOTE

One of the worst nightmares that can happen to an administrator is to find that his or her servers have been turned into spam gateways—literally passing spam along at breakneck speed. Many companies are currently offering software products that act as Anti-Spam Gateways, which eliminate spam, phishing attempts to gain passwords and other sensitive information, and many viruses before they move beyond the server. The primary benefit that most of these products offer is that they come preconfigured with very little for the administrator to do other than tweak a few settings during installation. Aside from this simplification, they offer little that is not available in SpamAssassin, and it is highly recommended that you investigate this open-source solution and its possibilities before purchasing a similar product.

Antivirus Tools

Conventional wisdom is that Linux is virtually virus-proof. This is true, for the most part, but perhaps not forever. Virus writers, from the script kiddies to the more professional criminal types, like to use Outlook as a transmission vector for their tools. Some have even called Outlook a virus-spreading mechanism that also delivers email.

As more people use Linux to get their everyday work done, the evil ones will try to rise to the challenge. How well they succeed depends on how ready for them Linux users (and developers) are when they arrive.

No antivirus tools are installed by default with openSUSE Linux. When you configure your mail server, you can configure Postfix to work with the Mail Delivery Agent called AmaViSd, which will, in turn, work with most antivirus tools.

The most prominent open source antivirus is ClamAV, and several commercial tools are also available for Linux, including F-Prot and Sophos.

References

- http://www.postfix.org/start.html—The Postfix home page. Be sure to click the Web Sites link on the menu to find a mirror site close to you.
- http://www.seaglass.com/postfix/faq.html—The Postfix mailing list FAQ, maintained by Kyle Dent, author of *Postfix: The Definitive Guide*.
- http://www.sendmail.org—The Sendmail home page.
- http://fetchmail.berlios.de—The Fetchmail home page.
- http://www.paulgraham.com/spam.html—Paul Graham's original essay, "A Plan for Spam," outlines the theory of Bayesian filtering.
- http://spamassassin.apache.org—SpamAssassin home page. Check out the wiki pages for downloadable custom rulesets.
- http://crm114.sourceforge.net/—The CRM114 antispam tool home page.
- http://bogofilter.org—Eric Raymond's Bogofilter project.
- http://www.nidelven-it.no/articles/introduction_to_thunderbird_5—A good introduction to spam filtering with Mozilla Thunderbird.
- http://www.iki.fi/era/procmail/mini-faq.html—The Procmail FAQ.
- http://pm-doc.sourceforge.net—The Procmail Documentation Project. See the PM-Tips page for sample rulesets/recipes and many other good ideas.
- http://www.clamav.net—Home of the open source Clam antivirus program.

CHAPTER 16

Collaborating with Others

IN THIS CHAPTER

- Getting News from RSS WebFeeds
- Usenet News Today
- Choosing a Usenet Newsreader
- Collaborating with Wikis
- Hosting Electronic Mailing Lists
- Working with Instant Messengers and Internet Relay Chat
- References

So far we have talked a lot about Linux being network-aware. Perhaps the main benefit of computer networking is to advance the ability of humans to network. When humans work together, amazing things get done. openSUSE includes a multitude of tools to help you work with other people, whether your collaborators are on the other side of your office or on the other side of the planet.

Several types of collaboration tools are included in openSUSE, but you can break them down into two groups:

- Asynchronous communication—Mailing lists, Wikis, and Usenet news
- Real-time communication—Internet Relay Chat, instant messaging, and video conferencing

The advantage of asynchronous communication (that is, communication in which people involved appear at different times to participate) is that it shrinks the physical distance between participants. People do not have to be in the same room at the same time to get things done. Someone in New York can post a message on a global mailing list or newsgroup, and some hours later, someone in Bangladesh, who was sleeping when the New Yorker posted, can respond.

The advantage of real-time communication is that it shrinks the response time. With everyone (virtually, at least) in the same room at the same time, questions can get answered instantaneously.

In this chapter, you will learn about all these methods. We covered the basics of email in the previous chapter, so you know how electronic mailing lists work from the user's end, but that's not all there is to know. openSUSE has three packages that will manage your own mailing lists: Majordomo, mlmmj, and Mailman.

Usenet newsgroups have been part of the fabric of the Internet nearly as long as email and took hold well before the World Wide Web was invented. Although Usenet now has an even bigger problem with spam and malware than email, there remain thriving and helpful communities of Usenet readers and writers who can help you get answers to a multitude of questions for the price of a well-crafted question. Tap into Usenet with one of the news-reading tools discussed here, and then consider hosting your own NNTP server.

More recently, a new collaborative information tool has arisen on the Web. Wikis, short for WikiWiki Web, are web pages that any registered user can edit. Wikis can be places for sharing knowledge and brainstorming ideas, within your team or with your audience. You'll learn more about creating your own wiki pages in this chapter, too.

Real-time communication tools have moved from the realm of teenage time wasters into serious collaboration tools for business. Chat and instant messaging technologies are now used to provide technical support for computer problems, confirm whether marketing and development are in agreement about a product, and even engage in complex business conversations and planning. In this chapter, you'll learn about the variety of Linux tools you can use to engage in this activity.

Getting News from RSS WebFeeds

You learned a little about webfeeds in Chapter 14, "Creating Basic Websites." Feeds are bits of code that allow websites to notify you when new content is up. They come in two flavors, Really Simple Syndication (RSS) and Atom, though virtually all applications that read webfeeds can process both formats. Webfeeds represent one of the first popular applications of the eXtensible Markup Language (XML), the stricter big brother of HTML.

Most webfeeds, as with most websites, are text-based, but feeds can also carry multimedia attachments with sound and video ready to be played on your computer, or transferred to your portable music player. This technology has given rise to the podcast industry, where everyone from TV and radio networks to your friend down the street is delivering news and commentary on most every topic under the sun.

You need an application called an aggregator to collect and read webfeeds from across the Web. If you see a little orange square on a site, this indicates a webfeed is available. Clicking this icon lets you "subscribe" to the site's feed, though you often have to go through a few extra steps to complete the process, depending on your browser and your aggregator. We'll cover these idiosyncrasies in this section.

Only recently have dedicated webfeed aggregators begun appearing in Linux. The latest versions of the Firefox and Opera browsers both have aggregators built in. Akregator for KDE is gaining converts, and Liferea for GNOME is getting there, too. Many audio players have aggregator features that support podcasts as well. You read about those in Chapter 10, "Sights, Sounds, and Other Fun Things." There are also several excellent online aggregators.

Aggregators in Browsers

Both Firefox 2 and Opera 10 have their own simple aggregators that you might find useful.

In the Firefox toolbar, you'll see an item called "Latest Headlines," with the orange webfeed icon. Clicking this item offers a drop-down selection of current headlines from a variety of news sources. Click on any one to be transported to the originating page for that headline. This is a Firefox "Live Bookmark."

When Firefox arrives at a site with a syndicated feed, the same orange button appears in the address line of the browser. Click this icon to add the feed as a Live Bookmark. This is stored with the rest of your bookmarks. When you go to a Live Bookmark, it looks like a folder with the orange icon, with headlines inside the folder. Click a link to go to the permalinked page for that headline.

Opera reads webfeeds in a couple of ways. Subscribing to a feed for reading in a browser window is as easy as clicking the XML button in the address line for a site. Opera will ask you if you want to subscribe; click Yes, and the current headlines will appear. The display is somewhat bland, as it uses the browser's e-mail interface (Figure 16.1), but click the link under the headline, and the story will appear in a new tab. Opera will check for new headlines each time it opens. By default, Opera will also check for new updates every three hours. This is configurable for each feed in the Manage Feeds dialog box under the Feeds menu.

TIP

One advantage of the Opera email interface for webfeeds is that you can add a label to an article for future reference. Select an article and click the Label icon. Mark it as a to-do, as Valuable, or just Funny.

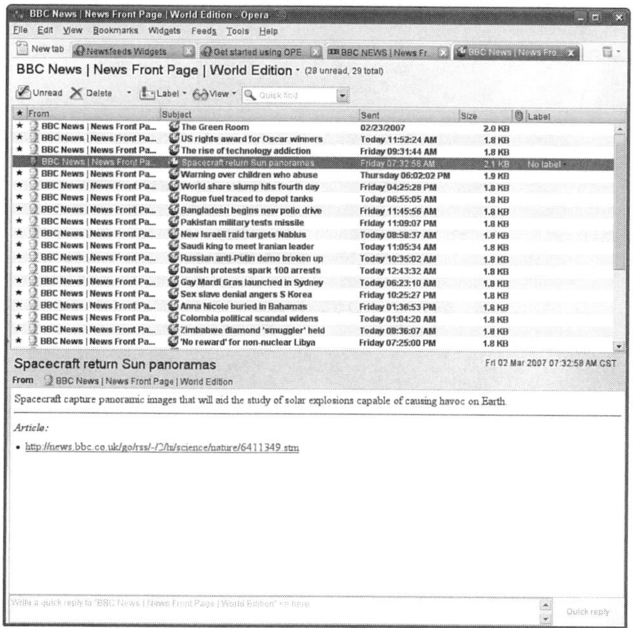

FIGURE 16.1 Opera displays webfeeds in its built-in mail reader.

Some websites have also created Opera Widgets that display alongside Opera when it is open. See http://widgets.opera.com/newsfeeds/ for a current list. See the Opera section of Chapter 13, "Using the Internet: Browsing the Web and Writing Email," for more on Opera Widgets.

Standalone Aggregators

As always, each Linux desktop environment has an aggregator designed for it, though they all work in both environments. Akregator is the default KDE aggregator, and it can be integrated with the Kontact personal information manager. Liferea (the Linux Feed Reader) and Blam! are written for GNOME. RSSOwl is an aggregator written in Java that looks pretty good too.

Akregator

Akregator can function alone or as part of the Kontact personal information management suite for KDE. If you decide to include it in Kontact (it is optional, and not loaded by default), it will open only as the Feeds module in Kontact.

When you first run Akregator in openSUSE Linux, it includes a few sample feeds on Novell, SUSE Linux, and KDE. You can choose to view all available articles in one window, or select each feed separately. Akregator will update all feeds whenever you start the application (this is configurable, if you don't have a permanent Internet connection), but you can click the down-arrow icons from the toolbar to check either the selected feed or all the feeds.

Content in a feed is set by the website owner, and can range from full-text articles to just a headline. In Akregator, click Complete Story to open a Konqueror tab that will take you to the originating website. Figure 16.2 shows the Article window with a tab on the right.

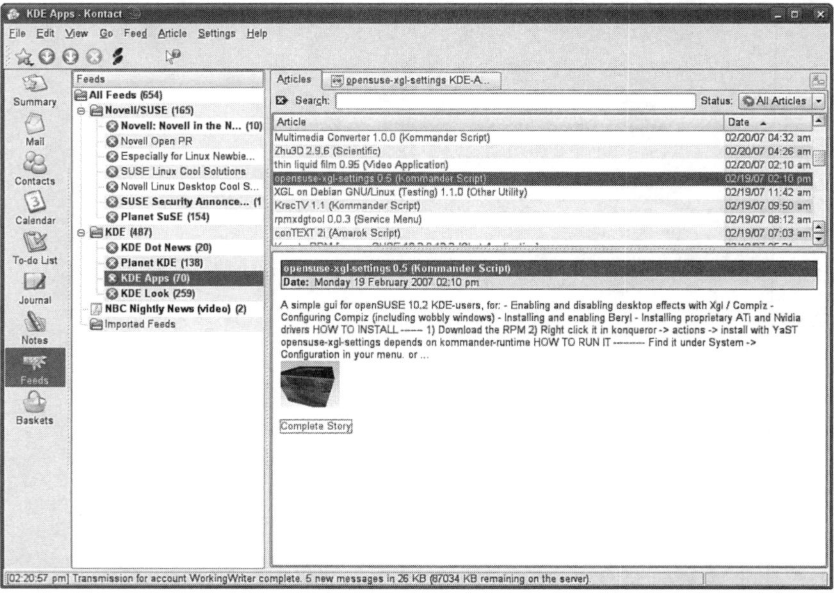

FIGURE 16.2 Akregator integrates with the Kontact personal information manager.

Adding new feeds to Akregator is easiest if you use Konqueror as your main browser. When you visit a site with a webfeed, the orange icon appears in the lower-right corner of the browser. Click the icon and the option to Add Feed to Akregator appears. Clicking this option adds the feed under the Imported Feeds folder by default, but you can drag this (or any) feed to another folder.

In other browsers, you will need to set up the browser to use Akregator, or copy and paste the URL for the feed into Akregator. In Firefox, for example, you have a pair of options. You can edit your Firefox preferences (in the Feeds) section to Subscribe to Feed with an application. Click Choose Application, and point to Akregator (/opt/kde3/share/applications/kde/akregator). The next time you click on the orange icon, a new screen will appear, asking if you want to subscribe using Akregator, or one of several online aggregators. Make your selection, and you're done.

Regardless of the browser you use, you can always use the cut-and-paste method of adding webfeeds. If you see a link to a feed on a website (usually marked with the orange icon, occasionally with just a text link mentioning RSS or Atom), right-click on it and choose Copy Link Location (or something similar, depending on the browser you're using). Open Akregator and click the Star icon in the toolbar. This opens the New Feed dialog. Paste the XML link in the Feed URL box and click OK.

TIP

The popularity of webfeeds began in the blogosphere, as bloggers began to read each other's material and link back and forth to each other. So if you're reading a blog in Akregator and click a link to another blog (or other site with a feed), you may find yourself wanting to subscribe to that other site too. This is easy to do in Akregator.

Look for the link to the feed on the page you're reading. Click the text link or the orange icon and drag it to the feed window. The New Feed dialog box will appear, with the URL already pasted. Click OK to add.

Podcast fans might find Akregator a little clunky to use. It will download attachments to a webfeed, but there is no automatic stream or download for multimedia files, and there's no simple way to designate a player once a podcast has been downloaded. The Amarok audio player handles podcasts better in KDE.

Blam!

Blam! (with the exclamation point as the focal point of its logo) is a simple looking GTK application designed more for folks who know what they want out of a feed reader/aggregator. It starts you off with a dozen open-source related webfeeds, which it calls Channels. It will import lists of feeds in the Outline Processor Markup Language (OPML) and let you add new channels manually (with copy-and-paste). It doesn't come with a Help file, so you are kind of on your own with this one.

Liferea

The Linux Feed Reader is a GTK application that offers the familiar clean GNOME look. It gives you about a dozen Example Feeds centered on GNOME and open source software to get you started.

RSSOwl

This Java-based cross-platform aggregator may be the best aggregator of all for the person who wants to see what this webfeed thing is all about. It comes with a tutorial that appears on first launch (but doesn't bother you again unless you pull it up from the Help menu) and a variety of Sample feeds covering more than just the tech world. The Welcome page even has a direct link to the support forums and mailing list for those who might be too intimidated to visit the project's Sourceforge page.

New users may stumble over the terminology RSSOwl uses for some items in its main screen. A Favorites folder may be easily understood by many, but not necessarily as the equivalent of all subscribed feeds. What is the difference between Aggregate All Favorites and Reload All Favorites when both appear as action buttons in the Favorites folder? The FAQ tells us that Aggregate lets you read all the feeds in a category at once, and Reload rechecks the sites and displays all items currently in the feed. Reload is good if you accidentally delete an article you wanted or to confirm that the site in question hasn't become more sporadic in posting.

These quibbles aside, RSSOwl is a powerful tool for reading, discovering and managing webfeeds. Individual feeds appear in tabs in the viewer. Clicking the link at the top of an article opens a Firefox tab by default to take you to the full article. The feed updates when you click on it in the Favorites window, unless you change the settings.

Perhaps the most intriguing features in RSSOwl are its Search for Newsfeeds and Discover Newsfeeds on a Website tools. Type in a search term in the newsfeeds and RSSOwl will scour the web for feeds related to the topic (see Figure 16.3). Import the entire list into your Favorites with two clicks (Import, then select–or create–a category for the result set).

If you're not sure whether one of your favorite sites has a feed, use the Discover Newsfeeds tool. Type in the site's address and RSSOwl will try to find a feed and display any feeds it finds. Choose one or more and Import into your Favorites.

RSSOwl supports podcasts, with a selection of a dozen of the best in the Samples. Click the Attachment link to open the file in Firefox.

A couple of other features help RSSOwl stand out. Find something interesting in your feed? Send a NewsTip email to a friend. Want to keep a copy of an article outside the reader? Go to the File menu and create a PDF version of the article.

Online Aggregators

If you switch between computers and operating systems frequently, you might like an online aggregator. The best of these is at http://www.bloglines.com. Bloglines works with most browsers. You can organize your feeds into subject folders and add and remove feeds with ease. Bloglines will even look at your current feed lineup and offer recommendations for new blogs that might interest you.

Google Reader, Rojo, and My Yahoo! all work under the same basic principle: pull a selection of feeds, display them on a page, and keep yourself informed.

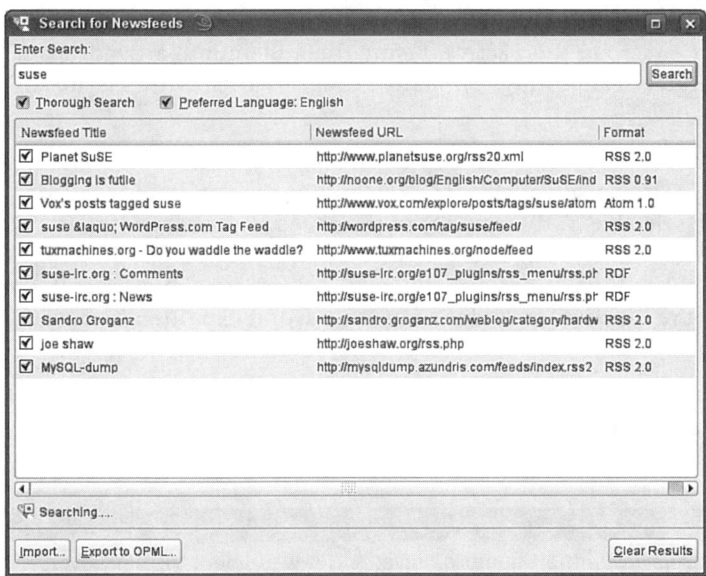

FIGURE 16.3 Find feeds on a particular topic with RSSOwl's Search for Newsfeeds tool.

Usenet News Today

When Usenet began, it was a genuinely new way for Internet pioneers to collaborate with each other. Instead of having to use hit-and-miss methods of finding electronic mailing lists of interest and import to your work, you could set up a server for public bulletin boards where everyone interested in some topic could drop in, find out the latest information (or "news") about that topic, and drop out again. Anyone who had news could post it there for everyone else's use. People could ask questions and get expert answers, from real people. No one was obligated to read every message, nor would irrelevant postings begin to clutter one's mailbox (at a time when disk space was at a premium). What could be better?

For a long time, nothing could. Newsgroups were created on most topics imaginable, organized hierarchically under a few basic categories: Computers (comp), Recreation (rec), Natural Science (sci), Society and Culture (soc), Debate and Controversy (talk), Miscellaneous (misc), and Usenet itself (news).

Anyone could propose to create a new group in these hierarchies, and there are democratic procedures in which users vote to approve new groups. This procedure grew oppressive for some people, leading to the rise of the Alternative (alt) hierarchy, where anyone could start a group, and many did (witness the existence of the alt.swedishchef.bork.bork.bork group).

Other hierarchies developed as hardware and software companies delivered Usenet support channels; colleges and universities set up internal newsgroups for students and faculty, and enterprising community-oriented geeks set up newsgroups for their local communities. Some are still functioning today.

Spam first raised its ugly head on Usenet when a pair of immigration attorneys posted an ad for their services in every newsgroup then active. Before the millennium arrived, spam had almost completely obliterated real postings on many groups. But many others are still quite useful.

Chances are good that your ISP offers at least some form of Usenet access. Contact them to find out the address of their Usenet server and the newsgroups they offer (also called their *newsfeed*). Many ISPs are selective in the content of their feed, especially when it comes to the alt groups. These are often seen as the seedier virtual neighborhoods, with pirated software, malware, and less-than-family-friendly text and images abounding. If there is a particular group you're looking for, and it's not included, it can often be added on request.

There are a few public news servers available, and you can find a list of them at http://freenews.maxbaud.net. Unfortunately, spammers often take advantage of this opportunity to peddle their wares, so be careful when using this.

USING GOOGLE GROUPS

Once upon a time, there was DejaNews, the Usenet archive, and it was good. Virtually every Usenet posting going back to the 1980s was included in this free web resource. Then the dot-com era collapsed and DejaNews was endangered. But who should come to the rescue, but the company working so hard to make the Web more useful to humans: Google.

Google Groups is a way to search through the Usenet archives with all the standard Google search tools and to get spam-free web access to all of today's Usenet as well. Google does, of course, place ads on the pages.

Just go to Google Groups (http://groups.google.com) and do a keyword search, or browse groups through the links. With free registration, you can subscribe to favorite groups and create your own public or private Google groups. Figure 16.4 shows the alt.os.linux.suse group in Konqueror.

One important difference from the DejaNews archive: Google Groups does not carry newsgroups where people post binary code or multimedia files. This excludes, among other things, the entire alt.binaries hierarchy. So you will need another Usenet reader to locate clip art posted to Usenet.

When reading Usenet postings, your client makes it easy to respond, either by email or as a public follow-up posting. Some clients support multiple "identities" for posting and emailing, so you can choose a different signature or return address.

CAUTION

Spammers use software "bots" to collect every email address they find on Usenet, so never post a real email address. Use something that a human can read, but a bot would have trouble with, like `mynameNO@SPAMmyISP.com`.

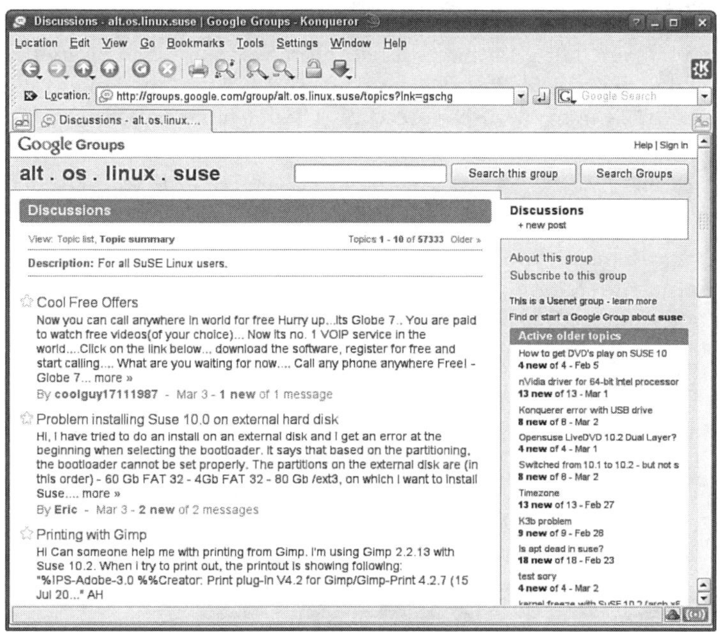

FIGURE 16.4 Google Groups gives you a searchable and browsable Usenet newsfeed on the Web. This is the alt.os.linux.suse group. The standard Google ads appear at the bottom of the page.

Choosing a Usenet Newsreader

Choices abound in reading Usenet in openSUSE. Many email clients can also deliver news. Several standalone clients are also around (Knode/Kontact, Pan, and several text-based choices). Some require you to be online when accessing news, others permit offline reading. Of course, there's also gnus for Emacs.

Mail/News Clients

Reading email and reading news are very similar tasks: Read and respond, perhaps save for later use. For this reason, the easiest way to keep up may be to use a mail client that supports reading Usenet.

Many email clients do this, including some of the best known: Mozilla Mail/Thunderbird, Evolution, Sylpheed, mutt, and pine. Setting them up to read Usenet is usually just a matter of identifying the Usenet server (often news.<ISPname>.com) and including login information, if authentication is required.

Reading news in a mail client is usually a plain-vanilla experience, without some of the fancier filters used by a standalone news client, but threads are usually supported (if they are supported in mail), and responding to a post operates the same way as email.

Support for binary transfers via Usenet, including images, multimedia files, and programs, tends to be a mixed bag. The yEnc encoding format is much more widespread in Usenet (see Chapter 15, "Managing Email Servers," for more on yEnc), and if your email client doesn't support it, you'll miss out. As many viruses spread via Usenet binaries, this can be a good thing.

Standalone GUI Newsreaders

Maybe your email client doesn't do news (for example, KMail), or you want something better adapted to the Usenet atmosphere (good binary transfer, bozo filters, and better ways to clear spam). Standalone newsreaders can be a good choice.

As with so many other GUI packages, there are standalone newsreaders for both KDE (KNode) and GNOME (Pan). You can include KNode inside Kontact if you want.

Pan

Pan runs much like the Windows newsreader Forté Free Agent, but is more advanced. You can read feeds from multiple servers, including the Novell Linux support groups (see Figure 16.5).

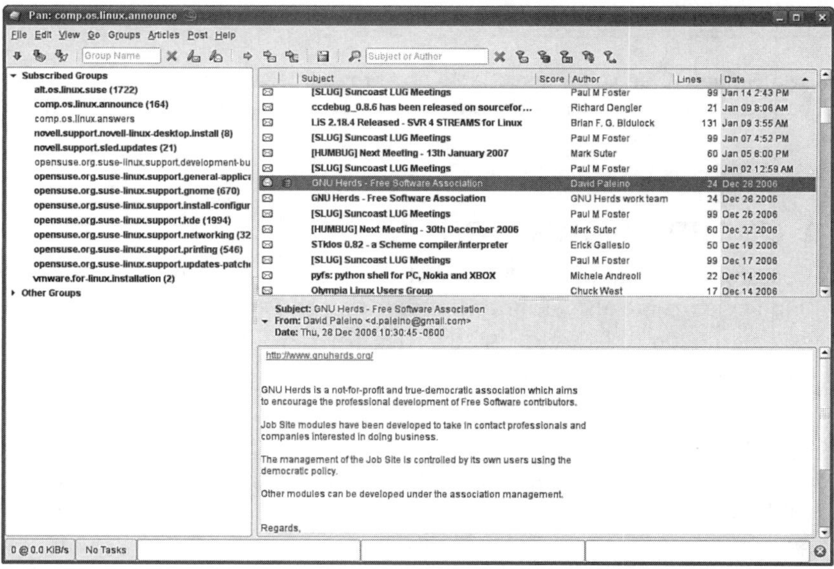

FIGURE 16.5 Pan is an easy-to-use graphical newsreader that was designed for GNOME but runs everywhere. You can choose to display groups, headers, and messages in a tri-pane format, as shown in this figure, or in tabs, with one pane showing and the others in the background.

Pan supports offline reading, so you don't have to tie up your phone line to read news if you have a dial-up connection. This is a multistep process, but one that is easy to get used to.

1. Download headers for the group(s) in which you're interested. The headers include (among other things) the subject lines for the postings, who posted, and how long a message is.
2. Select the thread(s) in the group that you want to read.
3. Download the message bodies and go offline (press L or go to File, Work Offline).

When you want to post a message, either by email or to the group, Pan gives you the choice to Send Now (if you're online) or Send Later (for offline use). The Send Later option is also good if you've just composed a really nasty flame and want time to reconsider. When you go back online, go to Post, Send Queued Messages to finish.

TIP

Pan messages marked Send Later are queued in the pan.sendlater folder. To edit or delete a message, choose Folders from the Show Groups pane. Select pan.sendlater, and you should see your message in the Headers pane.

Pan has excellent support for Usenet binaries and plays nicely with yEnc. The filters are a little difficult for an ordinary person to decipher, and there is no manual or online help.

KNode

KNode, although not identical to KMail, functions very much like it. As the only part of the Kontact suite not turned on by default, it might be considered something of a weakling; instead it is a fairly muscular client.

Figure 16.6 shows how to configure KNode to receive the official Novell support newsgroups, including the openSUSE and Ximian application groups.

TIP

There's an even easier way to subscribe to the Novell support groups: Open http://support.novell.com/forums/2su.html in Konqueror. Click any of the NNTP links on this page, and you'll be asked if you want to follow this link. Click Follow. KDE will open KNode automatically and download the current articles in the selected newsgroup.

Now click the up arrow in Konqueror, and you'll be taken to the main newsgroup page to subscribe to more groups!

Setting up a client to read a particular news server is not hard. Generally all you need is the server name and know whether you need to supply a password (that is, be authenticated) before using it. Some news servers are public, allowing anyone to connect, but most require some identification. By default, news servers use Port 119 to communicate with clients. Like your mail client, if you expect to keep KNode open for awhile and want to check for new articles/postings periodically, you can set the interval here. If you mostly want to read news offline, you should not turn on the interval check.

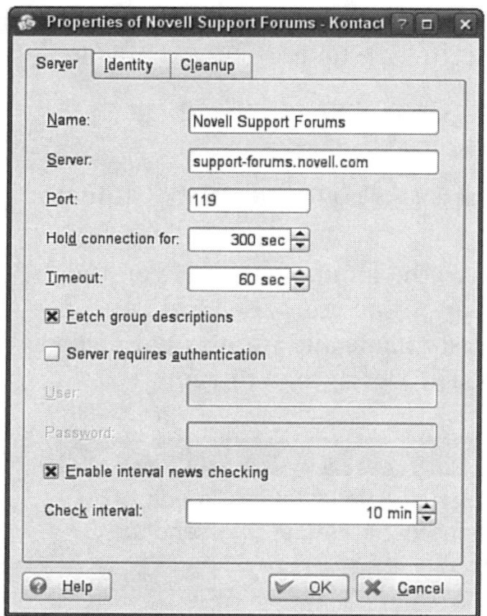

FIGURE 16.6 Configuring KNode for the Novell Support forums. News client server configuration screens are very similar to each other.

KNode also lets you specify an identity to respond to newsgroup articles on a per-account basis. Click the Identity tab to enter in a name, an email address for the From line, and (if you want) a different address in the Reply To field. KNode will use the default settings if you don't say otherwise.

Although not hopeless, KNode works better with text files than with binaries. KNode displays images and supports yEnc. Filters are easier to create than in Pan, especially if you have created filters in KMail.

Go to Settings, Configure KNode, Reading News. Click the Filters tab and you'll see the default filters. Suppose you post questions to Usenet, and you just want to see the follow-up articles to your question. To do this, click Add and follow these steps:

1. Name the filter **`Follow ups to my questions`**. Make sure the Show in Menu box is checked so that you can apply the filter easily.

2. Click the drop-down menu to change the Apply On setting to Whole Threads. Leave the Subject area as is.

3. Go down to the From area and type the placeholder variable **`%MYNAME`** into the box. The filter will then look for articles with your name, as defined in the Identities settings.

4. Click the Status tab and check the Has New Followups box, and then change the setting to True using the drop-down menu. Click OK to create the filter.

5. Now go to View, Filter (or click the Filter toolbar icon, which looks like a funnel), and select Has New_Followups to activate your filter on the current group.

Text-Based Newsreaders

Because there was Usenet almost before there were GUIs, many text-based newsreaders are still in use. Some are even under active development. Included with openSUSE are NetNews (nn), InterNetNews (inn), tin, slrn, and suck.

Before starting any of these, you need to set your news server as an environment variable. Do this as user, not as root. From the shell, type the following:

```
export NNTPSERVER=<YourNewsServerDomainName>
```

The next step is to view the groups on your server and subscribe to one or more. This is done by creating a .newsrc file. As an example, let's use slrn. Type the following:

```
slrn -f .jnewsrc - create
```

This configuration file, located at `/etc/slrn.rc`, is well commented and easy to customize.

When you create the .newsrc file, and, if necessary, log in, slrn will get all the groups available on the server. To subscribe to an interesting group, select it from the list and type a capital **S**. To just see your subscribed groups, type a capital **L**, followed by the Esc key, and then the number **1**.

Figure 16.7 shows slrn in action.

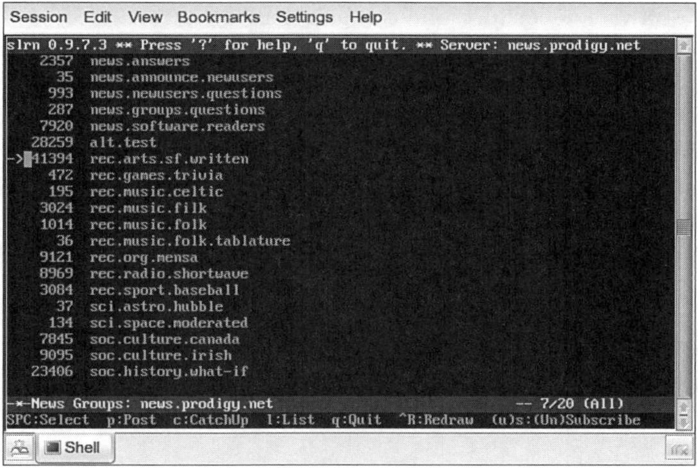

FIGURE 16.7 The text-based slrn newsreader displays a set of subscribed groups. Select a group and press Enter to read the messages.

Collaborating with Wikis

The WikiWikiWeb, taken from the Hawaiian expression for fast, quick, or speedy, was created by Ward Christopher as a way of tapping into the collective knowledge of his circle of friends and co-workers. It combines features of email lists, software documentation tools, and the simple structure of the Web to generate useful, accessible, and frequently updated and reviewed information.

The idea caught on, and people are collaborating with Wikis in all sorts of ways. The best known example of a successful and popular Wiki is Wikipedia.org. Its goal is to produce a basic compendium of human knowledge about most anything. As of February 2005, the English version of Wikipedia was approaching 500,000 articles produced, with at least some articles in some 20 other languages. It has spawned other projects, including WikiQuotes, the Wiktionary, and the Wikinews citizen journalism project.

Dozens of packages have been written to create Wikis with. These packages, called WikiEngines, have varying features. Like blog software, one WikiEngine should meet your needs and idiosyncrasies. Wikipedia and opensuse.org use the MediaWiki engine, which is built for heavy traffic. openSUSEOther engines are easy to get, with varying degrees of installation difficulty. See http://c2.com/cgi/wiki?ChoosingaWiki for help in selecting a package.

A Personal Wiki: Zim

Besides contributing your knowledge (or copy editing skills) at Wikipedia, one great way of experimenting with wikis is by creating your own. Zim is a Perl application that will do that for you. You don't need an active web server to use it, and it works pretty well out of the box.

Zim is included in the "guru" software depository, and can be installed via YaST. (See Chapter 21, "Keeping Your System Current: Package Management," for more information on setting up third-party repositories in YaST.) Once installed, go to the Office menu in KDE or GNOME, and you'll find Zim under Project Management.

Each time Zim runs, it will ask you to "open a repository," which may be more than a little disconcerting for the first time user. All it is really asking for is a name for a folder to contain your pages. Click Add and give a name to your wiki, as shown in Figure 16.8. You can have as many repositories/wikis as you want, so you can use each wiki to manage a particular project.

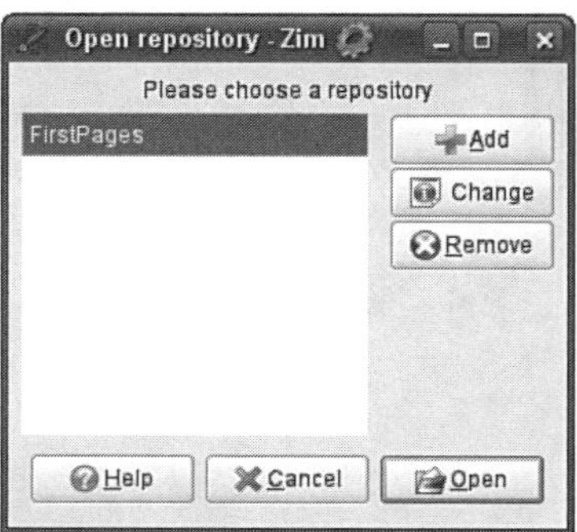

FIGURE 16.8 Create your own wiki pages with Zim.

When you create your repository, Zim displays a Home page, and notes the creation date, as in Figure 16.9. Treat Zim as something in between a simple text editor and a word processor. You can bold, indent, or underline text, and identify headings. Create bulleted lists by starting a line with an asterisk (*). Zim saves everything on creation, but you can still press Ctrl+S to save the file if you can't drop the habit.

What makes a wiki fast is the ease with which you can create a link. To create a new page on your site, simply put two brackets on either side of your page's title. That is, type the following in any page in Zim to create a new page called "My Wiki Practice Site":

```
[[My Wiki Practice Site]]
```

Zim will create the page and link to it. To link to a page outside this repository, put a colon between the left brackets and your text, like this:

```
[[:My Wiki Practice Site]]
```

FIGURE 16.9 A basic Zim page.

Standard URLs are automatically recognized and active links are created that will open in Firefox by default. The browser is configurable in the Preferences dialog box.

Zim pages can be opened in any text editor or word processor, so you can retrieve them and collate them any way you want. It comes with a few plugins you can activate in the Preferences, including a spell checker and a way to export your pages to a browser for printing.

This application was created mostly for organizing To-Do Lists, brainstorming, and pulling together notes for speeches, presentations and research projects. But you can probably come up with some ideas on your own. To see one of the things you can do with a Zim wiki, just click Help; you'll see a Zim wiki page, complete with the editing toolbar, but read-only.

MediaWiki

MediaWiki is a heavy-duty wiki application built to handle the thousands of visitors and editors to Wikipedia.org. It powers openSUSE.org as well, so it is no surprise that this package is included in the distribution.

While Zim keeps its data in simple text files, MediaWiki keeps its ever-changing data in a MySQL database (support for PostgreSQL was recently added, but is not as robust). You'll also need the Apache web server and the PHP scripting language loaded. All these packages, including MediaWiki, are installable from YaST.

Go to the YaST Software Management module and search for each package. If you happened to include the Web and FTP Server pattern in your openSUSE install, Apache is already in. MySQL is included in the Database Development pattern and PHP is included in the Web Development pattern. MediaWiki is not included in any pattern, so you must install it separately from the openSUSE installation.

NOTE

You'll find much more information about the foundation packages for MediaWiki in these chapters:

- Apache—Chapter 26, "Managing Web and FTP Servers"
- MySQL—Chapter 29, "Managing Databases"
- PHP—Chapter 31, "Creating Dynamic Websites"

Mediawiki stores its files in /srv/www/htdocs/mediawiki. Open a file manager and make a symlink from this directory to your ~/public_html folder, so that the Apache server can see the files.

Now connect to a MySQL database. Check in Chapter 29 to learn how to create a database (call it wikidb) and grant create, select, insert, update, delete, and lock tables permissions to a user.

You can run the Mediawiki installation script from your browser. Open http://localhost/wiki and the script should run. Tell MediaWiki how to connect to your database, and click Install.

When the installation is complete, you have a few housekeeping details to tend to, as follows:

- The installation script creates a file called LocalSettings.php in the Wiki/Config directory. This creates a serious security problem, as this file contains every piece of information MediaWiki needs to run, including the MySQL Root password. Move this file IMMEDIATELY to the main /Wiki directory, and then reset the file's permissions so that only the Owner can read and write the file (and make the Owner the Apache Owner).
- Finally, delete the entire /Config directory. You don't need it.

MediaWiki is now ready to meet the hordes wishing to collaborate on your project.

NOTE

As was mentioned earlier, MediaWiki was discussed only because it ships with openSUSE. Many other packages/WikiEngines are available, and you will want to use the one that best meets your needs. Visit http://c2.com/cgi/wiki?ChoosingaWiki to select a package for your implementation if you want to use something else.

Hosting Electronic Mailing Lists

Mailing lists are a traditional method of asynchronous electronic collaboration. They require no special skills or text formatting abilities from the user, and they can serve loads ranging from a small workgroup on a specific project to a global membership of thousands, even millions, of people interested in discussing the World Cup every four years. They are easy to administer, especially if the membership does not change much over time, and can help a website owner draw traffic with a touch of community.

The concept of an automated list is pretty simple: a list is an organized discussion among a group of people. To initiate a discussion (or thread), you can send a single message to the list management software, which then reflects the message to all list subscribers, that is, to all the people interested in the discussion.

Over the years, there have been several list management tools in use: L-Soft's Listserv, Majordomo, and Lyris, to name some of the best known. Recently, an open source package called Mailman has pulled an increasing share of the traffic.

For users, Mailman provides a consistent, web-based interface for managing their own participation, including subscribing/unsubscribing, getting a daily digest of postings, accessing the list archives, turning off the list for vacations, and so on. List administrators get many automated tools that make their jobs easier and less time consuming. Mailman is one of three list-management tools included in openSUSE (the others are Majordomo and mlmmj).

Mailman keeps track of all subscribers and watches for (and deals with) bouncing messages to some subscribers. It also generates the list archives, if the administrator asks it to.

There is always at least one administrator or moderator for any list—perhaps that is you. That person has access to a special, password-protected administrative web page; there, you can perform your list-god duties, including the following:

- Manually adding or deleting members, either because you're a nice person or your hand has been forced.
- Writing a Welcome message for new list members with the list ground rules.
- Setting the level of moderation for the list. Do you want to inspect every incoming message, or maybe just a new person's first few postings to certify they're not a spammer in disguise.
- Removing offensive messages from the archives.

Installing Mailman

YaST does most of the installation tasks, but there are a few configuration steps you must take before you can create a new list on your own system. These steps are explained in the `/usr/share/doc/packages/mailman/README.SuSE` file. The SUSE team assumes you are using Postfix as your MTA (see Chapter 15) and Apache as your web server (see Chapter 26).

1. In YaST's sysconfig editor (under System), go to Network, Mail, Mailman. (You can also edit `/etc/sysconfig/mailman` directly.) Identify the following items:

   - `MAILMAN_SMTPHOST`
   - `MAILMAN_DEFAULT_NNTP_HOST`
   - `MAILMAN_DEFAULT_EMAIL_HOST`
   - `MAILMAN_DEFAULT_URL_HOST`
   - `MAILMAN_VIRTUAL_HOSTS`

   and run `SuSEconfig -module mailman`.
2. Call `/usr/lib/mailman/bin/mmsitepass` as user root to set your site master password.
3. As root, edit `/etc/postfix/main.cf`. At the bottom of the file, you will see that YaST has already configured a default alias map: `alias_maps = hash:/etc/aliases, ...,`
4. Add this statement to the line: `hash:/var/lib/mailman/data/aliases`.
5. Return to the root shell and reload postfix with this command: `postfix reload`.
6. Finally, call `/usr/lib/mailman/bin/newlist mailman` as user root to create the master mailing list. This list is needed for the inner workings of Mailman. You will be asked to set up a password as the site administrator; make it easy to remember, but relatively hard to guess.

Now you can use the web interface to set up your list.

TIP

Need a host for your Mailman list? You can find a directory of free and commercial hosts at the Python-friendly Web Hosting page: http://www.python.org/moin/PythonHosting. Look for Mailman in the Services Offered column.

Running a Mailman List

Mailman files are stored in `/usr/lib/mailman/bin`. They are owned by root, but all members of the Mailman group have execute rights and can run Mailman commands, using either the web interface or from the shell.

Open your browser to http://localhost/admin to see the Mailman web interface. Now you can create and administer lists.

To run Mailman shell commands, change directories to `/usr/lib/mailman/bin` and then run your command. For example, to create a new list, type the following:

```
./newlist
```

The dot-slash is there because the commands are purposely left out of your path for security reasons.

When you create a new list, you'll be prompted to name the list (use all lowercase letters) and give the email address of the list owner. Mailman will send a confirming email to the owner you name. You establish the initial list password in this sequence as well.

You can find the documentation for Mailman in `/usr/share/doc/packages/mailman`. You'll find README files that cover potential problems with various mail transfer agents and operating systems and the current Frequently Asked Questions list. More formal documentation, tailored to different types of users, is at http://www.gnu.org/software/mailman/docs.html. You can read this online or download the PDF or plain-text versions.

Working with Instant Messengers and Internet Relay Chat

Real-time electronic communication takes two basic forms: Internet Relay Chat (IRC) is like live Usenet, where you go to a group (called a channel) and discuss a topic identified by that channel. Anyone can establish a channel, invite users to participate, set ground rules, and kick users out if they break the rules. Everyone on IRC has a "handle" used to identify them in the chat. Things are relatively anonymous.

Instant Messaging (IM) is a one-on-one process where users can chat with each other without having to visit an IRC channel. Popularized by America Online's Instant Messenger, several networks have since risen to facilitate instant messaging across the Net.

openSUSE users can choose from several clients to handle their real-time communication needs, both IRC and IM.

Internet Relay Chat (IRC)

Like email, the IRC protocol is fundamentally about text. The first IRC clients were based on the command line, and many of these are still in use. But just as plain-text email morphed into HTML-based mail with file attachments and GUI clients, so has IRC.

openSUSE includes a bunch of IRC clients. Among them: Ksirc (a.k.a. kdenetwork-irc) is the default KDE client (although Kopete works with both IM and IRC networks). Weechat is a text-based client available from the Guru YaST repository, and it works in all desktop environments. Xchat is the X Windows standard IRC client. Kvirc and Konversation are some other KDE-based clients, and tkirc is a command-line client based on the tcl-tk language. If you don't already have a favorite, try them all.

CAUTION

For security reasons, never run an IRC client as Root. For the most secure IRC experience, create a special IRC user and always launch your client as that user.

When encountering IRC for the first time, it can be a little intimidating. Unless you know exactly where you're going (as when someone invites you to a specific channel on a particular network), you have a multitude of choices.

Your first choice is the network server. Each client offers a wealth of public IRC servers to connect to (Kopete lists 49 in its wizard; Xchat lists 73). The default lists included with your client can be edited. If you know where you're going, you can also use the `/SERVER <HOSTNAME>` command. EFNet is the oldest IRC network, but there are many popular IRC networks, including Freenode (which is pretty big among coders and open source types), DALNet and Undernet. Depending on the client, you can connect to multiple servers simultaneously to participate in different channels. If you are looking for Linux support, check out ChatJunkiesNet.

Before joining a chat room, you should decide your nickname (or just plain "nick" in IRC). Use the `/NICK` command to identify yourself on IRC with up to 9 case-sensitive characters. You can change your nick as often (or as rarely) as you like.

Each server hosts multiple channels/rooms. These are topic areas and can vary constantly. Some channels are always present on a network; others are there only when something is scheduled. Use the `/LIST` command to see a list of all channels on your server. You can search the channel list for a topic (especially useful in one of the popular networks, because tens of thousands of channels may be open at any given moment); the exact search syntax will vary depending on your client. The list will tell you how many people are logged in on that channel at that moment and give you a description of what the channel is about. You can get a sense of the channel's conversational tone by the description. New users should probably stay away from channels that announce that "Lamers will be SHOT." Most channels are public, but you can set up private channels that require a password. This is configurable in your client. When you find a channel, use `/JOIN` to enter the channel.

TIP

Many open source project developers hang out in assorted IRC channels. This is a great source for support, if you need an answer NOW!

Look for SUSE developers at #suse on irc.freenode.com and user support at #sls-support, also on Freenode.

Check an application's website to see if they offer support via IRC and go for it! Googling "irc <application>" (no quotes) should work too.

After you have selected a channel, you can jump right in to the conversation. As you can see in Figure 16.10, the client should display a list of the participants' nicknames in one window, and postings will appear as scrolling text. Introduce yourself, ask a question, or just say "Hi!"

Your messages in the channel can be seen by everyone in the channel at that moment. You can send a private message to someone in the channel using the /MSG command. Type **/MSG <RecipientNick>** and your message in your client.

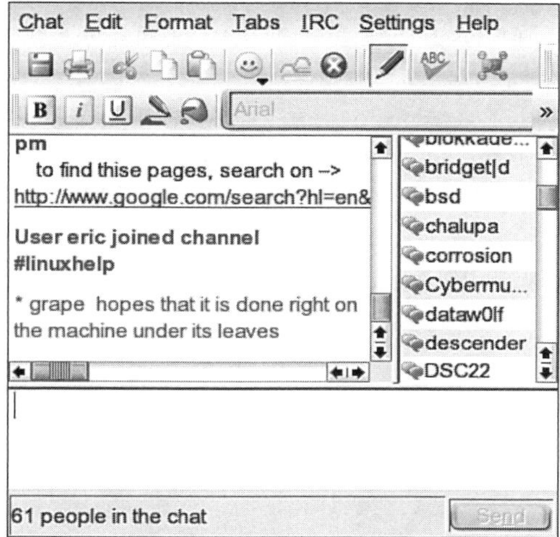

FIGURE 16.10 An IRC channel window. Postings scroll down in the upper-left pane, and participants are listed in the upper right. Post your message in the bottom editor.

NOTE

IRC can be a pretty nasty environment. Given the relative anonymity of its participants, things can happen here that are not rated PG. Language can be crude, and folks can be in chat rooms for every reason imaginable. You may want to watch out if someone starts a conversation asking for your "a/s/l" (age, sex, location). Visit http://www.irc.org/fun_docs/nocuss.html for a humorous take on the language issue, with a few tips on IRC netiquette.

When in IRC, the Golden Rule applies very well. Be respectful to other chatters, don't write in flashing ALL CAPS (even if you want to show off all the things your client can do), and ignore the idiots who act inappropriately.

To leave a channel, use the **/LEAVE <channel>** command. To end your IRC session, type **/QUIT**.

Linux Instant Messaging

Instant messaging should be much simpler than IRC, and it can be. The central problem is the multitude of proprietary IM protocols. The three dominant players—AOL Instant Messenger/ICQ, MSN Messenger, and Yahoo Messenger—all use different methods to connect users of each of their clients.

As long as you and everyone else you want to IM are on the same network, all you need is one account. If you have one friend on a different network, you have to get another account, possibly with another username or password to configure.

You have two ways to solve this dilemma: get a single IM client that supports all the protocols or have all your friends adopt the open-source Jabber protocol and use a Jabber client.

Kopete and Pidgin (for KDE and GNOME, respectively) are multiprotocol instant messengers that can run all the previously mentioned systems and leave you active for hours on end. SIM (the simple instant messenger) is an ICQ-only client (as is the command-line licq).

The Pidgin (formerly GAIM) configuration window in Figure 16.11 shows the protocol choices you have.

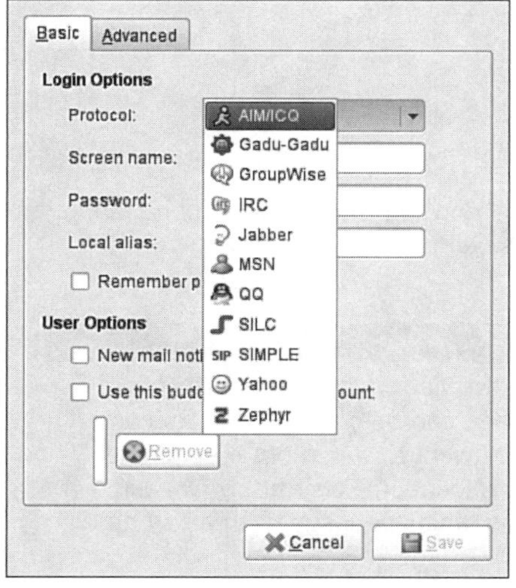

FIGURE 16.11 Pidgin supports several instant messaging protocols. Choose from the configuration menu.

Jabber is designed to be a universal web-standard IM protocol. Someday the others should all adopt it, but that won't happen soon. If more people used Jabber clients, the day might be hastened.

References

- http://akregator.kde.org—The Akregator webfeed reader for KDE/Kontact.
- http://liferea.sourceforge.net— Liferea, the Linux Feed Reader.
- http://www.rssowl.org—RSSOwl, the Java-based feed aggregator.

- http://groups.google.com—Google Groups. Read Usenet on the Web and create groups of your own.
- http://www.isc.org/index.pl?/products/inn—The InterNetNews Usenet server and reader.
- http://slrn.sourceforge.net—"s-lang read news"; the slrn newsreader.
- http://kontact.kde.org/knode—KNode newsreader in Kontact and KDE.
- http://pan.rebelbase.com—The Pan newsreader for GNOME.
- http://c2.com/cgi/wiki?WikiWikiWeb—WikiWikiWeb, Ward Cunningham's original collaborative site.
- http://c2.com/cgi/wiki?ChoosingaWiki—Choosing a WikiEngine, with help from Ward Cunningham's assembled masses.
- http://www.mediawiki.org—The assembled knowledge behind MediaWiki.
- http://zwiki.org—ZWiki, a Zope-based wiki engine included in earlier versions of openSUSE Linux. Docs still in progress.
- http://zopewiki.org/ZopeAndApache—Getting Zope and Apache working together. Helpful when hosting ZWiki on Apache.
- http://twiki.org—Another popular Wiki engine.
- http://en.wikipedia.org—The Wikipedia home page, perhaps the best example of how wikis work.
- http://www.list.org—Home of the Mailman list manager.
- http://www.greatcircle.com/majordomo—The Majordomo list manager.
- http://www.siliconexus.com/MajorCool—The web interface for Majordomo.
- http://www.irchelp.org—The place to get help with Internet Relay Chat.
- http://www.irc.org/links.html—IRC clients, channels, networks, and bots. Find them here.
- http://tldp.org/HOWTO/IRC—The Linux IRC mini-HOWTO.
- http://suse-irc.org/news.php—Web home of the #suse channel at irc.freenode.net.
- http://kopete.kde.org—Kopete, the KDE instant messenger and IRC client.
- http://www.jabber.org/user/userguide—The Jabber user guide, for learning about this open-source IM protocol. Jabber.org also hosts a public IM server for you to connect with.
- http://xchat.org—The Xchat home page.
- http://licq.sourceforge.net/—LICQ, the mother of all Linux instant messengers.

- http://pidgin.im —This IM client started as gaim, an AOL Instant Messenger (AIM) clone, but now supports most other IM networks as well.
- http://widgets.opera.com/newsfeeds—These widgets that supplement the Opera web browser display or manipulate newsfeeds.
- http://www.bloglines.com—The Bloglines online webfeed reader.
- http://freenews.maxbaud.net—Locate free, public Usenet news servers here.
- http://support.novell.com/forums/2su.html—Support forums for openSUSE at Novell.
- http://www.gnu.org/software/mailman/docs.html—User manual and other documentation for the Mailman mailing-list manager.

CHAPTER 17

Secure File Transfer

IN THIS CHAPTER

In the early days of the Internet, one of the really cool things about it was the capability to transfer files and programs from one computer to another. Using the File Transfer Protocol (FTP), anyone with a modem could connect with and download massive repositories of text files, shareware and freeware applications. People still use FTP all the time, although it is often obscured through the many graphical FTP clients. As you learned in Chapter 3, "Installing openSUSE," you can even install openSUSE Linux with the help of FTP.

FTP's ease of use comes with a hidden price, however. FTP is not a secure protocol. Virus-laden files and other malware can be easily uploaded to FTP servers and spread across the Internet. Unencrypted passwords and email addresses can pass through the network to be harvested by spammers and others with bad intent.

Fortunately, you can use new, more secure applications to get the benefits of FTP in a more secure environment. The Secure Shell (SSH) includes `sftp`, a more secure FTP client, and `scp`, the Secure Copy client. Both programs make file transfer safer and are still easy to use.

Another way of moving files around the Internet is by means of peer-to-peer technologies such as BitTorrent and Gnutella. These technologies are apparently as controversial as they are popular, but they use very simple methods of moving data across the network.

This chapter will look closely at file transfer software available in openSUSE Linux, using FTP and peer-to-peer technologies. In Chapter 26, "Managing Your Apache Web Server," you'll also learn about creating a secure FTP server with openSUSE Linux.

Choosing a File Transfer Protocol (FTP) Client

FTP uses a client/server model to move files across a network or across the Internet. It allows for the display of remote file directories. With the right permissions, users can open and edit files on remote directories with FTP as well.

By itself, FTP poses a security risk for both client and server, in part because it allows for login information, including usernames and passwords, to be entered (as well as sent across the network) via clear text. Thus, "anonymous" FTP became a standard practice on the Internet. If clients are not given credentials to use to attach to and manipulate stored data on the FTP server, clients can connect to an FTP site with a generic account by using "anonymous" as the username. Over time, it became customary to give the user's email address as a password. This would allow you to log on, but with general rights given to that of an anonymous user. Today, in addition to anonymous FTP, openSUSE Linux users can be more secure in their file transfers by using the Secure FTP client that comes with OpenSSH, the free version of the Secure Shell. This section will help you use sftp and other FTP clients.

Text-Based FTP Clients

It's good to use a text-based FTP client to learn what is actually going on in a file transfer. Dragging and dropping a file from one place to another is a fine way to simplify what is going on, but to understand the half-dozen commands that are being executed when you drag that file over can help you troubleshoot problems.

YaST installs LukemFTP as the default file transfer client for openSUSE Linux. This client was written for the NetBSD version of UNIX, and it works quite well. It replaces the standard FTP client, so you can use all the standard FTP commands.

Common FTP Commands

The following are the most common commands used in a typical FTP session. Be aware that after you have connected with a remote server, most shell navigation commands (`cd`, `ls`, and `pwd`, especially) work nicely.

Starting and Stopping

- `ftp`—This command starts the FTP client. You cannot connect without typing this first.
- `open`—This command connects with the remote FTP site, using either the IP address or the domain name. Type **`ftp`** at the prompt before using this command.
- `close`—This closes your connection, but stays in FTP so that you can log in to another server.
- `bye`—This command closes your connection, exits FTP, and returns you to your shell prompt.
- `quit`—Same as `bye`. This command closes the connection, exits FTP, and returns you to the shell prompt.

File Types

- `ascii`—Sets a transfer as ASCII text. Use this when sending or receiving text files only.
- `bin`—Sets a transfer as binary. Use this when uploading programs, images, or compressed archives. Also make sure that any program, image, or archive you download is marked with this tag. Some Windows clients upload files as ASCII by default; these are useless when downloaded later.

Actions

- `get`—Initiates a download of a single file from the remote server to your machine. Syntax: *`get <filename>`*.
- `put`—Initiates an upload of a single file from you to the remote machine. Syntax: *`put <path/filename>`*.
- `send`—Same as `put`.
- `mget`—Initiates a download of multiple files from the remote machine to your machine. Accepts wildcards as an argument. See also `prompt`. Example: *`mget *.png`*.
- `mput`—Initiates an upload of multiple files from you to the remote machine. Like `mget`, it takes wildcards as an argument. See also `prompt`. Example: *`mput *.png`*.
- `prompt`—This is an interactive command that gives you some control over `mgets` and `mputs` with wildcards. Prompt will ask you before you transfer if you want each matching file. This is especially good if you have a slow connection and find yourself downloading a duplicate, or otherwise unwanted, large file. This option is turned on by default.
- `hash`—Tells FTP to give you a progress bar of hash marks (#) to indicate how the transfer is going.

FTP includes many other useful commands, which can vary from server to server. If you want to check whether a server supports a particular command, run help after you have connected to your site. You'll get a list (but not a description) of available commands.

TIP

For full descriptions of FTP commands, consult the info page for FTP: **`info ftp`**. To really dig deep, read the comments in the source code, available on the openSUSE Linux DVD.

Using `lftp` Instead of Plain `ftp`

The `lftp` command is not included with a default openSUSE Linux installation, but can be installed by YaST. This can be useful if you have a dial-up connection and a transfer stalls or your connection dies in midtransfer. This package supports restarted downloads (as long as the server does, too) and can also support multiple downloads in a single session with job control.

Using `wget`

`wget` is a useful tool for managing noninteractive transfers, such as mirroring remote directories. It works using standard protocols such as FTP and HTTP, and also secure protocols such as HTTPS. Its non-interactivity might not appear to be a blessing, but this feature enables you to download files in the background or write scripts using `wget` to back up a directory to a remote location. This utility also supports restarted downloads.

Check out the online documentation at http://www.gnu.org/software/wget/manual.

Using `sftp` for Secure File Transfers

The Secure FTP client, `sftp`, was developed as part of the OpenSSH secure shell project to tighten up security problems in some of the fundamental Internet programs. SSH replaced `telnet` as the remote-connection tool of choice for many users, and `sftp` does the same for file transfers.

The goal of `sftp` is not so much to manage the file transfer itself, but to securely transmit login information. This way, files that don't belong in an anonymous FTP directory can still be accessed by those who need them. Instead of connecting with a standard FTP server, `sftp` connects to the `sftp-server` component of OpenSSH, allowing for username and password encryption when you log in. `sftp` does not include all the built-in commands that standard FTP does (you can't use wildcards, for example), but the subset is still quite useful.

If you are concerned that the transfer itself should be secure, you can use the `scp` (secure copy) command instead of `sftp`. For this, you'll need to have explicit access to the remote host and also need to know the structure of the file system (that is, where the directory you want to transfer to is located). Secure file transfers are slow because the bits are encrypted, but the lack of speed is well compensated by the peace of mind accompanying the security of the transfer.

Returning to `sftp`, you can use this only if the remote server has OpenSSH installed. See more on OpenSSH in Chapter 25, "Setting Up Networks and Samba," in the section "Securing Network Services." Secure FTP access is turned on by default in OpenSSH.

Chances are you'll want to use `sftp` in interactive mode. Enter the IP address or remote hostname with the command to access the remote machine:

```
sftp <IP address>
sftp docs.protek.edu
```

By default, the remote machine will recognize you as the current user on your machine. If you have a different username on the remote machine, use the command a little differently:

```
sftp mmccall@docs.protek.edu
```

It will now connect to `docs.protek.edu` and identify you with the new username.

`sshd` is usually configured to run on port 22, and this is where `sftp` tries to connect by default. Some servers can be configured to listen on a different port number, and you can specify that port using the `-o` switch:

```
sftp -oPort2221 mmccall@docs.protek.edu
```

Now you are connected and see a command prompt on the remote machine. To see exactly what commands are available, type **`help`** or a question mark (**?**) at the prompt. Proceed with your session and `quit` at the end.

GUI FTP Clients

openSUSE Linux includes just one standalone graphical FTP client, the GNOME-based gFTP. KFTPGrabber is also popular (and available from the Guru YaST repository). Of course, all the web browsers (Konqueror, Epiphany, Mozilla, Galeon, and Opera) have FTP clients built in as well. Konqueror in file-management mode (and the Nautilus file manager for GNOME) also has no problem connecting to a remote server and transferring files. Just type the URL for the remote machine into the Location box.

Using gFTP

The gFTP client for GNOME makes it easy to transfer files from any remote host. When you open it up, you'll see your home directory in the left panel (as you can see in Figure 17.1). When you connect to a remote site, its home directory will appear in the right panel.

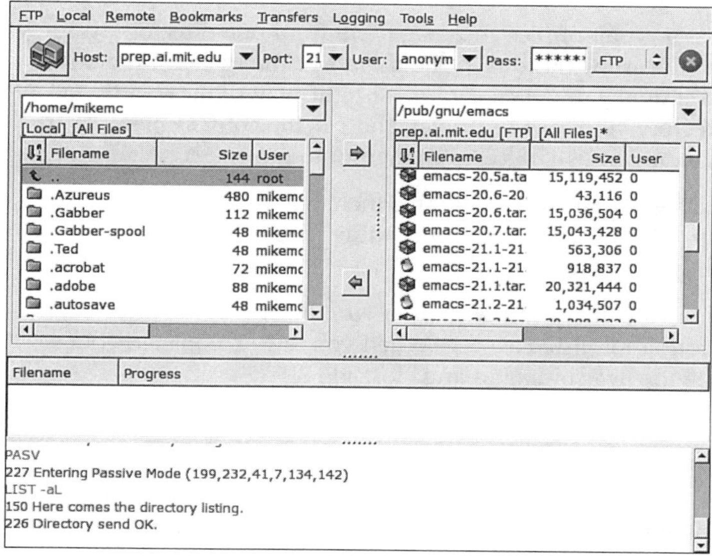

FIGURE 17.1 gFTP simplifies file transfer with side-by-side directories and drag-and-drop ease.

The program comes with bookmarks for some of the largest FTP file repositories, including the openSUSE FTP servers, so you can browse around for interesting files if you're so inclined. If you already know the site you want to connect to, make the connection by typing the address and the additional information into the Host field. After you have connected, you can go to the Bookmarks menu to add this server to your bookmarks for easy access later.

By default, gFTP is set up for anonymous access and delivers your local email address (<username>@linux.local) as the password. You can change the default address in the Options menu, located under FTP. The program also supports sftp and other SSH protocols. To check the settings for secure transfers, go to the FTP menu, and then select Options, SSH.

Figure 17.1 shows the Emacs directory on the GNU project server at the Massachusetts Institute of Technology. At the bottom of the screen, you can see the text stream noting the commands that have been entered. You cannot directly type commands into this window, but all the standard commands are available from the menus. The right-click context menus work well, too.

As always with Linux systems, the default transfer type is Binary, so if you are uploading or downloading a text file, go to the FTP menu and select Ascii.

NOTE

Use the ASCII transfer option only if you are moving plain-text files readable with a text editor. Word processing and spreadsheet files are binaries.

To start a transfer, select a file or group of files and drag them from one directory window to the other. You can also use the arrow buttons in the middle of the screen if the download directory is displayed. You must use the cd command to display subdirectories in either window. Select the directory you want to display and use the context menu or the Local or Remote menus (depending on what you're changing) to run the command.

The directory listings are sortable by any of the columns included, so if you want to see the latest additions at the top, click the Date column heading. The columns are also resizable if you can't see everything you want.

When a file is being transferred, it is listed in the transfer window under the directory listings. It will have progress information listed as well. When you have completed your transfers, press Ctrl+Q to issue the bye command and close gFTP.

Using KFTPGrabber

Many KDE users prefer using Konqueror to manage remote file transfers and local file-management tasks. If you are more comfortable with a traditional FTP two-panel interface or simply have trouble wrapping your mind around the idea that remote files are just another directory structure, KFTPGrabber can help. Essentially it opens a pair of Konqueror windows that appear side-by-side, with a set of FTP-specific menus to help you along.

You can install KFTPGrabber (and many other KDE packages not included in the openSUSE DVD) from the Guru YaST repository. See Chapter 21, "Keeping Your System Current: Package Management" for information on adding repositories to YaST. As with gFTP, KFTPGrabber supports bookmarks for your favorite FTP sites. It does not have any default bookmarks, but the Edit Bookmarks screen will import gFTP and other bookmarks with just a couple of clicks. From the Edit Bookmarks screen, click Import. Figure 17.2 shows this dialog box.

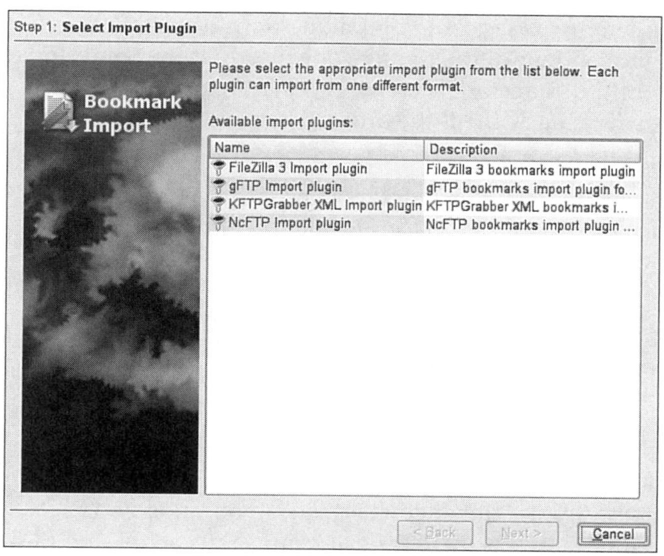

FIGURE 17.2 Import favorite FTP sites to KFTPGrabber from another FTP client with this dialog box.

Click File, New Session to begin multiple connections and transactions. By default, when you exit KFTPGrabber, it leaves an icon on the taskbar. This is configurable in the Settings. It also supports `sftp` and the other SSH protocols. One helpful tool is the two-click Compare Directories operation, which can help in doing remote backup operations and website updates.

17

Peer-to-Peer File Transfer

As controversial as it is popular, peer-to-peer (P2P) file sharing is unlikely to go away anytime soon. As long as Linux serves the "Information wants to be free" crowd (which will be forever), there will be Linux P2P tools.

Two general types of file-sharing protocols exist:

- The traditional, Napster-style model, where files are uploaded and downloaded from one computer to another.
- The BitTorrent model, where large files or packages are downloaded faster by allowing bits to come from several sources and combining them at the end.

Note that all types of files can and do circulate on file-sharing networks, including perfectly legal open-source software. Indeed, openSUSE and several other Linux distributions provide BitTorrent downloads for CD/DVD images. At the same time, be aware that any file can be easily renamed and shared, so that the innocent-looking .wav sound effect you pick up may be replaced by an active virus.

In this book, we're not going to examine the legal and moral questions of P2P file sharing. We note that, as of this writing, four of the top five downloads at the Sourceforge open-source development center (http://sourceforge.net) are file-sharing clients. Whether (and how) you choose to use these tools (as with all the other tools mentioned in this book) is entirely up to you.

For whatever reason, openSUSE Linux no longer includes most peer-to-peer clients in the basic distribution; the exceptions are the standard BitTorrent client and the KTorrent application. In this section, you will learn about several file-sharing clients of each style.

NOTE

Some of these clients are not in the 64-bit openSUSE Linux distribution.

Napster-Style File Sharing

While recording industry legal attacks against the original Napster application and network have transformed the original concept, there are still many applications and file-sharing networks that have sprung up to meet consumer demands, especially for electronic music files.

Gnutella, eDonkey/Overnet, and FastTrack (a.k.a. KaZaa) are perhaps the best known of the file-sharing networks to rise since Napster's fall. What makes them similar to Napster is the user's side of the process. Here is what a user does to get a file:

1. A user goes online to locate and download a copy of a file (for example, an MP3 music file).
2. The client connects to the P2P network and searches for the requested file among the shared directories of computers online at that moment.
3. The client then displays a list of matching files and a little bit of information about the computer the file is on (mainly download speed).
4. The user selects one copy from the list, and the client downloads the file from the selected computer.

The good thing about the system is that no matter what you're looking for, chances are someone on your network has it. The downside of this model relative to BitTorrent is that you're a prisoner of your partner's connection: No matter how fast your broadband or LAN is, if the person you're sharing with has a flaky dial-up that is only online an hour a day, that's the connection you get. If your client finds another copy of the file on another, faster computer, it will start a new download, but this can mean your hard drive begins to fill up with a bunch of partial downloads of the same file.

KMLDonkey is the KDE-based GUI for MLDonkey, a traditional P2P client that is looking for interoperability with several of these networks. GTK-Gnutella is its GNOME counterpart. They are both a little troublesome to work, but you should be able to avoid some of the pitfalls with this guide.

KMLDonkey

MLDonkey is a multi-network P2P client, which wants to work with all file sharers the world over. It began as a client for the eDonkey2000 network, now known as the Overnet, but now supports (to varying degrees) the Gnutella and FastTrack networks. KMLDonkey is the GUI front for this client.

As a would-be KMLDonkey user, you must first go to the MLDonkey website (http://www.mldonkey.org) to download the core package and the server lists. Several stable versions of the core MLDonkey package are stored here as tarballs. Download the latest and install it into your home directory. Those who want to ride the bleeding edge can download and compile from CVS here, too. The server lists are included in the mlnet package (in some places, mlnet is also defined as the core).

When both files have been downloaded, extract the MLDonkey tarball into your home directory. Then extract MLNet into the MLDonkey directory. Now run KMLDonkey, either from the Internet menu, or from the shell. If your servers don't appear (or you get a Failed to Connect message), run the MLNet file manually. The servers should now appear in the KMLDonkey window, and you should be on your way.

When you connect to the Donkey network servers (the default setting), the main KMLDonkey screen should look like Figure 17.3.

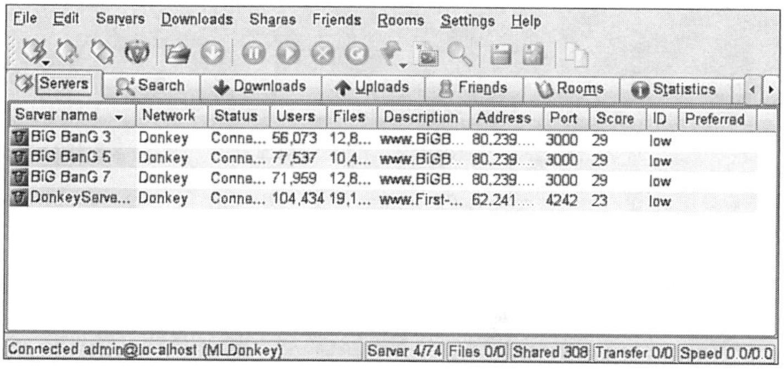

FIGURE 17.3 KMLDonkey displays the servers to which you are currently connected.

Click the Search tab to look for a file. Enter your search keyword(s) at the top and any modifiers further down. The categories are mostly self-explanatory, but if you are looking for an MP3 file, you may want to set a minimum bitrate. This indicates the relative sound quality of a music file. A bitrate of 128 is equivalent to a standard CD recording. The higher the bitrate, the bigger the file, so if you set your max size at 500KB and a bitrate of 128KB, you may see files that last only a few seconds.

These are file *sharing* networks, so do your part by designating at least one directory on your system for access to others (and probably not more than that). By default, KMLDonkey shares the Incoming directory where it places its own completed downloads. You can add more by going to the Uploads tab and right-clicking anywhere. Choose Share Directory from the context menu and type the path into the dialog box. Unfortunately, there is no Browse button in this dialog box, so you must type the full path.

17

GTK-Gnutella

Gnutella was one of the first decentralized networks to be created. Written by a developer at Nullsoft, the creators of the Winamp MP3 player for Windows, Gnutella was released under the GPL, and officially available for only one day. Nullsoft's owners, then called AOL/TimeWarner, were not pleased by this offering. A community of developers quickly formed to work on the code, and many clients have since been developed to support the Gnutella network.

The Gnutella2 network was created in 2003 and is designed to be a faster and a more efficient protocol than the original Gnutella protocol. Both networks still function.

GTK-Gnutella is a GUI client based on the Gimp Toolkit. It functions much like MLDonkey, but accesses only the two Gnutella networks.

The GTK-Gnutella interface is not exactly a thing of beauty, but it runs nicely. Like KMLDonkey, it first displays the servers to which you're connected. To search for something, click in the New Search box and type your keyword(s). You'll be taken immediately to the Search Results window, which you can see in Figure 17.4.

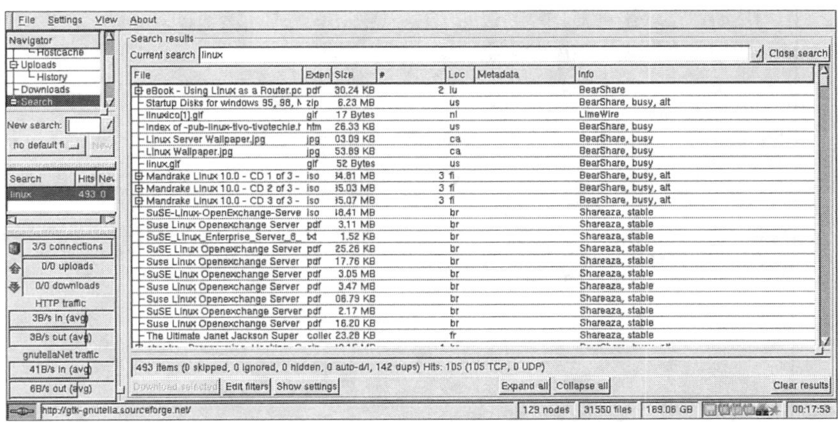

FIGURE 17.4 The GTK-Gnutella Search Results window. Select your file(s) to download from this list. Note that the Search box on the left displays all your active searches and the number of hits it has generated.

You can modify your search in this window. Click Edit Filters. Not especially user-friendly, these filter dialog boxes are nonetheless pretty easy to understand. You can set filters for size and name, along with several other parameters.

Select the file(s) you want to download from the search list and click the Download Selected button at the bottom to begin downloading. Searches remain active as long as GTK-Gnutella is running, and whatever main window you're in, you can always see the current results of your search in the Search window below the New Search box.

Settings are also fairly technical in the way they are presented, but if you are not sure what a setting will do, try mousing over the setting; often you'll see a ToolTip with an explanation or hint.

Wrangling the BitTorrent

Whatis.com describes the most important advantage of BitTorrent as follows: "Rather than having to send a download to each customer requesting it, the distributor or holder of content sends it to one customer who in turn sends it to other customers who together share the pieces of the download back and forth until everyone has the complete download. This makes it possible for the original server to serve many requests for large files without requiring immense amounts of bandwidth."

For the most part, BitTorrent is the sharing format of choice for big collections of archived text, books, and audio and video clips, including entire taped concerts and movies. With SUSE Linux 10, Novell joined the ranks of Linux distributors offering BitTorrent downloads of its ISO images, making it just a little easier to pull down that 3.1GB package. This has continued with the openSUSE community edition.

BitTorrent works a little differently from the traditional file-sharing arrangement discussed in the preceding section. It goes something like this:

1. Someone with content to share creates a *.torrent file to wrap the content in. This is done in the BitTorrent client. This person is referred to as the Seed.
2. An announcement is made on a website or mailing list that this torrent (or set of torrents) is available, with instructions given on finding its location.
3. People who want this file point their BitTorrent clients toward the seeded file.
4. Any other clients that have the file (or some pieces of it, depending on the client) and that are online contribute bits to every other client that is downloading the same file. This eases the load on the Seed and speeds the download for each client because more bits are coming down at the same time.
5. When a download is complete, it's proper form to remain online and keep your client open for awhile so that others can benefit. The client monitors the upload/download ratio and often can turn itself off when you have uploaded as many bits as you've downloaded (that is, a ratio of 1:1).

Finding torrents is not always an easy task. One site that attempted to be a BitTorrent content clearinghouse shut down after the Motion Picture Association of America threatened a lawsuit. The safe choices are downloading from official sources and getting music from trade-friendly artists (think jam bands: Phish, Grateful Dead, Leftover Salmon, String Cheese Incident, and others). An excellent site for downloading legal music torrents is http://bt.etree.org (this is the BitTorrent part of this large music-trading community).

Azureus, the Java BitTorrent Client

The most manageable BitTorrent client for Linux is a bit of open source Java code called Azureus. Named for a species of frog notable for its blue coloring, Azureus is easy to install and easy to work with.

Install Azureus the easy way through the Packman YaST repository, or head to the download page at http://azureus.sourceforge.net/_download.php. Download the appropriate client for your system (choose between the GTK and Motif versions for Intel x86 processors, or the specific versions for AMD64 or PowerPC processors). You will get a tarball that you can open with your favorite archiver.

Extract the tarball into your home directory, where it will create an `/Azureus` subdirectory. That's all you need to install the program.

To set up Azureus the first time, you need to run the program from the shell. From the home directory, type **`./azureus/azureus`** to start the Configuration Wizard. The wizard will identify your connection speed and adjust if necessary. Click Next to continue.

The next wizard screen tests the BitTorrent listen port to see if it is available. Click Test to run the test. If it fails, you need to reconfigure the Firewall in YaST or your hardware router to permit regular BitTorrent operations. See the next Tip for more detailed information.

TIP

BitTorrent works best when other clients have direct access to your bits. BitTorrent clients now communicate best through one port in the range 49152–65534. The Azureus Configuration Wizard will give you a random port to test. If you're using the openSUSE Firewall, you have to configure it to open the port. Go to the YaST Security and Users module and click Firewall. When you get to the Firewall Configuration page, click Allowed Services. Click the Advanced button in the lower-right corner to open the port. Type in the recommended TCP port and click OK to return to the main page. Click Next to view the current settings, including your changes. If this is correct, click Accept to confirm your changes.

If you have a hardware router that is your Internet gateway (as is often the case with broadband connections), you may have to configure that to permit BitTorrent communications as well. Visit http://www.portforward.com/routers.htm for helpful information on configuring several popular routers for BitTorrent.

BitTorrent clients will work even if you can't get the listen port open, but your upload/download speeds will suffer.

The last screen in the Configuration Wizard asks where to store your `.torrent` files. Accepting the defaults is perfectly OK. Click Finish to open Azureus.

When you have completed the installation, go back to the Azureus download site to get (via BitTorrent) the latest Java Runtime Environment (JRE). As with the Azureus client, click the appropriate client for your system. The difference is that Azureus will now open up to manage the download instead of your browser. You may even see the Upload Speed column activate as someone else uses some of the bits you've already downloaded.

TIP

When installing any new Java product, it's a good idea to check for a new JRE. Not everyone will have a convenient link like Azureus does. Go to http://www.java.com/en/download to get the latest and greatest. After the new JRE is installed, go to YaST and remove the earlier version.

Azureus has several plug-in enhancements for your BitTorrent experience and a simple Installation Wizard to obtain and maintain them. Go to the Plugins menu and select Installation Wizard. Select By List from Sourceforge.net to see all the plug-ins downloadable from the Azureus site. Click the plug-in name for a description of the tool, and check the box to install it. Click Next, and then Finish to begin the download. After it's installed, the Azureus Update Manager will automatically keep both the main program and any installed plug-in current. You'll also notice that plug-ins download into your torrent directory, and you become a seed for the next plug-in download.

KTorrent

KTorrent is the recommended client for openSUSE downloads and the only peer-to-peer client remaining in the standard openSUSE distribution. As you would guess, KTorrent integrates well into your KDE desktop, placing an icon on your taskbar for processing downloads while you're occupied with other tasks.

This client has a built-in search engine (based on Konqueror) that distinguishes it from other BitTorrent clients. To set this up, go to Settings, Configure KTorrent and click Search. You can enter a BitTorrent aggregator manually, or just click Update from Internet to get a new set.

Now click the Search tab, and enter your search term(s) into the box. By default, the Ktorrents engine is selected, but you can use the drop-down menu to change that if your first search isn't successful. Figure 17.5 shows some results from a search on Phish. Click the title to see a list of places that should have the file you're looking for. Click one, and the download page for that set of files will appear. Click the link to get your torrent.

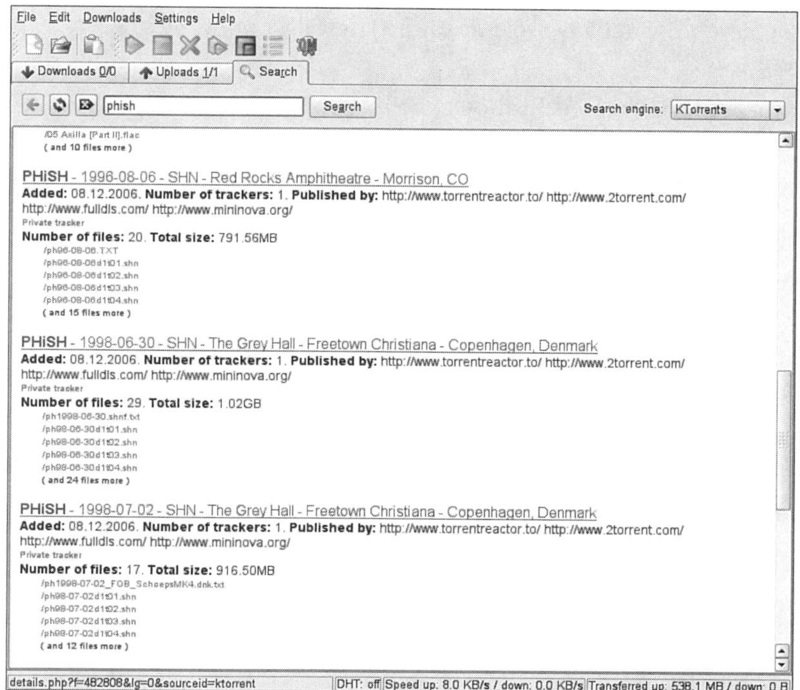

FIGURE 17.5 Search for torrents with KTorrent's Search tab.

References

- http://www.cert.org—The Computer Emergency Response Team. The place to go to learn about current security holes, and the latest virus alert email.
- http://www.openssh.org—The open-source Secure Shell home. OpenSSH includes the Secure FTP client.
- http://www.gftp.org—The GNOME FTP client.
- http://www.kftp.org—A KDE-based FTP client.
- http://www.ncftp.com/ncftp/doc—Documentation for the NcFTP client and server.
- http://wget.sunsite.dk—Wget, the GNU tool for non-interactive (scripted) file transfer.
- http://enterprise.linux.com/article.pl?sid=04/12/20/1910209—A pithy description of what you can do with wget.
- http://www.gnutelliums.com/linux_unix—A list of Unix/Linux Gnutella clients.
- http://gtk-gnutella.sourceforge.net—GTK-Gnutella.
- http://bittorrent.com—Bram Cohen's BitTorrent home page.
- http://azureus.sourceforge.net—Azureus, the Java BitTorrent client.
- http://www.java.com/en/download—Download the latest Java Runtime Environment here.
- http://www.portforward.com/routers.htm—Get help opening your hardware router for BitTorrent.
- http://gift.sourceforge.net—The GiFT open-source FastTrack peer-to-peer project.
- http://apollon.sourceforge.net—A GUI for GiFT.
- http://kmldonkey.org—KMLDonkey GUI client.
- http://mldonkey.sourceforge.net—The home of MLDonkey, where you can download the core program. Front page links to all the file-sharing networks the client supports.
- http://www.ktorrent.org— The KTorrent project.
- http://wiki.etree.org/index.php?page=BitTorrent—The eTree BitTorrent FAQ page, with much good information on BitTorrent clients, how BitTorrent works, and where to find content.

PART IV

Basic System Administration

IN THIS CHAPTER

CHAPTER 18

Managing Files, Volumes, and Drives

IN THIS CHAPTER

In the next four chapters, we will go over the system administration tasks you will have to know, whether you are managing a 1,000-seat network or a single system—your own.

Nearly everything you do in this chapter will be as Root/SuperUser. This is because you're dealing with important system-related issues. As noted previously, when you are working with Root powers, you can do wonderful things quite easily. It is also just as easy to blow your system away. Take care.

Here you will learn about the different file systems openSUSE Linux can use to format your drives and other storage devices. You'll learn about Logical Volume Management (LVM) and how to mount drives and add peripheral storage devices, such as a USB key chain storage device, to your system.

Sometimes it's hard to find a file or directory on a big system. Do you wonder if an application you heard about at the Linux User Group meeting is installed on your system? From the standard shell file-finders to the brand new Beagle graphical desktop search tool, you can find things relatively easily with the Linux tools you'll learn about in this chapter.

We'll also tell you about GNU Parted, the partitioning tool included with openSUSE Linux. This information is essential for Linux newbies, and old hands might pick up something new, too.

Choosing a File System

It's always good to remember that in Unix/Linux, a file system is not just the hierarchy of files and directories accessible through the shell or a GUI file manager.

File systems include the disk format type and the metadata surrounding files and directories. Because everything in Linux is a file with properties, permissions, and other attributes, everything attached to the system (printers, mice, keyboards, files on network servers, remote machines, FTP servers, and so on) is part of the file system.

When we talk of choosing a file system, though, we're talking about disk formats. The Linux kernel and openSUSE can work with many file systems. Table 18.1 shows the variety.

TABLE 18.1 Linux Compatibility with Various File Systems

Name	Description	Run Linux Natively	Read from Linux	Copy/Move Files
ReiserFS	Formerly the default SUSE Linux file system. Journaled file system.	Y	Y	Y
ext2	Extended file system. Default for many older Linux systems.	Y	Y	Y
ext3	ext2 with journal. Default for openSUSE.	Y	Y	Y
JFS	IBM Journaled file system.	Y	Y	Y
XFS	Journaled file system originally for SGI IRIX, ported to Linux.	Y	Y	Y
Minix	The file system Linus Torvalds ported to the x86 platform.	N	Y	Y
NFS	Network file system.	N	Y	Y
FAT12	DOS floppy disk format.	N	Y	Y
FAT16	MS-DOS File Allocation Table.	N	Y	Y
FAT32/vfat	Windows 9x file system.	N	Y	Y
NTFS	Windows NT/2000/XP. NTFS > Linux only.	N	Y	
HFS	Macintosh Hierarchical file system.	N	Y	Y
ISO9660	CD-ROM file system.	N	Y	Y
UDF	Universal Disk Format for DVD-ROM.	N	Y	Y

Understanding the Physical Structure of a Disk

All these file systems organize data on a disk in largely the same manner.

The differences between them, especially among the Unix/Linux file systems, are usually related to the speed of retrieval. Disks are organized (or formatted) in blocks. The first block of any disk is the boot sector, which contains a very short program (a few hundred bytes), which will load and start running the operating system.

In the case of a dual-boot system, a bootloading program, such as lilo or grub, will be stored there. All other blocks (sometimes called clusters or sectors) contain the operating system, all your application files, and all your data files that constitute your life.

In Unix and Linux, each block is 1024 bytes by default. A block contains several smaller bits of data:

- A superblock, with redundant information about the complete file system.
- More redundant file system descriptors, useful for reliability and disaster recovery. Also explains why it's really hard to recover when you remove/delete a file in Unix/Linux. All the redundancy disappears, too.
- A bitmap of the block.
- A bitmap of the inode table (see the paragraph following this list for more on inodes).
- Information from the inode table.
- The data itself.

An inode contains all the information needed to identify a file—its attributes and permissions, its location(s) on the disk, its owner, the timestamps—except the filename itself (which belongs to the directory).

There is one inode for every file. The inode table performs the same function as the DOS File Allocation Table (FAT). It keeps track of where files are located on the disk for easy retrieval.

Working with ReiserFS

ReiserFS version 3 was the default file system for SUSE Linux up to the 10.2 release. Created from the ground up by Hans Reiser, it is safer and faster than the old default ext2 file system.

It is a *journaling file system,* meaning it has a file (a journal) that records changes to the file system. Should you have a system crash, a power surge, or some other mishap leading to an unexpected (that is, involuntary) shutdown, recovery will be less traumatic. ReiserFS was the first journaling file system included into the Linux kernel, and it has been supported since kernel version 2.4.1 in January 2001.

If you've ever had Microsoft Windows crash or freeze up, you'll know the pain and agony associated with a non-journaling file system.

Following the unexpected shutdown, Windows runs its ScanDisk program over your entire hard drive, checking for both bad disk sectors and reestablishing where every file snippet is physically located on the disk. Because broken links might occur, you may have orphaned clusters, a common problem that will result in a loss of data.

Although Linux is a much safer OS with far fewer software-related crashes, Linux users have not been entirely exempt from the involuntary shutdown. When this happens under the ext2 file system, the fsck program also scans the entire file system to make sure no data is lost in the crash. It could also take its time in processing the drive before you can log in.

The journal file makes it tremendously faster and easier to confirm that the disk is not damaged and that data is not lost. The journal knows what changes (saving new data, creating new files, deleting files, updating, and so on) were made to the disk since the last normal shutdown and tells the disk scanner where they are physically located on the disk. The scanner confirms that the location is not damaged and proceeds. This process does not guarantee that no data will be lost in this situation (the journal does not know what you typed since the last save before the crash), but it is in much better shape.

ReiserFS also manages blocks much differently than the Extended Filesystem (ext2, ext3), allowing many small files to share a block. This speeds retrieval and should display small files faster.

Its chief weakness is a problem only for people converting an existing ext2 or ext3 file system to ReiserFS. You must back up all your data and reformat the drive before installing ReiserFS. If you are installing openSUSE Linux for the first time on your computer, this is nothing to worry about.

NOTE

The next generation of the ReiserFS, Reiser4, was released in early 2005. The file system, with financial help from the Defense Advanced Research Projects Agency (DARPA), has some advanced security features. These are outlined on the Namesys website: http://www.namesys.com/v4/v4.html#enh_security.

The Extended File System (ext2, ext3)

The ext2 file system was the standard and default throughout the early years of Linux kernel development. Hardly anyone used anything else until very recently. When ReiserFS first produced a journaling file system, Red Hat and others worked to bring journaling to this file system, and ext3 was added to the kernel as of v2.4.16 in November 2001. ext3 became the default SUSE file system with the release of openSUSE 10.2.

ext3 and ext2 are nearly identical except for the journal file. If you are installing openSUSE Linux over an existing ext2 file system, you might want to use ext3 instead of ReiserFS. The chief advantage of the ext3 file system is that it will automatically recognize files on ext2, and reformatting is not required.

JFS and XFS

IBM's original Journaling File System (JFS) and the XFS file system from SGI (formerly Silicon Graphics, Inc.) are file systems that were designed for other Unix versions now ported to Linux. JFS was the file system of choice for AIX users. SGI created XFS to be the basis for its IRIX systems.

JFS introduced journaling to Linux and has its own version of `fsck` to handle problem boots. XFS claims superior performance than either JFS or ReiserFS. Perhaps one of these will work for you.

Choosing a File System

Don't fret endlessly over what file system to choose. All the file systems discussed here are excellent. It is a one-time decision, though. There is some pain involved with changing file systems after installation, especially when moving from ext2 or ext3 to ReiserFS. If you are connected to an existing AIX or IRIX network or you are transitioning from one of these enterprise Unixes, stick with the file system you have.

Otherwise, selecting the default ext3 is probably your best choice.

Creating and Managing File Systems with Partitioner

The first, and perhaps only, time you have to create a new file system on your Linux computer is when you first install the operating system. You learned the basics of how to do this in Chapter 3, "Installing openSUSE."

If you add a second hard drive, or have set up a series of mount points that you decide to adjust in one way or another, you can go to the YaST Partitioner tool to handle this task for you.

NOTE

Until GNU Parted came along, partitioning in Unix and Linux was handled by the standard `fdisk` shell utility. It works a little differently from its DOS namesake, but performs the same essential tasks: creating and modifying the partition table.

The main difference between `fdisk` and Parted/YaST Partitioner, aside from the GUI, is that `fdisk` does not preserve existing data. If you tell `fdisk` to make the root partition 10GB smaller and create a new partition where the old one was, `fdisk` will do exactly that. If there was data sitting on a block in the last 10GB, it will be overwritten.

Feel free to use `fdisk` from the shell if you prefer, knowing its limitations.

18

Expert Partitioner (EP) is a GUI version of GNU Parted integrated into YaST. If you have used either of the Windows third-party partitioning products—PartitionMagic or Partition Commander—you will find EP familiar.

It simplifies the partitioning process and can adjust the partition table without harming existing data. You should know what you're doing before you begin, however. There is a reason it's called *Expert* Partitioner.

CAUTION

Unless you are working with new or otherwise empty drives, Expert Partitioner can ruin some data or even your entire hard drive. This is a very rare occurrence, but if you're making changes to your partition table in the middle of a thunderstorm, power surges can mess things up badly.

Always back up at least your most important files before using EP, even if you are not planning to touch that mount point! And use an Uninterruptible Power Supply (UPS) whenever you have important data of any kind on your computer. This is the minimum protection you need.

Using Expert Partitioner

Now that all the warnings are out of the way, we can begin to work with EP. It is actually a very simple tool. To open it, go to YaST, System, Partitioner. YaST will repeat the warnings you've seen in this section and make you click Yes before opening the tool.

There you will see your current partition table laid out, as shown in Figure 18.1.

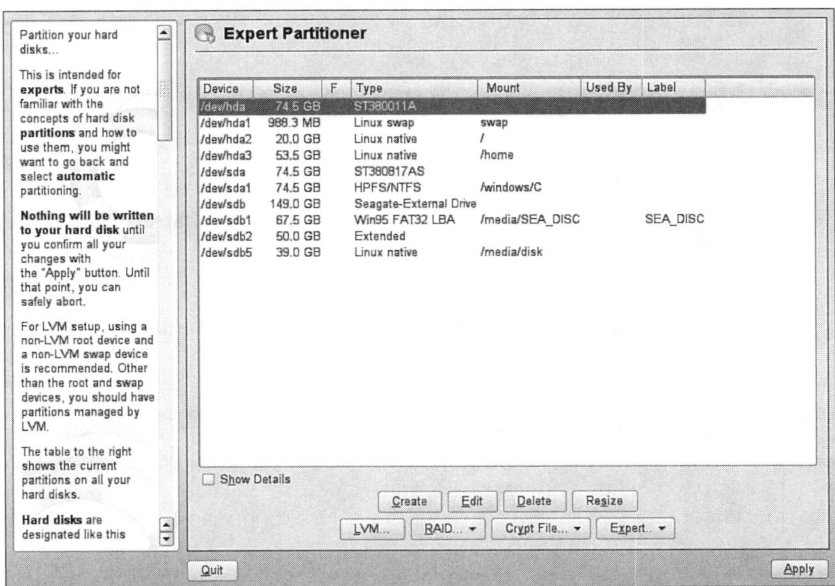

FIGURE 18.1 Expert Partitioner lets you resize existing partitions and create new ones. The initial screen displays your current partition table.

It's a good idea to have a hard copy of all this information, so write it down in your notebook before making any changes.

In Figure 18.1, you can see that two physical hard drives are on this system: an IDE drive, `/dev/hda`, and an SATA drive, `/dev/sda`. Each drive is 74.5GB after formatting. `/dev/hda` has two Linux partitions, Root (/) and Swap; `/dev/sda` has one Windows (NTFS) partition, seen here as `/windows/C`. The Start and End numbers are the block numbers, showing where on the disk each partition/mount point begins and ends.

NOTE

DOS/Windows (and practically all BIOS programs) support only four primary partitions on a drive. Dual-boot systems have a particular problem with this setup. To get around this limitation, use the idea of turning one primary partition into an extended partition that allows you to create multiple logical partitions, making more efficient drives by making smaller sectors/blocks. There are few limitations on the number of logical partitions inside an extended partition.

You can install openSUSE Linux into an extended partition; this is what YaST does by default. Linux file systems support up to 15 partitions/mount points.

Writing this information down is yet another safety valve in case of emergency, because you can reconstruct the table with the accurate start and end blocks if necessary.

At the bottom of the screen are eight action buttons that correspond to the task at hand. With EP, you can do the following:

- Create a new partition from empty space on the disk.
- Edit an existing drive or partition.
- Delete an existing partition or drive (and all the data on it).
- Resize a partition to make it larger or smaller.
- Manage a logical volume (this is covered later in this chapter).
- Create or manage a RAID volume structure (this is covered in Chapter 20, "Managing Data: Backup, Restoring, and Recovery").
- Encrypt a partition.
- Reread or delete a partition table (under the Expert button).

The following sections walk you through these tasks.

NOTE

When you're working with Expert Partitioner, you can do some experimentation without making changes to your system. Nothing you set up in the EP interface becomes final until you click Apply from the main window (refer to Figure 18.1).

Creating a New Partition

Click Create to set up a new partition. Depending on your setup, you will be asked what disk to create the partition on and whether it is a primary or extended partition (see the preceding Note). EP then displays the Create Partition dialog box, shown in Figure 18.2.

Figure 18.2 shows the default settings for this dialog box. In addition to the default ext3, you can format the new partition as ext2, ReiserFS, JFS, XFS, or as increased Swap. You can also create a FAT partition readable by Windows. The contents of the Options dialog box changes depending on the file system you choose.

A new partition can use only unformatted space on the physical drive. By default, EP will have this partition fill up the remaining free space, but you can choose to leave some space unformatted (and perhaps ready for another partition) by entering either a specific end cylinder or (as indicated) the size of the partition in megabytes (MB) or gigabytes (GB).

TIP

Check the Encrypt File System box to encrypt all new files created or moved into your new partition. See "Encrypting a Partition or Files" later in this chapter.

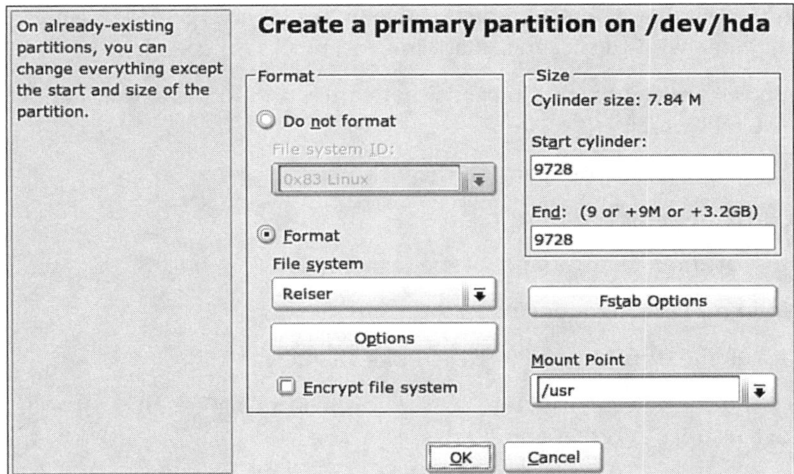

FIGURE 18.2 The Create Partition dialog box lets you set all the necessary options for a new Linux partition.

The Fstab Options button lets you set up Journaling mode (Ordered is the default), whether a user can mount this partition (No is the default), and whether to mount the partition automatically at startup (Yes is the default). You'll learn more about the fstab file in the "Mounting a File System" section.

The last section is the mount point definition. Use the drop-down menu or type in a mount point as well.

TIP

If you're adding a FAT partition, make `/windows/D` (or another drive letter) the mount point.

Click OK to confirm your choices.

Editing a Partition

When you select an existing partition and click Edit, the dialog box is nearly identical to Figure 18.2. All the options are editable except for the size parameters. You must use the Resize tool to change that.

Why would you edit a partition? If you want to use the Logical Volume Manager (LVM), at least one partition must have the type Ox8e or Ox83. You can set that in this dialog box. You may also want to change the fstab settings for a partition without editing the file by hand. Or you may want to change the mount point for one reason or another, especially with a nonroot partition.

Deleting a Partition

There are only two reasons to delete a partition with EP: You've copied off all the data and want to recover the space for something else entirely, or you have a non-root mount point that you don't want to treat as a separate partition anymore.

The latter situation can occur when you define a mount point for `/usr` or `/home` to get a faster response from the disk, and the results are disappointing. In that case, move all the files back to the / partition before deleting the mount point.

To use EP to delete a partition, first unmount it with the `umount` command at the shell prompt. Open EP. Select the partition. Click Delete. You may get a warning, especially if you haven't unmounted or if you accidentally selected the / partition. EP will then mark the partition for deletion. The delete action will not be final until you click Apply. After you do that, the partition will be gone, and the space will be available. See the section on `umount` later in this chapter.

Resizing a Partition

This is the trickiest part of the EP process and is the special trick of GNU Parted. The standard Linux fdisk program creates, edits, and deletes partitions. But fdisk, like its DOS/Windows counterpart, is destructive when it performs its functions. fdisk will cheerfully create a new partition where some old data is lying around, but that data will be no more when it's done.

EP will shrink an existing partition, taking care to preserve existing data and not overwrite it. You can then create new partitions on the empty space remaining.

To resize a partition, select the partition in EP and click Resize. The Resize dialog box (see Figure 18.3) appears.

Use the slider, the spin box, or type in the size (in gigabytes) you want your new partition to be in the Unused Disk box. The second, bottom graphic will show what the disk will look like after the resizing takes place.

If you change your mind, click Do Not Resize to return the settings to where they were. If you are ready to proceed, click OK. The partition will be marked for resizing.

When you have confirmed your intention to resize the large partition, use Create as previously described to create the new partition(s) to fill the newly created space. After you've done that, click Apply to implement the new changes. You can turn back at any time before you click Apply.

Encrypting a Partition or Files

If you run a business with your computer, you probably have some files that are more sensitive and valuable than others. You want to protect this information from prying eyes. Setting permissions and other access control tools is an important method of securing these files, but some things need even more security. This is especially true with data on laptops and removable hard drives.

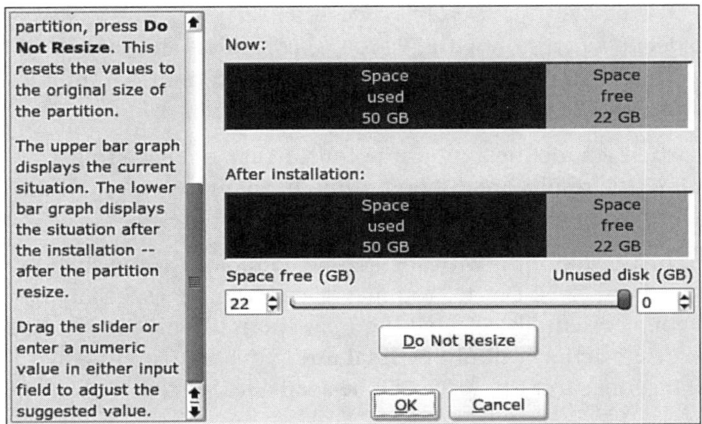

FIGURE 18.3 Expert Partitioner shows you the amount of space being used by your partition. Use the slider or type in the size you want your new partition to be.

openSUSE Linux makes it possible, and relatively easy, to set up an area where files are encrypted within that space. You can set off an entire partition or create an encrypted file system within single files.

You have the option of creating encrypted partitions during the installation process, but you can also do this within EP.

CAUTION

Don't use EP to encrypt a running file system! Adding encryption will destroy any data on a running partition. Always resize another partition and then create a new, encrypted partition with the process outlined in this section.

To create a single encrypted file to hold secure data, click Crypt File, Create Crypt File in the EP dialog box. Another dialog box (see Figure 18.4) appears.

Enter the path to the file to create along with its intended size. This is set to 50MB by default. Remember that this will be just one file, holding a spreadsheet with your balance sheets, for example. You want this file to be big enough to hold a growing file, but not so big that it encroaches on your capability to store other files. A good rule is to estimate how big that spreadsheet could get over the lifetime of your computer, and then double it.

SUSE recommends accepting the proposed settings for formatting and the file system type (that is, formatting for ext3). Specify the mount point. Decide whether the crypto file system should be mounted during boot in the fstab options. Click OK to mark this file for creation. EP will put this file at the end of the current partition. Your encrypted file will not be created until you click Apply at the end of the process.

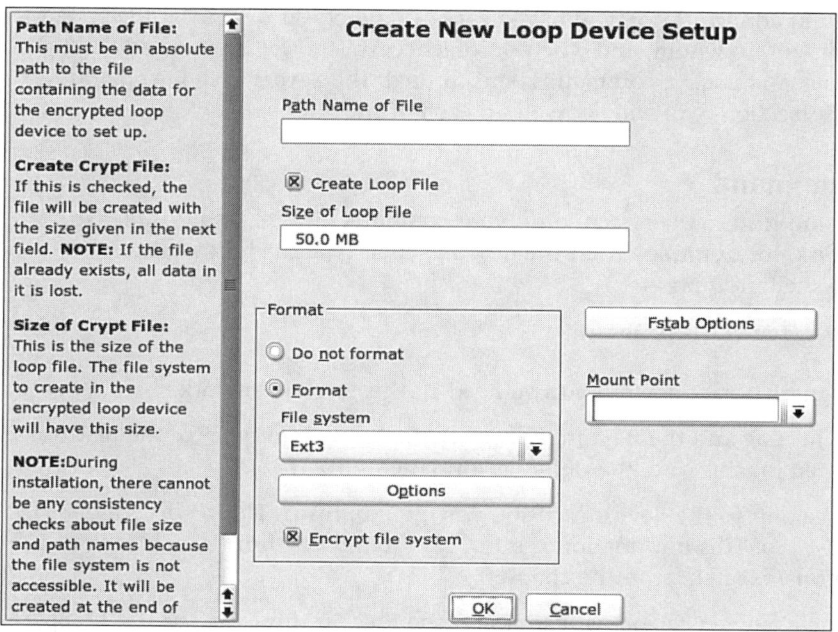

Path Name of File:
This must be an absolute path to the file containing the data for the encrypted loop device to set up.
Create Crypt File:
If this is checked, the file will be created with the size given in the next field. NOTE: If the file already exists, all data in it is lost.
Size of Crypt File:
This is the size of the loop file. The file system to create in the encrypted loop device will have this size.
NOTE:During installation, there cannot be any consistency checks about file size and path names because the file system is not accessible. It will be created at the end of
Create New Loop Device Setup
Path Name of File
Create Loop File
Size of Loop File
50.0 MB
Format
Do not format
Format
File system
Ext3
Options
Encrypt file system
Fstab Options
Mount Point
OK
Cancel

FIGURE 18.4 Use this dialog box to create a single file to hold secure data. When entering the pathname, do not point to an existing file unless you have it backed up.

To access an encrypted partition, you must use the `mount` command to make the partition visible. You will be asked to supply the password. See the section on the `mount` command later in the chapter.

Expert Functions

Two Expert functions round out the EP tasks. If you suspect that the partition table is not showing up correctly in the EP window, click Reread Partition Table.

It's not even close to being a common occurrence, but a bad label can get attached to a disk. If you're having otherwise weird problems on your system, disposing of the label can be a last option. Delete Partition Table and Disk Label is the equivalent of waving the white flag and saying goodbye. Along with the bad label, everything else on that partition will disappear as well. Always back up before running this one.

Mounting a File System

A Linux system doesn't really care what is attached to it at any given moment. Do you want to connect to a printer down the hall, a co-worker's laptop in Australia, a backup mirror on the corporate server in Shanghai, or a floppy disk in your own machine? No problem—with the `mount` command and the right permissions, all these devices and file systems will appear on your system as if they were all just another part of your computer.

If you are the system administrator, you have near-absolute power over what file systems appear on your system, to whom, and when. In practice, this power is exercised through the use of the mount and umount commands, and through the /etc/fstab file governing file systems. In this section, you will learn about each of these tools.

The mount Command

The mount command loads a file system onto your computer and makes it visible. To mount a floppy disk, for example, insert the disk and then type the following (as SuperUser) at the shell prompt:

```
mount -t vfat /dev/fd0 /media/floppy
```

This is how the syntax breaks down (and you need all this to make it work):

- Type (-t)—This flag and the next item identify the file system type for the platform to be mounted (in this case, the floppy is formatted for FAT32).
- File system—Point to the device partition you are mounting. Floppy disks are, by default, /dev/fd0. This information is set by and retrievable from /etc/fstab (see the section on /fstab later in the chapter).
- Mount point—Where fstab actually looks for the files. In this case, /media/floppy.

It is a good idea to have all your peripheral file systems (floppy drives, hard drives, USB and serial-port file storage devices, CD-ROM, DVD, and CD-RW drives) connected when you install openSUSE Linux. Why? YaST can then identify all these devices and build your /etc/fstab file automatically.

The umount Command

Most of the time after you have mounted a hard drive or partition, you'll keep it mounted. You're always accessing it. Removable storage media are different; you'll often pop one in, work on files (or copy/move them to your hard drive), and pop it out again. In Linux, this is a little more complicated process.

After you have mounted a floppy as described in the last section, before you can put another floppy in the drive, you must unmount the drive. To do this, you must use the umount command (without an N):

```
umount /media/floppy
```

or

```
umount /dev/fd0
```

Before unmounting any file system, make sure that no processes are using files on that file system. You will get an error message if that's the case.

In some rare cases, umount will not complete its task, or the error message points to a process that has stopped. If you cannot unmount a drive and you are certain that no processes are working on that drive, use `umount -f` to force the drive to unmount.

TIP

When KDE starts, it mounts any attached storage volumes and puts an icon in the taskbar for these drives. To unmount a portable volume, click the icon and select Safely Remove. You can also use this icon to open a Konqueror window to access the files.

Using `/etc/fstab` to Automatically Mount File Systems

The default file system mount behavior is set by the FileSystem TABle, or `fstab`. YaST sets this up during the initial installation. You can modify it directly in a text editor (as Root) or use Expert Partitioner's partition editing tool. After you understand the structure of the file, it will be much easier to hand-edit `etc/fstab`, but EP's fstab options page offers a friendlier interface if you are reluctant to hand-edit critical files.

TIP

You can view, but not edit, your fstab file in KDiskFree. This tool lets you see your current disk usage, device type, and mount point. You can mount unmounted file systems as well.

Here is a busy `etc/fstab` file, containing several drives and partitions, along with a CD-RW.

```
/dev/hda2  /             reiserfs  acl,user_xattr       1 1
/dev/sda1 /windows/C     ntfs       ro,users,gid=users,umask=0002,nls=utf8 0 0
/dev/hda1 swap           swap       pri=42              0 0
devpts     /dev/pts      devpts     mode=0620,gid=5     0 0
proc       /proc         proc       defaults            0 0
usbfs      /proc/bus/usb usbfs      noauto              0 0
sysfs      /sys          sysfs      noauto              0 0
/dev/cdrecorder       /media/cdrecorder     subfs
fs=cdfss,ro,procuid,nosuid,nodev,exec,iocharset=utf8 0 0
/dev/fd0              /media/floppy         subfs
fs=floppyfss,procuid,nodev,nosuid,sync 0 0
```

Each line in the `fstab` file represents another device, file system, or hard drive. The order of items in each line is identical, with six fields altogether. You would guess (correctly) that all the items included in the `mount` syntax discussed earlier appear here. In order, they would be File system, Mount Point, and Type. The other items are various options that you did not set in the earlier simple example of the `mount` command.

The fourth field indicates the mount options for that file system, separated by commas. For example, the Windows drive, `/dev/sda1`, mounts as read-only (`ro`) and all users can mount the drive. If the `user` flag is not set, only Root can mount the file system. `/dev/_cdrecorder` includes the `exec` option, which allows you to run binaries from the CD drive. The / (Root) partition uses an Access Control List (ACL) to determine whether binaries can be executed. This means permissions are set at a lower, more fine-grained level than just allowing anyone with access to the partition to execute programs.

The other options listed here are generally specific to that file system. To see all the options that can be used here, see the `mount` and `fstab` man pages.

The last two fields (in the example, all are marked 0 0 except for /, which is 1 1) are digits that other programs use. The fifth field tells `dump`, a venerable Unix backup program, whether to back up the file system when it is run: 1=Yes, 0=No.

The last field tells the file system repair tool `fsck` how to interact with each file system: 0=Never, 1=Run at a designated time, and 2=Run periodically, but less often than the 1s.

You should not have to edit `/etc/fstab` more than once, but if you have problems with the OS not seeing a file system (CD won't run, can't copy files from a floppy or Zip disk, for example), this is usually the place to start troubleshooting.

Logical Volume Management (LVM)

The dilemma in partitioning has always been how large to make each partition (also known as a volume). Too often, you just accept a default, or make a wild guess about how much space you'll need for the data you plan to put on your partition. One day, you'll find yourself painfully short of space on one volume, while having a ton of room on another. Wouldn't it be great to have some space that you could allocate on-the-fly, even while a partition was already mounted? Logical Volume Management (LVM) is a relatively new technology that allows you to use disk space from multiple drives in a single logical volume.

The LVM module in YaST is located under the System page. When you open it the first time, it asks you to create a Volume group. It's best to accept the default and create a System group, but allocate as much space as you want for your Volume group.

A Volume group identifies the Physical Volumes (PVs) on your system. These are the building blocks for your Logical Volumes (LVs). To create a new LV, click Add under the logical volume pane. You will need to specify a size and a file system (like ReiserFS). Click Finish to mount the new volumes.

When it's time to resize your LVs, return to this module. Select the volume you want to shrink and click Edit. Make this volume smaller, and then select the volume you want to expand. Edit it.

LVM works on any Linux file system and can also be used to create more swap space. With this in mind, let's discuss how you find files within your file system.

Finding Files

From time to time, you will need to locate a particular file in your file system. With openSUSE Linux, you have a variety of tools available to do this. We'll discuss how to use the find, locate, which, and whereis commands, as well as several graphical utilities to track down files.

Using find

The find utility does just what its name implies. It's used to find files in your computer's file system. The syntax for using find is as follows:

```
find path search_pattern
```

One of the advantages of find is that you can use a variety of search patterns. You can search for a filename, for a specific file type, for files of a particular size, for files that were modified at a certain time, and for files owned by a particular user or group.

These search patterns are created using the following command-line options:

- -name "*<file_name>*"—This option allows you to search for a filename. You can use a specific filename, or you can use a wildcard pattern.
- -size + or - *size*—This option allows you to search for files that are smaller than or larger than the specified size.
- -type *type*—This option allows you to specify whether you are looking for directories , files (f), or symbolic links (l).
- -ctime + or - *days*—This option allows you to search for files that were modified more or less than a specified number of days ago.
- -group *group_name*—This option allows you to search for files that are owned by a specific group.
- -user *user_name*—This option allows you to search for files that are owned by a specific user.

For example, suppose you wanted to find a file named myfiles that you think resides in the /home/tux directory on your system. You could enter **find /home/tux -name "myfile"** at the shell prompt. The find utility will then search the /home/tux path for any file named myfile, as shown in Figure 18.5.

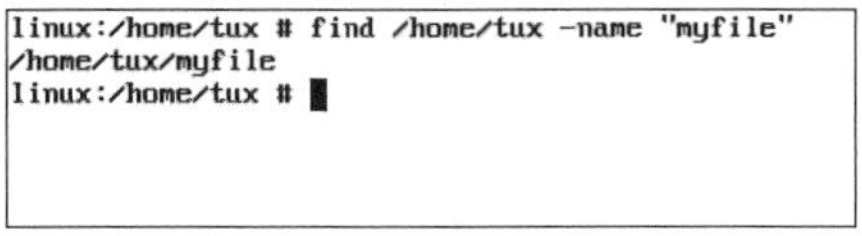

```
linux:/home/tux # find /home/tux -name "myfile"
/home/tux/myfile
linux:/home/tux # █
```

FIGURE 18.5 Using find to search for files.

The `find` utility, by default, searches all subdirectories beneath the path specified. In the preceding example, you could also enter **`find / -name "myfile"`** at the shell prompt and it would find the `/home/tux/myfile` file (although it will take much longer). For more information about how to use find, enter **`man find`** at the shell prompt.

In addition to `find`, you can also use the `locate` utility to search for files. Let's look at this utility next.

Using `locate`

The `find` utility works great for locating files in the file system. However, it has one drawback. It finds files by searching through each and every directory beneath the path specified in the command line. This process can be quite slow. For example, if you were to use `find` to create a search that searched for a specific file from the top of the file system, it may take 10 to 15 minutes (possibly longer) to complete.

As an alternative, you can use the `locate` utility to search for files. The `locate` utility operates using an entirely different search mechanism. Instead of searching through directories, it looks for the specified file within its own database of files that are stored in the system.

The `locate` utility is part of the `findutils-locate` package. Before you can use `locate`, you must use YaST to install this package on your system, as shown in Figure 18.6.

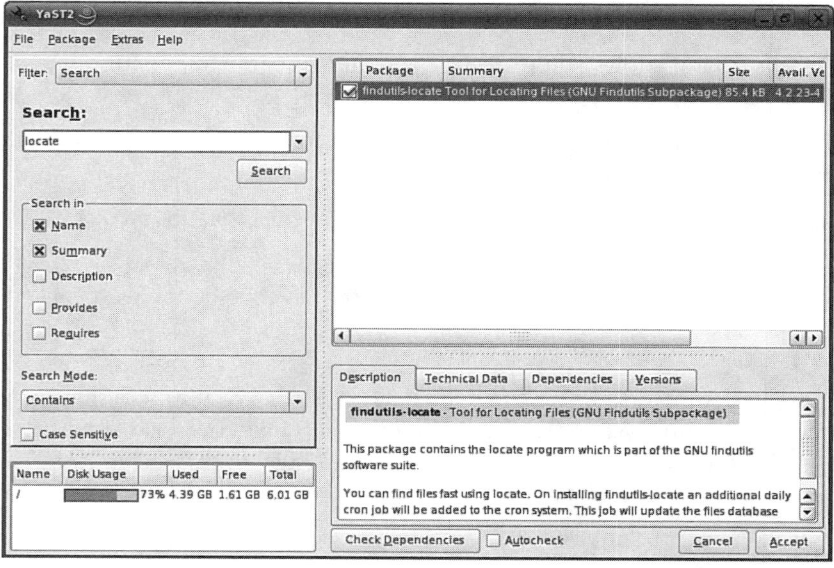

FIGURE 18.6 Installing *locate* packages.

After these packages are installed, a database is created in `/var/lib` called `locatedb`. A listing of files in your file system is stored in this database. This database is automatically updated every day. If necessary, you can also manually update it by running the `updatedb` utility from the shell prompt.

With the database updated, you can use the `locate` utility to search for files within it. The syntax for using `locate` is relatively simple. You simply run `locate` and specify the name of the file you want to search for, as shown next:

```
locate file_name
```

For example, if you wanted to search for the `myfiles` file, you would enter **`locate myfile`**, as shown in Figure 18.7.

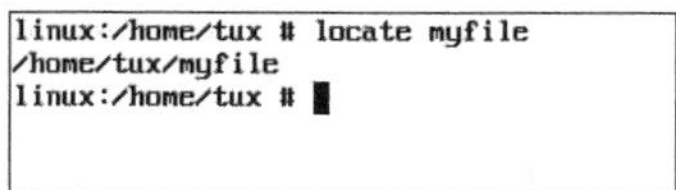
linux:/home/tux # locate myfile
/home/tux/myfile
linux:/home/tux #

FIGURE 18.7 Using *locate* to find files.

As with `find`, you can view the man page for the `locate` utility to learn more.

In addition to `find` and `locate`, you can also use the `which` command to search for files. Let's review this command next.

Using `which`

The `which` utility is a handy command for finding the executable files used by system commands. The `which` utility searches for files in a manner similar to the `find` utility. However, `which` searches for files only in the directories contained in the `PATH` variable.

At this point, you've probably noticed that you can run system commands, such as `which`, `locate`, `find`, `cp`, `rm`, and `cd`, regardless of what your current directory in the file system is. That's because the executable files for these commands reside in directories that are included in the `PATH` variable. You can see a listing of these directories by entering **`echo $PATH`** at the shell prompt, as shown in Figure 18.8.

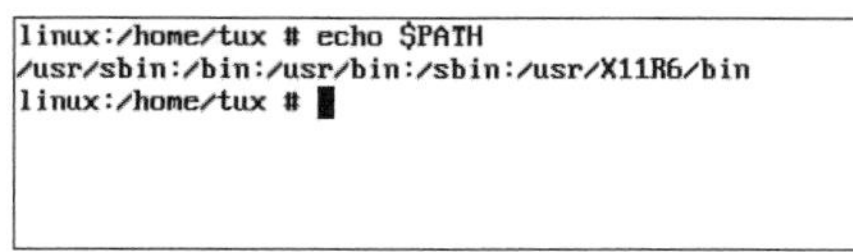
linux:/home/tux # echo $PATH
/usr/sbin:/bin:/usr/bin:/sbin:/usr/X11R6/bin
linux:/home/tux #

FIGURE 18.8 Viewing directories in the *PATH* variable.

The `which` utility is used to generate a search that is limited to the directories in the `PATH` variable. For example, if you wanted to find out where the `cp` executable resides, you would enter the following:

```
which cp
```

The `which` utility then returns the path where `cp` is located, as shown in Figure 18.9.

```
linux:/home/tux # echo $PATH
/usr/sbin:/bin:/usr/bin:/sbin:/usr/X11R6/bin
linux:/home/tux # which cp
/bin/cp
linux:/home/tux # █
```

FIGURE 18.9 Using *which*.

When working with system commands, you can also use the **whereis** utility. Let's explore this command next.

Using whereis

Like which, the whereis utility is used to find the location in the file system where system commands reside. However, it can return much more information about the file than which can. It not only returns the location of the file, but also the location of the man page file and the source code file (if it exists).

The syntax for using whereis is relatively straightforward. Enter

whereis *command*

For example, if you wanted to get information about the rm command, you would enter the following:

whereis rm

The whereis utility then returns the relevant data, as shown in Figure 18.10.

```
linux:/home/tux # whereis rm
rm: /bin/rm /usr/share/man/man1/rm.1.gz /usr/share/man/man1p/rm.1p.gz
linux:/home/tux # █
```

FIGURE 18.10 Using whereis.

If you want to limit the output provided by whereis, you can use the following syntax:

whereis *option command*

The options you can use include the following:

- **-b**—Returns only the location of the command in the file system.
- **-m**—Returns only the name and location of the command's associated man page files.
- **-s**—Returns only the name and location of the command's associated source code file.

In addition to these command-line utilities, openSUSE Linux also includes graphical utilities that can be used to search for files. Let's look at these next.

Using kfind

The first utility we will explore is `kfind`, which is a graphical version of `find` that runs within the KDE shell. To use KFind, go to the Applications Menu, then System, File System, Find Files/Folders. The screen in Figure 18.11 is displayed.

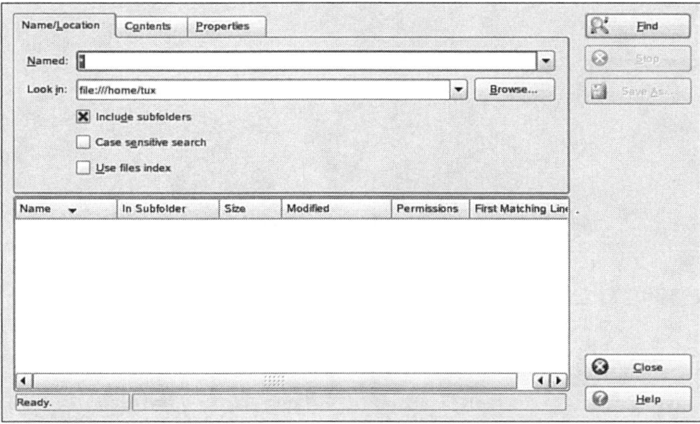

FIGURE 18.11 The *kfind* interface.

Within this interface, you can configure and execute complex search operations. To do this, complete the following:

1. In the Named field, enter the *name* of the file you want to search for. You can use wildcard characters such as * and ? to expand your search results.
2. In the Look In field, enter the *path* in which `kfind` should begin its search.
3. If you want `kfind` to search for the specified file in subdirectories within the specified path, mark Include Subfolders.
4. Select Find. The results of your search are displayed in the field below the search criteria, as shown in Figure 18.12.

In addition to `kfind`, you can also use a new, more advanced graphical search tool on openSUSE Linux: Beagle.

Using Beagle

Beagle is a search tool that can be used to find different types of information from a variety of data sources associated with your user account. It was originally developed by the Ximian team, and so has been integrated into the last few SUSE Linux releases. Beagle can search your personal documents, text files (including source code), email, browser history, instant messages, web pages on the Internet, man pages, help files, and media files.

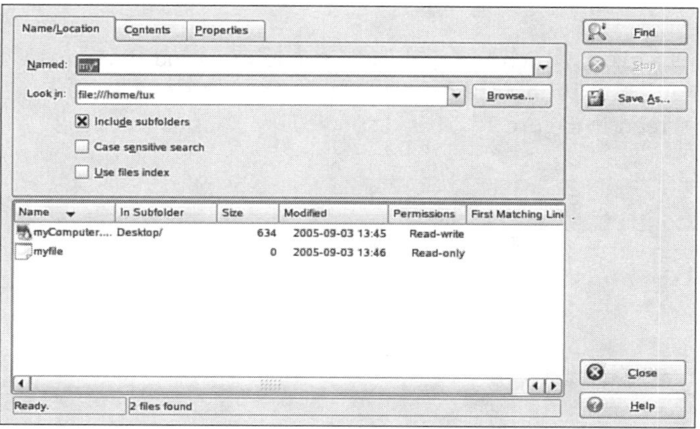

FIGURE 18.12 `kfind` search results.

Configuring Beagle

Beagle is installed by default when you install openSUSE. The Beagle-index package is installed with both GNOME and KDE base patterns, and KDE throws in its Beagle front end, called Kerry.

After you have Beagle installed, the next thing you need to do is start the daemon. It's important that you understand that the Beagle daemon operates in a different manner from other system daemons with which you may be familiar. Most other daemons run as either your root user or another specialized user account.

The Beagle daemon, on the other hand, is run from within your individual user account. This is because Beagle searches for data that exists within your own user space. To start the Beagle daemon, open a terminal session and enter **`beagled`** at the shell prompt. The daemon will run in the background and begin automatically indexing content available to your user account. You can also turn the Beagle daemon on in the YaST Runlevel Editor; see Chapter 22, "Managing the Boot Process and Other Services," for more information.

If you want to customize how the daemon behaves, you can run the Beagle configuration utility by entering **`beagle-settings`** from the shell prompt. When you do so, the screen shown in Figure 18.13 is displayed.

TIP

Both desktop search tools, Beagle-Search (GNOME) and Kerry (KDE), offer access to beagle-settings for the shell-shy.

Under the Search tab, you can configure whether `beagled` automatically starts searches and indexing as well as the hotkey sequence required to open the search window. You can configure what `beagled` will index by selecting the Indexing tab, shown in Figure 18.14.

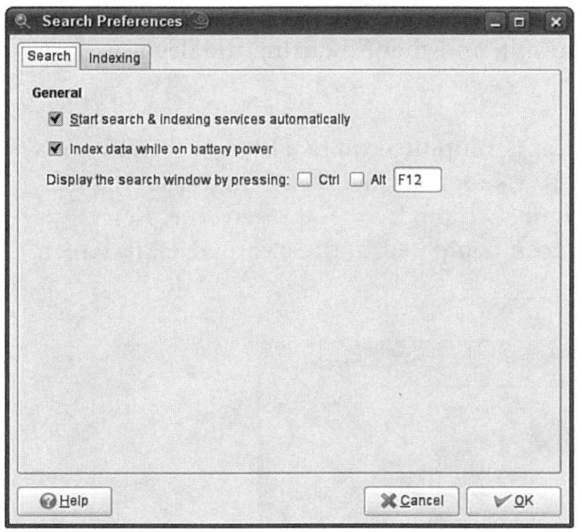

FIGURE 18.13 Configuring Beagle indexing and search behavior.

FIGURE 18.14 Configuring content to be indexed.

Under this tab, you can configure specific directories that should be indexed and other directories that should not be indexed. By default, all subdirectories of the directories specified are included. As the daemon is running, you can see the content it has indexed by entering **`beagle-index-info`** at the shell prompt.

Beagle will conduct its searching and indexing operations in the background and run with a low priority so that it doesn't take up excessive amounts of CPU time or hard disk bandwidth. In this mode, the indexing operation could take many hours to complete. However, you can force `beagled` to run at a higher priority and complete the index process much faster. This is done by stopping the daemon, entering **`export BEAGLE__EXERCISE_THE_DOG=1`** at the shell prompt, and then restarting the daemon.

Searching with Beagle

Using Beagle to search for desktop information is simplified quite a bit by the GUI tools supplied by each desktop environment. GNOME's tool is called just beagle-search, and KDE's is called Kerry. They offer a similar interface, though as is so often true, Kerry (Figure 18.15) offers a more detailed, busy screen compared to the clean GNOME screen (Figure 18.16).

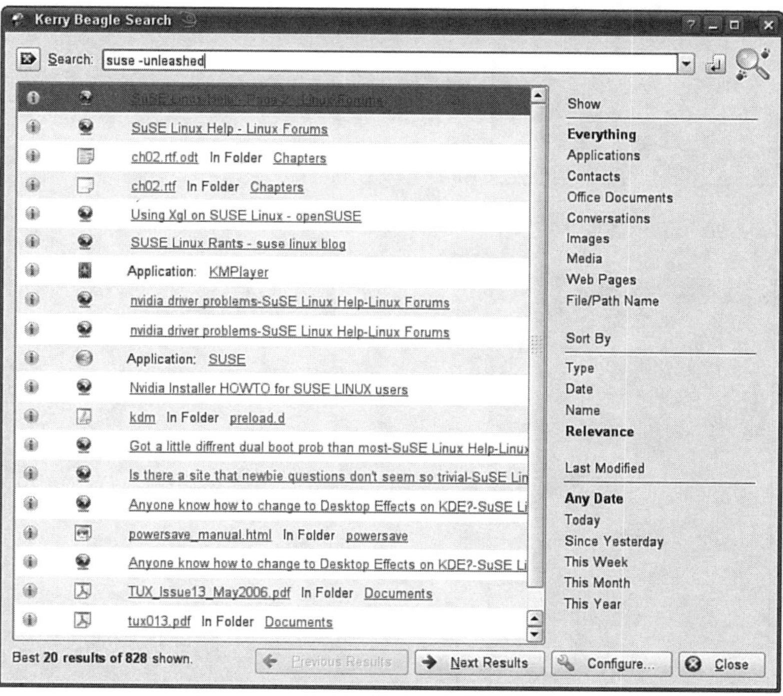

FIGURE 18.15 Kerry offers an easy way to sort search results.

Beagle is about finding information, not necessarily files. You can search just for files, but Beagle's power is searching through your Web cache, email, and documents to find what you're really looking for. If you know you read about a study where wine from purple grapes cured cancer, use Beagle to find out if you saved the reference somewhere on your system.

Both Beagle search tools are located in the System, File System area of the Applications menu. Click Search (with the magnifying glass icon) to get the GNOME Beagle-Search. Kerry also helpfully provides a taskbar icon, with a red bandanna wrapped around the Beagle's neck.

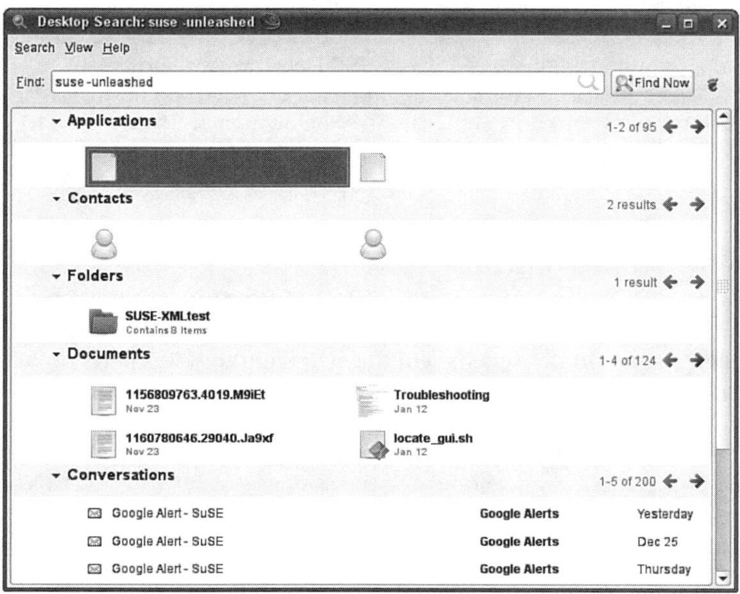

FIGURE 18.16 GNOME's beagle-search sorts results by document type.

While Beagle is a powerful search, it helps to have some experience and savvy with web searches. This is especially true with common terms. The GNOME tool offers a list of helpful Quick Tips when you load the application. If you use two terms, like "purple grapes" without the quotes, Beagle will search for both terms (a Boolean AND). Entering "purple grapes" with quotes will find items with that phrase in it, while entering "purple OR grapes" (no quotes, capital OR) will show everything with either the word purple or the word grapes in the text.

With this in mind, let's now discuss some more advanced tasks you can perform with your Linux file system.

File System Manipulation

For some people, reading books and going to lectures or discussions are the best way to learn new things. For others, playing around on a system is the way to go. If you want to see for yourself how things work in different file systems, try creating a file system using the loopback file system—a special file system that lets you accomplish this interesting and useful feat. You can use the file system you create to experiment with and practice almost all the shell commands found in this chapter with no fear of damaging your system.

TIP

To do this on a larger scale, you can install a basic openSUSE Linux system into the Xen virtual machine. Pick a file system, don't install the graphical end, and you have another playground apart from your working system. See the Xen section of Chapter 11, "Going Cross-Platform," for details.

Creating a File System for Testing

People who run Linux tend to be a tinkerer's lot. They like to try new things and are not afraid of getting under the hood and plumbing the depths of their computers to see what exactly is going on. Although many Linux users have multiple machines (and parts of machines) cluttering up the house, most people have just one computer with a single hard drive to play with. If you then have data on that computer that is really important, you don't want to blow away your operating system on a regular basis after an experiment goes awry. This is perhaps the reason the loopback file system was born. With this handy tool, you can create an image file containing the file system of your choice, and mount it—leaving your real file system alone and safe.

You could do this exercise on a floppy or other removable drive, but if you want ample room to play in, working off a hard drive is a better way.

Step 1—Make a Blank Image File

Use the `dd` command to create a file with a block size of 1,024 bytes (a megabyte) and create a file that is 10MB in size. You should have enough free space on your drive to accommodate a file that size, of course. You need 10,000 blocks of 1KB (1,024 bits) in this 10MB file, so here's what you type:

```
Dd if=/dev/zero of=/tmp/test-img bs=1024 count=10000
```

The shell responds with

```
10000+0 records in
10000+0 records out
```

Step 2—Make a File System

Now we need to make the system think the file is a block device instead of an ASCII file, so we use `losetup`, a utility that associates loop devices with regular files or block devices. You will use the loopback device `/dev/loop0. losetup /dev/loop0 /tmp/test-img`.

Then format the file with an `ext3` file system:

```
mkfs -t ext3 -q /tmp/test-img
```

If prompted that test.img is not a block device, enter **y** to proceed anyway.

Step 3—Mount the Test File System

Your test file system is ready to go, except that you can't do much with it until it is mounted on your system. Let's start with a mount point, then.

```
mkdir /mnt/image
```

Now we can mount it:

```
mount -o loop /tmp/test.img /mnt/image
```

After mounting the file system, look at it with the `df` command:

```
df -h /mnt/image
```

And get this response:

```
Filesystem      Size    Used    Avail    Use%    Mounted on
/tmp/test-img   10M     1.1M    9M       2%      /mnt/image
```

To unmount the image:

```
umount /mnt/image
```

You can even back up the image, in case something happens while you're playing:

```
cp /tmp/test-img test-img.bak
```

When you've confirmed that you have a mounted image file, you can create directories, copy files to it, delete files, attempt to recover them, and, generally speaking, do anything you want with this file system. It's a playpen where you can learn valuable lessons with no risk. If you somehow irreparably damage the file system on the image, unmount it, delete it, and start over, perhaps with that backup you just made. So have fun!

Let's now discuss how to mount a read-only partition on a running system.

Mounting a Read-Only Partition on a Running System

From time to time, you may need to mount a partition in your file system in such a manner that you can view the data that it contains but not be able to make changes to it. This can be accomplished by mounting the partition in *read-only* mode. You can do this in two ways. The first is with the mount command. At the shell prompt, enter

```
mount -r device mount_point
```

For example, if you had a partition at `/dev/sda3` and you wanted to mount it at the `/extra` directory, you would enter the following:

```
mount -r /dev/sda3 /extra
```

This is shown in Figure 18.17.

```
linux:/ # mount -r /dev/sda3 /extra
linux:/ # mount
/dev/sda2 on / type reiserfs (rw,acl,user_xattr)
proc on /proc type proc (rw)
sysfs on /sys type sysfs (rw)
tmpfs on /dev/shm type tmpfs (rw)
devpts on /dev/pts type devpts (rw,mode=0620,gid=5)
usbfs on /proc/bus/usb type usbfs (rw)
/dev/fd0 on /media/floppy type subfs (rw,nosuid,nodev,sync,fs=floppyfss,procuid)
/dev/sda3 on /extra type reiserfs (ro)
linux:/ #
```

FIGURE 18.17 Mounting a partition in read-only mode.

In Figure 18.17, you can see that the /dev/sda3 partition is mounted in the /extra directory. Notice that when the mount command is subsequently issued without arguments, the mounting for /dev/sda3 is shown with a (ro) designation, indicating that the partition is mounted read-only.

In addition to using mount, you can automatically mount the partition read-only using your fstab file. Simply add ro to the mount options field, as shown in Figure 18.18.

With this in mind, let's now look at mounting an image file as a floppy disk device.

```
/dev/sda2          /                 reiserfs   acl,user_xattr          1 1
/dev/sda1          swap              swap       defaults                0 0
proc               /proc             proc       defaults                0 0
sysfs              /sys              sysfs      noauto                  0 0
usbfs              /proc/bus/usb     usbfs      noauto                  0 0
devpts             /dev/pts          devpts     mode=0620,gid=5         0 0
/dev/cdrom         /media/cdrom      subfs      noauto,fs=cdfss,ro,procuid,
nosuid,nodev,exec,iocharset=utf8 0 0
/dev/fd0           /media/floppy     subfs      noauto,fs=floppyfss,procuid
,nodev,nosuid,sync 0 0
/dev/sda3          /extra            reiserfs   noauto,acl,user_xattr,ro 0
0
~
~
~
~
~
~
~
~
~
~
~
-- INSERT --                                             9,82          All
```

FIGURE 18.18 Mounting a partition in read-only mode using fstab.

Examining a Floppy Image File

Earlier in this chapter, you learned how to mount floppy disks on your openSUSE Linux system. Using the loopback filesystem, you can also mount an image file as a floppy disk. This is done by completing the following:

1. Open a terminal session.
2. Switch to your root user.
3. Create the image file by entering **dd if=/dev/zero of=floppy.img bs=512 count=2880** at the shell prompt.

4. At the shell prompt, enter **losetup /dev/loop0 floppy.img**.
5. Format the file using the MSDOS file system by entering **mkdosfs /dev/loop0** at the shell prompt.
6. Mount the image file as a floppy by entering **mount -t msdos /dev/loop0 /media/_floppy**.

This process is shown in Figure 18.19.

```
linux:~ # dd if=/dev/zero of=floppy.img bs=512 count=2880
2880+0 records in
2880+0 records out
1474560 bytes (1.5 MB) copied, 0.051337 seconds, 28.7 MB/s
linux:~ # losetup /dev/loop0 floppy.img
linux:~ # mkdosfs /dev/loop0
mkdosfs 2.11 (12 Mar 2005)
linux:~ # mount -t msdos /dev/loop0 /media/floppy
linux:~ #
```

FIGURE 18.19 Mounting an image file as a floppy.

Before ending this chapter, we need to discuss one more topic: working with character and block devices. Let's look at this next.

Managing Files for Character Devices, Block Devices, and Special Devices

As you've probably noticed as we've gone through this chapter, every device in your openSUSE Linux system is represented as a file in the `/dev` directory. Your hard disk drive is represented as a file, such as `hda` (IDE) or `sda` (SCSI). Your floppy disk drive is represented as a file, such as `fd0`. Even your CD-ROM drive is represented by the `cdrom` file, which is actually a symbolic link to another file, such as `hdb` or `hdc`. These files allow your hardware devices to function as one of the following device types:

- Character devices—Character devices transfer data in a serial fashion, one piece of information at a time. Modems, keyboards, mice, and terminals are examples of character devices.
- Block devices—Block devices are those that, unlike a character device, provide a degree of random access to the data they contain. Hard disk drives, floppy disk drives, and CD/DVD drives are examples of block devices.

18

Every device in your system needs a driver for the Linux kernel to be able to interface with it. For example, your IDE hard disk drive needs a driver; all SCSI devices in your system need a device driver as well. An important point to remember is that multiple devices of the same type can be serviced by the same kernel driver. For example, if you had three SCSI hard drives in your system, a single instance of the SCSI kernel driver can manage the three physically separate devices.

The Linux kernel keeps track of these different devices using *major* and *minor* device numbers. These numbers are assigned to each device's associated file in /dev. The major number indicates the type of device associated with the file. For example, consider the files displayed in Figure 18.20.

```
brw-rw----   1 root disk  3,   0 Aug 28 14:37 /dev/hda
brw-rw----   1 root disk  3,   1 Aug 28 14:37 /dev/hda1
brw-rw----   1 root disk  3,  10 Aug 28 14:37 /dev/hda10
brw-rw----   1 root disk  3,  11 Aug 28 14:37 /dev/hda11
brw-rw----   1 root disk  3,  12 Aug 28 14:37 /dev/hda12
brw-rw----   1 root disk  3,  13 Aug 28 14:37 /dev/hda13
brw-rw----   1 root disk  3,  14 Aug 28 14:37 /dev/hda14
brw-rw----   1 root disk  3,  15 Aug 28 14:37 /dev/hda15
brw-rw----   1 root disk  3,  16 Aug 28 14:37 /dev/hda16
brw-rw----   1 root disk  3,  17 Aug 28 14:37 /dev/hda17
brw-rw----   1 root disk  3,  18 Aug 28 14:37 /dev/hda18
brw-rw----   1 root disk  3,  19 Aug 28 14:37 /dev/hda19
brw-rw----   1 root disk  3,   2 Aug 28 14:37 /dev/hda2
brw-rw----   1 root disk  3,  20 Aug 28 14:37 /dev/hda20
brw-rw----   1 root disk  3,  21 Aug 28 14:37 /dev/hda21
brw-rw----   1 root disk  3,  22 Aug 28 14:37 /dev/hda22
brw-rw----   1 root disk  3,  23 Aug 28 14:37 /dev/hda23
brw-rw----   1 root disk  3,  24 Aug 28 14:37 /dev/hda24
brw-rw----   1 root disk  3,  25 Aug 28 14:37 /dev/hda25
brw-rw----   1 root disk  3,  26 Aug 28 14:37 /dev/hda26
brw-rw----   1 root disk  3,  27 Aug 28 14:37 /dev/hda27
brw-rw----   1 root disk  3,  28 Aug 28 14:37 /dev/hda28
brw-rw----   1 root disk  3,  29 Aug 28 14:37 /dev/hda29
--More--
```

FIGURE 18.20 Major and minor numbers.

In Figure 18.20, the `ls -l` command has been used to display the various IDE device files in /dev, denoted as hda. Notice in the middle of each line in the output of ls that two numbers are displayed. The first number is the major number. All IDE devices have a major number of 3. (SCSI devices have a major number of 8.) The major number identifies which device driver the kernel should use to interface with the particular device.

You will also see a second number listed in the middle of each line of the output of ls. This is the minor number. For example, device file hda has a major number of 3 and a minor number of 0. The minor number identifies the specific node of the device. In Figure 18.20, you can see that device hda1 (the first partition on the master IDE hard drive on the primary IDE channel) has a major number of 3 and a minor number of 1.

In addition, the output of ls, as shown in Figure 18.20, indicates the type of device represented by each file. This is indicated by the first character of each line. Notice that each hda line in Figure 18.21 begins with a `b`. This indicates that the IDE hard disk drives are block devices. By way of comparison, refer to Figure 18.21.

The tty devices shown in Figure 18.21 are serial devices. Accordingly, they have a `c` as the first character in each line of the output of ls, indicating that these files represent character devices.

You can create your own character or block device files. This is done with the `mknod` utility. The syntax of mknod is as follows:

```
mknod file_name device_type major_number minor_number
```

```
linux:/ # ls -l /dev/tty1*
crw-rw----  1 root tty 4,  1 Sep  5 17:36 /dev/tty1
crw--w----  1 root tty 4, 10 Sep  6 09:47 /dev/tty10
crw--w----  1 root tty 4, 11 Aug 28 14:37 /dev/tty11
crw--w----  1 root tty 4, 12 Aug 28 14:37 /dev/tty12
crw--w----  1 root tty 4, 13 Aug 28 14:37 /dev/tty13
crw--w----  1 root tty 4, 14 Aug 28 14:37 /dev/tty14
crw--w----  1 root tty 4, 15 Aug 28 14:37 /dev/tty15
crw--w----  1 root tty 4, 16 Aug 28 14:37 /dev/tty16
crw--w----  1 root tty 4, 17 Aug 28 14:37 /dev/tty17
crw--w----  1 root tty 4, 18 Aug 28 14:37 /dev/tty18
crw--w----  1 root tty 4, 19 Aug 28 14:37 /dev/tty19
linux:/ #
```

FIGURE 18.21 Viewing character devices.

For example, you could create a new character device named echo with a major number of 33 and a minor number of 0 by entering the following at the shell prompt:

```
mknod /dev/echo c 33 0
```

Major number 33 (character) is reserved for serial cards. You can view a complete list of major numbers and the type of devices they are associated with by viewing the `/usr/_src/linux-kernel_version/Documentation/devices.txt` file on your openSUSE Linux system.

References

- http://www.tldp.org/HOWTO/Filesystems-HOWTO.html—Always the place to begin. The file systems HOWTO.
- http://en.wikipedia.org/wiki/Filesystem—Wikipedia on how file systems work in various operating systems.
- http://en.wikipedia.org/wiki/Comparison_of_file_systems—Helpful chart on differences between file systems, with links to the Wikipedia articles on each file system.
- http://www.namesys.com—The group in charge of ReiserFS.
- http://batleth.sapienti-sat.org/projects/FAQs/ext3-faq.html—The Linux ext3 FAQ list. Differences between ext2 and ext3, as well as troubleshooting problems.
- http://oss.sgi.com/projects/xfs—The XFS for Linux site.
- http://www-106.ibm.com/developerworks/linux/library/l-fs9.html—An IBM DeveloperWorks article on XFS.
- http://www-106.ibm.com/developerworks/edu/os-dw-linuxjfs-i.html—A JFS tutorial; free registration with DeveloperWorks required.

- http://sources.redhat.com/lvm2—The Logical Volume Manager home page.
- http://www.tldp.org/HOWTO/LVM-HOWTO—The LVM HOWTO page.
- http://usalug.org/phpBB2/viewtopic.php?p=33142—Tuning up IDE hard drives with hdparm. A useful tutorial.
- http://www.gnu.org/software/parted—The GNU Parted home page.
- http://beagle-project.org—Home of the Beagle Desktop Search tool.
- http://www.freeos.com/articles/3921—A basic introduction to the Logical Volume Manager. Includes command-line instructions for building logical volumes.

CHAPTER 19

Managing Users, Managing Security

IN THIS CHAPTER

The heart of Linux security is determining who can use what file and what kind of use is permitted. This is not all there is to making Linux a more secure system, but ultimately, what is the purpose of computer security? Keeping the bad guys out of your files.

In this chapter, you will learn about setting up user accounts and creating and managing groups that work together. There are decisions to make about user passwords: Does the user select them, or does the administrator? How strong must passwords be? How often to change them? In this chapter, you'll get advice about security. In short, you'll learn about the human side of system administration.

This stuff is particularly important for system administrators in a multiuser office setting, but even if you are working by yourself, you will need to become familiar with permissions and passwords. This is the area where trouble often starts, and it's the first thing to check when you can't run something.

User Accounts and Permissions

All Linux systems require one administrator, the Root, and at least one generic user, who can be the same person. The Root is, as noted often here, all powerful. Generic users can be restricted to the point of being able to read only a single file, or have full run of the system as the SuperUser (su). This section will help you better understand how the permissions system works, beyond what you learned in Chapter 5, "Getting Started with openSUSE."

Setting Up User Accounts in YaST

The first user account is set up during the openSUSE installation. Adding users is a simple task in YaST.

In YaST, go to Security and Users, then User Management. YaST will review the current user accounts and display them in the first screen (see Figure 19.1).

Besides the standard operations of Adding and Deleting users, you can perform several user-related tasks from this screen:

- Change passwords and access rights for existing users
- Allow some users to log in without a password
- View and edit system users (more about this in the next section)
- Set default permissions and groups for new users
- Set password encryption standards
- Configure user-related information for Lightweight Directory Access Protocol (LDAP), Samba, Network Information Service (NIS), and Kerberos services

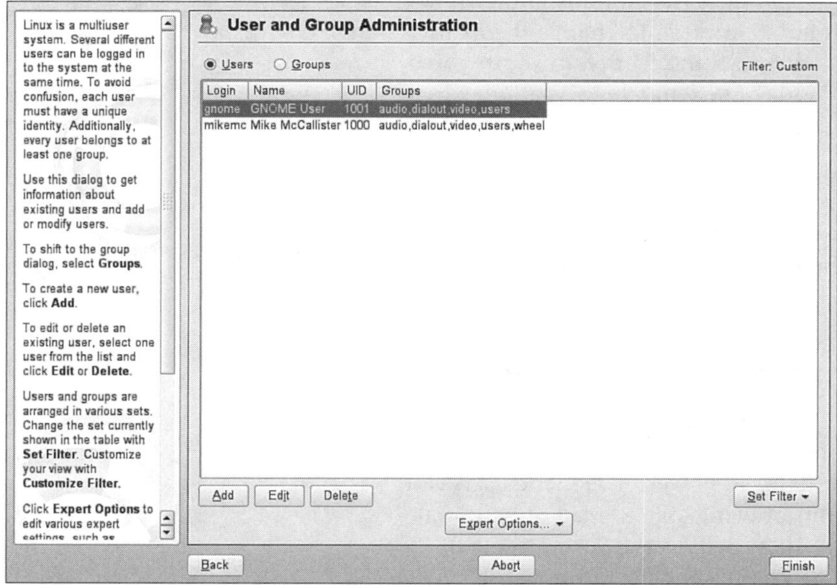

FIGURE 19.1 The YaST User and Group Administration tool.

You will explore some of these options later, but for now you'll create a new user. In this example, you're going to create a user called drone77. Click Add. Figure 19.2 will appear.

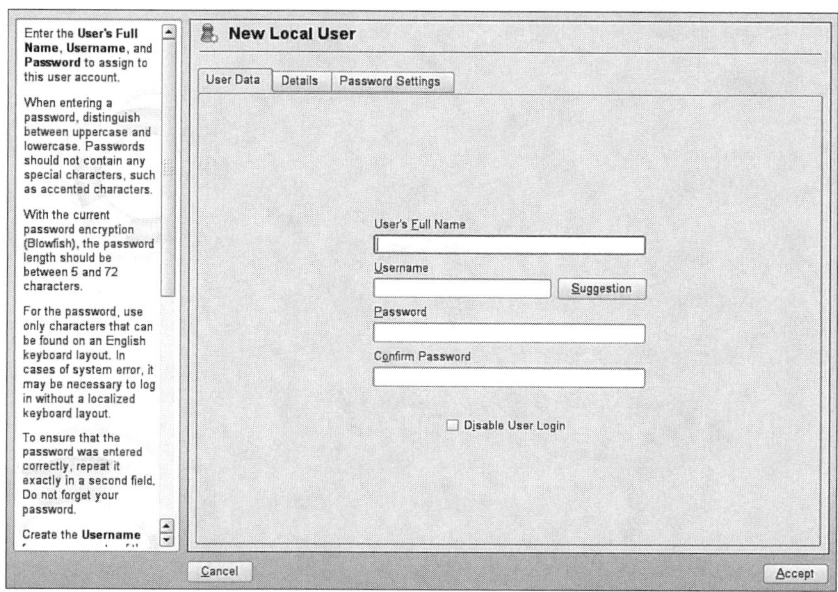

FIGURE 19.2 Set username and password in the first Add a New Local User screen.

YaST asks for the user's full name. This is not required, but YaST will use this information to provide a suggestion for the system username. Because we already have a username picked out, enter **drone77** on the User Login line. Type an initial password for this user. The Help pane on the left offers some pointers. The password must be between 5 and 72 characters; it is case sensitive (so mix in some capital letters) and can include spaces and just about any character on the keyboard.

To give drone77 a chance to select his own password, you need to set the expiration date. Click the Password Settings tab and Figure 19.3 opens.

The default settings are for a system in which passwords are set once and never changed. This is OK for a single-user system with a modem connection to the Internet, but it's a bad idea if you have an always-on connection, such as a DSL or cable-modem connection.

Frequent changes of your users' passwords is another way of staying one step ahead of the attackers. A good rule is to reset passwords every 3–6 months. drone77 is set to change passwords every 90 days.

TIP

Setting the Minimum Number of Days for the Same Password item for greater than 0 prevents users from changing passwords when forced and then immediately changing them back.

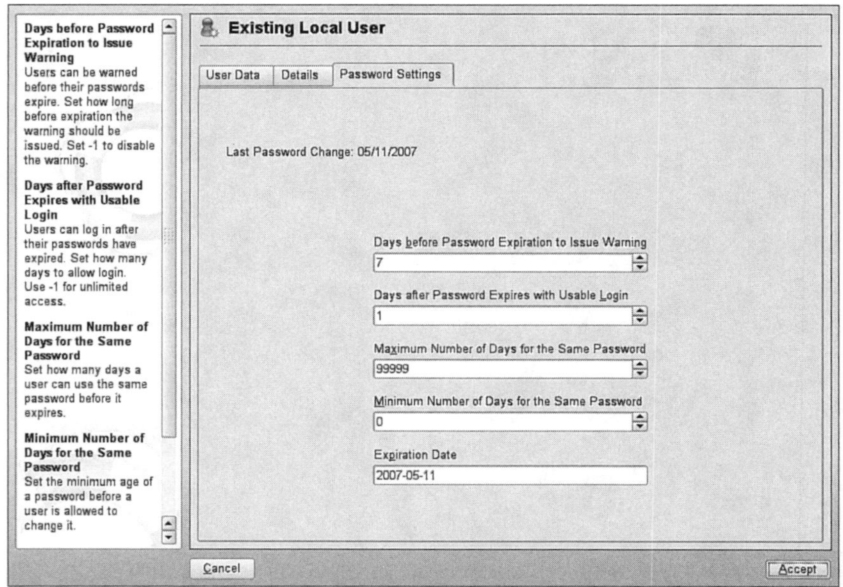

FIGURE 19.3 Let the user set a password on first login with these settings.

To let drone77 choose a password on login, you must set the Expiration Date for today (in the YYYY-MM-DD format) and set the Days After Password Expires with Usable Login to 1 or 0. The Days Before Password Expiration to Issue Warning can stay at the default, but can be adjusted to your preference. The system will then prompt drone77 to change passwords. When that happens, you should return here to delete the Expiration Date.

Click the Details tab to review the other defaults associated with this user. These default settings are generally OK, but there may be items to adjust. In this dialog box, you can set the following:

- User ID (UID)—Every user must have an ID number. Generic users must have UIDs greater than 499; YaST starts at UID 1000 to be safe. You can change this if you want, but do this only when you create the account. Ownership rights are associated with UID numbers, so changing the number will orphan any files outside of the user's home directory.
- Home Directory—By default, this is `/home/<username>`, but you can change this here. The best reason to change the home directory is if this user is really just a "persona" of another user (like you, for example), who wants to have a single `/home` directory to store data in.
- Home Directory Permission Mode—By default, permissions for files in the `/home directory` are set at 755 (rwxr-xr-x). If you would like other system users to have Write permission, change this to 775.
- Additional User Information—This line is for `finger` information. For privacy's sake, leave this blank (see "Changing User Information" in Chapter 5).

- Login Shell—This is the default shell for this user. By default, it's `bash`. Use the drop-down menu, which has the path to every installed shell on the system, to change shells.
- Default Group and Additional Group Membership—By default, YaST assigns users to the Users group and also to the Dialout and Video groups. You'll learn more about assigning groups in the next section.

When you're through adjusting these settings, click Accept to add this user to your system. drone77 should now appear on the list of Local Users. Click Finish to return to YaST.

System Users

Some applications need to own their files and processes to function securely. This is accomplished by creating *system users*. These are usually the daemons that always run in the background (`man`, `lp/print`, `mail`, `news`, and `bin`), but also include a few other applications, such as `MySQL` and the `Games` user. System users do not log in or have home directories, but they have passwords. They also have control over files that other generic users do not have. System users belong to their own group; that is, bin belongs to the Bin group.

View the list of system users in the User Administration screen by clicking Set Filter and selecting System Users. You should never have to configure these yourself, even as Root.

RWX: Understanding Permissions

Most of the practicalities of setting permissions were covered in Chapter 5. The focus there is on the *hows* of permissions. It's just a question of assigning Read, Write, and eXecute permissions to the Owner, Group, and World groups. You can do this either from the shell, using the `chmod` command, or in a GUI file manager. From the shell you can use octals or letter switches.

In this section, the focus is on *why* you want to set permissions in a particular way. Consider that permissions are the heart of security, as previously mentioned, and start with trying to think like a black hat—a would-be attacker. How can you use these three switches—RWX—to your advantage?

- Read—The safest permission to grant is Read. Giving Read access to a file allows viewing the contents of a file. Read access to a directory allows access to the list of files in that directory. In most cases, someone viewing a file (with bad intent or not) is harmless. But what if it's a critical document that needs to be kept from prying eyes? You probably want to encrypt the file as well, but removing the Read option is another step. What if an attacker wants to see if a file known to have a security hole is on your system? An attacker (or a software bot) can do that with World Read access to that directory.
- Write—Giving Write access to a file allows someone to change the content of a file. Write access to a directory means permitting renaming or deletion of existing files and creation of new files in that directory. It's a little easier to see the danger. Give World Write access to your web-server directory, and your site is a prime candidate

for defacement. Give an attacker Write access to your `.login` file (even without Read access), and someday you won't be able to login because that filename will have been changed. These types of things probably don't happen often, but they are the kinds of mistakes that happen frequently enough to be troublesome.

- Execute—Theoretically, any file in Linux can be made executable by setting this permission. In practice, executable files are standard programs or files that can be used as scripts. In a directory, execute rights are also called *search permissions*. It means you can use the directory's name when accessing its files.

Who Needs What? Managing Groups

Groups are the easy way to handle the need-to-know issues that always crop up when dealing with users on a network. Create a group when there is a set of people who need to have similar permission to work on particular files or directories.

As with users, there are two types of groups in openSUSE: Local and System. Generally speaking, Local groups are composed of real-life users, and System groups are for managing applications and their files.

Every user on a openSUSE system is assigned to the Users group, so common permissions can be set up for everyone. By default, all users are also assigned to the Dialout and Video groups, although this can be changed in YaST.

Adding Groups

Adding a new Local group to your system is very much like adding a user. From the YaST Security and Users section, choose Group Management. You can also come to this page directly from the User Management page by clicking the option button. On this page, you will see the existing Local groups (by default, just the Users group). Click Set Filter and then click System Groups to look at those groups instead.

To define a group of writers on this system, click Add to display the screen shown in Figure 19.4.

NOTE

When you are working with Group Administration in YaST, you are actually editing the `/etc/group` file that stores information about groups on the system. YaST also backs up the old file (as `/etc/group.YaST2save`) when it makes changes, so you can revert to the old file if you need to.

In addition to YaST, the SuperUser can use several commands to manage groups; `groupadd` (to add a group), `groupdel` (to delete a group), `gpasswd` (to set a group password), and `grpck` (to check `/etc/group` for typos) are among the most commonly used.

You can also edit this file directly (as the SuperUser). Back up the file first, as YaST does, and run `grpck` afterward.

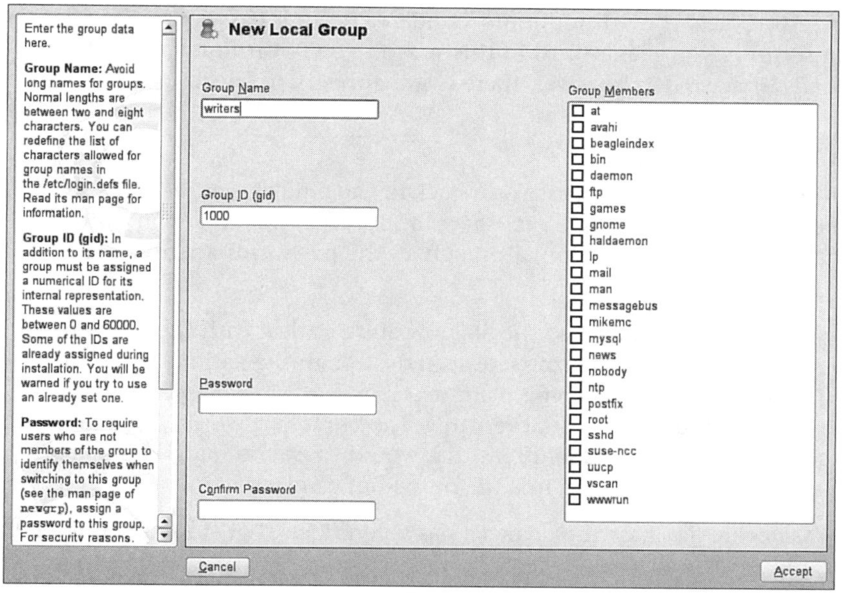

FIGURE 19.4 Adding a Writers group.

This process is straightforward. The only thing you have to do is to name the group and identify its members from the list of local and system users on the right. If you want to set a group password for extra security, define that here as well. YaST sets the default Group ID (GID) number starting at 1000. You can change this, but there's no real need to.

When you have checked the box of the members of the group, click Accept to create the group and return to the main page. You should see the Writers group on the list of Local Groups, along with its membership. You can add and remove members through this screen, and also through the User screen.

NOTE

Because the User and Group Administration tools share the same page, the Expert Options button appears in both. Except for the Write Changes Now option, nothing here really applies to groups. Use Write Changes Now if you are switching to the User Administration page before leaving YaST.

Click Finish to confirm your changes and close this window. Now you can choose to restrict some files and directories to the Writers group by assigning those files and directories to the Writers group and setting appropriate permissions.

Passwords: The First Line of Security

Studies have shown that one of the leading causes, if not the primary cause, of system break-ins is an easily broken password. openSUSE aims to help the system administrator train all users (even if there's only one) in password integrity and safety.

The YaST Security Settings lets you set minimum standards for user passwords and offer additional ways of securing your passwords. In this section you'll learn how to configure these to your best advantage. First, however, there is some theory to cover.

The `passwd` and `shadow` Files

A user isn't a user until he or she has a password. Back in the old days, all user passwords in Unix and Linux were stored in a single `/etc/passwd` file, accessible to anyone with Read access. That's still true, after a fashion, although all the passwords are now marked with an X.

In the mid-1990s, John F. Haugh II created the Shadow Suite to deal with the problem of readable passwords, and support for the software spread through the various Linux distributions by 1998. The idea is simple: Keeping plain-text passwords in a single file with World Read access makes it too easy for attackers to get access to passwords. Although making `/etc/passwd` unreadable is one solution, that would cause too many problems. The solution is to put real user passwords in a file only Root can read.

Both `passwd` and `shadow` are database files. `passwd` has seven fields that store the following for each record or user:

- Username
- Password (or holding place)
- UID
- GID
- Finger information
- Path to the home directory
- Default shell

That is, every field included in the YaST User Add screen.

`shadow` has nine fields for each record/user and shares just one with `passwd`: the username. The other fields are as follows:

- Encrypted password
- When the password was last changed, expressed as the number of days after January 1, 1970; also known as the *epoch*.
- The number of days before the password can be changed.
- The number of days before the password must be changed.
- The number of days the user gets before being warned the password is about to expire.
- The number of days after a password expires that the account is disabled.

- The number of days (if any) since the epoch that the account has been disabled.
- The last field is reserved for future use; that use has yet to be determined.

These fields are set in the Password Settings dialog box for each user.

Selecting Passwords

Passwords have become a way of life with just about every computer user. There are system login passwords, web portal passwords, online banking passwords, ATM passwords—the list goes on, possibly forever. Yet it is undeniable that you need all these passwords to protect yourself, your money, your files, and all the other things that we password-protect.

Your Linux files are only as secure as your password, so it's important to select passwords carefully. Following are some very basic tips on making your passwords secure:

- Choose something easy for you to remember, but hard to guess.
- Don't use your name, address, birthday, or other well-known fact about you as a password. The story goes that heiress Paris Hilton had her cell phone's address book hacked when she used her favorite pet's name as a password hint. System administrators have been known to check user passwords with a personnel file in their hands, using birth dates, spouse's names, and the like. An unusual combination of some of these characters can be successful, though.
- The longer the password, the better. By default, your system password must be at least five characters. Using the Blowfish password-encryption standard (see the next section for more information on this), your password can be up to 72 characters. It's hard to remember that many, however.
- Always remember: Passwords are case sensitive. Use a combination of upper- and lowercase letters in nontypical locations. It's OK to start your password with a capital letter, but throw some in the miDdLe too.
- Always use a combination of letters, numbers, and special characters. `T3st1n@` is much better than `te$ting`.

The trick is not getting too comfortable with one password, or endless variations on a single theme. Even if you've got what you think is a bulletproof password, come up with a couple more. You just never know when a password-cracking script will get lucky.

19

User Authentication Settings with Pluggable Authentication Modules (PAM)

To quote the Linux-PAM System Administrator's Guide:

> It is the purpose of the Linux-PAM project to separate the development of privilege granting software from the development of secure and appropriate authentication schemes. This is accomplished by providing a library of functions that an application may use to request that a user be authenticated.

In short, Pluggable Authentication Modules (PAM) extend the traditional Unix/Linux principle of doing one thing well. If an application needs to confirm (authenticate) a user, they can access the PAM libraries, instead of creating their own mechanism to do so.

NOTE

The Linux-PAM documentation is included in the openSUSE Help Center.

The YaST Local Security Settings serve as the GUI front end for PAM. Go to Security and Users in YaST and then to Local Security. On the first page, you can choose from three default configurations: Home Workstation (a standalone personal or family computer not connected to the Internet), Networked Workstation (for networked computers, either with other machines on a local area network or with an Internet connection), or Network Server (the highest level of security). Chances are you will want the Networked Workstation option as a base. You can certainly leave things at that, but perhaps you want to tweak the settings.

Table 19.1 shows the differences in settings between the three default configurations.

TABLE 19.1 YaST Default Security Settings

Setting	Level 1 Home Workstation	Level 2 Networked Workstation	Level 3 Network Server
Checking New Passwords	N	Y	Y
Test for Complicated Password	N	N	N
Password Encryption Method	Blowfish	Blowfish	Blowfish
Minimum Acceptable Password Length	5	5	6
Minimum Days to Password Change Warning	0	1	1
Maximum Days to Password Change Warning	99999	99999	99999
Days Before Password Expires Warning	7	14	14
Ctrl+Alt+Del	Reboot	Ignore	Ignore
Shutdown Behavior	All Users	Only Root	Only Root
Delay After Incorrect Login Attempt	1	6	3
Record Failed Logins	Y	Y	Y
Record Successful Logins	Y	Y	Y
Allow Remote Graphical Login	N	N	N
User ID Limitations	1000–60000	1000–60000	1000–60000
Group ID Limitations	1000–60000	1000–60000	1000–60000
Setting of File Permissions	Easy	Easy	Secure
User Launching UpdateDB	Root	Nobody	Nobody
Current Dir in Root's Path	Y	N	N
Current Dir in Path of Regular Users	Y	N	N
Enable Magic SysRq Keys	N	N	N

To change any of these defaults, you must click Details. YaST will walk you through the four pages of settings.

Some of these items may be perplexing. Read the helpful descriptions for each setting in the left pane of the screen when deciding how to handle each setting. The following list looks at a few:

- Password Plausibility Test—Enforces some of the rules for passwords suggested in the previous section.
- Password Encryption Method—There are three. By default, YaST chooses the Blowfish method at all three levels. This open-source algorithm was developed by security expert Bruce Schneier in 1993 and is faster and safer than the other two choices. Data Encryption Standard (DES) encryption was developed by the U.S. government in the mid-1970s and was the original free encryption algorithm. Passwords using this method are limited to eight characters. MD5 transforms a data string of any length into a shorter, fixed-length value. No two strings of data will produce the same hash value.
- UpdateDB—This program runs daily and works with the `locate` program to quickly find files. If Root runs `UpdateDB`, all files are updated. If the system user Nobody runs `UpdateDB`, only files that Nobody has access to are updated.
- Magic SysRq—The SysRq key is usually located next to the Scroll Lock key on your keyboard. When used with the Alt key, it can permit an orderly shutdown of a crashed system. The bad news is that someone with remote access to your healthy system can bring it down instantly. Given the rarity of system crashes, it is better to leave this disabled.

Monitoring User Activity

Monitoring user activity is part of the sysadmin's duties, and an essential part of tracking how system resources are being used. If you have multiple users on your openSUSE system, and especially if you don't, you should become familiar with some of these monitoring tools.

As the all-powerful sysadmin, you can monitor nearly everything your users do on the computer, held back only by the hours in the day. Fortunately for all concerned, even the Bastard Operator From Hell doesn't have time to do this. Any good sysadmin will check in periodically, just to keep the invaders at bay.

Shell Tools for Watching Users

The `acct` system accounting package is essential to pull together all the commands you'll need to keep tabs on your system. There are a bunch of handy tools there including `sa`, `accton`, and `lastcomm`.

You may need to start the `acct` service at startup. To do this, log in as SuperUser and type the following:

```
/etc/init.d/acct start
```

openSUSE will now track resource usage in the `/var/run/utmp` and `/var/log/wtmp` files. You can access these files with the following commands.

The `w` command will tell the sysadmin who is logged in, where he or she is logged in at, and what they are up to. No one is able to hide from the SuperUser. The `w` command can be followed by a specific user's name to show only that user—by default, it will show all current users.

The `ac` command provides information about the total connect time of a user measured in hours. It accesses the `/var/log/wtmp` file for the source of its information. To generate a list of users with their login hours, type the following:

```
ac -p
```

Even if you're a sole user, if you log in and out religiously, you might find this command useful. To get a list of total hours logged in on the system for a calendar day, type the following:

```
ac -d
```

TIP

Interestingly, a phenomenon known as timewarp can occur. An entry in the wtmp files can jump back into the past, and ac will show unusual amounts of time accounted for users. Although this can be attributed to some innocuous factors having to do with the system clock, it is worthy of investigation by the sysadmin. It can also be the result of a security breach.

The `ac` command can prove itself most useful in shell scripts when you want to generate reports on operating system usage to show management what OSs your users run.

The `last` command searches through the `/var/log/wtmp` file and will list all the users logged in and out since that file was first created. The system user `reboot` exists so that you might know who has logged in since the last reboot. A companion to `last` is the `lastb` command, which shows all failed, or bad, logins. It's useful to determine if a legitimate user is having trouble, or if someone is trying to break into your system. The hoped-for result of `lastb` is always a message telling you that the btmp log does not exist—meaning there have been not bad/attempted logins.

Letting Mortals Play at Wizardry: SuperUsers

It has been said here frequently that it is generally a bad idea to log in as Root and do work. Too much damage can be done, and if you're connected to the Internet, you can actually lose control of your system to an attacker. Nonetheless, there are tasks and operations that can be done only by Root, and you may find yourself needing to be Root on a daily basis. Fortunately, there is a built-in solution to this problem: becoming the SuperUser.

There are two ways to perform Root tasks while being logged in as a generic user. The su command allows anyone with the Root password to become Root. In a larger system, Root can also assign specific tasks to users without handing out the Root password by implementing the sudo command.

Changing User Identity with su

When you run YaST to make changes in your configuration, you are first asked for the Root password. You have just used su to become Root.

Whether the task is installing software, troubleshooting problems, or handling some other system-related issue, you will need this command sooner or later.

NOTE

Although most often run on a system to gain SuperUser access, su is not the SuperUser command. It stands for "Substitute User," and you can log in as any other system user with the correct password.

To run su from the shell prompt, use this syntax:

```
su <option> <username> <arguments>
```

Typing **su** by itself means you want to log in as Root, and you'll be prompted for the Root password. You'll also retain your own environment settings. To gain Root's environment, type **su -**.

To run a single Root command from the shell and return to your user prompt, use the -c switch. Try something like this:

```
su root -c chmod 600 /etc/shadow
```

When you have completed your Root tasks, type **exit** to return to your user prompt.

Using sudo to Grant Root Privileges

When you're the system administrator of a large system with lots of users, you don't want to give out the Root password to everyone who wants to install software on his or her computer. You can solve this problem with SuperUser Do, or sudo.

You configure sudo by editing /etc/sudoers with the special visudo editor. As you might guess, visudo is a version of vi made for use with this file. It checks for parsing errors in your edits, so you should definitely use this, rather than your regular editor (even if you normally work with vi). You may want to return to the vi section of Chapter 5 to review some of the commands if you are not familiar with this editor.

Run su to log in as Root before running visudo. To begin, run visudo with no arguments; that is:

```
visudo
```

The default /etc/sudoers file appears in the shell, looking something like this:

```
# sudoers file.
#
# This file MUST be edited with the 'visudo' command as root.
#
# See the sudoers man page for the details on how to write a sudoers file.
#

# Host alias specification

# User alias specification

# Cmnd alias specification

# Defaults specification
Defaults targetpw    # ask for the password of the target user i.e. root
%users ALL=(ALL) ALL # WARNING! Only use this together with 'Defaults targetpw'!

# User privilege specification
# You should not use sudo as root in an SELinux environment
# If you use SELinux, remove the following line
root    ALL=(ALL) ALL

# Uncomment to allow people in group wheel to run all commands
# %wheel    ALL=(ALL)    ALL

# Same thing without a password
# %wheel    ALL=(ALL)    NOPASSWD: ALL

# Samples
# %users  ALL=/sbin/mount /cdrom,/sbin/umount /cdrom
# %users  localhost=/sbin/shutdown -h now
```

Before editing sudoers, you may want to review the man pages for both sudoers and visudo (sudo itself has a man page as well) for instructions on how to use these files.

Feel free to uncomment any of the default lines to activate them. Instead of editing the default lines, you should add new lines (with a comment to document what you want to do). The basic format of a sudoers line is this:

```
<user> <host_computer>=<command>
```

The user can also be a group; so, for example, to grant permission to the Writers group to run YaST Online Update, add this line:

```
writers ALL=/sbin/yast2
```

To grant the Writers group this same permission without having to enter a password, add this line:

```
writers ALL=/sbin/yast2 NOPASSWD: ALL
```

When you're finished editing, type **:q** to save changes and return to the shell prompt. Type **exit** to return to your user prompt.

Once configured, sudo is very easy to use. Anyone in the Writers group should now be able to type this command to run YaST:

```
sudo /sbin/yast2
```

Depending on how you set it, writers may be prompted for their own user password to confirm membership in the group.

References

- http://tldp.org/LDP/sag/html—The Linux System Administrator's Guide.
- http://tldp.org/HOWTO/User-Authentication-HOWTO—Setting up passwords.
- http://tldp.org/HOWTO/HOWTO-INDEX/admin.html#ADMSECURITY—The Linux security HOWTOs all in one place. Be sure to read over the Security-HOWTO for an overview.
- http://www.tldp.org/HOWTO/Shadow-Password-HOWTO.html—Explains the shadow password system.
- http://www.novell.com/coolsolutions/feature/11685.html—A brief but nice overview of permissions and how to set them in Nautilus/GNOME.
- http://www.gratisoft.us/sudo—The sudo program lets you delegate specific administrative tasks to particular users without turning over the Root password.
- http://www.kernel.org/pub/linux/libs/pam—Pluggable Authentication Modules in Linux.
- http://www.ncsa.uiuc.edu/UserInfo/Resources/Hardware/IBMp690/IBM/usr/share/man/info/en_US/a_doc_lib/aixbman/admnconc/pam.htm—This guide to PAM under IBM's flavor of Unix is helpful to Linux users, too.
- http://www.ibm.com/developerworks/linux/library/l-sc7.html—This article on "Practical Linux Security" offers an interesting take on handling users.
- http://searchenterpriselinux.techtarget.com/originalContent/0,289142,_sid39_gci928466,00.html—This Linux Security Learning Guide is a handy set of articles and links on the range of security topics. A free registration is required to access the guide.
- http://www.schneier.com/blowfish.html—The Blowfish encryption algorithm home page.
- http://linuxgazette.net/issue81/vikas.html—A summary of the Magic SysRq process.

CHAPTER 20

Managing Data: Backup, Restoring, and Recovery

IN THIS CHAPTER

Maybe you've heard it a hundred times before, but it's still true: You will lose data one time or another. It's a question of *when*, not *if*.

Bad things happen to good data. A group of computer users in an office working on a Linux file server share data in a folder named SHARE. One of the users accidentally deletes a very important file in that folder that all other users use. No fear—because you backed up the system; a quick restore will be able to get that file back in place, as long as the backup was originally successful. This chapter is about preparing for that eventuality.

Preparing for Preventing Data Loss

Backing up data is not fun. It takes time and resources, and 99.999 percent of the time, it's not productive. For one person, it can be hard to justify taking the time to back up data, buy new storage media, and make sure your existing backups still work. However, the day your hard drive decides to join the scrap heap is the day that all that time pays off. That's when you're reminded that backups are like insurance; you hope you never need it, but when you need it, you're really happy it's there.

The trick is knowing how much to back up, what to back up, and how often to back up. This section will help you sort out these issues before you start.

How to Lose Data

When you think about it, data stored on a computer is a fragile thing. It is nothing but ones and zeros stored electromagnetically on a cheap metal platter. The storage industry does a fine job of protecting those digits, but it's almost a wonder that users don't lose more data than they do.

Aside from the times when you consciously press the Delete key or type **`rm`** `<filename>` at a shell prompt, when you talk about data loss, that data loss is usually an unintended consequence stemming from various causes. Mother Nature is often at the root of the problem: thunderstorms leading to electrical power surges, tornadoes, floods, hurricanes, and fire can all make data disappear or become useless in an instant.

Floppy disks are fragile things. They can get bounced around enough to damage the disk and corrupt files. Consider the unstable, buggy program you're using to create new data. When it hangs or crashes, you get a message warning you that `All unsaved data will be lost`.

Hard drives do die. Manufacturers even use a rating system of Mean Time Between Failures (MTBF) to quantify the number of hours a hard drive should function. And using wildcards to remove batches of unwanted files can result in wanted files disappearing, too.

Too often, however, data loss results from what technical support people call (privately) "keyboard-to-chair problems"—good old human error. As long as there are humans, no matter how intelligent they happen to be, they will do some not-so-intelligent things that can result in some level of data loss. Backups minimize the risk from all these causes of data loss.

Assessing Your Needs and Resources

In many ways, deciding on a backup strategy is predicated on the answers to two simple questions: What files do I need to back up, and how often do those files change?

The answers get down to a more critical question that lies beneath: What data is important to me?

When you have those issues settled, the question then becomes: What can I afford to spend, in both time and money, to protect that important data? The answers to these questions diminish in importance if you have access to massive amounts of bandwidth or empty warehouses that can store terabytes of data in every square foot of the property. That probably does not describe you, however.

Some backup methods take longer than others, and the same is true for restore methods.

Consider the situation where you have to restore everything. Can you afford to be down as long as it takes to restore using your method? If it's just your machine, will you have to sit there swapping disks in and out every few minutes, or can you automate the process?

These are the questions that will help you formulate your backup strategy. After you have that strategy, it's important to practice it religiously and test it periodically.

Whatever strategy you select, make sure to carry out these practices with similar fervor:

- Have more than one copy of critical data at all times.
- Label the backups using some consistent method (by date or by type of file).

- Store backups in a secure area with consistent temperatures.
- Store critical data somewhere offsite. If all your backups are in your house, and the house catches fire, you're in trouble.
- Try restoring from a backup regularly to make yourself comfortable with the process, and test the medium you're using.
- Test your media. Problems with the CD or defects with the tape can mess things up.

Choosing a Backup Strategy

Everyone's situation is different, but we can make some generalizations about different types of users and their backup strategies.

- Home users—The critical issue for home users is not rebuilding the operating system and applications. With the openSUSE installation DVD, reinstalling the base packages for your system should take about an hour. What is critical is preserving your home directory and your configuration files. Backing up email is optional, depending on the volume and how important you think it is. Configuration files are generally stored in the `/etc` directory, so backing up `/home` and `/etc` is your primary task. If you have applications installed outside of YaST, you should back these up as well. Unless you have critical projects in the works, a weekly backup to a CD-RW or some other external storage drive is all that's required.
- Small Office/Home Office (SOHO)—Like home users, SOHO users can focus on keeping the data in the home directory secure, along with configuration files, business-related mail, and applications installed outside of YaST. SOHO users need to be more rigorous about backups than ordinary home users, because the consequences are greater. Daily backups of important files are a good idea. Because files stored on tape drives are faster to restore than other media, you may want to consider investing in a tape drive, although CDs may be just as good. Redundant drives may also be possible for you.

Many backup strategies are used today, but in this section we'll review some of the more popular ones. Tweak any one of them for your own purposes.

CAUTION

If you are running Windows and Linux on the same computer, don't back up both file systems in one fell swoop. Back up your Linux files with a Linux tool and then do your Windows files in Windows.

YaST System Backup will also back up your partition table. See "Using the YaST System Backup" later in this chapter for details.

Simple Strategy

If all you need is to back up a few small documents and some configuration files, you only need a floppy disk or two. Copy the files directly.

You can now spend less than $100 for a portable hard drive that connects to your computer's USB port for quick, easy, and reliable transfer of gigabytes of data. You can use a folder synchronizing tool to copy all new files to this drive as often as required. Similarly, USB flash "keychain" drives are small enough to fit in a fire-resistant box for good basic security.

With a CD-RW or DVD-RW on hand, you should be able to use K3b to burn the entire home directory for all your users to a single 700MB CD.

Though this technology is aging, if you have a Zip drive or other high-capacity floppy, you can choose to back up the entire Documents directory for each user, plus the `/etc` directory for all your configuration files. Zip disks come in 100, 250, and 750MB varieties.

The beauty of this strategy is that you can back up files on the spot, simply by copying every changed or new file to your chosen medium, although this is harder to do with a CD. It becomes problematic when your backups grow beyond a single disk. At that point, you'll want to adopt a more formal strategy, as in one of those included in the following sections.

Full Backup Periodically

This is the standard backup process where you archive everything to your chosen medium on a weekly, biweekly, or monthly basis. The frequency depends on the importance of the data and how often it changes. Ideally, you can perform this backup to a designated network server, but depending on how much room your files take up, multiple CDs or DVDs may work.

The best way to do this is with archiving software, which is discussed later in the chapter.

Full Backups with Increments

This is the standard corporate backup routine used in medium-to-large networks. There's no technical reason smaller businesses can't do this, but it may be less necessary. With this strategy, you make a full backup to a tape weekly and back up new and changed files every day.

There are two ways of defining what is "new and changed"—that is, what to include in an incremental backup. The easiest way to do this is to have a single tape (Level 1) reference the last full backup (Level 0) each day. This way, you have to keep track of only two tapes. The danger is that if a lot of things change during a given week, you may run out of tape.

The alternative is to have separate incremental tapes for each day. If you perform your full backup on Friday night, your first increment is Saturday, and it references the full backup. You then remove Friday's tape and insert Sunday's tape, which will include changes since Saturday, and onward to Thursday. So if someone comes to you and asks for the file they accidentally deleted on Wednesday, you can easily find Tuesday's backup tape and restore from there.

It's best to use a professional backup solution, such as Amanda or BRU, for these complicated backups. As a system administrator, then, all you have to worry about is changing tapes. The software handles the actual backup.

Choosing Your Backup Medium

Leaving aside the warehouse full of terabytes, you need to decide how to store your backed up files. Making a copy of all the files on your hard drive and storing it on another partition on the same drive may be useful in some situations, but not when the drive goes bad.

Given this reality, you must choose another medium to which to back up your files. This section gives you a brief overview of your choices and includes some suggestions to help you find the right one for you.

Mirrors and RAID Arrays

A redundant array of inexpensive disks (RAID) setup offers a system administrator a great opportunity to have a real-time permanent copy of everything on a particular hard drive. Mirrors are additional volumes that contain an exact copy of whatever data is stored on the parent volume. Whenever an operation writes data to the parent volume, it is immediately written to the mirror volume as well. If the parent disk were to fail, the mirror disk can immediately take over, ensuring that data isn't lost. With relatively inexpensive hard drives available, this can be a great solution because, as we learned earlier, drives will always eventually fail.

Be aware, though, that mirrors don't check for corrupt files on the parent. They will write corrupt files to their disks as easily as they write good files.

For more information on setting up RAID arrays, see "Setting Up Mirror Disks and RAID Arrays" later in this chapter.

Removable Storage Media

Using some type of removable media is the standard backup solution for home and SOHO users. Although the 1.4MB floppy disk is slowly disappearing from the computing landscape, other more robust choices can make backups less of a painful experience. Anything that helps users get into the backup habit is a good thing.

Besides ordinary floppies, the following choices exist for removable storage.

Zip Drives

openSUSE has excellent support for the large capacity floppy drives from Iomega. Coming in 100, 250, and 750MB sizes, these drives can play a role in your backup strategy. These drives also have a choice of connections, serial and USB, which make the drives quite portable. The drive-and-disk combination can be more expensive than comparable CD-R/RW combinations. Zip disks also have a history of experiencing the "click of death," with a sudden wiping of the disk. This is not so much of a problem with newer drives, but it still happens.

USB Keychain Drives and Solid-State Portable Drives

Keychain drives (called that because they are so small you can attach them to a keychain) are so cool you might have trouble thinking of them as part of a serious backup program.

Depending on what deal your favorite electronics or office-supply store is offering this week, you can get up to 2GB for about $100, and often much cheaper. Plug the drive into a USB port and copy any files you want. Keychain drives use flash memory to store data. USB-based portable hard drives are also coming down in price, with 80GB of storage for about $100, and 400GB for less than $500. openSUSE will identify these drives as SCSI storage and mount them like any other volume on your system.

The key thing to remember about both types of drives is that you really need USB v2.0 to make the transfer time worthwhile. Older computers with USB 1.0 ports cannot take advantage of the tremendously higher speeds of the new ports. If you have room for another PCI card in your machine, you can add USB 2.0 ports to your system.

FireWire Drives

These portable drives use a different interface (IEEE 1394) than the USB drives do, but are otherwise similar. The interface is popular with portable music players and digital cameras. Most of these drives were created for the Macintosh platform, but the Linux kernel supports them.

CD-RW and Recordable DVD

For newer computers that have some kind of built-in recordable CD or DVD drive, it's hard to debate other choices for your backup. CD-R disks hold 700MB of data and cost less than a dollar; CD-RW (Read-Write) disks are only a little more for the same amount of space.

CDs are durable, compact, and provide a mountable file system. This makes them more versatile than tape for restoring files. They are less fragile than Zip drives and use a more mature technology than the keychain drives. Transfer speeds vary depending on the drive, but all are acceptable. You still have to be careful not to scratch the disk, but they can be protected by jewel cases.

Recordable DVD drives are also now becoming part of new PC installations. DVDs can hold up to 4.4GB of data, and cost around $2. The only issue is that there are two incompatible formats for recordable DVDs: DVD-RW and DVD+RW. You need to know what format your drive supports and buy the appropriate disks. Lately, DVD±RW drives have become available that allow you to use either format.

openSUSE provides several command-line tools to burn CDs and DVDs. The k3b utility gives you an excellent GUI interface for these applications, whether you run KDE or GNOME, and supports both DVD formats. To run k3b, use your desktop menu, or simply open a terminal session and enter **k3b** at the shell prompt.

Network Storage

Although enterprise-level systems can take advantage of Network Attached Storage (NAS) setups, where the backup storage volumes are on the network directly, rather than needing to be restored to a server, there are other options for the rest of us:

- Your Internet Service Provider (ISP) may offer some file storage, either as part of a website package, or straight out.
- Some commercial storage space companies (such as www.xdrive.com) offer space for a monthly fee.

- Google's Gmail service offers 2 gigabytes of mail storage for free. Richard Jones has written a program that converts some or all of that space into a working Linux file system. Find it at http://richard.jones.name/google-hacks/gmail-filesystem/gmail-filesystem.html.

Tape Drive Backup

Tape drives have been the standard corporate backup medium for a long time. The TAR archive format for Unix, which groups individual files into a single tarball for easy retrieval, stands for *Tape ARchive*. Tape cartridges can hold up to 70GB of data (more if the data is compressed), although capacities can vary.

Tapes are very reliable when maintained, but they do degrade over time. Tape drives can and do fail as well.

CAUTION

Tape drives can be fragile and must be cleaned, aligned, and maintained regularly. Do not risk your data by neglecting these tasks.

Using the YaST System Backup

As always, YaST is here to help simplify the backup task. It will not back up your entire drive, but it can get all the critical files you need to boot your system if your system fails. You can use this tool to create several backup profiles, depending on your strategy.

The System Backup and Restore System tools are both located in the YaST System page. You'll learn more about the Restore tool later in the chapter.

The first time you start System Backup, you will get a blank page. You must first create a backup profile. Go to Profile Management and click Add to create a new profile, as shown in Figure 20.1. You'll be asked to name the profile.

In this section, you learn how to make an initial backup to the home directory for later burning to CD. The first Add Profile screen, Archive Settings, explains a little about the process and asks you where you want to store your backup. Type the full path and name the file in the File Name line, as shown in Figure 20.2.

If you have the Network File System (NFS) running and can back up to a remote volume, click the Network button and select the NFS Server name and your directory in the appropriate boxes.

By default, YaST compresses your system files with the GNUZip (gz) tool and places all the compressed files into a Tape ARchive (TAR). You can also choose to compress with the newer bzip (bz2) archive format, or leave the files uncompressed in another TAR wrapper. If you are using Access Control Lists (ACL), YaST advises using the star format for the subarchives. There's no harm in selecting the defaults, but bzip gets slightly better compression rates than GNUZip.

Click Next to continue.

In the Backup Options screen (see Figure 20.3), you are defining files that won't be backed up. By default (and there isn't really any way to change this), YaST backs up every file from packages that have changed since installation. Checking the Backup Files Not Belonging to Any Package box backs up everything, including data files. The Check MD5 Sum Instead of Time or Size option uses the MD5 hash algorithm to determine whether a file has changed. MD5 transforms a data string of any length into a shorter, fixed-length value. No two strings of data will produce the same hash value. If you don't check this box, YaST will use the last modified date or a changed size to determine whether a file has changed. The latter backup will be faster, but perhaps not as accurate.

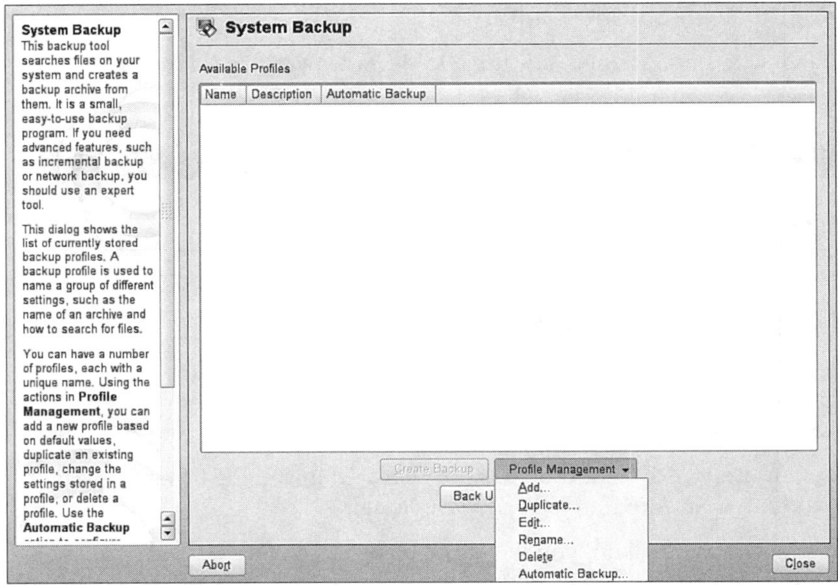

FIGURE 20.1 Click Add from the Profile Management menu to create a new profile.

TIP

You can (and perhaps should) have separate backup profiles for packages, data (files not belonging to any package, with your `~/Mail` directory excluded), and mail (with `~/Mail` included). See the Search Constraints screen to learn how to take directories out of the backup.

If you want to see a list of the files to be backed up before YaST completes the backup, check the Display List of Files Before Creating Archive box. To add a description of this particular backup profile, type in the appropriate box.

If you have a dual-boot system, and the boot manager sits on your hard drive, it is a good idea to back up your partition table. This is not done by default. Click Expert at the bottom of this screen, and then check Back Up Hard Disk System Areas. Clicking Options shows that Back Up Partition Tables is checked automatically when you choose to back up the system areas. If you have the default ext3 file system, you can use the Options to back up critical areas of the file system as well.

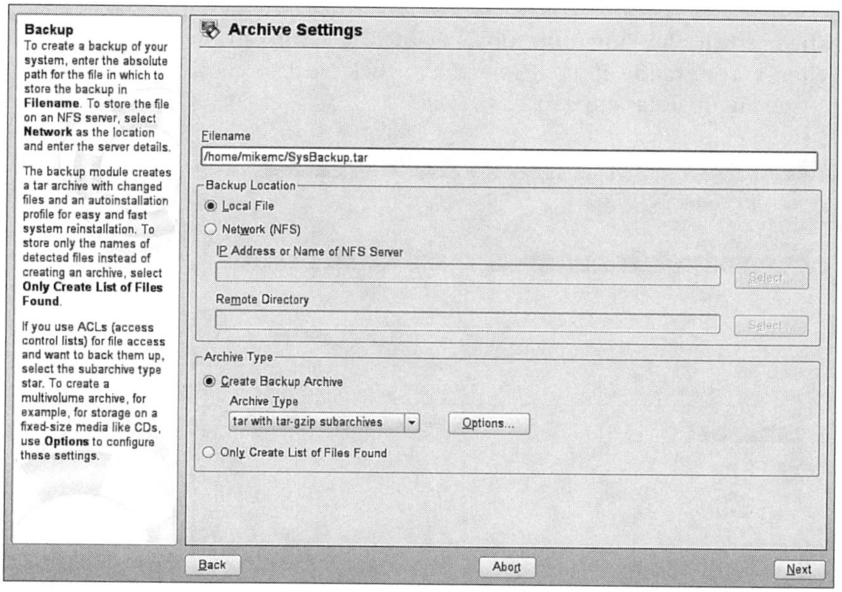

FIGURE 20.2 Define the location for your backup file and choose the type of archive you want to use in this screen.

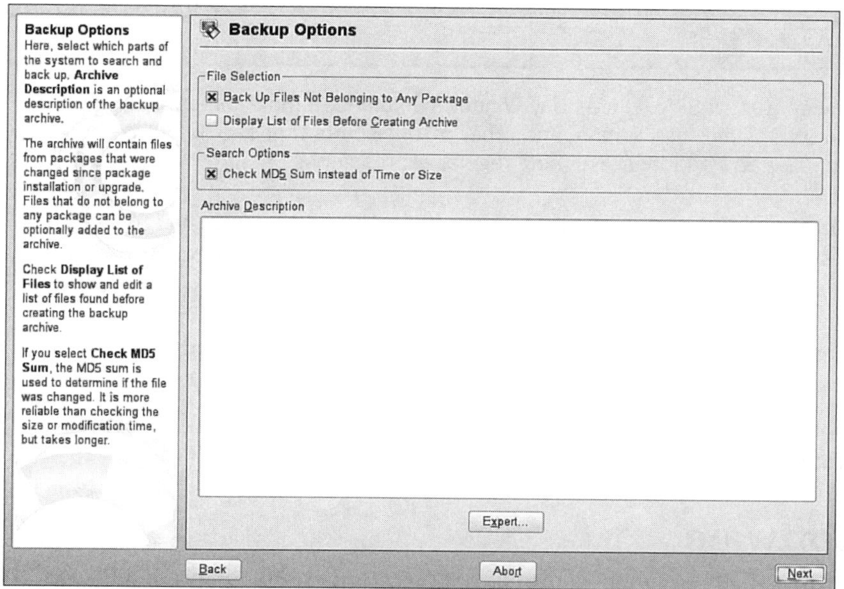

FIGURE 20.3 The Backup Options screen defines files that will not be backed up, rather than files that are backed up.

20

By default, YaST stores the backup archive while it's being built in the `/tmp` directory. You can change this in the Expert options, but you should only need to do this if that directory is exceedingly low on space.

When you've finished setting the Expert options, click OK to return to the Backup Options screen. When you've made all your selections, click Next to continue. The Search Constraints screen (see Figure 20.4) appears.

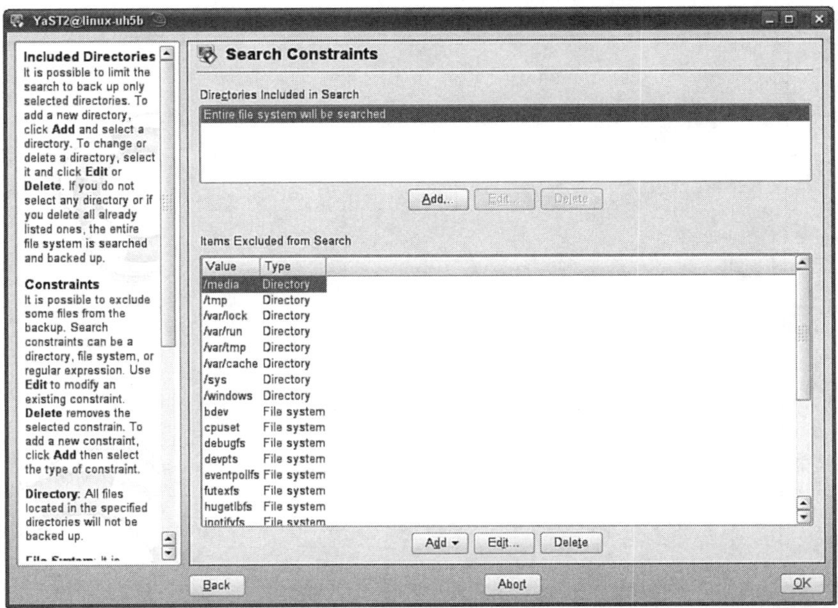

FIGURE 20.4 By default, YaST excludes any Windows volumes, remote directories, the /var directories that store transient information, and other mount points that should not be backed up. You can edit this list and add files matching regular expressions.

The final screen in the Backup Wizard lists directories and file systems to be ignored in the backup process. By default, directories that store transient system information and alien file systems such as CDs and floppies that happen to be sitting in their respective drives, Windows volumes, and remote directories are not backed up. You can add or delete any directory or file system to or from this exclusion list. You can also exclude files matching a defined regular expression.

Click OK to complete the backup profile. You will return to the main System Backup screen. Click Create Backup to begin the process.

Backup Software

YaST System Backup covers only vital system files. Many other tools exist to help you back up your more ordinary Linux files. They range from the simple command-line archiver TAR to commercial, industrial-strength products like Arkeia and BRU. In this section, you'll learn more about archiving with `tar` and two GUI applications, File Roller and Ark, that will help create archives for backup purposes.

ARCHIVES AND COMPRESSION FORMATS

Perhaps you've heard of the National Archives, the building in Washington, D.C., where the original Declaration of Independence and millions of other documents are stored. And perhaps you're wondering what that has to do with backup files.

Like the National Archives, the TAR format keeps important files safe and together. It puts a wrapper around a group of files that you designate. Their relationship can be as tight as a group of files that form an executable program or as loose as "the files I want to back up."

If your backup medium is limited in space, you can use a compression program to squeeze out redundant information to shrink a file to take up less space. Programs such as GNUZip and bzip use an algorithm to take text like the word *redundant* to note that it has a pair of Ds and Ns and reduces the size of that word by 11 percent. Taken over an entire document file, these algorithms can save a lot of space counting instances of letters, spaces, and other characters.

You can use TAR and the other compression programs with the shell or use a GUI client. By default, openSUSE uses the GNOME Archive Manager to work with archives, but the KDE Ark program works at least as well.

Backups with `tar`

The Tape Archive utility, `tar`, is one of the oldest in the Unix toolkit. It masterfully follows the Unix philosophy of "do one thing well." That thing is grouping files together in one easy-to-transport package. For doing backups, `tar` offers a simple command-line solution. This command archives the whole `/etc` directory and places the archive in the current directory:

```
tar cvf etc.tar /etc
```

These options create a new archive with the filename `etc.tar` that copies all files in the `/etc` directory to the archive. Note that `tar` is verbose in telling you what it's doing; that is, you'll see a stream of filenames rolling down the shell as each is added to the archive.

If you add the z switch to this command—that is

```
tar cvfz etc.tar /etc
```

you will also compress the files with `Gzip`. Similarly, adding the `j` switch would use the `bzip` formula.

The `tar` utility can also be used to back up data directly to a tape drive. Most tape drives use a SCSI interface and are accessed through `/dev/stx`; where *x* refers to the number of the tape drive in the system (st0, st1, st2, and so on). For example, if you have a single SCSI tape drive in your system, you would access it through `/dev/st0`.

To create a backup job and send it to the tape drive, complete the following:

1. Using YaST, make sure your tape drive was detected during boot and that the correct driver was loaded. Usually this isn't a problem, especially if you use a widely recognized SCSI board in your computer (such as those from Adaptec).
2. Insert a tape in your tape drive and wait for it to load and queue up.
3. Open a terminal session.
4. At the shell prompt, type `tar options /dev/stx <path_to_be_backed_up>`. For example, to create an archive of the /home directory (and all its subdirectories) on the first SCSI tape drive in the system, you would enter **`tar -cvfz /dev/st0 /home`**. If the size of the archive exceeds the capacity of your tape, you will need to remove the **`-z`** option and add the **`-M`** option. This will allow the tar archive to span across multiple tapes.
5. When the job is complete, you can rewind the tape and eject it at the command prompt using the `mt` utility. This is done by entering **`mt -f /dev/st0 rewoffl`**. The `mt` utility can also be used to perform a number of other tasks with magnetic tapes, such as erasing, rewinding, and fast forwarding. Check out the man page for `mt` for more information.

A key component of an effective backup strategy is to make sure backups occur regularly. Using the `crond` daemon, you can configure `tar` to automatically back up your system at a set time each day (usually later at night when you aren't using the system). This relieves you of the responsibility of remembering to manually start the process. Invariably, the day you forget to run a backup is the day you will end up needing it. Review the `tar` man page to discover the power and flexibility of this utility, and then put it to work in your backup scheme.

Using Ark

Ark is a very easy-to-use application that can create or open plain and compressed archives in several formats: `tar`, `gzip`, `bzip`, `zip`, `rar`, and `jar`, to name just a few. It's the default archive tool if you're using your openSUSE system with a KDE shell. As with many applications designed for KDE, it will work under GNOME as well. To create a new archive using Ark, complete the following:

1. In the new KDE menu, go to Applications, Utilities, Archiving, Ark (assuming you're using KDE).
2. Select File, New.
3. In the Create New Archive screen, enter a *name* for the archive in the Location field.
4. In the Filter field, select the type of archive you want to create. Most of the time, you will probably want to create a gzipped tar archive.

5. Select Save.
6. To add data to the archive, select either Action, Add File or Action, Add Folder. Select the file(s) to be archived.
7. Wait while the files are added to the archive.

Alternatively, you can also create an Ark archive by right-clicking files from within Konqueror and selecting Compress, Compress as archive_name.tar.gz from the menu. The new archive will be created and saved in the location you specify.

After it is saved, you can open any existing archive and add files to it. This is helpful if you have some files in other directories. Figure 20.5 shows you how an existing archive appears in the Ark window.

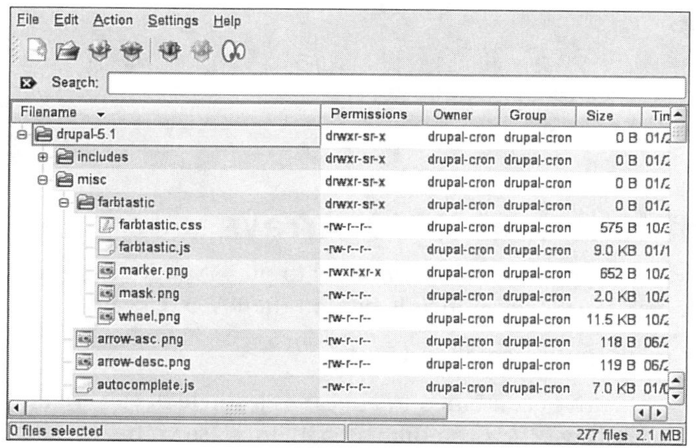

FIGURE 20.5 The Gzipped archive for the Drupal content management system in an Ark window.

Using GNOME File Roller

File Roller is the default archive tool for the Mozilla browsers, regardless of your preferred desktop environment. It integrates well with Nautilus, the GNOME file manager, allowing for drag-and-drop adding of files to new archives.

If you open Nautilus and then File Roller in the same desktop, you can drag files from Nautilus to File Roller. The archiver then asks if you want to create a new archive with the selected files. Click Yes to open the dialog box you see in Figure 20.6.

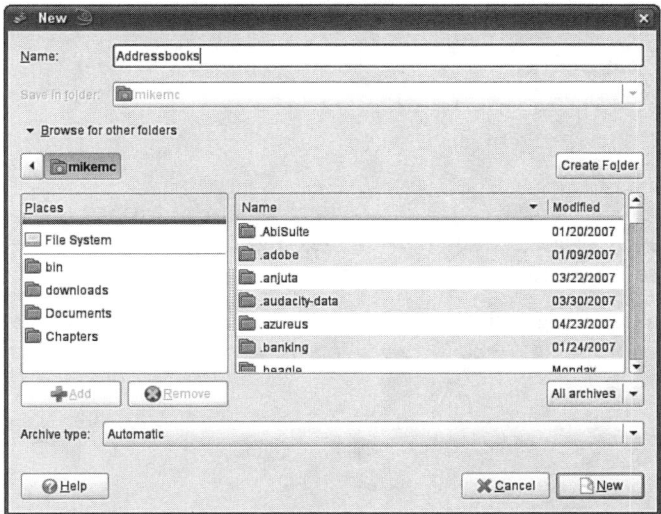

FIGURE 20.6 Save a new archive in File Roller.

Setting Up Mirror Disks and RAID Arrays

If you have two or more hard drives in your computer, one way to preserve files is to have one drive act as a mirror for another. This is the principle behind the RAID concept.

There are several levels of RAID arrays implemented in Linux:

- RAID-0 (stripe mode)—Multiple drives combined to appear as a single device. Data is saved in small stripes on each drive. This can dramatically increase your system performance because large chunks of data are split up between the drives and read or written concurrently. Unfortunately, RAID-0 doesn't offer any form of data protection. If problems arise on one drive in the array, files on both drives can become corrupted.

- RAID-1 (mirror)—Data is saved redundantly to all drives in a mirrored array. Instead of splitting data between drives, an exact copy of data being written is saved on multiple drives in the array. Each drive contains a mirror of every other drive. Mirroring doesn't improve system performance. However, your chances of retrieving a file stored in a mirrored array are excellent. With most RAID-1 controllers, a mirrored drive can be configured to instantly take over in the event that the main drive in the system fails; this provides a high degree of data protection.

- RAID-4—This array has three or more striped drives included, with one of them storing parity information. The parity information makes it easier to reconstruct data if one drive in the array fails. In essence, it creates an array that provides the speed of a striped array along with the protection of a mirrored array.

- RAID-5—This is the same as RAID-4, but parity information is distributed evenly among the drives. As with RAID-4, RAID-5 provides the benefits of both RAID-0 and RAID-1. RAID-5 is more commonly implemented than RAID-4. RAID-5 boards are usually much more expensive than RAID-0 or RAID-1 boards.
- RAID-0+1—Although this is not an official RAID level, many newer RAID controllers provide you with the option of creating a mirrored striped array using four hard disk drives. This provides the speed and redundancy benefits associated with RAID-5, but at a much lower cost.

It's important to note here that RAID can be implemented in two ways:

- Via hardware—With hardware RAID, you install a special disk interface into an expansion slot in the system to which your hard drives are attached. All RAID configuration tasks are completed using the BIOS of the RAID board. The RAID board itself represents the entire array to the operating system as a single hard disk drive. Using a RAID board generally provides faster performance than a software RAID solution (although at a higher cost).
- Via software—With software RAID, your system's hard disk drives are connected using the standard, non-RAID interface in your system. The operating system, then, is used to create a RAID array using these disks. Software RAID is usually much less expensive than hardware RAID, but is also considered to provide slightly slower performance.

openSUSE will support either type of RAID implementation. In fact, setting up a software RAID array on openSUSE is quite simple with the YaST Expert Partitioner.

CAUTION

It is always best to set up a RAID array when first installing openSUSE so that nothing can happen to your existing data when you're working with the Expert Partitioner.

The steps outlined here apply when you have purchased a drive to serve as your mirror drive after your initial installation. Be sure to back up critical files before starting this process. You will be changing the partition table for your system as part of the setup.

Before installing the new drive, you should convert your Root partition to change the SystemID. Start Expert Partitioner by going to YaST, System, Partitioner. Select your Root partition (marked Linux Native /) and click Edit. In the resulting dialog box, click Do Not Format. Use the drop-down menu to change the File System ID to 0xFD Linux RAID. Click OK to confirm. Click Apply to convert the File System ID.

When the conversion is complete, shut down the system and install the new drive. openSUSE should recognize the new hardware and ask how to format it. At this point, you want to create your RAID array (see Figure 20.7).

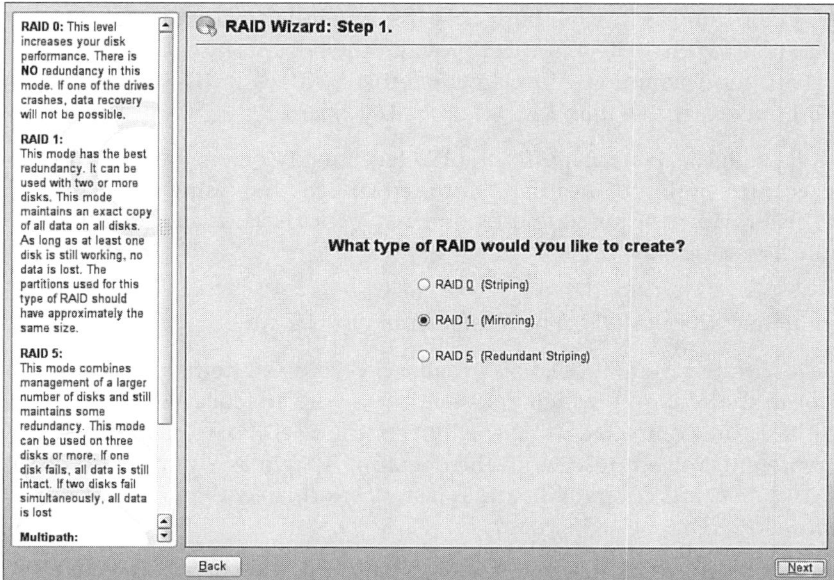

RAID 0: This level increases your disk performance. There is NO redundancy in this mode. If one of the drives crashes, data recovery will not be possible.
RAID 1: This mode has the best redundancy. It can be used with two or more disks. This mode maintains an exact copy of all data on all disks. As long as at least one disk is still working, no data is lost. The partitions used for this type of RAID should have approximately the same size.
RAID 5: This mode combines management of a larger number of disks and still maintains some redundancy. This mode can be used on three disks or more. If one disk fails, all data is still intact. If two disks fail simultaneously, all data is lost
Multipath:
RAID Wizard: Step 1.
What type of RAID would you like to create?
RAID 0 (Striping)
RAID 1 (Mirroring)
RAID 5 (Redundant Striping)
Back
Next

FIGURE 20.7 Define the RAID type in the first screen.

CAUTION

Although it's technically possible to create a software RAID array using two partitions on the same hard disk drive, you should *never* do this. The mirrored or striped partitions should always be located on different disks.

You will create a mirror. Click Next to continue.

The second screen (see Figure 20.8) allows you to define the drives you want to mirror. For this example, we created a dummy drive. In a real scenario, the mirror should be at least as large as the active drive. Select both partitions and click Add to create the mirror. Click Next to continue.

The final screen in the RAID Wizard sets options for the mirror (see Figure 20.9). For a mirroring (RAID 1) operation, there's no reason to shift from the defaults. To confirm the settings and return to the main Expert Partitioner screen, click Finish.

When you have finished with the RAID Wizard, click Apply to create the RAID array.

If you chose to use a hardware-based RAID array, you won't have to complete any of these steps. The RAID board will present the array to openSUSE as a single hard disk drive. Simply partition and format the logical drive just as you would a physical hard disk drive.

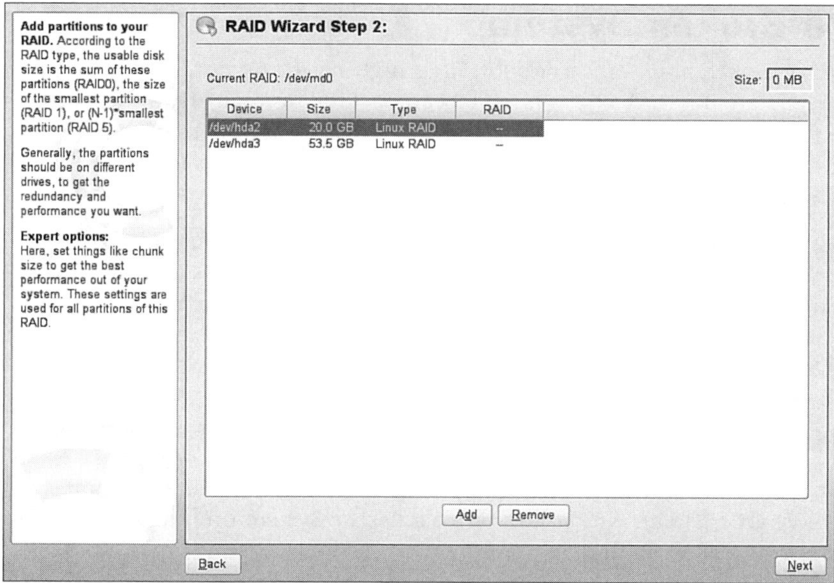

FIGURE 20.8 Add partitions to mirror each other in this screen.

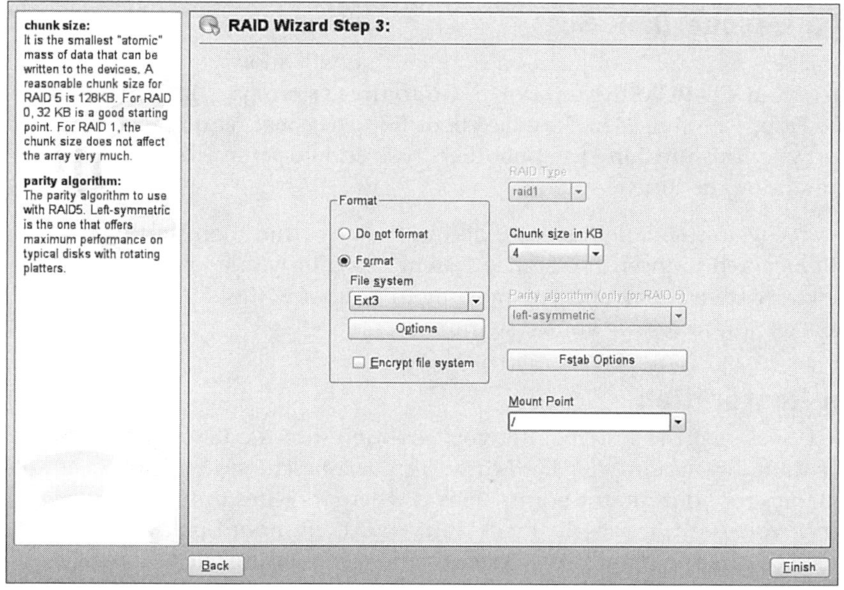

FIGURE 20.9 Set options for the mirror drive in the final RAID screen.

20

Rescuing a Broken System

When your system is broken and you can't boot, it's a nightmare you don't want to confront. But here you are. Fortunately, you have been backing up regularly and have an archive to restore from. In this section, you'll learn how to get your system back in shape.

Booting from the openSUSE DVD

The openSUSE installation disk included with this book is bootable and can get you into Rescue mode. First, make sure your BIOS is set to boot from your system's CD/DVD drive before the hard drive. Insert the openSUSE DVD into the drive, and boot. You may select Manual Installation to enter special boot parameters under Boot Options, but do this only if you know what you're doing. As you boot from the DVD, you will be asked to select the correct language and keyboard layout.

Select Start Installation or System in the main menu.

Select Start Rescue System and identify where the rescue system is located. By default, this is the CD. If you have access to an NFS volume with a Rescue System on it, choose this option. If you have a set of Rescue floppies, see the next section to learn that process.

The Rescue System starts. You can log in as Root with no password. Skip to the "Using System Restoration" section to see what to do next.

Booting from a Rescue Disk Set

YaST will let you make a series of boot disks on floppies that will allow you to boot the rescue system when your CD-ROM drive is down. Go to the System page in YaST to locate the Boot or Rescue Floppy module. The Standard boot floppy system requires seven floppy disks. When you finish making the boot disks, you should return to YaST to make a separate disk containing the Rescue system.

When you need to recover, insert the first boot disk in the drive and then start your computer. You will be asked to insert the Rescue system disk after you boot. As with the DVD boot, the Rescue System starts, and you may log in as Root without a password. Proceed to the next section to restore your system.

Using System Restoration

Regardless of how you started the system, after you've gotten into the Rescue system, there is work to be done. To mount your hard drive from the Rescue system, you need to know the device names for your mount points. This is where it comes in handy to have an accessible copy of your `/etc/fstab` file. By default, your Root mount point is `/dev/hda1`. You need to carefully mount the system step by step, using the following method. Type the following command:

```
mount /dev/hda1 /mnt
```

This gives you access to the full Root partition. If you have set any other mount points (except for Swap, which is not important here), mount them under the `/mnt` point as well, as in this command to mount the `/usr` partition:

```
mount /dev/hda2 /mnt/usr
```

If you have simply misconfigured a configuration file to cause the boot problem, you should now be able to go to `/etc` and locate the file to reedit back to health. You also have the option to use YaST System Restoration to retrieve a backed up file. Follow these steps to use System Restoration.

NOTE

Depending on the state of your system, you may get the graphical YaST, where the images in the upcoming figures come from, or the shell version. The menus, however, are identical.

If you prefer to work in a graphical environment (and you can run X), type **`startx`** to run the X Window System and your preferred environment. Otherwise, just type **`yast`**.

Use the down arrow to go to the System module, tab to the components side, and then arrow down to System Restoration. Press Enter to start the module. Figure 20.10 shows the first Restore screen.

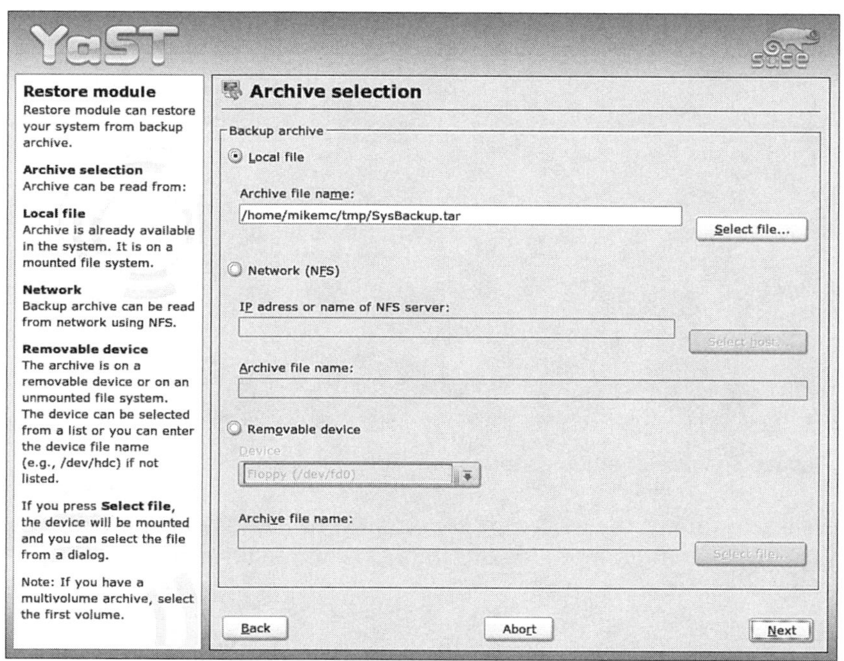

FIGURE 20.10 Locate your System Backup file in this screen.

20

Use this screen to locate your System Backup file. In this instance, it's a local file; use the Select button to locate the file. If you have burned the backup to CD or Flash drive, use the Removable Device option to show that (make sure the disk is in the drive first). Click Next to continue. YaST will read the contents of the backup archive file.

The second screen gives you some basic information on the archive: when it was created, where it is located, and any comments you made about the archive when you created it. To see a list of the packages and files you backed up, click Archive Content. This is just a list; selecting files and packages to restore happens in the next screen.

By default, YaST restores packages to the / directory (that is, its original location), runs SUSEConfig to make sure everything's in order after the restoration, and reloads your bootloader (if you have one). If you have a good reason to change any of these options, click Expert Options to make those changes. Click Next.

In the final screen, you can select the package(s) and files to restore. By default, YaST restores everything (see Figure 20.11). Choose Deselect All, Select Files to choose your package(s) yourself.

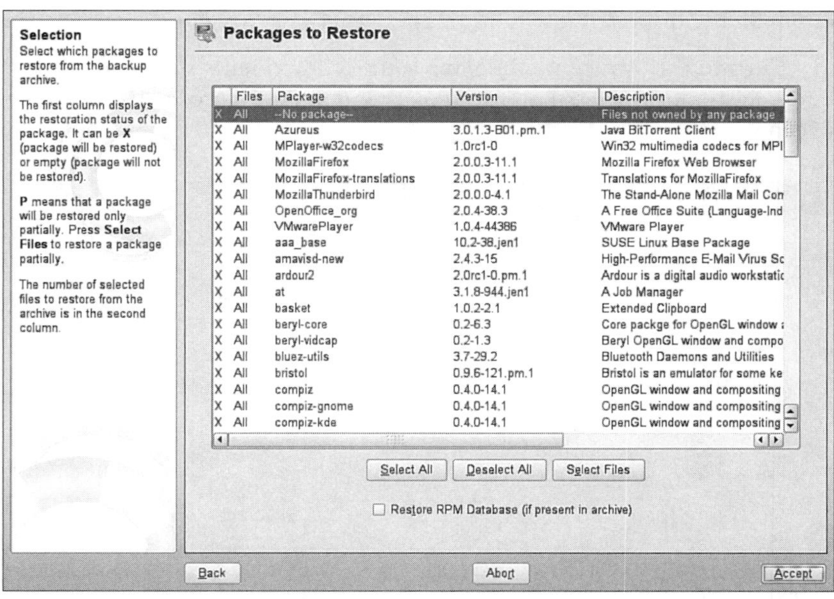

FIGURE 20.11 Choose package(s) and files to restore in the final screen.

When you're finished selecting files, click Accept to restore your files. When the process is complete, you return to the shell prompt. Remove the CD from the drive, and type **`reboot`** to reboot the system normally.

References

- http://www.tldp.org/HOWTO/Linux-Complete-Backup-and-Recovery-HOWTO—How to back up your system to support a bare-metal recovery.
- http://www.tldp.org/LDP/sag/html—The Linux System Administration Guide. See Chapter 12 on backups.
- http://www.tldp.org/HOWTO/Ext2fs-Undeletion.html—Undeleting files from an Ext2/3 file system.
- http://tldp.org/HOWTO/Software-RAID-HOWTO.html—Learn about software-based RAID arrays in Linux.
- http://amanda.sourceforge.net—The Amanda home page.
- http://linuxgazette.net/104/odonovan.html—An excellent and easy-to-understand article on using rsync and cron for automated backups.
- http://www.k3b.org—The home of K3b, the KDE CD/DVD burning tool.
- http://richard.jones.name/google-hacks/gmail-filesystem/gmail-filesystem.html—The GMailFS program, which allows you to convert your gigabyte of Gmail storage into a working Linux file system.
- http://www.bluehaze.com.au/unix/cdbkup.html—Using a shell script to back up to CD.
- http://www.mondorescue.org—A rescue tool that can produce bootable CDs to restore a broken system.

CHAPTER 21

Keeping Your System Current: Package Management

IN THIS CHAPTER

- Installing Software with YaST
- The Basics of the Red Hat Package Management System (RPM)
- Updating Your System with openSUSE Updater
- Updating Your System with Smart
- Compiling Software from Source
- References

OpenSUSE Linux makes hundreds of Linux applications available to you with just a few clicks of your mouse. Many of these are installed along with your system, but you can install many more at any time.

New and updated applications are released constantly. Most applications developed for Linux are not produced by a single company needing to get out a new version on a given date to make this quarter's sales projections. They are released when they are ready.

When security issues are discovered in an application, patches can appear within hours. Keeping up with all these changes could be an administrative nightmare, but openSUSE Linux makes it easy for you. YaST is, after all, Yet another Setup Tool. The Software Management and Online Update modules are designed to make it easy to install the tools you need and keep them as up-to-date as possible.

openSUSE Linux even offers a choice of two update managers, the openSUSE Updater (also known as YaST Software Management or Zypper) and the Smart Package Manager.

In this chapter, you'll learn everything you need to know about installing, removing, and updating your system and its applications.

Installing Software with YaST

You got a taste of how YaST installs software during the initial system installation. You chose a desktop environment (KDE, GNOME or Other), and perhaps adjusted the

Software installation settings. YaST then assembled the packages included in your selection and installed them.

Sooner or later, you will need an application not included in that standard system installation. Unless that application is brand new, chances are you'll find it on the openSUSE Linux DVD. This means you're just a few minutes away from having it installed on your system.

Follow these steps to install any new software package(s) from the openSUSE Linux installation disk.

After inserting the openSUSE Linux installation DVD, start YaST. Enter your SuperUser password and YaST will open to the Software page. Click Software Management. After reading the current package setup, and checking other installation sources (more about these later), YaST displays the Search page (see Figure 21.1):

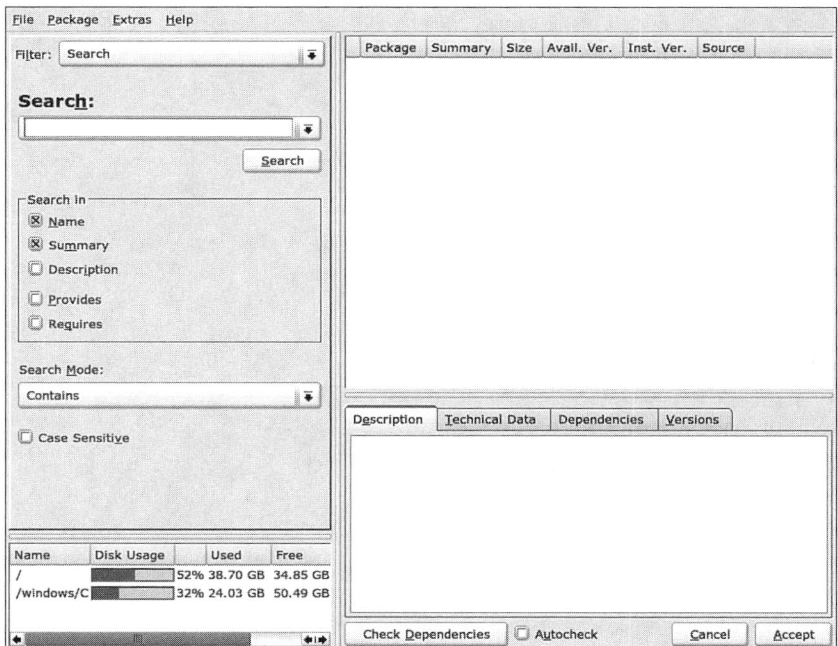

FIGURE 21.1 Search for a specific package or type of package in this YaST screen.

This is a standard search page, and it is excellent for finding specific applications, either by name or function. You can use Search if, for example, you want to see what Perl modules you have installed and what others are included in the distribution. Enter perl- into the Search box (the hyphen is there because all Perl module packages use the syntax perl-<module name>).

Sometimes you might want to explore the DVD for interesting applications or to look for a particular type of program. You have two options for this type of search: Package Groups and Patterns. Use the drop-down Filter menu to display the Package Groups (see Figure 21.2).

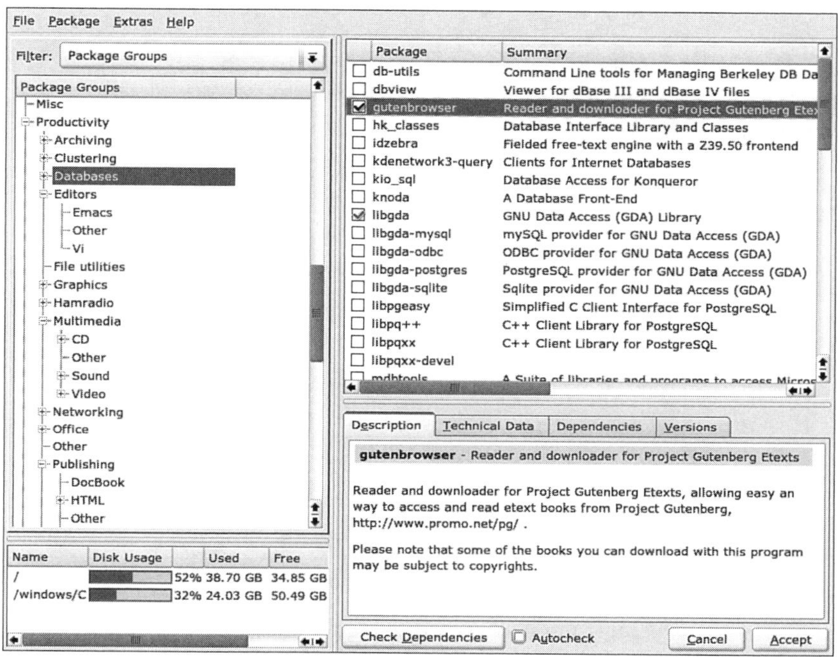

FIGURE 21.2 Use the Package Groups filter to browse through a list of similar or complementary applications.

With Package Groups, everything is organized in a tree by type of application. Click a branch to see all the relevant packages. Some branches are further subdivided for a narrower selection, but the Multimedia branch displays everything in CD, Sound, Video, and Other.

Patterns were introduced in openSUSE 10.2, and are especially useful to new users. You may know, for example, that you want to set up a web server on your system, and so click the Apache package to install it. YaST will automatically add any other packages Apache needs to run on the system (thanks to the Red Hat Package Management (RPM) system that checks for dependencies), which is good. It will not, by itself, select all the packages you need for a "typical" web server. Patterns are an attempt to overcome this weakness.

Choose Patterns from the Filter menu, and you'll see a list of different functions in the upper left pane (Figure 21.3) Scroll down to Web and LAMP Server and select it. A set of packages appears in the upper right pane, with descriptions of each package in the lower right pane. If you check the box next to Web and LAMP server, most of the packages inside the pattern will be marked for installation. You still have the option of choosing to install or not install specific packages, but you likely won't run into an error message when trying to engage some feature you thought would be in the main application.

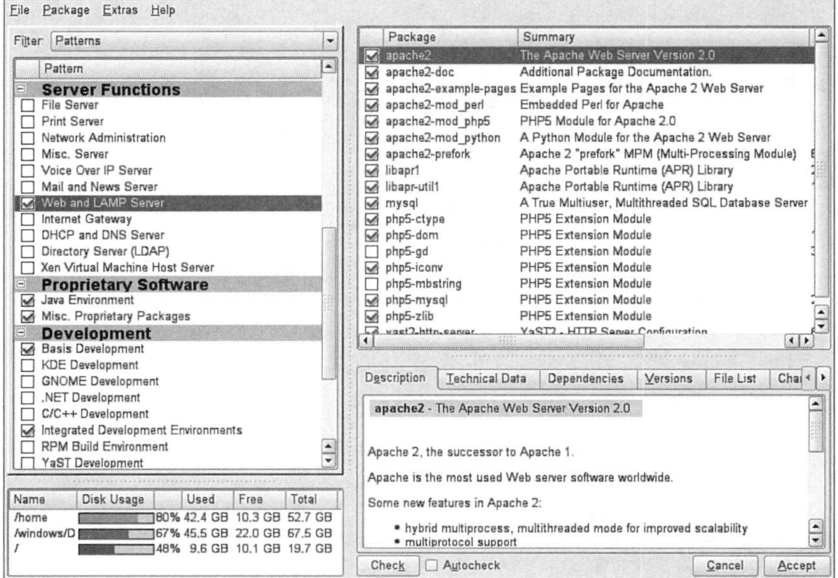

FIGURE 21.3 Patterns help you select the packages you need for common computing tasks.

Whatever filter you choose, YaST will show all the matching packages in the upper-right pane, with pertinent details. Click any individual package for a more detailed description of that package in the lower-right pane. Installed packages will be checked. To install any others, check the box. You can also right-click any package and choose from the following menu options (these will vary depending on whether the package is installed or not):

- Install—Selecting this option will install the package.
- Do Not Install—Selecting this option specifies that the package should not be installed.
- Keep—Selecting this option specifies that a previously installed package should remain installed and not be modified.
- Delete—Selecting this option uninstalls the package.
- Update —Selecting this option specifies that the already installed package be updated with the version residing in the installation source.
- Taboo—Never Install—Selecting this option specifies that the package is to never be installed.
- Protected—Do Not Modify—Selecting this option specifies that the package is already installed and should not be modified.

You can also configure special installation options without right-clicking the package using the check box. Clicking the check box next to an installed package once displays the Update icon, which is really a reinstall. Double-clicking the check box marks the package for removal. Some installed packages appear in red type; this means that the version you have installed now is newer than the package on the DVD. Choosing Update on these packages will revert the current version to the version on the DVD.

When you have finished choosing packages, click Accept to complete the installation. Occasionally, you'll see one of two additional screens. One screen tells you that some other packages will be installed in addition to your selected packages to satisfy some dependencies (see more about dependencies in the next section, "The Basics of the Red Hat Package Management System (RPM)"). The other screen indicates that one or more of your selections will conflict with an existing package and offers suggestions about how to deal with the conflict.

YaST then installs the selected packages (see Figure 21.4), processes any other requests made in this session, and runs SUSEConfig to make sure everything's in order. When completed, YaST asks whether you want to install any other packages. Click Install More to do so or click Finish to close the Install module.

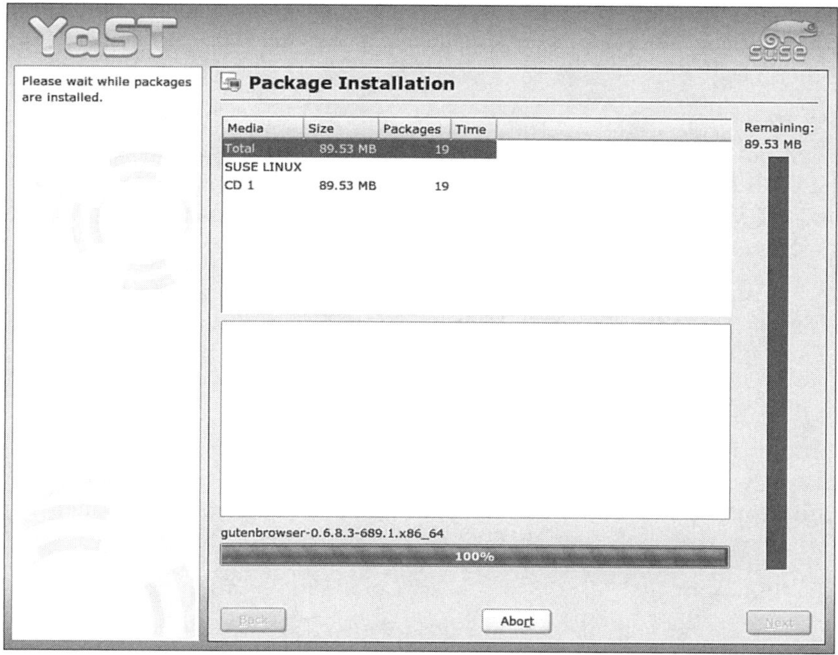

FIGURE 21.4 YaST installs the selected packages.

You can also use YaST to install a package from the command line. To do this, you must first know the name of the package you want to install. When you do, enter the following:

```
yast -i package_name
```

For example, if you wanted to install the dosbox package, you would enter the following:

```
yast -i dosbox
```

Just as when using the Software Management module, installing a package from the command line performs a dependency check and automatically installs any dependent packages required.

After installing any new package, you should always run Online Update to check for updated versions of the software. This protects your system against any bug or security problem that may have been discovered and fixed since the last openSUSE Linux release; it often gives you new features, as well.

You'll learn more about your online update options later in this chapter.

Managing Software Installation Sources

In the preceding example, you used YaST to install additional packages from the openSUSE installation disk. However, you can use YaST to specify other locations from which packages should be installed. You can select an FTP or HTTP server on the Internet, a server on your local network, or a directory on your local hard drive (assuming packages have been copied there).

The YaST openSUSE 10.3 install program even offers to add the basic installation sources. This means you don't have to hunt down your installation DVD when you need new software. This solution is best if you have a broadband Internet connection. You can also do this later in the YaST Software section. Click Additional Product Repositories, and select from the choices on the screen.

Having an alternative installation source can be a lifesaver when you need to install a new package, but have misplaced or damaged your openSUSE Linux CDs. Installing from the Internet also ensures that the packages you are installing are the most current available.

Let's take a look at how to add a YaST installation source. Complete the following:

1. Open a web browser and navigate to http://en.opensuse.org/Additional_YaST_Package_Repositories. This website provides a listing of third party sites you can use as installation sources. Scroll down the list to find one you like.

2. Right-click the link for openSUSE 10.3 and select Copy Link Location from the menu.

3. Start YaST and provide your SuperUser password.

4. In YaST, select Software. You will see a module in the right pane called Software Repositories, as shown in Figure 21.5.

5. Select Software Repositories. The screen in Figure 21.6 is displayed. Notice in Figure 21.6 that your CD or DVD drive is included in the list of installation sources by default.

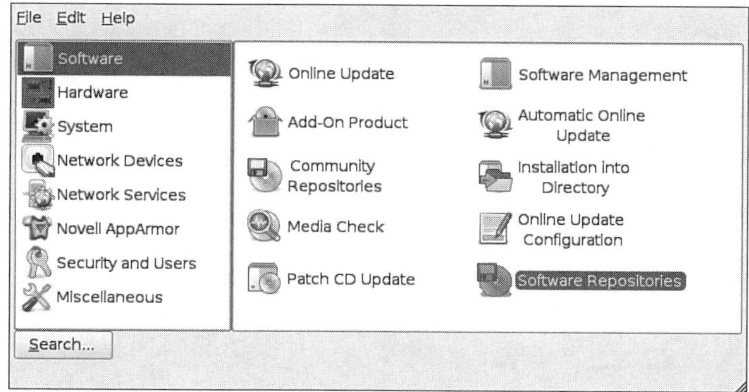

FIGURE 21.5 The YaST ISoftware Repositories module.

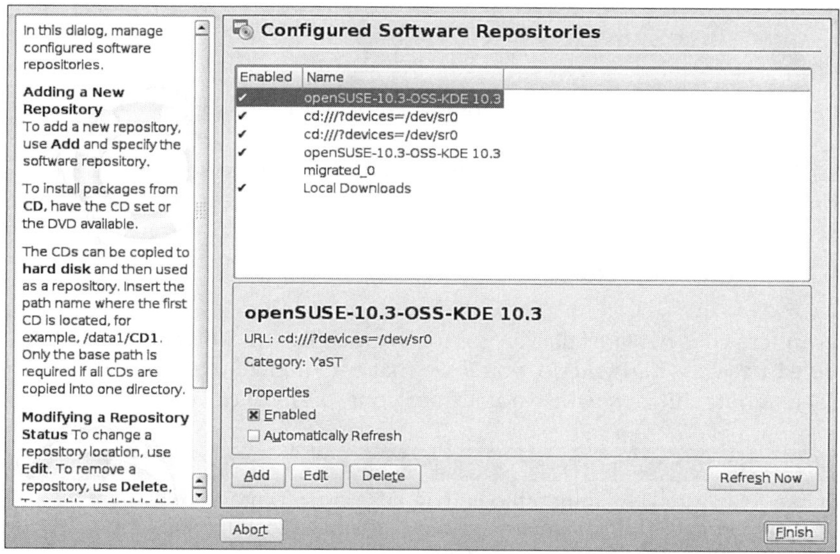

FIGURE 21.6 Setting the installation source.

6. Click Add, and the Media Type screen (Figure 21.7) appears. Choose Specify URL, click Next, and paste the URL for your the site you selected. You can also name the repository if you like.

   When you click Next, YaST probes the source to confirm it has the installation packages and creates the package database on your system. This can take some time, especially if you have a slow connection.

7. You should see the mirror site added as an additional installation source.

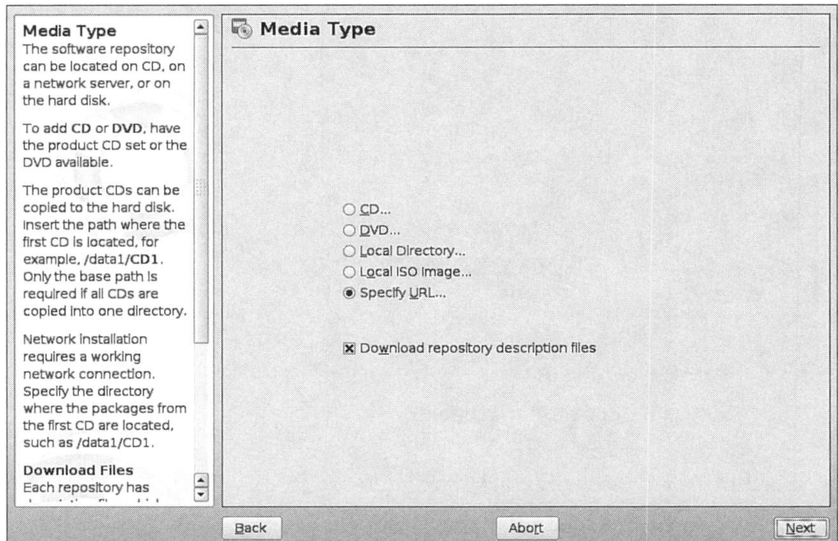

FIGURE 21.7 Choose the type of media or URL for your new installation source.

8. Check the Enabled button to have YaST Software Management list software from this repository each time it runs. If you want YaST to check for new and updated software from this repository automatically, check the Automatically Refresh box.
9. Select Finish to confirm your settings.

At this point, you can test your new installation source by opening the Software Management module in YaST. When you do, you'll see that the module retrieves its package information from the remote mirror site instead of from your local CD or DVD drive.

TIP

Are you one of those folks who likes to ride the cutting edge of software development? Add the openSUSE Factory to your installation sources. This isn't recommended for production machines, as the latest untested packages are included here. You can pick up newer stuff this way, though often at a cost of less stability on your system. Find out more at http://en.opensuse.org/Factory.

With this in mind, we need to relate a little background about applications and packages.

The Basics of the Red Hat Package Management System (RPM)

The RPM system was inaugurated in 1995 to manage applications in Red Hat Linux 2.0. It was the successor to a collection of Perl scripts that functioned as the earliest Linux packaging tools. Rewritten in the C language in 1996, it quickly became the de facto standard for managing application installations for several distributions, including (open)SUSE Linux.

The basic idea behind RPM is to have a single pristine archive of an application's source code that can build packages for different systems and that can track new versions. An RPM database of all available applications is installed on your computer (in /var/lib/rpm) and is accessed by YaST and other configuration tools to determine exactly what is on your system, what might be new and updated, and what files each package provides that another package might need to run properly.

This last part, the dependency resolver, is one of the features that made RPM so successful among Linux developers and distributors. When you look at a package in YaST, click the Dependencies tab in the lower-right corner. Here, under Provides, is a list of every file included in the package. After the Provides list, the Requires list tells you every file that this package needs to run, and the Prerequisites list tells you what needs to be installed before you install this package (down to the minimum version number, if necessary). Next up is the list of packages that this package will replace or make obsolete. You have to hope that some other package doesn't require one of these; if it does, you'll get a warning. Finally, there is a list of conflicts; installing this package will create problems for applications on this list.

RPM packages are now more secure, as packagers can include digital signatures encrypted with GNU Privacy Guard (GnuPG). All packages produced by openSUSE Linux are signed, so you know they are genuine.

NOTE

Interested in packaging your own software with RPM? See Chapter 28, "Programming Tools."

Downloading RPM Packages Outside of YaST

openSUSE Linux is known for including the largest number of application packages of the major Linux distributions, but it doesn't include every application ever created. Because Linux developers come up with new ideas all the time, there's always something new to try as well.

You can download and install just about any RPM package from any source and run it on your openSUSE Linux system. It's possible that new packages may have some ill effect on your system's stability, but that's rare, especially with RPMs.

When you visit a software repository like freshmeat.net, you can see dozens of new and updated applications posted daily. Many developers build RPMs for their applications to make things relatively easy for users to install. Some even build separate RPMs for Red Hat and openSUSE users.

You should create a single directory for your downloaded files. It should be in your home directory. Set up your browser(s) to download all files to that directory. You should do this because you can then add that directory to YaST's installation sources and directly install new RPMs in YaST.

To add your ~/download directory to YaST's installation sources, follow these steps.

1. Open YaST. Select Software, Software Repositories.
2. Click Add. Select Local Directory from the Media Type screen.
3. Type in or browse to the ~/download directory. Click OK to confirm.
4. The directory should appear in the main window.

Now when you download an RPM package to that directory, you can open YaST's Software Management module and install that package.

TIP

KDE/Konqueror users get a bonus convenience when downloading RPMs with the Konqueror web browser. After it is downloaded, Konqueror displays an Install with YaST button. Click it to run YaST's Install module.

In GNOME Nautilus, right-click on any RPM and select Open With, then Install Software (or Smart Package Manager, if this is installed) from the context menu to get this same functionality.

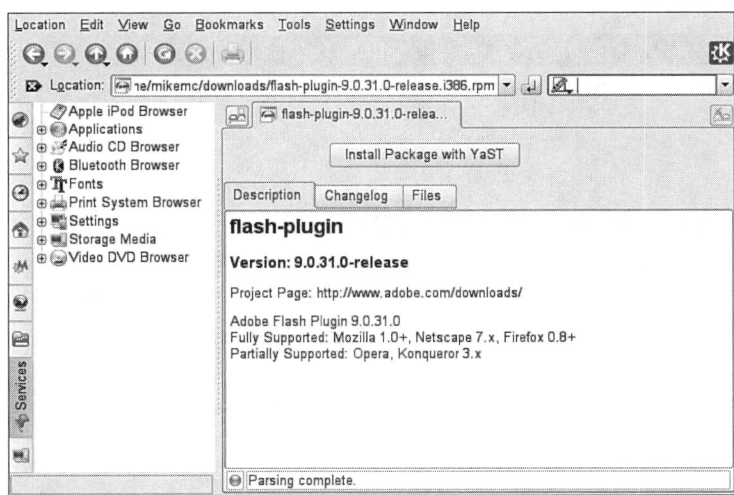

FIGURE 21.8 Install RPMs directly from Konqueror with the Install Package with YaST button.

Updating Your System with openSUSE Updater

An Internet connection is all you need to keep your openSUSE Linux system current. This section tells you about using the openSUSE update system to maintain your system in tip-top shape. Every package posted to a YaST server has been tested by SUSE staff to ensure that it works correctly with your system.

Running the openSUSE Update System

For the most control over the update process, run Online Update manually. You can choose which server to access and which applications to update. You can also get more information on the patch applied to the application. It takes a little time, but it is not especially complex.

For a long time, SUSE maintained just a few online update servers, in Germany and in a few other European locations. Online Update always checked for a new list of servers whenever it opened, but the list rarely changed. In early 2004, many more update servers came online, and YOU delivered a geographic list to users.

You will first want to set up and configure your update server. Go to the YaST Software page, and select Online Update Configuration. The first time you use this tool, you will register your copy of openSUSE Linux with Novell. After that, you will just change your update server.

In the first screen, select Configure Now, and have the Hardware Profile and Optional Information boxes checked. Click Next to have YaST find a nearby server.

YaST will check your update server and display a list of packages with new updates. Security-related updates will be checked automatically, and you can select from the remaining choices. Click Accept to begin the download and installation process.

When you have configured your update server, go to Online Update to check for updates. YaST will compare its list of currently installed packages to the packages in the Update Server. This can take some time if you have just reconfigured your update server. If there are updates available, you'll see a screen similar to Figure 21.9. At the top of the screen is the list of available updates. Security updates are marked in red.

You can see a detailed description of each patch in the left middle pane. In the case of security patches, this describes the problem solved by the patch. For more mundane updates (bug fixes, new releases, and other patches unrelated to system security), the level of detail in the descriptions runs the gamut. Click Accept to download and install the updated packages.

Online Update will download and install the selected packages, giving you an onscreen progress report (see Figure 21.10). When the download is complete, click Finish to run SUSEConfig and return to the YaST Control Center.

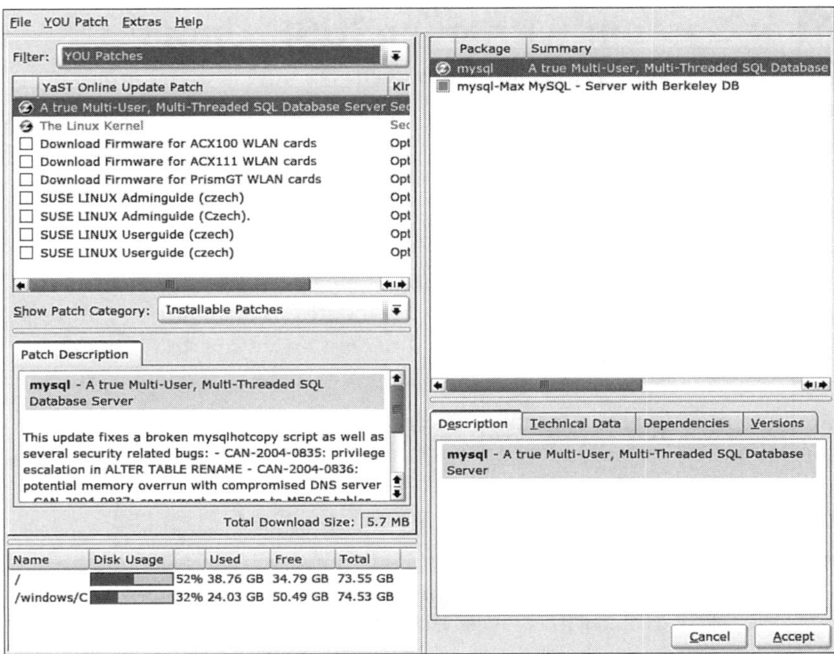

FIGURE 21.9 The YOU Update screen lists security updates (marked in red) with detailed descriptions of the problem the fix solves.

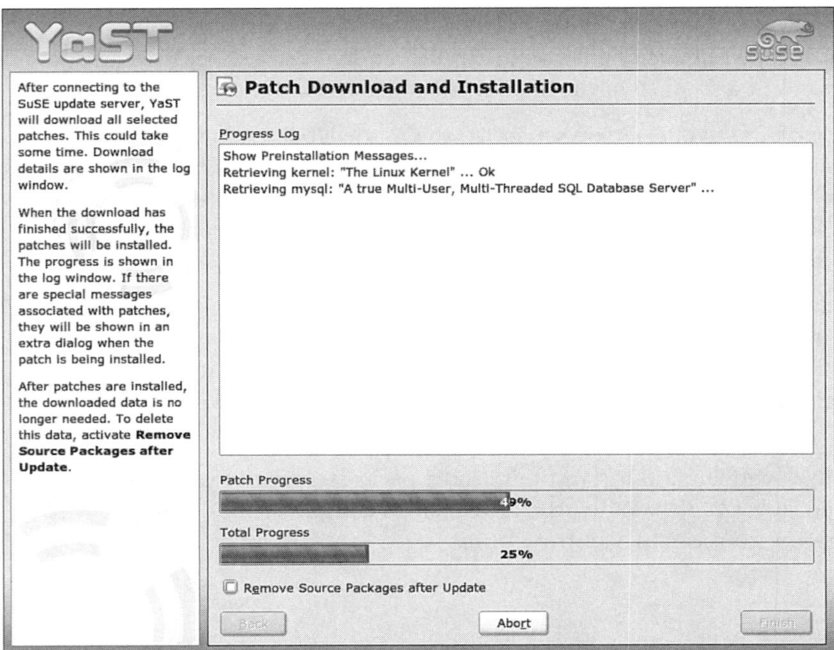

FIGURE 21.10 The progress bar keeps you informed on the download and installation process.

That's all there is to it. With the exception of kernel updates, you should never have to reboot the system to complete an update.

Using the Online Updater to Monitor Update Servers

Wondering what that blue circle is in your taskbar? The openSUSE Updater tool will work overtime to see that you're currentwith all updates. It changes colors to tell you what's up, and will also post a message when there is a new goodie available.

Right-click on the Updater icon to set how often Updater should check the update server. The default is 24 hours; use the arrows to move that interval up or down.

TIP

Can't find the openSUSE Updater icon? From the KDE menu (or the main menu in GNOME), go to System, Desktop Applet to start openSUSE Updater.

Updating Your System with Smart

Users of Debian Linux and its descendants (Ubuntu, Xandros, and the like) can be a little smug about their package management system, the Advanced Package Tool (APT). Using APT to install most packages from the command line involves typing **`apt-get install <package>`** and APT does the rest.

Developers for the Brazilian Linux distribution Conectiva first created apt4rpm to bring the benefits of APT to RPM-based distributions. Eventually the vision grew to try coming up with a single package management system that could support various methods of updating Linux systems, a "smart" package manager. And this is what we have, the Smart Package Manager.

NOTE

APT is still available in openSUSE as a command-line-only application. Find it in the System/Packages group in YaST Software Management. It is not under active development, however.

Smart works a lot like the YaST package management system. Set up your software repositories, require a SuperUser to install or updte packages. Check the repositories regularly, and pull the new packages along with any other dependent packages down when the arrive. Offer a command line interface. What makes Smart perhaps a better choice is its speed and ease of use.

The first time you run Smart (and supply the SuperUser password), it will automatically find and set up several popular repositories (called Channels in Smart), so you don't have to look for places to download from. It will also access the RPM database to see what you have installed already. These are indicated by a green box next to the package name (as in Figure 21.11).

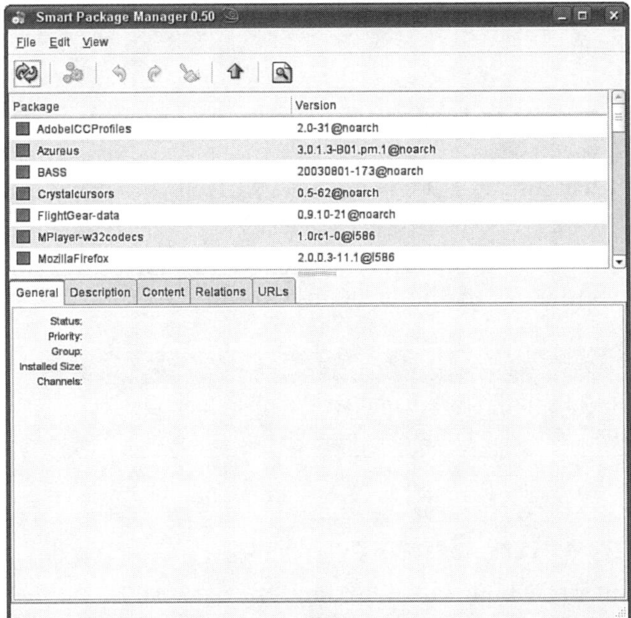

FIGURE 21.11 Installed packages are marked with a filled in box in the Smart Package Updater.

To see what's new for your system, click the Update Channels icon (which looks like a pair of arrows chasing each other in a circle). This update will take a few minutes, depending on how many packages have changed and your connection speed. When the update is complete, go to the View menu and click Hide Old. The list will update to show only packages that are newer than the ones on your DVD, including upgrades from your installed packages and packages not on the openSUSE DVD. If you just want to update currently installed packages, uncheck Hide Old and check Hide Non-Upgrades.

Check the box next to the package you want to install or update and Smart will tell you if other packages need to be installed with it. When you've completed your selections, click the Apply Marked Changes icon (the gears) to begin the download. Smart will first display all the changes to be made so you can back out if necessary.

A progress bar will mark each package, and the overall process. When the download completes, Smart will "commit the transaction;" that is, install or update the package(s). If the install generates any messages, these will appear in a separate log window.

Finally, Smart will update its cache, which is the key to its speedy display. When this is finished, you can explore the database some more, install more packages, or exit out.

Adding a new channel is very similar to adding an installation source to YaST. Go to the View menu and select Channels. You'll see the current list of channels. Click New, and select Read Channel Description from URL. Supply the URL and click OK. Smart will find the repository information, and handle the setup.

Want to install RPMs from a local directory? Again, click New from the Channels screen. Click Provide Channel Information, and point to the appropriate directory.

Compiling Software from Source

Some programs are too complex or too specialized for the programmer to go through the trouble of creating RPMs. Thus, the programmer archives the source code in a tarball and sends it out. Often, simply extracting the code into an appropriate directory is all that's needed to make the application work, as you've seen with several of the blogging tools in Chapter 14, "Creating Basic Websites," and the Azureus BitTorrent client in Chapter 17, "Secure File Transfer."

Other programs must be compiled before they can work. This section will help you do this. Before beginning, you will need to have the GNU Compiler Collection (gcc) installed to handle this task.

First, when compiling new source code, create a new subdirectory in your home directory called source. This will let you compile your code as a user and help prevent any bad (or even malicious) code from harming your system.

Now the task is to extract the archive into the new ~/source directory. You can do this in GNOME File Roller or Ark for KDE, but it will be faster from the shell. Change directory to the ~/download folder (or wherever your source archive is sitting). Depending on the archive format of the original file, type one of the following commands:

```
tar xzvf <package>.tgz -C ~/source
tar xzvf <package>.tar.gz -C ~/source
tar xjvf <package>.bz -C ~/source
tar xjvf <package>.tar.bz2 -C ~/source
```

The first two are different extensions for a tar/gnuzip archive, whereas the last two were archived using bzip. The -C switch extracted the archived files to the ~/source directory. If you are not sure what archiving method was used, use the file command to help you determine the format. Type **`file <package>`**.

Now change to the extracted program directory under the ~/source directory. Look for a file called something like README or INSTALL (and usually named in ALL CAPS so that you can find it more easily). This file will have detailed instructions on how to compile and make the program work. Chances are that these instructions will be some variation on the Configure/Make/Make Install process. This means you will first run a script called configure, as follows:

```
./configure
```

This script confirms that all dependencies are met and the build environment is solid. When this script runs successfully, compile the program with the make utility included in gcc:

```
make
```

Finally, log in as the SuperUser and install the program with the same make utility:

```
make install
```

This should safely install your new source program.

References

- http://www.novell.com/coolsolutions/feature/16592.html —A screenshot-filled YaST tutorial.
- http://www.suse.de/~sh/YaST2-Package-Manager—Written to explain the big changes in YaST with v8.1, there's a lot of good information here on how YaST works.
- http://www.rpm.org—Home for information on the Red Hat Package Management system. The site includes an online version of Ed Bailey's 2000 book, *Maximum RPM*.
- http://labix.org/smart—Home of the Smart Package Manager. Downloads, FAQs, mailing list, etc.
- http://packman.links2linux.org—Excellent repository for packages not yet included in the official distribution. Download directly or use APT.
- http://rpmfind.userfriendly.net/—A U.S. mirror for the RPMFind search engine.
- http://rpmseek.com—Find more RPM packages here.
- http://freshmeat.net—A giant repository of Linux and other open source software, organized by date received. Thus, the freshest meat is at the top.
- http://en.opensuse.org/Additional_YaST_Package_Repositories—Find more installation sources for openSUSE packages here.
- http://en.opensuse.org/Factory—The openSUSE Factory repository. If you want to live on the cutting, if unstable, edge of openSUSE development, untested RPMs are located here.

PART V

Advanced System Administration

IN THIS PART

CHAPTER 22

Managing the Boot Process and Other Services

IN THIS CHAPTER

- Understanding the Boot Process
- System Services and Runlevels
- Controlling Services at Boot with the YaST Runlevel Editor
- Manually Starting and Stopping Services
- System Monitoring Tools
- References

To begin understanding how your Linux computer works, you need to know how it starts. Booting in Linux is a three-step process; during this process, the computer's basic input/output system (BIOS) starts the machine's hardware without a care as to what operating system its owner (you) wants to run.

It hands control of the machine to a boot manager (such as LILO or GRUB), which does care about finding at least one operating system on the machine.

Finally, you tell the boot manager what file system to run, and it does. The Linux kernel then manages the rest of the session.

In this chapter, you learn exactly what you need to know about the Linux boot process. Some of this information applies to other operating systems, but in this chapter, we focus on starting up and booting openSUSE Linux.

Determining which services run in a Linux box partly depends on what purpose(s) the Linux box is intended to serve. Its system state, or *runlevel*, controls what starts and what doesn't. Ultimately, you have the power, as SuperUser, to define which services run when.

You'll walk through a boot process to see exactly what happens when your computer starts up. You will use the YaST Runlevel Editor to manage services. You'll also look at some of the tools you can use to monitor your system and keep it in tip-top shape.

Understanding the Boot Process

All x86-type computers, whether running processors from Intel or AMD—no matter what operating system they have—start up the same way. BIOS software that sits on a specialized chip activates all the circuitry on the motherboard, and occasionally other hardware connected to the motherboard, and then goes looking for a boot manager—a piece of software code that starts an operating system. This boot manager code can sit on a hard drive (where it's called the Master Boot Record, or MBR), a floppy disk, a CD-ROM, or even on another computer if the system is using the network file system (NFS). This bootloader software tells the BIOS where the Linux kernel is located, how to load it into memory, and how to start it.

Starting to Boot: BIOS to Boot Manager

If all goes well in the hardware initialization, the BIOS locates a special hexadecimal value written to the volume, which makes the volume bootable.

The order in which it looks for this is in the BIOS settings, which you can access by pressing a certain key or key combination while the BIOS is still in command. The traditional order was floppy disk, hard drive, and then some other place. In recent years, bootable CD-ROMs joined the BIOS options and now should be first on the list.

Any modern BIOS should be able to search a variety of devices to find a bootable volume, but the BIOS always stops looking upon finding the first bootable volume. This is why it's a good idea to remove your openSUSE Linux installation CD after adding new software to your system. If you don't, the next time you boot will be to the CD. This is presumably why the CD now has Boot from Hard Drive as the default option on its opening menu.

NOTE

Your BIOS will alert you with a series of beeps if it finds a hardware problem that makes your system unbootable. Each motherboard manufacturer has a different system of generating those beeps, so consult your motherboard manual to learn the code, or contact your PC vendor or manufacturer to try to fix the problem.

When the BIOS finds the bootloader code, it then looks for the MBR, the first sector on the hard drive. This is the most important sector on the disk because the bootloader code (just 446 bytes) and the partition table (64 bytes) reside there. Having properly initialized the hardware, the BIOS can now place the bootloader code into memory and hand over the boot process to the bootloader. The bootloader code that sits in the MBR has one job—to start the full bootloader program, GRUB by default, and load it into memory.

Choosing a Boot Manager: GRUB Versus LILO

You may not realize it unless you are dual booting multiple operating systems, but after your BIOS starts firing up the fan, the microprocessor chip, and the power supply, a boot manager, or *bootloader*, takes over the process until the kernel starts up.

Linux supports a variety of open-source and proprietary boot managers, but you can install only two with YaST: the Grand Unified Bootloader (GRUB) and the Linux Loader (LILO). GRUB has been the default bootloader for SUSE Linux since v8.2, but LILO still runs quite a few systems, and you may want to use it instead.

LILO succeeded `loadlin` as the primary Linux bootloader and seems to be in the long process of being superseded by GRUB. LILO carries out its single task, booting to a file system, well. It is not quite as flexible or as configurable as GRUB. Nonetheless, it is still the default bootloader for systems in which the Root partition is installed on CPU-dependent RAID controllers (such as many Promise or Highpoint controllers), Software RAID, or a Logical Volume (LVM) managed disk.

The chief difference between the two bootloaders is in how they find and load file systems. LILO looks for a file system based on where the partition table says it is. GRUB can read and identify several file systems (ext2, ext3, ReiserFS, JFS, XFS, Minix, and DOS).

In YaST, the Boot Loader Settings module is on the System page. You can set LILO as the default if you want in the Boot Loader Installation tab (see Figure 22.1) and set many other options in the Section Management screen (Figure 22.3).

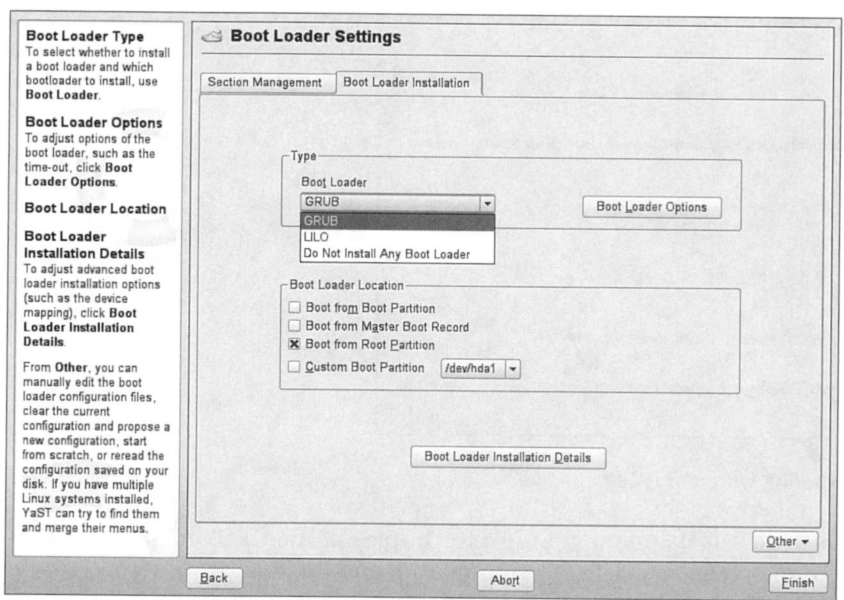

FIGURE 22.1 Select and configure your bootloader.

By default, GRUB displays a menu, allowing you to boot openSUSE Linux from the hard drive, from a floppy drive, or into *fail-safe* mode. Fail-safe mode loads a kernel version with a set of parameters that makes it possible to boot with some hardware problems. If there's another operating system on your computer, GRUB will list this on your boot menu as well. After 8 seconds, GRUB will boot the first item on the menu; that is, it will boot openSUSE 10.2.

NOTE

At the bottom of the GRUB menu, you can specify options for the kernel, if you are so inclined.

You can see how each process builds on the previous one, allowing different operating systems to work on the same hardware.

The GRUB menu you see is controlled by the GRUB configuration file, which is located at `/boot/grub/menu.lst`. A sample `menu.lst` file is shown in Figure 22.2.

NOTE

You can also view and edit the menu.lst file in the YaST Boot Loader module as well. Click Other in the lower-right corner of the screen, and select Edit Configuration Files from the menu. Use the drop-down menu to view /boot/grub/menu.lst.

```
# Modified by YaST2. Last modification on Sun Feb 18 15:38:20 CST 2007
default 0
timeout 8
##YaST - generic_mbr
gfxmenu (hd0,1)/boot/message
##YaST - activate


###Don't change this comment - YaST2 identifier: Original name: linux###
title openSUSE 10.2
    root (hd0,1)
    kernel /boot/vmlinuz root=/dev/hda2 vga=0x31a resume=/dev/hda1 splash=silent showopts elevator=
    initrd /boot/initrd


|
###Don't change this comment - YaST2 identifier: Original name: floppy###
title Floppy
    rootnoverify (hd0,0)
    chainloader (fd0)+1
    makeactive


###Don't change this comment - YaST2 identifier: Original name: failsafe###
title Failsafe -- openSUSE 10.2
    root (hd0,1)
    kernel /boot/vmlinuz root=/dev/hda2 vga=normal showopts ide=nodma apm=off acpi=off noresume
edd=off 3
    initrd /boot/initrd
```

FIGURE 22.2 Working with *menu.lst*.

The first portion of `menu.lst` defines options for the display of the GRUB menu, such as the color scheme of the menu, the default menu option, and the number of seconds (timeout) before GRUB runs the default menu option.

Following the display options is a list of items that will be displayed in the GRUB menu. Each menu item begins with "title." Notice in Figure 22.2 that this particular GRUB menu will display three items:

- openSUSE 10.2
- Floppy
- Failsafe—openSUSE 10.2

The remaining lines tell GRUB where to find the operating system files needed to run Linux. These include the following:

- root—This command sets the current root device to the specified device.
- kernel—This command loads the primary boot image from the boot image file.
- initrd—This command loads an initial ramdisk for the boot image.

To configure how GRUB boots your system, you can either manually edit `menu.lst` with a text editor, or you can use the YaST System, Boot Loader module, shown in Figure 22.3.

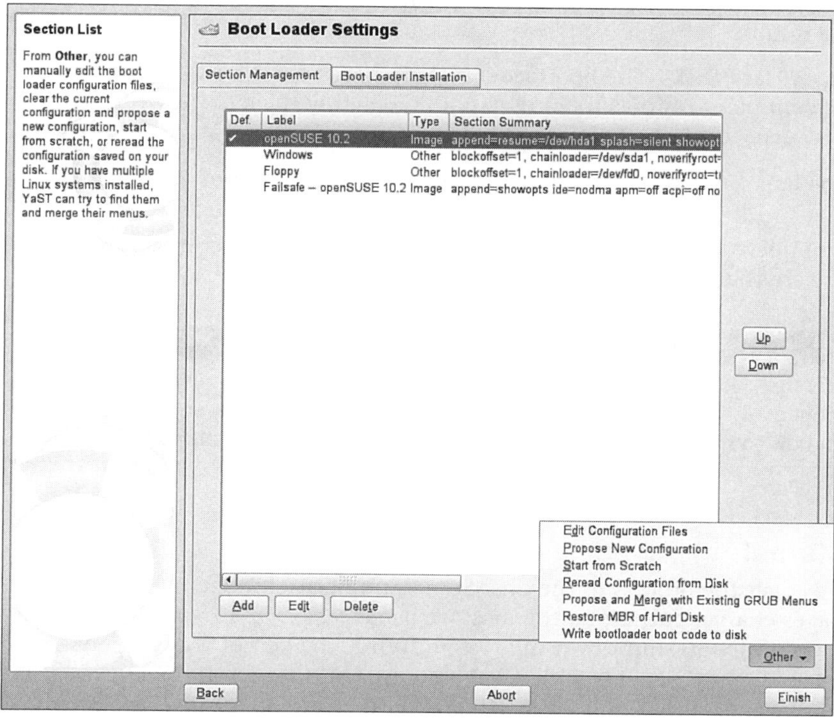

FIGURE 22.3 Configuring GRUB in YaST.

The Boot Loader Settings have become much more automated in openSUSE. You can still edit your configuration files manually if you have the desire, but the options you have to let YaST handle the task are greater. To see these options, click Other to see a drop-down menu with your configuration options (Figure 22.3). If you have trouble booting with GRUB, this is the place to come. The options include the following:

- Edit Configuration Files—Manually edit the `/boot/grub/device.map` (identifies physical drives), `/boot/grub/menu.lst`, and `/etc/grub.conf` (specifies how grub loads) files. For experts only.

- Propose New Configuration—If you're having trouble, this is probably the first option to select. YaST takes another look at your system, and suggests modifying `menu.lst`.
- Start from Scratch—Delete everything in the Section Management window before applying another option. All configuration files are backed up, so this isn't a permanent deletion.
- Reread Configuration from Disk—Pull up the current configuration, either live or backup.
- Propose and Merge with Existing GRUB Menus—If the live configuration file(s) differ from the current backup, check both files and propose the best configuration based on the results.
- Restore MBR of Hard Disk—The bootloader code is stored on the Master Boot Record. This command restores the original MBR, deleting the current GRUB configuration (`/etc/grub.conf`).
- Write bootloader boot code to disk—Restore the new /etc/grub.conf to the MBR.

When you have completed your changes, click Finish to write the new configuration to your system. These are the settings that will govern your next boot.

NOTE

In addition to manually editing the `menu.lst` file and using YaST, you can also use the GRUB shell to configure how your system boots. Simply enter **`grub`** at the shell prompt. To learn how to manipulate GRUB from the shell, see the grub man page.

Loading the Kernel

When GRUB hands over the process to the openSUSE Linux kernel, it leaves the scene. The kernel now takes charge, putting up the message `Uncompressing Linux...`; it is present and available to you until you shut down the system. While the kernel boots, openSUSE Linux puts up a nice blue wallpaper to hide all the boring text that scrolls by as the kernel initializes first your peripheral hardware, then the hard drive and attending file systems, followed by the serial ports. Press the Esc key to watch the boot process unfold.

As a user, or even as an administrator, you don't have much direct interaction with the Linux kernel. You run applications, which occasionally interact with the kernel to get things done. In the kernel's view of things, an application is simply a process, one of many it deals with. The father of all processes, which the kernel loads soon after the kernel itself loads, is called `init`, located in the `/sbin` directory. The rest of the boot process (and later, the shutdown process) is really handled by `init`, not the kernel. All other processes are started by `init` or one of its child processes. `init` is centrally configured by the `/etc/inittab` file.

After activating the serial ports, the kernel runs a series of boot scripts, located at `/etc/_rc.d/boot.d`, which activates (and, if required, mounts) still more devices and local file systems.

Then `boot.clock` sets up the system clock, `ldconfig` identifies the current time zone, and local networking interfaces are turned on via `boot.sysctrl`, `boot.localnet` (for the loop-back interface), and `boot.isapnp`.

Finally, the kernel's System Boot Control declares

```
The system has been set up
```

and runs `/etc/init.d/boot.local`. This program invokes the appropriate runlevel for the system. There is much more on runlevels in the next section, but a standard networked desktop will launch Runlevel 5 as it hits the home stretch of the boot process.

At Runlevel 5, networking services are started and various other services and the system logs come online. The sound driver, keyboard maps, CUPS printer interfaces, mail transfer agent, and `xinetd` Internet services come next.

Finally, the kernel starts the X Window System and the display manager (KDM by default) that allows the user to log in. Logging in loads the desired desktop, and you're done.

NOTE

To closely examine your most recent boot process, open `/var/log/boot.msg` in a text editor, or open the YaST View Startup Log module from the Miscellaneous page.

System Services and Runlevels

There are several ways to start and stop services. openSUSE Linux uses the *runlevel* method that originated with Unix System V. Runlevels determine when, or if, a service runs. They also determine the order in which services are started.

Runlevels, generally speaking, identify the type of use for the computer. Table 22.1 explains the different runlevels in openSUSE Linux; notice that they correspond somewhat directly to the basic choices of software installations presented to you during the initial installation of openSUSE Linux.

The minimum installation is roughly equivalent to Single User Mode, Runlevel 1, whereas the minimum graphical install corresponds to Runlevel 3. The gluttons who want a graphical desktop use Runlevel 5.

TABLE 22.1 Runlevels

Runlevel	Description
0	System Halt, system shutdown.
1	Single User, or rescue, mode. Only root can log in.
2	Local Multiuser mode without remote networking.
3	Full Multiuser mode with network.
4	Not used.
5	Full Multiuser mode with network and X display manager (also fail-safe mode when booted directly from the boot prompt).
6	Reboot.

While the system is running, you can actually change your current runlevel. When you change runlevels, all services essential to your current runlevel are stopped and the services essential to the new runlevel are started.

To do this, enter the `init` command at a shell prompt, followed by the runlevel number to which you want to switch. For example, if you want to switch from Runlevel 5 (complete with X and a desktop environment) to Runlevel 3 (the minimal graphical environment), you would complete the following:

- Open a terminal session and switch to your root user account.
- At the shell prompt, run the init script for Runlevel 3 by entering **`init 3`**.

When you do this, `init` consults the `/etc/inittab` configuration file and runs `/etc/_init.d/rc` with 3 (the new runlevel) as a parameter. The `rc` utility runs stop scripts for every service that is missing a start script in `/etc/init.d/rc3.d` but that has a stop script in `/etc/init.d/rc5.d`.

Stop scripts have filenames that begin with K (for "kill"), and start scripts begin with S (for "start"). The numbers following the letter indicate an order for each script to be executed. This prevents files with some dependencies from crashing before they stop.

After all the unnecessary Runlevel 5 scripts have been stopped, the start scripts run for services needed in Runlevel 3 but not in Runlevel 5.

When you installed openSUSE Linux, you were given the option to set your system's default runlevel. By default, this is Runlevel 5. This is usually the best option for most users. However, suppose it isn't the right choice for you. Suppose you want to use your openSUSE Linux system as a server (which it can do very well), and you don't want the CPU spending unneeded cycles redrawing your graphical screens. You would prefer it to boot, by default, to a text-based prompt while retaining the capability to run your graphical desktop when needed. In this situation, Runlevel 3 would be a better choice.

You can set your default runlevel in two ways. First, you can edit your `/etc/inittab` configuration file with a text editor, as shown in Figure 22.4.

Notice that about three-fourths of the way down the screen, a line reads as follows:

```
id:5:initdefault:
```

This line specifies which runlevel your system should boot to by default. If you want to change this to Runlevel 3, you should complete the following:

1. Open a terminal session and switch to your root user account.
2. At the shell prompt, enter **`vi /etc/inittab`**.
3. Arrow down to the `id:5:initdefault:` line in the file.
4. Press Insert.
5. Change the 5 to a **3**.

6. Press Esc.
7. Enter **:exit**.
8. Reboot your system.


```
#
# /etc/inittab
#
# Copyright (c) 1996-2002 SuSE Linux AG, Nuernberg, Germany.  All rights reserve
d.
#
# Author: Florian La Roche, 1996
# Please send feedback to http://www.suse.de/feedback
#
# This is the main configuration file of /sbin/init, which
# is executed by the kernel on startup. It describes what
# scripts are used for the different run-levels.
#
# All scripts for runlevel changes are in /etc/init.d/.
#
# This file may be modified by SuSEconfig unless CHECK_INITTAB
# in /etc/sysconfig/suseconfig is set to "no"
#

# The default runlevel is defined here
id:5:initdefault:

# First script to be executed, if not booting in emergency (-b) mode
si::bootwait:/etc/init.d/boot

"/etc/inittab" 97L, 2926C                                    1,1           Top
```

FIGURE 22.4 Editing the `/etc/inittab` file.

When the system boots, it will enter Runlevel 3, as shown in Figure 22.5.

```
Setting current sysctl status from /etc/sysctl.conf
net.ipv4.icmp_echo_ignore_broadcasts = 1
net.ipv4.conf.all.rp_filter = 1
                                                                        done
Enabling syn flood protection                                           done
Disabling IP forwarding                                                 done
Disabling IPv6 forwarding                                               done
Disabling IPv6 privacy                                                  done
                                                                        done
System Boot Control: The system has been                                set up
System Boot Control: Running /etc/init.d/boot.local                     done
INIT: Entering runlevel: 3
Boot logging started on /dev/tty1(/dev/console) at Thu Sep  8 13:59:21 2005
Master Resource Control: previous runlevel: N, switching to runlevel:   3
Starting D-BUS daemon                                                   done
Starting irqbalance                                                     failed
Initializing random number generator                                    done
Starting resource manager                                               done
Starting VMware Tools services in the virtual machine:
   Switching to guest configuration:                           done
cat: /proc/pci: No such file or directory
   DMA setup:                                                  done
   Guest operating system daemon:                              done
Setting up network interfaces:
    lo
    lo        IP address: 127.0.0.1/8                                   done
Waiting for mandatory devices:  eth-id-00:0c:29:59:38:13
19 17
    eth2      device: Advanced Micro Devices [AMD] 79c970 [PCnet32 LANCE] (rev 10)
    eth2      configuration: eth-id-00:0c:29:59:38:13
    eth2      DHCP client NOT running
    eth2      IP address: 192.168.1.33/24 (DHCP)
    eth2      IP address: 192.168.1.33/24
_
                                                                   SUSE Linux
```

FIGURE 22.5 Booting into Runlevel 3.

When it's finished booting, your system will display a simple, text-based screen asking you to authenticate. After logging in, you can optionally start your graphical environment by entering **startx** from the shell prompt.

The second way you can change your default runlevel is with YaST. If you're not comfortable using Linux text editing tools, you can let YaST do the work for you. To change your default runlevel using YaST, complete the following:

1. Start YaST and navigate to the System, System Services (Runlevel) module.
2. Select Expert Mode. The screen in Figure 22.6 is displayed.

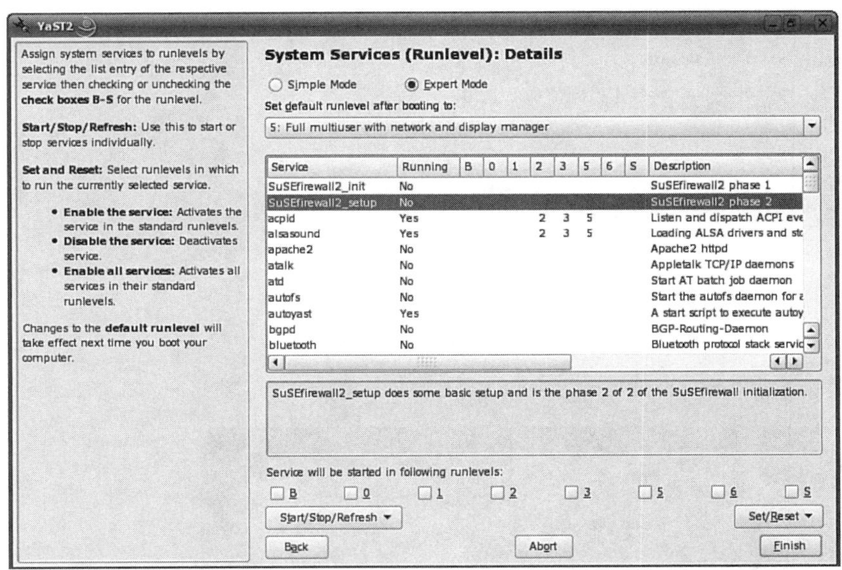

FIGURE 22.6 Changing the default runlevel in YaST.

3. In the Set Default Runlevel After Booting drop-down list, select the default runlevel for your system.
4. Select Finish.

The next time you restart your system, it will boot to the default runlevel you configured.

Controlling Services at Boot with the YaST Runlevel Editor

YaST provides a startlingly easy way for system administrators to manage which services run at boot. The YaST Runlevel Editor module is easy to understand and gives you important information about each service. The start/stop process is nothing more than a mouse click.

How wonderful, you're thinking. A nice change. Experienced system administrators may cringe a little, though. It is so easy to destroy your system. The help text to the left of the Runlevel Editor, shown in Figure 22.7, offers a relatively calm warning: The `Runlevel Editor` is an expert tool. Only change settings if you know what you are doing, otherwise your system might not function properly afterwards.

That's fine as far as it goes. The Caution box coming up next may be closer to the point.

CAUTION

You can render your system unbootable if you do not take particular care when starting new services, and especially when stopping existing services. Using the Runlevel Editor in Expert Mode is potentially more dangerous. Don't change the runlevel for a service without very good reason. Always review the changes you made before closing the Runlevel Editor. They will not take effect until you reboot your computer, so you can prevent catastrophic errors if necessary.

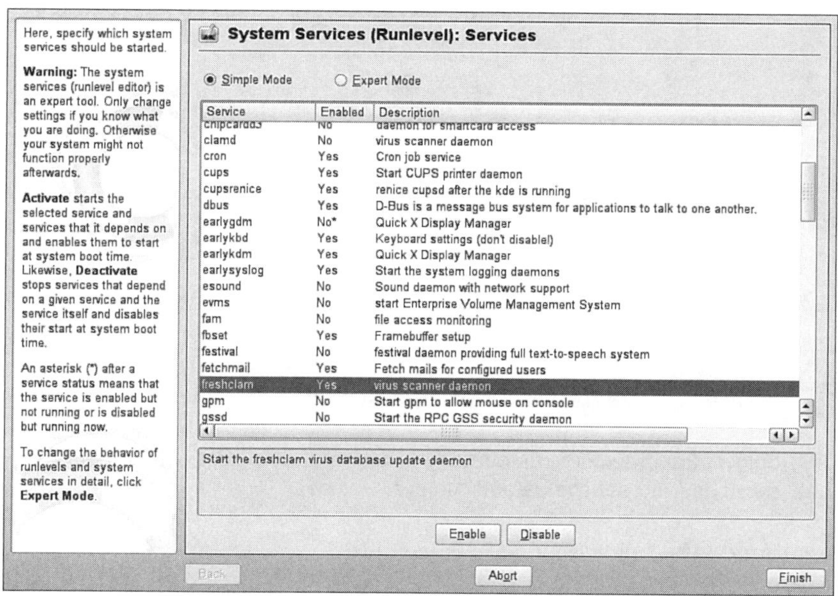

FIGURE 22.7 The YaST Runlevel Editor makes it incredibly easy to turn services on and off. Great care must be taken so that you do not disrupt your system's functioning.

Using the Runlevel Editor

When you open the Runlevel Editor module from the YaST System page, a list of all available services appears. The second column tells you whether this service currently is loaded at boot, and the third column offers a brief description of each service. Click a service, such as `freshclam` in Figure 22.8, and see a more detailed description in the bottom pane.

To start a service when you next boot your system, select it from the list and click Enable. To turn a service off, select it and click Disable. Review your changes and click Finish to confirm them. Reboot your computer to force the changes.

Expert Mode

Click the Expert Mode button to display the additional options (see Figure 22.8). The first thing you may notice are the boot scripts and other services listed here. When in Expert Mode, you really need to know what you're doing, and you get much less hand holding as far as descriptions of each service.

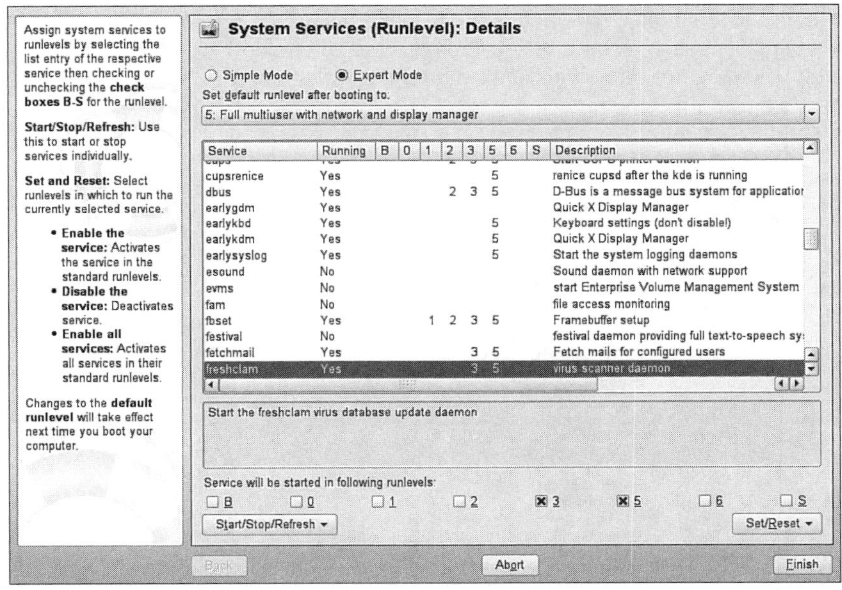

FIGURE 22.8 The Runlevel Editor Expert Mode lets you start and stop services, set different runlevels for individual services, and set the default runlevel on boot.

In Expert Mode, you can do the following:

- Change the default runlevel on boot.
- Identify which service can run on each runlevel, from boot to shutdown and everything in between.
- Start, stop, or restart any service without rebooting.
- Enable all services on boot.

As in Simple Mode, the editing process is straightforward. Use the drop-down menu to select the default runlevel. Select a service to make changes. Click the Start/Stop/Refresh menu to act on a service now: Start a service not currently running, Stop a running service, or Refresh (stop, if necessary, then start) a service.

Use the check boxes near the bottom of the screen to change the runlevel of a selected service. B runs a service at boot. S runs a service at shutdown.

Notice that when you change from Simple Mode to Expert Mode, the second column changes from Enabled to Running. This lets you use the Start/Stop/Refresh menu. The Set/Reset menu lets you enable or disable individual services and adds a third option: Enable All Services.

Make your changes, review them carefully, and then click Finish to confirm your changes.

Manually Starting and Stopping Services

If you change the configuration file for a particular service, you usually have to stop and restart the service to use the new configuration. When making changes to the X server, it is often worthwhile to change from Runlevel 5 to Runlevel 3 to test the changes, and then switch back to re-enable the display manager. This way, if you make a mistake, you can fix it and get it right without having to reboot every time.

To stop, start, or restart any service, open a shell as the SuperUser. To see if your ALSA sound server is running, type the following:

```
/etc/init.d/alsasound status
```

The script will report its status. It should report

```
ALSA sound driver loaded.                  running
```

To stop and restart the service, type

```
/etc/init.d/alsasound restart
```

and the following should appear:

```
Shutting down sound driver                  done
Starting sound driver:  via82xx             done
Restoring the previous sound setting        done
```

As noted in the previous section, you can also use the YaST Runlevel Editor in Expert Mode to start, stop, or restart any service.

System Monitoring Tools

openSUSE Linux and the two desktop environments offer several tools, both graphical and shell-based, to help you manage and monitor your system.

KSysGuard

Windows users sooner or later become familiar with the Task Manager tool, if for no other reason than to close out some application that is "not responding" to the user or the operating system. Those who make the switch to openSUSE Linux will feel comfortable the first time they open the KDE equivalent: KSysGuard. The good news is you rarely, if ever, have to run this program to make a program behave (or, failing that, go away).

Although KSysGuard looks like and behaves much like Task Manager, *do not* press Ctrl+Alt+Delete to bring it up. The famous "Three Finger Salute" just brings up a shut-down dialog box. You can launch this application from the shell by typing **`KSysGuard`** or going to System, Monitors in the KDE menu.

KSysGuard offers two types of information by default in its tabbed window. The System Load tab (see Figure 22.9) gives you a graphical view of several system processes. You can adjust the information this tab displays using the menus on the left side. The Process Table (see Figure 22.10) has a list of every process currently running on your system, with many details on its status. If you find an application hung up, you can locate its process(es) here and (with the right permissions) kill it.

NOTE

If a problem application is owned by Root, you can write down the Process ID (PID) number, log in as SuperUser in a shell, and type `kill <PID>` to end that process.

Even better, launch KsysGuard as the SuperUser by going to a shell prompt (or pressing Alt-F2) and typing kdesu ksysguard. Now you can kill any process.

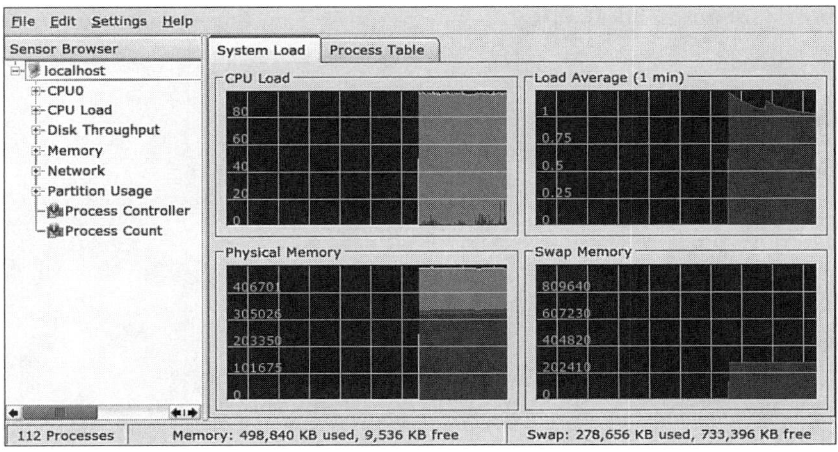

FIGURE 22.9 See what's happening on your system with the System Load monitors in KSysGuard.

To add a new set of monitors to KSysGuard, go to the File, New menu (or press Ctrl+N) and select a set of monitors from the menu on the left.

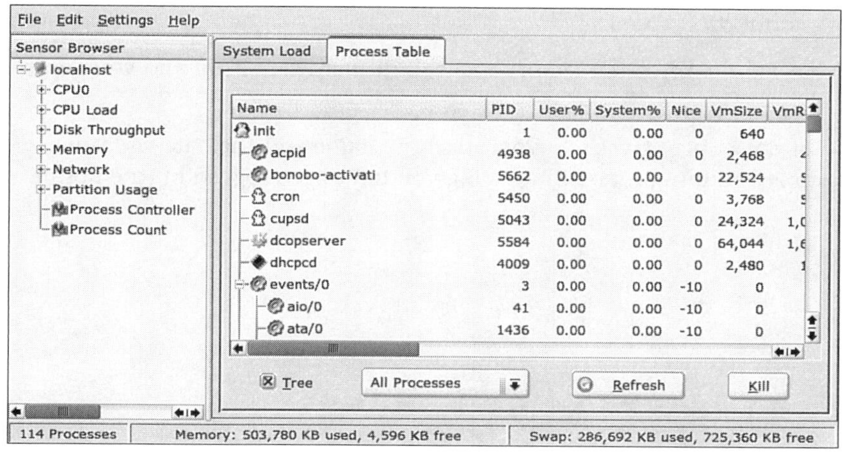

FIGURE 22.10 Kill problem applications in the Process Table.

KDiskFree and KwikDisk

Short on disk space? Need to know when to modify your partitions or logical volumes? KwikDisk can sit in your KDE system tray and tell you what disks are currently mounted and how much space each has remaining. By default, it will also pop up a warning box when a disk is getting full.

To put KwikDisk in your tray, right-click in an empty spot on the tray. Choose Add Application to Panel, System, Desktop Applet to find KwikDisk.

KwikDisk is the watchdog for a larger program, KDiskFree, which gives you similar information from your `/etc/fstab` file and lets you mount and unmount drives with a right-click.

GKrellM

This is an oddly wonderful little program that can be geek eye candy as well as a very powerful and informative tool at your disposal.

GKrellM (see Figure 22.11) is a GTK-based monitor. The name comes from the aliens in the 1956 science fiction movie *Forbidden Planet*. Bill Wilson, GkrellM's author, relates that "the Krell had a room with wall to wall meters for monitoring their power systems, and that is what I was thinking of when I came up with the GKrellM name."

By default, the program will pull information from the `/proc` directory and tell you several important things about your computer, including the following:

- What sort of use your CPU is getting.
- The number of users (both "live" and system) logged in and the processes running.
- When the hard drive is being accessed, and for how much data at a time.

- Your network connection speed.
- A graph of your Random Access Memory usage, both hardware RAM and your Swap partition.
- The very top of the display gives you your machine name and the date and time. On the bottom is a running total of how long you have been logged in (the uptime total).

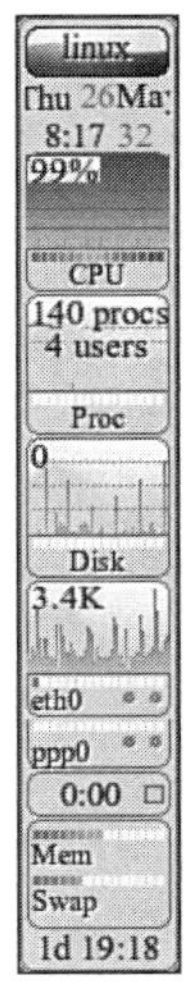

FIGURE 22.11 GKrellM helps you visualize what is happening on your computer.

Right-click any monitor to configure that monitor. Right-click on an edge to bring up the GKrellM Configuration screens. Insert any monitor you'd like from the lengthy list of choices.

GKrellM has been blessed with devoted users who have written plug-ins for nearly everything you might like to do with the application. And in its eye-candy role, there are themes you can download to change colors and some behaviors. Access all these at the application website, http://www.gkrellm.net.

References

- http://tldp.org/LDP/LG/issue70/ghosh.html—This Linux Gazette article, "Bootstrapping Linux," offers great detail on the BIOS and MBR.
- http://www.lostcircuits.com/advice/bios2/1.shtml—"The LostCircuits BIOS Guide." The site itself is a bit ad heavy, but there is excellent information on various BIOS settings.
- http://www.techarp.com/freebog.aspx—"The Definitive BIOS Optimization Guide," another excellent site with plain-language explanations of many BIOS settings. Useful no matter what OS you use.
- http://www.ibm.com/developerworks/linux/library/l-slack.html—Joe Brockmeier explains the Slackware Linux boot process, which is not so different from openSUSE Linux.
- http://linux-newbie.sunsite.dk—"The Linux Newbie Administrator Guide." Very helpful, if getting a little dated.
- http://www.troubleshooters.com/linux/grub/grub.htm—"GRUB from the Ground Up," a fine explanation of how to create a GRUB boot floppy and boot it on a disabled machine.
- http://www.gnu.org/software/grub/manual—The GRUB manual in various formats.
- http://tldp.org/HOWTO/LILO.html—The LILO Mini HOWTO.
- http://tldp.org/LDP/lame/LAME/linux-admin-made-easy—"Linux Administration Made Easy." See Section 4.8 on booting with LILO.
- http://www.linux.com/article.pl?sid=04/05/17/1832239—A brief review of KSysGuard.
- http://docs.kde.org/stable/en/kdebase/ksysguard—"The KSysGuard Handbook."
- http://members.dslextreme.com/users/billw/gkrellm/gkrellm.html—The home of GKrellM.
- http://www.gkrellm.net—The GKrellM site. Get add-ons and more information.

CHAPTER 23

Securing Your Machines

IN THIS CHAPTER

It's an old story, but it will remain true for the foreseeable future: The only method of keeping a computer 100% secure is to lock it in a room and never turn it on. The one thing computers do best is also the most dangerous thing about them—they collect, store, and display information. Your job as a system administrator is to ensure to the best of your ability that particular bits of information are displayed only to the people and machines to which you want those bits displayed.

With its permission-based file system, Unix and Linux make a good start on protecting your data from the bad guys. However, the more connections your computer makes to other computers—first to a local area network, then to a wide area network, and finally to the Internet—the more chances your data have to be compromised.

In today's world of interconnected computers and "always-on" access to the Internet, the importance of maintaining a secure computer has never been greater. There may be some truly dangerous cyber-terrorists out there working at bringing down society as we know it, but these are not the people from which you have to protect your machine on a regular basis. The ordinary computer user has to put up with the script kiddies (young folks who want to prove their alleged computer prowess by running prewritten programs that break into other people's systems), disgruntled employees, and fast-spreading viruses and worms. Unfortunately, that's more than enough to keep you busy for quite some time.

In earlier chapters, you've learned some basic skills for protecting your computer with permissions (Chapter 19, "Managing Users, Managing Security"), fighting viruses (Chapter 15, "Managing Email Servers"), and transferring files securely (Chapter 17, "Secure File Transfer"). In this chapter, the focus is on other tools to protect yourself and your information. You also will become prepared for the worst and acquire some idea of what to do when your carefully laid security strategy is somehow penetrated.

Understanding Computer Attacks

There are many ways to divide up the types of computer attacks, but perhaps the easiest to understand is the internal attack, where someone has access to a computer on the local area network. This is in contrast to the external attack, which occurs over the Internet. The distinction is important because it clarifies the relative danger your system is in. Chances are excellent that your local network is protected quite well by the system of permissions, along with the trust you place in your users to not damage the system. Unless you are in the habit of hanging around with the bad guys and giving them access to your system, you shouldn't have to spend a great deal of time protecting your system against your users.

It's that outside world that you must worry about most. In a world—and Internet—filled with millions upon millions of people, some percentage (usually small) will be evil. The Internet makes it possible for machines to connect on a vast scale, and any single machine can be attacked by people located anywhere on the planet. Within minutes of making first contact with the Internet, some machines can be attacked, although usually not successfully. Don't let your machines be counted among the victims.

This situation is not a result of malicious users lying in wait for your IP address to do something interesting. Instead, canny virus writers have created worms that exploit a vulnerability, take control of a machine, and then spread it to other machines around them. As a result, more attacks today are the result of these autohacking tools. There are really only a handful of truly evil individuals out there; however, as with most human endeavors, if you're really the target of someone's attack, you probably cannot prevent it without a massive effort.

Scripts come in another flavor as well: prewritten code that exploits a vulnerability and gives its users special privileges on the compromised machine. These scripts are rarely used by their creators. They get posted online for the aforementioned script kiddies, who use them to invade vulnerable systems and brag about it to their friends.

Your job as a system administrator is to keep your computers and local networks from being compromised by worms, script kiddies, and the more serious attacks conducted by more experienced criminals. Your users (even if it's just you) want to use the computer to accomplish great things and not worry about the firefights outside. Wearing your sysadmin hat, you can accomplish this task.

Regardless of the source of the attack, you can follow a five-step checklist to secure your openSUSE Linux box:

1. Assess your vulnerability. Decide what machines can be attacked, what services they are running, and who has access to them.

2. Configure the server for maximum security. Install only what you need, run only what you must, lock down applications to make sure they cannot be misused, and configure a local firewall.

3. Secure physical access to the server.

4. Create worst-case–scenario policies.
5. Keep up to date with security issues.

You'll learn more about each step in the following sections. You must implement all the steps.

Assessing Your Vulnerability

It is a common mistake for people to assume that switching on a firewall makes them safe. Although there's no question that switching on a firewall is an important step to take, it is not a solution and never has been. Each system has distinct security needs, and taking the time to customize its security layout will give you maximum protection and best performance.

The following are the most common security mistakes people make:

- Installing every package—openSUSE Linux 10.3 has three gigabytes of software included in the distribution. If a machine is not going to be an FTP server, you probably don't need to have the server installed on it. YaST makes it easy to configure your installation so that you can remove unnecessary packages and get the ones you will use.
- Enabling unused services—Do you really require the capability to access your system remotely? Do you want people to upload files to your machine? If not, don't run SSH or FTP. Always think about what you use, whether that service is open to the Internet, and whether you need it.
- Disabling the local firewall on the grounds that your server already has a firewall installed—When it comes to firewalls, more is better. Your computer is your castle. Put up a wide moat with a long drawbridge, followed by a thick wall, followed by another thick wall 10 feet away from the first one. Make it hard to access, and it won't be worth the time it takes for your attacker to continue.
- Letting your machine give out more information than it needs to—Earlier we talked about the unfortunate, if inevitable, demise of `finger` as a useful tool to find out about other users on the network. Now it's just another way to hack into someone's system.
- Keeping the door to the server room unlocked—Less common in IT shops these days, but still a bad idea. Even if your sysadmins live in the server room (and with Linux servers, that really shouldn't be—they work best unattended), the room should be locked whenever no one is inside.
- Being careless with your wireless network—Wireless networking is convenient and helpful, but the standards were not developed with security in mind. Someday, this is likely to improve. However, we're not there yet.

After you have ruled out these common problems, you're on to the real problem. How can the bad guys attack your machine? What can people access from the outside? This comes down to the question of what applications and services face the Internet and what are the ports on which they run.

The best way to find answers to these questions is through the `Nmap` networking utility. This little tool will scan the ports of any machine on your network, or all of them, and tell you which ones are open at that moment. Any service you have installed that responds to `Nmap`'s query is pointed out and you may, in turn, choose to lock down ports that should not be open.

openSUSE Linux does not install `Nmap` by default, but you can install the command-line version and a GUI front-end called `Nmap-gtk` (also known as nmap-front-end) through YaST. Other GUIs are available at the Nmap website, http://www.insecure.org/nmap.

Although you can use the shell version, it is much easier to configure and see the results of `Nmap`'s work in the GUI (See Figure 23.1). It is also better to run `Nmap` as the SuperUser, because you will get more information that way. To launch `Nmap-gtk`, log in as the SuperUser and type **`nmapfe &`**.

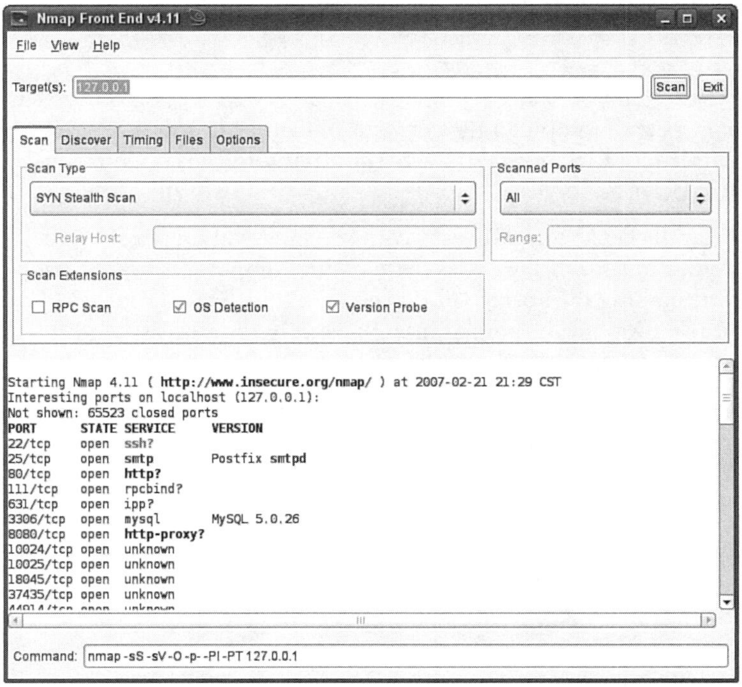

FIGURE 23.1 *Nmap* scans ports to see what is open and vulnerable.

The best way to run `Nmap`, especially the first time, is to use the SYN Stealth scan (on by default when you launch it as SuperUser) with OS Detection and Version Probe on. By default, `Nmap` scans the localhost (127.0.0.1), but you can add or change targets by typing the IP address(es) into the Target(s) edit box. The first time you run `Nmap`, you should click the Scanned Ports box to change the scan range from a few default ports; select All from the drop-down menu. This scan takes a few seconds longer (but the scan shouldn't take more than a few minutes altogether), but it gives you a more complete picture of your status. As you adjust your options in the GUI, you'll see the actual shell command being built at the bottom of the window. You could, if so inclined, copy this command to a text file and run it as a shell script later on.

When you have made your selections, click Scan. `Nmap` tests each port to determine whether it responds. If it does, `Nmap` asks the application at that port for version information and displays that information to the `Nmap` screen. You then get results like those displayed in Figure 23.1. Ideally, there will be no surprises on the list. If there are surprises, or you decide that there are some unnecessary services on the list, you can take action.

You can log your `Nmap` scan by going to Save Log in the File menu and choosing a location from the menu. To view the log file later, go to Open Log from the File menu.

If you just have one or a few machines on the network, you probably need to run `Nmap` only once a year, or if you suspect your system is compromised. Sysadmins of larger networks should run `Nmap` regularly as part of their general maintenance regimen.

CAUTION

Peer-to-peer file sharing networks such as Gnutella and BitTorrent usually require you to open ports on your firewall to speed up, or even access, the network. Recognize that you may be compromising your security when you participate in these networks. Be wary when downloading files from these sources. As of this writing, no significant worm has propagated itself through peer-to-peer networks, but it could easily happen. Not every file with a certain name contains the content you may be expecting after you get it downloaded.

Protecting Your Machine

After you have disabled all the unnecessary services on your system, what remains is a core set of connections and programs that you want to keep. Don't think you're done, though. It's time to consider what to do about your wireless network and the physical security of your servers.

Securing a Wireless Network

Wireless networking under the 802.11 standards is not built with security in mind. The practice of *wardriving*, where folks drive around with wireless-equipped laptops looking for a hotspot, tells you most of what you need to know about the security of the average wireless network. It's one thing to use random wireless hotspots to surf the Web on the road; it's quite another to intercept packets of data transferring across someone's wireless network. This is potentially a serious problem that you need to be concerned about. Great progress has been made in the last few years, but this problem has not been solved yet. If an attacker is in your neighborhood and knows the frequency that your network uses, you have a nightmare on your hands. It should also be noted that the encryption standard of most wireless NICs is weaker than you need and should not be considered part of your security plan.

TIP

Whenever you are running on a wireless LAN, always run Open-SSH tools to protect yourself and your data. SSH passwords are not transmitted as plain text, and your sessions are encrypted.

This is especially true if you are accessing public WiFi access points. Many hosting providers don't (or haven't until recently) provided secure email, and your username/password combination is sent in plain text across the network every time you check your mail.

If you have your own network, it should be secured with the Wired Equivalent Privacy (WEP) algorithm. You want not only to protect your personal workstation/desktop/whatever information, but also your credentials on any servers to which you connect.

Whether or not your network is wired, the better the physical security of your computers, the more secure your network will be. Keep wireless transmitters (routers, switches, and the like) as close to the center of your building as possible. Do your own wardriving around the building to see if anyone just walking around can access your network, and shut things down tighter if you can.

It does not take much to hook up a wireless access point to a legitimate network hub; whoever does this can compromise your entire network. Be wary and scan for wireless access points regularly.

Another Word on Passwords and Physical Security

This is one of those messages that is difficult to emphasize too much: Secure passwords and secure machines are the first line of defense against electronic break-ins. Follow the password rules outlined in Chapter 19, especially if you're the Root user. Having access to the Root account is the holy grail for an attacker. Protect that account and that password with everything you have. Enforce the password standards mercilessly on your users as well.

If you are the sysadmin on a company openSUSE Linux server, be aware that changes in people's employment status can create problems for you. Former employees are often the source of attacks on servers. Have a policy in place for what happens to user accounts when someone leaves your company. That policy need not be draconian, but it should be fair to all concerned. Make sure everyone knows what it is, and enforce it consistently.

Configuring the SUSE Firewall

If you connect to the Internet, even with a modem and dial-up connection, you need a firewall to protect you from attack. Fortunately, openSUSE Linux includes an excellent firewall to help you. Go to YaST Security and Users and click the Firewall module to start the process. This module offers seven configuration screens, but you don't have to work with every one to turn the firewall on.

The Start-Up screen (see Figure 23.2) tells you whether the firewall is currently running, and asks if you want to start the firewall automatically when booting (the default and highly recommended setting).

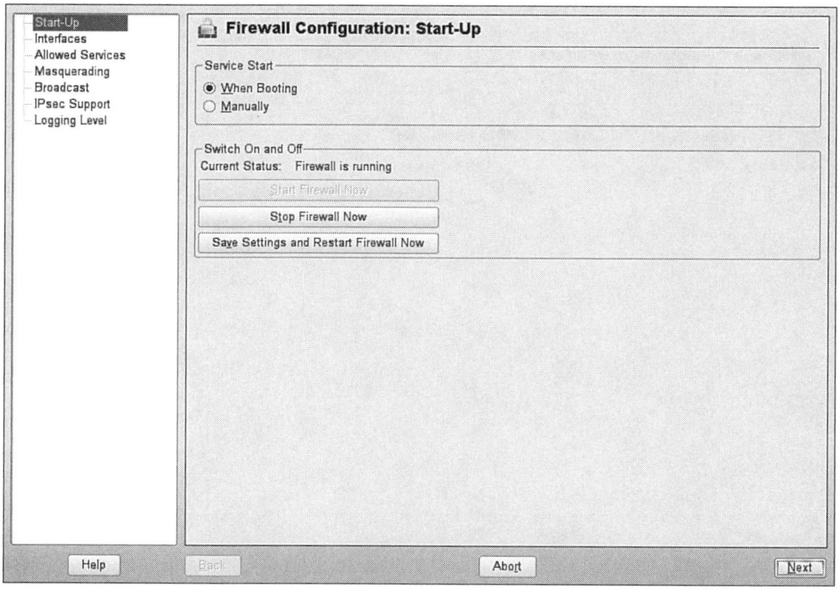

FIGURE 23.2 Turn the SUSE Firewall on and off in the Start-Up screen.

The Interfaces page displays the network cards and modems that face the outside world. YaST should already have identified these pieces of hardware in the Network Devices module. What's new here is the Zone Configuration column, which tells the firewall how the hardware interacts. In Figure 23.3, you'll notice that neither the DSL Connection nor the Ethernet card is configured in any zone. The DSL Connection is OK as is, but let's change the Ethernet card's setting.

Select the card, and click Change at the bottom. A popup will appear with information on the card. Click the drop-down menu to change the assigned zone and select Internal Zone.

You get three choices in this dialog box (these choices reappear in the Allowed Services page as well):

- Internal Zone—Your internal network. Services running through devices in the Internal Zone are not blocked by the firewall.
- External Zone—Services in this zone face out to other networks. By default, the firewall doesn't let anything through devices in the External Zone (though this is configurable elsewhere).

- Demilitarized Zone—The DMZ is for services that are intended to face out to the External Zone. If you have a web or mail server active that you want the world to see, but other things that you don't (like your personal mail on the system), assign the device here.

Click OK to confirm your changes.

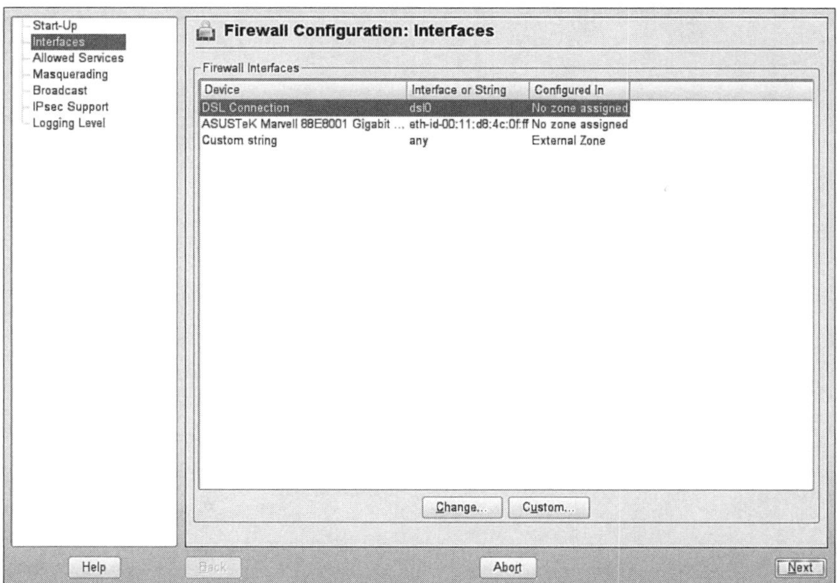

FIGURE 23.3 Select your LAN interface and Internet interface on this screen.

The Allowed Services page (see Figure 23.4) is used mainly for systems with active server components that need ports open to communicate with their clients. If you are using a web server (Apache or similar), a mail server, or any other server on the list, check the appropriate box. If you want other computers on your LAN to have only the same access to services on your computer that the rest of the Internet has, check Protect Firewall from Internal Zone.

NOTE

If you install a server package through YaST Network Services, the install wizard will always ask you to open the firewall so that it can function properly.

If an Internet application needs a specific port opened, you can click the Advanced button to open that port.

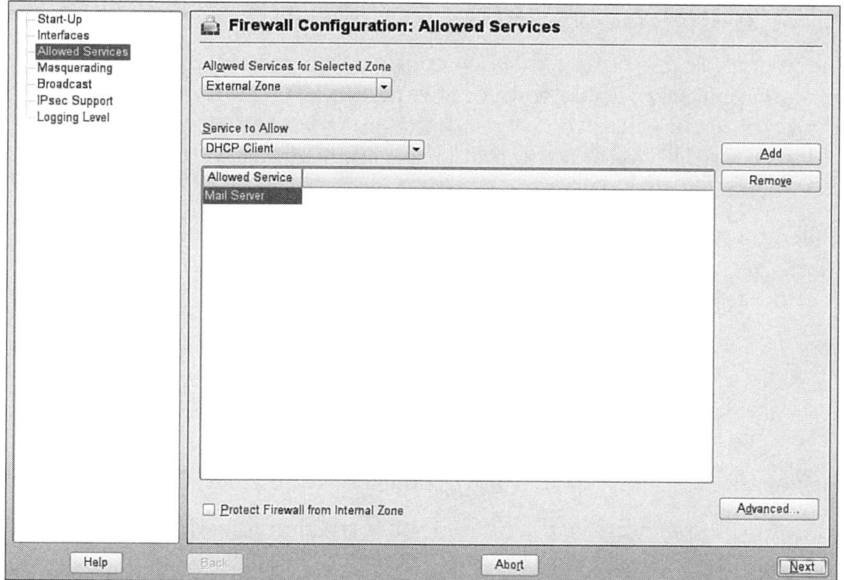

FIGURE 23.4 Open ports for any servers on this screen.

CAUTION

Whenever you open a port in your firewall, you are drilling a hole through which an attacker can breach. There is always a good, specific reason for opening a particular port. Make sure you have a good reason before you drill the hole.

The Masquerading page lets you set up masqueraded IP addresses on your system. This is discussed in Chapter 25, "Setting Up Networks and Samba."

If you need to send messages to every computer on your network or you want your CUPS print server to be available to others, visit the Broadcast page to set up these services.

IPsec is a method of securing encrypted messages within the network and between networked machines. Go to the IPsec page to enable IPsec to send and receive encrypted packets within a data stream.

The last screen sets up the information the firewall logs contain. Unless you are trying to troubleshoot a specific problem, it's a bad idea to log every packet, or even every dropped packet. Stick to the defaults here.

When you have finished configuring the firewall, click Next. A summary page with the current settings will appear. Review it, and click Accept to activate the firewall with your new settings.

The configuration file adds a script to the boot process so that the firewall loads each time you boot. To turn off the firewall, reopen the module to the Start-Up page. Click Manually under Service Start, and click Stop Firewall.

Protecting Applications with AppArmor

Firewalls protect machines by preventing access via ports on your PC. A firewall can be configured to allow an application access to the network, but if a security hole is found in that application, your whole machine could be at risk. AppArmor is a Novell-created application that tries to ensure that your Internet-facing applications do the things they were intended to do—and nothing else.

AppArmor is installed by default in openSUSE Linux and creates basic profiles for other installed applications. You should create an AppArmor profile for every outward facing application, such as the following:

- Web browsers
- FTP programs
- Servers of just about every type (web, mail, news, FTP, and file-and-print)
- Any applications that run on your web server (like blogs and wikis)
- Even applications that play Internet radio and other streaming media

YaST simplifies the process of adding profiles, at least somewhat, with the Add Profile Wizard. Go to the Novell AppArmor page and click Add Profile Wizard. You'll be asked to identify an application to profile first. You can either type in a program name or browse your hard drive to find the executable file. Click Create to start the wizard. Figure 23.5 appears.

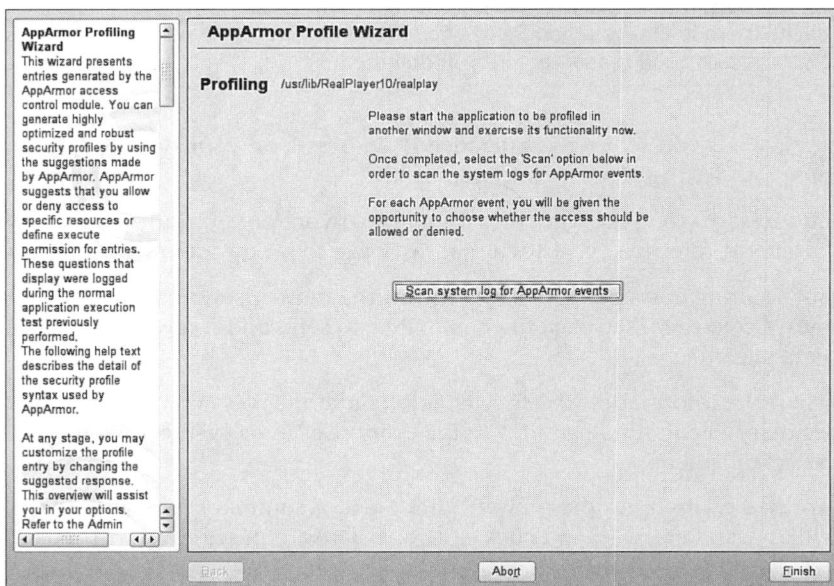

FIGURE 23.5 The AppArmor Add Profile Wizard.

The wizard asks you to start the named application and have it do something that accesses the network. When you've done that (you don't have to exit out of the application, but there's no harm in doing so), click the button in the middle of the Add Profile Wizard screen. YaST will scan the system logs for events triggered by the selected application. Beginning with the launch of the application, you will learn what sorts of things get logged in a typical program run. This may surprise you, especially if you're not a programmer to begin with. You'll be asked to allow or deny every event in the log. The first time through, assuming you believe the application is behaving normally, you should allow the event.

When the wizard finds a call to an executable (see Figure 23.6), you will usually get four options:

- Inherit—The standard choice; this allows the executable to run.
- Profile—Create a special profile for this application and allow it to run or not based on that profile.
- Unconfined—Tells AppArmor to ignore this resource, regardless of what the profile ordinarily says.
- Deny—Don't run this.

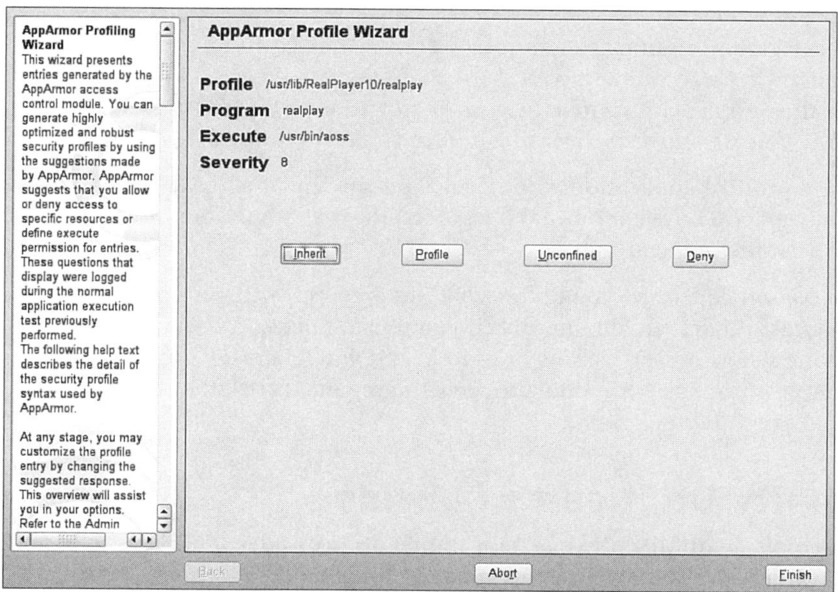

FIGURE 23.6 Click Inherit to allow an executable to run.

When the application wants to read a file, you may get options about the location from which to obtain the file, as in the RC configuration file in Figure 23.7. Clicking Glob here adds a third option, home/*/*. Click Edit to further define the location.

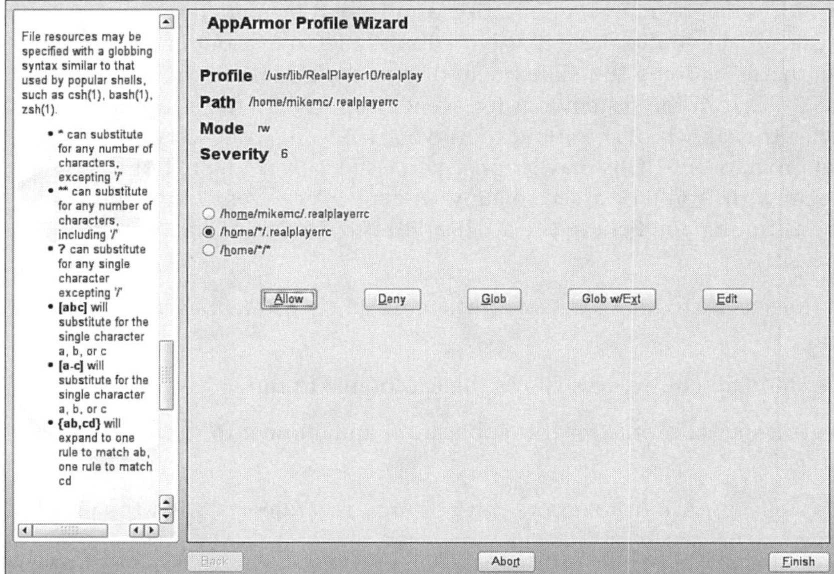

FIGURE 23.7 Help the wizard find the proper configuration file.

Determining an application's normal functioning can be a time-consuming process, but eventually all events will be accounted for and the main wizard screen will reappear. Click Finish to confirm this profile. Unfortunately, you are not asked if you want to create another profile, but you are asked to confirm whether you really want to leave.

When you update a profiled application, you should run the Update Profile Wizard to keep AppArmor in the loop on what normal operations for that application are. You can also add and edit a profile manually.

AppArmor runs a daily report to let you know what's happening with your profiled applications. You can adjust the schedule to hourly (if you're paranoid and/or have an application that is behaving suspiciously), weekly, or monthly (if you're already buried in reports). Use the AppArmor Reports module to view the reports, or ask that they be emailed to you and two other people.

Other Security Utilities to Consider

In addition to the tools mentioned thus far, you should also consider adding some basic Linux security tools to your toolbox. These include the following:

- Tripwire—This is one of the best file system monitoring tools around. It records information about important files (such as checksums) in a database. If anything changes in those files, Tripwire will catch the change when it runs (configure it as often as you like with cron) and will alert you. More information on Tripwire can be found at http://www.tripwire.org.

- Snort—This is a sniffer that monitors network packets and can be used to alert you to suspicious activity. Acting as an intrusion detection system, it can offer you the first warning that a possible attack is underway. More information on Snort can be found at http://www.snort.org.
- PortSentry—Like Snort, PortSentry acts as an intrusion-detection system by looking for suspicious activity. It differs from Snort in that it tries to find this activity by focusing on attempts aimed at the local computer and not on the network as a whole. It also offers the capability to block ports, and thus functions as a firewall as well. More information on PortSentry can be found at http://sourceforge.net/projects/sentrytools.

NOTE

Although it has been implied, it is important to note that any network is only as strong as the weakest element on it. To have a secure network, it is important to keep all workstations secure.

What to Do if You've Been Hacked

Humor books aside, it is never fun trying to come up with worst-case scenarios, and it's even less fun trying to figure out how to survive them. Thinking about the day someone breaks into your carefully protected, what-seemed-secure network and compromises your system is harder still. Yet thinking about it ahead of time can ease the stress of that day and can also put that day further into the future.

You can take courses and even get certified in disaster recovery management, also called business continuity. The suggestions offered here just scrape the surface. However, the following are some ideas to help you think out and plan for the day that no one wants to come—and how to survive and recover from it. The job you save may be your own.

- If at all possible, don't just shut the network down. If the attack has ended, you let the attacker know you're on to him by yanking the cord. Give the security team a chance to catch the perpetrator if he returns.
- Not everyone needs to know you've been attacked. If the attack came from inside, it wouldn't be a good idea to tell all the employees.
- Head over to http://www.rootkit.nl/projects/rootkit_hunter.html and pick up a copy of the Rootkit Hunter. Rootkits are programs attackers leave behind so that they can mess you up again. The programs are designed to hide themselves, but this application can help you find them. The bad news is that if a rootkit is found, you have to wipe the machine and start over.
- After you've thought about it and decided the compromised machine is not really required on the network, take the machine offline. You may decide that the chances of your attacker coming back are slim, and so you don't want to try luring him or her back.

- Start reviewing your log files, and store them somewhere else. Because log files can be edited—they are just text files, after all—there may still be useful information in them that can help you track down the attacker.
- Check `/etc/passwd` for unauthorized users. Although you should be using `shadow` to store your genuine user passwords, invaders often create new users in `/etc/passwd` in hopes that some applications just check that file to confirm permissions. If you see a user you don't recognize or can't verify, remove it immediately.
- Run `lsof` to obtain a list of open files. The `-p` option can be used to specify a process ID number (such as a suspected user's shell) to limit the display to only those open files associated with them.
- Run `ps aux` to check for unusual programs running on the system, and watch your `cron` job listing, too.
- Check on `/srv/www` and make sure all your web pages are present, accounted for, and unchanged.
- Check the contents of `.bash_history` in each of your user's home directories. Look for attempts to log in as the SuperUser or Root. If you find them, don't put that user under suspicion automatically; that user may have just been the unlucky account the attacker reached.
- If you have a prior relationship with a security company, call them in right away. They can find things in the log files that an untrained observer won't.
- Bring those backup tapes back and start checking them. Just because you noticed this attack doesn't necessarily mean it was the first time.
- If you haven't done so already, develop a more formal disaster recovery plan!

Keeping Up to Date on Linux Security Issues

It's no surprise that computer security is a hot topic on the Web. You can find a lot about it in the technology news sites and most Linux-oriented news sites as well. Two sites you should be familiar with are the following:

- LinuxSecurity.com—This is primarily a news service that scours the Web for security-related information and commissions articles for its site as well. Every Monday morning, you can get the Linux Security Week newsletter in your inbox, with all the security warnings issued in the previous week so that you can keep your system safe. The site also hosts Security HOWTOs, a glossary of security terms, and the comments and forums you expect on a PHP-driven website.
- SecurityFocus.com—This is possibly the best general site on computer security; it is also the host of the famous BugTraq mailing list. This extremely high-traffic list is often the first place the public learns of newly exposed application vulnerabilities. The site also hosts a Focus on Linux list and offers an RSS feed for its news content and vulnerability announcements.

To keep up with the latest security updates for openSUSE Linux, keep your favorite update application in your desktop taskbar, too. This will help you keep your system as secure as the SUSE/Novell engineers can make it.

References

- http://www.insecure.org/nmap—The `Nmap` home page. There is a lot of general information about network security here, as well as official and user-generated documentation.
- http://www.rootkit.nl/projects/rootkit_hunter.html—Analyze whether an attacker left behind tools to wreak more havoc on your system.
- http://www.novell.com/linux/security/apparmor—The official Novell AppArmor page.
- http://en.opensuse.org/AppArmor—AppArmor on openSUSE.
- http://www.securityfocus.com—Keep up with security issues on all platforms.
- http://www.linuxsecurity.com—Focus on Linux security problems and solutions.

CHAPTER 24

Kernel and Module Management

IN THIS CHAPTER

Previously, you learned what happens when you start your Linux computer: The BIOS wakes up all the electronics on the motherboard and finds a bootloader. The bootloader checks the hard drive to find a kernel. The kernel does everything else. But what is a kernel?

Stripped to its essentials, the kernel really is the operating system. It is the piece of software that allows humans to interact with otherwise inanimate pieces of plastic, silicon, and other precious metals. The Linux kernel is Linux. Distributions such as openSUSE, Debian, Fedora Core, and Ubuntu package different sets of applications, update mechanisms, and configurations. They are all Linux because they distribute the Linux kernel that was released by Linus Torvalds and developed by an amazing crew of kernel hackers.

In this chapter, you will learn how to get your hands on the kernel source, how to manage kernel modules, how and when to patch the kernel, and how to troubleshoot problems with the kernel.

The vast majority of openSUSE users will find that the precompiled kernels provided by the SUSE engineers will more than satisfy their needs. These kernels are available through YaST (as is the kernel source code). openSUSE is designed for the tinkerer, though. If you think you can be a kernel hacker, openSUSE can help you find out.

Even if you're a little fearful of the idea of messing with the kernel, you should read the first two sections of this chapter to know a little bit about the history of the kernel and how it works. Someday, you just might pick up a brand-new piece of hardware for which a Linux driver was added to the kernel snapshot last week. Go all the way through this chapter, and you'll know exactly what to do to get it working.

Linus's Baby: The Linux Kernel

At the bottom of most Linux-related web pages and at the front of this (and just about every other) Linux book, there is a notice: Linux is a registered trademark of Linus Torvalds. In most cases in the larger world, posting such a notice is just another silly requirement imposed by lawyers on publishers and web designers. For this book, at least, it is but one way to acknowledge the debt we all owe to the Finnish programmer who started it all.

While the GNU Project to develop a free Unix-based operating system had been working on a functioning kernel for years, Torvalds wanted to do his computer science homework at home. So in August 1991, he ported the teaching operating system called Minix to the Intel 80386 platform and offered the code to readers of the Usenet newsgroup, comp.os.minix.

The Linux Source Tree

The kernel source code lives in a group of directories called the kernel source tree. This tree's structure is important because the process of compiling the kernel is automated.

When you compile a kernel, `make` is actually running a series of scripts. The scripts, `makefiles`, expect to find pieces of the kernel code in specific places. If they are not there, the makefile breaks, and the kernel is incomplete. You will learn how to compile a kernel with `make` later in the chapter.

You don't need the kernel source code on your system for Linux to run—you just need the compiled kernel binaries for that. If you ever want to compile a kernel, you need to install the `kernel-sources` package from YaST.

The sources are stored in `/usr/src/linux`, which contains several directories; the most important for you is the Documentation directory. In these files, you should find about everything you need to know about the kernel and its various modules. In the subdirectories, you'll find text files with detailed information about all the various drivers for peripherals, file systems, and networking tasks patched into the kernel. These documents are written for programmers, but the advanced user can often glean much useful information as well.

Types of Kernels

There was a time when Linux kernels were monolithic—a single block of code containing all the instructions for the processor, motherboard, and other hardware.

When changing hardware, you had to recompile the kernel to include the drivers for the new piece and remove the old drivers. This was important because unnecessary kernel modules took up memory, which was at a premium.

As the kernel code grew larger and the number of devices that you could add to a computer increased, recompiling became a nearly unbearable chore. So kernel hackers developed a new building method to solve the problem. Device drivers became modules that could be loaded and unloaded into the kernel when you needed them. With this modular approach, all the kernel code could be compiled at once, with most of the code compiled into modules. Adding new hardware involved loading a module in place of rebuilding the whole kernel.

The standard Linux kernel has some drivers compiled inline, as part of the kernel itself. These are the drivers required during the boot process. Kernel modules are loaded after login.

NOTE

Commonly, drivers for SCSI disk drives that you intend to boot are inline. If they aren't, you couldn't access the drive.

Ingenuity has gotten around this problem of needing inline drivers, however. You can use `initrd` to start a RAM disk. This creates a small kernel and the appropriate device driver, which accesses the device and loads the actual kernel. You'll learn more about this later in the chapter.

Some code can be only inline or in a module (for technical reasons), but most code can be compiled either way. With fast modern processors and cheap memory, the performance differences are negligible, but they are of concern when installing Linux on an older, slower machine.

When compiling a kernel, you select inline or modular loading during the `make config` step that you'll learn more about later. Unless you have a specific reason to do otherwise, you should always choose modular loading when asked.

Managing Modules

When you are using a modular kernel, you need to load and unload the modules automatically whenever possible. You may need to pass parameters, such as memory addresses or interrupt codes, on to modules when you load them. In this section, you'll learn about the tools Linux offers to manage your kernel modules.

Use any of these module management tools to get your kernel to bend to your will. All of them have man pages to help out, if necessary.

- `lsmod`—Just as `ls` provides a list of files and directories, `lsmod` gives you a list of loaded kernel modules. This is usually a long list, so you should develop the habit of piping the command through `less`, which is the GNU pager.
- `insmod`—Load (insert) a specified module into the kernel. If the module you want to load is installed in a directory other than under `/lib/modules`, be sure to specify the full path when running this command. Several options are offered for this command; the most useful is `-f`, which forces the module to be loaded.
- `rmmod`—Unload (remove) a specified module (or more than one) from the running kernel.
- `depmod`—Creates a dependency file (`/lib/modules/<kernelversion>/modules.dep`) for individual modules. Many kernel modules need other modules to load first; that

is, they are dependent on another module to work. During the system boot, `depmod -A` is run very soon after the kernel starts up to sort out the order in which modules load. The `-A` switch is there so that a new dependency file is created only when there is a change in modules.

- `modprobe`—Perhaps the most used module tool, `modprobe` combines `insmod` and `rmmod`. `modprobe` uses the dependency file created by another tool, `depmod`, to automatically load or unload (with the `-f` switch) a module.
- `modinfo`—Get a module's name, author, license type, and perhaps other information from a module's object file—that is, if the author included any information in the object file. Modules contributed by SUSE engineers include information on whether the module is officially supported.
- `/etc/modprobe.conf`—Not a command, but a file that contains module variables. These variables control how `modprobe` and `depmod` behave.

When to Recompile

There was a time when all users were warned to take a blood oath never to recompile a SUSE kernel. The SUSE engineers had worked endlessly to make sure everything worked just so and had the best device drivers you could get. Compiling new modules into this carefully balanced and functional kernel could lead to disaster.

Today, openSUSE is designed to be an "enthusiast's" (read "tinkerer's") version of the operating system. So as a user, you are almost expected to want to tweak every setting to squeeze the most performance and individuality you can out of your computer. There's even a kernel-of-the-day directory on the SUSE server that is accessible for any user. Don't ever use this on a production system, but if you *really* like the bleeding edge of development, you can be there every day.

Nonetheless, the vast majority of openSUSE users can (and should) rely on the kernel shipped (and occasionally updated) by SUSE. Those engineers have not been slacking on the job; they still work endlessly to make sure your system is as stable and as high performing as it could possibly be. When security holes are discovered in the kernel, a patched kernel will be in the YOU servers almost instantly.

TIP

To learn more about SUSE's process in building kernels, check out `/usr/src/linux/_README.SUSE`. This file is included in the `kernelsources` package.

When should you violate the Don't Recompile a SUSE Kernel rule? You are permitted to come up with your own exceptions, but these three are probably the best reasons:

- To accommodate a really new, or obscure, piece of hardware.
- To update your entire system before a precompiled kernel is available. That is, you need a newly released kernel with a device driver that will finally solve a longstanding printer problem.

- If you are running SUSE on an older computer and you need to optimize the kernel to run on the older hardware.

As noted earlier, you can pick up RPM packages for new kernels by way of the SUSE kernel-of-the-day repositories. Include this repository in your package manager's configuration file, or use YaST to get it. This will simplify the installation process.

CAUTION

Always back up data before manually compiling a new kernel. You never know what can happen when you are essentially upgrading your OS.

After your new kernel is installed, reboot your system to load the new kernel.

NOTE

When you use YaST to install a new kernel (whether you're doing it yourself or YOU is getting a security patch), YaST will warn you about running the `lilo` bootloader before rebooting. It is safe to ignore this warning if you are using `grub`, the default openSUSE bootloader.

Kernel Versions

In the preceding section, I mentioned the kernel-of-the-day repository. The very existence of this place gives you a sense of the pace of development of the kernel. As new features are added, bugs are fixed, and new technology is incorporated into the code base; new iterations of the kernel are coming out all the time.

This is the reason why kernel version numbers are so complicated. With most applications, versioning is a relatively simple operation, with a major version number indicating lots of new features (or, in the case of commercial applications, at least enough to justify paying for an upgrade), and one or two digits after the dot indicating bug fix updates. Linux kernels are a different story.

For example, openSUSE 10.2 shipped with kernel version 2.6.18.2-34. You can break this version number down into these sections:

- Major version—Currently at 2.
- Minor version—Currently at 6. Even-numbered minor versions are stable kernels; development releases are odd numbered.
- Sublevel number—This is the current iteration of the kernel. If you visit www.kernel.org, you'll see it listed as the stable version. This number changes much more often than the first two. In this case, it's 18.
- Extraversion level—This number represents the work the SUSE engineers have done with the latest patch. Here, it's 2, but the dash indicates that there have been 34 small patches added since 2.6.18.2. Generally, this work addresses code issues in the stock kernel and additional hardware support.

To see what kernel version you're running, type `uname -r` at the shell prompt.

NOTE

Alan Cox has taken on many responsibilities within the kernel hacking team, including leading the team as maintainer. One of those tasks (though not one he's formally assigned to) is releasing periodic ac patches distinguished by the -ac marker at the end of the kernel version. Stored and downloadable at http://www.kernel.org/_pub/ linux/kernel/people/alan/, these patches include hints at what's being cooked up by the team working on the test kernel. Experimenters can join in the testing.

Getting New Kernel Sources

The Linux kernel has always been available free for the download. You can obtain kernel tarballs with your favorite FTP client or web browser from ftp.kernel.org or (preferably) one of the 99 (and counting) mirrors listed at http://www.kernel.org/mirrors. A kernel compressed by `bzip2` is around 35MB, while the same tarball compressed with `gzip` is around 42MB.

In the v2.6 download directory, you will find a plethora of download choices (see Figure 24.1 for a browser-eye view).

linux-2.6.18.3.tar.g..>	18-Nov-2006 22:38	248
linux-2.6.18.3.tar.sign	18-Nov-2006 22:38	248
linux-2.6.18.4.tar.bz2	29-Nov-2006 14:38	40M
linux-2.6.18.4.tar.b..>	29-Nov-2006 14:38	248
linux-2.6.18.4.tar.gz	29-Nov-2006 14:38	50M
linux-2.6.18.4.tar.g..>	29-Nov-2006 14:38	248
linux-2.6.18.4.tar.sign	29-Nov-2006 14:38	248
linux-2.6.18.5.tar.bz2	01-Dec-2006 19:21	40M
linux-2.6.18.5.tar.b..>	01-Dec-2006 19:21	248
linux-2.6.18.5.tar.gz	01-Dec-2006 19:21	50M
linux-2.6.18.5.tar.g..>	01-Dec-2006 19:21	248
linux-2.6.18.5.tar.sign	01-Dec-2006 19:21	248
linux-2.6.18.tar.bz2	19-Sep-2006 23:56	40M
linux-2.6.18.tar.bz2..>	19-Sep-2006 23:56	248
linux-2.6.18.tar.gz	19-Sep-2006 23:56	50M
linux-2.6.18.tar.gz...>	19-Sep-2006 23:56	248
linux-2.6.18.tar.sign	19-Sep-2006 23:56	248
linux-2.6.19.1.tar.bz2	11-Dec-2006 14:40	41M
linux-2.6.19.1.tar.b..>	11-Dec-2006 14:40	248
linux-2.6.19.1.tar.gz	11-Dec-2006 14:40	51M
linux-2.6.19.1.tar.g..>	11-Dec-2006 14:40	248
linux-2.6.19.1.tar.sign	11-Dec-2006 14:40	248
linux-2.6.19.tar.bz2	29-Nov-2006 17:20	41M
linux-2.6.19.tar.bz2..>	29-Nov-2006 17:20	248
linux-2.6.19.tar.gz	29-Nov-2006 17:20	51M
linux-2.6.19.tar.gz...>	29-Nov-2006 17:20	248

FIGURE 24.1 This selection of a kernel mirror FTP directory shows the variety of download options.

These include all the sublevel versions of the 2.6 kernel, compressed with different tools, along with digital signature files (with the `.sign` extension) to validate the kernel as official. Patch versions, with just the patches from that iteration, are also stored here (you'll learn about these in the next section). The directory also has changelog files for each iteration, indicating the changes from the previous release.

To download a full kernel, select the version you want in the compression format you're most comfortable with. The openSUSE GUI archive programs can handle both `gzip` and `bzip2` formats, so you can get the smaller `bzip2` file.

After it is downloaded, move the package to a directory other than `/usr/src` (keeping it in your download directory is perfectly fine) and extract it to your home directory. From the shell, the command for a `bzip2` file is **`tar -xjvf linux-2.6.10.tar.bz2`**, and for a `gzip` archive, type **`tar -xzvf Linux-2.6.10.tar.gz`**.

TIP

Use your Tab key to take advantage of your shell's file-completion feature when extracting a downloaded kernel. In the preceding example, type **`tar -xjvf linux`** and then press Tab to complete the filename.

Once the source tarball is unpacked, you will see a new directory with the correct kernel version number. Copy or move this directory (as the SuperUser) to `/usr/src`. Create a symbolic link (also known as a `symlink`) of `linux-2.6` to the new kernel. From the shell, type the following:

```
rm /usr/src/linux-2.6
ln -s /usr/src/linux-2.6.10 /usr/src/linux-2.6
```

When you create this symlink, you can get creative, allowing multiple kernel versions to be compiled and tailored for different functions. Change the symlink to the kernel directory you want to work on.

CAUTION

The correct symlink is critical to have `make` work properly. Always have the symlink point to the version of the kernel sources you're working with.

Patching the Kernel

If you have a slow modem connection to the Internet, downloading a whole kernel may be quite a chore. As previously mentioned, the kernel mirror download directory will also have smaller patch files with only the changes since the last iteration.

NOTE

You need to have an installed `kernel-sources` package from the openSUSE disk (or another full version of the kernel source in `/usr/src/linux`) to use patch files.

However, in doing this, you may be trading one chore for another. If you are using version 2.6.13, for example, and the patch containing the module you need is version 2.6.18, you can't just apply the 2.6.18 patch file and go on your merry way. You must apply all the intermediate patch files, in the order they were released (first 2.6.14, then 2.6.15, and on up to 2.6.18).

For simplicity's sake, download your patches to a `/patch` directory in the source tree. You will need Write privileges on the directory to do this.

If you need to patch several versions at once, as in the previous example, there is help. The `patch-kernel` script is located in the `/usr/src/linux/scripts` folder. This script applies all the necessary patches to bring your kernel up to the latest version.

TIP

Before running the `patch-kernel` script, back up your existing kernel source files, just in case something goes wrong.

The syntax for the `patch-kernel` script is as follows:

```
patch-kernel <source-dir> <patch-dir> stopversion
```

The source directory defaults to `/usr/source/linux` if you don't specify it here, and the patch directory defaults to the current working directory. So if you are patching version 2.6.13 to version 2.6.18, and the patches are all in `/usr/src/linux-2.6.13/patch`, type this:

```
scripts/patch-kernel /usr/src/linux-2.6.13 /usr/src/linux-2.6.13/patch
```

The script applies all the patches in the `/patch` directory and then creates a 2.6.18 code tree. If you're working from a clean stock kernel, you should have an error-free process. If something goes wrong, the script will create files with the patch number with a `.rej` extension (or just a # sign), indicating which patch failed. If this happens, you need to troubleshoot it yourself, which is a task best saved for the experienced C programmer familiar with the kernel source.

Whether you have assembled the kernel from the openSUSE disk by downloading a full version or a patch, you are now ready to compile this new code tree.

Compiling the Kernel

When you've downloaded a fresh kernel, or patched your existing sources, you need to compile the new kernel to use the new functionality. *Compiling* from source means transforming human-readable text/code into binary, machine-readable form. Compiling a kernel also means taking those binary files and putting them where they belong in `/boot` and `/lib` and then notifying GRUB (or LILO) of the changes.

The good news is that you have your old buddy `make` to automate nearly the whole compile process for you. By following these steps, you can compile and install a custom kernel just for you.

1. Back up your data, just in case.
2. Make sure you have a working boot disk with the old kernel on it, just in case something goes wrong. See the following note to learn how to create one.

NOTE

Before making any changes to your current, running kernel, make sure you have a backup copy. SUSE recommends using the installation CD to boot in an emergency, but what if the CD drive is inaccessible? It's good to have a floppy backup as well.

YaST once allowed you to make a boot disk directly, but the kernel has grown too large to fit on a single floppy; this size problem complicates the task. However, it is still possible to create a bootable kernel with seven floppies, using this process:

If you need to format the disks first, use this command:

```
fdformat /dev/fd0u1440
```

Mount the openSUSE DVD (for example, to `/media/cdrom`):

```
mount -tiso9660 /dev/cdrom /media/cdrom
```

Change to the boot directory on the DVD:

```
cd /media/cdrom/boot
```

Create the boot disk with the following command:

```
dd if=/media/cdrom/boot/bootdisk of=/dev/fd0 bs=8k
```

The README file in the DVD's `/boot` directory will give you more information on including kernel modules on additional floppies.

---

3. Back up the `.config` file, if it exists, just in case. Type (as SuperUser) **`cp .config .config.bak`**.
4. Run `make mrproper` to prepare the kernel source tree, cleaning out any old files or binaries. `make mrproper` will delete the `.config` file. Restore it.
5. Edit the makefile to change the EXTRAVERSION number.
6. Modify the kernel configuration file with `make xconfig` (or the interface of your choice).
7. Run `make dep` to create code dependencies used later in the process.
8. Run `make clean` to prepare the sources for actual compilation.
9. Run `make bzImage` to create a binary image of the kernel.

24

NOTE

Several `make` directive choices exist to create this image, but the most common are the following:

- `zImage` makes an uncompressed kernel image.
- `bzImage` creates a compressed image. Some BIOS's cannot parse large images, and this image accommodates that requirement.
- `bzDisk` creates a compressed image and places it on a floppy disk for testing purposes. Make sure you have a floppy in your drive before running this directive. You won't be prompted.

10. Run `make modules` to compile any modules your new kernel needs.
11. Run `make modules_install` to install the modules in `/lib/modules` and create dependency files.
12. Run `make install` to automatically copy the kernel to `/boot`, create any other files it needs, and modify the bootloader to boot the new kernel by default.
13. Open a text editor and verify the changes made to `/boot/grub/grub.conf`; fix if necessary. If you happen to be running LILO as your bootloader, check `/etc/lilo.conf` and rerun `/sbin/lilo` if you make any changes.
14. Reboot and test the new kernel.

Troubleshooting Problems

Compiling a kernel is a complex operation, and things can go wrong. Chances are, you will see error messages printed on the screen when something does go wrong. Some of these messages will show up in the `/var/log/messages` file, which you can look at in any text editor. Other messages may appear in other error logs as well. First thing: Don't panic! Many (if not quite all) problems can be solved with proper research.

Errors During Compile

It's rare that a kernel doesn't compile, but there's always a chance that something slips through the testing process.

A more likely scenario is that the compile crashes before completion when you attempt to experiment with new and untested code. Trying to add support for a newer device to an older kernel can also sometimes result in a compile crash.

It's also possible for you to end up with a *tainted kernel*. A tainted kernel is one where you have introduced a module that isn't covered by the GPL or similar license. This can happen when you're using hardware that requires a proprietary module (such as Nvidia display adapters). If you compile the kernel with one of these proprietary modules, you will see taint warnings.

Should you run into this situation, you're down to two options: Remove the offending module and wait for a solution from the kernel hackers, or try fixing the error yourself.

Most folks might want to take the safer course and wait for a fix, but if you think you might like to help hack the kernel, this is your opportunity. Finding a solution not only solves your problem, it might help millions of users down the road.

If you run into this problem and want to explore it, your first step is to contact the maintainer of the kernel section that did not compile. Go to `/usr/src/linux/MAINTAINERS` to find the person in charge. Ask if the team is aware of your problem. If necessary, you could post a problem to the appropriate mailing list, but before doing this, look at the If Something Goes Wrong section of the `/usr/src/linux/README` file.

Runtime Errors, Bootloader Problems, and Kernel Oops

If the kernel compiles, but crashes after you restart your computer, you have runtime errors. Error messages will appear on the screen (you can see them after you've turned off the SUSE boot screen by pressing Esc) or in the `/var/log/messages` file. Bootloader problems will be displayed on the screen, without a log file. *Kernel oops* are errors in a running kernel, with the errors written to `/var/log/messages`.

In these situations, Google is your friend. Chances are quite good that someone else has seen the error message(s) you have and that documented solutions are out there. Head to your favorite search engine and type in the error message with quotes around it. Be aware that Google has a 10-word limit on search terms, so you may need to focus on the keywords in the error message.

Most problems that surface after compiling a new kernel are bootloader-related. If you are running the LILO bootloader and forget to run `/sbin/lilo` after configuring the new kernel, it will have problems. See the LILO mini-HOWTO at the Linux Documentation Project (http://www.tldp.org/HOWTO/LILO.html) for diagnostic aids and solutions to most LILO problems. The GRUB manual is also online, at http://www.gnu.org/software/grub/manual/.

Kernel Tuning with `sysctl`

As the kernel developed over time, developers sought a way to fine-tune some of the kernel parameters. Before `sysctl`, those parameters had to be changed in the kernel configuration and then you had to recompile the kernel.

The `sysctl` utility can change some parameters of a running kernel. It does this through the `/proc` file system, which is a virtual window into the running kernel. Although it might appear that a group of directories and files exist under `/proc`, that's only a representation of parts of the kernel; these parts are referred to as variables. We can display a list of the variables as shown in the following shell command sequence:

```
sysctl -A
```

```
kernel.HZ = 1000
kernel.min-timeslice = 1000
kernel.def-timeslice = 21000
kernel.ngroups_max = 65536
kernel.printk_ratelimit_burst = 10
kernel.printk_ratelimit = 5
kernel.panic_on_oops = 0
kernel.pid_max = 32768
kernel.overflowgid = 65534
kernel.overflowuid = 65534
kernel.pty.nr = 5
kernel.pty.max = 4096
kernel.random.uuid = 7e576126-6356-4159-afd3-4de6a0227736
kernel.random.boot_id = 152ee742-ef9d-49c5-a271-cb98662ddc7e
kernel.random.write_wakeup_threshold = 128
kernel.random.read_wakeup_threshold = 64
```

This is just a partial listing of some kernel settings—the whole list runs about 20 pages. For this reason, you may want to pipe the command through `less`, which is the GNU pager.

NOTE

To see the full list of variables, enter **`sysctl -A`** at the shell prompt. You can learn more about working with the kernel by reviewing the kernel API documentation at http://kernelnewbies.org/documents/kdoc/kernel-api/linuxkernelapi.html.

If you want to change a value, use the `-w` (write) switch:

```
sysctl -w kernel.pid_max=35000
```

We've increased the maximum PID (process ID) number with this command. This change is good only for the current session. If you find a setting is useful, save it to the `/etc/sysctl.conf` file. The syntax is identical to the shell command:

```
kernel.pid_max=35000
```

This tool is more interesting to kernel hackers than to most users, but it is a potentially powerful tool.

References

- http://www.kernel.org—The Linux Kernel Archives, the place to find the latest kernel and more information.
- http://www.kernel.org/mirrors—Download the kernel from a server near you.
- http://www.gnu.org—GNU's not Unix. The home of many kernel-related projects. Get software and documentation here, and a healthy dose of free-software philosophy.
- http://www.gnu.org/software/make/manual/make.html—The `make` manual. This utility is much more than a source-code build environment.
- http://kniggit.net/wwol26.html—"The Wonderful World of Linux 2.6," a guide to the latest version of the kernel by Joseph Pranevich.
- http://www.kernelnewbies.org—For people who want to try their hand at kernel hacking. The Kernel Newbies host an IRC chat channel, #kernelnewbies, and a wiki from this site.
- http://tldp.org/LDP/lki—"Linux Kernel 2.4 Internals Guide." Get more in-depth about how the kernel works.
- http://tldp.org/HOWTO/HOWTO-INDEX/os.html#OSKERNEL—These HOWTOs explore the kernel in several ways.
- http://www.minix3.org/—The home of the new version of Linux's parent OS.
- http://jungla.dit.upm.es/~jmseyas/linux/kernel/hackers-docs.html—Its origins are similar to those of a FAQ document, but this annotated "Index of Documentation for People Interested in Writing and/or Understanding the Linux Kernel" is more of a reference guide, with pointers to an abundance of useful kernel information.
- http://kerneltrap.org—"Your Ultimate Source for Kernel News."
- http://www.gnu.org/software/grub/manual—The GRUB manual.
- http://www.tldp.org/HOWTO/LILO.html—The LILO mini-HOWTO.

CHAPTER 25

Setting Up Networks and Samba

IN THIS CHAPTER

Before it was known for almost anything else, Linux made its name in networking. Your Linux computer can connect with almost any operating system under the sun—MacOS (both flavors), all Unix flavors, and even Windows (with Samba's help). Linux servers easily and quickly can be deployed in heterogeneous networks and will run pretty much forever without a crash or reboot.

openSUSE differs from SUSE Linux Enterprise Server (SLES) mostly in that SLES tends to offer a more server-friendly implementation—often with older but more stable packages. openSUSE has more than enough power and flexibility to manage your home or small-to-medium business servers. This chapter will help you get going.

You will learn some basic Linux networking concepts and how to configure your network interface cards (NICs) and other network devices with YaST.

Networking with TCP/IP

Unix networking is based on the same stack of protocols that powers the Internet (well, perhaps it's the other way around): the Transmission Control Protocol/Internet Protocol (TCP/IP) suite. In addition to the two namesake protocols, the TCP/IP suite includes the User Datagram Protocol (UDP).

The purpose of these protocols is to move data around in *packets*. These are tiny little chunks of data created at the transmitting end and moved at the speed of light toward the receiving machine. Packets move faster and more accurately to their destination than one hunk of data would. Under TCP/IP, all data travels via IP packets from one IP address to another IP address.

TCP provides a connection-based protocol, allowing two network hosts to establish a dedicated communication path between themselves. When a TCP connection is made, the data stream is broken up by IP into packets, and it travels to the second machine. TCP then reassembles the packets back into a whole stream, figures out what type of data it is, and approaches the appropriate port for that data type (port 110 for POP email servers, as an example).

Where does UDP fit in the scheme of things here? It is a connectionless protocol. Applications that use UDP just choose a destination and start sending. UDP is usually used for small amounts of data or on fast and reliable networks. Some peer-to-peer networks also use UDP.

TCP/IP Addressing

Here is one thing you should get straight at the beginning of your networking studies: local area network (LAN) addressing is distinct from Internet addressing, even if they are based on the same protocol stack. This can lead to some level of confusion, in part because in Unix, even a standalone computer that never interacts with another machine still has a loopback IP address.

Internet IP addresses (also known as "public" IP addresses) are assigned by an addressing body like the American Registry for Internet Numbers (ARIN), which is the body in charge of IP addresses for the United States. Internet Service Providers (ISPs) and other entities requiring blocks of IP addresses apply to ARIN and similar institutions. The addressing body then assigns the requested blocks, which are, in turn, assigned to the ISP's subscribers. These addressing bodies are needed because every machine on the Internet at a given moment requires a distinct IP address. You'll see later, when you learn about DHCP, that one IP address can represent any number of physical machines.

LAN IP addresses are assigned by the system administrator so that each physical machine attached to the network has a distinct address. As a result, your computer can have three identities or addresses at once: its loopback address (the one-computer network), its LAN address (and if a computer can connect to several networks, it can have several LAN addresses), and its public Internet address.

> **NOTE**
>
> Learn more about setting up loopback connections in Chapter 12, "Connecting to the Internet."

Standard TCP/IP addressing under version 4 of the protocol is expressed as a series of four decimal numbers separated by dots, as in `187.0.15.255`. These represent a 32-bit binary value, and each of the four sets of numbers is called an *octet*. Each octet includes a number range from 0 to 255. The first octet usually signifies the *class* to which the network belongs. There are three classes of networks:

- Class A networks have a first octet in the range of 1–126, and the last three octets define the host. Each Class A network has up to 16,777,214 hosts. Of these, a first octet of 10 is reserved for local networks (127.0.0.0 is reserved for the loopback range).

- Class B networks have a first octet in the range of 128–191. In this range, the first octet of 128 is also reserved for local networks. The first two octets belong to the network, the last two to the host. There are 16,382 Class B networks, with 65,534 possible hosts.
- Class C networks have a first octet in the range of 192–223. In this range, the first octet of 192 is also reserved for local networks. The first three octets belong to the network, with only the last octet belonging to the host. Thus, there are 2,097,150 possible Class C networks, but each network can have only 254 hosts.

Two other network classes are irrelevant to this discussion: Class D network addresses are reserved for multicast addresses, and Class E addresses are experimental.

These classes are standard, but a *netmask* also defines your network class. The netmask shows what part of an IP address represents the network and which represents the host. Common netmasks for the different classes are the following:

- Class A—255.0.0.0
- Class B—255.255.0.0
- Class C—255.255.255.0

There's more information on netmasks in the "Network Organization" section later in this chapter.

The allocation of IPv4 addresses is reaching the breaking point. Class A networks are full. Class B is nearly there, and you can guess where Class C is, too. Something needed to be done, and it was. Welcome Internet Protocol, version 6.

NOTE

Many years ago, it was thought that we would run out of IP addresses in a very short time. This led to the need and demand for IPv6. What was not anticipated or foreseen, though, was the creation and widespread adoption of technologies, such as Network Address Translation, which enable multiple clients to share the same IP address. Because of their extensive use, the transition to IPv6 has moved much slower than it otherwise would have.

The Next Step: Internet Protocol, Version 6 (IPv6) Addressing

It's easy to see the need for IPv6. Just think of how many different machines you use to access the Internet today: desktop PC, laptop, personal digital assistant, or cell phone with email and Web access. Thinking about getting a Voice over IP (VoIP) phone? Now consider the prospect of widespread Internet use in the global South: Brazil, China, India, and South Africa. All these devices need addresses, as do the smart houses and web-enabled refrigerators that are quickly becoming a reality.

IPv6 fixes this problem by using 128-bit addresses using hexadecimal numbers, producing a truly mammoth number, equaling 3.4×10^{38} potential addresses. Instead of four octets, IPv6 addresses have eight hexadecimal groups. Four groups belong to the network and four groups belong to the host.

Like the global transition to the metric system, moving to IPv6 has been a long process. The initial standard was adopted in 1994, but the vast majority of Internet connections still use the old standard. Many networking utilities, firmware, and parts of some (non-Linux) operating systems will need rewriting to fully support IPv6.

You can use IPv6 to set up your internal network. All flavors of SUSE Linux support IPv6, and openSUSE 10.3 includes many utilities to use the new network. Consult the Linux+ IPv6 HOWTO at http://www.tldp.org/HOWTO/Linux+IPv6-HOWTO for more information.

Ports

Network servers rarely have just one dedicated task. For example, a web server might handle standard pages and secure pages, and perhaps an FTP volume as well. For this reason, applications are assigned *ports* by the Internet Assigned Numbers Authority (IANA) to make direct connections for specific services. Ports are unique numbers used within a TCP/IP packet that designates packet traffic for a specific application. These ports help TCP/IP distinguish services so that data gets to the right application. You've seen references to these ports elsewhere in this book: Web browsers access port 80, POP email clients look for port 110 to get mail, FTP servers use port 21, and BitTorrent uses port 6881. You can see these common ports in the `/etc/services` file and online at http://www.iana.org/assignments/port-numbers.

As a system administrator, you can assign ports on your server to different applications. You can do so by editing the server's configuration file. This can occasionally thwart remote attacks on a common port, but it requires you to notify your legitimate remote users to connect to the new port instead of the common port.

Network Organization

The bigger your network gets, the more problematic the organization of your addressing becomes. If you have fewer than 254 devices needing an IP address, you're pretty much home free with a Class C network. But after that, it can get interesting. There are some workarounds, though, which is what this section is about.

Subnetting

Class A and B networks can include separate networks called *subnets*. These subnets are specified in the second octet (in Class A networks) or in the third octet (in Class B networks). One computer with an address of 172.19.25.0 and another of 172.19.120.5 would be on the same Class B network (172.19), but on different subnets. These two computers would need a router or switch to communicate. Subnets can be useful to separate workgroups.

Netmasks

Subnet masks, or just plain netmasks, are used by TCP/IP to show which octets are owned by the network and which are owned by the host. You saw the standard netmasks earlier in the chapter. You can use customized netmasks to organize subnets to fit your needs. Even if you have a single Class C address, you can use netmasks to create subnets. You don't have to use an entire octet to represent a network, you can subdivide an octet to produce your own subnets.

Here's a simple example of using a unique subnet mask for a network. Instead of the standard Class C address which uses three octets to represent the network portion of the IP address, we'll add a part of the fourth octet to be used in the subnet mask. To determine the number of bits to add to the subnet mask, you must first determine the number of subnets you need to create in your network. If you want four subnets, you'll need to add two bits of the host address to the subnet mask (since two binary bits are required to produce four unique values).

There are eight bits within the fourth octet to use, so we'll take the top two bits as the network subnet, and the bottom six as the host address. To create the new subnet mask, you set all of the network bits to one. Setting the network bits to one in the fourth octet now produces 11000000, which is a value of 192 in decimal. This makes your new subnet mask 255.255.255.192.

When you use the entire octet as a subnet mask, assigning host IP addresses is easy. The downside to using only part of an octet in the subnet mask is that now assigning IP addresses becomes tricky. Only part of the fourth octet is now used as the host IP address. Table 25.1 demonstrates how to assign addresses to hosts on the new subnets.

TABLE 25.1 Assigning Host Addresses on a Subnet

Subnet bits	Host bits	Decimal IP address
00	000000 to 111110	.0 to .63
01	000000 to 111110	.64 to .127
10	000000 to 111110	.128 to .191
11	000000 to 111110	.192 to .254

In this network subnet, you can create four subnets, each containing 64 hosts. You'll notice that in each subnet, the host address of all one's (111111) is not used. This is a special address, reserved for local broadcasts to all hosts on the local subnet.

Network Address Translation (NAT)

NAT is a service that makes it possible for a server to translate between hosts on a network using private addresses and one or more public addresses. Usually, the router running NAT supports all the clients on a network segment and shares a single registered IP address among all of them. This allows the hosts to essentially hide behind the router, and a firewall is created at the network layer.

Hardware Devices in Networking

Standalone PCs require several hardware devices to network with other PCs, servers, peripherals, and the outside world. This section reviews the most essential and explains how to get networking going on your system.

Network Interface Cards (NICs)

Unless a computer can interface with a network, there is no network. That's what NICs are for. Each NIC has a unique address known as the Media Access Control (MAC) address that identifies the NIC. This hardware address is used by DHCP and several other protocols to identify a machine. NICs come in several flavors, depending on the method (or *topology*) they use to connect with other NICs. With the exception of some wireless NICs, openSUSE Linux supports nearly every card on the market, regardless of topology. These topologies are discussed in the sections that follow.

Token Ring

This is one of the older networking technologies. It was developed by IBM. As you would think, the network is set up in a ring, with each host passing around a single token. When a host receives the token, it can transmit data. The maximum transfer speed of a token ring NIC is 16Mbps (16 million bits per second). It uses an *unshielded twisted pair* (UTP) cable.

10BaseT Ethernet

There are other forms of Ethernet NICs, but this was the standard for a long time. Ethernet hosts link in a star pattern to a hub at the center. The hub must be within 100 meters of any host. Data goes through the hub to all the hosts, but packets are processed only by the appropriate host. Transfer speed is 10Mbps. 10BaseT also uses UTP cable.

100BaseT Ethernet

This simple upgrade to the 10BaseT standard is easy for administrators to handle, offering much faster transfer rates than 10BaseT with little more exertion than replacing NICs and hubs. As you might guess, 100BaseT NICs have a transfer speed of 100Mbps. It requires Category 5 UTP cable.

Fiber Optic and Gigabit Ethernet

If you are building a network for the first time or have a big budget, you should consider these cards. Fiber optic cable is relatively expensive, but it delivers data much faster and at longer distances than standard copper wire solutions. This is due, in part, to fiber's capability to transmit digital data directly without needing to convert the data to analog for transmission across metal wires. Gigabit Ethernet delivered over fiber optic cable transfers data at 1000Mbps.

Wireless NICs

With all the hype and discussion of wireless networking, it's easy to forget that wired networks are still faster. Nonetheless, the convenience and cost can make wireless very attractive even for networking desktop PCs. This is especially true for new networks where the wiring is not already in place.

As with any new technology, Linux support is not yet 100 percent, but it is catching up quite nicely. There's more on wireless networking later in this chapter.

Network Cable

In practical terms, there are two general types of network cables in use today: UTP and fiber optic. Six categories of UTP cable are available, and each has a different purpose:

- Category 1—Your telephone wire, used for voice transmission.
- Category 2—A token ring cable, with a transfer speed of 4Mbps.
- Category 3—A 10BaseT cable, with a transfer speed of 10Mbps.
- Category 4—Modern token ring networks, with a transfer speed of 16Mbps.
- Category 5—The most widely used UTP cable today. Transfer speed is up to 100Mbps.
- Category 6—This cable also has a transfer speed of 100Mbps and comes in two forms: stranded, for runs up to 25 meters, and solid, for runs up to 100 meters.

Fiber optic cable is used frequently in wide area networks (WANs) because it will transmit data up to 62 miles at 100Mbps. It is free of electromagnetic interference, and it is more secure.

Hubs

Hubs connect several hosts in a star network topology. They can have any number of connection ports, but typically they come in 4-, 8-, 16-, 24- and 48-port configurations. Hubs allow you to easily expand a network. Need more connections? Just buy another hub. Hubs can even connect with other hubs through an *uplink* port; the connected hubs then act as a single hub. Troubleshooting problems is also a little easier because if one host goes down, it doesn't take the whole network down with it.

Routers and Bridges

Routers and bridges connect your network to its subnets and to other networks. They do this by using different methods.

Bridges, or *dumb gateways,* are used to filter network data contained within a subnet. Often an application server resides on the same subnet as multiple clients. Traffic from the clients to the server will propagate to every hub on the subnet, regardless of whether the server is located there.

To solve this problem, bridges can be added between hubs within a subnet. A bridge blocks traffic that is not intended for a specific device on the subnet. This can greatly reduce the amount of traffic on hubs within the subnet, allowing you to add more devices within a subnet.

Routers are designed to connect networks to other networks and the Internet. They filter data so that you can block certain ports that you don't need. Routers tend to be more expensive than bridges, but for home and small business use, DSL packages often come with routers for around $100.

Switches

Switches combine the versatility of hubs with the network traffic control of bridges by internally bridging each port on a hub. With bridges, traffic control was at the hub level. With switches, traffic control is at the individual hub port level. This can reduce the amount of traffic sent out on hub ports to individual workstations. Only traffic destined for the network device on that port is forwarded.

Not only do switches help alleviate network traffic, but also they provide a simple level of network security. If individual workstations are plugged into switch ports, the workstations will see only the traffic that is destined for the workstation. The traffic from the other workstations on the switch is not forwarded to the port. This prevents unsavory users from installing network monitoring software on a workstation and snooping on other workstations' traffic.

Wireless Access Points

By far, one of the biggest advances in modern networking technology is the wireless network. Wireless networks allow devices to roam freely around an area and maintain network connectivity. A wireless access point is used to relay network signals through the airwaves to remote workstations, laptops, PDA's, and even servers.

Wireless access points have both distance and speed limitations. Currently most access points are limited to around 90 feet distance, and they can provide up to 54Mbs network speed.

One disadvantage of wireless networks is security. While wired networks restrict who can access the network (a device must be plugged into a switch or hub port), wireless access points broadcast your network signal anywhere the air waves travel, including outside your house.

Wireless networking protocols provide for signal encryption, allowing you to configure basic security protection for your data. Only devices that are configured with the correct encryption key are allowed to access the network.

Initializing New Network Hardware

If YaST does not automatically identify your card, you can set this up manually in the Network Cards module. Open YaST, go to Network Devices, Network Cards. The Network Settings screen pops up.

Any detected cards are displayed in the list, along with their assigned IP address (or DHCP, if they use DHCP to obtain an IP address automatically from the network). You can edit or delete the detected network cards or add a new one if your network card was not autodetected during installation. Figure 25.1 shows an example of the Network Settings window.

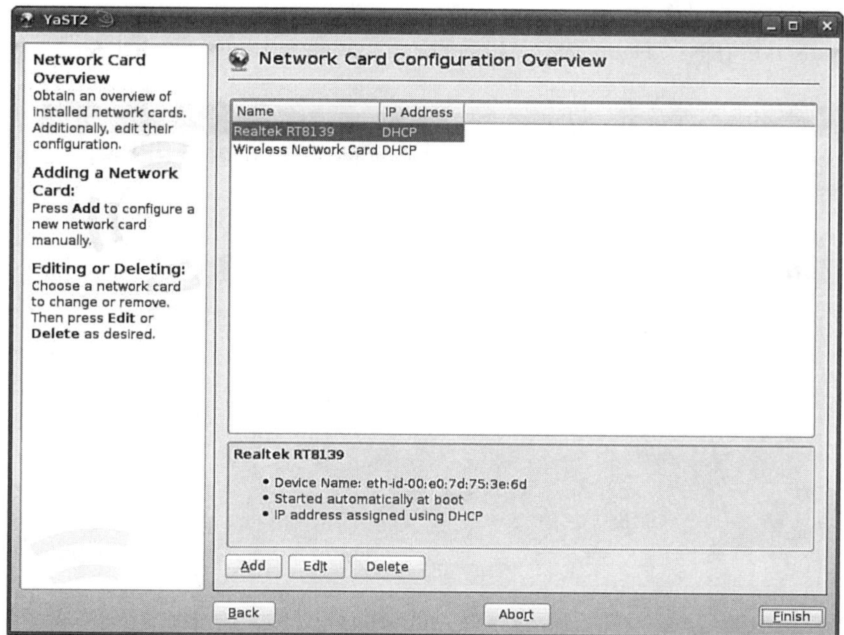

FIGURE 25.1 Edit detected network cards or add new network cards manually.

Click the Global Options tab to set your network controller. There are two methods used to control network devices on the openSUSE 10.3 system. The NetworkManager application provides a fancy, graphical front end for you to start, stop, and monitor network interfaces from your desktop. The NetworkManager appears as an icon on the KDE system tray. Clicking the icon displays the status of all network cards.

The second network setup method is the ifup command line program. If you do not want to use the graphical NetworkManager method, this program can be used manually from the command line to manually start and stop network devices. For most users, the NetworkManager method is much easier to use, and it should be selected.

To add a new card, return to the Overview tab and click Add, and then provide the necessary information to select the driver for your NIC. If your NIC is connected either by PCMCIA (typical for laptops) or USB, click the appropriate box. Click Next to continue.

After selecting the network card driver, you must configure the IP address information. Figure 25.2 shows a NIC configured for DHCP.

To set up the NIC with a static address, click the appropriate button. Enter the static address; you'll see the subnet mask is set for `255.255.255.0` by default. You can change this if you like.

Click Host Name and Name Server to give the machine a name on the network and to identify a domain name server (DNS). Figure 25.3 will appear. Change settings and click OK.

NOTE

You can also access this screen through the DNS and Host Name module under YaST Network Services.

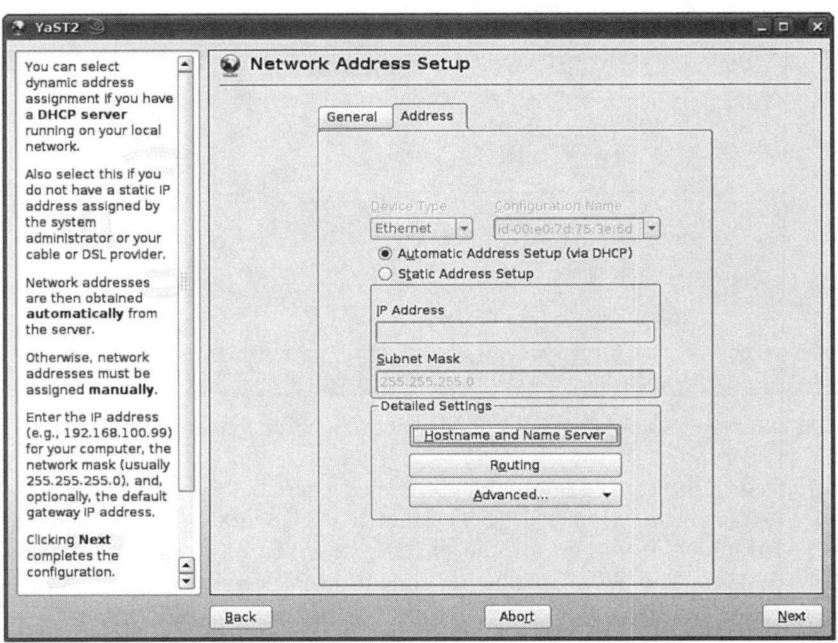

FIGURE 25.2 Addressing for this card is handled by DHCP. You can also use this screen to set up a static address or configure this machine as a router.

In the Advanced Settings, you can set a Maximum Transfer Unit (MTU) for this card, choose when to load the NIC if you don't want it to start at boot, and allow users to adjust NIC settings in the Detailed Settings menu. You can also add multiple addresses through aliases. Unless you have specific reasons for doing any of the above, you shouldn't, because the defaults will work well.

Click Next to return to the main screen and click Finish to confirm your settings. You will need to reboot to activate your card.

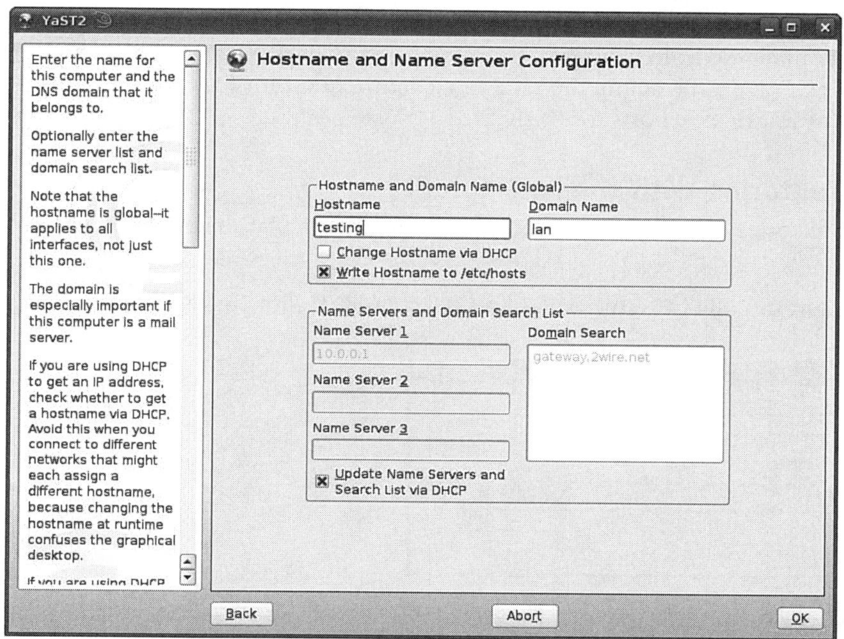

FIGURE 25.3 Give this machine a name and identify a domain name server for its Internet connection.

Using the Network File System

The Network File System (NFS) is a way for different computers on the same network to share files transparently, as if volumes and directories were all on the same computer. If a user happens to work on multiple machines, NFS allows that user to log in and access the home directory using any computer on the network.

Any computer on the network can have an NFS server, an NFS client, or both. The necessary packages are installed by default with openSUSE.

Starting and Configuring the NFS Server

To start the NFS Server on any network computer, run the NFS Server module in YaST Network Services. On the first screen, click Start NFS Server and check the Open Port in Firewall box, if necessary. Click Next to identify (export) directories to other machines.

To include a directory on the server, click Add Directory in the middle of the screen. Enter the full path of the directory or browse to it. Click OK and you will see some options. By default, all hosts on the network can see this directory, but you may limit that.

25

The options box includes the default permissions: `ro` (read-only), `root_squash` (prevents Root from another machine from changing permissions on your files), and `sync` (which requires the server to save a file before replying to a client request for it). Other options can be set here; consult man exports to see them.

Importing Directories with the NFS Client

Adding shared directories from an NFS Server to work on a particular machine is a snap in YaST.

Open the NFS Client module in Network Services. Click Add. Figure 25.4 appears.

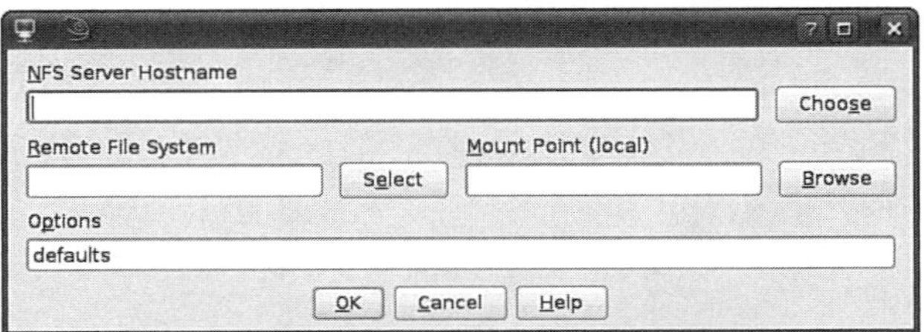

FIGURE 25.4 Add the NFS server to your file system with this dialog box.

Enter the NFS server hostname (or click Choose to search for servers on the network). Select a shared directory in the Remote Filesystem box and name a mount point (perhaps `/nfs`) on your local system. Click OK to confirm your choices, and click Finish to edit your `/etc/fstab` file to include the remote directory among the mount options for this machine.

Playing Nice with Microsoft Windows Using Samba

It may not be inevitable anymore, but there just might be one computer, or 100, running Microsoft Windows on your network. Despite vastly different file systems, it is possible, even easy, to enable those Windows machines to access files on the Linux machines, and visa versa. The Linux Samba program uses the Server Message Block (SMB) protocol to perform this miracle.

The following sections describe how to set up and configure Samba in openSUSE to interact with Windows networks.

Samba Client

The most basic function is to allow your openSUSE system to access Windows shares on your network. The Windows shares can be shared by either Windows workstations within a Microsoft network workgroup or even a Windows server within a Microsoft network domain.

The Samba client software is loaded by default in openSUSE 10.3. You can instantly browse your network for Windows shares by clicking the Network Browsing icon on the desktop. The Network Browsing icon starts Konqueror in remote mode, allowing you to scan the network for several types of remote filesystems:

- SLP services—Remote hosts using the Service Location Protocol, which is a standard Internet protocol for network resources to identify themselves on the network.
- SMB Shares—Remote hosts using the Microsoft proprietary protocol used for sharing folders and printers on the network
- Zeroconf services—Remote hosts using a relatively new network standard for network applications to advertise themselves on the network.
- Add Network Folder—Allows you to directly map to a Webfolder, FTP address, Microsoft network shared drive, or Secure Shell (ssh) connection.

If you know the network resource to which you want to connect, you can use the Add Network Folder icon to map directly to it using its Microsoft network name (`\\server\sharename`).

To browse for available Microsoft networks, click the SMB Shares icon. A new Konqueror window appears, showing any Microsoft workgroups or domains found on the network, as shown in Figure 25.5.

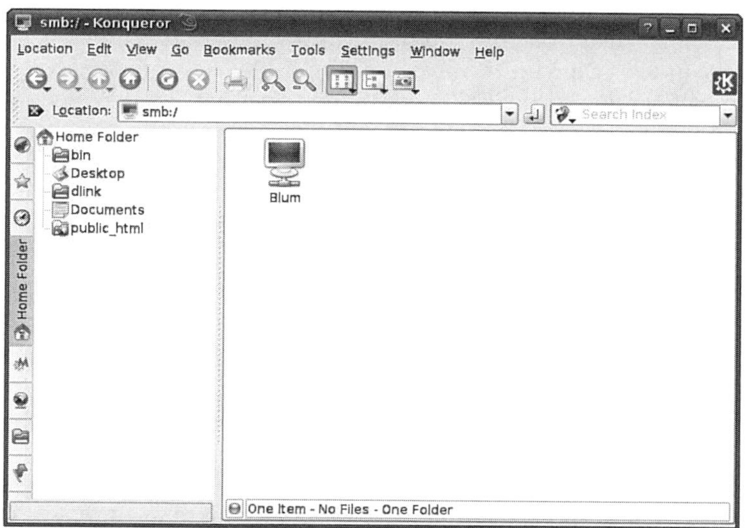

FIGURE 25.5 Browsing for Microsoft workgroups and domains.

Click the workgroup or domain you wish to browse. Another window appears, showing icons for each of the workstations or servers sharing resources in the workgroup or domain. Clicking an individual workstation or server produces another window, showing the individual shared resources offered by that system, as shown in Figure 25.6.

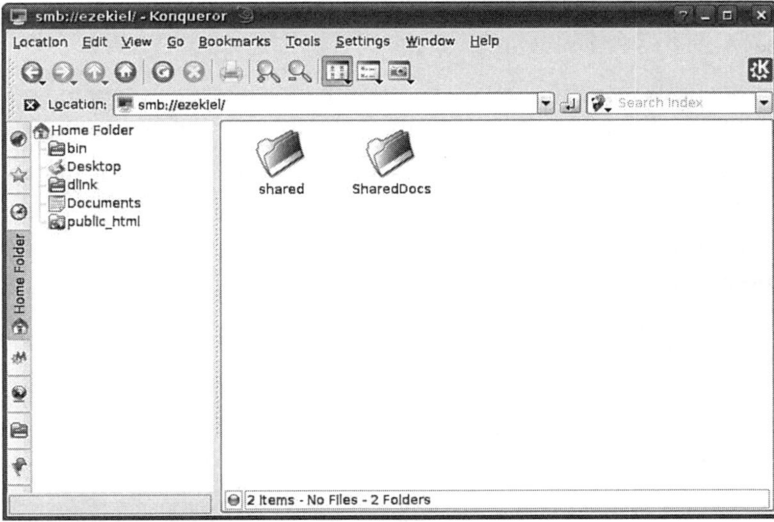

FIGURE 25.6 Displaying shared resources on a workstation.

Clicking a shared resource displays the contents of the shared resource (assuming you have permission to view the resource).

You can also configure the Samba client to allow you to log into a Microsoft Windows network domain using the Windows Domain Membership icon in the Network Services section of YaST. This feature allows your openSUSE workstation to act just like a Windows workstation by logging into the domain using a user account. Logging into the Windows domain allows you to have access to domain resources just as if you were on a Windows workstation.

Samba Server

Not only does Samba allow you to connect to Microsoft network resources, but also it allows your openSUSE system to act like a Windows server, sharing folders and printers on the network. This feature is not installed by default, so you must do a little bit of configuring to get it going.

Installing the Server

To install and configure the Samba server software, start YaST, select Network Services, and click the Samba Server entry. The Initializing Samba Server Configuration window appears, as shown in Figure 25.7.

The first time you select this feature, openSUSE will attempt to load the necessary Samba server software elements. The method used depends on the method you used to install openSUSE. If you used the CD method, YaST will ask you to insert the appropriate installation CDs.

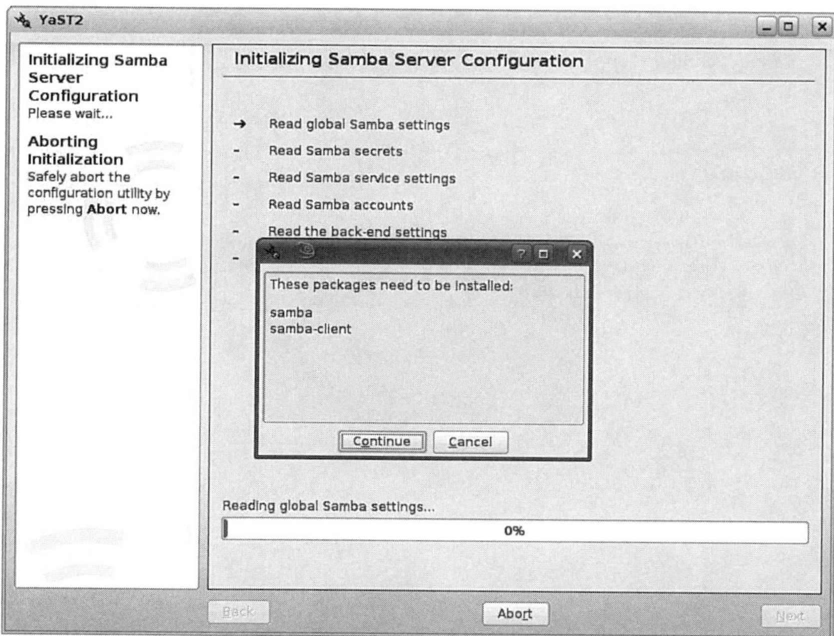

FIGURE 25.7 Starting the Samba Server configuration.

Once the Samba software is installed and the configuration files are read, the installer goes through two wizard windows, allowing you to configure the Samba server:

1. Select a workgroup or domain to which to add the server.
2. Choose if the server will be a Primary Domain Controller (PDC) for the domain or a member server. Each domain must have one PDC defined, and it can be either a Windows server or a Samba server.

After these configuration windows, the main Samba Configuration window, shown in Figure 25.8, appears.

The Samba configuration window has three tabs that divide the configuration features:

- Start-Up—Allows you to set if the Samba server starts automatically when the openSUSE system boots, as well as whether or to open a firewall port to allow remote devices to access the Samba server.
- Shares—Allows you to configure and enable shared folders on the server. After a shared folder is defined, you can enable and disable it using this control.
- Identity—Allows you to change the workgroup or domain name, as well as the server function (PDC or member server) configured earlier in the process.

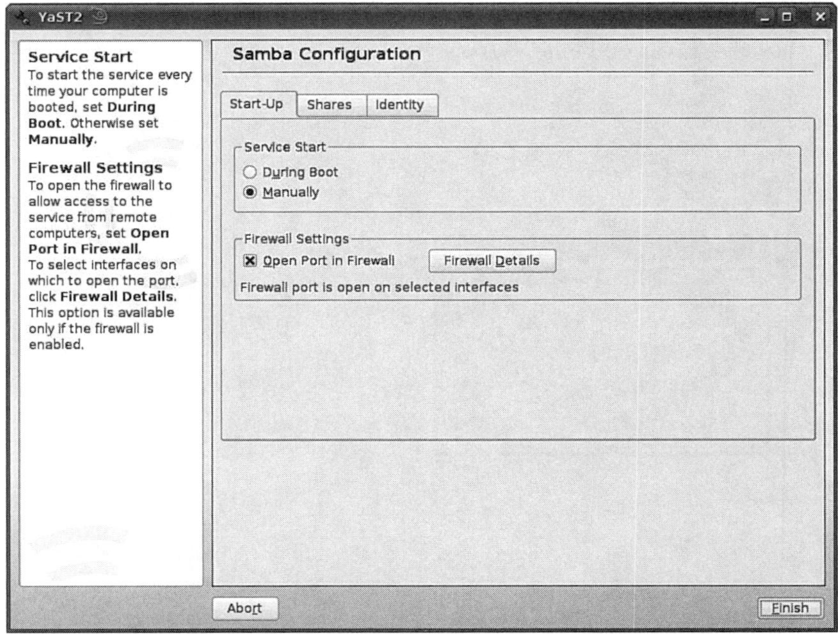

FIGURE 25.8 The Samba Configuration window.

By default, openSUSE creates shared folders for each individual user's home directory (called homes), as well as shares for access to all of the user directories (users) and group directories (groups). You can configure each share to be either Read-Only or Writable for remote network users. Be careful when sharing folders on a public network, as you do not want to provide easy access to your important data.

There are two important features that you must configure on the Identity configuration tab. Under the Advanced Settings dropdown box, there are two features:

- Expert Global Settings
- User Authentication Settings

The Expert Global Settings feature allows you to set configuration parameters for the Samba server. One important parameter that is left out of the default configuration is the `ENCRYPT PASSWORDS` parameter.

This parameter allows users on Microsoft Windows workstations and servers to connect to shares on the openSUSE system. Click the Add button, and select the `ENCRYPT PASSWORDS` option from the list of available parameters to use. You must then check the checkbox next to the parameter to ensure it is set.

The User Authentication Settings allows you to configure how the Samba server tracks user accounts and passwords. By default, it is set to use a password file, similar to how system accounts are handled. Unfortunately, the password file location is not defined in the configuration.

Highlight the smbpasswd file entry, and then click the Edit button. Type in the full pathname of the smbpassword file: /etc/samba/smbpasswd.

After saving these configuration items, you can click the Finish button to allow the Samba server wizard to save the configuration.

Configuring User Accounts

Before you can connect to shared folders or printers on the Samba server, you must specify user accounts that can be used to log into the Samba server. The Samba server is configured to use its own user and password file. Both files are located in the /etc/samba directory.

The smbuser file maps openSUSE system accounts to Samba accounts. By default, the root openSUSE system account is mapped to a Samba account called administrator. This is the default privileged account used on Windows workstations and servers. Users logged in as administrator will connect to the Samba server as the root user account.

You can also map individual openSUSE user accounts to other Windows accounts in this file. Each user account is stored on a separate line in the format:

```
user = mapping
```


where user is the openSUSE user account, and mapping is the Windows account mapping. Obviously, you do not need to map Windows accounts to openSUSE accounts if they are the same.

The next step is to assign a password to the Samba account. The smbpasswd program is used to assign passwords to Samba accounts. The first time a Samba account is created, you must use the -a option:

```
testing:/home/rich # smbpasswd -a rich
NEW PASSWORD:
RETYPE PASSWORD:
testing:/home/rich #
```

Once the account is created, you can log in from any Windows workstation or server using the user account/password combination. If you are already logged into the Windows workstation or server using the account and same password, you won't even be asked to enter it when you map to a Samba resource!

Starting the Samba Server

If you selected to start Samba automatically, the server services (smbd and nmbd) are started, and they will start every time you reboot the openSUSE system. If you selected to start Samba manually, you must manually enter two commands at the command line for it to start:

```
rich@testing:~> su
password:
testing:/home/rich # rcsmb start
testing:/home/rich # rcnmb start
```

Note that you must be root user to start the Samba server services. You can change to the Root user account using the su command line command.

The first command starts the Samba SMB service, allowing remote Microsoft (and Samba) clients to connect to shared resources. The second command starts the Samba browsing service. This service advertises your Samba server on the Microsoft network. You do not have to advertise your Samba server, thus providing a small level of security. Only clients who know your server and share names would be able to map to the Samba shares.

The Samba software provides a few command line tools to manage the Samba server. The smbstatus command can be used to quickly view any clients that are currently connected to shared resources on the server:

```
testing:/etc/samba # smbstatus

Samba version 3.0.23d-6-1083-SUSE-SL10.2
PID     Username      Group         Machine
---------------------------------------------------------------
 5029   rich          users         daniel       (10.0.1.33)

Service      pid     machine       Connected at
------------------------------------------------------
rich         5029   daniel        Tue Jan  9 21:03:36 2007
IPC$         5029   daniel        Tue Jan  9 21:03:28 2007

Locked files:
Pid          Uid         DenyMode   Access      R/W        Oplock
SharePath   Name    Time
--------------------------------------------------------------------------------
---------
5029         1000        DENY_NONE  0x100001    RDONLY     NONE
/home/rich   .   Tue Jan  9 21:03:36 2007

testing:/etc/samba #
```

The individual network clients are identified, as are any files on the system that are currently in use.

The smbclient command provides a quick command line method for connecting to Microsoft network resources. You can use it to list the shares on your Samba server:

```
linux:/home/rich # smbclient -L localhost -N
Domain=[MYDOMAIN] OS=[Unix] Server=[Samba 3.0.23d-6-1083-SUSE-SL10.2]

        Sharename       Type      Comment
        ---------       ----      -------
        profiles        Disk      Network Profiles Service
        users           Disk      All users
```

```
        groups          Disk      All groups
        print$          Disk      Printer Drivers
        netlogon        Disk      Network Logon Service
        IPC$            IPC       IPC Service (Samba 3.0.23d-6-1083-SUSE-SL10.2)
Domain=[MYDOMAIN] OS=[Unix] Server=[Samba 3.0.23d-6-1083-SUSE-SL10.2]

        Server                   Comment
        -----.                   ---.
        TESTING                    Samba 3.0.23d-6-1083-SUSE-SL10.2

        Workgroup                Master
        -----.                   ---.
        MYDOMAIN
linux:/home/rich #
```

The -L command line option specifies the address of the remote server to access (in this case, the localhost), and the -N option specifies to list all available resources (shares and printers) available on the server. This simple command allows you to quickly view what's available on the network from a specific server.

25

Securing Network Services

SUSE Linux uses xinetd, the eXtended Internet Services Daemon, to secure network services and to keep the bad guys out.

xinetd is a more secure version of the original Internet Services Daemon, inetd. It is designed in particular to protect your network from denial of service (DoS) attacks. A DoS attack occurs when someone tries to saturate a server's resources with repeated requests for services. You can limit the number of incoming connections with xinetd to something manageable.

To configure xinetd, go to the YaST Network Services page and select the xinetd module. YaST is actually reading from and writing to the /etc/xinetd.conf configuration file. Here you can set up your access control lists to allow (or deny) particular IP addresses and domain names from making requests on your network.

You can also restrict access to only some services with xinetd.

As an administrator, you should always know the services that you are offering the reason for such. Security on a server and security on a workstation are often approached from two different angles—this need not be the case, but it does provide two opposing views of how to approach the issue.

On a server, often all services are turned off and then only the ones that are needed are turned on. For example, when the server needs to host a web site, the appropriate services for that application are turned on. The downside to turning off all of the services is that you may go overboard and block applications in use. If users balk that they cannot access something they have a legitimate need to, you can turn on the appropriate service. Of course you should first ascertain that they really should be able to use that application. Services are enabled one at a time as needed until it is known exactly what the server needs, and this configuration then becomes the set of offerings for the server.

With a workstation, often you start with a host of services enabled. You then start turning them off one a time until you get to the point where you are unable to do the desired task. You then enable the application service in question once more.

Both approaches work and are useful in different scenarios. The key to both is careful research and good documentation.

References

- http://arin.net—The American Registry for Internet Numbers, the body that assigns public IP addresses for the United States.
- http://www.ietf.org/rfc.html—Search for, or get a list of, Internet Engineering Task Force Requests for Comment.
- http://www.deepspace6.net—A resource clearinghouse for information on Linux and the new IPv6 Protocol. Good links and documentation pages.
- http://www.tldp.org/HOWTO/Linux+IPv6-HOWTO—The Linux IPv6 HOWTO.
- http://www.ietf.org/rfc/rfc2460.txt—The IPv6 Standard document.
- http://linuxreviews.org/features/ipv6—Interesting article on "Why You Want IPv6."
- http://www.iana.org/assignments/port-numbers—Learn what ports are assigned to what applications at the Internet Assigned Numbers Authority site.
- http://directory.google.com/Top/Computers/Software/Internet/Servers/Address_Management/Dynamic_DNS_Services/—The place to find Dynamic DNS service providers.
- http://www.isc.org/sw/dhcp—The keepers of the SUSE Linux default DHCP server package and the optional client. You can view the current DHCP README file online at the ISC site.
- http://dhcp-monger.est-unique.net/wakka.php?wiki=Welcome—The DHCP-Mongers Wiki. Read man pages, search the mailing lists, and submit new information.
- http://nfs.sourceforge.net—The Network File System project page, including FAQ list.
- http://www.samba.org—The Samba home page. See the "HOWTO" collection and "Samba-By-Example Guide" in the Documentation section.
- http://wi-fi-jiwire.com—Find a wireless hotspot wherever you may be at this site, sponsored by the WiFi Alliance trade group.
- http://standards.ieee.org/getieee802—Get the official IEEE standard document for any 802.xx networking specification here. This runs the gamut from Ethernet (802.3) to WiFi (802.11) and beyond.

- http://portal.suse.com/sdb/en/2002/11/wavelan.html—Wireless network setup from the SUSE Support Database.
- http://www.hpl.hp.com/personal/Jean_Tourrilhes/Linux/Wireless.html—Good material on Linux wireless networking.
- http://www.securityfocus.com/unix—This comprehensive security site offers security news, mailing lists, and even some firewall rule sets.
- http://www.linuxsecurity.com—Get the weekly "Linux Advisory Watch" and "Linux Security Week" newsletters to keep up with the latest information and patches. Tutorials for beginners and articles for security professionals.
- http://www.insecure.org—The home of the nmap security scanner.
- http://www.ethereal.com—The freeware Ethereal network protocol analyzer and packet sniffer.

CHAPTER 26

Managing Web and FTP Servers

IN THIS CHAPTER

With the exception of peer-to-peer services, when you get information, documents, software, and other goodies from the Internet, chances are you are visiting a web or FTP server. Your openSUSE system can easily perform either of these functions. This chapter will help you to do that.

Most of the chapter is focused on the most popular web server platform on the Web, the open source Apache server. You'll learn a little bit about some open source and commercial Apache alternatives, some of which are included on the openSUSE DVD. Finally, there's an introduction to the Very Secure FTP server to help you transfer files more safely (both for your system and the clients who approach).

What Is Apache?

There is no World Wide Web without web servers, more accurately called *httpd* servers. And there is no more popular web server than the open-source Apache server. In Chapter 14, "Creating Basic Websites," you played a little bit with Apache in setting up a test system for your website and blog. Here we will go into more detail on the topics of setting up and administering your web server.

In the beginning, there was the National Center for Supercomputing Applications (NCSA). Although the World Wide Web was first invented by Sir Tim Berners-Lee while he was at the Conseil Européen pour la Recherche Nucléaire (CERN) in Switzerland, the Web could not become what it is today without two practical additions: a server and a browser. The pioneers for both these applications were at NCSA at the University of Illinois.

A web server is nothing more than an application that runs silently in the background, listening for incoming requests from another computer for a particular document. After it receives a request, the server responds with the document, using the Hypertext Transfer Protocol (HTTP). The NCSA developed the first popular server application, HTTPd, but eventually lost interest in the project. Development on HTTPd formally ended in 1998.

A group of users and developers continued to work on the open-source code for HTTPd, fixing bugs and adding features in a haphazard way. Things were formalized when Bob Behlendorf and Cliff Skolnick set up a site where these HTTPd patches could all go. Before long (or so the legend goes), "a patchy server" got a formal name, Apache.

Marc Andreessen and others on the HTTPd team also worked on NCSA Mosaic, the first successful browser application. Andreessen went on to produce a commercial application, Netscape Navigator, that built on the Mosaic code.

Over the years, Apache has become by far the most popular web server application. Netcraft has been monitoring server usage since October 1995, when HTTPd was still number 1. Apache has been the most popular server since October 1996 and has steadily increased its market share.

The Apache Software Foundation (ASF) was incorporated in 1999 as the official guardians of the project. Today it has a board of directors elected annually by ASF members. It hosts two dozen web-related software projects that share the open-source Apache License.

The Apache 2.0 web server was released in 2002 and is included in your openSUSE Linux DVD. You can also download source code directly from the project website, http://httpd.apache.org/download.cgi, and build it yourself.

Installing Apache

You can install Apache through YaST, just like any other package. This is by far the easiest way. During the basic openSUSE install, if you click the Web and LAMP Server pattern, Apache v2.2.3 will be added to your base installation. Otherwise, open the YaST Software Management module and select the Pattterns filter at the top of the left pane. This will get you to the Web and LAMP Server pattern. When you search for Apache in YaST, you'll see a couple dozen packages, including several modules and Perl scripts that are optional but that may be useful to you.

When you install Apache 2.x, you will need one of the multiprocessing module (MPM) packages to run the server. The MPM is the component responsible for listening for network connections, accepting the request, and passing it to children processes for handling. There are two module packages available, apache2_prefork and apache2_worker, but only one can be loaded into the server at a given time.

The apache2_prefork package is installed with the Web and LAMP Server pattern. This MPM handles requests using forked processes. The more advanced worker MPM handles requests using threads and is more geared toward use on a multiprocessor system. The worker MPM also has been known to wreak havoc with some older modules. It's important to select the correct MPM based on your needs and hardware.

Be sure to install the `apache2-example-pages` as well (it's included in the pattern). This will let you test whether Apache is working immediately after installation.

If you prefer to get under the hood and see exactly what is going on, however, you can still compile your web server from source code.

Building Apache from the Source Code

You can get the latest stable source code from the Apache download site at http://httpd.apache.org/download.cgi. This page will point you to a mirror site that changes constantly. You can choose from a tarball, called `httpd-<version-number>.tar`, compressed with either gzip or bzip2. These archives are a few megabytes each and should not take too long to download, even with a dial-up connection.

CAUTION

Installing Apache from source can be a difficult task. Before attempting to do this, you should be very comfortable with your knowledge of your system and how all the various parts work together. You should know what to do in case of a problem. Much less can go wrong when you install via YaST, or even by using the standard Red Hat Package Managers (RPMs), and you can always uninstall an errant RPM package. That is not the case with source code.

After the download is complete, you should extract the archive into a safe temporary directory, such as `/tmp`. The archive creates a new `httpd_<version-number>` directory to store its files. This directory will contain a README file, a LICENSE file, and an INSTALL file.

The README file lists introductory information about the httpd server itself, where to find the latest version and documentation, acknowledgements, and whom to contact if you want to become involved or report a bug. The LICENSE file enumerates the terms and conditions for use and redistribution of the server software. The INSTALL file gives a quick overview at the installation process. Be sure to check out these files before attempting to build Apache.

Apache relies heavily on the use of autoconf and libtool, and although you could compile Apache the old-fashioned way by editing Makefile templates, you'll find it easier to use the `configure` script that comes in the tarball. To do this, open a shell (as a regular user), change directories to the location of the extracted tarball (that is, `/tmp/httpd_<version-number>`, if you're following along), and then type the following command:

```
./configure —help
```

The script will output a list of configuration options you can use to fine-tune the compile process and Apache's setup. After you've read through the list and determined which options best suit you, run the configure script again:

```
./configure —prefix=/usr/local/httpd2 —with-mpm=prefork —enable-so  \
     —enable-rewrite
```

The files will be placed in `/usr/include/apache2` by default when the compiled httpd is installed, so you may want to specify a different directory using the prefix option as I did earlier. Keeping Apache's binary files, scripts, configuration files, and modules all together is a good idea and makes things easier if you later need to upgrade or remove the server.

The configure script generates the necessary Makefile to compile the server. Type **`make`** to begin compiling the source code. After the code has been compiled, log in as the SuperUser and type **`make install`** to complete the installation and install the files under the directory you specified with configure's prefix option.

You can now configure your server. See the "Runtime Server Configuration Settings" section later in this chapter for ways to do that.

TIP

If you have already installed Apache and want to upgrade to a newer source version, try creating symlinks from the old installation to the new extracted directory.

Starting and Stopping Apache

Now you've installed Apache with its default configuration. SUSE Linux provides a default home page, `/srv/www/htdocs/index.html`, in English and several other languages to test whether Apache is working properly. The proper way to run Apache is to have the web server run after the system has booted, the network is configured, and any firewall is loaded. The YaST Runlevel Editor takes care of this for you. This module is located on the YaST System page. See "Using the Runlevel Editor" in Chapter 22, "Managing the Boot Process and Other Services."

TIP

In the Advanced mode of the Runlevel Editor, make sure Apache is set to load at Runlevels 3 and 5.

After that is done, open any browser to http://localhost. If you have installed the sample pages package, you should see Figure 26.1.

You can also use a wrapper script, `apachectl`, to start and stop the Apache server without having to reboot the entire machine. This comes in handy when you tweak httpd's configuration and need to restart the service for the changes to take effect. The script is found in the same directory as the httpd binary and in its simplest incantation, followed by `start`, `restart`, `graceful`, or `stop`:

```
./apachectl start
```

Intuitively, `start` and `stop` will start and stop the server, respectively. You can use `restart` to stop and immediately start the server again, or use `graceful` to give Apache a chance to finish any tasks it's performing before stopping (a graceful stop).

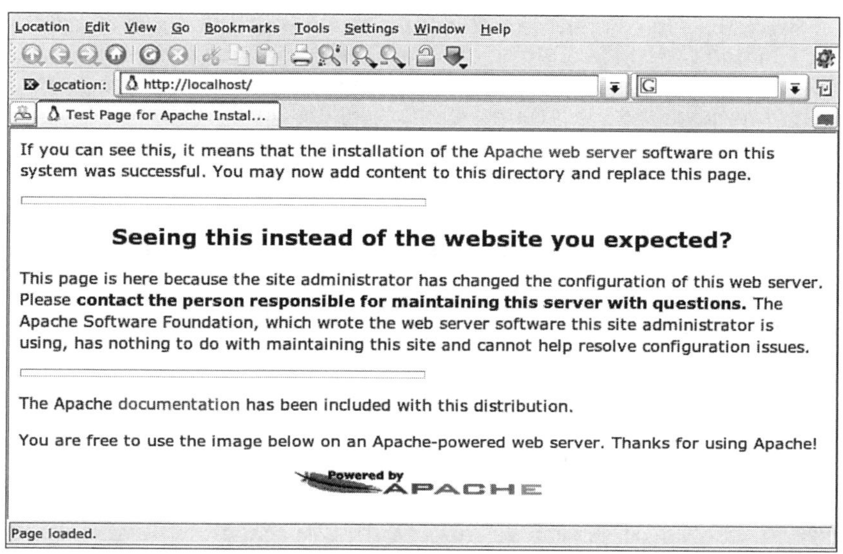

FIGURE 26.1 If Apache is installed correctly, you'll get this test page when pointing a browser to http://localhost.

Runtime Server Configuration Settings

Running Apache with its default settings should suit most uses. There are some tweaks you can make to customize Apache to your own liking or needs. If you installed Apache using YaST, Apache's standard configuration file is stored in `/etc/Apache2/httpd.conf`. If you installed Apache manually, the `httpd.conf` file will reside in the etc subdirectory of whatever you specified as Apache's base directory using configure's prefix option. You can either use SUSEConfig or edit this file directly to customize your server.

The SUSEConfig editor is located on the YaST System page. To configure Apache, go to Network, WWW, Apache2. Open the tree (click the + sign) to view the settings. These include the following:

- `APACHE_HTTPD_CONF`—Use this setting to specify a different configuration file than the default `httpd.conf`.
- `APACHE_MPM`—Multiprocessing modules are compiled into Apache and handle tasks such as network and process management. Remember, Apache can use only one MPM at a time. You can have both MPMs installed, but this setting determines which MPM is used. By default, SUSE Linux installs the `prefork` MPM.
- `APACHE_SERVERADMIN`—Useful only if `APACHE_SERVERSIGNATURE` is set to `email`. This setting lists the administrator's email address. The default is `webmaster@`<hostname>, where <hostname> is taken from the `HOSTS` file.
- `APACHE_SERVERNAME`—This is an important setting, especially if the server is open to the Internet and not just your LAN. Use this to define your fully qualified domain

name, such as www.susefan.com, because this is the name your server will return when pinged. You don't need to set this if the machine's canonical name (that is, what SUSE calls your machine) is fine with you; Apache will use this by default. If you administer your own DNS (see Chapter 27, "Managing Domain Names," for information on how to do that), be sure to add an alias for your host. Otherwise, ask the manager of your DNS (your ISP, for example) to set this name.

- `APACHE_CONF_INCLUDE_FILES`—Create a custom configuration file and name it `httpd.conf.local`. Use this setting to have Apache use the custom configuration file in addition to the default. You can add multiple files separated by spaces.
- `APACHE_CONF_INCLUDE_DIRS`—Suppose you have a server application and its configuration file installs to a directory other than `/etc/Apache2`. Use this setting to allow Apache to read this configuration file. You can add multiple directories separated by spaces.
- `APACHE_MODULES`—This is where modules installed by YaST are activated. Look over the Description text for hints on various modules.
- `APACHE_SERVER_FLAGS`—This is the equivalent of starting Apache from the command line with various switches to turn features on and off. Review the Apache man page to see a list of switches/flags you can enter here.
- `APACHE_START_TIMEOUT`—By default, if the kernel tries to start Apache during boot, and Apache does not start in 2 seconds, it will report a timeout. You can extend this time (if, for example, you have some security features added that will slow response time) here.
- `APACHE_SERVERSIGNATURE`—This starts a footer at the bottom of any server-generated error page. By default, this includes the server name and Apache version number. If you want to include a contact point for the user to find you, set this to `email` and enter an email address at `APACHE_SERVERADMIN`. If you prefer that nothing appear, set this to `no`.
- `APACHE_LOGLEVEL`—This defines what gets entered into the server logs by setting the minimum level. By default, this is set at `warn`, so only problems that generate warnings (or worse) are entered. Informational messages are screened out. You should change this only if you are trying to troubleshoot a problem that might generate a lower-level message.
- `APACHE_ACCESS_LOG`—The location of your access log. Who is visiting?
- `APACHE_USE_CANONICAL_NAME`—This is turned off by default; turn it on so that Apache delivers the ServerName listed earlier. Use the DNS setting to let the domain name server handle requests for the server name.
- `APACHE_SERVERTOKENS`—This tells Apache how much information it delivers about itself when asked. The default is the OS on which it is running. You can set this higher or lower.
- `APACHE_EXTENDED_STATUS`—You can get additional information in your server status reports with this option turned on, but recording it will slow the server down some.

- APACHE_BUFFERED_LOGS—Use this to get Apache to store several log entries in memory and write them together to disk, rather than writing them after each request. On some systems, this may result in more efficient disk access and hence higher performance. It may be set only once for the entire server; it cannot be configured per virtual host.
- APACHE_TIMEOUT—This is how long, in seconds, Apache attempts to process a request before giving up. By default, this is set at 300 seconds (5 minutes).

Additional Settings in `httpd.conf`

Most important Apache settings can be configured in /etc/sysconfig, but some must be edited in Apache's own configuration file, /etc/Apache2/httpd.conf. Consult the Apache documentation for a listing of all the settings, also called directives, but you should consider changing the following defaults:

- DocumentRoot—This should be set to the top directory from which you want to serve files. The default is /srv/www/htdocs.
- MaxClients—The maximum number of concurrent clients (that is, visiting browsers). The default is 150, but it probably should be set with consideration to the amount of traffic you expect.
- Port—Where Apache listens for traffic. This is set by default at port 80, the assigned port for HTTP traffic. This also may be set to port 8080 depending on your intended setup.
- Directory—Set directory permissions with this directive.
- DirectoryIndex—The file(s) Apache looks for when a request is made for the index or listing of a directory. Several documents can be listed (so you can list such files as index.php, index.shtml, index.htm, index.txt, and so on), and the server will return the first one in the list that it finds. If none of the documents exist, then, depending on how you've configured things, Apache may try to generate its own directory listing.
- UserDir—In every user's home directory, there is a subdirectory called public_html. To have Apache recognize files in this directory, set it here. The address for these pages would be http://<servername>/~<username>.

26

File System Authentication and Access Control

You may have some documents in your web directory that you don't want the whole world to have access to. From a user's standpoint, you've often come across pages that require a password or that simply tell you that you aren't authorized to use this page. In this section, you'll learn how to protect parts of your site from prying eyes through user authentication and authorization.

Restricting Access with `allow` and `deny`

Apache lets you restrict access to your site based on IP addresses or hostnames. This is done through directives in `httpd.conf` called `allow` and `deny`.

Suppose you plan to host an `apt` package repository at `susefan.com/pub/`, but you don't want anyone outside of `susefan.com` downloading its files with a browser. You would add these lines to `httpd.conf`:

```
<Location /pub>
    SetHandler pub
    Order deny, allow
    Deny from all
    Allow from susefan.com
</Location>
```

Note the four statements. First, we told Apache that when someone tries to access the `/pub` directory, it needs to check whether the person is allowed. Then we set the order for Apache to check—first process the `deny` statements and then the `allow` statements. In this case, the statements are easy to follow: Deny everyone, unless the request originates from a host within the `susefan.com` domain.

You can describe your limits for either `deny` or `allow` in six ways:

- `all` affects everyone.
- A full or partial IP address, such as 192.168.1.101 or 192.168.1. This is preferred over a domain name because it's faster to process.
- A full or partial host or domain name, such as `susefan.com`. This is a little slower than an IP address because Apache must do a DNS lookup to confirm the host.
- A network/netmask pair such as 192.168.1.0/255.255.1.0.
- A network address in the classless interdomain routing (CIDR) form, such as 192.168.1.0/24.
- An environment variable, such as env=allowed_hosts.

Authentication

Many organizations have a members-only section of their website where information is stored that the rest of the world can't access. To see the information in such a restricted area, users must prove they are authorized to do so, usually by providing a username and password.

Apache Basic Authentication is the most common authentication method used, probably because it is quite straightforward in its approach. When someone attempts to access a protected page, Apache asks for a username and a password. It then verifies the username and password and if successful, Apache serves the request.

CAUTION

Basic Authentication does not encrypt the password when you type it in, so don't use valuable passwords (such as your login password) for your protected page.

Similarly, webmasters should not use Basic Authentication for highly sensitive data. You have the option of using Apache Digest Authentication (which is more secure, but not always supported by browsers) using SSL/TLS or finding some more secure means of making the data available to a selected group. Consult the Apache documentation for information on Digest Authentication.

The first step in implementing Basic Authentication is to create a plain-text list of usernames and passwords. This is done using `htpasswd2`, a script included with the Apache2 package and installed to the same directory as httpd and apachectl. You should store these passwords away from your main Apache installation directory, making it harder for rogue applications to find them, so make a new directory (as the SuperUser) to hold this file, such as `/usr/local/httpd2/passwd` first.

NOTE

Basic Authentication is implemented with the `mod_auth` module. In the unlikely event that you get a `command not found` error message when running `htpasswd2`, make sure this module is installed.

When you have created this directory, type this command to create a new hidden password file, with the first user included:

```
./htpasswd -c  /usr/local/httpd2/passwd/.htpasswd mikemc
```

You'll be prompted twice for this user's password:

```
New password:
Re-type new password:
Adding password for user mikemc
```

To add new users to this file, use the same command without the `-c` switch (which creates a new file):

```
./htpasswd /usr/local/httpd2/passwd/.htpasswd newuser
```

Next, you need to tell Apache to refer to `.htpasswd` when serving a protected page. You do this in one of two ways: directly through `httpd.conf` or by creating a new `.htaccess` file. The `.htaccess` file should be located in the directory you want to protect; in the example used in the `allow/deny` section, this would be `/pub/.htaccess`. In `httpd.conf`, you would create a new section labeled `<Directory /pub>`. Either way, the syntax is the same. Use these four directives:

```
AuthType Basic

AuthName "Members Only"

AuthUserFile /usr/local/httpd2/passwd/.htpasswd

Require user mikemc
```

Here the `AuthType` is Basic because we're using Basic Authentication (the option would be set to Digest if mod_auth-digest was used). The `AuthName` can be anything and identifies the realm or category of that page. In this case, all pages with the `AuthName` Members Only would have the same password. Thus, when the browser went to another page marked Members Only, it could deliver the same password without forcing the user to retype it in an endless series of pop-up dialog boxes. The `AuthUserFile` points to the `.htpasswd` file containing the usernames and passwords. The `Require` directive specifies the user(s) allowed to access the page.

If, instead of one person having access to a resource, you want to create a group of users with the same level of access, create a group file named `.htgroup` in any text editor with the Group Name and a list of users. Save it in the same directory as `.htpasswd`. The `entry in .htgroup` file should look like this:

```
Members: mikemc robsh ltorvalds svillinski
```

The concept of the two files is similar to Linux's `/etc/passwd` and `/etc/group` files; `.htpasswd` stores each username and password hash, and `.htgroup` aggregates usernames into logical groups. Each group member needs to have a password listed in `.htpasswd` before access is allowed.

Now edit your `.htaccess` file so that your group has access.

```
AuthType Basic
AuthName "Members Only"
AuthUserFile /usr/local/httpd2/passwd/.htpasswd

AuthGroupFile /usr/local/httpd2/passwd/.htgroups
Require group Members
```

Everyone in the Members group would now have access to all pages with the Members Only realm.

NOTE

You can create as many groups as you want in your `.htgroups` file. Each entry is a single line listing all its members together, separated only by a space.

Apache Modules

It should not surprise you that the patchy server does most of its work through modules. After all, it's this very modular design that has enabled it to become a powerful, flexible web server. Some 50 core modules are included in the Apache2 package, and a couple dozen more are included in the SUSE Linux distribution. All are installable with YaST. In addition, nearly 400 modules are stored in the Apache Module Registry at http://modules.apache.org.

The following is but a brief sampling of the modules available for Apache:

- bw_mod—Limits the number of simultaneous connections and bandwidth usage for virtual hosts and directories.
- mod_auth_mysql—Adds MySQL database-based authentication.
- mod_bt—Extends Apache to handle the BitTorrent protocol and act as a tracker.
- mod_clamav—Scans files for viruses with ClamAV before serving them to the client.
- mod_ftpd—Extends Apache to handle FTP transactions.
- mod_gnutls—An alternative to mod_ssl that provides the capability to use SSL/TLS.
- mod_mono—Serves ASP.NET client applications in a non-Windows environment with Mono.
- mod_perl—Processes embedded Perl code before serving a document.
- mod_php5—Processes embedded PHP code before serving a document.
- mod_python—Processes Python code embedded in the page before serving a document.
- mod_rewrite—Manipulates URL addresses according to rules written using regular expressions.
- mod_ruby—Processes Ruby code embedded in the page before serving a document.
- mod_so—Enables usage of modules linked at runtime in contrast to those only statically compiled.
- mod_ssl—Adds the capability to establish and communicate across SSL/TLS connections.
- mod_websh—Processes Tcl code embedded in the page before serving a document.
- mod_xslt—A filter that transforms XML files into other formats on-the-fly by applying XSLT stylesheets.

Each module adds new directives that can be added to your configuration files. Make sure the module is compatible with your Apache installation, though. Changes made to Apache between versions 1.3.x and 2.x break some modules. All that information, including the module's installation procedures and the new configuration directives they make available, can be found either in the module's or Apache's documentation.

Virtual Hosting

Apache lets you host several domains with a single instance of the server, a process referred to as *virtual hosting*. This service can be a godsend for the system administrator overseeing an installation with limited resources, such as hardware, static IP addresses, or even time to monitor several server setups. Virtual hosting is implemented through several directives included in `httpd.conf`.

> **NOTE**
>
> The `mod_vhost_alias` module is another virtual hosting tool included with the core Apache package. It is designed for use by ISPs and other large sites.

There are two ways to implement virtual hosts in Apache: name-based and IP-address–based hosting. This section covers both options.

In either case, you must first tell Apache the IP addresses that have multiple domains associated with them. You can either use a specific IP address or the `*` variable to indicate that Apache should consider any request it receives as a candidate for virtual hosting. Open `httpd.conf` and type

```
NameVirtualHost *
```

Name-Based Virtual Hosting

According to the HTTP/1.1 specification, when a client seeks out a document from a server, it includes the expected domain in its request. Although various domains may resolve to the same IP address with a DNS query, the domain names in the HTTP requests will still be different. This is the basic principle of name-based virtual hosting.

This type of virtual hosting (also known as *vhosting*) is the easiest and most popular way to handle hosting multiple domains. With this method, you need only one IP address to host several domain names. Apache receives a request, examines it to identify the desired domain, and obliges with the proper page.

You'll need to add `VirtualHost` sections in the configuration file for each domain name after the NameVirtualHost directive. For example, if you want to host a personal site at www.YourName.com and a second site, www.susefan.com, this is how you would enter them in `httpd.conf`:

```
<VirtualHost *>
    ServerName www.YourName.com
    DocumentRoot /srv/www/htdocs/YourName.com
    ServerAdmin webmaster@YourName.com
    ErrorLog /var/log/apache2/www.YourName.com-error_log
    CustomLog /var/log/apache2/www.YourName.com-access_log common
</VirtualHost>
```

```
<VirtualHost *>
    ServerName www.susefan.com
    DocumentRoot /srv/www/htdocs/susefan.com
    ServerAdmin webmaster@susefan.com
    ScriptAlias /srv/www/htdocs/susefan.com/cgi-bin
    ErrorLog /var/log/apache2/www.susefan.com-error_log
    CustomLog /var/log/apache2/www.susefan.com-access_log common
</VirtualHost>
```

CAUTION

Although SSL/TLS have not been discussed, it is still worth mentioning that Apache cannot distinguish different security certificates for name-based virtual hosts. This is because SSL/TLS operate at a socket level, and the request has already been encrypted by the time Apache receives it. This may cause warnings to be triggered by the client's browser, depending on the common name listed by the certificate. In these cases, IP-Address–Based virtual hosting is recommended.

As the server receives the request, it will scan through the configuration file seeking a virtual host entry's ServerName or ServerAlias directive that matches the expected domain. If no matching entry can be found, the first virtual host is used. The virtual host first inherits the directives set earlier in the `httpd.conf` file and then overrides those explicitly set for the host.

In the preceding example, www.YourName.com will use whatever ScriptAlias value is defined in the base configuration, whereas www.susefan.com will use `/srv/www/htdocs/susefan.com/cgi-bin`.

IP-Address–Based Virtual Hosting

Hosting multiple IP addresses is a little more complex than hosting multiple names, but it is more widely supported. All but a very few ancient browsers (that is, those browsers that support only HTTP/1.0) support name-based vhosts, but if you want to be universal, this is the way to go.

NOTE

Kernel support for multi-IP-hosting, called IP aliasing, must be enabled for these commands to work. This is the default setting for openSUSE Linux.

Setting up IP-based vhosting is a two-step process. First, you must identify the addresses to use. As the SuperUser, run `ifconfig` to find the Internet address (listed here as `inet addr`) attached to `eth0`, your Ethernet connection. It should show up similar to the following:

```
inet addr:172.26.1.33
```

Then use ifconfig to bind more addresses to the network interface:

```
/sbin/ifconfig eth0:0 172.26.1.40
/sbin/ifconfig eth0:1 172.16.1.41
```

Now you can enter the same VirtualHost statements in httpd.conf as you did when using names, with changed:

```
<VirtualHost 172.26.1.40>
    ServerName www.YourName.com
    DocumentRoot /srv/www/htdocs/YourName.com
    ServerAdmin webmaster@YourName.com
    ErrorLog /var/log/apache2/www.YourName.com-error_log
    CustomLog /var/log/apache2/www.YourName.com-access_log common
</VirtualHost>

<VirtualHost 172.26.1.41>
    ServerName www.susefan.com
    DocumentRoot /srv/www/htdocs/susefan.com
    ServerAdmin webmaster@susefan.com
    ScriptAlias /srv/www.htdocs/susefan.com/cgi-bin
    ErrorLog /var/log/apache2/www.susefan.com-error_log
    CustomLog /var/log/apache2/www.susefan.com-access_log common
</VirtualHost>
```

Dynamic Content

Active content on a web page can range from a simple form or opinion poll, to a search-engine results page, to a portal with personalized news content.

Apache offers three methods of generating active content: common gateway interface (CGI) scripts, server-side includes (SSI), and active content modules such as mod_perl.

Chapter 31, "Creating Dynamic Websites," covers the creative end of making active content. This section is a brief introduction into the nuts and bolts of delivering this content to users.

CGI Programs

CGI is a specification that allows a web server to execute programs and scripts that reside on the web server and return their output back to the client. CGI programming is the most common method of generating dynamic content for the web. Almost any language can be used, although Perl, Python, and C tend to be the most popular.

The easiest (and most secure) way to activate the CGI capabilities of Apache is to create a special directory that will contain all the scripts, and specify it using the ScriptAlias directive. Traditionally, the name of the directory is cgi-bin. Apache will try to run any file that resides in that directory.

Remember, these programs must be executable by the system Apache user. When you place your programs there, the permissions must be set to permit this:

```
chmod 755 program.cgi
```

Another way to enable CGI is to add `+ExecCGI` to the directory's Options directive and then set a handler for files with certain extensions. These changes can be made either in the `http.conf` or `.htaccess` file:

```
Options +ExecCGI
AddHandler cgi-script .cgi .pl
```

In the preceding code, files in the directory with a `.cgi` or `.pl` extension will be handled as CGI scripts. Apache will execute the scripts and return the results to the requesting client.

Depending on your security requirements, you can also add this code:

```
<Files *.cgi>
     Options +ExecCGI
     SetHandler cgi-script
</Files>
```


Server-Side Includes

SSIs are specially crafted comments called *elements*, which are embedded in a web page and interpreted by Apache. They can be used to include the contents of other files, display environment variables (such as the current date and time) or a file's timestamp, and produce program outputs.

To enable SSI, _mod_include must be available to Apache, and you must add `+Includes` to the directory's Options directive either in `http.conf` or in `.htaccess`:

```
Options +Includes
```

There are then two methods for identifying a file for processing as an SSI document. The first is to specify a file extension, traditionally `.shtml`, and associate a handler to process files that end with that extension:

```
AddType text/html  .shtml
AddHandler server-parsed  .shtml
```

The directives may be placed in either the `http.conf` or a `.htaccess` file. When set, Apache will process all files with the `.shtml` extension for SSI elements before returning the results to the requesting client.

The second method for identifying a file is by turning on the XBitHack directive and setting the execute permission bit on any SSI file. Again, they may be set either in `.htaccess` or `httpd.conf`.

```
XBitHack on
```

With `XBitHack` turned on, Apache will parse all files that the user has permission to execute, regardless of the file's extension.

Active Content Modules

If you find yourself writing a lot of CGI scripts in a particular interpreted language, it might be beneficial to see if a module exists that integrates the language's interpreter with Apache. For example, you would probably do better in the long run using the `mod_perl` Apache module instead of processing your Perl-powered pages through CGI. When you call a script from Apache, the Perl interpreter process starts, does its work, and then eventually stops. You can just imagine what that does to your system's resources if you have 20 scripts running simultaneously, even if just for a few seconds. When you channel those scripts through a module, everything is handled by one native interpreter. This makes everything go faster—and safer.

The downside is that `mod_perl` is much fussier about errors. Apache doesn't really mind if you don't release a resource programmatically, because it shuts down the script before that becomes a problem. In a module, errors accumulate and become real problems. The upside is that you will become a better programmer as a result of fixing all these problems.

Some languages are specifically designed to be run through an Apache module, such as PHP. PHP can be used to process scripts through CGI; the language's documentation encourages the use of an Apache module over the CGI implementation.

openSUSE Linux provides Apache modules for four scripting languages: `mod_perl`, `mod_python`, `mod_php5`, and `mod_ruby`. See Chapter 30, "Using Perl and Python," and Chapter 31 for more information about using these languages.

Other Web Servers

Apache may be number one in the web server business, but it is not the only one. Aside from IIS (a commercial web server product from Microsoft), several general-purpose web servers can run on Linux. Specialized web servers, such as the Zope application server, and J2EE application servers, also run on Linux.

This section covers some of the server products that will run on openSUSE Linux.

thttpd

This tiny server (only 129KB), included in openSUSE Linux and installable via YaST, aims to be a simple, small, fast, and secure web server. It's not as feature rich as Apache or other server applications, but it does support CGI, Basic Authentication, virtual hosting, and bandwidth throttling.

Caudium WebServer

The Caudium WebServer is on par with Apache but again with different strengths and weaknesses. It is a non-forking, threaded web server. It offers a web-based configuration interface, templating with the RoXen Macro Language (RXML), Pike code embedding, and the Supports Database, a method through which the requesting browser's capabilities can be identified without using JavaScript in the web document. Caudium is not distributed with SUSE, but its source code can be downloaded from the project's home page.

Xitami

Xitami is a small, multi-threaded and modular web server application that can also handle FTP requests. It supports direct support for CGI scripts written in Perl, Awk and Python, Basic Authentication, virtual hosting, on-the-fly server configuration, and server-side XML processing. Xitami is not distributed with SUSE, but the project's source code can be downloaded from its website.

Zope

Zope is an open-source web-application server written mostly in Python. It is included in SUSE Linux and is installable via YaST.

Zope is an excellent content management framework and is geared toward serving dynamic pages. Zope can do its own web serving and has many of the same modules to do its work that Apache does, but it is often used together with Apache.

The best thing about Zope as a web server is that the simple web-based interface makes configuration much easier than with Apache.

ColdFusion

Adobe's ColdFusion server bills itself as a fast way to create powerful web-based applications. It can run as a standalone application server, integrate with Apache, or work in conjunction with other J2EE solutions to serve CFML documents. The main benefit of the ColdFusion server is its Java underpinnings, which allow developers to use third-party Java code in their Internet applications, and tight integration with other Adobe technologies. Free trial and developer versions are available from the company's website.

TomCat

The TomCat servlet container is part of the Apache Foundation's open-source Jakarta project and embodies the industry's standard implementation for the servlets and JSP interfaces. It can be configured as a standalone application server or integrated with Apache to serve JSP pages. TomCat can handle CGI and SSL requests when acting as a standalone server. Other benefits are its Single Sign On feature and web-based configuration interface. TomCat5 is included in openSUSE and can be installed via YaST. You can also download itfrom the project's website.

JBoss

JBoss started out as a container for Enterprise JavaBeans (EJB) and has developed into a full-fledged application server for Java programs. Now owned by Red Hat, JBoss remains open source (licensed under the LGPL) and remains one of the most popular application servers out there. The JBoss wiki also claims JBoss "is also the point of entry for thousands of newbie Java developers." Install JBoss 4 via YaST, or through the project website.

Building an FTP Server

FTP is a client/server process. In Chapter 17, "Secure File Transfer," you learned about the client side; that is, how to locate and download files from FTP servers on your network or the Internet. In this section, you will learn about openSUSE Linux's Internet file-serving capabilities.

As alluded to before, two types of FTP servers exist: Authenticated (or *standard*) servers and Anonymous servers. A standard FTP server requires a valid username and password to give access. Anonymous FTP allows anyone access.

Anonymous servers are convenient for users, but can pose a security threat if not cared for. Fortunately, openSUSE Linux uses logical permission schemes and a default configuration that makes it difficult for you to make mistakes.

openSUSE Linux users can build both types of FTP servers, but this section will focus on securing an anonymous server with the Very Secure FTP server package, vsftpd.

Configuring xinetd for Secure File Transfer

Starting an FTP service in openSUSE is relatively simple, thanks to YaST. Go to the Network Services section and click Network Services (xinetd). xinetd allows you to apply individual access policies for different network connection requests, such as FTP.

To turn VSFTP on xinetd, first click the Enable button at the top of the Network Services Configuration screen. The various services that can be controlled by xinetd become active and are no longer grayed out. Check the Status column—you can start or configure any of the services marked with three dashes (—-). The dashes indicate that a service is inactive; any services that are running now are labeled ON and are also configurable.

Depending on what you have installed, you should see two Services labeled `ftp`, and both should be inactive. Click `vsftpd`, and then click Toggle Status (On or Off) at the bottom. Figure 26.2 displays the screen.

An X should appear in the Change column on the left. Click Finish to start the Server.

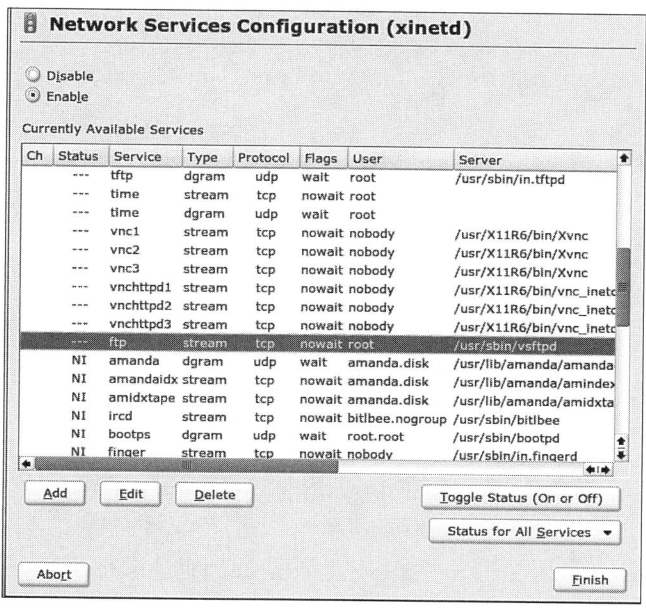

FIGURE 26.2 Start the Very Secure FTP server in YaST Network Services.

Configuring Secure File Transfer Servers

The Very Secure FTP main configuration file, `vsftpd.conf`, is located in the `/etc` directory with the rest of the configuration files. You can edit it as Root. The default settings are designed for minimum setup of an Anonymous server. The Anonymous FTP User Settings section of this file sets up the rules for these users. Following are some suggestions:

- If you want to remove Anonymous access and make it an authenticated server, set anonymous_enable to NO.
- To allow Anonymous download of only files that the World (Others) have Read access to, set anon_world_readable_only to YES.
- To allow Anonymous users to upload files to your server, set anon_upload_enable to YES. This line is commented out by default.
- To allow Anonymous users to create directories, set anon_mkdir_write_enable to YES. Otherwise, set to NO. This line is commented out by default.
- To allow Anonymous users to write (edit and delete) files in the public directories, set anon_other_write_enable to YES. Otherwise, set to NO.

You can make many adjustments while reading this file. Read the man page for vsftpd.conf (or visit http://www.vsftpd.beasts.org/vsftpd_conf.html for the HTML version).

References

- http://www.apache.org—The Apache Software Foundation umbrella site. Access all Apache projects from here.
- http://httpd.apache.org—The place to start for information on the Apache Web Server. Includes news, downloads, and FAQs. Check the Docs subproject for a PDF user's guide.
- http://modules.apache.org—The Apache Module Registry. Locate modules to install and contribute modules you've created.
- http://www.apachetoday.com—A little cluttered and ad ridden, but ServerWatch's Apache Today site is still an excellent source of Apache news and tutorials.
- http://tldp.org/HOWTO/HOWTO-INDEX/apps.html#SERVERHTTP—An index of web server-related HOWTOs, mostly dealing with Apache, but a few others, too.
- http://susefaq.sourceforge.net/faq/apache.html—The Unofficial SUSE FAQ list includes useful SUSE-specific Apache information. See the FTP section as well.
- http://www.securityfocus.com/infocus/1818—"Apache 2 with SSL/TLS: Step-by-Step," This article helps you secure your server with SSL.
- http://news.netcraft.com/archives/web_server_survey.html—The monthly Netcraft survey of popular web servers. As this is being written, about 60 percent of the Web runs on Apache.
- http://modpython.org—Home of the `mod_python` Apache module.
- http://hoohoo.ncsa.uiuc.edu/cgi/—Information on the common gateway interface.
- http://modruby.net—The `mod_ruby` page.
- http://www.acme.com/software/thttpd—Home of `thttpd`.
- http://caudium.net/—The Caudium WebServer home page.
- http://www.xitami.com/—The Xitami website.
- http://www.zope.org—All the latest and greatest from the Zope community.
- http://www.adobe.com/products/coldfusion—The ColdFusion product page at Adobe.
- http://www.houseoffusion.com—A ColdFusion user community. Includes mailing lists, news, and assorted other resources for ColdFusion users.
- http://tomcat.apache.org—The Java Servlet and JSP server released through the Apache Free Software Foundation.
- http://labs.jboss.com—The hub of activity for the JBoss application server. You can download the main application and related projects. There's a wiki with FAQs, archived webcasts, and a ton of other information.
- http://www.vsftpd.beasts.org—The Very Secure FTP server.

CHAPTER 27

Managing Domain Names

IN THIS CHAPTER

- Essential DNS Concepts
- DNS Hierarchy
- Configuring DNS with YaST2
- Hosts File
- Basic DNS Tools
- Configuring Name Servers with BIND
- Logging
- Summary
- References

The domain name system (DNS) is the lifeblood of the Internet. Without DNS, we would all be forced to remember TCP/IP addresses to get to websites, get to our email, buy merchandise, or look up information in a search engine. To go to www.novell.com to learn more about SUSE, for example, you would have to remember 130.57.5.25. Why attempt to remember a set of numbers such as this when you can remember www.novell.com/_linux? The DNS brings a level of simplicity into surfing the Web and doing work with openSUSE. In this chapter we will learn how DNS is used with openSUSE. Of course, there are ways around this—by editing your HOSTS file, for example, to make the lack of DNS bearable by adding a local DNS database to your personal system—but for the most part, if you don't want to update this file each time you want to use DNS, make certain you implement a DNS server in your enterprise so that you can remember www.novell.com, instead of 130.57.5.25.

In Chapter 12, "Connecting to the Internet," you learned how to connect to the Internet. In Chapter 25, "Setting Up Networks and Samba," you learned about TCP/IP fundamentals. In this chapter, you will build on the concepts of the Internet and TCP/IP and learn about the DNS, how it is configured on your openSUSE system, and how to modify it if needed. In this chapter, you will also learn how to set up openSUSE as a DNS client in YaST, edit DNS configuration files, use tools such as nslookup to gather information, and finally, learn the fundamentals of using Linux as a DNS server.

Essential DNS Concepts

The DNS is a distributed and hierarchical database whose function is to resolve hostnames to IP addresses. As mentioned earlier, this is really the only reason DNS is used. As a matter of fact, using DNS adds latency and complexity to any configuration management you need to do, such as changing the DNS information itself. Because the DNS database is distributed, those changes need to replicate through the DNS system, whether it is hosted locally within your network privately, is a public DNS server communication with other public DNS servers to replicate changes, or a hybrid of both. DNS is worth every ounce of issue you may derive from it, so let's start by taking a look at how to configure it locally on your openSUSE system so that you can use and test it.

In the following example and illustration, DNS will be shown step by step and simplified as much as possible, although entire books are dedicated to the subject because of its depth and complexity.

In this example, your hostname is the website www.novell.com. Suppose that you would like to visit the Linux section of the website to find out more about openSUSE. The website's IP address is 130.57.5.25. You are currently on a home laptop running openSUSE. You open a web browser and attempt to visit the www.novell.com site by entering the easy-to-remember Uniform Resource Locator (URL) of www.novell.com. Consider the following steps, shown in Figure 27.1, that are taken when you enter a domain name into your web browser:

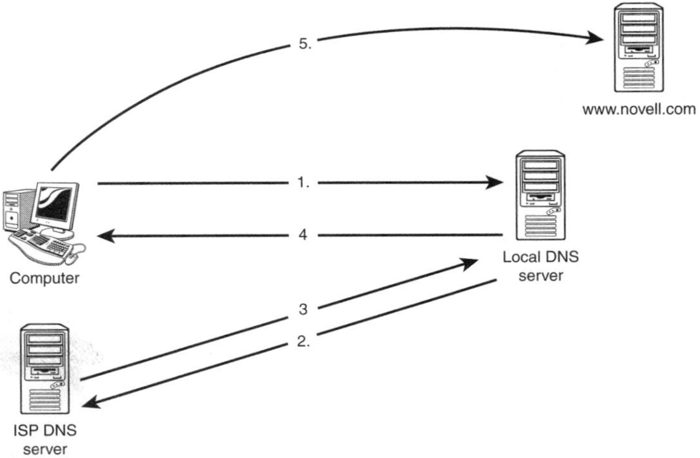

FIGURE 27.1 Viewing a simple DNS design.

1. Your local system (with help from you, of course) wants to get to www.novell.com. To do this, it needs to know what Novell's website IP address is and because it does not, it asks its locally configured hosts file to resolve the DNS name: novell.com. This local system currently does not have any entries in the hosts file; therefore, the manually configured DNS server (the local DNS server) will attempt to resolve it.

2. This is the first time this site has been requested; therefore, the domain is unknown by the local DNS server and the request needs to be forwarded from the local DNS server to the ISP's DNS server, which does know that www.novell.com resolves to 130.57.5.25. The ISP's DNS servers are public servers.

3. After the full URL of http://www.novell.com is placed in the Location field, requested by the browser, and resolved to an IP address of 130.57.5.25, that information is then cached in the local DNS server so that if this request is again brought up, it will be quicker to resolve.

4. Now that www.novell.com has been resolved to the local DNS server, the answer of 130.57.5.25 is given to the client.

5. The client now can connect via the Internet to the www.novell.com website and browse it for openSUSE help or other information.

In this scenario, you had a DNS server and a DNS client. In this chapter you will learn how to set up and install openSUSE to handle both server and client tasks. The DNS client is the host that is requesting DNS information that is provided by a DNS database, either local to the system itself (hosts), as shown in Figure 27.2, or on a server configured to provide such information. First, let's view the local database on the openSUSE system. You can find the HOSTS file off the root of the operating system, in the `etc` directory. (Later in this chapter, you will learn how to configure this with YaST.)

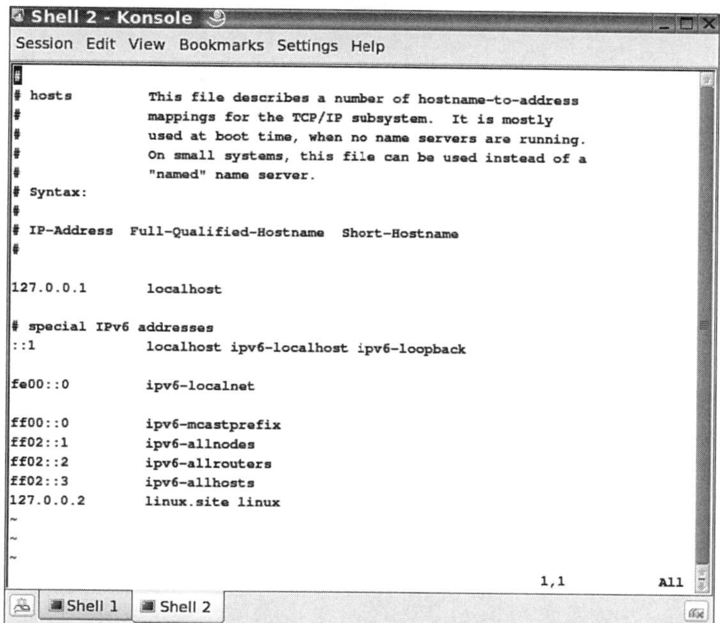

FIGURE 27.2 Viewing a Linux HOSTS file.

The server with BIND installed is called a DNS server. Let's continue discussing what DNS is, its inner workings, and how it works with Linux.

DNS Hierarchy

After you understand how the DNS is used for communication, you should also understand how it's entered as a URL into a computer web browser such as Konqueror. Figure 27.3 shows a standard web browser with a URL inserted.

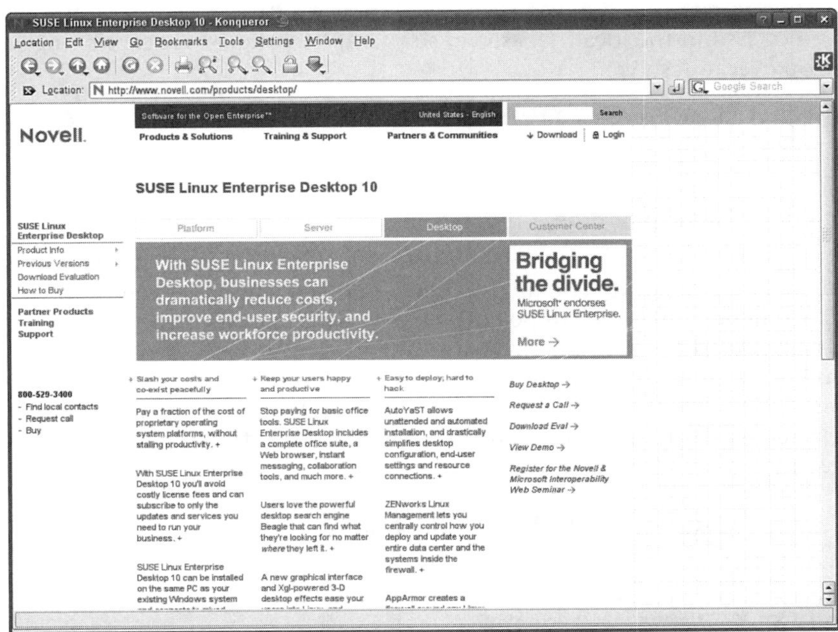

FIGURE 27.3 Finding help online.

To understand the DNS, you have to understand what it is you are looking for when you enter a URL such as the one shown here. For instance, the URL for Novell's home page for SUSE Linux Enterprise is found in the location field as the following:

```
http://www.novell.com/linux/
```

Because URLs and web browsing are not this chapter's focus, let's just quickly review them so that we can get into DNS in more detail. First is the protocol that you will be using, which is HTTP (Hypertext Transfer Protocol).

HTTP is nothing more than a protocol that is used to transmit files over the World Wide Web (WWW) using port 80. The entry www.novell.com is a fully qualified domain name, or FQDN. An FQDN consists of a host, a domain name, and a top-level domain (TLD). These are all shown in the URL www.novell.com. In this example, www is the host (this entry is not always required), novell is the second-level domain, and the .com is the TLD. Although it's not seen, a period also follows .com, which would make the FQDN appear as www.novell.com. The trailing period shows the root. You do not have to add this period, but it's okay if you do. Most people don't even know that it exists. Some browsers append the entry, and some ignore it; either way, it works.

TLDs are explained as follows. In Figure 27.4, you can see a few TLDs with second-level domains following.

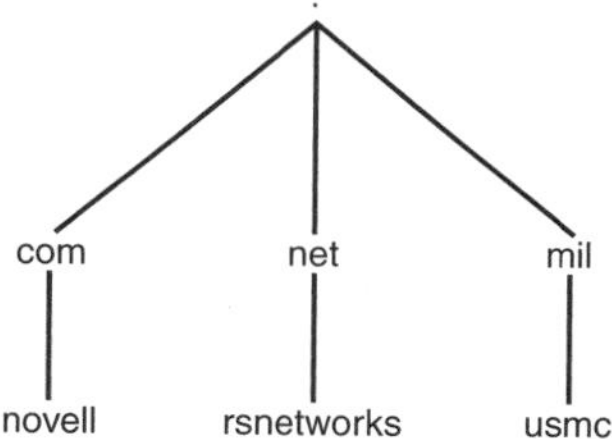

FIGURE 27.4 Viewing a sample DNS hierarchy.

For this example, take a look at the following three URLs:

- http://www.novell.com
- http://www.rsnetworks.net
- http://www.usmc.mil

You may see after you enter some of the URLs (www.usmc.mil, for example) that although it works, it is replaced by a different URL in the Location field of your web browser. In this example, www.usmc.mil has been redirected to a new, longer URL. Both URLs lead to the home page, or index page, of the website; the URL is being redirected by the web server's internal configuration.

In these examples, the highest level of the DNS hierarchy is Root. A single period (.) represents the Root domain, as shown in the illustration.

You can also see that the TLD is .com, .net, and .mil. In the early 1980s, about a half-dozen main TLDs were designated for use. Domain names may be registered in three of the most commonly used TLDs, which are .com, .net, and .org. There are many others, but most serve limited purposes. Table 27.1 lists some of the most common TLDs.

TABLE 27.1 Common Top-Level Domains

Domain	Description
.com	The TLD of .com represents the word "commercial.' It is the most widely used and accepted domain name in use today—worldwide.
.net	The TLD of .net represents the word "network." It is most commonly used by Internet Service Providers (ISPs), hosting companies, or other businesses that are directly involved in the infrastructure of the Internet.
.org	The TLD of .org represents the word "organization." It is used mostly by not-for-profit groups.
.edu	The TLD of .edu represents the word "education." It is used mostly for colleges, schools, and educational facilities worldwide.
.mil	The TLD of .mil represents the word "military." It is mostly used to denote military branches, such as the Navy and the Marine Corps.

TABLE 27.1 Continued

Domain	Description
.biz	The TLD of .biz represents the word "business." It is used mostly to show a small-business website, although most times, .com is preferred only because it's more commonly known to the general public.
.info	The TLD of .info represents the word "information." It is used mostly to show informational-based websites such as directories, phone books, or any other form of service that provides information to the general public or private groups.
.gov	The TLD of .gov representsthe word "government." It is used mostly to show government agencies and departments.

NOTE

The original seven TLD were .com, .edu, .gov, .int, .mil, .net, and .org. In 2001 and 2002, the other entries were introduced. In addition to these, countries have always had TLDs available for their use as well—.au for Australia, and so on. In recent years, a few countries have opted to make their domains available for use by anyone—these include .tv for Tuvalu, .ws for Western Samoa, and .cc for the Cocos Islands.

Note that these are just guidelines; you can purchase and use just about any URL as long as it is available. You may find, just by the fact that the domain name is not available for sale, that many of your good ideas for names are already taken.

NOTE

You can find more information on TLDs at the following URL: http://www.icann.org/tlds/.

Now you should feel very comfortable with the DNS hierarchy when you see a URL such as www.novell.com.

DNS maps friendly names to IP addresses. It is similar to a phone book, pairing hostnames and IP addresses much in the same way as people's names are paired with their telephone numbers. The internal structure of that phone book is the DNS hierarchy. Now that you understand how DNS is structured, let's dive into the internals of it.

Zones

The DNS database contains zones. These are called *zone files,* which contain resource records (explained in the next section). A DNS zone file is also a database. There are two standard zone types: forward lookup zones and reverse lookup zones. A forward lookup zone allows for a resource-name-to-IP-address resolution. This is what we did in looking up the IP address of www.novell.com.

A reverse lookup zone, if you haven't already guessed, does the opposite, which is allowing for IP-address-to-resource-name resolution. If you only had an IP address, a reverse lookup identifies the hostname. Both zones need to be built, created, and managed by a system administrator. The reverse lookup zone is contained in a domain known as `in-addr.arpa`.

Records

When you're building a DNS infrastructure, the hierarchy is pretty straightforward. You have the TLD, the second-level domain, and a zone database created on the DNS server. A database is not worth much, of course, without records. Records are nothing more than files that hold data that the DNS server queries. Each domain that is created always contains resource records containing information about the DNS infrastructure you are managing, especially by default. Some records are made by default when you install DNS for the first time. There are many types of DNS database records. The most common database record is the A (Address) record, which maps a hostname and an IP address. This is the primary method of DNS resolution. A records are responsible for most of the DNS communication and resolution in use with DNS. The DNS forward lookup zones are populated with a variety of resource records. The most common resource records are listed in Table 27.2.

TABLE 27.2 Commonly Used DNS Records

A (Address) record	The Address record contains the hostname to IP address mapping for the particular host. The majority of the records in the zone will be host A Address records.
PTR (Pointer) record	The Pointer record is used for reverse lookups. This file is merely a pointer to another location.
MX (Mail Exchanger) record	The Mail Exchanger record identifies the domain's preferred mail servers.
CNAME (Canonical Name) record	Also known as an *alias*. Canonical Name must be used with an existing A record; it provides an alias type name to map to the original A record's IP address.

Now that you understand the fundamentals of DNS and how it works for you as a client, let's look at how to configure it on openSUSE.

Configuring DNS with YaST2

Configuring DNS with YaST is an easy process when you configure the client. Remember from our earlier discussion that the DNS resolution process is used for simplicity, allowing a client to use an easy-to-remember name instead of what it really needs to use, which is the IP address. You use the domain name; the client (when configured properly) gets that information from its local database (hosts) or from an external distributed one, such as DNS. To configure your client with DNS, you will need to know the following from your ISP or your local systems administrator:

- The IP address of the DNS server(s)
- The correct domain name(s)

That's it! It's that simple to set up DNS on your local client. It's even easier if you have Dynamic Host Configuration Protocol (DHCP) in use. DHCP can be used to automatically update the DNS information on your client if you have a DHCP server installed on your network. Chances are good that your ISP will provide you with the DNS information you need through its DHCP server.

To configure DNS manually, use the following steps.

1. Open YaST and navigate to the Network Services menu in the YaST Control Center. Select DNS and Host Name, as shown in Figure 27.5.

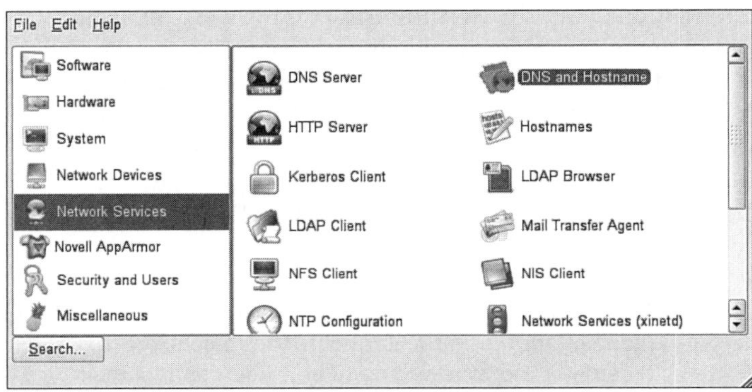

FIGURE 27.5 Configuring DNS with YaST.

2. When you open YaST, YaST will take a moment to initialize its network configuration. The first time you are entering this section of YaST, you may be prompted to edit DNS information manually. A warning will pop up to let you know that although you may be getting ready to make a manual entry, the DNS information was already configured by DHCP, as shown in Figure 27.6.

3. You can choose to either Accept or Modify the contents. Accepting will gray out all configurable sections except for the host and domain name sections at the top of the DNS configuration window. If you click Modify, you will be given a chance to edit the settings manually. If you are unsure of what you are doing, you may want to write down the settings you are changing so that you have a way to get back to the original configuration. If you change your DNS settings, it's likely you will no longer be able to access the Internet anymore from your openSUSE system.

4. To manually change the settings, select Modify. The Host Name and Server Configuration screen appears (see Figure 27.7).

5. Use this dialog box to define a new hostname and domain name for your computer. By default, YaST will write the new name to your `/etc/hosts` file, but you can change that behavior by unchecking the box. If you do not write the name to your hosts file, other DNS servers will be able to resolve your IP address to the new name only when the machine is on the network.

6. To manually set the name servers your machine uses to translate hostnames into IP addresses, uncheck the Update Name Servers and Search List via DHCP box. Identify

the Name Server(s) you want to use and/or the domain search listing, perhaps as is laid out in Figure 27.7.

7. Click Finish to confirm your new settings. When you finish, you will be able to use those settings when attempting to resolve names on the Internet, such as www.novell.com.

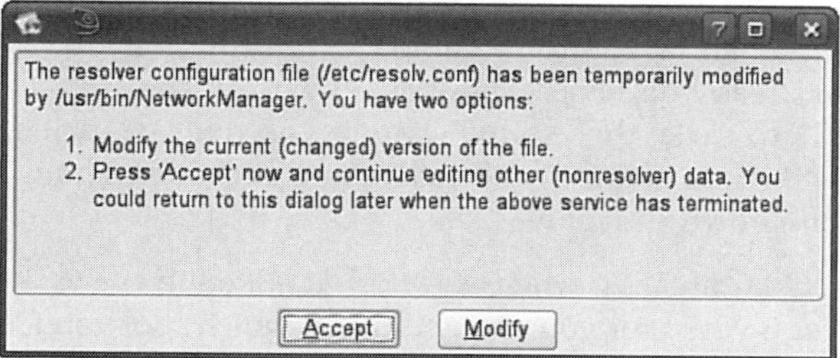

FIGURE 27.6 Viewing a DNS resolver warning.

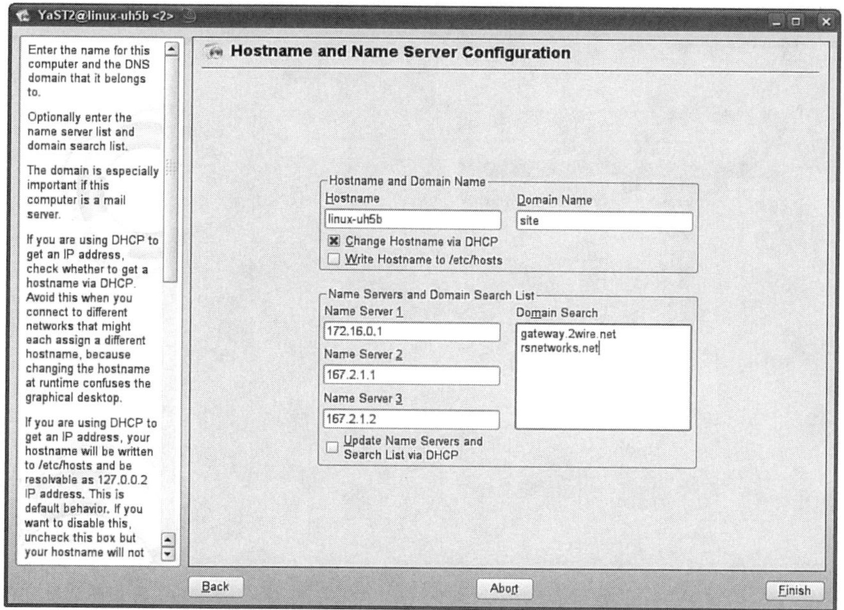

FIGURE 27.7 Host Name and Name Server Configuration page.

A name server is a computer that translates hostnames into IP addresses, and that is what the name server seen here are doing. If you remember the example in the beginning of this chapter, this section should make more sense—you are configuring the client to get its information from one of the three servers listed here. Why three? Usually you would have a primary, a secondary, and a tertiary name server from which to get information. For disaster recovery purposes, it's common to have more than one single DNS server on which to rely. Relying on a single DNS server means all your eggs are in one basket, and if an egg cracks, you are out of name resolution! As you can see from this simple example, it's common to have multiple DNS server settings on which to rely.

The domain search list is the list of domain names where hostname searching begins—and hopefully ends with the proper name resolution applied to the client. You can add multiple names in the search list, although it's commonly seen, and used, with only one domain name.

Hosts File

Multiple files on your openSUSE system will allow you to modify DNS information. To work with the hosts file, which we have already discussed and worked with in the `/etc` directory, we will look at how to use YaST to make those same changes. As you saw earlier, open YaST and navigate to the Network Services menu in the YaST Control Center. Then select Host Names. A dialog box opens as shown in Figure 27.8.

In this section, you can change the hosts file from YaST, whereas we saw it edited in the vi editor before. You can do either, whichever is easier for you, depending on which tool you feel the most comfortable using to make your edits. If you are new to Linux, you should attempt to learn both, although the YaST way is easier than the vi editor at the shell prompt.

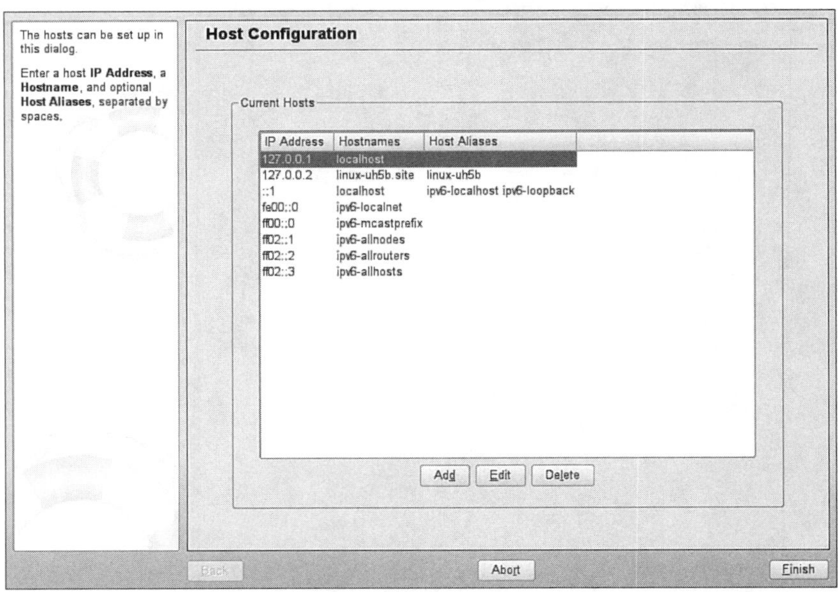

FIGURE 27.8 Viewing the Host Configuration in YaST.

Basic DNS Tools

To test your new DNS configuration, you can attempt to access the Internet, or if you want to be a little more technical, you can use tools such as `nslookup` or `dig`. In this section of the chapter, you'll take a look at both tools.

The `dig` tool has been around for a long time on Unix systems and serves a very important function. `dig` (the Domain Internet Groper) is a Unix-based program that allows users to learn information from a DNS site by querying it. You can see from Figure 27.9 that `dig` has, in fact, found quite a bit of information on www.novell.com.

NOTE

In Figure 27.9, the default gateway address has been blackened out to protect the identity of the system. You will not see a black bar on your screen as you do here.

You can also use `nslookup`, a tool that you may be familiar with when using Microsoft Windows products, such as Windows XP. openSUSE also uses the `nslookup` command as follows:

```
linux:~ # nslookup

> www.novell.com

Server:         172.16.0.1

Address:        172.16.0.1#53
```

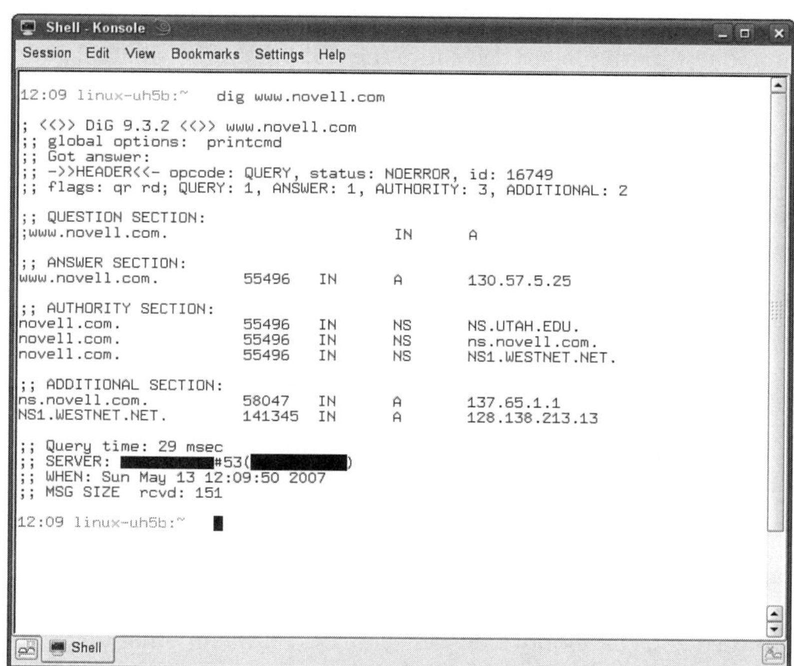

Shell - Konsole
Session Edit View Bookmarks Settings Help
12:09 linux-uh5b:~ dig www.novell.com
; <<>> DiG 9.3.2 <<>> www.novell.com
;; global options: printcmd
;; Got answer:
;; ->>HEADER<<- opcode: QUERY, status: NOERROR, id: 16749
;; flags: qr rd; QUERY: 1, ANSWER: 1, AUTHORITY: 3, ADDITIONAL: 2
;; QUESTION SECTION:
;www.novell.com. IN A
;; ANSWER SECTION:
www.novell.com. 55496 IN A 130.57.5.25
;; AUTHORITY SECTION:
novell.com. 55496 IN NS NS.UTAH.EDU.
novell.com. 55496 IN NS ns.novell.com.
novell.com. 55496 IN NS NS1.WESTNET.NET.
;; ADDITIONAL SECTION:
ns.novell.com. 58047 IN A 137.65.1.1
NS1.WESTNET.NET. 141345 IN A 128.138.213.13
;; Query time: 29 msec
;; SERVER: #53()
;; WHEN: Sun May 13 12:09:50 2007
;; MSG SIZE rcvd: 151
12:09 linux-uh5b:~
Shell

FIGURE 27.9 Using dig.

The non-authoritative answer follows:

```
Name:   www.novell.com
Address: 130.57.5.25
```

The next step is to use the set command, which will show you all of your DNS server assignments. By typing **set all**, you can see your primary, secondary, and other DNS servers, as well as other settings changes you can make with this command:

```
Default server: 172.16.0.1
Address: 172.16.0.1#53

Set options:
  novc                  nodebug           nod2
  search                recurse
  timeout = 0           retry = 3         port = 53
  querytype = A         class = IN
  srchlist = gateway.2wire.net
> exit
```

You can type **exit** and select a carriage return to quit. This will bring you back to the Linux prompt so that you can work again at the shell prompt. These tools will help you to verify and test your DNS service, either locally or against a DNS server.

Now that you understand some of the fundamentals of the DNS and have learned how to configure it on a client and test it, it's time to delve into the real power of openSUSE and turn it into a DNS server.

Configuring Name Servers with BIND

Before we dig (pun intended) deeper into how to configure DNS as a server-based service on your openSUSE system, a word on the service itself—BIND.

BIND stands for Berkeley Internet Name Domain (or Daemon). BIND is software developed by the University of California at Berkeley, as the name implies. BIND is a full service DNS solution that allows clients to get name resolution information as requested. Although an entire book can be dedicated to Unix- and Linux-based DNS, for purposes of this chapter, we will not get too involved with BIND's history and current status. In this section we will cover the basics. If you want more information, the following URLs explain DNS, BIND, and how to configure BIND to the smallest detail:

- http://www.tldp.org/HOWTO/DNS-HOWTO.html
- http://www.isc.org/index.pl?/sw/bind/

BIND is one of the most used and commonly seen forms of DNS on the Internet today. In fact, most service providers use only BIND because of their lack of trust and the proprietary nature of the Windows-based DNS server products.

Now that you are familiar with BIND, let's look at how to configure your system with it. Up until now you have worked with openSUSE as a client of DNS. Next, you will make openSUSE function as the server that the clients query to get their DNS resolution information. Let's look at how this is done.

First, you need to verify that DNS is installed on your openSUSE system. To verify, open up YaST. On the left pane of the YaST Control Center, select Software. Then select Software Management. In Figure 27.10, you can see in the DHCP and DNS Server pattern whether BIND is installed. Here, for this example, it has already been installed.

NOTE

If you try to open the YaST DNS Server module without BIND already installed, YaST will offer to install it for you.

Next, you need to configure DNS. To configure DNS manually, you can use YaST to install the base system and then configure it as well. To get to the DNS configuration pages, open YaST and navigate to the Network Services menu in the YaST Control Center.

You can use the DNS Server module of YaST to configure a DNS server for your local network. When you start the module for the first time, a wizard will prompt you about making changes on your forwarder. A forwarder is used to send your request to the next server that will be able to answer the request and then cache it on the forwarding server, which will most likely be "Internet facing" and have a publicly assigned IP address.

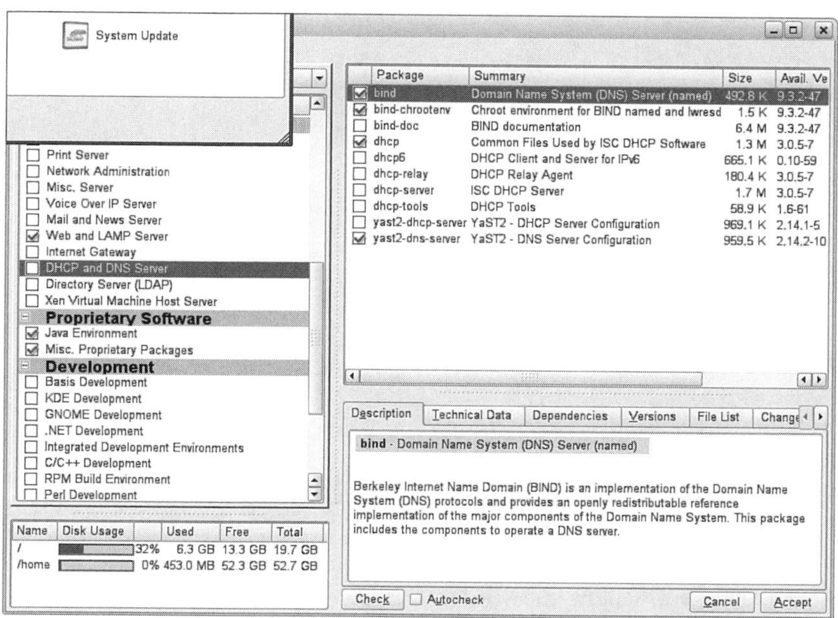

FIGURE 27.10 Using YaST to install DNS.

Next, consider the following. Because you've set up the client, you are now setting up the server. If you remember from previous examples, the DNS server, if not a root server, will still need to get its information from a public Internet-based DNS server. The server you are creating now with your openSUSE system is a local DNS server that will be used in your local environment (or network), and it will have to query another DNS server for its name resolution information because it is not a public Internet-based DNS server. You can, in fact, set it up as an Internet-based DNS server, but because doing so is outside the scope of this book, this chapter will not be able to cover all those details in depth. There are many more steps to configuring a DNS solution, and there are many ways you can set it up, allowing you to meet just about any name resolution scenario placed before you.

To set your openSUSE system as a Local DNS server, you can bypass the forwarder configuration by clicking Next. You do not have to set a forwarder. Remember, a forwarder is nothing more than setting your local DNS server as a non-root DNS server that will query a root server if it does not know the answer to a query. When you starting the module for the first time, see the dialog box shown in Figure 27.11, DNS Server Installation: Forwarder Settings.

Click Next to enter the other DNS server configuration settings areas, such as where you will build new A records.

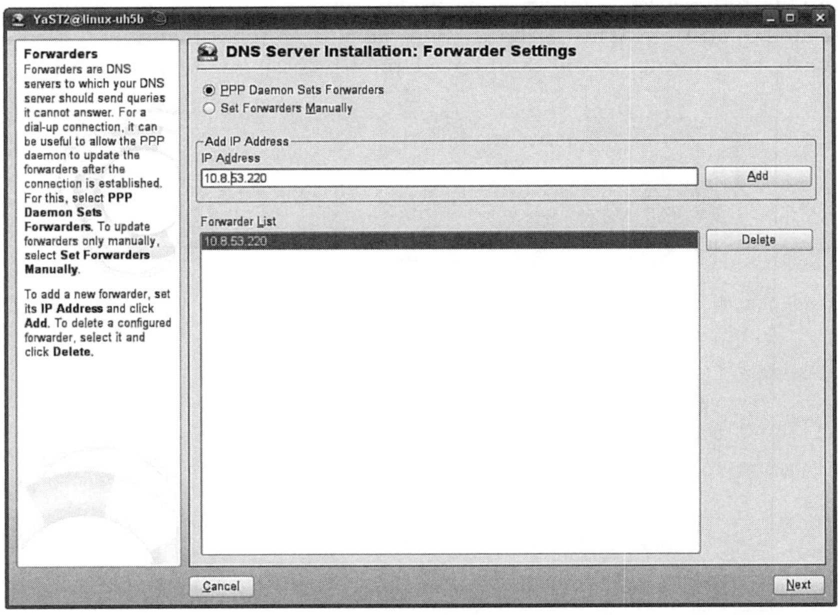

FIGURE 27.11 Changing the forwarder setting.

After you have clicked Next, you will be shown the DNS Zone section where you can add a new zone. A default of example.com is shown in Figure 27.12.

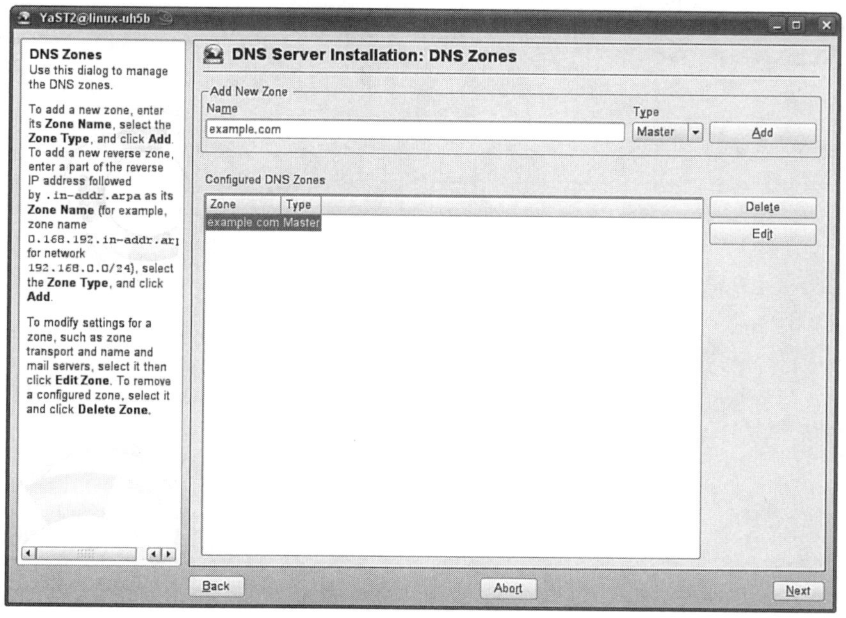

FIGURE 27.12 Viewing DNS Zone information.

This particular dialog box consists of several parts and is responsible for managing of zone files, adding new zones, or removing a zone. To add a zone, add or change the current zone name of example.com. The type of zone will be the master because it's the first zone you are making. After you make more zones, you will be given an option to make a slave domain. A slave is a DNS server that will get its main information from the master server. Read and writes can be done on the master; the slave is read-only and gets its configuration information from the master.

To add a reverse zone you have to know to add the extension to your zone, such as 10.1.1.in-addr.arpa. The name must end in `.in-addr.arpa` and you will need to add this manually. Select Edit Zone to configure other settings of an existing zone. To remove a zone, you can select Delete Zone. If you decide to edit a zone, you can select Edit Zone.

Inside the zone, you can change many settings, such as adding records. To add a simple A record so that you can have basic name resolution, click the Records tab and add a new resource record. (Resource records were covered earlier in the chapter; now you can add one manually.) To add a record, add the hostname (without the domain name) to the Record Key. The Type is an A record (the Domain Name Translation). The Value is the IP address you want to use. By clicking Add, you will have successfully added your first resource record beyond what may have been made during the installation, such as the SOA record, or Start of Authority, which is a record that will indicate the start point or point of originating authority for information stored in the zone just created. The SOA resource record is the first record created when adding a new zone. This is a great example of a record that is made for you (see Figure 27.13).

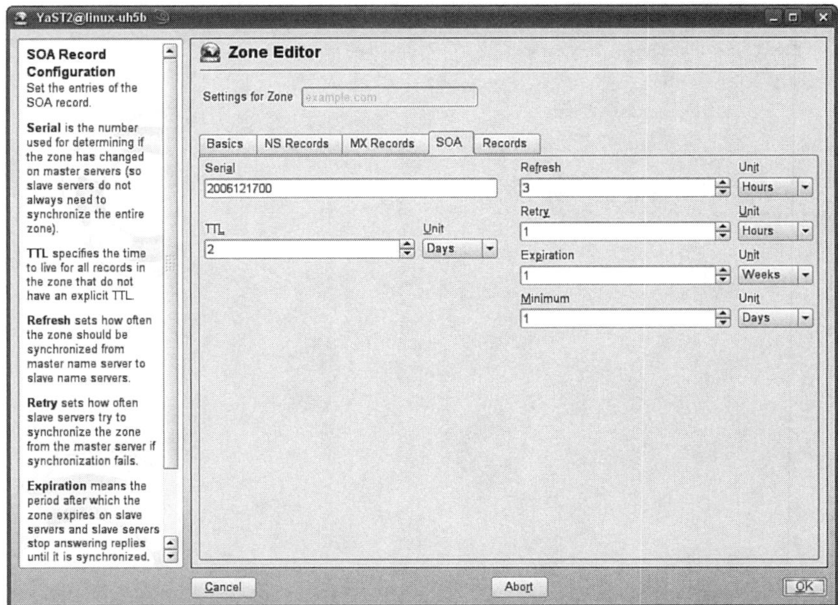

FIGURE 27.13 Using the Zone Editor.

Now that you understand how to add records and adjust the zone file database, click Back to go back to the original DNS Zones configuration page. You can also click OK to finish, but you are not quite finished with your configurations.

Clicking Next from the DNS Zones dialog box will bring you to the Finish Wizard. The reason why you didn't want to bypass this screen by clicking OK is that you want to modify the DNS server startup options and behavior. For instance, do you want the server started now, or when you boot up? Or do you want to set it for manual start? Either way, you can adjust these settings in the DNS Server Installation Finish Wizard. When you're done, click Finish to run your new DNS server. You can also click Expert Options to get more options to choose from, including a section where you can adjust your logging settings, which is covered next.

Logging

Now that you have your DNS Server installed, you will want to set up logging so that you can help find problems and aid your troubleshooting process if needed. Generally speaking, you may be able to get away with turning on logging only as needed, to save space. The better alternative is to leave logging on, but then you must check and analyze the log often to identify issues and problems. When you have completed your check, save the old log files.

There are many things you can log, as shown in Figure 27.14, and there are multiple options from which you can choose.

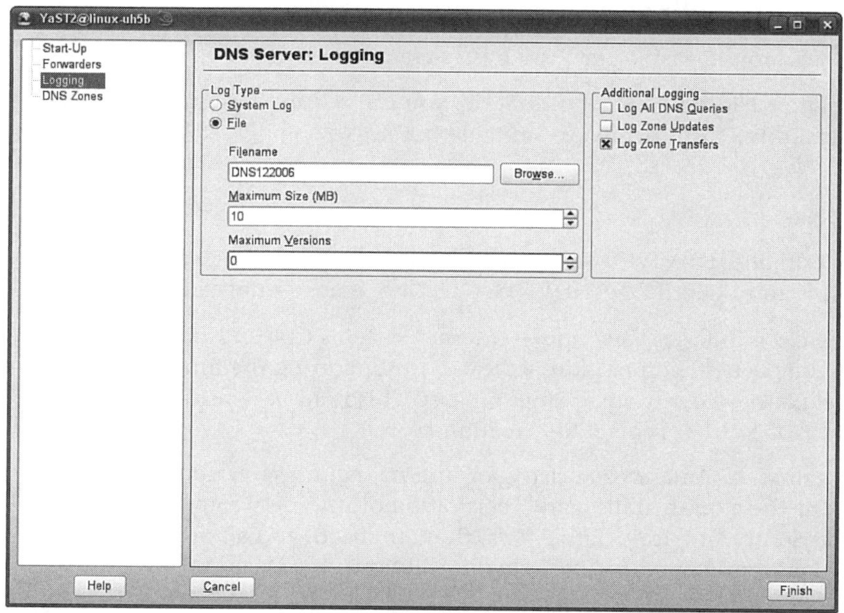

FIGURE 27.14 Viewing SUSE log settings.

To specify the location where the logging data is stored, look under Log Type in the DNS Server Logging dialog box. By clicking the Browse button, you can select a new location to store the file. It's recommended that you click Browse anyway and make a new directory called `DNSLOG`, for example, so that you can save all your files in one location. As a handy side note, from the example shown here, I have named the file in a way that dates it, because if you save files, you will need a way to recall what files have what information in them. You'll also need to know when they were created so that you have a way to track back to a specific time or date. Either way, make sure you have a system in place that allows you to organize your data so that it's easy to retrieve.

If you choose Log to a System Log, you can now log to the system log, which is stored in `/var/log/messages`. Also, make sure you set the log correctly, including its size, which should be set to about 5–10MBs, depending on how much information you want to store based on your logging selections. Zone transfers are the only entries to be logged, and they are being logged to an independent file named DNS122006, which stands for DNS log, 12 (month of December), and the year 2006. You can use any example that comes to mind, or use this one if it works for you and your business or personal needs.

Summary

Remember that DNS is nothing more than a naming system and protocol used not only by companies worldwide in their internal networks, but also for the publicly accessible Internet. DNS is used to add a human quality to finding data on the network. To a machine, searching an IP address like 130.57.5.25 is no big deal. However,

27

www.novell.com is much easier for humans to remember than a set of numbers. You can move domain names around easily, but IP addresses are not so portable.

There is much to know about DNS; like openSUSE, you can set up the system as a DNS client or a DNS server. YaST will help you configure both.

References

- http://www.tldp.org/HOWTO/DNS-HOWTO.html—The Linux Documentation Project. This is an in-depth DNS HOWTO with DNS general information as well.
- http://www.isc.org/index.pl?/sw/bind/—Internet Systems Consortium, Inc. (ISC) is a nonprofit public benefit corporation dedicated to supporting the infrastructure of the universal connected self-organizing Internet. This is an in-depth DNS/BIND HOWTO with DNS/BIND general information as well.
- http://www.arin.net—American Registry for Internet Numbers. A nonprofit registry responsible for the administration and registration of Internet Protocol (IP) numbers in North and South America, South Africa, the Caribbean, and all other regions administered currently managed by Network Solutions, Inc.
- http://www.iana.org/—Internet Assigned Numbers Authority. IANA is a government-funded authority that assigns and distributes international domain names and IP numbers or Internet addresses and oversees the Internet software protocols of the officially sanctioned root servers.
- http://www.internic.net/—A registry responsible for name assignment within the following TLDs: COM, EDU, NET, GOV, and ORG.
- http://www.icann.org/tlds/—The Internet Corporation for Assigned Names and Numbers.

PART VI

Programming

IN THIS PART

CHAPTER 28

Programming Tools

IN THIS CHAPTER

- Basic Programming in C Under Linux
- Building Applications with Eclipse
- Using the KDevelop Integrated Development Environment
- Using Anjuta to Create GNOME Applications
- Using the GNU Compiler Collection
- Managing Collective Software Development with CVS and Subversion
- Creating RPM Packages
- Other Linux Programming Resources
- References

Although GNU/Linux is many things, it has been and always will be a programmer's plaything. The GNU Project began with a C compiler and a text editor. Linux began as a porting project. Although the intertwined projects have grown considerably beyond their hobbyist roots, they will never completely outgrow them.

In this and the next few chapters, you'll learn about the tools openSUSE Linux provides both the beginning programmer and the most seasoned software engineer. From simple compilers to full-blown integrated development environments (IDEs), Linux can help you program in dozens of languages and in an environment best suited to your style.

Open-source development isn't always a solitary task, however. Concurrent Versions System (CVS) and Subversion each make it easier to collaborate with others. And after you've created a quality program, you may want to make it readily available and easy to install for the public at large. For that, there are several solutions, most notably the Red Hat Package Manager (RPM).

This is not a book on how to program complex software programs, and novices should not expect to learn more than the barest rudiments in this and subsequent chapters. Learning programming is a worthwhile, if challenging, pursuit. It is also one of the best ways to give back to the Linux community for all the wonderful applications you're using with your copy of openSUSE Linux. If you are intrigued by what you read in this and in the coming chapters, there are more than a few good books on the subject, some of which will be highlighted here.

This chapter focuses on some of the tools available for programming in C, C++, and Java. You'll also learn about a trio of Linux IDEs: Eclipse, KDevelop, and Anjuta. You'll see how CVS and Subversion can be used to manage your source code and collaborate with other programmers. Finally, you'll learn how you can use RPM to disseminate your final product.

Basic Programming in C Under Linux

Unix and the C programming language have been partners from the very beginning. The vast majority of Unix and Linux code (including the Linux kernel) is written in C, and that tradition continues. C is a platform-neutral language; the code is not dependent on any particular system architecture.

C is a language that uses a compiler to transform your code to something machines can read directly. Interpreted languages, such as Perl and Python, need a separate program known as an *interpreter* to run.

You first enter your C program's statements (called *source code*) into a text file. This code is then fed to a *compiler* that translates the source code you've written into a binary file—the ones and zeros that the machine can read. Often, a *linker* is used to connect the program with other system libraries or with other programs.

As you saw in Chapter 5, "Getting Started with openSUSE," openSUSE Linux offers a variety of text editors. Most contain special features for programming in assorted languages, such as highlighting commands in different colors and checking for mismatched parentheses and brackets. Programmers will also find the following essential tools in openSUSE Linux:

- The GNU Compiler Collection, which will compile and link programs written in seven programming languages.
- The GNU Debugger (`gdb`), which identifies and helps you troubleshoot problematic code.
- The Make utility, which pulls multiple source-code files into a single working package.
- Autoconf, which allows a programmer to create customized compiling and installation configurations for a program's source code.

NOTE

These programming tools are not installed by default when you install openSUSE Linux. You can easily get them using YaST, and they must be installed before any of the programs mentioned in this chapter will work on your system.

The easiest way to install multiple programming tools in YaST is to use the Patterns tool. Open the Software Management module, and select the Patterns filter from the drop-down menu at the top. Scroll down to Development, and you will see a variety of languages and tools to choose from. See Chapter 21, "Keeping Your System Current: Package Management" for more information on installing software with YaST, including Patterns.

A Simple C Program

C program source code files come in two types: *header*, or *include*, files and programs or procedural files. Standard C program files have a `*.c` extension and contain at least one *function*. Functions are a set of commands a program carries out to accomplish its tasks.

Header files have an `*.h` extension and carry variable descriptions, declarations, and other data common to all source files in the project.

Writing simple programs in C is a six-step process:

1. Open your favorite text editor.
2. Type the source code.
3. Save the file with the appropriate extension (`.c` for a program or `.h` for a header file).
4. Repeat Steps 2 and 3 as necessary if your application's source code will be broken down into multiple files.
5. Compile the program with GCC.
6. Run the program and then debug any problems.

Since time immemorial, the first program taught to students of a new language is called "Hello World" and consists of printing those two words on your screen. It's a short program, but its aim is to demonstrate the basic syntax of the language. We will follow the steps listed previously to write a "Hello World" program in C.

Open your favorite text editor and write the following source code text, exactly as you see it. Press Enter to insert a new line after the final brace.

```
#include <stdio.h>
int main(int argc, char* argv[]){
    printf("Hello, World.\n");
    return 0;
}
```

Details vary from editor to editor, but chances are good that your braces are highlighted in color, as is the quoted phrase. Now save this file as a plain text document named `hello.c` to a `source` directory, either in Home (`/~/source`) or in Documents (`/~/Documents/source`).

You'll read more about the GNU Compiler Collection (gcc) and other more basic tools for programming in C and other languages later in the chapter. Because most software is developed with tools that combine editors with linkers, compilers, and source control tools in integrated development environments (IDEs), we'll detour for a while to cover the main IDEs included in openSUSE Linux.

28

Building Applications with Eclipse

IBM has been a big backer of Java since the language was born in the mid-1990s, and possibly even a bigger backer of Linux and open-source software since the turn of the twenty-first century. It isn't a big surprise that as a result, the IBM-sponsored Eclipse development platform is open source and works well in Linux.

The Eclipse IDE began as an environment for building applications in the Java language. Because it is endlessly extensible with plug-ins, much more can be done with it. Developers regularly use it to program in Python, PHP, and other languages.

With the release of Eclipse SDK 3.2, called the Callisto release, various projects devoted to different development arenas have organized in the Eclipse community. Mature projects within the Eclipse ecosystem include:

- Business Intelligence and Reporting Tools (BIRT)
- Data Tools Platform for creating database connectivity software
- Device Software Development Platform for creation of embedded software for non-computer devices
- Eclipse Modeling Project for producing modeling frameworks
- Tools Project for more and better language tools
- Test and Performance Tools Platform (TPTP), which created benchmarking and QA tools
- Web Tools Platform, creating JavaServer Faces, AJAX, J2EE and Web Standards tools

This list grows and mutates regularly. If there is a type of development you're interested in doing, chances are excellent you'll be able to find a community of developers building tools within the Eclipse framework.

Installing and Updating Eclipse

The Eclipse package that you install with YaST contains these core features: the Eclipse Java Development Tool (JDT), the C/C++ Editor, the Equinox Rich Client Platform, the Plug-In Development Environment (PDE), and the Eclipse Software Development Kit (SDK). openSUSE Linux also includes the Ant build application, the JDI debugger, the JUnit testing framework, and a refactoring tool. Other plug-ins are installable through the Eclipse Update Manager, a YaST-like tool that checks for new software versions and installs them.

NOTE

The Eclipse community plans a major, annual simultaneous release of most projects early each summer. As of this writing, the Europa simultaneous release is set for June 2007.

To open the Update Manager, open Eclipse (from the Development, Integrated Environments menu). Go to the Help menu. Select Software Updates, and then Find and Install. Choose Search for New Features to Install from the wizard screen. Click Next.

TIP

Before using the Eclipse Update Manager with openSUSE Linux, there's some business to take care of.

When YaST installs Eclipse, all the files and directories are owned by Root with the group set as Root. The average user has access only by default, but the Eclipse Update Manager needs write access to create and update files in the `/usr/share/eclipse` directory.

You solve this problem by logging in as the SuperUser and creating a new system user called **`eclipse`**, and a group of the same name, with the new user as its only member.

Finally, because Root owns this directory and its branches, you need to adjust the permissions for `/usr/share/eclipse`. Go to this directory and type **`chgrp -R eclipse *`**. This makes the `eclipse` group responsible for the directory and all its subdirectories. Now you can use `chmod` to allow this group to read and write files in the same directories: `chmod -R 661 *`. You should now be able to run Update Manager without any trouble.

The second screen offers a list of repositories for new and updated Eclipse software. Each major project keeps its own repository that may not appear on this list by default. To add the Web Tools Project update site, for example, click New Remote Site and add this URL in the box: **http://download.eclipse.org/webtools/updates/**.

As with most update managers, Eclipse uses mirror sites to lighten the load on any one server. You can select a mirror yourself, or save time and have the manager select mirrors. Check the Automatically Select Mirrors box at the bottom of this screen, and click Finish to begin the update.

The Update Manager will contact each source and offer a list of new and updated packages from each repository. Check a box to download and install a package. You may get an error message indicating some dependency issues. You don't have to scrounge through the list to resolve these issues, though. Just click Select Required on the right side of the window.

Update Manager uses a tree hierarchy, so if you check the Web Tools Platform Updates box, it selects all the available tools from this site. Click Next to accept the open source Eclipse Foundation license. The last step in the wizard asks where you want to install the updates. By default, everything is stored in `/usr/share/eclipse`. Change this if you like with the Change Location button. Click Finish to begin the download.

You can have the update run in the background while you work on a project, but Eclipse will have to restart when the update is complete. View the progress in the bottom of the IDE. The Update Manager will ask you before it restarts.

Using the Eclipse Workbench

The first time you run Eclipse, you'll get a Welcome screen. Feel free to walk through the tutorials and examples offered there, and when you're done, click Workbench at the bottom of the screen to get started.

TIP

Eclipse uses the Firefox browser to deliver its online help, including the Welcome to Eclipse tutorials. If you don't have Firefox installed, or if you prefer a different browser, go to Preferences in the Window menu in the Eclipse Workbench. Under General, choose Web Browser and identify your preferred application. Eclipse finds Konqueror, and you may use the New dialog box to add other browsers to the list.

In Figure 28.1, you can see a sample "Hello World" program written in Java in the Eclipse Workbench. This program could just as well have been written in any text editor, but the Workbench gives you quite a lot at your fingertips to make the project easier.

In the upper-left corner is the Package Explorer, which lets you move around and open files in your project editor. The editor is in the center. You can have any number of files open in the editor at any given moment, but only one active at a time. You'll see any others in a tab in this area. In the upper-right corner is the Outliner, which shows each element in the active program. Clicking any item in the Outliner highlights that element in the editor.

Across the bottom, Eclipse watches for problems in your code and flags them for you. If your program displays some text on your shell (also known as the console), it will display a Console tab as well.

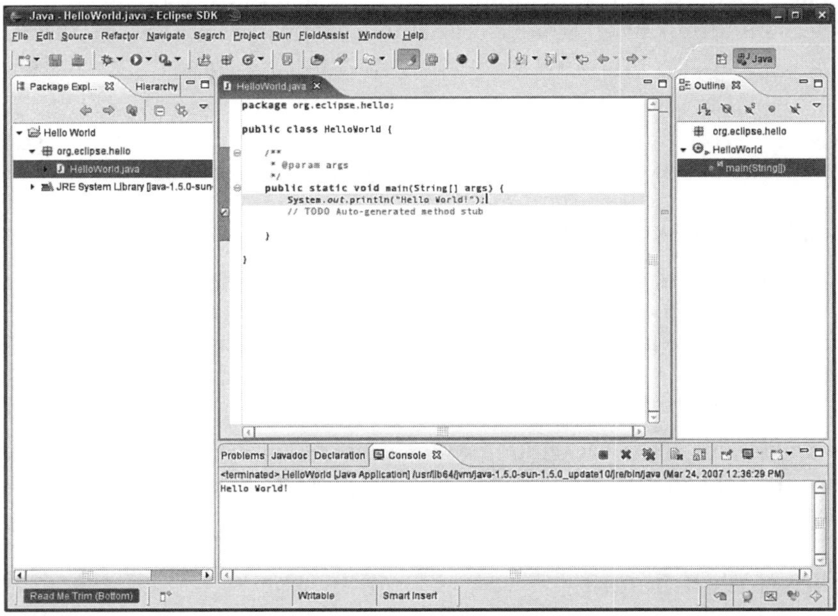

FIGURE 28.1 The Eclipse Workbench puts many tools at your fingertips.

Creating a Small Java Application in Eclipse

Perspectives are a set of related views and windows that help complete the task at hand. Each Perspective is tailored to a specific task. The current Perspective is indicated in the upper-right corner of the workbench, above the Outliner. By default, Eclipse displays the Java Perspective.

You can change Perspectives by going to the Window menu and selecting Open Perspective. The default list of choices changes depending on the Perspective you're starting from, but you can always display the entire list of Perspectives with the Other option. Once you have a Perspective displayed, you can further customize this view by maximizing windows, adding others, and closing some (if you find a particular setup useful, you can save a custom Perspective as well from Window, Save Perspective As). Begin by selecting the Java Perspective. Eclipse will respond by moving the default windows around a little bit to set up the Java Perspective layout.

For our "Hello World" example, you will need a new project to store your code in. Go to File, New, Project (or use the New Project toolbar button), and a wizard appears. Create a new Java Project, and name it **`Hello World`** (spaces are permitted in project names). You can further specify build settings, but that's for projects more complex than this one and the defaults will suit us fine.

Now your program (actually a Java class) can be created. Go to File, New, Class to launch the Class Wizard. Name it **`HelloWorld`**, but this time with no space. You should also define a package, because the use of the default package is discouraged (a package puts the class in a folder with related classes). The convention for the Eclipse Platform is to use **`org.eclipse`** as the default; for this one, use **`org.eclipse.hello`**. Check the Public Static Void Main box to create a void main method stub, and then click Finish. You'll see the result, `HelloWorld.java`, in the Java editor window.

The `Main()` function needs something to do. In the Outliner, click `main(string[])`. You'll see `main` highlighted in the editor. Go to the end of the line (with the left brace) and press Enter. Type **`System.out.println("Hello World!");`**. The Eclipse editor will offer syntax suggestions as you type; if you're feeling lazy, go ahead and select from your options. When complete, your code should resemble the following:

```
package org.eclipse.hello;

public class HelloWorld {
    public static void main(String[] args) {
        System.out.println("Hello World!");
    }
}
```

Notice that in the editor's title tab, there's a small asterisk to tell you there is unsaved content. When you've finished entering your code, go ahead and save your work either with File, Save or the Ctrl+S key combination.

Now it's time to run the program. Make sure `HelloWorld.java` is selected in the Package Explorer window on the left. Go to Run, Run As, Java Application. If all has gone well, you should see the Console window open on the bottom, as shown in Figure 28.1, displaying `Hello World`. If you have any problems, you can use the Debug view to help you sort it out.

Eclipse offers you an easy way to export your project when it's time to finally release it. To export our new Hello World application as a JAR file, make sure the Hello World project's root is selected in the Package Explorer pane and select File, Export. The Export Wizard will appear.

The first step of the wizard will prompt your for the type of export; select Java, JAR file, and click Next. Continue through the steps, ensuring that you set the export destination for your archive, and specify the main entry class. Eclipse will package your application and you can share it now with whomever you please.

Using the KDevelop Integrated Development Environment

KDevelop began as an IDE to rapidly produce C++ code for use in KDE projects. Since its inception it has grown to support 13 compiled and scripting languages. It is not part of the standard openSUSE Linux installation, but you can install the necessary packages in YaST.

KDevelop automates many of the tasks needed to create new programs. In fact, you won't even need to write anything yourself to produce a "Hello World" program in several languages! You will, however, get a sense of how such a program is built in the real-world KDE environment. Let's walk through the process of creating quality, free GUI software for KDE.

Begin by opening KDevelop. It is (or rather, they are) located in the KDE menu under Development, Integrated Environment. When you get to this menu, a selection of language-specific choices for KDevelop appears. For purposes of this example, we'll use the multi-language IDE.

A clean screen appears. Go to the Project menu and select New Project. A wizard appears. You'll see the array of available languages and default projects. Open the C++ tree and then the KDE branch. Scroll down to Simple KDE Application. When you select this option, a screenshot and description will display in the right panel, as shown in Figure 28.2.

Name the project **`KHello`**. Note that the Final Location line will revise itself. If you don't already have a `source` directory in your home directory, use the Browse button to create one. You'll then be asked whether to make this destination the default. This is up to you. Click Next to continue.

The second screen sets general information about you, the developer, and defines the license this program will carry. By default, KDevelop selects the GPL, but you can use the drop-down menu (as shown in Figure 28.3) to choose another license if you like.

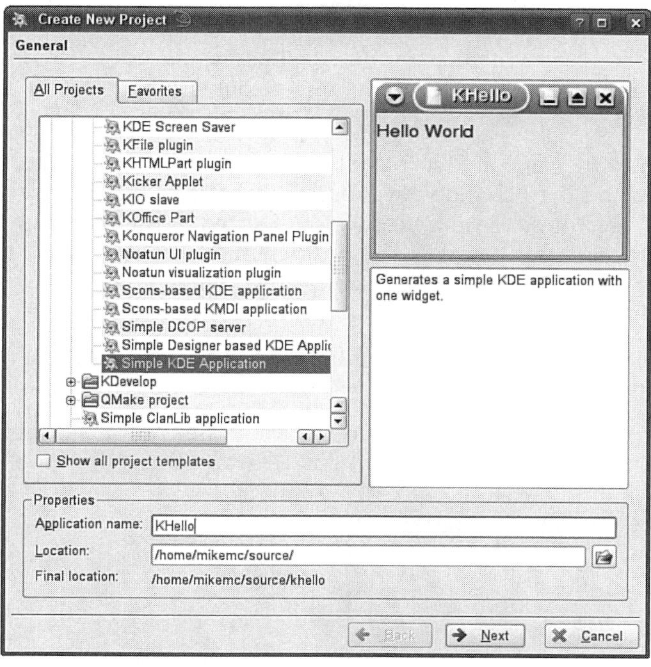

FIGURE 28.2 Select a project and name it in the first KDevelop New Project Wizard screen.

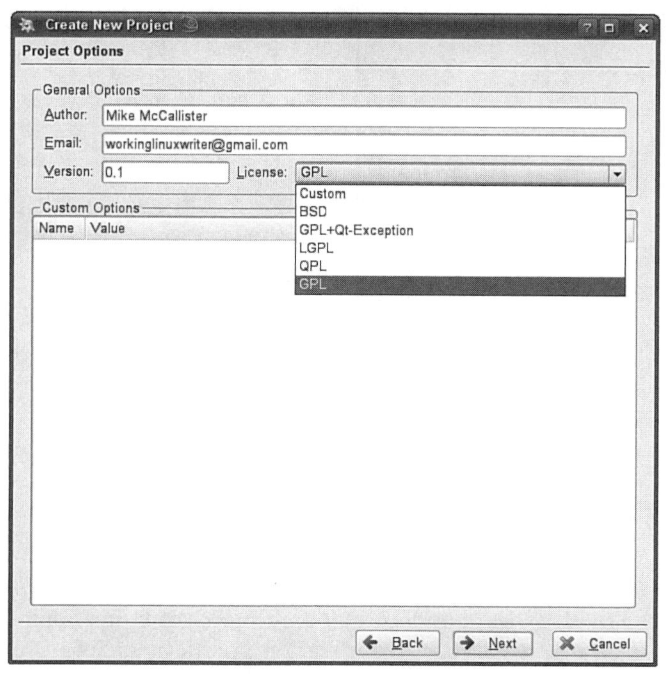

FIGURE 28.3 Choose from a variety of open-source licenses.

28

KDevelop pulls your name and email address from your KDE settings, but these fields are completely editable. It is a very good idea to include a valid email address, if not necessarily your primary one, with your free software, so users can contact you with bug reports and the like. Click Next to continue.

The third screen asks you to identify the version control system you're using, if any. The fourth and fifth screens set up your header file and your program template. Both include the standard GPL announcement, regardless of what license you selected in the previous screen. You may want to edit or delete this if you are using a different license (you may also add other text to your header file or CPP file in these templates). When you are finished editing the templates, click Finish to create `KHello.cpp`.

KDevelop displays its code in what it calls the IDEAl user interface (see Figure 28.4). You can adjust this in the Settings if it's not to your liking.

If you use Execute Program from the Build menu, KDevelop will ask to run Automake and Configure first. This is good practice. KDevelop will do that and then run the application.

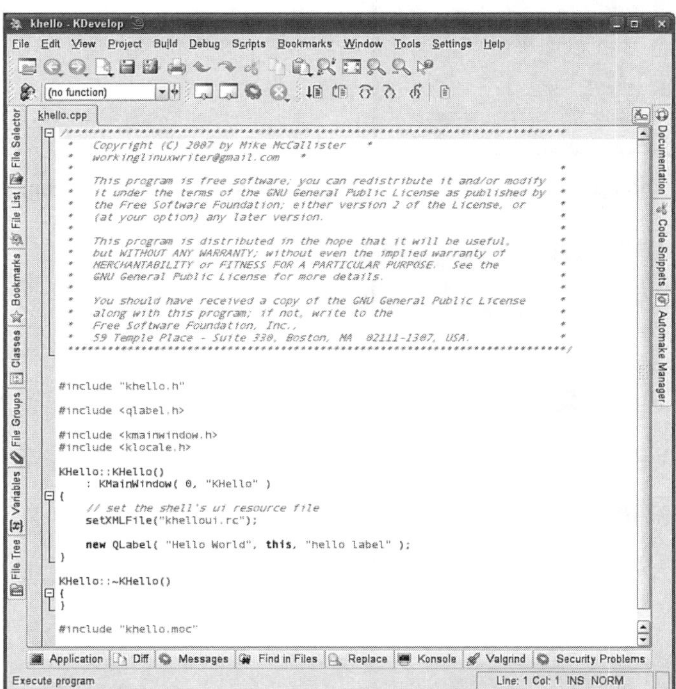

FIGURE 28.4 KDevelop generates a complete "Hello World" KDE program in C++ and displays it in this window.

After the program runs, click the File Selector tab on the left side of the KDevelop window. These files were all created by the wizard and are standard pieces of Linux applications. Click any file and it will open in the editor. In your real programs, be nice to your users. Modify the `INSTALL` file if users need to do something unusual to get your program working. Include `README` information and `NEWS` on this version's progress. If you have specific plans for the program, by all means share those plans in the `TODO` file.

Using Anjuta to Create GNOME Applications

Anjuta is a relatively new tool to help create GTK+ and GNOME applications with C and C++. It works with the Glade-2 GUI generator for GTK/GNOME and other packages to create nice-looking GNOME applications. As we saw with KDevelop, writing a Hello World application here won't require us to write any code. We'll get a sense though of how an application can be written in Anjuta.

You can install Anjuta with YaST, but the package dependency information is incomplete, so it does not install all the packages it needs. To be safe, try installing the `-devel` packages in the YaST Development libraries. Under Install and Remove Software, click the Package Groups display from the drop-down menu at the top. Go to Development, Libraries, GNOME. Many packages there will be called `<PackageName>-devel`. These packages contain all the necessary files to create (that is, develop) new programs.

When you open Anjuta, you have the choice of creating a new project, importing an existing project, or opening an existing Anjuta project or file. Click the Application Wizard button to begin a new project, and, after an introduction page, the screen shown in Figure 28.5 appears.

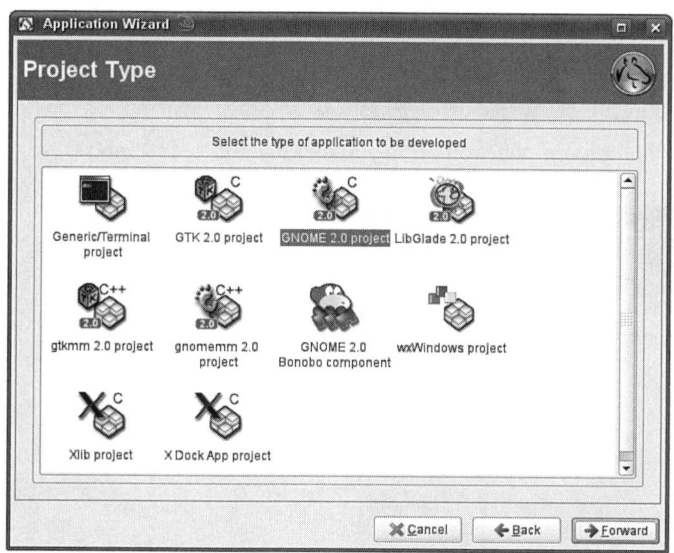

FIGURE 28.5 Select a new project type in the first screen.

In the second screen (see Figure 28.6), you select the name of the project and the language to be used. Project names are one word and are duplicated in the Project Target box.

The third screen asks you to describe your project. You can be pretty long-winded if you choose. In the final settings screen (see Figure 28.7), you set up where to put your program in the GNOME menu, as well as several other items. Enabling `gettext` support allows you to internationalize your application with other human languages. You may also specify an icon for your application if you want it to appear in the GNOME Application menu.

Confirm the settings you want the project to have and apply them to generate Yet Another Hello World program. Anjuta now runs its own Autogen program, which generates a `configure` file based on the wizard settings (see Figure 28.8).

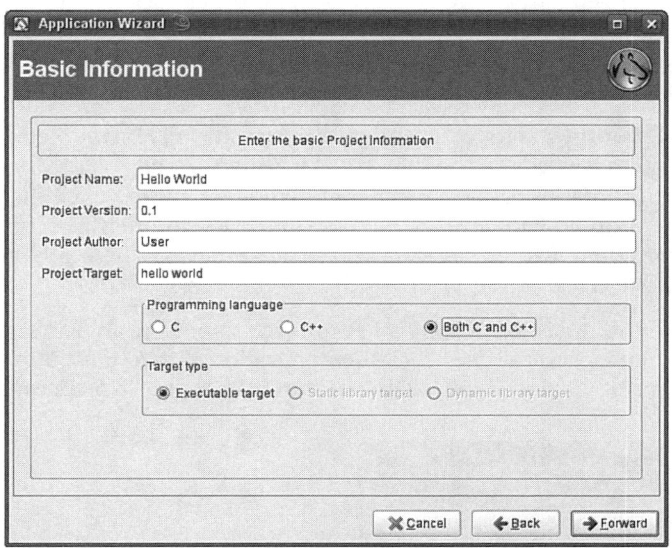

FIGURE 28.6 In Anjuta, project names are one word, and you can code in both C and C++.

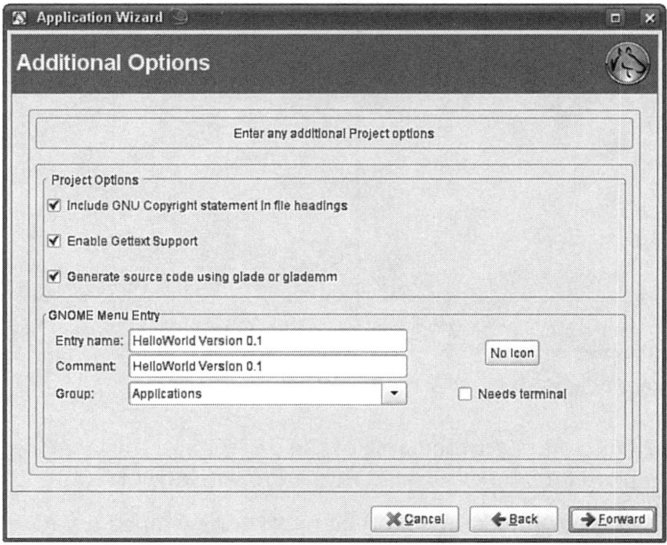

FIGURE 28.7 Make final adjustments and choose an icon in the project settings here.

After Anjuta has generated the source code and a configure script, you must compile and build the application before you can run it. Go to the Build menu and select Build (or Build All, if you have more than one file). After the application has been compiled and built, from the same menu, select Execute. You should see a terminal pop open with "Hello World!" and instructions on how to close the window.

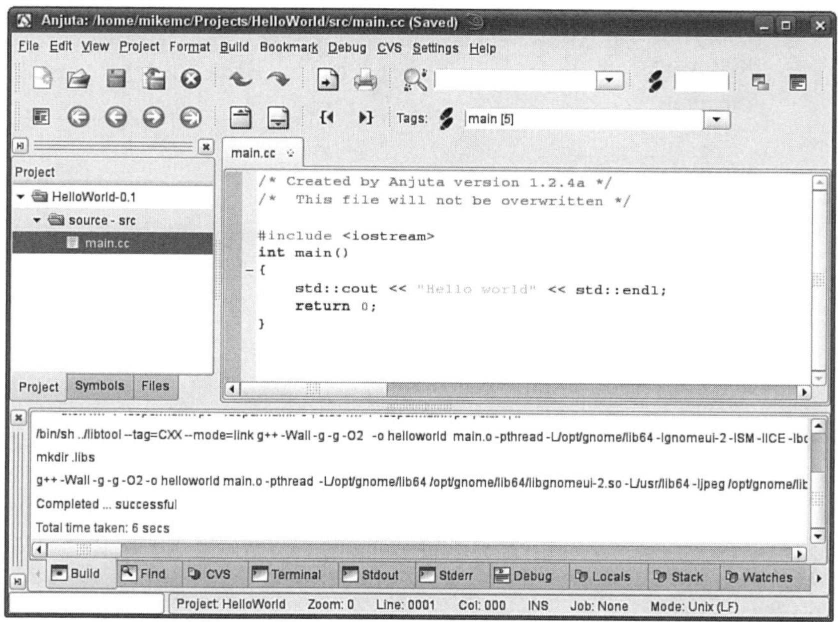

FIGURE 28.8 When Anjuta generates source code, you still must compile, build, and execute the code.

Using the GNU Compiler Collection

The GNU C Compiler (GCC), first written by Richard Stallman in 1987, has grown over time to support six other languages: Ada, C++, Fortran, Java, Objective-C, and Objective-C++. This is why the official name changed to the GNU Compiler Collection. Version 4.0 came out in April 2005.

Open a shell, change to the directory you saved your program to, and compile your program:

```
gcc -o hello hello.c
```

TIP

Your editor may have a direct link or command to run the compiler, so you can test your program without leaving the editor. Consult the editor's documentation.

TIP

The GCC determines which compiler to use based on the file extension of your source code. Table 28.1 shows common extensions for the supported languages. You can override this behavior by using the `-x` option (see **`man 1 gcc`** for more information).

TABLE 28.1 GCC Expected File Extensions for Source Codes

Language	Extension
Ada	Source: .ads, .adb
C	Source: .c
	Header: .h
C++	Source: .C, .cc, .cp, .CPP, .cpp, .c++, .cxx
	Header: .H, .hh
Fortran	Source: .F, .FPP, .fpp, .r
Objective-C	Source: .m
	Header: .h
Objective-C++	Source: .M
	Header: .h

The compiler creates an executable program called `hello` from the source file, `hello.c`. Heed any warnings you may get from the compiler. If you get any, you've mistyped something or forgot to press Enter (new line) at the end of the code. If necessary, compile again until you get a fresh prompt with no feedback. GCC delivers only bad news; if things work, it just does its thing.

If you look in the directory you will see a new file called `hello` with no extension. Now you can run the program:

```
./hello
Hello, World.
```

What did you do? You saved the source code with a `.c` extension to note what language this code is written in. The compiler created the executable `hello` (the name specified by the `-o` option), and then you executed the program. Because the program is not located in one of the standard executable directories, `usr/bin` or `/usr/local/bin`, you must use the dot-slash execute command in the directory where the program is located.

Additional GCC language front ends exist for Pascal, Modula-2, Modula-3, Mercury, VHDL, and PL/I; these are developed by teams separate from the GCC team and are not available via YaST. The Objective-C++ component is also missing from SUSE. You can access these languages at http://gcc.gnu.org/frontends.html.

Managing Collective Software Development with CVS and Subversion

The original revision control system (rcs) utility has features to manage small application projects, but when an application grows larger or is maintained by several developers, a better tool is needed. The Concurrent Versions System (CVS) arose to manage a corps of far-flung open-source developers and files that can potentially change on a minute-by-minute basis.

CVS controls the source code by storing it exclusively in one place, called a *repository*, and setting rules for access to the files. A CVS repository from the client perspective is like an FTP site or other remote access directory. It contains all the files in a particular development project. The difference between CVS and FTP is that a CVS repository is like a library (what leaves the library comes back to the repository), and FTP is like a bookstore (where you keep everything you take out). To work on a file or set of files in any source control environment (CVS, Subversion, or something else), you must check them out of the repository and check your changes back in (or *commit* your changes, in the CVS vernacular). The administrators of the repository can decide whether more than one person can check out a file at a time, how to process multiple changes, when to build the new version of the application, and what files will be included.

With CVS, you can get a complete record of changes in files without having multiple copies taking up space on your hard drive or server volume. Source files can be compared against the list of changes between versions, and any version can be reconstructed for review. Because any version can be reconstructed at any time, bugs can be tracked more easily and better test cases can be developed.

Incidentally, version control isn't good only for software projects. Any electronic file that undergoes frequent revisions or that is grouped with other files in a larger entity (for example, a book and its chapters) might do well to exist in a repository. It is reasonably simple to create a CVS repository on your local drive.

Create a base directory for all your CVS projects, such as **~/cvsroot**. Then point CVS to that directory:

```
cvs -d ~/cvsroot
```


You can now add files and directories (projects) to `cvsroot`, which can, in turn, be versioned over time using CVS. The six key CVS commands are the following:

- `add`—Commit a new file to the repository.
- `import`—Add a batch of new files or projects to the repository.
- `checkout`—Get a file to edit.
- `commit`—Return an edited file to the repository.
- `remove`—Make files currently in the repository disappear (other copies may exist elsewhere, however).
- `update`—In a local repository, confirm that everything is current. In a remote repository, get the latest changes in your working directory.

CVS isn't perfect, however, and in 2001, some CVS developers moved to another project, Subversion, which they hoped would solve some of CVS's nagging problems. This project, designed to eventually replace CVS as the open-source project management tool of choice, released version 1.0 in 2004 and has won many converts.

Both CVS and Subversion work in substantially the same way. Subversion adds several new features, including the capability to track versions of directories, a binary differencing algorithm, and more efficient branching and tagging of new versions of files.

Both CVS and Subversion are command-line applications, but Cervisia provides a GUI front-end to CVS and Subversion for KDE users. It can be used either as a standalone application or integrated into a Konqueror window. Cervisia allows you to connect to your repository and update and work directly with it. Eclipse also has a CVS plug-in that works the same way.

Creating RPM Packages

You have created this wonderful piece of software that you want to share with the rest of the Linux world. Because you are a kind and considerate programmer, you want to make it easy for non-programmers to install and run it on their systems. The best way to do this, especially on an openSUSE Linux system, is to build an installation package with RPM.

You learned the basics of the RPM system in Chapter 21. That section looked at RPM from the user's standpoint: the standard way of installing software on openSUSE Linux. In this section, you'll get a brief introduction to how to create RPM packages from your source code. You'll find a more detailed approach, with everything you need to know, by reading Ed Bailey's *Maximum RPM* at http://www.rpm.org/max-rpm.

You can make an RPM package out of any program for which you have working source code. This means you can use programs you have created, but also any other open source program you think needs an RPM. Helping to package new RPMs for a project is an easy, excellent way to contribute to the open-source community. The process is quite simple:

1. Obtain the source code for the application.
2. Build the program source.
3. If necessary, make a patch including any changes required to build the code successfully if the original would not build on your system.
4. Ensure that the necessary RPM-specific directories exist somewhere on your system: `BUILD`, `SOURCES`, `SPECS`, `RPMS`, and `SRPMS`.
5. Create a spec file for your package.
6. Build the RPM package.
7. Test the package.

As a sample project, let's make an RPM for the "Hello World" application you wrote using KDevelop.

Making a Spec File

Because you already have a working KHello program compiled from source, the first three steps in the process are complete. The key step is creating the spec file that tells the `rpm` application how to install KHello on someone's system. The spec file can be created using any text editor.

There are eight sections in an RPM spec file: a header, a prep section, a build instruction section, an installation section, file cleanup, pre- and post-installation and optional uninstallation scripts, a list of files in the package, and a changelog.

The header section gives a basic description of the package and has a number of elements. Following is our header section for KHello:

```
Summary: "Hello World" for KDE
Name: khello
Version: 0.1
Release: 1
Copyright: GPL
Group: Applications/Games
Source: /home/mikemc/source/KHello/KHello.tgz
Distribution: SuSE Linux

%description
KHello prints the words "Hello World" in a KDE window.
```

The summary element is a one-line description of our RPM package. The application's name and version are identified using name and version, respectively. A release number is used to identify sequential bug fixes if the extent of the recoding doesn't warrant a version increase. The program's licensing can be specified with copyright. The group element is used to identify which section under the K menu a shortcut icon will be placed.

The source element should point to a pristine copy of our source code (without any patches applied). More than one file can be specified by using source0, source1, source2, and so on. If you did need to apply a patch, those should be listed in the same manner as the source code using the `Patch` element.

The `%description` allows us to insert a complete description of what our application does; it can take up more than one line if necessary.

With our header section complete, we can now turn our attention to the prep session. The prep session consists of an `sh` script to prepare the working directory and source code. We can also use predefined RPM macros to perform common tasks. All we'll need to have in our prep section is a reference to RPM's `%setup` macro:

```
%prep
%setup
```

If you had a patch file, you would also want to reference the `%patch` macro on a separate line after `%setup`.

The Build section is relatively straightforward. You should put any commands here that you would need to use to build the software after you had untarred the source, patched it, and `cd`ed into the directory. This is just another set of commands passed to `sh`, so any legal `sh` commands can go here (including comments).

Your current working directory is reset in each of these sections to the top level of the source directory, so keep that in mind. You can `cd` into subdirectories if necessary.

```
%build
make
```

The Install section works much the same way as Build. Ideally, you can run `make install`, but if the Makefile doesn't provide the capability to automatically install an application, it will be necessary to write the `sh` script to accomplish this here.

```
%install
Make install
```

The Cleanup section is used mostly for testing purposes. Use the `%clean` macro to remove any leftover files from the `BuildRoot` directory before running a second time.

You can run pre- or post-installation scripts by using the `%pre` or `%post` macros in this section. Similarly, you can run scripts before or after an uninstallation using `%preun` or `%postun`.

All the files included in your package must be listed in the Files section. You will generate a file list in your first test build, which you can then copy to this section. There are also some macros to help with this listing, which you can find at http://www.rpm.org/RPM-HOWTO/build.html.

The last section of the spec file is a changelog, listing new features and fixes in this version. Each entry begins with a standard string:

```
*date +"%a %b %d %Y" <YourName> <YourEmailAddress>
```

A subsequent line begins with a—and lists the changes. For our example, because you're just at the first version, type something like **`First version`**. You can enter anything, but the changelog should be as informative as possible.

```
%changelog
*Fri Sep 30 2005 mikemc mikemc@susefan.com
- Created first version.
```

Save this file in the KHello directory, and you're just about ready to go.

Listing Files and Generating Patches

The contents of `%files` are critical because if a file is not listed, it will not be included in the final RPM package. One way to generate a good file list for your spec file is to get the source to build cleanly without using RPM. To do this, unpack the sources and preserve the directory by changing its name to `KHello.orig`. Then unpack the source again so that you have two directories. Go into the KHello source directory and build it.

If you had to edit any code, you'll need a patch. After you get things to build, clean out the source directory from any files that were made from the `configure` script. Then `cd` back out of the source directory to its parent. Use the diff utility to create a patch file:

```
diff -uNr KHello.orig KHello > KHello-bugfix.patch
```

This will create a patch for you that you can use in your spec file. Note that the `bugfix` that you see in the patch name is just an identifier. You might want to use something more descriptive as to *why* you had to make a patch. It's also a good idea to look at the patch file you are creating before using it to make sure no binaries were included by accident. Afterward, copy the file list generated by the build into your spec file.

Building and Testing Your RPM Package

Now that you have a useful spec file, it's time to copy your files to their proper place in the RPM directories created earlier and build your RPM. The original sources and patches should be copied to the SOURCES directory and the spec file is copied to the SPEC directory.

Build the RPM by entering into the SPEC directory and issuing this command:

```
rpm -ba khello.spec
```

The command will build both a binary RPM and a source RPM. If you want only a binary package built, use the `-bb` argument instead, or use `-bs` if you want only a source package.

RPM will use the `BUILD` directory to compile the application from the source code and patches and then place the finished binary package file in RPMS. The finished source package file will be placed in SRPMS. With some good fortune, you should now be able to change into the RPMS directory and run `rpm -ivh khello.rpm` to install your new package.

If possible, try installing the package on at least one other computer. After you have successfully built your RPM, register at freshmeat.net and announce your new application!

Other Linux Programming Resources

This very brief introduction to the tools of programming cannot possibly scratch the surface of what you need to know to get started in the field. If you have further interest in programming, here are a few of the better books on bookstore shelves:

- *Sams Teach Yourself C++ in 21 Days*, by Bradley Jones and Jesse Liberty
- *The C++ Programming Language*, by Bjarne Stroustrup
- *Sams Teach Yourself C in 21 Days*, by Bradley Jones and Peter Aitken
- *The C Programming Language*, by Brian W. Kernighan and Dennis M. Ritchie
- *Sams Teach Yourself Java 2 in 21 Days*, by Rogers Cadenhead and Laura Lemay
- *Eclipse Kick Start*, by Carlos Valcarcel
- *Eclipse in Action*, by David Gallardo, Ed Burnette, and Robert McGovern

References

- http://gcc.gnu.org—Home of the GNU Compiler Collection.
- http://gcc.gnu.org/frontends.html—Front ends for other languages available for GCC.
- http://www.gnu.org/software/autoconf—The Autoconf configuration utility.
- http://gcc.gnu.org/java—GCC's Java compiler, GCJ.
- http://subversion.tigris.org—The very well-designed Subversion site.
- http://svnbook.red-bean.com—The online book, *Version Control with Subversion.*
- http://ximbiot.com/cvs/wiki—The CVS wiki that replaced cvshome.org.
- http://www.linux.ie/articles/tutorials/cvs.php—A somewhat cheeky CVS tutorial.
- http://www.eclipse.org—The hub of the Eclipse community. Everything you need to get going and keep going.
- http://www.eclipse.org/projects—Check on the current status of (and get involved in) all the Eclipse subprojects here.
- http://www.eclipseplugincentral.com—The place to find your needed Eclipse plug-ins, with news, too.
- http://www-128.ibm.com/developerworks/eclipse/downloads—The IBM Development Packages for Eclipse. Includes free bundles for the Web Tools Project, testing and modeling tools, and an Enterprise bundle with everything.
- http://planeteclipse.org/planet—A collection of blogs by Eclipse developers.
- http://www.kdevelop.org—News, forums, documentation, and a real-time chart indicating the number of downloads per hour of this IDE.
- http://anjuta.sourceforge.net—The GNOME/GTK+ IDE.
- http://www.digitalfanatics.org/projects/qt_tutorial—Tutorial for C++ developers to learn Qt.
- http://doc.trolltech.com—The official reference documentation for current and recent versions of Qt.
- http://wiki.rpm.org—Home for information on the Red Hat Package Management system. Head for the Docs page for online versions of two books on RPM.
- http://tldp.org/HOWTO/RPM-HOWTO—An excellent guide to creating an RPM.
- http://www.rpm.org/max-rpm—Ed Bailey's *Maximum RPM* article.
- http://www.rpm.org/RPM-HOWTO/build.html—Macros that help with generating a file list.

CHAPTER 29

Managing Databases

IN THIS CHAPTER

- What Is a Relational Database?
- Implementing MySQL
- Implementing PostgreSQL
- Using openSUSE Database Clients
- References

In this chapter, we look at database creation and client access with openSUSE Linux. Databases can be considered digital phonebooks—when there is a need for highly organized storage of a massive amount of information, a database is called for. There are very special requirements associated with databases; therefore, it shouldn't seem strange that it takes special software to create a storage system that is highly organized by items such as fields, records, and tables. Databases (if optimized and running properly) can store massive amounts of data, such as logging information for a web server. The blending of Apache web server software, the PHP scripting language, and the MySQL database engine is basically what fuels most of today's website development. PHP will be covered in Chapter 31, "Creating Dynamic Websites."

This chapter is only an introduction to these two technologies. Entire publications have been dedicated to the topic of building databases, especially with MySQL and PostgreSQL, two of today's hottest web-based database technologies in use.

This chapter covers the installation and configuration of both MySQL and PostgreSQL and discusses two popular Open Source database client applications, OpenOffice.org Base and Rekall.

What Is a Relational Database?

A database is a collection of information organized in such a way that a computer program can quickly select desired pieces of data based on a query that you provide. As previously mentioned, databases are the storage sites for the world's data.

Database services are based on a client/server model. In openSUSE Linux, you can install components based on that model for both the client and the server portions of the database. You can install a complete database server by installing the full-featured MySQL or PostgreSQL installation packages in YaST. You can then use various database clients to access the database server running on your system.

By installing the server, you install the software needed to run, operate, and manage database protocols such as SQL. SQL stands for Structured (or Standard) Query Language; it is a standard language for accessing and manipulating databases. SQL defines statements that can be used to retrieve and update data in a database, such as `SELECT`, `UPDATE`, `DELETE`, `INSERT`, and `WHERE`.

You can access a database server in various ways, such as by the command prompt using the mysql command or by using graphical client software such as OpenOffice.org Base or the Rekall database client program.

Before getting too far into this chapter, we need to discuss how databases work. There are two general types of databases: flat-file databases, which are much like your `/etc/passwd` file, and relational databases, which are much more complex and require much more structure to organize them. Flat-file databases are poor performers and are not truly scalable. A flat-file database is the opposite of a relational database, which is hierarchical. Relational databases, on the other hand, are specialized to handle large amounts of data. They are scalable, which means that they grow well, unlike their flat-file counterparts.

Relational databases are organized by fields, records, and tables. In a relational database, a field is a single piece of information. A record is one complete set of fields, and a table is a collection of records. This is essentially what makes up the logical structure of databases.

In a database, each table is identified by a name, such as *Contacts*. Each table contains records, also called rows, that contain the actual database data. For example, suppose we were to define a table called Contacts and create the following three records:

```
Last          First      Address            City           State
Coughanour    David      578 E. 200 N.      Santaquin      Utah
Johnson       Brian      113 N. 1111 E.     Rigby          Idaho
Corry         Jason      57 E. Wrangler     San Antonio    Texas
```

Using the SQL language, you can create queries that return specific data from the database. For example, suppose you were to compose the following query:

```
SELECT Last FROM Contacts
```

The database would return the following data:

```
Last
Coughanour
Johnson
Corry
```

In addition to creating queries, the SQL language allows you to update, insert, and delete records. This is done using the following commands:

- `SELECT`—Retrieves information from a table
- `UPDATE`—Modifies information in a table
- `DELETE`—Removes information from a table
- `INSERT`—Adds new data to a table

In addition to manipulating data within a table, SQL commands can also be used to manage the table itself. This is done using the following commands:

- `CREATE TABLE`—Creates a new table
- `ALTER TABLE`—Modifies an existing table
- `DROP TABLE`—Deletes an existing table

A key feature of a relational database is that you can create relations between tables, which enables you to create powerful interrelated data sets. A relational database is also known as a relational database management system (RDBMS). RDBMS is a type of database management system (DBMS), but focuses on the relational model just discussed.

When you install the database server with YaST, you can create the system of database tables where the data will be stored and organized in a way that information can be managed efficiently. If data is managed this way, it is quick to retrieve and easier to manage, mine, and control.

Implementing MySQL

MySQL is quite possibly the most popular Open Source relational database server available. Many Internet websites use MySQL as the backend database system for storing data for online shopping. While it doesn't quite yet have as many features as some commercial database server packages, it is best known for its simplicity and quick data access speeds.

This section describes how to install and configure the MySQL database server on your openSUSE system. Following that, a short example is shown on how to create a test database and tables for an application.

Installing MySQL

The default openSUSE 10.3 configuration does not install the MySQL database server. As long as you have the installation CD-ROMs or a connection to the Internet, you can install it quickly and easily using the YaST Software Management module, as shown in Figure 29.1.

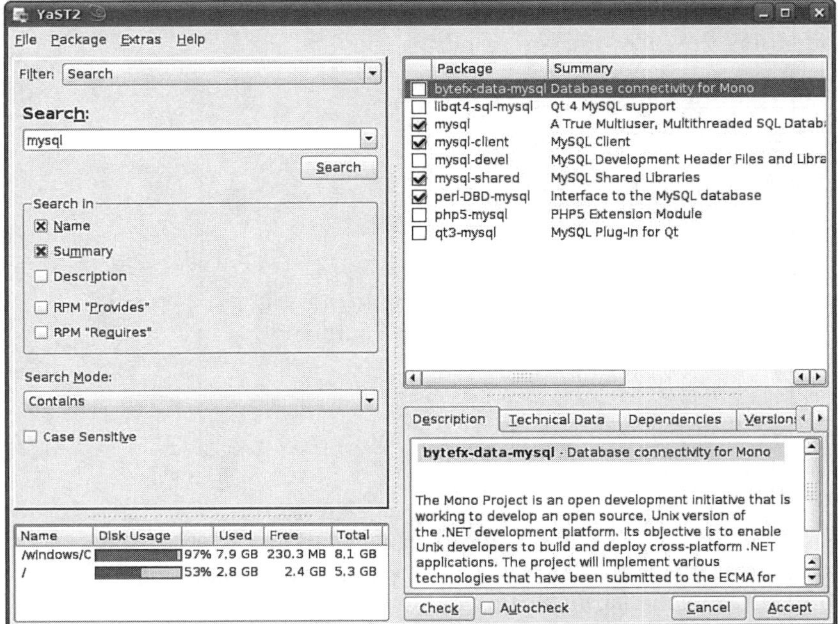

FIGURE 29.1 Using YaST to install MySQL.

To install MySQL on your system, complete the following:

1. Run YaST and navigate to Software, Software Management.
2. In the Search field, enter **mysql**; then select Search.
3. In the Package column, select the following packages, as shown in Figure 29.1:
   - mysql
   - mysql-client
   - mysql-shared
   - perl-DBD-mysql

There are many other MySQL-related packages that you could install. Most of these packages, such as apache2-mod_auth_mysql, are used to enhance the functionality of the MySQL service. You can, optionally, install these packages as well using the same technique as installing the main MySQL package.

When you are done with your installation, you are highly encouraged to run the YaST online update so that you can install any recent patches that have been released for the MySQL database. These include new tools, security fixes, and software patches that may be available. You may also be interested in viewing the www.mysql.com web site for the latest version of the product. You can download the source files in an RPM package and install the latest version if your needs require it.

After installing MySQL, a number of initial configuration tasks must be completed before you can begin working with your first database table. We'll look at these tasks next.

Completing MySQL Initial Configuration Tasks

After installing the MySQL packages, you will need to do the following tasks:

- Start the MySQL server
- Secure the MySQL superuser account
- Create MySQL user accounts

The following sections discuss how to do each of these.

Starting the MySQL server

The MySQL database consists of many files and directories stored in the /var/lib/mysql directory. The openSUSE MySQL server installation creates the base database directory and a special user account (called mysql) that has access to the database directory. The MySQL server process runs in the background and controls access to the database. All access to the MySQL database must be through the server process.

You can choose to either manually start the MySQL server process when you want the MySQL server active or allow openSUSE to start it as part of the boot up sequence so that it runs at all times. The openSUSE install includes a startup script file to start the MySQL server process. This script is used whether you manually start the server or choose openSUSE to start it automatically.

To manually start the MySQL server, as the Root user, use this command:

```
testing:~ # /etc/init.d/mysql start
```

The mysql startup script is located with the other openSUSE startup scripts in the /etc/init.d directory. The start option instructs the script to attempt to start the MySQL server process. The first time the MySQL server starts, it must initialize the database files within the /var/lib/mysql directory structure:

```
rich@testing:~ > su
password:
testing:~ # /etc/init.d/mysql start
Creating MySQL privilege database...
Installing all prepared tables
/usr/sbin/mysqld: Can't read dir of '/var/lib/mysql/.tmp/' (Errcode: 2)
Fill help tables
/usr/sbin/mysqld: Can't read dir of '/var/lib/mysql/.tmp/' (Errcode: 2)
PLEASE REMEMBER TO SET A PASSWORD FOR THE MySQL root USER !
To do so, start the server, then issue the following commands:
/usr/bin/mysqladmin -u root password 'new-password'
/usr/bin/mysqladmin -u root -h linux.lan password 'new-password'
See the manual for more instructions.
```

```
You can test the MySQL daemon with the benchmarks in the 'sql-bench' directory:
cd sql-bench ; perl run-all-tests

Please report any problems with the /usr/bin/mysqlbug script!

The latest information about MySQL is available on the web at
http://www.mysql.com
Support MySQL by buying support/licenses at http://shop.mysql.com
Starting service MySQL                                                    done
testing:~ #
```

Note that you must be the Root user to run the startup script. The MySQL server starts, initializes the database files, and then runs in the background waiting for clients to access the server. After the server is started for the first time, the database files do not have to be initialized, so the startup message is much shorter (you'll also see a few error messages when the server is run for the first time, since these files don't exist yet). To manually stop the MySQL server, just issue the `stop` command from the startup script:

```
testing:~ #/etc/init.d/mysql stop
Stopping service MySQL                                                    done
testing:~ #
```

If you want the MySQL server to start automatically when you boot the openSUSE system, you can enable it in the System Services. To do that, start YaST, select the System icon, and then the System Services icon. The currently configured system services appear, as shown in Figure 29.2.

If you've installed MySQL using YaST, an entry is automatically made for the mysql server. Just select it, and enable it to be started by the system. The next time you boot, openSUSE will automatically start the MySQL server.

Secure the MySQL Superuser Account

Once the MySQL server is up and running, you'll want to perform a couple of housekeeping tasks. The MySQL database maintains its own user accounts for controlling access to the database. The administration account is called (not surprisingly) `Root`. Unfortunately, by default, the `Root` user account has no password assigned to it. You should assign a password to the account immediately after installing the server to prevent unauthorized connection to your database.

NOTE

It's important that you understand that MySQL has its own user accounts that are separate from your openSUSE Linux system's user accounts. MySQL maintains its user accounts in a special database, separate from the openSUSE Linux system. Even though MySQL uses an account named Root, it's not the same as the Root account on your Linux system. The MySQL database runs on your system as a Linux system user account named mysql, which is created when the MySQL packages are installed. You'll see a little later on how to create your own MySQL user accounts.

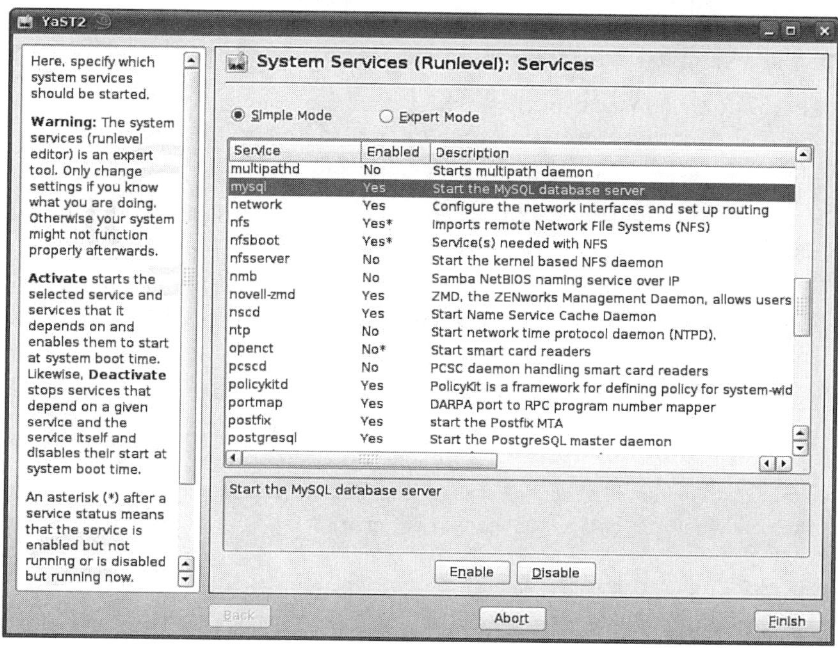

FIGURE 29.2 Configuring system services to start.

The `mysqladmin` command line utility is used to change the password for the Root user account:

```
rich@testing:~ > mysqladmin -u root password 'testing'
rich@testing:~ > mysqladmin -u root -h testing.lan password 'testing'
rich@testing:~ >
```

Notice that you do not need to be the Root system user to use the `mysqladmin` program. All of your access is performed within the MySQL database structure. The `-u` option specifies the database user account to use for access.

There are two entries required for changing the Root user password. MySQL tracks user access by remote location. In the second entry, the `-h` option is used to specify the domain name of the host. The MySQL user system allows you to allow a user to have access from one location, but be blocked from accessing the database from a different location. This feature allows you to control from where users can access the database.

By default, all accounts are created for access from the `localhost` location. However, if the user accesses the database from a TCP/IP connection from the local host, you should also have an entry for the complete hostname (`testing.lan` in the above example) . This results in two entries for each user from the local host.

Create MySQL User Accounts

The Root user account has complete access to everything in the MySQL database system. This is intended purely for administration purposes. It is not recommended to run your database application using this account. Instead, you should create other user accounts for users to use when accessing database applications.

Creating user accounts is done from within the MySQL database system. MySQL uses internal system tables that contain information on all database objects, including user accounts. To create new user accounts, you must create new entries in the system tables.

The default MySQL installation includes a simple command line client that allows you to access the MySQL database. With the `mysql` command line client, you can enter simple SQL commands for the server and view the results returned.

When using the `mysql` client, you must specify the database name to which to connect, as well as the MySQL user account to log in as. The MySQL system tables are stored in the database named mysql, so you'll want to connect to that database:

```
rich@linux:~> mysql mysql -u root -p
Enter password:
Reading table information for completion of table and column names
You can turn off this feature to get a quicker startup with -A

Welcome to the MySQL monitor.  Commands end with ; or \g.
Your MySQL connection id is 1 to server version: 5.0.26

Type 'help;' or '\h' for help. Type '\c' to clear the buffer.

mysql>
```

Now that you are logged into the MySQL server, you can view the existing user accounts configured using simple SQL statements:

```
mysql> select user,host,password from user;
+------+-------------+-------------------------------------------+
| user | host        | password                                  |
+------+-------------+-------------------------------------------+
| root | localhost   | *A43F8E65F6CFE4B13261D9488E30765AE60C6B98 |
| root | testing.lan | *A43F8E65F6CFE4B13261D9488E30765AE60C6B98 |
|      | testing.lan |                                           |
|      | localhost   |                                           |
+------+-------------+-------------------------------------------+
4 rows in set (0.04 sec)

mysql>
```

The user accounts are maintained in the `user` system table, which has lots of fields. This simple query displays the user accounts, the host from which they are allowed access, and the encrypted password. Notice that, as expected, there are two entries for the Root user. The blank entries are the default user values to ensure that any user accounts not configured are denied access.

Adding a new user account in MySQL is as simple as using the SQL INSERT command:

```
mysql> insert into user (user,host,password) values ('rich', 'localhost', '');
Query OK, 1 row affected (0.00 sec)
mysql> insert into user (user,host,password) values ('rich', 'testing.lan', '');
Query OK, 1 row affected (0.00 sec)
mysql>
```

Because we don't want to add data for all of the fields in the user table, we must specify the fields we are populating. After the INSERT commands are executed, the new user account exists, but there is no password assigned, which prevents the account from logging in. The next step is to assign a new password for the user account.

This is done using the UPDATE SQL command, along with the special MySQL PASSWORD() function, which encrypts the password using the MySQL encryption method:

```
mysql> update user set password = PASSWORD('testing') where user = 'rich';
Query OK, 2 rows affected (0.00 sec)
mysql>
```

NOTE

It is extremely important to remember the WHERE part of the UPDATE SQL command to limit which user account gets the password change. Without it, the password on every user account will be changed. That would be bad, especially if you have lots of users.

Since MySQL version 5 you can also use the CREATE USER command to add a new user account and assign a password all in one step:

```
mysql> create user 'mytest'@'localhost' identified by 'test';
Query OK, 0 rows affected (0.00 sec)
mysql>
```

You can use the SELECT command to query the user table and verify that the new user entries have been entered correctly. Once a normal user account is created, you are ready to start creating some database objects for your application.

Creating Databases and Tables

The MySQL server has the ability to maintain multiple databases simultaneously. Clients can access each database separately from the same MySQL server. It is a good idea to create a different database for each application the server supports. This helps ensure data doesn't get mixed up between applications, and it also helps prevent users from accidentally assigning the wrong permissions to the wrong data.

The following sections show how to create a new database on the MySQL server and how to insert new application data into the database.

Creating the Database

A mysql session can connect to only one database at a time, restricting access to only the database objects (such as tables and views) configured within that database. You can view the existing databases on a MySQL server using the special show databases command from any database:

```
mysql> show databases;
+——————————+
¦ Database           ¦
+——————————+
¦ information_schema ¦
¦ mysql              ¦
+——————————+
2 rows in set (0.00 sec)
mysql>
```

To create a new database, use the CREATE SQL command:

```
mysql> create database test;
Query OK, 0 rows affected (0.00 sec)
mysql>
```

Once a database is created, if you want to connect to that database, you need to use the CONNECT command:

```
mysql> connect test;
Connection id:    2
Current database: test

mysql>
```

After a database is created, you must grant users permission to view and/or alter the objects within the database. The GRANT SQL command is used to assign specific permissions to database objects to individual users. To allow a user to have complete control over a database, you can use the all keyword:

```
mysql> grant all on test.* to rich;
Query OK, 0 rows affected (0.04 sec)

mysql>
```

This command grants all permissions for any object in the test database to the user account rich. This effectively enables him to act as an administrator for the database. However, he doesn't have full access to the MySQL server. This is a common way to create localized superusers for database applications.

Connecting to the Database

Once a new database is created, you'll want to be able to log into the database and start manipulating data. To log into the test database using the `mysql` client, you would use the following command:

```
rich@linux:~> mysql test -u rich -p
Enter password:
Reading table information for completion of table and column names
You can turn off this feature to get a quicker startup with -A

Welcome to the MySQL monitor.  Commands end with ; or \g.
Your MySQL connection id is 6 to server version: 5.0.26

Type 'help;' or '\h' for help. Type '\c' to clear the buffer.

mysql>
```

The `-u` option specifies the user account to use, and the `-p` option instructs `mysql` to query for a password. Now the user `rich` is connected to the test database and can start entering SQL commands.

Creating Tables

As mentioned earlier, in a relational database, all data contained within the database is arranged in tables. The `CREATE TABLE` SQL command is used to define the data fields and format of each table:

```
mysql> create table employees (
    -> empid int not null,
    -> lastname varchar(30),
    -> firstname varchar(30),
    -> salary float,
    -> primary key (empid));
Query OK, 0 rows affected (0.04 sec)

mysql>
```

The employees table was created using five data elements. You can use the `show tables` command to view all of the tables in a database:

```
mysql> show tables;
+----------------+
| Tables_in_test |
+----------------+
| employees      |
+----------------+
1 row in set (0.00 sec)

mysql>
```

29

To view the individual records in a table, use the SELECT SQL command:

```
mysql> select * from employees;
Empty set (0.00 sec)

mysql>
```

The new table was created, but doesn't have any data in it yet. To add data records, use the INSERT SQL command:

```
mysql> insert into employees values (1, 'Blum', 'Rich', 25000);
Query OK, 1 row affected (0.03 sec)

mysql> insert into employees values (2, 'Blum', 'Barbara', 45000);
Query OK, 1 row affected (0.00 sec)

mysql>
```

To check if the data was inserted correctly in the table, use the SELECT command again:

```
mysql> select * from employees;
+-------+----------+-----------+--------+
| empid | lastname | firstname | salary |
+-------+----------+-----------+--------+
|     1 | Blum     | Rich      |  25000 |
|     2 | Blum     | Barbara   |  45000 |
+-------+----------+-----------+--------+
2 rows in set (0.00 sec)

mysql>
```

As expected, the data appears in the table. Your application is well on its way. Next we'll look at how to use the PostgreSQL database server.

Implementing PostgreSQL

PostgreSQL is yet another Open Source database package that has attained popularity in the Linux world. The claim to fame for PostgreSQL is that it implements many of the advanced database features that the commercial products do, such as views, stored procedures, triggers, and hot backups. Unfortunately, at the present time, it does so at the expense of data access speed (PostgreSQL is not known for its speediness). If you are looking for advanced database features in a free software package though, PostgreSQL is definitely the way to go.

This section describes how to install and configure the PostgreSQL server on your openSUSE system. Following that is a brief example of creating a database and table within PostgreSQL.

Installing PostgreSQL

As with MySQL, the PostgreSQL server can be installed using the YaST Software Management wizard, as shown in Figure 29.3.

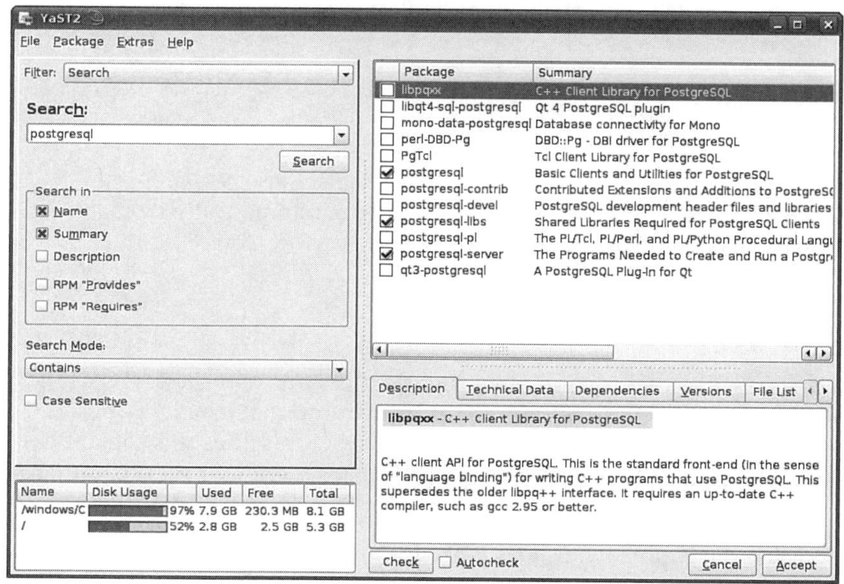

FIGURE 29.3 Using YaST to install PostgreSQL.

To install PostgreSQL on your system, complete the following:

1. Run YaST and navigate to Software, Software Management.
2. In the Search field, enter **`postgresql`**; then select Search.
3. In the Package column, select the following packages, as shown in Figure 29.3:
   - postgresql
   - postgresql-libs
   - postgresql-server

Just as with the MySQL package, the openSUSE installation also includes several other PostgresQL packages, mostly used for developing application programs that access a PostgreSQL server.

After installing the PostgreSQL server package, you again have the option to manually or automatically start the PostgreSQL server. To manually start the server, use the postgresql startup script located in the standard area:

```
testing:~ # /etc/init.d/postgresql start
Initializing the PostgreSQL database at location /var/lib/pgsql/data done
```

```
Starting PostgreSQL                                          done
testing:~ #
```

Just as with MySQL, the first time the PostgreSQL database server is started, the data area in /var/lib/pgsql is initialized. To manually stop the PostgreSQL server, use the stop command:

```
testing:~ # /etc/init.d/postgresql stop
Stopping PostgreSQL                                          done
testing:~ #
```

You can use the System Services function to set PostgreSQL to automatically start at boot up. From YaST, select the System icon and then the System Services icon. Find the PostgreSQL item, and then enable it to autostart.

Accessing PostgreSQL

In openSUSE, the PostgreSQL server is configured slightly different than the MySQL server. If you remember, the MySQL server maintains its own internal database of users that can be granted access to database objects. While PostgreSQL also has this capability, the openSUSE implementation utilizes the existing openSUSE system user files to authenticate PostgreSQL user accounts.

While this can sometimes be confusing, it does make for a nice clean way to control user accounts in PostgreSQL. Another major difference for PostgreSQL is that the administrator account in PostgreSQL is called postgres, not Root. The openSUSE PostgreSQL installation automatically creates a system account called postgres and assigns it an unknown password so that you can't log into the system with it.

Similar to MySQL, PostgreSQL uses a command line client to interact with the server. The PostgreSQL command line client is called psql.

The psql client passes the system login information of the account and runs it to the PostgreSQL server for authentication. Unfortunately this means that you must be logged in as the postgres system account to access the postgres PostgreSQL administrator account. The easiest way to do that is with the Linux su command:

```
linux:~ # su postgres
postgres@linux:/root> psql -U postgres
could not change directory to "/root"
Welcome to psql 8.1.5, the PostgreSQL interactive terminal.

Type:  \copyright for distribution terms
       \h for help with SQL commands
       \? for help with psql commands
       \g or terminate with semicolon to execute query
       \q to quit

postgres=#
```

Now you are logged in with the postgres database superuser account. Similar to the MySQL show commands, PostgreSQL uses a series of special, non-SQL meta-commands to view database information. The four most used meta-commands are:

- \l to list the databases
- \c to connect to a database
- \dt to list the tables within a database
- \q to exit the database

While logged in as the postgres superuser, you can create a new database for the PostgreSQL server. The standard CREATE DATABASE SQL command is used to create new databases:

```
postgres=# create database test;
CREATE DATABASE
postgres=# \c test
You are now connected to database "test".
test=#
```

After creating the database, use the \c meta-command to connect to it. You can create database objects only while you are connected to the database.

User accounts in PostgreSQL are called Login Roles. The postgres superuser can create new Login Roles and grant permissions to database objects to them. Remember though, the openSUSE implementation of PostgreSQL uses the openSUSE system password files to authenticate Login Roles, so your PostgreSQL Login Roles must match an existing openSUSE user account:

```
test=# create role rich login password 'testing';
CREATE ROLE
test=# grant all on test to rich;
GRANT
test=#
```

Now you can log in to the test database using the system account rich:

```
rich@testing:~> psql test
Welcome to psql 8.1.5, the PostgreSQL interactive terminal.

Type:  \copyright for distribution terms
       \h for help with SQL commands
       \? for help with psql commands
       \g or terminate with semicolon to execute query
       \q to quit

test=>
```

Because I was already logged into openSUSE as the user `rich`, all I needed to do was run `psql` with the name of the database to connect to. With the new database created, and a user account with access to the database, you are ready to start playing with data!

Creating Tables

Once you are in the PostgreSQL database, it is just a matter of using standard SQL commands to create tables and insert data:

```
test=> create table employees (
test(> empid int4 primary key not null,
test(> lastname varchar,
test(> firstname varchar,
test(> salary float4);
NOTICE:  CREATE TABLE / PRIMARY KEY will create implicit index "employees_pkey" for
table "employees"
CREATE TABLE
test=>
```

This command creates the new `employees` table. To verify that it has been created, use the `\dt` meta-command:

```
test=> \dt
          List of relations
 Schema ¦   Name    _¦ Type  ¦  Owner
----+------.+---.+-----
 public ¦ employees ¦ table ¦ rich
(1 row)

test=> select * from employees;
 empid ¦ lastname ¦ firstname ¦ salary
---.+------+------.+----
(0 rows)

test=>
```

The table exists and has no data. Now you can put data into the table using the `INSERT` command:

```
test=> insert into employees values (1, 'Blum', 'Rich', 25000);
INSERT 0 1
test=> insert into employees values (2, 'Blum', 'Barbara', 55000);
INSERT 0 1
test=> select * from employees;
 empid ¦ lastname ¦ firstname ¦ salary
---.+------+------.+----
     1 ¦ Blum     ¦ Rich      ¦  25000
```

```
      2 ¦ Blum       ¦ Barbara    ¦  55000
(2 rows)

test=>
```

The data was successfully added to the table. As you can see, using the PostgreSQL and MySQL database servers is very similar. That is the whole point behind the SQL standard. Once you know the proper SQL commands, you can work in almost any relational database server.

While database servers are great for large applications that must manipulate thousands of records, using a large database server is sometimes overkill. If you are interested in creating small, simple personal databases, openSUSE provides other options for you. The next section describes two of those options and shows you how to use them.

Using openSUSE Database Clients

The openSUSE Linux distribution includes a few different database client programs for your use. While not as sophisticated as the MySQL and PostgreSQL database servers, they can come in handy when creating small personal databases.

The OpenOffice.org Base database client is installed by default in openSUSE 10.3. The installation CD-ROMs also include the popular Open Source Rekall database client. The following sections describe how to use them for your personal databases.

OpenOffice.org Base

The OpenOffice.org suite of office productivity tools is an Open Source project that mimics the functionality of the Microsoft Office suite of software. One of the core packages in Microsoft Office is the Access database client. Microsoft Access provides a graphical front end for users to easily create tables, queries, and reports without having to know any SQL statements.

Base supports both an internal database file format (similar to the Access .mdb file structure) as well as the capability to connect to a remote database server (such as MySQL or PostgreSQL). Base is configured in openSUSE to use the internal database file. If you want to use Base to connect to your MySQL or PostgreSQL server, will need to download and install the MySQL or PostgreSQL Java Database Connectivity (JDBC) drivers.

The OpenOffice.org Base program mimics the functionality of Access by providing the same graphical front end features for creating tables, queries, and reports. To start Base, click the Applications menu area, then select Office, then Database, then OpenOffice.org Base (Database). The Base Database Wizard, shown in Figure 29.4, appears.

In the database wizard, you must select to use the embedded HSQL database engine for your database file. After selecting the database file and location, the main graphical window appears, as shown in Figure 29.5.

FIGURE 29.4 The OpenOffice.org Base Database Wizard.

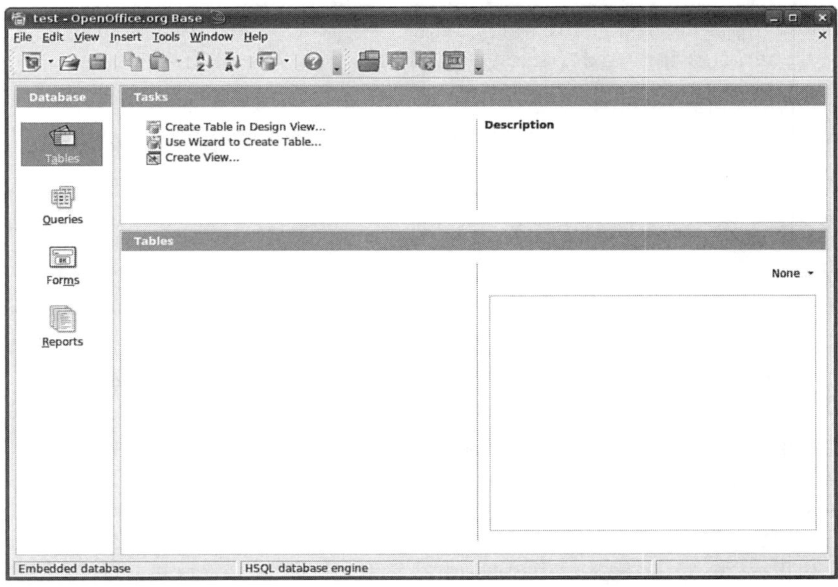

FIGURE 29.5 The Base main window.

From this window you can create new tables using either the design view (which looks amazingly similar to the Microsoft Access table design view) or the Base table wizard. You can also use the design or wizard methods to create new queries, forms (for inputting data into tables), and reports (for displaying data).

Once a table is created, you can use the graphical table viewer to view and insert data in the table, as shown in Figure 29.6.

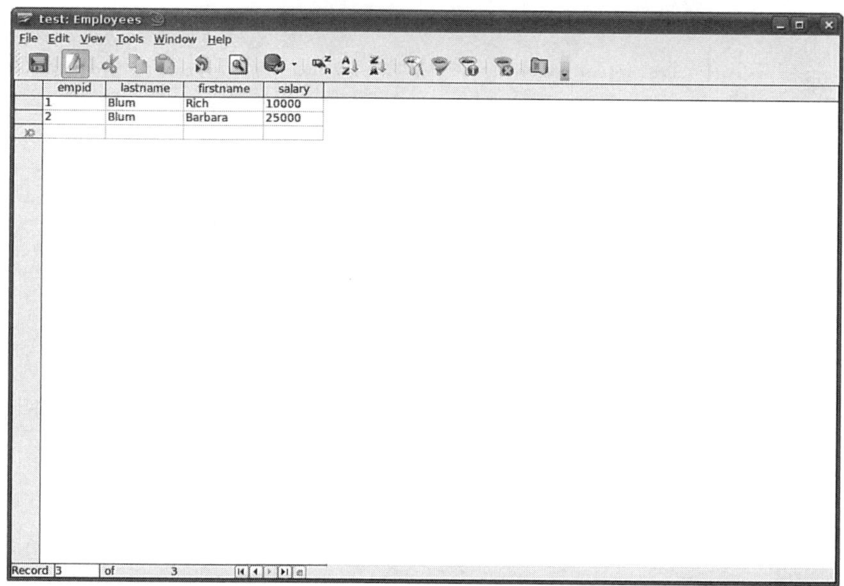

FIGURE 29.6 Viewing data using the Base table viewer.

If you have experience using Microsoft Access to create databases, you'll feel right at home working with OpenOffice.org Base.

Rekall

While OpenOffice.org Base is a full-featured database client application, sometimes all you need is a simple database client to create a few tables to hold data. The openSUSE Linux 10.3 includes such a product.

The Rekall database client is a more simplistic database client, providing the basics without all of the bells and whistles of OpenOffice.org Base. While it also has the capability of using JDBC to connect to a MySQL or PostgreSQL database server, it is configured by default to use its own XBase database file format (which may sound familiar if you remember the old PC DBASE database product).

While not installed by default, it is easily installed using the YaST Software Management screen.

Search for the Rekall packages in Software Management. There are two packages that must be installed:

- rekall—The core graphical application
- rekall-sqlite—The SQLite database driver
- rekall-xbase—The XBase database driver

When Rekall is installed, it appears in the same Database menu area as Base (under the Office section). The first time you run Rekall, it goes through an installation wizard which allows you to set a few default values:

- Whether to use a single window mode (SDI) or a multiple window mode (MDI)
- Whether to use the older scripting method or the newer macro method of automating functions
- Whether to prompt to verify insert, update, and delete database functions

After the installation wizard completes, the main Rekall window appears with no databases shown. Clicking the New button starts the Database Connection Wizard, as shown in Figure 29.7.

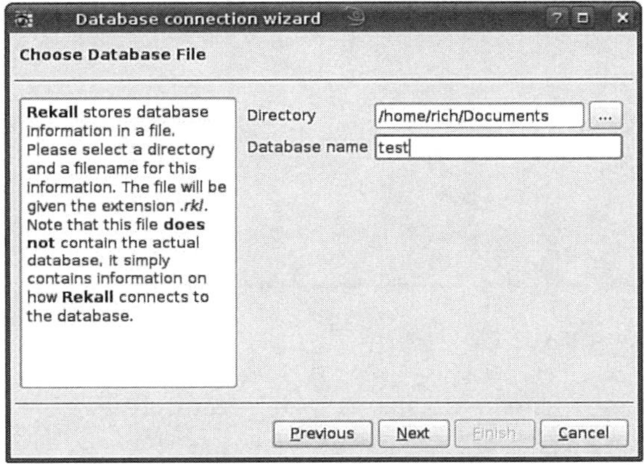

FIGURE 29.7 The Rekall Database Connection Wizard.

The wizard prompts for information related to the specific database:

- The directory to store the database file
- The name of the database
- Where to store database objects (in the database file or separately)
- The database driver
- A directory to store the individual database tables

Once you have completed the information in the wizard, the main Rekall database window appears, as shown in Figure 29.8.

As you can see in Figure 29.8, the Rekall graphical display contains the same elements as the OpenOffice.org Base program (tables, queries, forms, and reports); note, however, that they are not as fancy. Just as in Base, there are simple views that are used to design new tables, queries, forms, and reports.

While not as fancy as Base, Rekall provides all the basics of a personal database system. If you are running openSUSE on a less-powerful system, Rekall may be just the right thing for your database needs.

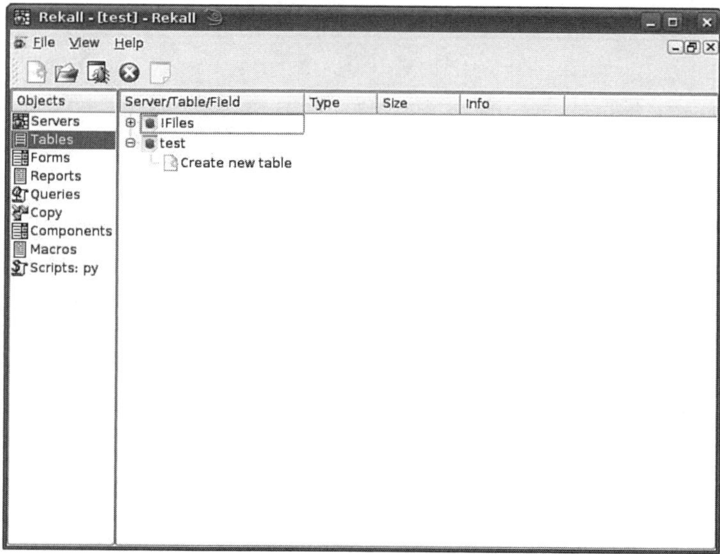

FIGURE 29.8 The main Rekall database window.

References

- http://www.mysql.com/—The MySQL database home page, with news, downloads, and documentation.
- http://dev.mysql.com/doc/—MySQL database home page's documentation repository. If you want to learn more about MySQL, visit the documentation center.
- http://www.postgresql.org/—PostgreSQL database home pages. PostgreSQL is one of the world's most advanced open-source databases supporting almost all SQL constructs, including subselects, transactions, user-defined types, and so on.
- http://www.postgresql.org/docs/—PostgreSQL database home page's documentation repository. You can start here to find a wealth of PostgreSQL information available online. This section of the website contains current and archived manuals for PostgreSQL users and administrators.
- http://www.openoffice.org—The OpenOffice.org home page. You can learn all about the features of Base from the online documentation.
- http://www.rekallrevealed.org—The Rekall home page. Provides information on the features and abilities of the Rekall database client.

CHAPTER 30

Using Perl and Python

IN THIS CHAPTER

- What Is Perl?
- Working with Perl
- Perl Programming
- Perl Modules and CPAN
- The Future of Perl
- What Is Python?
- Working with Python
- Programming in Python
- Python Modules
- Python IDEs and the Interactive Shell
- References

The primary open-source, web-development tools are often lumped together as a makeshift suite called LAMP: Linux, Apache, MySQL, and Perl/Python/PHP. Linux and Apache provide the base to deliver your web-based application; MySQL provides convenient data access, and scripting languages such as Perl, Python, and PHP handle much of the heavy lifting involved in working with the data and presenting it to the end user.

The massive growth of the Web in the early 1990s fueled an interest in getting interesting things online quickly. The common gateway interface (CGI) offered developers a way to produce dynamic content and add interaction to the Web by allowing a user to remotely execute a remote script or program on the server and returning the results. Many programmers had experience with Larry Wall's Practical Extraction and Report Language (Perl), so it was a natural choice to use in CGI programming. Perl quickly became the language of choice and it continues to play an important role in today's Internet.

Perl can be a difficult language to learn, but it is easy to use after you understand how it works. It is highly flexible, with more than one way to do just about anything. That flexibility is what makes it a little complicated.

Python is younger than Perl, but they have many things in common. They are both interpreted languages, have active cultures that center around the language and the philosophy behind it, and within their respective cultures, fun is a big component. Python is object oriented and has a cleaner syntax than Perl. Python has contributed substantially to the Web, not only as a scripting language, but also serving as the building blocks for applications such as Zope and BitTorrent.

In this chapter, you'll get an overview of both languages and learn how to begin using them in openSUSE Linux.

What Is Perl?

Perl is an interpreted scripting language written in the mid-1980s to help system administrators automate some of their tasks. It has grown from there. It is essentially a procedure-based language, but it does support object orientation.

Because of its power and flexibility, Perl goes by many nicknames: the Swiss Army Chainsaw, bash on steroids, and so on. What is interesting about Perl is that nearly all of its code and syntax is borrowed from other languages. If you're well versed in computer languages, you'll likely see pieces of C, bash, BASIC, awk, and sed reflected in Perl.

You might be surprised at how ubiquitous Perl is on your system. Do a file search for `*.pl` on your entire system and you are likely to find hundreds of Perl scripts with this extension. Look at the directories in which these files sit, and you'll see how critical Perl is to this operating system and its application developers.

There are two guiding principles in the Perl movement. The phrase "Perl makes easy things easy, and hard things possible" highlights both the simplicity of Perl, and the power of Perl. The phrase "There Is More Than One Way To Do It" (TIMTOWTDI, also known as the "Tim Toady" principle) is used to show the versatility of the Perl language, often providing several ways to solve a programming probelm. Remember these ideas and you will go far.

Working with Perl

Perl is an interpreted language, which means the Linux system can't run a Perl program by itself. Linux must run an external program to interpret the Perl commands and execute them. In Linux, the program used to interpret and execute Perl commands is (obviously) `perl`.

Due to its popularity (and the fact that many system scripts use it), the `perl` program is installed by default in all Linux distributions (including openSUSE). You can use two methods to invoke the `perl` interpreter:

- Manually on the command line
- Automatically within the Perl script

You can manually run the `perl` interpreter program directly from the command line to process a Perl script. Here's a simple Perl script to experiment with:

```
# This is a simple test Perl script
print "This is a test script.\n";
```

This simple two line script incorporates a comment line (lines starting with a pound sign), which is ignored by Perl, and a single line of actual Perl code. The `print` command sends a string to the default standard output, which is the console when running interactively.

Notice the odd looking character on the end of the string. The `\n` character represents a carriage control, allowing the cursor to move to the next line on the display. The `echo` command in bash shell scripts automatically adds the carriage control character when displaying text. The Perl `print` command behaves similar to the C language `printf` command, and it requires that you manually add the carriage control character.

Once the script is created and saved, you can run it using the `perl` interpreter:

```
rich@testing:~> perl test.pl
This is a test script.
rich@testing:~>
```

When manually using the `perl` interpreter, you can invoke several command line options to control the behavior of the interpreter. The most popular options are `-w`, which produces warnings about any errant syntax you have in your Perl code, and `-d`, which invokes the Perl debugger:

```
rich@testing:~> perl -d test1.pl

Loading DB routines from perl5db.pl version 1.28
Editor support available.

Enter h or `h h' for help, or `man perldebug' for more help.

main::(test.pl:1):      print "This is a test script\n";
  DB<1>
```

The debugger allows you to interactively step through the Perl script line by line, examining the results as each statement is executed. This is extremely handy when trying to find a bug in a large script.

The automatic method of running Perl scripts is accomplished by directly defining the Perl interpreter within the script itself (just as with a shell script in Chapter 8, "Shaking Hands with Your Shell"). The first line in a Perl script must tell the shell what program to run to process the commands. For Perl, this is the `perl` interpreter, which is normally located in the `/usr/bin` folder. After that, you can enter your Perl commands:

```
#!/usr/bin/perl
# This is another simple test Perl script
print "This is the second test script.\n";
```

30

This enables you to run the Perl script by itself on the command line (or from within another shell script). Before you can do that though, you must ensure that the Perl script file is set with execute permissions:

```
rich@testing~> chmod +x test2.pl
rich@testing:~> ./test2
This is the second test script.
rich@testing:~>
```

Now the Perl script can be run directly from the command line prompt, or even from within other shell scripts.

Perl Programming

Just like any other programming language, Perl has specific rules for handling things such as variables, operators, and expressions. This section describes some of the nuances you'll need to know about to program with Perl.

Perl Variables and Data Structures

Variables in Perl come in three types: scalar, arrays, and hashes:

- Scalar variables are those that hold a single value. Scalars are preceded by a $ sign in the code. Some assignment statement examples using scalar variables are

```
$x = 5;
$pi = 3.14159;
$animal = "dog";
```

- Arrays are numerically indexed lists of scalar data. Arrays are identified in Perl by the `@` sign. An example of an array is

```
@months = ("January", "February", "March", "April", "May", "June", "July",
     "August", "September", "October", "November", "December");
```

- Hashes are collections of scalar values arranged in key/value pairs. Hashes are identified with a `%` sign. An example of a hash is

```
%birthdays = ("mom" => "SEP 06", "jean" => "JUN 01", "marc" => "JUN 16");
```

Scalars can be strings or numbers and can change from one type to the other, depending on the operator. If an operator expects a number, Perl will see the value as a number, and if an operator expects a string, Perl will see a string. This lets you concentrate less on the difference between numbers and strings, as long as you get the operator right (you'll learn about operators in the next section).

Arrays follow the same syntactical conventions as scalars. Each scalar value that makes up an array can be referred to as `$<array>[index#]`, where, in this case, # is a numerical index. The index begins at 0, meaning that the first item in the list is 0, the second is 1, and so on.

Hashes were originally called *associative arrays*. The => identifier is called a *fat comma* because it behaves much like a comma in other contexts. In fact, commas could be used to define the preceding hash, but the fat commas make it more legible. Compare:

```
%birthdays = ("mom", "SEP 06", "jean", "JUN 01", "marc", "JUN 16");
```

Operators and Other Statements

Programming has always been about manipulating data, so you can't do much with all these variables unless you have some operators to work on them. There are three main types of operators in Perl: comparison, compound, and arithmetic operators.

Comparison operators compare the value of one operation or statement with that of another to see if the overall statement resolves to either "true" or "false." A different course of action can be followed within the program, depending on how statements resolve. Table 30.1 lists the comparison operators offered by Perl. You'll notice that the operators are different for numerals and strings.

TABLE 30.1 Perl Comparison Operators

Meaning	Numeric Operator	String Operator
Equal to	==	eq
Less than	<	lt
Greater than	>	gt
Less than or equal to	<=	le
Greater than or equal to	>=	ge
Not equal to	!=	ne
Returns -1 if less than, 0 if equal, and 1 if greater than	<=>	cmp
Range between first and second operands	..	–
Matched by regular expression		=~
Not matched by regular expression		!~

Compound operators are largely identical to Boolean operators and can be combined with other operator types into more complex forms of results. These are listed in Table 30.2.

TABLE 30.2 Perl Compound Operators

Meaning	Operator
Logical AND	&&
Logical OR	;;
Logical NOT	!
Group these compound statements	()

Arithmetic operators can be used to perform all sorts of mathematical operations on variables. These are listed in Table 30.3.

TABLE 30.3 Perl Arithmetic Operators

Meaning	Operator
Raises x to the y power	x**y
Calculates the remainder of x/y	x%y
Adds x to y	x+y
Subtracts y from x	x-y
Multiplies x times y	x*y
Divides x by y	x/y
Negates y	-y
Increments y by 1 and uses value	++y
Uses value of y and then increments by 1	y++
Decrements y by 1 and uses value	—y
Uses value of y and then decrements by 1	y++
Assigns value of y to x	x=y

Regular Expressions

Many Linux applications use regular expressions to simplify searches. In Perl, regular expressions have been taken to the level of an art form.

Statements with regular expressions use several of the same symbols that wildcards and operators use, but for slightly different reasons. Regular expressions use symbols to match patterns in text.

Some folks suggest that Perl regular expressions even represent a small programming language of their own. When you open the `perlrequick` man page (a brief introduction to regular expressions in Perl), this idea is reinforced by using a "Hello World!" example. To find the word `World` in "Hello World", use this line in a Perl script:

```
print "It matches\n" if "Hello World" =~ /World/;
```

This script tells Perl to find (=~) the expression `World` in the `Hello World` string and then print the words `It matches` with a newline (`\n`) if it is found.

Any scalar can be matched against a regular expression in a script. This offers a wealth of possibilities to locate and manipulate data. The trick is learning the shorthand involved in getting it. This shorthand includes the *metacharacters* that represent search terms and operators. It's because regular expression patterns are made up of metacharacters that some people find cryptic and difficult to decipher.

Table 30.4 shows you some of the primary metacharacters and their uses in Perl. If you are familiar with regular expressions and wildcards in the shell or other applications, watch carefully for differences in Perl's metacharacter usage.

TABLE 30.4 Some Perl Metacharacters

<table>
<tr><th>Meaning</th><th>Metacharacter</th></tr>
<tr><td>Match any single character (except a newline).</td><td>.</td></tr>
<tr><td>Match the preceding character(s), any number of times.</td><td>*</td></tr>
<tr><td>Match the preceding character(s), one or more times.</td><td>+</td></tr>
<tr><td>The preceding character(s) may not be in the string, but it will still match if the other requirements are present.</td><td>?</td></tr>
<tr><td>Boolean OR statement.</td><td>|</td></tr>
<tr><td>Text matches if a tab character is present.</td><td>\t</td></tr>
<tr><td>Pattern matches if it is at the beginning of a line.</td><td>^</td></tr>
<tr><td>Pattern matches if it is at the end of a line.</td><td>$</td></tr>
<tr><td>Match a letter, number, or underscore.</td><td>\w</td></tr>
<tr><td>Match a number.</td><td>\d</td></tr>
<tr><td>Match any whitespace character such as a space, tab, or newline.</td><td>\s</td></tr>
<tr><td>Escape any metacharacter into an ordinary character.</td><td>\</td></tr>
</table>

In addition to searching and matching text segments and character patterns, regular expressions can also be used to validate user input. The form of expected input is expressed as a regular expression against which the input is compared.

```
my $email = <STDIN>;
print "Input is in valid format" if
    $email =~ \[A-Za-z0-9._%-]+@[A-Za-z0-9._%-]+\.[A-Za-z]{2,4}\
```

This is just a taste of how to use regular expressions in Perl. Read over the `perlrequick` and `perlretut` man pages for a more in-depth look, or check out *Teach Yourself Regular Expressions in 10 Minutes* by Ben Forta and published by Sams Publishing.

Perl Command Line Arguments

As with shell scripts, Perl allows you to extract arguments entered on the command line when the script is run. Perl places any supplied arguments into the array `ARGV`. You can reference each individual argument using the appropriate array element (in Perl, arguments start at zero).

Here's an example of a using an argument in a Perl script:

```
#!/usr/bin/perl
# leap.pl - determine if a specified year is a leap year
if ($ARGV[0])
{
   $year = $ARGV[0];
   if (( $year % 4 == 0) xor ( $year % 100 == 0 ) xor ( $year % 400 == 0 ) )
   {
      print "$year is a leap year\n";
```

```
   } else
   {
      print "$year is not a leap year\n";
   }
} else
{
   print "Sorry, you did not provide a year.\n";
}
```

The `leap.pl` script accepts a year value as a single argument on the command line and then determines if the year is a leap year. The argument is extracted from the array as `$ARGV[0]`, and assigned to a variable. That's not absolutely necessary, but often it is easier to work with a real variable name within the program rather than carry the ugly argument names around. The first `if` statement checks to make sure that an argument was included on the command line. If not, a warning message is displayed and the script exits.

If a year was included on the command line, its value is assigned to the variable `$year`. The standard tests for a leap year are then performed within another `if` statement. First, the year is checked if it is divisible by 4. Years that are divisible by 4, but also by either 100 or 400, are not leap years. The Boolean `xor` function is used to ensure that the year can only be divisible by 4.

The answer is displayed using the standard `print` command. Notice that the `$year` variable is included in the output within the string.

Perl Modules and CPAN

The Unix philosophy of creating and using small programs that do one thing well, often in conjunction with other similar programs, has led to the largely modular design of even the most complicated applications. So it is with Perl. Perl does much of its work through modules that plug in to the Perl environment. Many Perl modules are installed with the basic Perl installation, and dozens more are optionally installable through YaST.

One important component included in the base Perl installation is the marvelous CPAN.pm module. CPAN.pm makes it easy to download and install other modules from CPAN, the Comprehensive Perl Archive Network. CPAN is a large repository of Perl modules, reusable code, and documentation. There you can find more Perl goodies than you can imagine.

CPAN is always accessible from the Web at http://www.cpan.org, and you can search and download modules directly with your browser. But for ease of installation, the Perl CPAN module can't be beat.

Log in as SuperUser and type

```
perl -MCPAN -e shell
```

The first time you run CPAN, you'll go through a configuration dialog. Accepting the default configuration options is usually the right thing to do, but you'll still want to read through everything carefully. You can always modify the configuration later on if you have to by entering **`o conf init`** at the `cpan>` prompt.

After configuring your system, CPAN will ask about your location and find a nearby download mirror. This speeds up your transfer and doesn't use as much bandwidth. After you've selected one or more mirror sites, you will see the `cpan>` prompt. You can now search CPAN for something useful.

Let's look for an update for SpamAssassin. Type **h** to see a list of available commands. Reading the help screen, we see that regular expressions can be used to search for a specific module. To search for our updated package with the regular expression, `spam`, type

```
m /spam/
```

TIP

On each visit to the CPAN mirror, run the command reload index to ensure that you can access the latest modules to hit the mirror.

The CPAN module searches the database for modules that fit and then lists the matching modules. Among them is the `Mail::SpamAssassin` module (and several child modules). To download and install this module, type

```
install Mail::SpamAssassin
```

CPAN will download the module, configure it for your system, and run `make` and `make install` all at once. If you prefer to download now and install later, use the `get` command instead of `install`. The `h` or `?` command is always at your side to help you decide what to do next.

TIP

The CPAN module offers a command history if ReadLine support is enabled. If it is, you can use your up and down arrows to repeat or edit a recent command.

When you have found and installed all the modules you want, type **q** at the `cpan>` prompt to quit the module and return to the SuperUser prompt.

The Future of Perl

Perl 6 has been under development since the year 2000 and may be near release when you read this. It is a nearly complete rewrite of the interpreter's code, with numerous changes. The biggest change is the new Parrot interpreter, through which all Perl 6 code will pass. This virtual machine is designed to support not just Perl 6, but Perl 5, Python, and several other scripting languages as well.

The following are a few highlights of the effects on the core Perl language itself:

- Perl 6 will be more strongly typed, allowing you to specify both the storage type and implementation type of a variable.

- Sigils (all those funny symbols used in regular expressions) will be simplified. In the new version of Perl, sigils will cease to be adjectives and become an indivisible part of the nouns themselves.
- Case statements are simpler, too. How does one single control statement sound? It's called `given`, and it is used like this:

```
$val = 'G4';
given $val {
 when 'A4' { print "paper" }
 when 'B4' { print "prior" }
 when 'C4' {  die "BOOM!" }
 default  { print "huh??" }
}
```

Many Perl 6 features can already be accessed using various Perl 5 modules available from CPAN.

What Is Python?

It's still a defining image. In May 2000, *Linux Journal* did a special supplement on the Python language, and the editors wanted to do something fun for the cover. There wasn't the budget for the Knights Who Say "Ni," the Minister of Silly Walks was unavailable, and perhaps they couldn't find a cross-dressing lumberjack for a photo shoot. Yet they needed something Pythonesque to get the right mood. Someone remembered a sketch with an organist in the middle of a field near the ocean, and a legend was born. The supplement featured a long side-shot of a man sitting at a (computer) keyboard with his bowtie on—and nothing else. And the letters poured in.

There may have been some folks who didn't get it (indeed there will always be some folks who don't get it), but one thing that Python (the language) and the people who use it aim to do is dispel the myth of the humorless geek. The language is named, after all, for the immortal stars of the British sketch show *Monty Python's Flying Circus*. Yet for all the silliness inherent in Python culture, the language is responsible for some very hardworking tools.

Quality assurance teams for both computer hardware and software use Python scripts to get their products ready for release. Search engines (including Google) use Python to perform their tasks. Web designers and bloggers use Python-based tools Zope and Plone to generate their content. Top-flight scientists in geophysics, electromagnetics, and fluid dynamics use the SciPy library in their research.

Python programmers are very productive because the language is easy to grasp, and it doesn't take much to get going. It puts an emphasis on creating human-readable code and being explicit about what is going on in the code. The language handles many housekeeping activities, such as I/O, memory management, data typing, and variable binding, with aplomb.

The next section tells you a little bit about programming in Python and the tools available to you in openSUSE Linux.

Working with Python

Python is also an interpreted language and requires an interpreter to execute Python scripts. Unlike Perl though, the Python interpreter also includes an interactive mode. Typing the command python on the command line invokes the interpreter in interactive mode:

```
rich@testing:~> python
Python 2.5 (r25:51908, Nov 18 2006, 09:59:15)
[GCC 4.1.2 20061115 (prerelease) (SUSE Linux)] on linux2
Type "help", "copyright", "credits" or "license" for more information.
>>>
```

The interactive prompt is now waiting for you to type Python commands:

```
>>> print "This is a test"
This is a test
>>> 2 + 2
4
>>>
```

To exit from the interactive interpreter, press Ctl+D. This returns you to the normal command line prompt.

Entering Python commands directly into the interpreter is not an easy way to program. Alternatively, you can store your Python commands in a text file and then include the filename on the command line:

```
rich@testing:~> python test.py
This is a test
rich@testing:~>
```

Similar to shell and Perl scripting, you can also invoke the Python interpreter from within your scripts:

```
#!/usr/bin/python
# Running a Python script
print "This is another script test"
```

As with other scripts, you must make the script file executable before you can run it on the system:

```
rich@testing:~>chmod +x test2.py
rich@testing:~> ./test2.py
This is another script test
rich@testing:~>
```

The script runs as expected from the command line.

Programming in Python

While Python acts like a typical scripting language, it was designed to be much more. The Python language provides many features found in higher-level languages such as high-level data types, structures, and built-in error checking. The following sections describe some of the programming features found in Python.

Python Variables and Data Structures

Python has four variable types: scalars, lists, tuples, and dictionaries:

- Scalar variables are those that hold a single value, much the same as in Perl. Although unlike Perl, numeric and string types are segregated and no extra symbols are prefixed to variables in Python. Examples of numeric and string scalar variable assignments are

  ```
  x = 5
  pi = 3.14159
  animal = "dog"
  ```

- Lists are numerically indexed lists of objects. They can be made up of any combination of things you choose, such as scalar data, dictionaries, tuples, and even other lists. An example of a list assignment is

  ```
  months = ["January", "February", "March", "April", "May", "June", "July",
  "August", "September", "October", "November", "December"]
  ```

- Tuples are almost identical to lists, except they are immutable. That means unlike a list, which you can change and modify any way you like, you cannot change a tuple.

- Dictionaries are associatively indexed arrays comparable to Perl's hashes. They are a collection of objects or values arranged in key/value pairs. An example of a dictionary assignment is

  ```
  birthdays = {"mom" : "SEP 06", "jean" : "JUN 01", "marc" : "JUN 16" }
  ```

Indentation

Every programming language has a way of organizing code so that it appears in readable chunks. Examples of these separators include whitespace, braces, and explicit line terminations (such as the semicolon in C). Python uses indents as a formal part of the language, and lines end with a hard return.

The rules on indentation are simple. Be consistent in how you indent. Use the same number of spaces to indent a block of code. If you need a statement that spans more than one line, use the backslash (\) to continue the line. Here's an example of Python's indentation rule at work:

```
file = open("./data.txt", "r")
while 1:
  line = file.readline()
```

```
  if not line:
    break
  print line,
file.close
```

Python's indentation rules may take a little getting used to if you're coming from another programming language such as Perl, but they will make your code more readable and thus easier to maintain. With any project, it's good to keep in mind that you may not always be the person in charge of the code, and memory fades, so make it readable at all times.

Extreme Object Orientation

In Python, *everything* is an object. They have identities, types, and values, but also inherent properties and methods. For example, you can determine the index of a given substring using a string object's index method:

```
import string
greeting = "Hello World! It's nice to meet you!"
location = greeting.index("nice")
print location
```

You can create your own objects with the `class` statement. User-defined classes can have class variables and class methods, which govern all instances of the class. Each instance of a class can, in turn, have its own instance variables that don't apply to other instances.

Python Command Line Arguments

Passing command line arguments to a Python program is slightly different from Perl. Because Python in a modularized language, it uses modules for everything, including how it interacts with the command line.

The `sys` module is required to interact with the system. It contains the `argv` array, which passes command line arguments to the script. Here's an example of using the `argv` array to process command line arguments:

```
#!/usr/bin/python
# determine if a specified year is a leap year
import operator, string, sys
if (len(sys.argv) == 2):
   year = string.atoi(sys.argv[1], 10)
   by4 = year % 4
   by100 = year % 100
   by400 = year % 400
   if (operator.xor(by4 , operator.xor(by100, by400))):
      print sys.argv[1] + " is not a leap year"
   else:
      print sys.argv[1] + " is a leap year"
else:
   print "Sorry, you did not provide a year."
```

30

As you can see from this example, Python is a little more complicated than Perl when using command line arguments. The command line argument is placed in the `sys.argv` array as element 1 (not 0 as in Perl). Unfortunately, Python is very specific about data types. The command line arguments are all captured as string values.

Because the program needs to use the command line argument as an integer value, it must be converted. The `string` module provides the `atoi` function, which converts ASCII strings to integer values. After assigning the new integer value to a variable, the calculations can begin.

However, in Python, special mathematical operators (such as the Boolean XOR) are also functions, and must be used as functions instead of operators. This requires importing the `operators` module and rewriting the if statements to use the `xor()` function.

Python Modules

All object-oriented programming languages include libraries that contain pre-built classes that are useful to programmers. The Python programming language is no different.

In Python, class libraries are called modules. A module contains classes and functions that can be called from within a Python script. The standard Python installation includes a library of standard modules that are built into the interpreter. To reference classes and functions from the module, you must define the module name within the script using the `import` command, as was demonstrated in the previous section.

Here is an example of using the SMTP module to easily send a mail message from your Python script:

```
#!/usr/bin/python
# program to send simple mail message
import smtplib, string, sys, time

From = string.strip(raw_input('From: '))
To = string.strip(raw_input('To: '))
Subject = string.strip(raw_input('Subject: '))
Date = time.ctime(time.time())
Header = ('From: %s\nTo: %s\nDate: %s\nSubject: %s\n\n'
          % (From, To, Date, Subject))
Text = "This is a test message"

server = smtplib.SMTP('localhost')
result = server.sendmail(From, To, Header + Text)
server.quit()
if result:
    print "problem sending message"
else:
    print "message successfully sent"
```

This sample program imports four standard modules. The `smtplib` module provides SMTP functions, the `string` module provides string functions, the `sys` module provides functions that interact with the system, and the `time` module provides modules for getting the time from the system.

The script uses mail program on the local system to send the created message. If you do not have your mail system configured, this script won't work. The `raw_input()` function from the `sys` module is used to retrieve input from the user required for the e-mail message, and the `strip` function is used to remove any blank spaces before or after the entered strings.

Besides the standard modules, there are a host of other modules available for just about any type of programming function you can think of. Scanning the Web for the term "Python modules" produces thousands of code modules freely available to incorporate into your own applications.

Python IDEs and the Interactive Shell

Several IDEs are available to help developers write their scripts and programs. Although many are cross-language, some are primarily written for working with Python. Two such examples of the latter are IDLE and SPE.

IDLE, short for Integrated DeveLopment Environment, is part of the basic Python distribution. It is coded in Python itself and uses the Tkinter toolkit to create its graphical interface. Don't let its barebones appearance fool you, however; IDLE offers syntax highlighting, smart indents, a multiple-undo history, a partial debugger, call tips, and an interactive shell.

A very popular Python IDE is SPE, which stands for Stani's Python Editor. It's written in Python and uses wxPython as its interface toolkit. SPE offers more features than IDLE, including sticky notes, a regular expressions assistant, a UML viewer, and a class explorer window. SPE is not included in openSUSE, but can be downloaded from its site.

Other cross-language editors used for Python development include jEdit (a popular IDE written in Java), Eclipse, and Anjuta (both discussed in Chapter 28, "Programming Tools").

Calling `python` from a console with no command-line arguments will start Python's interactive shell, so you don't need to fire up a full-fledged IDE or even a text editor to test out your ideas in Python. You can enter statements at the shell prompt and it will immediately interpret them. Sending an EOF character (usually the Ctrl+D key combination) will exit the interactive shell.

References

- http://www.perl.com—News, articles, blogs and the like.
- http://www.perl.org—Links to the Perl universe.
- http://www.cpan.org—CPAN is the place to download modules and other gotta-have Perl stuff. If you write something useful, upload it here.
- http://use.perl.org—Find out about conferences, user group meetings, and assorted fun facts.
- http://learn.perl.org—Where to begin with Perl online. Tutorials, book recommendations for all levels of expertise, and a beginner's mailing list.
- http://www.tpj.com—Archives for The Perl Journal, a monthly magazine focused on Perl programming.
- http://www.pm.org—PerlMongers user groups.
- http://dev.perl.org/perl6—The Perl 6 hub. Get overall design information here and the latest on development of Perl 6 and the Parrot interpreter.
- http://python.org—The center of the Python universe. Just about everything Python links here.
- http://www.pythonware.com/daily—The Daily Python; Python news and comment from around the Web and the blogosphere.
- http://wiki.python.org/moin/BeginnersGuide—For new programmers, a Python guide.
- http://docs.python.org/tut/tut.html—This tutorial promises to teach you Python in an afternoon.
- http://www.amk.ca/python/howto—A collection of Python HOWTO documents, including how to use regular expressions in Python.
- http://www.die-offenbachs.de/eric/index.html—Home for the Eric Python IDE.
- http://www.pyzine.com—An online archive of Python technical articles.
- http://en.wikipedia.org/wiki/Python_programming_language—A long and detailed entry, and a worthy introduction to the Python language.
- http://pythonide.stani.be/—Home of Stani's Python Editor.
- http://www.jedit.org/—A programmer's text editor written in Java that offers support for Python development.

CHAPTER 31

Creating Dynamic Websites

IN THIS CHAPTER

- Using PHP
- Setting Up an Interactive Site with Drupal
- Setting Up a Web-Based Community Forum
- References

Websites that remain stagnant and don't change will most likely suffer and lose traffic. See it once and you never have to go back. Give a user a reason to come back—news, community, downloading, commentary—and not only will one person keep coming back, her friends will visit, too. You'll get links from other places, and then Google finds you faster. It's a simple formula.

You could manually code large chunks of the site every day, but a far easier solution is to use PHP, the PHP Hypertext Preprocessor, to easily create and maintain lively, interactive sites that people will want to visit regularly. Some 20 million domains use PHP to generate their sites, and the number increases nearly every month.

In Chapter 14, "Creating Basic Websites," you created a basic static website with tools included in openSUSE Linux. In this chapter, you'll learn how to use PHP to make that site more interactive and appealing. You'll use the PHP-based Drupal framework to ease the process of building your site. Then you'll let your users talk among themselves with a forum.

Using PHP

PHP is the result of another lazy programmer's effort to simplify his life. Back in 1994, Rasmus Lerdorf wanted to eliminate some of the drudgery associated with updating his personal web page. Lerdorf wrote some Perl scripts to generate HTML tags based on some C code. In June 1995, he announced the existence of the Personal Home Page (PHP) tools, version 1.0, in a Usenet CGI newsgroup. Those tools have since evolved into a full-fledged scripting language with a powerful engine, Zend, and a large community of developers hacking the code. You can read more about the history of PHP at http://php.net/history.

The PHP Home Page at http://www.php.net defines PHP as "a widely used general-purpose scripting language that is especially suited for Web development and can be embedded into HTML. Much of its syntax is borrowed from C, Java, and Perl with a couple of unique PHP-specific features thrown in." It is open source and works on the server side to generate its content. PHP often works with databases such as MySQL and PostgreSQL to generate content.

PHP boasts a command-line interpreter as well as modules that work with just about any web server out there, but we will focus on PHP's `mod_php5` module for Apache. Similarly, PHP works with just about any database management system, but we will focus on MySQL.

PHP is extensible through the PHP Extension and Application Repository (PEAR) at http://pear.php.net, and the PHP Extension Community Library (PECL) at http://pecl.php.net.

Installing PHP

The core PHP package, mod_php, and many PHP extensions are installable through YaST, making it easy to use PHP on a local Apache server setup. The YaST Web Development and LAMP patterns will each install the core PHP package and a small set of modules. The core PHP package installs the basics of the language, which work from a command line. If you plan on using PHP in a CGI capacity, this is fine—but this isn't the recommended (or most beneficial) way. The apache2_mod_php5 package is an Apache module that will allow you to process and serve HTML pages with embedded PHP code. You'll want to install both the core and mod_php5 packages.

To confirm that PHP is properly installed on your system, open a text editor and write this line:

```
<?php phpinfo(); ?>
```

Save the file as `/srv/www/htdocs/test.php`. Now open a web browser to http://localhost/_test.php. Figure 31.1 should appear.

If you don't get the PHP info page, make sure the script was typed correctly, and then see if Apache is running by going to `http://localhost`. If Apache is not running, check the Runlevel Editor in YaST.

Look carefully at the info page. You will see which PHP extensions are installed, where your `php.ini` configuration file is stored (by default, it is in `/etc`), and a fairly detailed configuration report.

If you are using a web-hosting vendor, make sure that PHP5 is supported before uploading PHP pages to your site. Finding a host with PHP support should not be difficult, but many PHP-related websites, like the PHP Resource Index at http://php.resourceindex.com, include pointers to PHP-friendly hosts.

Before writing any PHP code, you should also check that your favorite text editor or IDE supports PHP code highlighting and the like. All the web-authoring tools included in openSUSE Linux (Bluefish, Quanta Plus, and Nvu) support PHP. Emacs need a separate php-mode, downloadable from Sourceforge.net (http://sourceforge.net/projects/php-mode). There are also PHP helper scripts for VIM at http://www.vim.org.

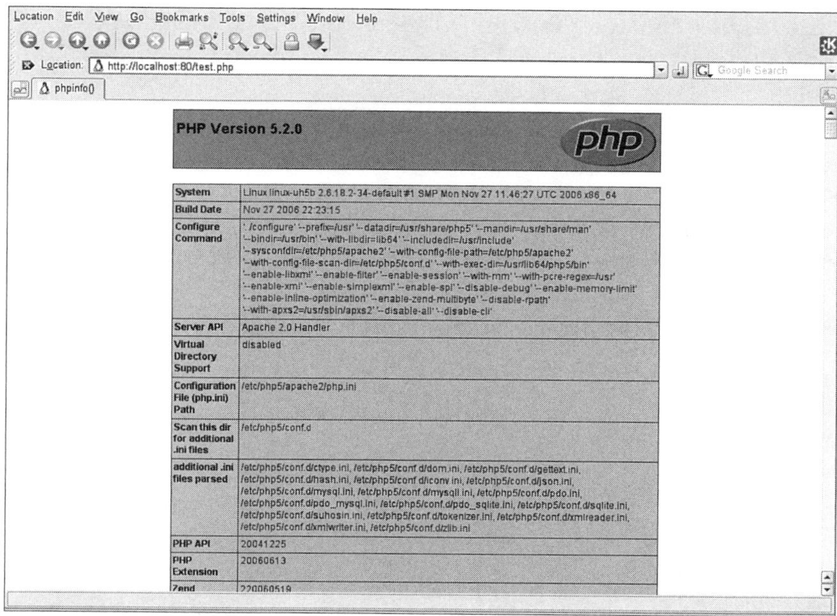

FIGURE 31.1 If PHP is properly configured on your system, this page should appear in your web browser after writing the test file.

Writing PHP Scripts

You've already written your first PHP script—the one-line `test.php` script you used to test your installation in the last section. There's more to learn, of course, and you will do that in this section.

The PHP interpreter basically treats any documents fed to it as text and echoes back the contents, unless it finds code set between special opening and closing tags. The neat thing is that you can embed your code in an HTML page and PHP won't touch your HTML. It will only process your code, and the end result is a final HTML document with the PHP code replaced with the resulting output. This is demonstrated in Figure 31.2.

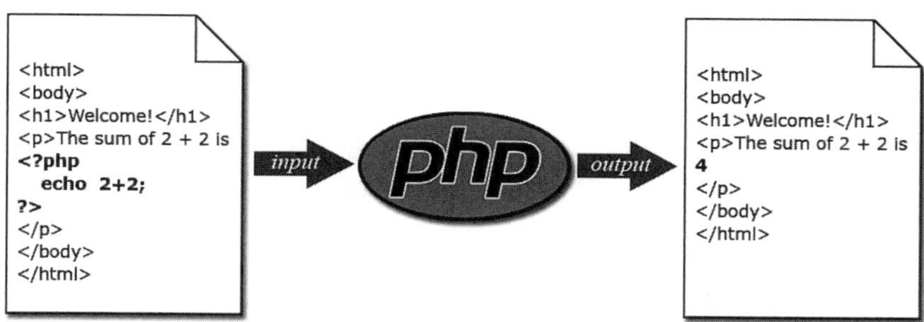

FIGURE 31.2 The PHP interpreter processes only your code that is delineated with <?php and ?>. The end result is a complete HTML document.

PHP's include function is used to import the contents of another file. This allows you to include other PHP scripts or even other HTML files into your scripts and use PHP to template your website:

```
<html>
<h1>Welcome!</h1>
<?php include "menu.html"; ?>
<img src="img/me.jpg" alt="picture of me" />
<p>Welcome to my website.  Here you'll learn all sorts of neat stuff about
me.  Here's some of the things that are going on in my life right now:</p>
<?php include "events.html"; ?>
<p>Thanks for stopping by!</p>
<hr />
<?php include "footer.html"; ?>
</html>
```

Variables are used in PHP to store information in memory that the script may need. They are identified by a $ and are not strictly typed like variables in other languages. This means a variable can hold a number, a string, or anything else that you may want to alias.

PHP also offers a variety of mathematical and logical operators to compare variables. By using them with PHP's flow control structures, you can write scripts that follow different paths, depending on the value of the variables. Table 31.1 shows some of the operators available in PHP.

```
<?php
  $forecast = "rain";
  $times = 17;
  if ($weater == "rain") {
      echo "I've already told you ";
      echo $times;
      echo " times... if it's going to rain you should bring your umbrella!";
  }
  if ($weather != "rain") {
      echo "Have a nice day!";
  }
?>
```

TABLE 31.1 Selected PHP Operators

Meaning	Operator	Example
Assignment	=	`$x = $y`
Add	+	`$x + $y`
Subtract	-	`$x - $y`
Multiply	*	`$x * $y`
Divide	/	`$x / $y`
Calculate the remainder	%	`$x % $y`

TABLE 31.1 Continued

Negation	-	-$x
Increment by 1	++	$x++
Decrement by 1	—	$x—
Equal to	==	$x == $y
Exactly equal to	===	$x === $y
Less than	<	$x < $y
Greater than	>	$x > $y
Less than or equal to	<=	$x <= $y
Greater than or equal to	>=	$x >= $y
Not equal to	!=	$x != $y
Logical NOT	!	!$x
Logical AND	&&	$x && $y
Logical OR	||	$x || $y
Group	()	($x = 5) && ($y = $z)

PHP also has looping structures that can be used to cycle through a section of code any number of times. This saves you the time of having to explicitly write the same section of code over and over. Here's an example that will zip through and write out all the numbers between 1 and 10,000—each on a separate line:

```
<?php
  $x = 1;
  while (x >= 10000) {
      echo $x;
      echo "<br />";
      $x++;
  }
?>
```

Many predefined functions are available in PHP to help manipulate data, explore strings of text, and even generate graphical images and PDF files. From its simple Perl days, PHP has grown to be a very useful and robust scripting language. I highly recommend exploring the documentation available at http://www.php.net to learn more about the power of PHP.

Adding More Functions to PHP

PHP can be extended in a similar manner as Apache, where a modular design permits adding new features and functionality by linking in new modules. The PECL library is a set of modules that can link into the language's core. The new functions they provide are then available as any of PHP's built-in functions.

PEAR is a collection of reusable, open-source code for use in your PHP applications. The code is organized as a selection of files that act as wrappers giving convenient access to various PHP functions or extending PHP in some way. The files are collectively known as a *package*.

Both PECL modules and PEAR packages can be installed using the pear utility, available through YaST. Calling `pear` without any arguments will display a list of commands `pear` understands. The install argument followed by the package or module name will install it; the uninstall argument similarly will uninstall the component.

```
./pear install Mail
downloading Mail-1.1.8.tgz ...
Starting to download Mail-1.1.8.tgz (16,196 bytes)
......done: 16,196 bytes
install ok: Mail 1.1.8
```

PHP 5 vs. v4

PHP version 5.0 was released in June 2004 and was included with SUSE Linux Professional beginning with version 9.3.

PHP 5 features enhanced support for Extensible Markup Language (XML), using the `libxml2` toolkit. Strong support exists for all XML-related technologies, but many are especially excited about the potential for ordinary users to create fully rendered PHP objects using the SimpleXML parser. With SimpleXML, you can read, write, or iterate over your XML file with ease to access elements and attributes.

If you're interested in building web services applications with PHP, there is new support for Simple Object Access Protocol (SOAP).

For programmers, the chief difference between the two versions is the improvements for object-oriented programming in the Zend Engine. PHP has had some object modeling available since version 3, but some experienced object-oriented programmers had problems when some objects would behave oddly.In PHP 5, among the changes welcomed by programmers used to working with objects are the following:

- You can use common access modifiers to limit access to certain classes and properties.
- Constructor and destructor methods of dealing with objects are more consistent and easier to use.
- A new `final` class declaration limits overloading inheritance.
- Objects are now passed by reference, not by value.
- Objects can be cloned with the `clone` keyword.
- Classes may have constant values.

Other new enhancements include extensions that add support for the SQLite portable database library and HTML Tidy, a marvelous tool that cleans up your HTML and other markup code. You can also download a new Perl extension to support writing Perl in your PHP documents.

If you're just getting started with PHP, rest assured that most every web host that supports PHP will support this not-so-new version at this point. On the other hand, if you have a bunch of PHP4 scripts and wonder if they're still useful, you shouldn't have to worry too much about that, either.

Visit http://www.zend.com/php5/whats-new.php for a more complete listing of the new features in PHP 5.

Setting Up an Interactive Site with Drupal

Drupal (pronounced DROOP-el) offers a powerful framework that makes creating the dynamic site of your dreams within the grasp of even novice website developers. With Drupal you can build heavily trafficked sites with frequently updated content, like http://www.TheOnion.com and http://www.LinuxJournal.com, multimedia sites like MTV.uk, and personal weblogs like the Italian guy who wanted to share his process of building a Linux-based Home Media Center.

Drupal 5 was released in January 2007, and in this section, you'll learn how to get started with this latest edition of Drupal.

Installing Drupal

As with our other examples, let's install Drupal to run on the Apache web server included with your openSUSE system. If you haven't done so yet, start Apache from the YaST Runlevel Editor. Be sure PHP is also installed on your system.

Download the latest version of Drupal from the drupal.org website. Extract the tarball into the ~/public_html directory.

Drupal is database-driven, so it is important to give Drupal access to a MySQL or PostgreSQL database before beginning the install. Create a Drupal user and database in your preferred database management system. In MySQL, this user should have SELECT, INSERT, UPDATE, DELETE, CREATE, DROP, INDEX, ALTER, CREATE TEMPORARY TABLES, LOCK TABLES permissions on the Drupal database. See Chapter 29, "Managing Databases" for more information. The Drupal tarball also includes text files with instructions on setting up your Drupal database in MySQL and PostgreSQL.

Make sure to have the database name, host name, username, and password handy, as the Drupal install script will ask for these items.

NOTE

If you're using a web host, check with your hosting service to see what you need to do to access the database.

When you have created your database and set the user permissions properly, it's time to install Drupal. Open your browser and go to http://localhost/<drupal-folder>/. You should see the Database Configuration page. You'll be asked how to connect to the database and other initial settings. When the install script finishes, you will see the Welcome page.

From this page, click Create the First Account. This will be the administrator of your site, with control over everything that happens. You can have multiple adminstrators on a Drupal site, but just like the system Root account, whoever has this account's password has all the power.

When you've created the First Account, login as the Administrator and complete the configuration steps. The Drupal community recommends creating a Files subdirectory in your Drupal install directory. This will hold various goodies (avatars, logos, multimedia, and such) that Drupal modules can access.

Be sure to look over the Administration pages to configure your site the way you want it. Define what users can do in Users Management > Access Control. Choose a theme for your site in the Site Building section.

Installing Drupal Modules

The Drupal community has contributed much of the power of this platform in the form of modules. Drupal has dozens of modules that can handle most any task in this new wave of the interactive web. Want to let random visitors leave public comments on items on your site? That's easy, and you can set time limits on the display too, among other things. Import blog postings using several engines (WordPress, Blogger, etc.)? Of course. Keep track of your organization's supporters and mobilize them for events and fund drives? Why certainly!

TIP

If you're building a site for any kind of organization that works in the political arena at any level, you'd be wise to check out the modules contributed to Drupal from CivicSpace Labs. Originally developed to build participation in election campaigns, these tools now are available to anyone.

Visit http://drupal.org/project/Modules/ to start exploring the modules available. You can Browse by category, name, and date contributed. Find the module you want and download it. Extract the module (which will come in its own folder), and upload it to your remote site (or your own public_html folder).

Check the INSTALL or README text files in the module's install folder to see if there's anything special you need to do before going live.

Now go to the Drupal Admin page. Go to Site Configuration, Modules to find the installable modules. Check the Enable box for your desired module(s), set permissions if necessary, and you're done.

Setting Up a Web-Based Community Forum

One of the best ways to keep users coming back to a site is to make the site more interactive and offer your visitors the opportunity to discuss the topic of your site through a bulletin board or forum system. PHP makes it easy to bring a forum into your site. One of the more popular bulletin board packages, phpBB, is free and available at http://www.phpbb.com.

Installing phpBB

To install phpBB, go to http://www.phpbb.com/downloads.php to get the latest version. You get a choice of archive formats, so choose any one. Extract the archive to `/srv/www/_htdocs`. It will create a `/phpBB2` directory.

Change the permissions on `/srv/www/htdocs/phpBB2/config.php` to `0666` so that everyone can read and write to this file. Then create a new MySQL database for phpBB. Create the user bbuser, set a password, and grant it full access privileges to the new database.

In a browser, type **`http://localhost/phpBB2/install/install.php`** into the address line. The installation portion of the system will appear, as illustrated in Figure 31.3.

Be sure to fill in all the requested information. Under Basic Configuration, make sure you have the correct database type listed. By default, it selects MySQL 3.x, but you will have MySQL 4.x installed on your system and an option to download 5.x from the MySQL website, www.MySQL.com. In Database Configuration, identify the database and the user you created for phpBB.

In the Admin Configuration section, tell phpBB how to identify you as the administrator of the bulletin board. At the bottom of the screen, click Start Install. The program will connect to your database and create the admin user for phpBB. Click Finish Installation.

For security reasons, you will now want to delete the `/contrib` and `/install` subdirectories. If these files are on the public web server, you put your entire bulletin board system at risk. When you've done this, refresh your browser to be taken to a sample forum page.

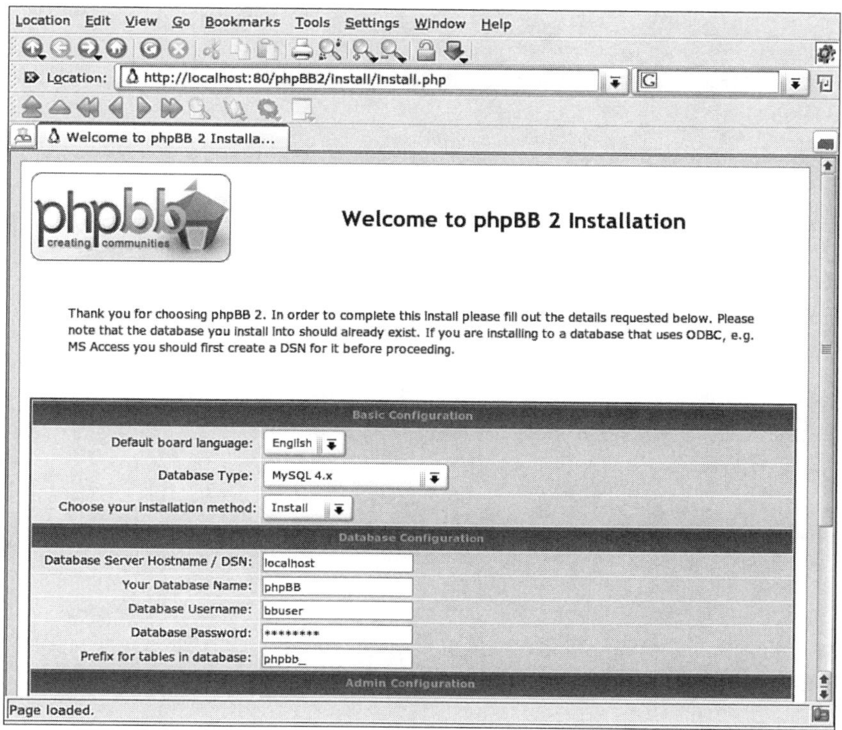

FIGURE 31.3 Start configuring your forum system with the Install page.

Configuring phpBB and Creating Forums

The initial phpBB setup includes a dummy domain name and description text, along with a Test forum. This is mostly to give you something to look at. At the bottom of the forum page, click Go to Administration Panel to begin configuring your bulletin board for real.

You'll be taken to the Admin Index, which will have very interesting stats about your forums when they go live. However, we want to start with the General Configuration settings, located under General Admin on the menu list on the left. In Figure 31.4, you'll see that the Site Name and Site Description have been adjusted. Most of the other defaults here are OK for an initial setup. Review everything else here and click Submit when you're happy.

Now it's time to create some forums. Under Forum Admin, click Management. You can set up categories and topics for your forums here. Type a category name, such as Wisconsin Baseball Today into the New Category edit box, and then click Create New Category.

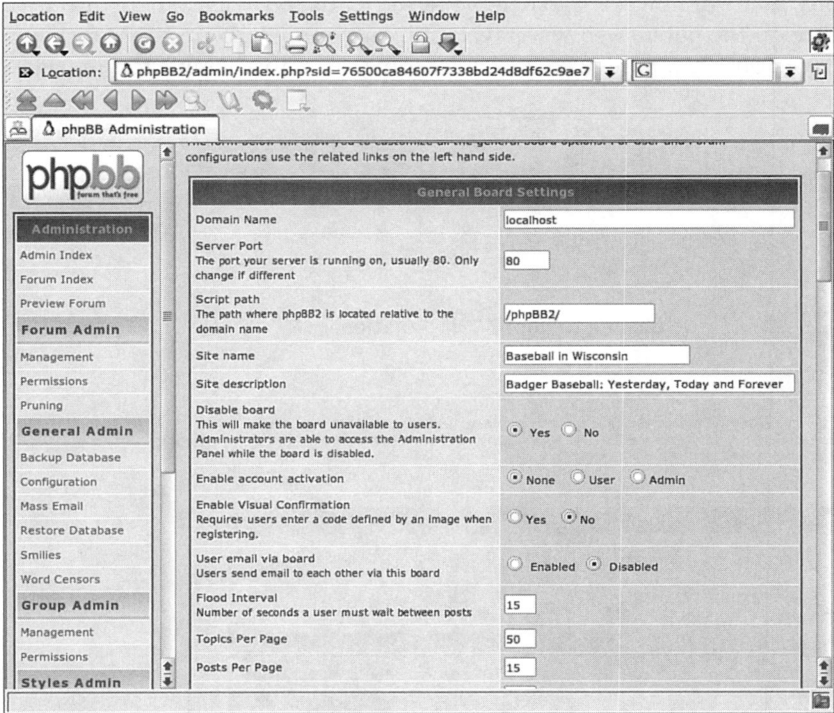

FIGURE 31.4 Give your forum a name and description, among other things, in the General Configuration settings.

You'll need to define some more specific forum topics next. Type a forum topic, such as Milwaukee Brewers, into the New Forum box (as shown in Figure 31.5) and click Create New Forum.

A dialog box appears (see Figure 31.6), where you can add a description for this topic. You may want to set some limits on the discussion in the Description as well. Review the other settings and click Create New Forum when ready.

After you've set up your real categories and topics, it's safe to delete the Test category. Click Forum Index under Administration, and you'll get a look at what visitors will see when they come by. It should look something like Figure 31.7.

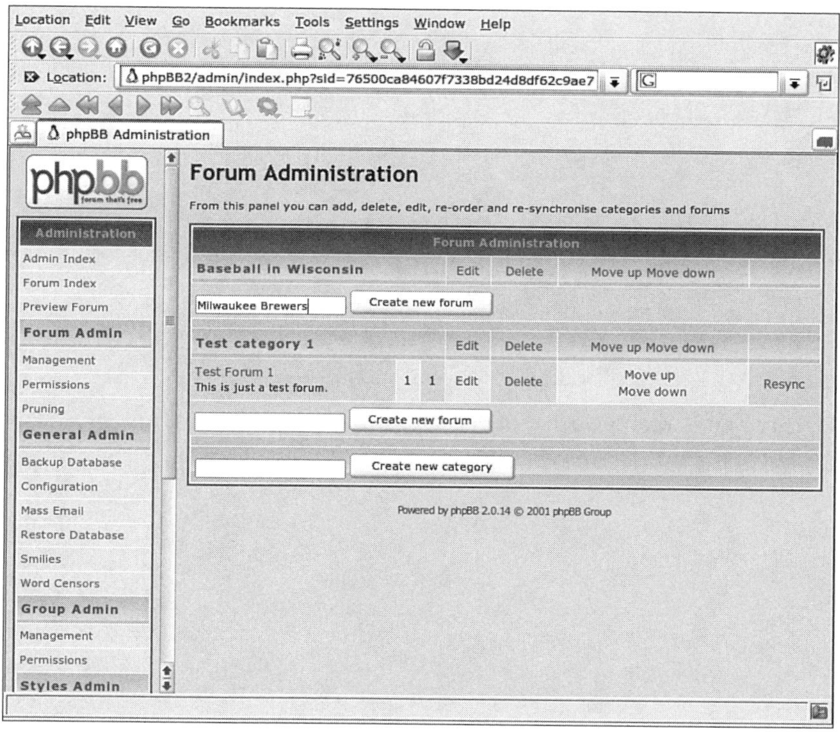

FIGURE 31.5 When you have a category for your forums, you need to define forum topics.

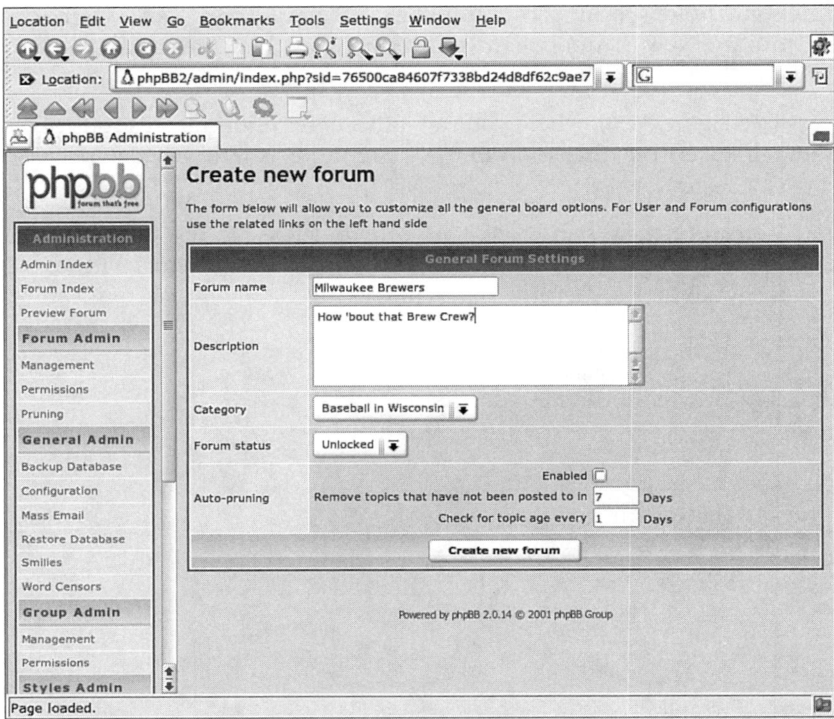

FIGURE 31.6 Describe your forum topic in this dialog box.

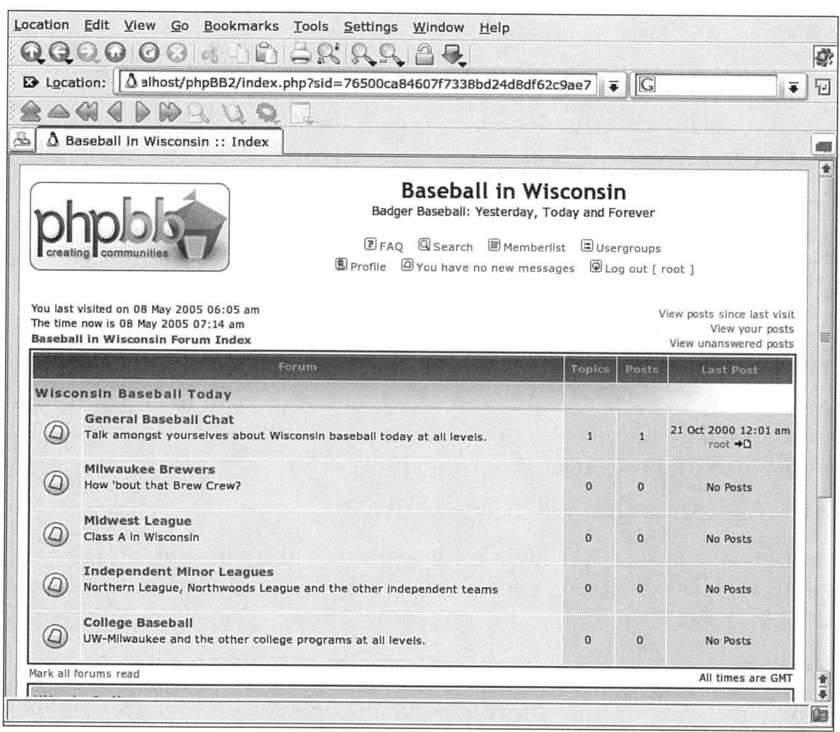

FIGURE 31.7 You're ready for visitors.

References

- http://www.php.net—The PHP home page.
- http://www.zend.com—Zend Technologies, owners of the Zend scripting engines at the heart of PHP 4 and 5.
- http://devzone.zend.com/node/view/id/1717—"The OO Evolution of PHP." A nice article describing the changes in object-oriented programming support in PHP5.
- http://www.phpbuilder.com—Tutorial and news site.
- http://codewalkers.com—A site offering tutorials, code, reviews, and support forums for programming with PHP and MySQL.
- http://php.resourceindex.com—The PHP Resource Index. The main draw for this site is the thousands of ready-made PHP scripts, functions, and classes. You can also find links to other tutorials and the larger PHP community.
- http://weberdev.com—More code, tutorials, and weblogs.
- http://www.hotscripts.com—Scripts for every webmaster's need, mostly in PHP, but also in Perl, Python, JavaScripts, and even some in C and C++. Updated constantly, this is a great place to look for something interesting.
- http://phpdeveloper.org—News and forums for all types of PHP coders.
- http://www.midnighthax.com/phpeditors.php—A filterable (by OS and license type) list of editors and IDEs that support PHP coding.
- http://forums.devnetwork.net—The PHP Developers Network web forums.
- http://www.planet-php.net—A collection of PHP-related weblogs.
- http://www.ibm.com/developerworks/edu/os-dw-os-php-pear.html—"A Step-by-Step Guide to publishing your own PEAR channels" from IBM DeveloperWorks.
- http://phpnuke.org—One of the original PHP-based content-management systems.
- http://drupal.org—The Drupal home.
- http://www.wordpress.org—The WordPress personal publishing system.
- http://www.phpbb.com—phpBB, a popular PHP-based community forum system.

CHAPTER 32

Performance Tuning

IN THIS CHAPTER

- Optimizing Services
- Using PowerTweak
- Tuning Hard Disk Drives
- References

Squeezing extra performance out of your hardware might sound like a pointless task, given how inexpensive hard drives and memory have become over time. To a certain degree this is true, for most folks at least. But as we've said before, Linux users are tinkerers at heart. Many of us will gladly spend hours to make our computers work harder, faster, and smarter. Like the amateur auto mechanics of generations past, a cottage industry of overclockers and performance zealots has risen among the hordes of geekdom. And with the capability that Linux and other open-source software gives you to look under the hood and see for yourself what's going on, you can find the way to squeeze that last bit of juice out of an application.

The amount of benefit you can get by optimizing your system varies, depending on what kinds of tasks you are trying to perform. Even with all the shortcuts built in to any modern word processor, no software tricks will make your fingers type any faster in OpenOffice.org under openSUSE than in Microsoft Word in Windows. In the next few pages, we will look at ways to get a little more oomph out of your openSUSE system.

You should understand that optimization is not an absolute term. You can do almost anything to improve performance for a computer or specific application, and still have room to get even more out of it. But after a while, the law of diminishing returns starts kicking in, and you start working too hard to get not much back. So use these tips and methods, but remember that the reason you want to improve your performance is not for its own sake. You want to get some work done, too.

Nowhere else is the auto mechanic metaphor more appropriate than among the folks who muck around at the lowest levels of their systems. These are the folks who break down specification lists and performance metrics and consider it a challenge to get more out of them than they were promised. This section is for these folks.

Before you undertake any of this type of work with Linux, keep a couple things in mind. First, perform a benchmark on your system before you start tweaking it. Your openSUSE DVD offers a pair of related command-line utilities for this task: `bonnie` and `bonnie++`. Aside from the programming languages each was developed on, there are few differences between the two utilities. `bonnie++` offers several more option switches.

Many other packages are available as well. If you visit http://www.freshmeat.net, you can search for the term **`"benchmark"`** and find a variety of packages. If you happen to be a programmer, you can probably develop your own benchmarking tests, and perhaps you want to offer those to the Linux community after they've been tested a few times on your own system.

Second, tweak one thing at a time. If something bad happens (and tweaking is all about finding the limits, after all), make it something that's easy to trace. Log in your book what works, what doesn't work, and what breaks. Then move on to the next thing.

If you're going to find the limits of your system, have two things ready at all times: a good backup of your important data and the batch of seven boot floppy disks to rescue your system if you need to. If you haven't yet, go to the YaST System page and launch the Boot or Rescue Floppy module to perform this absolutely essential task.

Let's begin by discussing how to optimize the services running on your system.

Optimizing Services

One of the most basic (and most frequently overlooked) tasks in optimizing the performance of a Linux system is to scrutinize the services it's running. Put very simply, the more services you have running, the slower the system will perform.

openSUSE is a true multitasking operating system. It's capable of running many process at the same time on a single CPU. However, the process of suspending one running process while running another one places a heavy load on the system CPU. The more times this happens, the slower the system runs. You can monitor how frequently this happens using the `vmstat` utility from the shell prompt. Sample output from `vmstat` is shown in Figure 32.1.

Notice under the System heading that there are two columns: in and cs. The in column displays the number of *interrupt requests* (either hardware or software generated) the CPU has processed each second. The cs column displays the number of *context switches* the CPU has had to deal with each second.

NOTE

An interrupt is a signal received by the CPU indicating that something (usually hardware) in the system needs its attention. A context switch occurs when the CPU has to suspend one running process and run another. Both of these events are CPU intensive.

```
linux:~ # vmstat 1
procs -----------memory---------- ---swap-- -----io---- --system-- -----cpu------
 r  b   swpd   free   buff  cache   si   so    bi    bo   in    cs us sy id wa
 1  0  57328   6836  10772  46488   18   16   461    71  302   262  7 18 55 21
 0  0  57328   6836  10772  46488    0    0     0     0  256   120  0  2 98  0
 0  0  57328   6836  10772  46488    0    0     0     0  251   107  1  2 97  0
 0  0  57328   6836  10772  46488    0    0     0     0  307   165  4  5 91  0
 0  0  57328   6836  10772  46488    0    0     0     0  251   104  0  1 99  0
 0  0  57328   6548  10808  46488    0    0     0    64  261   130  2 13 84  1
 0  0  57328   6548  10808  46488    0    0     0     0  251   103  1  0 99  0
 0  0  57328   6548  10808  46488    0    0     0     0  255   115  2  2 96  0
 0  0  57328   6548  10808  46488    0    0     0     0  251    95  0  2 98  0
 0  0  57328   6548  10808  46488    0    0     0     0  255   107  2  1 97  0
```

FIGURE 32.1 Using `vmstat` to view system performance.

A certain number of these events are unavoidable. For example, every time you move the mouse or type a key on the keyboard, you generate an interrupt request. However, the number of these events, especially context switches, can be reduced by running only those services that you actually need.

When your system was installed, the installation program made many assumptions about what services should be automatically run at boot. Most of these services are necessary for your system to run properly. However, some of them aren't. To see what's running on your system, open YaST and navigate to the System, System Service (runlevel) module, as shown in Figure 32.2.

For example, notice in Figure 32.2 that the Postfix MTA (Mail Transfer Agent) is configured to automatically start at runlevels 3 and 5. Postfix is a popular email daemon that is widely implemented by many organizations to provide a powerful mail solution.

However, on your personal openSUSE system, there's a pretty good chance that you don't need it, especially if you're using an external ISP for email services. In this case, you can stop the Postfix MTA and configure it to not start at boot, thereby reducing the load on your CPU. In this example, you can stop the service by entering **`rcpostfix stop`** at the shell prompt. Then you can use the Runlevel Editor in YaST to disable Postfix at boot.

CAUTION

Don't get too carried away shutting down services. You might be tempted to stop services that you don't recognize. Most of these services actually are needed for your system to run properly. Only disable a service after you have thoroughly researched what it does and are confident that it isn't required.

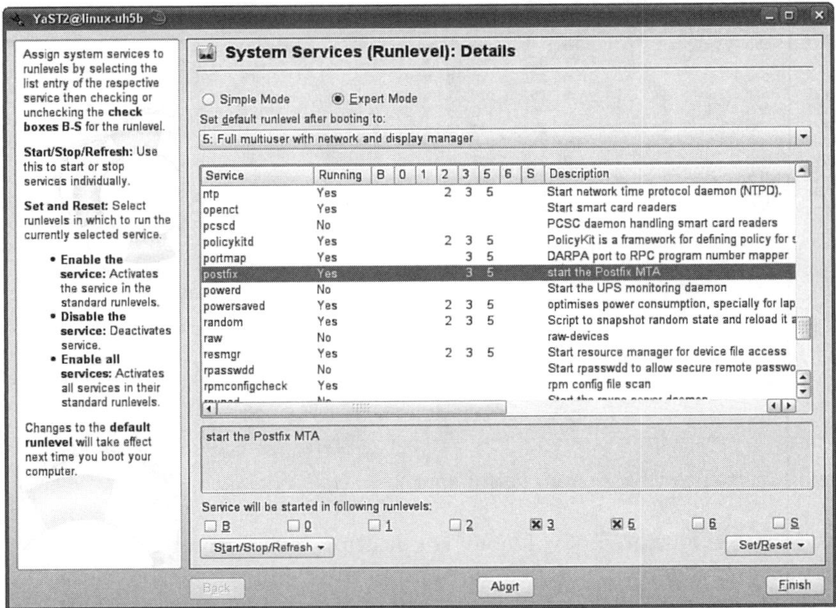

FIGURE 32.2 Viewing services configuration in YaST.

Tuning Hard Disk Drives

In addition to managing running processes and using PowerTweak, you should also consider tuning the performance of the hard disk drive in your openSUSE system. Read/write operations on the hard drive represent some of the most time-intensive operations your Linux kernel will have to complete as it goes about its business, to the point where hard disk operations can become a significant bottleneck in your system.

Hard disk operations are slow because hard disk drives themselves are inherently slow when compared to other storage devices such as RAM or SRAM cache. A hard disk drive is composed of mechanical devices—motors, platters, and actuator arms—that require a certain amount of time to complete their tasks.

However, there are some things you can do improve the performance of the drives in your system. The first aspect you need to consider is the type of drive you use in your computer. Let's talk about this topic next.

Choosing the Best Hardware

Not all hard disk drives are the same. The quality of the drive you choose can make a big difference in the overall performance of your system. When selecting a drive, you should keep the following points in mind:

- Drive interface—Most desktop systems sold today use Integrated Drive Electronics (IDE) hard drives. (The latest IDE drives are called Serial Advanced Technology Attachment [SATA] drives.) These drives are inexpensive to manufacture and can store a large amount of data, hence their popularity.

  Unfortunately, IDEdrives have some serious shortcomings that you should keep in mind. First, the IDE controller on the master drive requires a lot of CPU time to read or write data. Although IDE drives may have a high data-transfer rate, the CPU is going to have to do a lot of work to make it happen.

  Second, remember that both the primary and secondary IDE channels on your system can have two IDE devices connected to it, resulting in a total of four drives in a typical system. Keep in mind that many different types of IDE drives have been manufactured over the years. Early IDE drives transmitted data at around only 15MBps. Later-generation IDE drives can transfer data at speeds up to 133MBps. If you connect an older, slower drive to an IDE channel with a newer drive, the newer drive will slow down to the speed of the old drive. The entire channel will operate at the speed of the slowest device connected to it.

  Finally, attaching two devices to the same IDEchannel can slow things down because a single drive controller must manage two devices. If you choose to use IDE, you will get the best performance if you install a single device on each channel.

  If you want the best performance possible from your disk subsystem, you should consider using either a Serial ATA (SATA) or a small computer system interface (SCSI) disk controller and drive. Both of these systems address many of the shortcomings of IDE and provide better performance.

- Data transfer rate—Over the years, many types of hard disk interfaces have been manufactured. Some interfaces are faster than others with respect to the amount of data they can transfer. If you choose to use an IDEdisk interface, be sure to select either an ATA100 or ATA133 system.

  If you choose SCSI, you might find your choices a little more complicated. Over the years, a variety of SCSI standards have been implemented, including SCSI I, SCSI II, and SCSI III. Within the SCSI II and III standards, you can choose from Fast, Wide, and Fast/Wide options. Although the variations can get confusing, you'll get the best performance from a SCSI III Fast/Wide adapter and hard disk combination.

  If you go with SATA, you can choose between SATA/150, which transfers data at 150MBps, and SATA/300, which transfers data at 300MBps. As with the other disk options, the faster the drive and controller, the faster the performance of your system.

- Disk rotation speed—Remember that hard disks are mechanical devices. The speed at which data can be read or written is heavily dependent on how fast the platters inside the disk rotate. The faster the rotation speed, the faster the data can be read or written. Low-end, inexpensive drives rotate at around 3500 RPMs. Midrange disks rotate at around 5000 RPMs. Fast disks rotate at 7200 or even 10000 RPMs. The faster the rotation, the better your system performance will be.

After you've selected the best drive for your system, you can then tune your drive for its best performance. Let's talk about how to do this next.

Tuning Hard Drive Parameters at Boot

One way to tune your hard drive involves adjusting the settings in your BIOS. Every BIOS seems different, and so consult your motherboard manual before proceeding. Take every precaution, and make sure the BIOS sees all your drives. Change one setting at a time.

Linux does offer a limited means to interact with BIOS settings during the boot period (mostly to override them).

Other options include the following commands, which can be used to force IDE controllers and drives to be optimally configured. Your mileage may vary, but they have worked for some. You can get more information in the Bootprompt HOWTO at the Linux Documentation Project. Consider the following:

- `idex=dma`—This will force DMA support to be turned on for the primary IDE bus, where x=0, or the secondary bus, where x=1.
- `idex=autotune`—This command will attempt to tune the interface for optimal performance.
- `idex=ata66`—If you have ATA66 drives and controllers, this command will enable support for them.
- `hdx=ide-scsi`—This command will enable SCSI emulation of an IDE drive. This is required for some CD-RW drives to work properly in Write mode, and it might provide some performance improvements for regular CD-R drives as well.
- `idebus=xx`—This setting identifies the speed of your IDE bus. It can be any number from 20–66; set this manually if `dmesg` says that the bus speed isn't autodetected correctly, or if the bus speed is set in the BIOS to a different value (overclocked). Most PCI controllers will be happy with 33.
- `pci=biosirq`—Some motherboards might cause Linux to generate an error message saying that you should use this noun. Look in dmesg for it; if you do not see it, you don't need to use it.

These options can be sent to the kernel at startup by pressing F2 at the GRUB menu and entering your preferred options in the Boot Options Field. You can also use the YaST Boot Loader module to insert these parameters into `/boot/grub/menu.lst`. To do this, complete the following:

1. Run YaST and navigate to System, Boot Loader.
2. In the Section Management tab, select the menu item to which you want to add these options.
3. Select Edit.
4. In the Optional Kernel Command Line Parameters field, enter the *option(s)* you want to include.

5. Select OK.
6. Select Finish.

You can also use the hdparm utility to tune your drive. Let's talk about how to do that next.

The hdparm Utility

The hdparm utility can be used by the SuperUser to set and tune the settings for IDE hard drives. You would do this to tune the drives for optimal performance.

Once only a kernel patch and associated support program, hdparm now is included with openSUSE (though not by default; you must install via YaST). You should only experiment with volumes that are mounted as read-only because some settings can damage some file systems when used improperly. Evidence of this can be seen when typing the hdparm command without any arguments. This displays the program's help; look at all the options marked DANGEROUS.

NOTE

Setting the -u option to 1 can result in a significant boost in the performance of the system. However, some IDE drives don't support this parameter.

Running this utility is fairly straightforward. Type:

```
hdparm <option> <device>
```

To test an IDE hard drive, type:

```
hdparm -tT /dev/hda
```

Be sure to replace /dev/hda with the mount point of your hard drive (usually with a number to represent the partition you want to test, such as dev/hda1). hdparm will then run two tests—cached reads and buffered disk reads. A good IDE hard drive should be getting 400–500MB/sec for the first test and 20–30MB/sec for the second. Note your scores, and then try this command:

```
hdparm -a16 -d1 -u1 -c1 /dev/hda
```

After you've made these changes (and have taken another look at the Help to see what you're doing), test the drive again. The score for this test should be higher than the baseline -tT test. Run this command to use the new, faster settings on all subsequent boots:

```
hdparm -a16 -d1 -u1 -c1 -k1 /dev/hda
```

The -k1 option saves the settings.

Read over the man page for more information about the multitude of options previously listed. Be aware that the SUSE engineers do their best to optimize all the settings before shipping the distribution. Because they cannot anticipate every configuration, however, it's worth a try to see what you can get on your own, if you're so inclined.

Disabling File Access Time

Whenever Linux reads a file, it changes the last access time, which is known as the atime. This is also true for your web server. If you are getting hit by 50 requests per second, your hard drive will be updating the atime 50 times a second. If you don't really need to know when a file was last accessed, you can disable atime by modifying `/etc/fstab` to include the `noatime` attribute for the file system.

With an `ext2/ext3` file system, you can also use the `chattr` (change attribute) command to turn off atime changes (by directory) with this command:

```
chattr -R +A <directory_path>
```

The `-R` switch makes the command operate recursively throughout the subdirectories of the specified directory.

With this in mind, let's now discuss how to spread out the disk load on your system.

Spreading Out the Load

With a Linux system, certain directories and partitions are used more heavily than others. These include the swap partition, `/var`, `/tmp`, and `/home`. Placing all these on the same hard disk can slow down performance.

To increase performance, they should be spread across multiple hard disk drives. If possible, the performance can be increased by installing multiple hard drives in your system and creating separate partitions for `/var`, `/tmp`, and `/home`, distributing them (along with the swap partition) across the drives.

NOTE

In an ideal world, you would place each of these partitions on a separate hard drive to achieve the maximum level of performance.

Earlier you learned how read/write operations can slow a hard drive's performance. Distributing the read/write load across multiple drives allows multiple operations to occur simultaneously.

References

- http://www.textuality.com/bonnie—This is the home of the `bonnie` performance benchmark utility.
- http://www.coker.com.au/bonnie++—bonnie++ is a benchmarking tool for Linux file systems, with links to similar tools for RAID systems and SMTP servers.
- http://tldp.org/HOWTO/BootPrompt-HOWTO.html—Boot options for the Linux kernel.
- http://sourceforge.net/projects/hdparm—The home of hdparm.
- http://powertweak.sourceforge.net—This is the home of Linux PowerTweak. Some history and an overview of the project is available.

CHAPTER 33

Command-Line Master Class

IN THIS CHAPTER

- Command Line Basics
- File Management Commands
- System Management
- Combining Commands
- References

Throughout this book, we've talked a lot about getting things done in both GUI and command-line environments. It's not difficult to understand that for most users (and that's probably an understatement), the point-and-click interface is the best and easiest way to use a computer. Graphical desktop environments represent the future of Linux as an everyday operating system. Yet, the shell still represents the fastest and most powerful way to use a Linux computer. Once you have mastered the shell and its available tools, there's an amazing amount of stuff you can do with just a few keystrokes.

The Linux shell can be a black box for the average user. Actually, in most cases, it *is* a black box with a white cursor unless you're running the `rxvt` X terminal, where the colors are reversed. But in the hands of an experienced Linux geek, pipes and redirects and regular expressions and all the things that make the shell special can fulfill the promise of personal computing in ways that just don't compare to the GUI experience.

In the early days of Linux, one of the taglines used to bring people over described the promise of personal computing: "Put the power of a workstation in your PC." Before Linux matured, you had to spend tens of thousands of dollars to buy a machine that had enough resources to run a commercial Unix variant. Linux brought that power within reach of most users, and the seat of that power is in the command line.

This chapter aims to make you a master of shell arcana, at least on a small scale. There might be some repetition of earlier lessons, but repetition can be a good thing when learning something new. By the end, you'll be able to do a few amazing things, and perhaps acquire the taste to do more. Have fun!

Command Line Basics

This section starts off with a short review of the command line basics. Because the command line doesn't have any fancy GUI help available, understanding the basic format of commands and how to get information on commands helps to make life easier in the command line environment.

Command Format

All Linux commands follow the same basic format:

```
command -options arguments
```

The first item is obviously the command name. Most commands can be modified using one or more options. Options are used to modify the behavior of the command, such as to indicate whether the command will produce an output.

Options are usually a single character and are preceded with a dash (such as `-h`). Some commands though allow complex options that are complete words. These options are preceded by a double dash (such as `—help`). If there is more than one option, each can be listed either separately on the line (such as `-a -b -c`), or if they are single letter options, they can all be bunched together after a single dash (such as `-abc`).

Following the options, there may or may not be one or more arguments for the command to use. An argument provides information for the command, such as file names to copy or user accounts to add. Knowing what commands require what arguments can be tricky. Fortunately there is help in the man pages.

The man Pages

One great feature that openSUSE includes by default is the man pages for Linux commands. Don't worry—the man pages aren't a guy thing. They're the manual pages for all of the commands used in bash. As new software packages are installed, they usually include the appropriate man pages as part of the installation package. This makes it easy to reference help for installed programs on the system.

The man pages are displayed using the `man` command. To get the man pages for the `date` command, enter:

```
rich@testing:~> man date
```

You should see the man page for the date command displayed. There is lots of information available in the man pages. The man page divides command information into separate sections, as described in the Table 33.1.

TABLE 33.1 The man Page Sections

Section	Description
Name	Displays the command name and a short description
Synopsis	Shows the format of the command
Description	Describes each command option and argument
Author	Provides information on the person who developed the command
Reporting Bugs	Provides information on where to report any bugs found
Copyright	Information on the copyright status of the command
See Also	Refers you to any similar commands

You can step through the man page by pressing the space bar or by using the arrow keys to scroll forward and backward through the man page text. From the Synopsis and Description sections of the `date` command, you can see that there are lots of options for displaying the date in a variety of formats. If you use a root shell session, you can also use arguments to set the date of your system directly from the command line interface. To exit the man page screen, press `q` on your keyboard.

File Management Commands

The openSUSE system provides great graphical tools for managing files and directories on your system. However, once you become proficient in command line commands, sometimes it's quicker to open a command prompt and use the command line commands to manipulate files and directories. This section describes the command line commands necessary to manage files and directories on your system.

Viewing File Information

In the graphical world it is easy to see what files are available in a directory. They all appear as icons in the Konqueror window. However, to view specific file information, you have to look at a specific file's properties. In Konqueror, this requires right-clicking the file and selecting the Properties menu item. In the command line world, you can use the `ls` command to display all of the files in a directory and their properties at once.

Use `ls` without any options to get a plain list of files in the current directory. You can also use all the standard wildcards to find particular files or types of files:

```
rich@testing:~> ls *.txt
README.txt    license.txt    printer.txt  test.txt
info.txt      notice.txt     rpms.txt
rich@testing:~>
```

This produces a list of files with a `.txt` extension in the directory, but with no other information about the files. The `ls` command offers many ways to display file information. Here are some of the standard switches for `ls`:

- `-a`—Include hidden files
- `-h`—Display file sizes in kilobytes (K) and megabytes (M)
- `-l`—Displays the "long" listing, like the Details view of a GUI file manager
- `-r`—Reverse order
- `-R`—Recursively list directories
- `-s`—Shows file and directory sizes
- `—sort`—Sorts the listing

One of my favorite option combinations is `-sail`. Besides being easy to remember, it provides a wealth of file information in a single command:

```
rich@testing:~> ls -sail
total 200
131485 8 drwxr-xr-x 22 rich users 4096 2006-12-18 15:13 .
131073 4 drwxr-xr-x  3 root root  4096 2006-12-18 14:54 ..
131508 4 -rw———-  1 rich users   31 2006-12-18 15:08 .bash_history
131507 4 -rw-r—r—  1 rich users 1177 2006-12-18 14:54 .bashrc
131542 4 drwx———  7 rich users 4096 2006-12-18 15:07 .beagle
131498 8 drwxr-xr-x  2 rich users 4096 2006-12-18 14:54 bin
131525 4 drwxr-xr-x  3 rich users 4096 2006-12-18 15:05 .config
131557 4 -rw-r—r—  1 rich users   54 2006-12-18 15:04 .DCOPserver_linux__0
131558 0 lrwxrwxrwx  1 rich users   31 2006-12-18 15:04 .DCOPserver_linux_:0 ->
/home/rich/.DCOPserver_linux__0
131528 8 drwx———  2 rich users 4096 2006-12-18 15:05 Desktop
131512 4 -rw———-  1 rich users   26 2006-12-18 15:03 .dmrc
131504 8 drwx———  2 rich users 4096 2006-12-18 15:10 Documents
131500 4 -rw-r—r—  1 rich users  208 2006-12-18 14:54 .dvipsrc
131489 4 -rw-r—r—  1 rich users 1637 2006-12-18 14:54 .emacs
131494 4 -rw-r—r—  1 rich users 1332 2006-12-18 14:54 .exrc
131559 4 drwxr-xr-x  2 rich users 4096 2006-12-18 15:04 .fontconfig
131491 4 drwxr-xr-x  2 rich users 4096 2006-12-18 15:04 .fonts
132107 4 drwx———  2 rich users 4096 2006-12-18 15:12 .gconf
132108 4 drwx———  2 rich users 4096 2006-12-18 15:12 .gconfd
132172 4 drwx———  2 rich users 4096 2006-12-18 15:12 .gnome2
131560 4 -rw———-  1 rich users  189 2006-12-18 15:04 .ICEauthority
131501 4 -rw-r—r—  1 rich users  861 2006-12-18 14:54 .inputrc
131513 4 drwx———  4 rich users 4096 2006-12-18 15:04 .kde
131490 4 -rw-r—r—  1 rich users  164 2006-12-18 14:54 .kermrc
131629 4 drwx———  3 rich users 4096 2006-12-18 15:05 .local
131499 4 drwxr-xr-x  2 rich users 4096 2006-12-18 14:54 .mozilla
131488 8 -rw-r—r—  1 rich users 6043 2006-12-18 14:54 .muttrc
132103 4 drwx———  3 rich users 4096 2006-12-18 15:12 .ooo-2.0
131503 4 -rw-r—r—  1 rich users  925 2006-12-18 14:54 .profile
```

```
131492 8 drwxr-xr-x  2 rich users 4096 2006-12-18 14:54 public_html
131556 4 drwxr-xr-x  2 rich users 4096 2006-12-18 15:05 .qt
132200 4 -rw———-     1 rich users  304 2006-12-18 15:13 .recently-used
131523 4 drwxr-xr-x  2 rich users 4096 2006-12-18 15:04 .skel
132058 4 drwx———     4 rich users 4096 2006-12-18 15:09 .thumbnails
131502 4 -rw-r—r—    1 rich users  311 2006-12-18 14:54 .urlview
131655 4 drwxr-xr-x  2 rich users 4096 2006-12-18 15:05 .wapi
131511 4 -rw———-     1 rich users   50 2006-12-18 15:03 .Xauthority
131486 8 -rw-r—r—    1 rich users 7913 2006-12-18 14:54 .xcoralrc
131495 4 drwxr-xr-x  2 rich users 4096 2006-12-18 14:54 .xemacs
131497 4 -rw-r—r—    1 rich users 1940 2006-12-18 14:54 .xim.template
131506 4 -rwxr-xr-x  1 rich users 1365 2006-12-18 14:54 .xinitrc.template
131510 8 -rw———-     1 rich users 4499 2006-12-18 15:09 .xsession-errors
131487 4 -rw-r—r—    1 rich users  119 2006-12-18 14:54 .xtalkrc
rich@testing:~>
```


This format displays all of the hidden files (files starting with a period), directories, and normal files in the directory. It shows the total number of blocks the directory takes and detailed information about each file, such as the internal Linux index number, the block size, permissions, owner, group, and creation time. Getting all of this information at once from a GUI tool is next to impossible.

Managing Directories

The `ls` command displays the file information for the files located in the current directory. To display information in another directory, you could specify the full directory name on the `ls` command line (such as `ls /usr/bin`), but that can become tedious as well as confusing.

Moving around between directories in the graphical world is as easy as clicking on a directory name. In the command line world, it requires a command line command, `cd`.

By default, when you open a command line prompt session, you are placed in your home directory (/home/*username*). Each individual user on the openSUSE system has a unique home directory. The command prompt used in Konsole shows the current directory, which for the home directory is indicated by a tilde (~):

```
rich@testing:~>
```

To navigate to other directories on the system, you must manually change directories (thus the command name `cd`). To change to subdirectories of your home directory (such as your Documents directory), all you need to enter is the directory name:

```
rich@testing:~> cd Documents
rich@testing:~/Documents>
```

The new command prompt indicates that you are now in the Documents directory under your home directory. You can now use the `ls` command to view the files in that directory.

When you change directories at the command prompt, there are two different techniques you can use. The first is to type the absolute directory path. For example, to get to the Documents folder in Katie's home directory, you would type this command:

```
rich@testing:~> cd /home/katie/Documents
```

This command specifies the exact path to follow to get to Katie's Documents directory.

However, if you are just jumping back-and-forth between a couple directories in your own home directory structure, it can get tiring to have to type so much. Instead of typing the full pathname, you could use a relative directory path. Relative directory paths change directories relative to the directory you are currently in.

Linux uses a couple of shorthand symbols to indicate directories. The period (.) always represents the directory that you're in. Two periods (..) represents the parent directory of your current directory. You can use both symbols in command line commands to describe directory locations.

For example, if you're still in your Documents directory, you can get back up to your home directory by typing the following:

```
rich@testing:~/Documents> cd ..
rich@testing:~>
```

The .. placeholder comes in handy when moving between directories within your home directory. From your Documents directory, you can get to your Desktop directory using two different ways, by either using the complete path:

```
rich@testing:~/Documents> cd /home/rich/Desktop
rich@testing:~/Desktop>
```

or the shorthand method:

```
rich@testing:~/Documents> cd ../Desktop
rich@testing:~/Desktop>
```

The first command uses the absolute pathname to get to the Desktop directory (remember to use your user account name instead of mine). The second command uses the .. symbol to tell the `cd` command to go up one directory in the hierarchy (which from the Documents directory should be your home directory), and then to the Desktop directory. That is a lot less typing to deal with.

If you use the `cd` command all by itself on the command line, it'll return you to your home directory, no matter where you are on the system. This can come in handy when you're digging through the file system and are a few folders deep in an area.

Creating new directories is a pretty simple task with `mkdir`. Just type the command and the name of the new directory, and if you have write permission to the new directory's parent, it will create it without a word. If you are a lazy typist, be aware that `md` works just as well as the more formal `mkdir`.

Just don't get ahead of yourself. If you want to create two directories at once, this is not always possible. While it is quite permissible to create two new directories using `mkdir UserDocs Music`, `mkdir` will complain if you try to create `Music/CDs`, if the `Music` directory does not exist already.

But wait, there's a solution to this problem. Try this command:

```
mkdir -p /Music/CDs
```

With the `-p` switch, `mkdir` creates the parent directory, `Music`, and then the child, `CDs`.

Changing File Permissions

What you learned earlier about chmod can be greatly extended through one simple switch: `-c`. This instructs chmod to display a list of all the changes it made as part of its operation, which means we can capture the output and use it for other purposes.

This switch is not a command history, but that can be a good thing. If you want a file to have certain permissions, but are not sure what the current permissions are, you can run this command. If no results display, nothing changed.

Another interesting switch is the `—reference` switch. Say you want all files in the current directory to have the same permissions as /home/myfile.txt, you can run this:

```
chmod —reference ~/myfile.txt *
```

The `-R` switch (note the capitalization) makes your command recursive through all the files and subdirectories of the current directory. If you happen to have trouble writing new files to your `/home` directory, run **`chmod -R 600 /home`** to make all files and subdirectories read/write to their owner.

Listing File Contents

One of the first shell commands a Unix or Linux user learns is `cat`, which displays the contents of a file in the shell. This is useful both because you don't have to open a text editor or similar application to see whether a certain file contains a certain string, and because you can display the results of another command as text.

The standard use of `cat` is to display a file like this:

```
cat myfile.txt
```

There are two commonly used options that go with `cat`. You can include line numbering in `cat` by adding the `-n` switch. Adding `-s` displays one blank line at a time. This means if you have a file with a lot of blank lines interspersed with a few lines of text, `cat` will "squeeze" out all the extra blank lines, print a line of text, a blank line (which can represent many more blank lines), more text, another blank line, more text, and so on.

You can combine these two switches as well, as in this command, which displays the output of `/proc/cpuinfo` and shows you information about your CPU:

```
cat -sn /proc/cpuinfo
```

If you run this command yourself, you will see the list of items has each line numbered and a single numbered blank line at the bottom. The file itself may have as many blank lines at the bottom as it wants; `cat` will display (and count) only the first one.

Finally, you can use `cat` to string together multiple files, and then perform operations on all of them without having to cut and paste them all together, like this:

```
cat -s myfile.txt myotherfile.txt
```

Incidentally, some users are surprised to learn that `cat` does not abbreviate "catalog" or some other familiar word beginning with those three letters. `cat`'s job is to concatenate the contents of files, as we've seen in the last example.

There are times when the `cat` command is overkill. If you need to check the last few entries in a log file, it could take you quite a while to scroll through to the end of the file using `cat`. It would be nice if you could automatically jump to the last few lines in the file.

You can do this by reading active log files with `tail`. This command displays the last few lines of a file and updates as new lines are added. To have `tail` monitor your system log's security messages, try this:

```
tail -f /var/log/secure
```

The `-f` switch has `tail` follow the progress of the file and deliver each new message as it is generated. To keep it running as long as the log generates messages, add the PID number (which you can get from `ps`) of the log you're following and add it to the command thusly:

```
tail -f ----pid<PID#> /var/log/secure
```

This option outputs only those log entries that are produced by the specified process in the PID.

Searching Inside Files

`grep` is one of those legendary Linux tools, a tool that genuine wizards employ with regularity. It is unquestionably a powerful tool for finding things. You use it to find text of any sort, whether in files or in standard input. Standard usage is simple:

```
grep -r "some text" *
```

This searches through all the files in the current directory and its subdirectories for a string "some text." (The `-r` switch makes it recursive. Note that unlike `chmod`, the `r` here is lowercase.) When `grep` is finished, it will display matching lines along with the name of the file in which the line is contained. If you don't want to see the matching line, use the `-l` switch. This displays all the files with text that matches, but none of the matching text.

You can also use regular expressions for your search terms (see Chapter 29, "Managing Databases," for more on regular expressions).

Here are a few more useful switches:

- -v—Inverts your search, so `grep -v "some text" *` looks for files that do not contain the search phrase.
- -i—Changes grep's default case-sensitivity.
- -c—Delivers a count of matching lines without naming files or displaying lines. Works with -v as well to count non-matching lines.
- -n—Displays the line number of the matching line(s) in the file.

You'll see an important use for grep later when we look at piping together commands.

Copying and Moving Files

Managing your files and directories from the shell is pretty straightforward, and mastering the basics of cp and mv doesn't take much. But let's look at a couple of switches that will indeed help you.

To copy a file or group of files from one directory to another is simple:

```
cp *.txt ~/Documents
```

This copies all text files from the current directory to the `/home/<username>/Documents` directory. All well and good, but what if there's one text file already in /Documents with the same name as one of the files you're copying? Perhaps you ought to consider more creative filename conventions, but cp's default behavior in this instance is to overwrite the existing file.

One of two switches will solve this problem for you. The -i switch makes cp an interactive command and prompts you before overwriting an existing file. Perhaps even better (at least if you know the two files are really different versions of the same file) is the -u switch, which tells cp to only copy if it is newer than the file in the destination directory. This is also useful when synchronizing directories, say from your laptop to your desktop. Both of these switches work with mv, making it useful in both contexts.

One other thing about mv: It is the command you use to rename a file in Linux. Where you would normally include a destination path for your move operation, just type the new name. The shell will "move" the file to the new name:

```
mv myfile.txt mynewfile.txt
```

This command renames the file myfile.txt to mynewfile.txt. The moving part of the command comes into play if you move a file to a directory. The filename stays the same, but the location changes:

```
mv myfile.txt ~/Documents
```

This command moves the file from the current location to the Documents folder, keeping the same file name.

Deleting Files

Way back at the beginning of the book, you were warned about `rm`. If you have forgotten, it bears repeating. If you are logged in as Root, and type `rm -rf /`, you can kiss your system goodbye. While the best way to protect yourself against this eventuality is to log in as Root (or more precisely, as the SuperUser) only when you absolutely have to, there is a backup plan. You should implement this right away, too.

Sticky fingers at the keyboard are more of a problem than bad intentions when it comes to the problem of over-deleting. Using `rm -rf <directoryname>` is not necessarily evil, either. All you are doing is saying "Yes, I really mean to delete this directory (and everything underneath it with the `-r` switch), so don't warn me." But if you start typing the path `rm -rf /home/<formeruser>` and accidentally put a space after that first slash, you are indeed asking for trouble. You've gone from deleting the home directory of an old user to deleting / (the entire root directory) ...and then the old user.

The way to protect yourself is to include the `--preserve-root` switch every time you use `rm`. The `--preserve-root` switch prevents any remove operations from succeeding on the root directory. You aren't even required to remember this tip. Right now, just add this line to the `.bashrc` file in your home directory (and the .rc configuration file of any other shell you might use):

```
alias rm='rm —preserve-root'
```

Now you don't have to think about it again. Each time you run `rm`, it will know not to ever delete the / directory. That just about covers everything you'll need to know for working with files from the command line. The next section demonstrates a few handy commands that can be used to help you in your system administration duties.

Locating Files

One of the most frustrating times is installing a new application and then not being able to run it because you don't know where it was installed. If you remember from Chapter 8, "Shaking Hands With Your Shell," the shell attempts to find commands by traversing the `PATH` environment variable. If a program doesn't place the main executable file in a directory defined in the `PATH` variable, the shell will never find it.

There are three commands that can help you here:

- `find`
- `locate`
- `which`

The `find` command is the most basic of these commands. The format of the find command is:

```
find [-H] -[L] -[P] [path] [expression]
```

The `find` command scans the entire directory structure starting at the *path* you define, either skipping links (`-P`, the default), following all links (`-L`), or following links specifically indicated in the path (`-H`). The tricky part of the `find` command is the *expression*.

The expression defines what to find and what to do when it is found. There are way too many options available to list here (that's what the man pages are for). The most common expression items to use is `-name`, which specifies what you are looking for, and `-print`, which specified to print out the complete path of the found item. Here is a quick demonstration of a find command:

```
rich@testing:/home/rich # find / -name hosts -print
/etc/hosts
```

You can also use values to modify some options. For example, to display all files over 990kB in size, try the command:

```
find / -size +990k -print
```

The plus sign indicates you're looking for values larger than the one specified. Without it, `find` will only show files matching the value.

The `find` command is a good tool, but it can be startlingly slow. It must manually search through all of the directories in the path you specify. That's where `locate` comes in.

The `locate` command is just a wonderful tool, one that speeds the process immensely. This program uses a database that indexes your directory. The key to succeeding with `locate` is to update this database regularly.

NOTE

`locate` is the only command in this listing not installed by default in openSUSE Linux. You can install the `findutils-locate` package in YaST, however. When you install it, openSUSE Linux will automatically update the index database nightly. If you want to manually update the database during the day, just run the `updatedb` command included in the package.

All you have to do then is run this command:

```
locate <filename>
```

You will quickly get a list of every directory that file appears in. The only downside is that you can only search for a filename, not any other property of the file. Once you've found it, of course, you can use other commands to get more information about it if you need it.

Finally, there's the `which` command. This command helps you quickly (and I do mean quickly) find the location of shell commands (but only shell commands). Do you want to know the physical location of a command? Type `which mkdir`, and almost instantly you'll discover that the `mkdir` command sits in `/bin/mkdir`.

System Management

One of the areas where the command line commands really shine is in system administration. While there are a few GUI tools available for the system administrator, most experienced admins go straight for the command line toolbox.

This section covers some of the most commonly used admin command line commands. These commands help you quickly know what is happening on different aspects of your openSUSE system.

Disk Usage

The du command displays the size of each file and directory that is inside the current directory. Its most basic usage is as easy as it gets:

```
du
```

With this command, you get a long list of directories and the amount of space their files take up. Add the -a switch, and you get an even longer list, with the size of each individual file. One problem with this is that du outputs its sizes in bytes, which is excellent on the accuracy scale, but can get annoying if you have video files with tens or even hundreds of megabytes on the list. Coming to the rescue is the -h switch, making the results more human-readable, if perhaps not so precise. Big files now read as 27M (for megabyte).

Combining these two switches, along with the -c switch, which gives you a total size, gives you a very nice list of files and their sizes:

```
du -ahc /home/mikemc
```

The listing can be extremely long (especially if you have lots of files in your home directory). Often the easiest things to do is redirect the output of the du command to a text file. You can then browse the text file at your leisure, examining who's using the most space on your disks.

Disk Free Space

A big problem for system administrators is disk management. Knowing which disks are mounted, and how much disk space is available on each disk, is crucial in controlling your system. Running out of disk space on the root partition of your system is a major problem.

The df command is a simple way to see what is happening on each of the mounted disks:

```
rich@testing:~> df
Filesystem          1K-blocks      Used Available Use% Mounted on
/dev/hda3             7050802   2399319   4293234  36% /
udev                   127668       100    127568   1% /dev
/dev/hda4             9904349     36631   9364482   1% /home
/dev/hda1            21327868  12450016   8877852  59% /windows/C
/dev/sda1              994528    404432    590096  41% /media/USB DISK
rich@testing:~>
```

The output from the df command shows each physical partition that is currently mounted (even removable devices such as USB memory sticks). For each partition, the total amount of space, the space used, and the space available are all shown. And for the mathematically-challenged, it even calculates the percent of used disk space.

Running Processes

There aren't many commands more powerful than the ps command. It can tell you an extraordinary amount of things about your machine and how it runs. This command shows what processes are currently running on your Linux system. It can be a lifesaver when your system is running slowly. A quick glance at the processes running can often tell you what's happening.

By itself, the ps command is not too exciting. If you enter the ps command at the command prompt, you should see only two processes running: your bash session and the ps command you ran.

```
rich@testing~> ps
  PID TTY          TIME CMD
14445 pts/1    00:00:00 bash
14512 pts/1    00:00:00 ps
rich@testing:~>
```

This is because, by default, the ps command only shows the processes associated with your user ID and terminal ID (Konsole session). To see everything running on the system, you must use a few additional command line options. You can use the ps command man page to see what options are available.

Unfortunately, there's quite a bit of controversy in the Linux world about the ps command. At one time, there were different versions of the ps program floating around. Of course, each version of ps used different options to mean different things. To try to resolve this problem, the Linux community tried to make everyone happy and created a version of ps that combines all of the different version options into a single version.

This resulted in an odd situation were the ps command can use the same command line options both with and without a dash, and get different results. Perusing through the ps man page may help you decide which ps command option to use to get the information you need.

My favorite ps command options are a, e, l, and x (without the dashes). Because you can group command line options together in any order, this combination of options makes axle. Besides being simple to remember, this combination shows you all of the processes running on your system and just about everything you would ever need to know about them.

```
rich@testing:~> ps axle
F   UID   PID  PPID PRI  NI    VSZ   RSS WCHAN  STAT TTY        TIME COMMAND
4     0     1     0  15   0    740   284 -      Ss   ?          0:01 init [5]
1     0     2     1 -100  -      0     0 migrat S    ?          0:00 [migration]
1     0     3     1  34  19      0     0 ksofti SN   ?          0:00 [ksoftirqd]
```

```
1     0     4     1  10  -5      0     0 worker S<   ?          0:00 [events/0]
1     0     5     1  10  -5      0     0 worker S<   ?          0:00 [khelper]
1     0     6     1  20  -5      0     0 worker S<   ?          0:00 [kthread]
1     0     9     6  10  -5      0     0 worker S<   ?          0:00 [kblockd/0]
1     0    10     6  20  -5      0     0 worker S<   ?          0:00 [kacpid]
1     0    72     6  20  -5      0     0 worker S<   ?          0:00 [cqueue/0]
1     0    73     6  10  -5      0     0 serio_ S<   ?          0:00 [kseriod]
1     0   110     6  15   0      0     0 pdflus S    ?          0:00 [pdflush]
1     0   111     6  15   0      0     0 pdflus S    ?          0:00 [pdflush]
1     0   112     6  10  -5      0     0 kswapd S<   ?          0:00 [kswapd0]
1     0   113     6  20  -5      0     0 worker S<   ?          0:00 [aio/0]
1  1000  3781  3743  15   0  35400 17524 -      S    ?          0:00 konqueror [
1  1000  3788     1  15   0  29096 12536 -      S    ?          0:00 kpowersave
1  1000  3789     1  15   0  29920 14260 -      S    ?          0:00 kmix [kdein
1  1000  3796     1  15   0  28220 13220 -      S    ?          0:00 klipper [kd
0  1000  3814     1  15   0  41436 15736 stext  Sl   ?          0:02 beagled /us
1  1000  4043     1  15   0  26292 10408 -      S    ?          0:00 rssservice
1  1000  4046  3743  15   0  25888  6260 -      S    ?          0:00 kio_file [k
1  1000  4047  3743  15   0  51808  7920 -      S    ?          0:00 kio_http [k
1  1000  4048  3743  16   0  51808  7888 -      S    ?          0:00 kio_http [k
1  1000  4059     1  16   0  30980 13872 -      S    ?          0:00 korgac —mi
1  1000  4069  3743  15   0  32252 15396 -      S    ?          0:01 konsole [kd
0  1000  4070  4069  15   0   4528  1920 wait   Ss   pts/0      0:00 /bin/bash L
0  1000  4099  4070  16   0   2272   824 -      R+   pts/0      0:00 ps axle LES
rich@testing:~>
```

Wow, that's a lot of information! You should see some things you recognize, such as the `konsole` program running a command prompt session, the bash shell program, and of course, the `ps` program.

In Chapter 22, "Managing the Boot Process and Other Services," you saw the KSysGuard system monitor application display processes in a tree pattern, showing the relationships between processes. Think you can't get that in a shell? Wrong! Try adding the `f` option to produce the process hierarchy using ASCII art!

Finding System Hogs

One of the biggest headaches for system administrators is when the system is running slow. When you having dozens of users complaining, it is hard to even think straight about how to determine what is happening to the system.

The best tool in your command line toolbox is the `top` command. This command is another way to get a handle on what's happening on your system. More precisely, it seeks to identify the biggest resource hogs at a given moment, so if your system has slowed to a crawl, you can determine and terminate whatever process is killing your system. Here is an example of using `top`:

```
top - 14:55:40 up 11 min,  3 users,  load average: 0.16, 0.46, 0.45
Tasks:  96 total,   2 running,  94 sleeping,   0 stopped,   0 zombie
Cpu(s):  6.5%us,  2.7%sy,  0.0%ni, 88.8%id,  1.9%wa,  0.2%hi,  0.0%si,  0.0%st
Mem:    255336k total,  251416k used,     3920k free,     4040k buffers
Swap:   522104k total,      116k used,   521988k free,   111712k cached

  PID USER      PR  NI  VIRT  RES  SHR S %CPU %MEM    TIME+  COMMAND
 4270 rich      15   0 35048  12m 6840 S  7.9  4.9   0:01.89 beagled-helper
 3300 root      15   0 58700  12m 3908 S  0.6  5.1   0:18.12 X
 3814 rich      15   0 42016  15m 8956 S  0.3  6.4   0:02.32 beagled
 4069 rich      15   0 32252  15m  11m S  0.3  6.1   0:02.17 konsole
 4268 rich      21   0  2256 1020  772 R  0.2  0.4   0:00.08 top
    1 root      15   0   740  284  240 S  0.0  0.1   0:01.81 init
    2 root      RT   0     0    0    0 S  0.0  0.0   0:00.00 migration/0
    3 root      34  19     0    0    0 S  0.0  0.0   0:00.02 ksoftirqd/0
    4 root      10  -5     0    0    0 S  0.0  0.0   0:00.06 events/0
    5 root      20  -5     0    0    0 S  0.0  0.0   0:00.00 khelper
    6 root      13  -5     0    0    0 S  0.0  0.0   0:00.00 kthread
    9 root      10  -5     0    0    0 S  0.0  0.0   0:00.00 kblockd/0
   10 root      20  -5     0    0    0 S  0.0  0.0   0:00.00 kacpid
   72 root      20  -5     0    0    0 S  0.0  0.0   0:00.00 cqueue/0
   73 root      10  -5     0    0    0 S  0.0  0.0   0:00.02 kseriod
  110 root      15   0     0    0    0 S  0.0  0.0   0:00.00 pdflush
  111 root      15   0     0    0    0 S  0.0  0.0   0:00.05 pdflush
```

The top display sorts the running processes by CPU usage, memory usage, and runtime. It continually updates the display every five seconds (you can change that with a command line option). Once top is running, there are several interactive commands that you can use. Pressing the `spacebar` immediately updates the display. Pressing the `q` key exits the display, and pressing the `k` key allows you to enter the PID of the process you want to stop (kill).

You are best off running `top` as the SuperUser, because you never know who owns the bad-acting process. You don't actually need any switches to get `top` running properly. After you type `top` at the prompt, it will open and display a list of processes sorted with the most CPU-intensive tasks at the top. Unfortunately, those processes don't have names in the `top` display.

To kill the process at the top of the list, type `k` and enter the PID. You are prompted for a signal number (the manner in which you want the process killed), with 15 as the default. This signals the process politely, asking it to shut down. Those apps that are not wildly out of control comply with the request. If your unruly process doesn't terminate, repeat the process, only this time send the not-so-polite Signal 9 (terminate and terminate NOW).

Combining Commands

So far, we have been using commands individually, and for the most part, that's what you'll be doing in practice. What gives Linux its real power, though, is when users string commands together to build on the results of one tool to get even more done. There are even commands that serve as glue to hold these more complex tool chains together.

All the commands we have looked at here print their information to the screen, but the target can be flexible. There are two ways to control where output should go: piping and redirection. Pipes connect one program's output and the next program's input. Instead of displaying results on the screen, a command will send results to another program, which manipulates the information it gains to get even better results for the user. Output redirection works in a similar way, but works best when creating new files. We'll look first at pipes, and then at redirection.

There's a Freeciv game going on, and you need to know who's in it. Let's take two of the commands we learned about earlier in this chapter to find out:

```
ps aux | grep freeciv
```

What you did was create a list of processes live on the system right now. That list, including additional information about the processes (including the owner of each process), was sent to `grep`. It looked at that list and looked for lines containing the word "freeciv." `grep` then identified the matching lines and told you who owned the active clients, and who owned the server as well.

Earlier, we used `du` to develop a good list of all the files on the system. Wouldn't it be nice to have that in a file that we could then manipulate further down the road? Simple enough:

```
du -ahc /home/mikemc > du.txt
```

If we wanted a running total of who was playing Freeciv at any given moment, we could start a `cron` job to run our `ps ¦ grep` pipe, and then add a third command:

```
ps aux | grep freeciv > players.txt
```

Simple, yet a pretty good illustration of just what we can do by just combining a few commands.

References

- http://www.gnu.org—The spiritual home of the free-software OS movement. Learn much about command-line tools here.
- http://www.linuxdevcenter.com/linux/cmd—The alphabetical directory of Linux commands. Information on over 600 Linux commands.
- http://tuxfiles.org/linuxhelp/cli.html—Newbie-oriented help on assorted command-line topics.
- http://linuxcommand.org—You have Linux installed and running. The GUI is working fine, but you are getting tired of changing your desktop themes. You keep seeing this "terminal" thing. Don't worry, they'll show you what to do.
- http://justlinux.com/nhf/Shells/Basic_Console_Commands.html—More on the commands listed here.

Index

NUMBERS

A

B

C

D

E

F

G

H

I

J

K

L

N

O

P

Q–R

S

T

U

Z

REGISTER THIS BOOK

Register this book and unlock benefits exclusive to the owners of this book.

Registration benefits can include

- Additional content
- Book errata
- Source code, example files, and other downloads
- Increased membership discounts
- Discount coupons
- A chance to sign up to receive content updates, information on new editions, and more

Book registration is free and takes only a few easy steps:

1. Go to **www.samspublishing.com/register**
2. Enter the book's ISBN (found above the barcode on the back of your book).
3. You will be prompted to either register for or log in to samspublishing.com.
4. Once you have completed your registration or log in, you will be taken to your "My Registered Books" page.
5. This page will list any benefits associated with each title you register, including links to content and coupon codes.

The benefits of book registration vary with each book, so be sure to register every Sams Publishing book you own to see what else you might unlock at **www.samspublishing.com/register**

Related Linux and Open Source Titles

Ubuntu Linux 7.10 Unleashed

Andrew and Paul Hudson

ISBN-10: 0-672-32969-7
ISBN-13: 978-0-672-32969-2

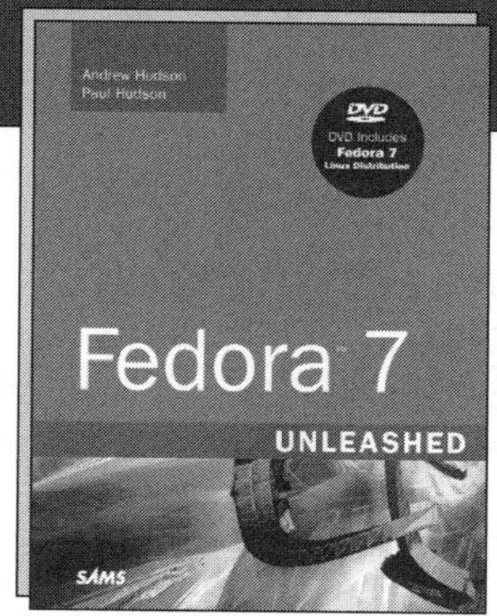

Red Hat Fedora 7 Unleashed

Andrew Hudson and Paul Hudson

ISBN-10: 0-672-32942-5
ISBN-13: 978-0-672-32942-5

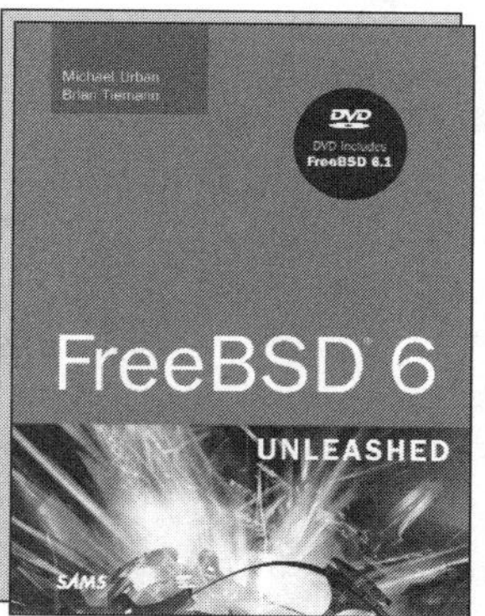

FreeBSD 6 Unleashed

Brian Tiemann

ISBN-10: 0-672-32875-5
ISBN-13: 978-0-672-32875-6

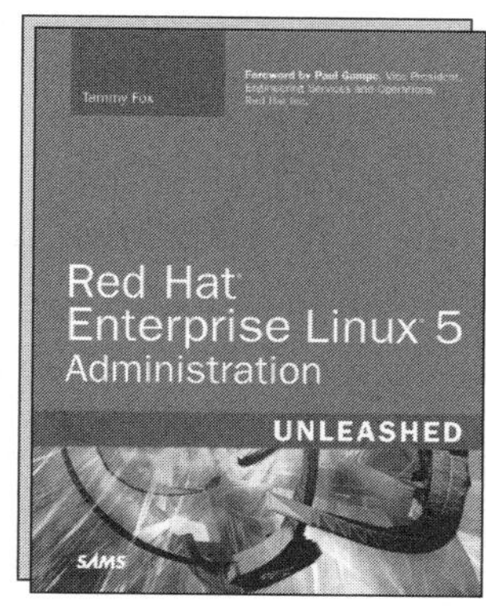

Red Hat Enterprise Linux 5 Administration Unleashed

Tammy Fox

ISBN-10: 0-672-32892-5
ISBN-13: 978-0-672-32892-3

Sams Teach Yourself PHP, MySQL and Apache All in One
Julie Meloni
ISBN-10: 0-672-32873-9
ISBN-13: 978-0-672-32873-2

Linux Phrasebook
Scott Granneman
ISBN-10: 0-672-32838-0
ISBN-13: 978-0-672-32838-1

MySQL Phrasebook
Zak Greant and Chris Newman
ISBN-10: 0-672-32839-9
ISBN-13: 978-0-672-32839-8

PHP Phrasebook
Christian Wenz
ISBN-10: 0-672-32817-8
ISBN-13: 978-0-672-32817-6

Apache Phrasebook
Daniel Lopez
ISBN-10: 0-672-32836-4
ISBN-13: 978-0-672-32836-7

SUSE Linux Enterprise Server 9 Administrator's Handbook
Peter Kuo and Jacques Béland
ISBN-10: 0-672-32735-X
ISBN-13: 978-0-672-32735-3

Linux Firewalls, Third Edition
Steve Suehring and Robert L. Ziegler
ISBN-10: 0-672-32771-6
ISBN-13: 978-0-672-32771-1

Linux Kernel Development
Robert Love
ISBN-10: 0-672-32720-1
ISBN-13: 978-0-672-32720-9

Sams Teach Yourself MySQL in 10 Minutes
Chris Newman
ISBN-10: 0-672-32863-1
ISBN-13: 978-0-672-32863-3

SAMS

www.samspublishing.com

What's on the DVD

The book's DVD-ROM contains the complete binary version of openSUSE 10.3—the equivalent of five CDs.

AMUSEMENTS

- FreeCiv
- KDE Game Collection
- Maelstrom
- SuperTux
- Xboard

DEVELOPMENT

Languages

- Bison
- Flex
- GCC
- Guile
- Java
- Mono
- Perl
- Python
- Ruby
- Tcl
- TK

Tools

- Ant
- Autoconf
- Automake
- cscope
- CVS
- DDD
- DejaGnu
- ElectricFence
- Expect
- GDB
- Libtool
- Ltrace
- Make
- Strace
- Subversion

DOCUMENTATION

- BIND Documentation
- HTML Documentation for the GNU C Library
- GNOME 2.x Desktop Documentation
- Qt 3 Development Kit and man pages
- Samba documentation
- Xen Virtualization documentation
- Online manuals for X11

HARDWARE

- a2ps
- ALSA
- Bluetooth firmware and libraries
- CUPS
- Printer filters
- GNOME Printing Architecture
- gPhoto
- GTKam
- hdparm
- klipsi
- LIRC
- mgetty
- motv (Video4Linux TV application)
- PCI Utilities
- SCSI Tools
- sendfax
- wireless-tools
- xpp
- XSane

PRODUCTIVITY

Archiving

- Bzip
- cpio
- konserve
- Pax
- Star
- Unzip
- Zip

Databases

- db-utils
- Knoda
- C++ Client Library for PostgreSQL
- Mergeant
- MySQL
- PostgreSQL
- Rekall
- SQLite
- UnixODBC
- XBase

Editors

- ed
- GNU Emacs
- AUC TeX
- flim
- Gedit
- jEdit
- JOE
- Mined
- ViM
- XSLIDe

File Utilities

- GNU Find
- KDE Utility Programs
- Midnight Commander
- Nautilus

Graphics

- AutoTrace
- Blender
- Dia
- Eye Of GNOME
- F-Spot
- GIMP
- GNUPlot
- GpsDrive
- ImageMagick
- Base Libraries for KDE Graphics Applications
- netpbm
- GNU Ocrad
- Skencil

Multimedia

- ALSA Tools
- amaroK
- arts
- aumix
- banshee
- cdparanoia
- CDRDAO
- Cecilia
- dvd+rw-tools
- FluidSynth
- K3b
- Kaffeine
- KDE Multimedia Applications
- RealPlayer
- Sound-juicer

Multimedia (continued)

- SOX
- Totem
- Xine

Networking

- Apache 2
- BIND
- BitTorrent
- Bogofilter
- Curl
- Dante
- DHCP client/server
- Dirmngr
- EPIC
- Epiphany
- Evolution
- Fetchmail
- Finger
- Flash Player
- FreeRADIUS
- GnomeICU
- GPG 2
- Grepmail
- htdig
- imap
- INN
- iproute2
- iptables
- iputils
- krb5
- Lynx
- Mailx
- Mozilla
- Mozilla Firefox
- MRTG
- mutt
- Netcat
- OpenLDAP
- Opera
- PHP
- Pidgin
- Pine
- PostFix
- PPP
- PPTP
- procmail
- Quagga
- RADVD